W9-COE-527

Why Access 95? Why the Beginner's Guide?

Access revolutionized the world of database development. Before Access appeared, databases were things that sat on giant mainframes at the end of corridors. With Access, though, the power of this unique form of data storage was brought to small businesses and the home user alike. The latest release of Access is blessed with many new features and wizards which means that the task of creating a professional application is made even more simple.

Access 95 has a lot to offer, so there's a lot to explain. The Beginner's Guide to Access 95 rises to that challenge. Using a relaxed and visual style, the book takes you quickly and painlessly to outstanding results. Create a great looking application that utilizes all the features of Access 95 without prior knowledge of databases. Motivating and entertaining at every stage, it's the book Access 95 deserves.

What is Wrox Press?

Wrox Press is a computer book publisher which promotes clear, jargon-free programming and database titles that fulfill your real demands. We publish for everyone, from the novice through to the experienced programmer. To ensure our books meet your needs, we carry out continuous research on all our titles. Through our dialog with you, we can craft the book you really need.

We welcome suggestions and take all of them to heart - your input is paramount in creating the next great Wrox title. Use the reply card inside this book or contact us at:

feedback@wrox.com

Compuserve 100063, 2152

http://www.wrox.com/

Wrox Press Ltd.
2710 W. Touhy
Chicago
IL 60645
USA

Tel: +1 (312) 465 3559

Fax:+1 (312) 465 4063

The Beginner's Guide to Access 95

Alex Homer

Wrox Press Ltd.®

The Beginner's Guide to Access 95

Published by Wrox Press Ltd. Site 16, 20 James Road, Birmingham, B11 2BA
Printed in Canada
1 2 3 4 5 TRI 99 98 97 96

Library of Congress Catalog no. 95-61788
ISBN 1-874416-82-6

Trademark Acknowledgements

Wrox has endeavored to provide trademark information about all the companies and products mentioned in this book by the appropriate use of capitals. However, Wrox cannot guarantee the accuracy of this information.

Credits

Author	**Managing Editor**	**Production Manager**
Alex Homer	John Franklin	Greg Powell
Editors	**Beta Testers**	**Design/Layout**
Chris Ullman	Deb Somers	Neil Gallagher
Gina Mance	Ian Wilks	Graham Butler
Graham McLaughlin		Damon P Creed
Gordon Rogers	**Proof Readers**	Eddie Fisher
	Melanie Orgee	Greg Powell
Technical Reviewers	Pam Brand	
David Skowronski		**Cover Design**
Nick Ajderian	**Index**	Third Wave
	Simon Gilks	

For more information on Third Wave, contact Ross Alderson on 44-121 236 6616
Cover photo supplied by The Image Bank

About The Author

Alex lives and works in the idyllic surroundings of the Peak District in Derbyshire, UK. A technical salesman for a national manufacturing company, his fascination with databases started with the Oric Atmos home computer - storing and analyzing details of customers and sales.

The first databases were home-grown in machine code and from there he graduated through many other database systems, including Reflex and various dBase clones.

Coming to Access with version 1, Alex has finally found a system with the power to provide all the long sought-after features. He continues to develop applications which aim to combine the latest technology with the real needs of the commercial world.

The Beginner's Guide to
Access 95

Summary Of Contents

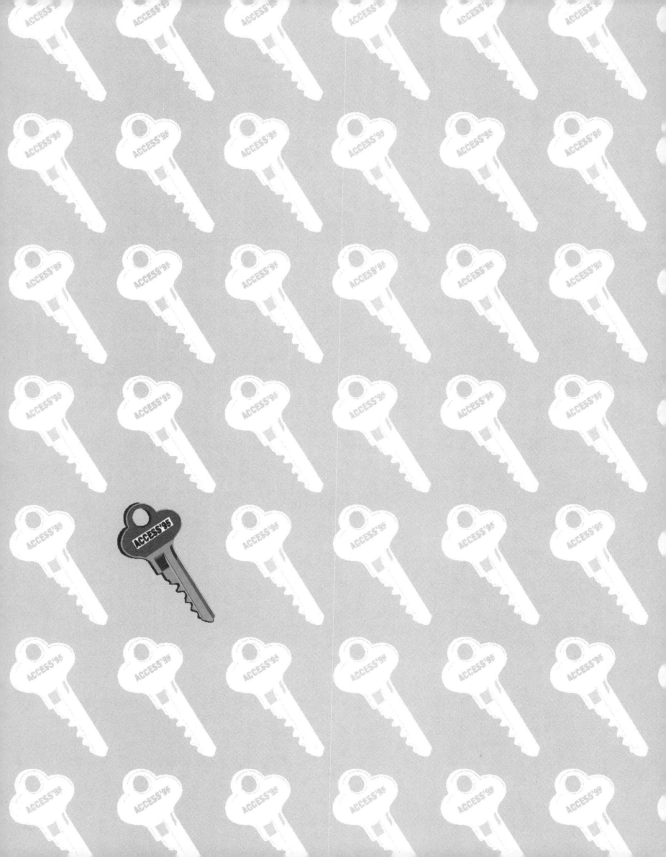

The Beginner's Guide to
Access 95

Table Of Contents

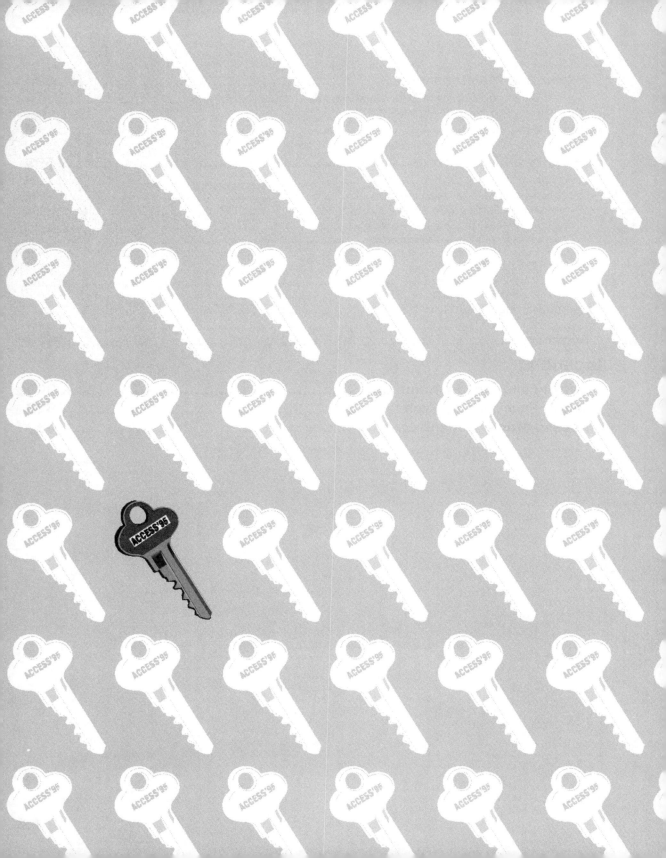

The Beginner's Guide to
Access 95

Introduction

Who's this Book For?

This book is designed to teach you how to create sophisticated databases in Microsoft's Access 95. There are two kinds of beginner who will benefit from this book:

- You're new to databases and you're starting with Access 95. This is a great place to start learning. We start off in familiar territory with an Excel spreadsheet, using well-known terms such as row and column. You'll learn how the spreadsheet terminology applies to Access 95 and then move straight on to explore database application development. If you've been put off in the past by long-winded and incomprehensible database terminology, this book will ease you into Access with the minimum of fuss. In order to master Access, you will, of course, have to learn the terminology and methods, but in this book you'll first be taught how to build your database application using approved methods and then you'll learn why what you've done is good practice.

- Alternatively, you have experience of another database such as Paradox or dBase, but have yet to get to grips with Access. The idea of relearning concepts you're already familiar with strikes you as tedious and a waste of your time. This book is still the one to take you into the world of Access 95. In this case, you might want to skip Chapter 1, and immerse yourself straight away in Access 95 database development.

What's Covered in this Book

The Beginner's Guide to Access 95 contains all the information you'll need to learn how to develop Access databases. By following the practical examples in each chapter, you'll quickly become proficient at creating tables, forms and reports, manipulating data and transferring and linking it to data in other applications. By the end of the book you will be able to create practical databases, tailored to your own specific needs.

Practice makes perfect and, in this book, we introduce an iterative approach that allows you to learn without effort. In Part 1, our aim is to start with a recognized concept, in this case an Excel spreadsheet, and use it as an aid to understanding databases. We then go on to examine the different objects that make up a database. In Part 2, you 'relearn' and build on the concepts you have covered in the first Part, seeing how they are used in a full-blown application. Finally, in Part 3, we look at some wider issues, including the interaction of the example application with other applications, Access 95's means for communicating with a database, and security.

To give you a real taster of what you will be doing, take a look at the following screenshot. This is the opening screen of the application that forms the basis of Part 2 of the book. By the time you have worked your way through the book, you will be more than capable of creating your own version of this database.

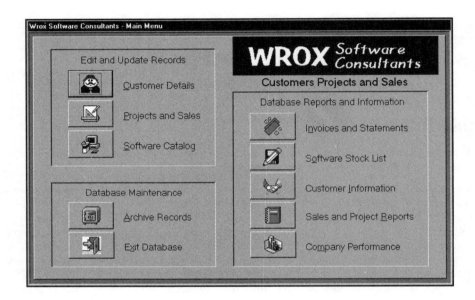

What we won't be teaching you is how to use Windows 95/NT - we're assuming that you have a basic knowledge of this software. Also, we won't be catering for 3.1 users because Access 95 will only run on a 32-bit operating system. At the moment, Windows 95 is probably a more popular 32-bit system than Windows NT, so the screen shots in the book are based on Windows 95. As a result, those of you using Windows NT will find that one or two of the directives, for example, closing windows, are different but you shouldn't find that this interferes in any way with the quality of the tutorial.

What You Need to Use this Book

Apart from a bit of time and a willingness to learn, you'll need access to a PC running Windows 95/NT and Access 95, and preferably a copy of Office 95.

In order to install and use the samples on the disk included with this book, you'll need a hard drive with at least 5 megabytes of free space. It's important to install the samples from the disk as these form a fundamental part of the learning process. The book is written with the assumption that you have your comp at hand and will try out the examples as directed.

To install the examples from the disk, place the disk in your A: drive and go to Explorer. Run the file **Setup.exe** by double clicking on it. The archive will create a new directory on your local drive named **BegAcc95** and extract all of the examples to this directory.

Conventions

We use a number of different styles of text and layout in the book to help differentiate between the different kinds of information. Here are examples of the styles we use and an explanation of what they mean:

Try It Outs - How Do They Work?

1 These are examples that you should work through.

2 Each step has a number.

3 Follow the steps through.

FYI Extra details, For Your Information, come in boxes like this.

- **Important Words** are in a bold type font.
- Words that appear on the screen, such as the table names, menu options and expressions that you type in, are a similar font to the one used on screen, e.g. the Project table.
- Keys that you press on the keyboard, like *Ctrl* and *Enter*, are in italics.
- All filenames are in this style: **WroxSoft.mdb**.
- Function names look like this: **IsNull**
- SQL code will be shown in the following format:

```
SELECT Customer.CustName Customer.Phone FROM Customer ORDER BY Customer.CustName;
```

Tell Us What You Think

We have tried to make this book accurate, enjoyable and honest. But what really matters is what it does for you. Please let us know your views by either returning the reply card in the back of the book, or by contacting us at Wrox Press. The easiest way is to use email:

feedback@wrox.com
http://www.wrox.com/
Compuserve: 100063,2152

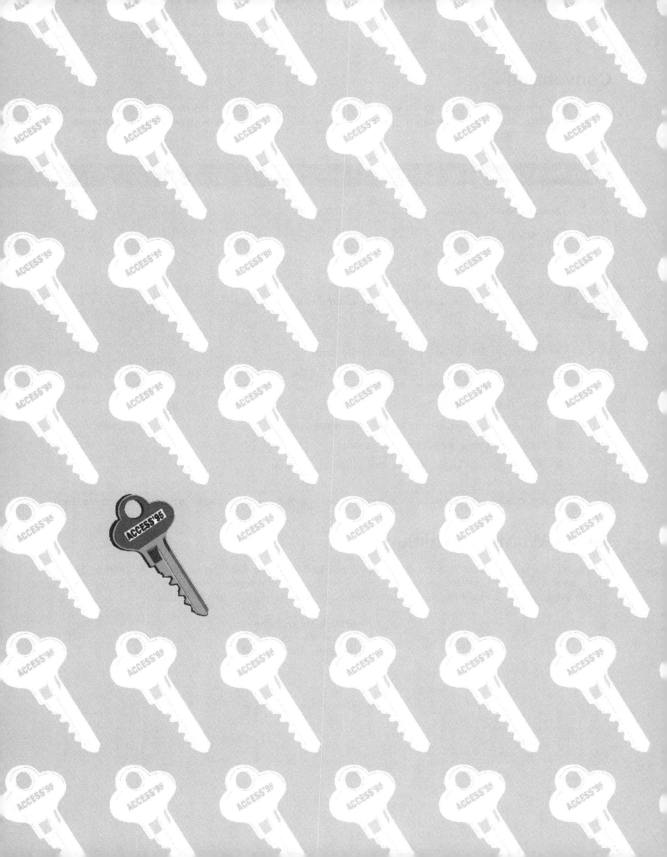

Understanding What Access Does

In Part 1, we look at how and why a database is a better source of information than other applications that you may be tempted to use to store data - such as spreadsheets. Today you need all the competitive advantage you can get to stay ahead of the crowd, and better information is at the root of all business aims. To quote a modern-day proverb: 'What you are giving me is data, what I need is information'. A well-designed database can extract the exact information you need from the reams of data you have to keep.

In Chapter 1 we'll take a look at how a spreadsheet can be used to store data, using Microsoft Excel as the example. In Chapter 2, we'll transfer the data from Excel to Access and, by comparing what the two applications can do, start to see the power that Access offers. In Chapter 3 we'll look at how we can extract information from our new database.

Chapters 4, 5 and 6 will look at how we can restructure the stored data and start to get some really useful information from it. Then in Chapters 7 and 8 we'll look at forms and reports to see how we can get new data in, and real information out, of our new database.

The techniques you learn in this first part will form the basis of all your future work in Access, so take the time to work through the examples and really understand what you are doing. By the end of the part, you will feel comfortable with the Access environment and be able to build and get information from simple databases.

So, without further ado, let's get started...

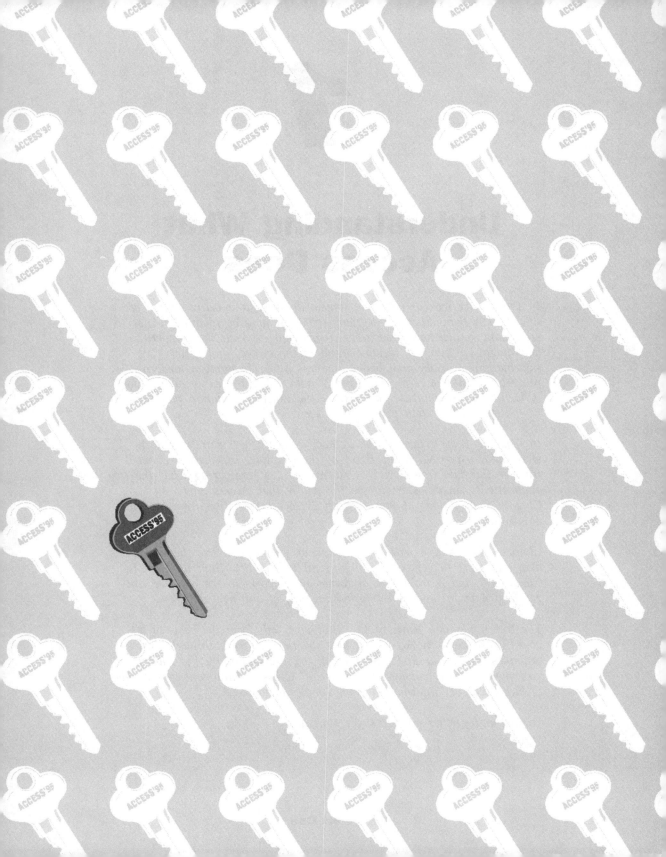

Reaching The Limits Of Spreadsheets

You've bought this book to learn Microsoft's database - Access - so it might surprise you to see that the first chapter is going to be about spreadsheets. Read on, though, and all will become clear. Our intention is to use this first chapter to prepare the ground for the rest of the book - to clarify exactly why you need a good database and what you are likely to want from it.

In this chapter, we are going to examine Access' capabilities by looking at the limitations of spreadsheets - this is, in our experience, the most common spring board into the database world. Spreadsheet data looks very much like the data in databases, and the concepts of rows and columns in Access are much easier to understand in the context of the rows and columns of a spreadsheet. If you've already used a database (dBase, Paradox), then you may wish to skip this chapter and start instead at Chapter 2.

Don't worry if you're unfamiliar with spreadsheets or haven't used Excel before - you should still work through the chapter as it'll provide a good indication of what you're aiming at with Access.

In this chapter we will cover:

- Using a spreadsheet for data storage.
- The Excel database functions.
- How Excel stores its data.
- Why Excel can't offer all the features we need.

Displaying Data in Excel

For the purposes of this first chapter, we are going to assume that you are familiar with the concept of a spreadsheet, and, in particular, that you know your way round Microsoft's spreadsheet, Excel. We make this assumption as many people will be using the Microsoft Office Pro suite, which includes both Excel and Access. Excel and Access have similar menu bars and use similar direct manipulation techniques for altering rows and columns. Like databases, spreadsheets are used as a data storage medium - but by comparing what you can do in Excel to what you no doubt would like to be able to do (and what you can do in Access), we will show you just how powerful and sophisticated Access is.

The disk that accompanies this book contains sample data from a fictitious software consultancy - Wrox Consultancy. We'll be using this data in examples throughout the book. The data is in the file **Accounts.xls** - this contains the spreadsheet that Bill Bright, our software consultant, uses to keep track of the work he does for his customers.

 Windows 95 allows you to use long and more descriptive names for disk files. It also hides the 'extension part' of a file name by default, so the file you see may be called simply **Accounts**, with the description **Excel spreadsheet..** We'll be using the full file names in this book - you can view these using the **My Computer** file manager (in Windows 95) if you prefer. Select **Options** from the **View** menu, and in the **View** tab of the **Options** dialog uncheck the last option - **Hide MS-DOS file extensions...**

So, let's start by having a look at the data that Wrox Consultancy stores.

Try It Out - Checking Out Wrox Consultancy

1 Double click on the Excel icon or select Microsoft Excel from the Start menu.

2 Select the File menu and use the Open option to load the Excel file **Accounts.xls**. This file is on the disk that accompanies the book (see the Introduction for details on how to install the files). Once you've loaded the file, select the sheet named Original.

	A	B	C	D	E	F	G	H
	Date	CustName	Address	Town	State	ZipCode	Phone	Fax
2	12-Jun-95	Aardvaak Ltd.	All Saints Street	Athens	OH	39812	216-376-1298	216-376-8811
3	23-Jun-95	Burger Queen	Constants Avenue	Houston	TX	30517	713-771-6727	713-771-6728
4	5-Jul-95	Education Dept.	The Offices, City Square	Chicago	IL	10745	312-712-8567	
5	16-Jul-95	Education Dept.	The Offices, City Square	Chicago	IL	10745	312-712-8567	
6	3-Jul-95	Cummings Intl.	124th Street West	Pittsburgh	PA	17265	412-455-6104	412-455-1399
7	20-Jun-95	J.R.Higgins	The Market	Green Bay	WI	61733	414-831-8812	414-831-7293
8	16-Jun-95	James Builders	2131 New Street	Phoenix	AZ	78034	602-281-3318	602-281-7318
9	23-Jul-95	Jonahs Boats	The Quay	Stocksville	FL	16734	305-711-8855	
10	8-Jul-95	Le Bistro	Rue Francais	Vancouver	WA	41322	206-133-8294	206-133-8295
11	30-Jun-95	Major Records	Third Avenue	Stocksville	FL	10015	305-711-7851	305-711-8531
12	18-Jul-95	Martha's Bar	Top Street	Clarksville	NY	54876		
13	18-Jun-95	Miracle Supplies	18th Avenue	Oakland	CA	10593	415-671-6633	415-671-8833
14	26-Jun-95	Miracle Supplies	18th Avenue	Oakland	CA	10593	415-671-6633	415-671-8833
15	13-Jul-95	Miracle Supplies	18th Avenue	Oakland	CA	10593	415-671-6633	415-671-8833
16	28-Jun-95	Pedro Mana	Calle Sebastione	St. Paul	MN	65109	612-401-1350	612-401-1388
17	20-Jul-95	Union Records	712 Main Street	Tampa	FL	51267	813-167-3520	813-167-3521
18								

Original / Projects / Customers / Contacts /

Project	HoursWorked	HourlyRate	TotalCharge	TaxRate	TaxDue	TotalDue	Paid
Accounts System	38	$50.00	$1,900.00	12%	$228.00	$2,128.00	Y
System Development	18	$65.00	$1,170.00	14%	$163.80	$1,333.80	Y
Schools Support	39	$50.00	$1,950.00	0%	$0.00	$1,950.00	
Schools Support	11	$50.00	$550.00	0%	$0.00	$550.00	
Robotics Installation	8	$75.00	$600.00	8%	$48.00	$648.00	Y
PC Upgrades	5	$85.00	$425.00	14%	$59.50	$484.50	
Accounts System	21	$50.00	$1,050.00	12%	$126.00	$1,176.00	Y
Navigation System	14	$45.00	$630.00	10%	$63.00	$693.00	Y
Menu Generator	4	$60.00	$240.00	15%	$36.00	$276.00	Y
Catalogue System	17	$80.00	$1,360.00	13%	$176.80	$1,536.80	
Menu Generator	6	$60.00	$360.00	15%	$54.00	$414.00	
Warehouse System	13	$70.00	$910.00	11%	$100.10	$1,010.10	Y
Warehouse System	11	$70.00	$770.00	11%	$84.70	$854.70	
Accounts System	11	$50.00	$550.00	12%	$66.00	$616.00	Y
Accounts System	38	$50.00	$1,900.00	12%	$228.00	$2,128.00	Y
Catalogue System	25	$80.00	$2,000.00	13%	$260.00	$2,260.00	

3 The spreadsheet contains columns where Bill stores the date, the customer's name, address, phone and fax number, and the type of project undertaken. He also keeps track of the number of hours worked, the hourly rate, the total charge, tax rate, tax due, and total due. The final column tells him whether or not he's been paid for the work.

4 The contents of the TotalCharge, TaxDue, and TotalDue columns are calculated automatically from values in the same row using formulae in these cells. Each month Bill uses the information to type out an invoice and statement for each customer and updates the last column when the payment arrives.

The data may not be enough to satisfy the tax man, but at least it'll give us a chance to show you how Excel can be used to manipulate data. Most other Windows spreadsheets will offer similar capabilities.

Account Management with Excel

So what are the tasks we need to accomplish in our day-to-day account management? We need to be able to:

 Sort the entries into a different order

 Find a particular entry quickly

 Filter the entries to show only the ones we want to see

 Sum the values in various columns

 Update the entries and add new ones

Of course, it would be nice if the system could produce our invoices, statements and financial reports automatically as well. However, that's something that Excel can't do. In fact, in this chapter we'll come across several things that aren't possible with spreadsheet programs. Access has the power to handle them, though, and as we progress through the book we look in more detail at how Access compares to Excel.

Sorting, Finding and Filtering in Excel

With Excel, you can sort the rows in a spreadsheet, find particular entries, and filter entries to display certain rows only. All these actions can be carried out quite easily using the functions in the Data menu.

Try It Out - Sorting

1 Click on any cell in the block of entries and select Sort from the Data menu.

2 Excel will display the Sort dialog box. Check that the Header Row option at the bottom of the dialog is selected. The name of the column by which the table is currently sorted then appears in the top group of controls.

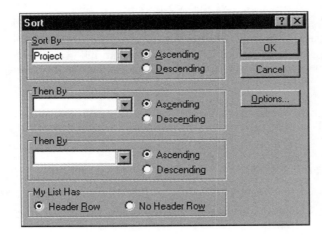

3 Click on the little arrow to the right of the top of the box labeled Sort By, and select Project. Make sure the Ascending check box is selected.

4 In the second box, select Date and Ascending.

5 Leave the third box blank.

6 Finally, click OK and the entries will be sorted according to the criteria you've just defined.

	A	B	C	D	E	F	G	H	I	
1	Date	CustName	Address	Town	State	ZipCode	Phone	Fax	Project	Hou
2	12-Jun-95	Aardvark Ltd.	All Saints Street	Athens	OH	39812	216-376-1298	216-376-8811	Accounts System	
3	16-Jun-95	James Builders	2131 New Street	Phoenix	AZ	78034	602-281-3318	602-281-7318	Accounts System	
4	28-Jun-95	Pedro Mana	Calle Sebastione	St. Paul	MN	65109	612-401-1350	612-401-1388	Accounts System	
5	13-Jul-95	Miracle Supplies	18th Avenue	Oakland	CA	10593	415-671-6633	415-671-8833	Accounts System	
6	30-Jun-95	Major Records	Third Avenue	Stocksville	FL	10015	305-711-7851	305-711-8531	Catalogue System	
7	20-Jul-95	Union Records	217 Main Street	Tampa	FL	51267	813-167-3520	813-167-3521	Catalogue System	
8	08-Jul-95	Le Bistro	Rue Francais	Vancouver	WA	41322	206-133-8294	206-133-8295	Menu Generator	
9	18-Jul-95	Martha's Bar	Top Street	Clarksville	NY	54876			Menu Generator	
10	23-Jul-95	Jonahs Boats	The Quay	Stocksville	FL	16734	305-711-8855		Navigation System	
11	20-Jun-95	J.R.Higgins	The Market	Green Bay	WI	61733	414-831-8812	414-831-7293	PC Upgrades	
12	03-Jul-95	Cummings Intl.	124th Street West	Pittsburgh	PA	17265	412-455-6104	412-455-1399	Robotics Installation	
13	05-Jul-95	Education Dept.	The Offices, City Square	Chicago	IL	10745	312-712-8567		Schools Support	
14	16-Jul-95	Education Dept.	The Offices, City Square	Chicago	IL	10745	312-712-8567		Schools Support	
15	23-Jun-95	Burger Queen	Constants Avenue	Houston	TX	30517	713-771-6727	713-771-6728	System Development	
16	18-Jun-95	Miracle Supplies	18th Avenue	Oakland	CA	10593	415-671-6633	415-671-8833	Warehouse System	
17	26-Jun-95	Miracle Supplies	18th Avenue	Oakland	CA	10593	415-671-6633	415-671-8833	Warehouse System	
18										
19										

How It Works

The three boxes in the Sort dialog box allow you to define the criteria for the sort. The spreadsheet entries will be sorted first by the column shown in the first box, then, if two entries are identical, by the column shown in the second box, and if there are still identical entries, by the column shown in the third box. In the above example, therefore, the entries are sorted first by project, and then, where the project type is the same for two or more entries, by date.

When you sort rows in Excel (or Access, for that matter), the final order depends on the type of data in the columns. If it's text, Excel sorts it into alphabetical order; if it's numbers it sorts into numeric order.

By default, Excel ignores case when sorting, so, for example, 'Education' and 'education' are sorted together. You can force Excel to sort in a **case-sensitive** way by clicking on Options... in the Sort dialog box and then checking the Case Sensitive box.

Ascending and Descending should be pretty self-evident. If you are sorting text entries in Ascending order, those starting with the letter A will be at the top of the list. If you sort in Descending order, your entries that start with A will be at the bottom of the list.

If a text entry starts with a space, and you sort in Ascending order, the entry will be placed at the end of the list. If you sort in Descending order, it will be at the beginning. Blank or empty cells are always sorted at the end of the list. If the cells contain formulae, they are sorted on the results (not on the actual text of the formula).

Finding

Finding an entry is also very simple. You can find an entry either by selecting Find from the Edit menu and using the Find dialog box, or by using a **filter**. The Find dialog allows you to search the whole sheet by column or by row, and to specify whether to match the case and whether the string you enter should match all or only part of the entry in a cell.

Try It Out - Finding an Entry

1 Select Find from the Edit menu and enter the word Aardvark into the dialog box that appears.

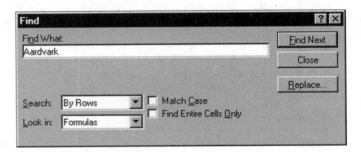

2 Click on Find Next and the next cell containing the word Aardvark will be highlighted.

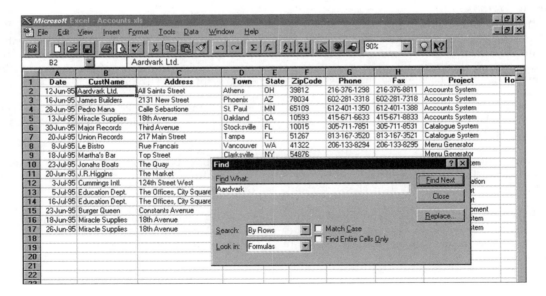

3   You can get rid of the Find dialog box by clicking the Close button.

Filtering

You can also find entries that match a certain criteria by using a filter. This filters out the rows that do not match the criteria you specify, displaying just the ones that do.

Try It Out - Filtering

1   Select Filter from the Data menu and then select AutoFilter.

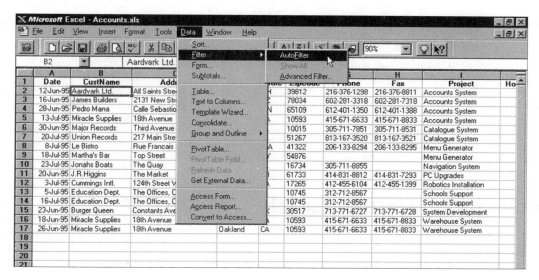

2   Access adds a drop-down button to the head of each column. Click on the arrow in the Town column and select Stocksville from the list shown.

A	B	C	D	E	F
Date ▾	CustName ▾	Address ▾	Town ▾	Sta ▾	ZipCoc ▾
12-Jun-95	Aardvark Ltd.	All Saints Street	Oakland	OH	39812
16-Jun-95	James Builders	2131 New Street	Phoenix Pittsburgh	AZ	78034
28-Jun-95	Pedro Mana	Calle Sebastione	St. Paul	MN	65109
13-Jul-95	Miracle Supplies	18th Avenue	Stocksville	CA	10593
30-Jun-95	Major Records	Third Avenue	Tampa Vancouver	FL	10015
20-Jul-95	Union Records	217 Main Street	(Blanks)	FL	51267
08-Jul-95	Le Bistro	Rue Francais	Vancouver	WA	41322

3   The entries will now be filtered to show only those whose Town field is Stocksville.

4 You can see which column has a filter applied, as the drop-down list button will have a blue, rather than a black, arrow. The numbers of the rows that are displayed are also in blue. To remove the filter, select Filter from the Data menu again, and then select Show All.

You could use a filter to see which customers haven't paid yet (to do this you would select (Blanks) from the Paid column list). You could also apply two filters together to find out how many customers in Stocksville haven't paid their bill. In fact, by using one or more filters to control which rows are displayed, you can pinpoint whatever information you need.

AutoFilter is the easiest way to quickly limit the rows that are displayed to those that match particular criteria, though there is also another method of filtering data. This involves using Advanced Filter, and we'll look at how to do this later in the chapter.

Manipulating Data in Excel

OK, so we've looked at how to display data according to our needs, but to manage the accounts effectively, we also need to be able to manipulate the data in a spreadsheet. We need to be able to perform calculations on the data we have, as well as update and add new entries.

Producing Subtotals

One of the most fundamental tasks we need to be able to carry out is the summing of entries. For example, our consultant may need to know how many hours he's worked. The tax man will also be interested in how much tax he's due to pay. Excel has a clever function which will produce subtotals automatically. Let's try it out.

Try It Out - Producing Subtotals

1 Turn off any filters that you still have, so that all the entries are visible (to turn off AutoFilter just select it again so the check mark on the menu disappears). Then use the Sort dialog to sort the entries by CustName, and then by Date.

14

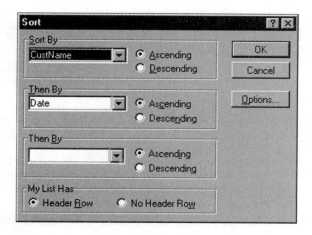

2 Select Su**b**totals from the **D**ata menu to display the Subtotals dialog.

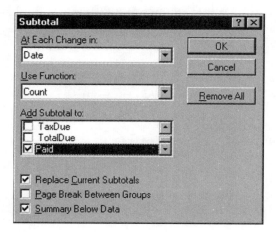

3 We're going to create a subtotal for each customer, so in the box labeled **A**t Each Change in, select CustName, and in the **U**se Function box select Sum.

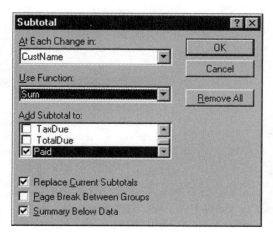

4 In the third section of the dialog, check the four boxes for HoursWorked, TotalCharge, TaxDue and TotalDue. You can leave the check-boxes in the bottom section set to their default values.

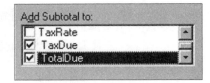

> **FYI** You can leave the boxes that are checked by default as they are if you like - it just means that you will get subtotals for these columns as well.

5 Click OK, and Excel will insert a subtotal row for each customer, showing the totals for that customer. It will also add a Grand Total line at the end showing the overall totals.

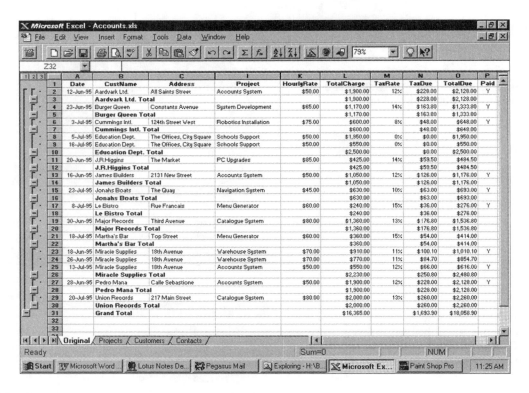

> **FYI** We have hidden some of the columns in the above screenshot so that you can see the subtotals. To keep the screenshot clear, we did this by placing the cursor between the gray column headers (where it changes to an East/West arrow) and then dragging to the left. However, if you want to hide columns, your best bet is to place the cursor in the top cell of the column to the right of the ones you want to hide, and then select **Split** from the **Window** menu. You can then use the scroll bars at the bottom to view the columns you want to see. You can remove the split easily by selecting **Remove Split** from the **Window** menu. (Remember this technique, as you'll use it Access later).

Filtering Subtotals

To produce the invoices at the end of the month, Bill Bright needs to know the totals for each customer excluding those entries that have already been paid. No problem...

Try It Out - Who Hasn't Paid?

1 First display the Subtotal dialog (select Su**b**totals... from the **D**ata menu) and then click **R**emove All to remove any existing subtotals.

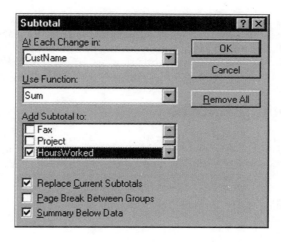

2 Turn on Auto**F**ilter and in the Paid list, select (Blanks) to display just the entries that haven't been paid.

	A	B	C	I	K	L	M	N	O	P
1	Date ▼	CustName ▼	Address ▼	Project ▼	HourlyRa ▼	TotalCharg ▼	TaxRal ▼	TaxDu ▼	TotalDu ▼	Pa ▼
5	5-Jul-95	Education Dept.	The Offices, City Square	Schools Support	$50.00	$1,950.00	0%	$0.00	$1,950.00	
6	16-Jul-95	Education Dept.	The Offices, City Square	Schools Support	$50.00	$550.00	0%	$0.00	$550.00	
7	20-Jun-95	J.R.Higgins	The Market	PC Upgrades	$85.00	$425.00	14%	$59.50	$484.50	
11	30-Jun-95	Major Records	Third Avenue	Catalogue System	$80.00	$1,360.00	13%	$176.80	$1,536.80	
12	18-Jul-95	Martha's Bar	Top Street	Menu Generator	$60.00	$360.00	15%	$54.00	$414.00	
14	26-Jun-95	Miracle Supplies	18th Avenue	Warehouse System	$70.00	$770.00	11%	$84.70	$854.70	
17	20-Jul-95	Union Records	217 Main Street	Catalogue System	$80.00	$2,000.00	13%	$260.00	$2,260.00	

3 Finally, repeat the operation with the Subtotal dialog to display just the totals for the unpaid entries.

	A	B	C	I	K	L	M	N	O	P
1	Date ▾	CustName ▾	Address ▾	Project ▾	HourlyRa ▾	TotalCharg ▾	TaxRal ▾	TaxDu ▾	TotalDu ▾	Pa ▾
5	5-Jul-95	Education Dept.	The Offices, City Square	Schools Support	$50.00	$1,950.00	0%	$0.00	$1,950.00	
6	16-Jul-95	Education Dept.	The Offices, City Square	Schools Support	$50.00	$550.00	0%	$0.00	$550.00	
7		**Education Dept. Total**				$2,500.00		$0.00	$2,500.00	
8	20-Jun-95	J.R.Higgins	The Market	PC Upgrades	$85.00	$425.00	14%	$59.50	$484.50	
9		**J.R.Higgins Total**				$425.00		$59.50	$484.50	
13	30-Jun-95	Major Records	Third Avenue	Catalogue System	$80.00	$1,360.00	13%	$176.80	$1,536.80	
14		**Major Records Total**				$1,360.00		$176.80	$1,536.80	
15	18-Jul-95	Martha's Bar	Top Street	Menu Generator	$60.00	$360.00	15%	$54.00	$414.00	
16		**Martha's Bar Total**				$360.00		$54.00	$414.00	
18	26-Jun-95	Miracle Supplies	18th Avenue	Warehouse System	$70.00	$770.00	11%	$84.70	$854.70	
20		**Miracle Supplies Total**				$770.00		$84.70	$854.70	
22	20-Jul-95	Union Records	217 Main Street	Catalogue System	$80.00	$2,000.00	13%	$260.00	$2,260.00	
23		**Union Records Total**				$2,000.00		$260.00	$2,260.00	
24		**Grand Total**				$7,415.00		$635.00	$8,050.00	

It's now a fairly easy task to prepare the invoices or statements for each customer on a word processor - you have all the information you need at your fingertips. You can even copy entries from the spreadsheet into your word processor using *Ctrl-C* and *Ctrl-V* in the normal way, to save on the typing. All in all, you've got a useful tool for controlling your business.

Updating and Adding Entries

There's still one item on our 'must have' list that we haven't covered yet - updating existing entries and adding new ones. Of course, with a spreadsheet it's easy to go to any cell and edit the contents, or to add another row at the end of the list. However, there is another way to do this.

There is an automatic data entry form in Excel that makes adding and updating entries very easy. Let's have a look at this now.

Try It Out - Entering Data

1 Remove any subtotals and turn off Auto<u>F</u>ilter.

2 Click on any cell within the range of entries and select F<u>o</u>rm from the <u>D</u>ata menu. Excel displays a dialog which contains all the column names and the values from the first row of entries. The calculated values (TotalCharge, TaxDue, and TotalDue) are not text boxes - you can't change the values in these. However, you can freely edit any of the others and the changes will be passed back into the spreadsheet automatically when you click the C<u>l</u>ose button.

3 The Find<u>P</u>rev and Find<u>N</u>ext buttons allow you to move through the entries. You can use the <u>C</u>riteria button to filter the entries to match a certain value for any of the columns and then scroll through only matching entries (this is discussed in more detail in the next section). You can also <u>D</u>elete an entry, or add a <u>N</u>ew one, using the buttons.

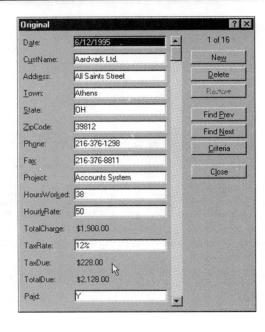

Using More Complex Criteria

We've already seen how to filter entries to show only those that match simple criteria - i.e. those where a particular field is a certain value. In the previous examples we displayed the rows that contained Stocksville in the Town column, or a blank in the Paid column. What happens, though, if you want to be more specific? For instance, how about finding all the projects you worked on after a certain date, or all the projects over a certain value?

You can't do this with the methods we've seen so far, but Excel does have two other methods: Advanced Filter, and the Criteria function we saw in the data form. We'll look at the Advanced Filter first.

Try It Out - Checking Out the Advanced Filter

1 Make sure you've closed the data form and turned off Auto Filter and any Subtotals you may have generated.

2 Place the cursor in any cell within the block of entries and select Filter from the Data menu, then Advanced Filter. Excel highlights the block of data and displays the Advanced Filter dialog.

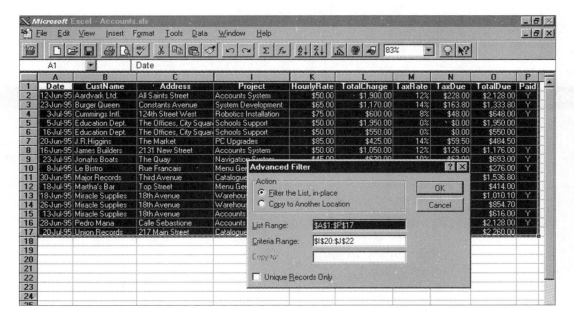

How It Works

This rather complicated dialog contains several controls.

The top two radio buttons allow you to specify the action you want to perform. Excel can either filter the list in place in the same way as it did when we used Auto Filter, or it can copy matching rows to a new location that you specify in the Copy to Another Location box. If you check the bottom radio button, only unique rows will be displayed - in other words if two rows are identical, it will only show one of them.

The remaining two boxes show the list range and the criteria range. The list range is set by default to the block of entries containing the cursor (remember, we placed the cursor in the block first), and the criteria box will probably be empty unless you've used Advanced Filter previously.

Excel automatically checks that the cells around the cursor form a 'list range' - you don't have to explicitly name the range first as you do in some spreadsheet programs.

 If you look on the spreadsheet, above the left hand corner of the grid and the blank square used for selecting the whole spreadsheet, you will probably see the current cell name. If a range of cells is selected, then you would get the name of the left hand cell of the range. Just as each cell has a name, such as A1 or B7, each range can have a name as well. It is possible to name ranges explicitly by highlighting the required area and then typing a name in this box.

Excel checks that each column contains data of similar type, and assumes that the range consists of all the cells up to the first blank row and column. Of course, you can enter a different list range by dragging over the spreadsheet with the mouse or typing in the range of cells or the name if one has already been defined.

Before you can actually apply the filter, you need to set up the criteria range which tells Excel what records you want to see. We'll do that now.

Try It Out - Using the Advanced Filter

We are going set a filter that displays only the rows for Accounts System projects that have a TotalDue amount greater than 1000. To do this we will enter the names of the columns that we want to use in the criteria in an empty row below the block of entries, together with the criteria that's to be applied.

1 Close the Advanced Filter dialog by clicking Cancel.

2 Enter the criteria as shown in the screenshot:

13	18-Jun-95	Miracle Supplies	18th Avenue	Oakland	CA
14	26-Jun-95	Miracle Supplies	18th Avenue	Oakland	CA
15	13-Jul-95	Miracle Supplies	18th Avenue	Oakland	CA
16	28-Jun-95	Pedro Mana	Calle Sebastione	St. Paul	MN
17	20-Jul-95	Union Records	217 Main Street	Tampa	FL
18					
19					
20		**Project**	**TotalDue**		
21		Accounts System	>1000		
22					
23					

3 Now place the cursor in the block of entries to be filtered and open the Advanced Filter dialog again.

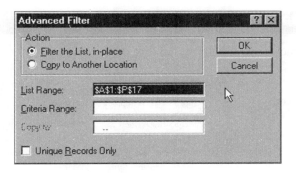

4 Place the cursor in the **C**riteria Range box (delete any value that is already there) and then drag the mouse over the criteria range on the spreadsheet (in the above screenshot this is the range B20:C21). Excel will automatically place the selected range into the dialog.

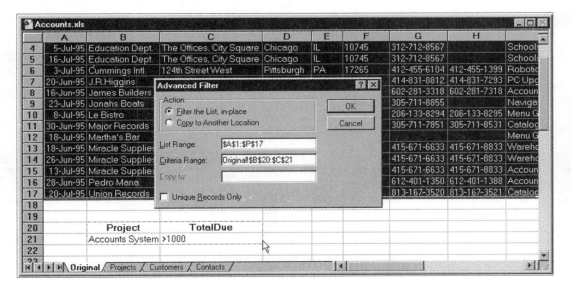

5 Now apply the filter by clicking the OK button.

	I	J	K	L	M	N	O	P
1	Project	HoursWorked	HourlyRate	TotalCharge	TaxRate	TaxDue	TotalDue	Paid
2	Accounts System	38	$50.00	$1,900.00	12%	$228.00	$2,128.00	Y
8	Accounts System	21	$50.00	$1,050.00	12%	$126.00	$1,176.00	Y
16	Accounts System	38	$50.00	$1,900.00	12%	$228.00	$2,128.00	Y
18								
19								

6 To remove the filter and show all the records again, simply select **F**ilter from the **D**ata menu, and then **S**how All.

21

Try It Out - ANDing and ORing

The criteria can be made more complicated by adding extra columns.

1 Add a column for Town and enter Phoenix in the cell below it.

13	18-Jun-95	Miracle Supplies	18th Avenue	Oakland	CA
14	26-Jun-95	Miracle Supplies	18th Avenue	Oakland	CA
15	13-Jul-95	Miracle Supplies	18th Avenue	Oakland	CA
16	28-Jun-95	Pedro Mana	Calle Sebastione	St. Paul	MN
17	20-Jul-95	Union Records	217 Main Street	Tampa	FL
18					
19					
20		**Project**	**TotalDue**	**Town**	
21		Accounts System	>1000	Phoenix	
22					
23					

2 Apply the filter with the new criteria range. Only the rows that match all three criteria will be displayed. In this case, the three criteria you specified are '**AND**ed' together - in other words, the row must match all three conditions before it's displayed (1st condition **AND** 2nd condition **AND** 3rd condition).

	A	B	C	D	I	L	M	N	O	P
1	Date	CustName	Address	Town	Project	TotalCharge	TaxRate	TaxDue	TotalDue	Paid
8	16-Jun-95	James Builders	2131 New Street	Phoenix	Accounts System	$1,050.00	12%	$126.00	$1,176.00	Y
18										
19										
20		Project	TotalDue	Town						
21		Accounts System	>1000	Phoenix						
22										

3 Now place each of the criteria on a different row below the column names and use the whole block as the criteria range.

	A	B	C	D	I
1	Date	CustName	Address	Town	Project
8	16-Jun-95	James Builders	2131 New Street	Phoenix	Accounts System
18					
19					
20		Project	TotalDue	Town	
21		Accounts System			
22			>1000		
23				Phoenix	
24					

4 Apply the filter. In this case, any entry that matches the first condition **OR** the second condition **OR** the third condition will be displayed.

	A	B	C	D	I	L	M	N	O	P
1	Date	CustName	Address	Town	Project	TotalCharge	TaxRate	TaxDue	TotalDue	Paid
2	12-Jun-95	Aardvark Ltd.	All Saints Street	Athens	Accounts System	$1,900.00	12%	$228.00	$2,128.00	Y
3	23-Jun-95	Burger Queen	Constants Avenue	Houston	System Development	$1,170.00	14%	$163.80	$1,333.80	Y
5	5-Jul-95	Education Dept.	The Offices, City Square	Chicago	Schools Support	$1,950.00	0%	$0.00	$1,950.00	
8	16-Jun-95	James Builders	2131 New Street	Phoenix	Accounts System	$1,050.00	12%	$126.00	$1,176.00	Y
11	30-Jun-95	Major Records	Third Avenue	Stocksville	Catalogue System	$1,360.00	13%	$176.80	$1,536.80	
13	18-Jun-95	Miracle Supplies	18th Avenue	Oakland	Warehouse System	$910.00	11%	$100.10	$1,010.10	Y
15	13-Jul-95	Miracle Supplies	18th Avenue	Oakland	Accounts System	$550.00	12%	$66.00	$616.00	Y
16	28-Jun-95	Pedro Mana	Calle Sebastione	St. Paul	Accounts System	$1,900.00	12%	$228.00	$2,128.00	Y
17	20-Jul-95	Union Records	217 Main Street	Tampa	Catalogue System	$2,000.00	13%	$260.00	$2,260.00	
18										
19										
20		Project	TotalDue	Town						
21		Accounts System								
22			>1000							
23				Phoenix						
24										

Note that you don't need to enter an equals sign if the entry is to match the value exactly, and you don't need to use quotation marks for text values. Simply enter the criteria value exactly as it would appear in the cell in the block of entries you're filtering.

Data Form

The other way of filtering records involves the data form we saw earlier.

Try It Out - Filtering Using the Data Form

1 First make sure you have removed the last filter, then click on any cell within the range of entries and select F**o**rm from the **D**ata menu.

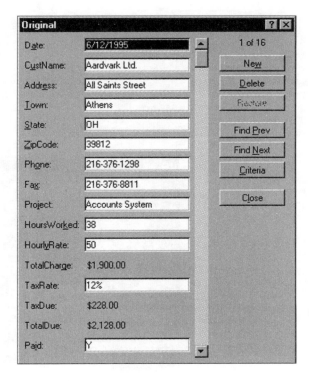

2 Click the **C**riteria button and Excel will display an empty text box for each column in the block of entries, this time including the calculated columns.

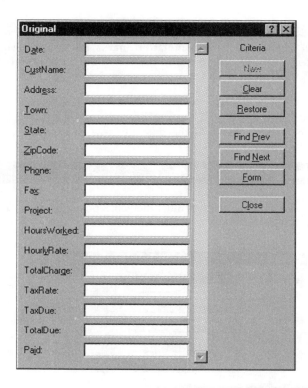

3 Enter Accounts System in the Project box and >1000 in the TotalDue box.

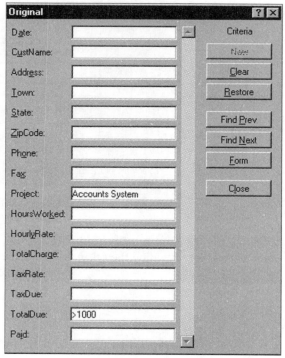

4 Click on the FindNext and FindPrev buttons. Excel will cycle through the entries, showing only those that meet the criteria you've just defined.

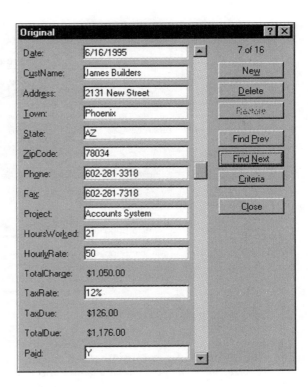

As you can see, when you filter the records using the data form, the criteria are ANDed. Note that Excel is not that helpful if there are no records that match the criteria you specify - it still displays the first record in the table.

So is Excel a Spreadsheet or a Database?

Well, to be honest it's a bit of both - things are never simple are they? What we've seen is a pretty competent way of manipulating a simple set of data entries. And it's true, at first glance, that there are several similarities between a spreadsheet and a database.

By nature, spreadsheets store items in cells, each being part of a row and a column. In database terminology, a block of cells is referred to as a **table**. In our example, each row of the table defines the different data items for one customer, and each column contains the values for one item, but for all the customers. If you are talking about a database, you would refer to each row as a **record**, and each column as a **field**. There are lots of other technical terms related to tables, but you don't need to worry about these for the moment.

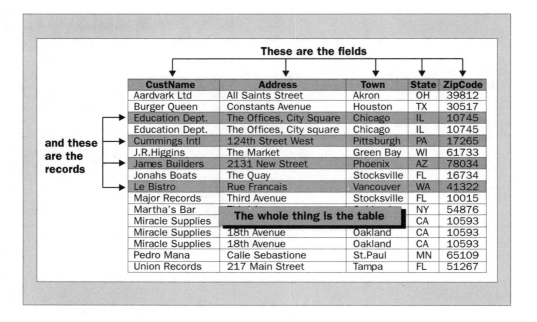

These are the fields

CustName	Address	Town	State	ZipCode
Aardvark Ltd	All Saints Street	Akron	OH	39812
Burger Queen	Constants Avenue	Houston	TX	30517
Education Dept.	The Offices, City Square	Chicago	IL	10745
Education Dept.	The Offices, City square	Chicago	IL	10745
Cummings Intl	124th Street West	Pittsburgh	PA	17265
J.R.Higgins	The Market	Green Bay	WI	61733
James Builders	2131 New Street	Phoenix	AZ	78034
Jonahs Boats	The Quay	Stocksville	FL	16734
Le Bistro	Rue Francais	Vancouver	WA	41322
Major Records	Third Avenue	Stocksville	FL	10015
Martha's Bar			NY	54876
Miracle Supplies			CA	10593
Miracle Supplies	18th Avenue	Oakland	CA	10593
Miracle Supplies	18th Avenue	Oakland	CA	10593
Pedro Mana	Calle Sebastione	St.Paul	MN	65109
Union Records	217 Main Street	Tampa	FL	51267

and these are the records

The whole thing is the table

In the previous examples, we manipulated the data using filters and produced subtotals. In effect, we were *querying* the data to gain information about it. In database terms these operations are referred to as **queries**, and we'll see how a 'true' database implements these in the next few chapters. Finally, we used a form to view and update the entries, and it should come as no surprise to learn that **forms** are the main method of interacting with the data in a database application.

Why You Need Access

OK, you have probably realized what's coming next. Yes - Excel does include several functions to enable you to manipulate data, but no - it's not sophisticated enough to handle all the tasks that you will need to perform if you're dealing with large amounts of data. For instance, imagine if you wanted to store the name of your contact at each company, and possibly include his or her home or mobile phone number? You could easily add extra fields (columns) to the spreadsheet, but as the number of fields increases, the whole thing becomes more and more unwieldy. It would soon become a major task just to fill in the extra fields for each record - and in many cases the phone number would be repeated just as the customer's name and address is. What if you had to include details of two or more contacts for each project - you would end up with even more columns. How many contacts should you allow for? Three, or even four?

One way round this is to split the spreadsheet into two or more smaller tables, placing each on a different page or sheet. You could store the details of each project on one page of the spreadsheet, the customer's address and phone number on another, and the details of your contacts on another. To make sure you know which projects and which contacts belong to each customer, you must include the customer's name in each of these tables. You can see this in the **Accounts** spreadsheet by looking at the sheets named Projects, Customers and Contacts.

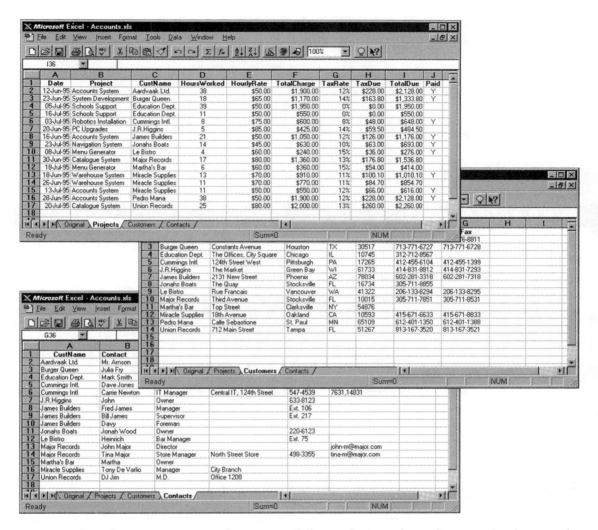

However, the information is now split up over different sheets and you have no simple way of seeing it all in one go. You have to move from one page to another to produce an invoice; if you want to follow up a project, you have to flip back and forth to find the contact's name and number, then match it to the particular project. Remember - the idea is to produce an application that's easy to use! You want to be able to automate your data storage so that eventually you can produce invoices and statements without having to keep switching from page to page and copying data into a word processor.

What would happen if your contact at a company changed? You would have to do a global find and replace for each occurrence of the contact. Also, all changes would then be lost unless you saved the spreadsheet, and a big spreadsheet can take quite a few minutes to save. In Access the updates are made immediately to the database and you don't have five minutes of finger tapping, like you do while you wait for Excel to get back to you.

And imagine how you'd go about getting *real* information from the spreadsheet, such as finding out what percentage of your time was spent on each type of project? Or perhaps your salespeople expect regular printed reports of sales to each customer in their territories. In Excel these types of query would require several complicated steps to effect, and you'd probably end up copying data into a new sheet just to analyze it. That's OK for a one-off inquiry, but it's hardly a profitable use of your time. Yes, Excel can perform some quite complex data analysis, but you're always tied to the spreadsheet background structure of rows and columns - sorting and displaying rows of data can hardly be thought of as sophisticated data manipulation in today's competitive business climate.

That's almost it for this chapter. We are going to move on to Access in the next chapter (patience!), so to leave things nice and tidy, we'll just close down the Excel spreadsheet.

Try It Out - Abandoning Excel

1 Select <u>C</u>lose from the <u>F</u>ile menu.

2 Do not save the changes you have made to the spreadsheet.

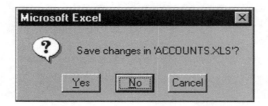

3 While you're at it, you might as well exit Excel altogether. After all, you've a much better tool at hand.

Summary

This chapter has given you an overview of some of the reasons that probably influenced your decision to learn Access. Spreadsheets are all well and good as accounting packages, but when it comes to data storage, their limitations are soon evident. Having hit some of the problems typically encountered when trying to store large amounts of data in a spreadsheet, and perform useful actions on it, you should now have a fairly good idea of what you want from Access, and thus of where this book is going.

In this chapter we have covered:

▶ How to manipulate data in Excel

▶ The limitations of Excel as a data storage medium

▶ Why you need Access

In the next chapter you'll see how you perform the tasks from this chapter in Access itself. It's time to load up your real database application and get down to business.

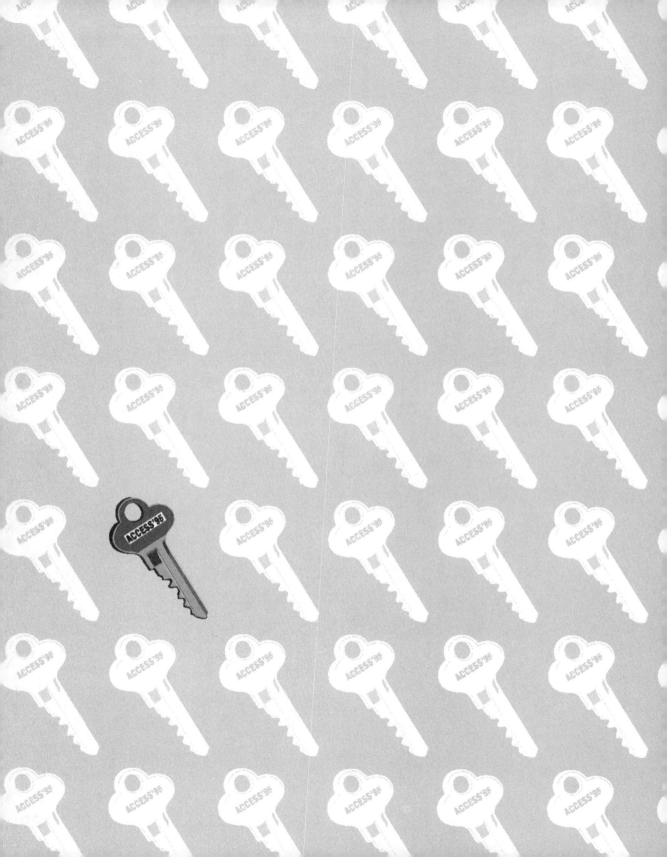

Importing The Spreadsheet Idea Into Access

In this chapter, we'll consider how you can move the Excel spreadsheet that we have just used into Access. This will give us the basis for the database application that we will continue to use throughout the book. In this chapter, we'll be looking at how we can do in Access what we did with Excel in Chapter 1.

We'll be covering:

- Importing Excel data into Access.
- Viewing and manipulating data in Access.
- Sorting, finding and filtering records.
- Viewing data in a form.
- Saving and printing the contents of the database.

So first, how do we get our existing data from Excel into Access...?

Importing Data from an Excel Spreadsheet

As you've seen, there's a limit to what you can do with data in Excel. If you want to be able to extract useful information from a large amount of data, you really need to place this data into a database. Luckily, Access allows you to capture data from a range of different spreadsheet programs, so it's not difficult to move the data we were using in the last chapter from Excel into Access. You must have a database open in Access before you can import data - we'll create a new one for this purpose.

Try It Out - Importing Excel Data into Access

Before we can start work, we have to create a new database. This is because, unlike word processors or spreadsheets, Access can't hold its data in memory. You have to create a database as a file on disk before you can work with it. (In an application like Word or Excel, you would start with a document called Untitled and only save it when you're ready.)

The following Try It Out may look long and complicated, but believe me, Microsoft have made the processes of creating a new database and importing data incredibly easy. They've done this by providing a team of **wizards** to do the hard work for you.

Access wizards are a series of screens provided by Microsoft to help you through some of the more complicated processes. There are wizards to import data, build tables, create reports etc. Wizards are great - you just click a button and the wizard will walk you through the necessary steps for that action. All you have to do is select the option you want at each stage.

So don't be put off by the length of the next example. It's really all just a matter of pointing and clicking.

1 Start Access by double-clicking on its icon, or selecting it from your Windows Start menu. The New Database window opens automatically. Select Blank Database.

You'll notice that when you open the New Database window, Access offers you the option to use the Database Wizard to create the new database. This allows you to select from a wide range of pre-defined database types, from order processing to recipe storage, and then modify it so that all the tables you need are built automatically. However, we're going to import our existing data, and along the way we'll learn how to create our own tables. If you're starting a new database for other uses, you'll find that the Database Wizard can save you time. We'll take a closer look at it later in the chapter.

2 Click OK. Access displays the File New Database dialog. By default, the database will be put in your My Documents folder. It's a good idea to put your databases in a separate folder from Access itself to avoid confusion with the many files that it stores in its own directory. Enter a name for the new database in the File name: box - call it Accounts.

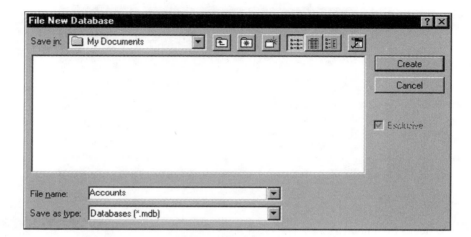

3 Click Create and Access will display the Database window with the name of our new database. The various lists in this window are empty because so far we've only created an empty database.

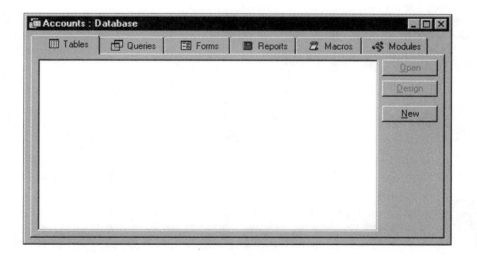

OK, so that's the first stage - creating the database. We can now set about importing our Excel data.

4 Choose the File menu, select Get External Data, and then click Import.

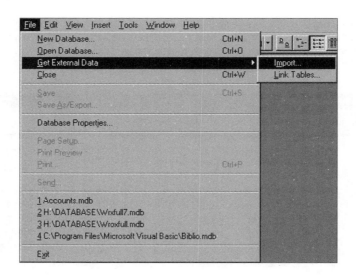

5 Access opens the Import dialog. Change to the BegAcc95 folder (where you installed the sample files from the disk) and select Microsoft Excel (*.xls) in the Files of type: box. The **Accounts** spreadsheet file will be shown in the list above.

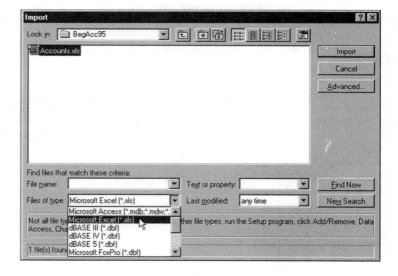

 Your list of file types may differ from those shown here if you've installed extra import filters, or if you changed the defaults when you installed Access. If you can't see all the file types shown here, run **Setup** again and install them from your Access program disks.

6 Select the **Accounts** spreadsheet and click Import. Access starts the Import Spreadsheet Wizard which will guide you through the process of importing the data. The first window allows you to select which parts of the spreadsheet you want to import - remember we used the sheet named Original, but there were others in the spreadsheet. Make sure that Show Worksheets is checked, and the Original sheet is selected. The window below shows the contents of this sheet - you can scroll through it to check that you've got the one you want.

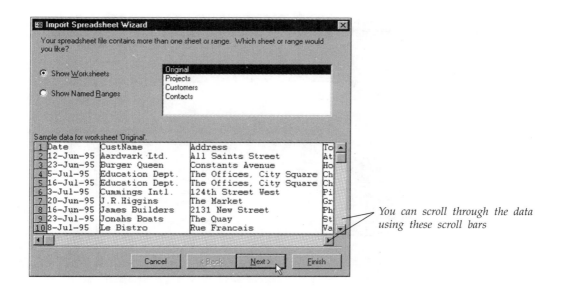

You can scroll through the data using these scroll bars

7 Click **Next>** and the wizard will move on to the next screen. Click the check box to confirm that First Row Contains Column Headings. The column headers that we had in the spreadsheet will then be displayed - Access will use these as the names of the fields in the new table.

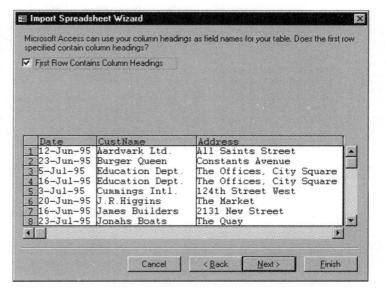

8 Click **Next>** again. This screen enables us to tell Access what type of data is stored in each column, so that it creates the right kind of field in the new table. There's no need to change anything here - just leave all the settings at their defaults.

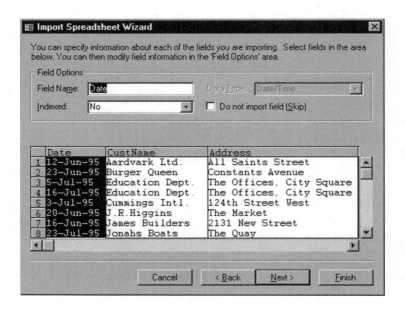

9 Click Next> again and you'll arrive at a window that allows you to specify a primary key. Don't worry about what this is at the moment - we'll reveal all in the next chapter. Just select No Primary Key for the moment and leave it at that.

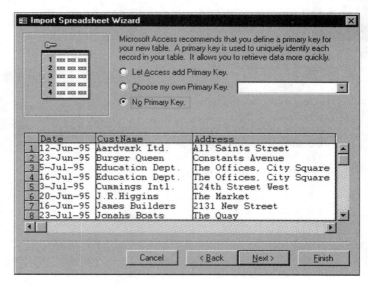

10 Click Next> once again and you'll reach the final screen.

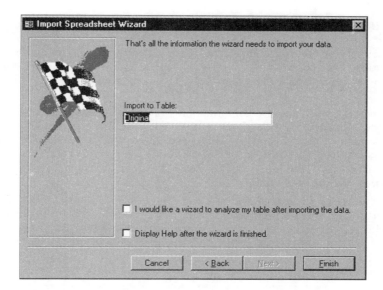

11 The Import Spreadsheet Wizard has now finished gathering information and needs to start importing data from the spreadsheet. To kick this off, just click Finish.

12 Once the import is complete, Access displays a message to tell you so. If there are any problems with the import it will tell you what happened. In our case, though, the data is imported successfully.

13 Click OK and you'll see that the Database window is no longer empty. It now contains a table called Original. You can view the data in the table by selecting it and clicking Open.

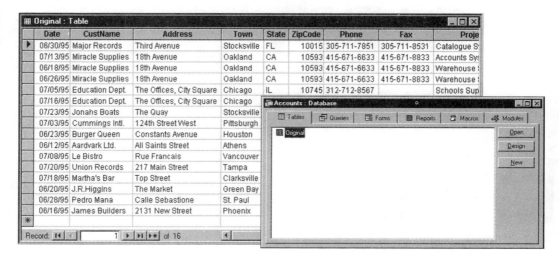

Note that if you saved the changes to your spreadsheet in Chapter 1, then Access will also import the criteria that we added below the table there. If this happens, just delete the extra rows from the top of the table - click on the gray selector bar on the left of the table, drag down to select the rows you want to remove, and press *Delete*. Access will ask you to confirm that you want to delete the records - click **Yes**.

Congratulations. You have now imported information from Excel into Access and created an Access version of the spreadsheet. If you look at the table, you'll see it contains all the information that we looked at in Chapter 1. Before we go any further, let's take a quick look at the main differences between the versions of the data.

Excel Tables Compared to Access Tables

The table in Access looks pretty similar to the Excel one, but if you look closely you'll see a few differences. For a start, there are no row (record) numbers in Access. You can no longer specify data as being in cell B5, or in a range named 'PhoneNumbers'. This may come as a bit of a surprise - especially if you've used other database programs before. We'll come back to this in Part 2.

	Date	CustName	Address	Town	State
▶	06/30/95	Major Records	Third Avenue	Stocksville	FL
	07/13/95	Miracle Supplies	18th Avenue	Oakland	CA
	06/18/95	Miracle Supplies	18th Avenue	Oakland	CA
	06/26/95	Miracle Supplies	18th Avenue	Oakland	CA
	07/05/95	Education Dept.	The Offices, City Square	Chicago	IL
	07/16/95	Education Dept.	The Offices, City Square	Chicago	IL
	07/23/95	Jonahs Boats	The Quay	Stocksville	FL
	07/03/95	Cummings Intl.	124th Street West	Pittsburgh	PA
	06/23/95	Burger Queen	Constants Avenue	Houston	TX
	06/12/95	Aardvark Ltd.	All Saints Street	Athens	OH
	07/08/95	Le Bistro	Rue Francais	Vancouver	WA
	07/20/95	Union Records	217 Main Street	Tampa	FL
	07/18/95	Martha's Bar	Top Street	Clarksville	NY
	06/20/95	J.R.Higgins	The Market	Green Bay	WI
	06/28/95	Pedro Mana	Calle Sebastione	St. Paul	MN
	06/16/95	James Builders	2131 New Street	Phoenix	AZ

Title bar: **Original : Table**

Record: 1 of 16

Current record — points to first record

Record selector

Blank record — ✳

Record navigation controls

The current record is marked with an arrow pointer on its **record selector** (the gray row marker on the left of the row where the row number would be in Excel). A new blank record is always available at the end of the list, and this is marked with an asterisk.

 Although the 'number' of the current record is shown in the record selector at the bottom of the table window, Access doesn't number the records in a table internally. We'll discuss how we refer to and manipulate individual records in Part 2.

At the bottom of the table window are the **record navigation controls**. You can use these to move to the first, last, next or previous record, or you can click on the record number and type in a new value to move to that record. There's also a <u>G</u>o To command on Access's <u>E</u>dit menu that you can use to move to a different record.

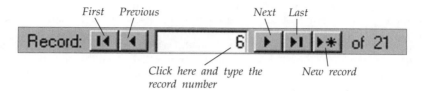

Now close this window down by clicking on the cross in the top right corner and you're left with the Database window.

The Database Window

The Database window is Access's nerve center. You'll be using this window constantly throughout your work with Access, selecting and creating new **objects** as you work with the database. By objects, we mean the various components that go to make up the database, such as tables, queries and forms.

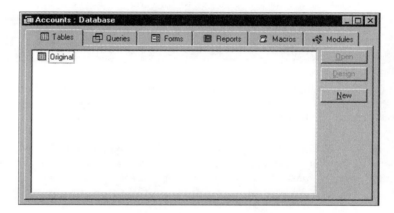

You use the tabs along the top to select each of the different types of object. The window can be re-sized so that it doesn't cover so much of the screen. In fact, once you become familiar with it, you can shrink it down until only the icons on the page tabs are visible. This makes working with the various objects, and switching between them, much easier.

As the Database window is so integral to what you do with Access, it's useful to be able to get to it quickly (you'll soon find that the window gets hidden under the mass of other windows you have open while you're working). This is where the toolbar comes in useful. If the Database window is minimized or hidden by other windows, you can always bring it to the front, and restore all other maximized windows to their default size, by clicking the Database window button on the toolbar. Alternatively, you can press the *F11* key, which can be used even if the Database window button is unavailable.

The toolbar buttons provide a lot of short cuts in Access, so it's well worth spending a couple of minutes familiarizing yourself with them. We'll have a quick look at them now.

Access Toolbars

There are often several different ways of carrying out an action in Access - you can use the normal menus at the top of the window, or the short-cut menus that appear when you click with the right mouse button on part of a window. However, the quickest way is to use the buttons on the toolbar. These change depending on what you're currently doing - as in other applications, there are different toolbars for each type of object (tables, queries etc).

Now that you have closed the table and just have the Database window on view, what you can see is the Database toolbar. This allows you to do things like create a new database, open an existing one, etc. It also has buttons for more advanced actions - we'll discuss these as we cover the different processes later in the book.

 FYI   Don't worry about remembering what all the different buttons do. Microsoft has made life easy by providing tooltips - text boxes that appear when you point the cursor at a button for a couple of seconds to remind you what each one does.

When you open up a table, the toolbar changes to the Table Datasheet toolbar. This has options for manipulating data.

There are several other toolbars which you will meet as you work with different objects. We're not going to show them all here. What's important is that you understand that there are different options available, depending on what you're doing at the time.

 FYI   Access toolbars can be hidden. If you can't see the toolbar, go to the **View** menu and select **Toolbars**. In the dialog that appears, look for the toolbar you want (e.g. **Table Datasheet**) and make sure it's marked with a tick. If not, click on it and it will appear, then click **Close**.

Datasheet View and Design View

In Access you can swap between **datasheet view** and **design view**. This may seem confusing at first, but it's actually quite intuitive. Datasheet view, as the name suggests, is where you view your sheet of data, i.e. where you can look at the table as a whole. In this view you can also create new records. Design view, on the other hand, is (surprisingly) where you design the table and create new fields and set the format and data types for each field. The terms will very soon be second nature to you - so don't let them worry you right now.

The first button on the Table Datasheet toolbar is the Select View button. This opens a list where you can toggle between the different views of an object. So, in Table Datasheet view, the button will switch to Table Design view, and in Table Design view, it enables you to switch to Table Datasheet view. We'll be using this a great deal in the next chapters.

Manipulating Data in Access

Remember the tasks we carried out on the data in Excel? Let's see if we can now do the same using our new Access database. As in Chapter 1, we want to be able to:

▶ Update the records and add new ones.

▶ Sort the records.

▶ Find a particular record.

▶ Filter the records to display only the relevant ones.

Updating and Adding Records

Updating and adding records is simple - Access behaves much like a spreadsheet in this respect.

Try It Out - Updating Records

1 Open up the table by selecting the Original table and clicking on Open.

2 Move the cursor to the record for Union Records (record number 12 if you're using the record navigation controls at the bottom of the window).

	6/12/95	Aardvark Ltd.	All Saints Stree	Athens	OH
	7/8/95	Le Bistro	Rue Francais	Vancouver	WA
▶	7/20/95	Union Records	217 Main Street	Tampa	FL
	7/18/95	Martha's Bar	Top Street	Clarksville	NY
	6/20/95	J.R.Higgins	The Market	Green Bay	WI
	6/28/95	Pedro Mana	Calle Sebastion	St. Paul	MN
	6/16/95	James Builders	2131 New Stree	Phoenix	AZ

3 The address is wrong. Change the street number from 217 to 712. Just click in the right cell and edit the number in the usual way (using *Backspace*, *Delete* etc)

Original : Table

	Date	CustName	Address	Town	State	ZipCode	Phone
	06/30/95	Major Records	Third Avenue	Stocksville	FL	10015	305-711-7851
	07/13/95	Miracle Supplies	18th Avenue	Oakland	CA	10593	415-671-6633
	06/18/95	Miracle Supplies	18th Avenue	Oakland	CA	10593	415-671-6633
	06/26/95	Miracle Supplies	18th Avenue	Oakland	CA	10593	415-671-6633
	07/05/95	Education Dept.	The Offices, City Square	Chicago	IL	10745	312-712-8567
	07/16/95	Education Dept.	The Offices, City Square	Chicago	IL	10745	312-712-8567
	07/23/95	Jonahs Boats	The Quay	Stocksville	FL	16734	305-711-8855
	07/03/95	Cummings Intl.	124th Street West	Pittsburgh	PA	17265	412-455-6104
	06/23/95	Burger Queen	Constants Avenue	Houston	TX	30517	713-771-6727
	06/12/95	Aardvark Ltd.	All Saints Street	Athens	OH	39812	216-376-1298
	07/08/95	Le Bistro	Rue Francais	Vancouver	WA	41322	206-133-8294
✎	07/20/95	Union Records	712│Main Street	Tampa	FL	51267	813-167-3520
	07/18/95	Martha's Bar	Top Street	Clarksville	NY	54876	
	06/20/95	J.R.Higgins	The Market	Green Bay	WI	61733	414-831-8812
	06/28/95	Pedro Mana	Calle Sebastione	St. Paul	MN	65109	612-401-1350
	06/16/95	James Builders	2131 New Street	Phoenix	AZ	78034	602-281-3318
*							

Record: ◄◄ ◄ [12] ► ►► ►* of 16

41

4 To save the changes, just move to another record.

Editing Fields

There is more than one way of editing the contents of the field. You can:

▶ Double-click on a word or drag the mouse over any part of the existing field to highlight a part of it, then amend the contents.

▶ Move the cursor to the left-hand edge of a field until it changes to a thick cross shape, then click to highlight all of the field and type in the new value.

▶ Click anywhere in a field and press *F2* to highlight the whole field, then type in the new value.

▶ Click in the field and edit in the normal way (using the *BackSpace* or *Delete* keys, etc.).

Once you start to edit a record, the record selector icon changes from an arrow to a pencil to indicate that the record has been changed, but not saved. You can edit several fields in the same record while the pencil is displayed, but the changes aren't permanent until the whole record is saved.

Indicates the current record   *Indicates an edited record which*   *Indicates a blank new record,*
                                   has not yet been saved   *ready for editing*

If you move to another field in the record and press *Escape* while the pencil marker is shown, all the fields will be returned to their last saved values - all changes will be abandoned. If you press *Escape* after editing a field, but before you move from that field, only the changes in that field will be abandoned. To abandon all changes in the record, press *Escape* again.

To save changes to a record, you just have to move to another record or close the table window. You can save the current record explicitly by selecting Save Rec**o**rd from the **R**ecords menu, or by using the shortcut key combination *Shift + Enter*. Once you have saved changes to a record, they are automatically saved to disk.

Adding and Deleting Records

Adding and deleting records in an Access database is equally easy - as you will see right away.

Try It Out - Adding and Deleting Records

You'll recall that a new empty record is always present at the end of the table, indicated by an asterisk.

1 Move to this empty record and type in a date. As soon as you start to type, Access changes the asterisk to a pencil to show the record is being changed, and adds a new blank record below.

7/18/95	Martha's Bar	Top Street	Clarksville
6/20/95	J.R.Higgins	The Market	Green Bay
6/28/95	Pedro Mana	Calle Sebastione	St. Paul
6/16/95	James Builders	2131 New Street	Phoenix
8/15/95			

2 Fill in some of the other fields either by typing in an entry or by using *Ctrl-C* and *Ctrl-V* (the shortcuts for copy and paste) to copy the contents of another field to the new record.

 FYI Notice that Access is a little more choosy than Excel when copying and pasting blocks of fields in one go. You may get a warning that you're editing more than one record, and be asked to confirm the changes.

3 Try creating a duplicate record - select a whole record by clicking the record selector (just as you would use the row selector in Excel) and then copy it to the blank record at the end of the table.

Click here to select the whole record

7/18/95	Martha's Bar	Top Street	Clarksville
6/20/95	J.R.Higgins	The Market	Green Bay
6/28/95	Pedro Mana	Calle Sebastione	St. Paul
6/16/95	James Builders	2131 New Street	Phoenix
8/15/95	James Builders		

4 The changes you made will have been saved to the database when you moved to a different record. To leave the database in its original state, select any new records you have created and press *Delete* - Access will ask you to confirm the operation before you lose them for good.

So now you've seen how to update, add and delete records. The next step is to see how you can control the way they're displayed...

Sorting, Finding and Filtering Records

Access provides two types of sort and filter method. This is designed to make it easier for users switching to Access from Excel - the simple methods are very similar to those we saw in Chapter 1 when we used Excel to handle our data. The advanced sort and filter methods, however, provide much more flexibility and, in the main, it's these we'll be concentrating on. But first, we'll take a look at the simple methods.

Simple Record Sorting

In Access, it's very easy to do a simple sort on a group of records. So easy in fact, that all it requires is two clicks of the mouse.

Try It Out - Simple Sorting

We'll sort the table into alphabetical order by customer.

1 Place the insertion point (cursor) anywhere in the CustName column.

2 Click the Sort Ascending button on the toolbar (or select Sort from the Records menu and then click Ascending). You can also right-click on a field and select Sort Ascending from the short-cut menu.

3 To sort into descending order, use the Sort Descending button, the Descending option from the Sort menu, or right-click and select Sort Descending - it's as easy as that.

Sorting by more than one column, as we did with Excel, is a little more complicated. We use filters for this.

Simple Record Filters

Access filters account for three toolbar buttons. There are also matching entries on the Records menu: Filter By Selection, Filter By Form, and Apply Filter/Sort. You can also select these options from the short-cut menu by right-clicking on the table.

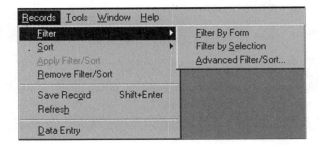

Filter By Selection uses any entries in the table that you've selected and shows only the records that have the same values in these fields. Filter By Form displays a grid of drop-down list boxes where you can select from existing entries in each field, or enter a criteria, to define which records will be shown. We'll try out both of these methods.

Try It Out - Filtering by Selection

1 If it's not already open, open the Original table by selecting it in the Database window and clicking the Open button.

2 We want to show only records for customers in California and New York. However, we can only select adjacent fields in the table. Click in the CustName field and click the Sort Descending button to sort the records. When we do this sort, the two records we want end up next to each other. This is by coincidence rather than by design (If this descending sort hadn't moved the records next to each other, we'd have been forced to sort by state and use AZ (Arizona) and CA (California) as the states for the filter).

3 Move the cursor over the left-hand edge of the State field (CA) of the record for Miracle Supplies until it changes to a thick cross shape. Click to select this field, then drag down to include the NY entry for Martha's Bar.

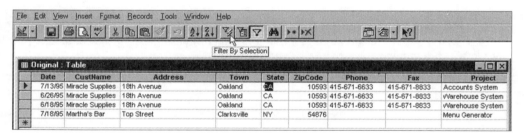

4 Click the Filter By Selection button on the toolbar, or select Filter from the Records menu and click Filter By Selection. Access displays only records which have the selected values, i.e. CA or NY, in the State field.

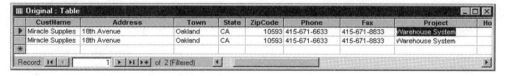

5 Now narrow the records down further by applying another filter to the result of the first. In the Project field, select an entry for Warehouse System by clicking at the left of the field, then click the Filter By Selection button again. Now only 2 of the 4 records are shown.

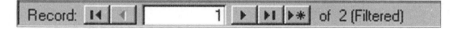

6 The record navigation controls also show you that a filter is applied.

7 To remove the filter, you just need to click one button. When a filter is applied, the Apply Filter button is shown depressed. If you place the cursor over this button, the tooltip shows Remove Filter. So this button is a toggle - just click it again to remove the filter. Alternatively, you can right-click and select Remove Filter/Sort from the short-cut menu that appears.

So filtering by selection involves highlighting the entries that you want to match in the displayed records. Filtering by form is a bit more flexible. Let's look at this method now.

Try It Out - Filtering by Form

1 With the table still open, click the Filter By Form button on the toolbar, or select Filter from the Records menu and click Filter By Form. You don't need to select any data in the table first - this method is similar to the AutoFilter we used in Excel.

Date	CustName	Address	Town	State	ZipCode	Phone
				"CA" Or		

Original: Filter by Form

2 The grid contains the filter from the last example. Click the Clear Grid button on the toolbar to clear it. This removes all the selected entries from the grid - including those lurking unseen off the edge of the screen window.

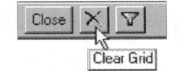

3 Now click in the State field to display its drop-down list box button. Click this button and select the entry for CA. Access will place this entry into the grid. Then go to the Project field and select Warehouse System.

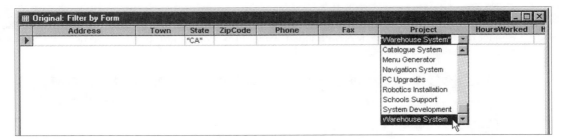

4 Click the Apply Filter button. Access will display only the records that meet these conditions - i.e. ones that have a customer in California who purchased a Warehouse System.

Date	CustName	Address	Town	State	ZipCode	Phone	Fax	Project
8/26/95	Miracle Supplies	18th Avenue	Oakland	CA	10593	415-671-6633	415-671-8833	Warehouse System
6/18/95	Miracle Supplies	18th Avenue	Oakland	CA	10593	415-671-6633	415-671-8833	Warehouse System

Original : Table

ANDs and ORs

If we filter by form, there are extra features that we can use. You'll remember that in Excel in Chapter 1, we were able to specify whether both condition A **AND** condition B should be met, or whether either condition A **OR** condition B should be met. The example above **AND**s the two conditions together - the record must contain CA **AND** Warehouse System. It won't surprise you, though, to learn that you can also **OR** in Access.

Try It Out - ORing in Access

1 Remove the above filter by clicking the Remove Filter button on the toolbar, or selecting Remove Filter/Sort from the Records menu. Then click Filter By Form to open the Filter window.

2 Click the Clear Grid button on the toolbar to clear the previous filter.

3 Now look at the bottom of the window. There's one tab marked Look for and other marked Or. With the Look for tab selected, click in the State field and select CA.

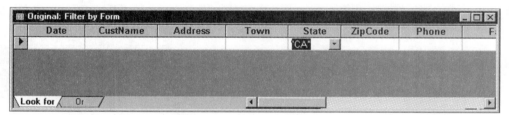

4 Then click the Or tab and select Warehouse System.

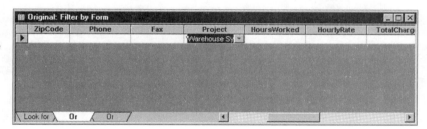

5 Finally click Apply Filter again. Access now shows all records that have either CA as the State **OR** Warehouse System as the Project.

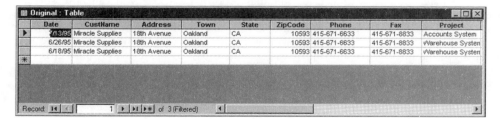

Filtering with Expressions

As well as selecting existing items from drop-down lists for a filter, we can also enter **expressions**. This means that, as in Excel, we can use comparisons to determine which records are displayed. Let's try this out.

Try It Out - Using Expressions

In this example we'll display only those projects that have a TotalCharge of more than $1000.

1 Click the Filter By Form and Clear Grid buttons to remove the current filter.

2 Go to the TotalCharge field and, instead of selecting an existing value, type in >1000.

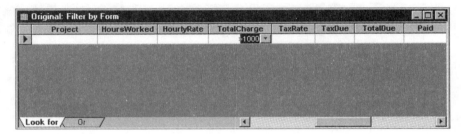

3 Click the Apply Filter button to display the result - only the projects where the total charge is greater than $1000 are shown.

Project	HoursWorked	HourlyRate	TotalCharge	TaxRate	TaxDue	TotalDue	Paid
Catalogue System	25	$80.00	$2,000.00	0.13	$260.00	$2,260.00	
Accounts System	38	$50.00	$1,900.00	0.12	$228.00	$2,128.00	Y
Catalogue System	17	$80.00	$1,360.00	0.13	$176.80	$1,536.80	
Accounts System	21	$50.00	$1,050.00	0.12	$126.00	$1,176.00	Y
Schools Support	39	$50.00	$1,950.00	0	$0.00	$1,950.00	
System Development	18	$65.00	$1,170.00	0.14	$163.80	$1,333.80	Y
Accounts System	38	$50.00	$1,900.00	0.12	$228.00	$2,128.00	Y

Record: 1 of 7 (Filtered)

This about covers it for the simpler filtering and sorting methods that Access provides. It's now time to look at the more advanced methods.

Advanced Sorting and Filtering Methods

Advanced Filter/Sort is, in effect, just another type of filter, but you can both sort and filter with it in one go. It uses a different window to specify the criteria and sort order and has a great deal more flexibility and power than the simpler methods we've been using which, after all, offered no real advantage over those we found in Excel. Once you've learnt how to use the advanced techniques, it's really much easier than trying to achieve the same effect using the simple methods. So fasten your seat belt, hold onto your hats, and we'll unleash the power of Access' Advanced Filter/Sort dialog.

Advanced Sorting

We'll start by looking at how to sort records using the Advanced Filter/Sort option. As you'll see, this offers us all the features that we had in Excel, together with even more flexibility.

Try It Out - Advanced Record Sorting

We'll kick off by sorting the records by more than one field. We want to sort first by project type and then by customer.

1   First remove any filters that have been applied to the table by clicking on the Remove Filter button on the toolbar or by selecting Remove Filter/Sort from the Records menu.

2   Select Filter from the Records menu and click Advanced Filter/Sort. The Filter window appears.

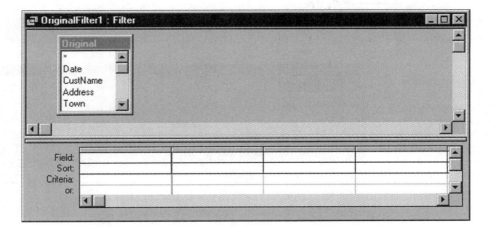

3   The information from the last criteria that was applied might still be present in the Advanced Filter/Sort window, so to clear all the current fields and criteria from the Advanced Filter/Sort window just click the Clear Grid toolbar button.

4   Click on Project in the list of fields that are at the top of the Filter window, and drag it down to the first box (labeled Field:) in the grid in the lower half of the window. The cursor will change shape as you do so.

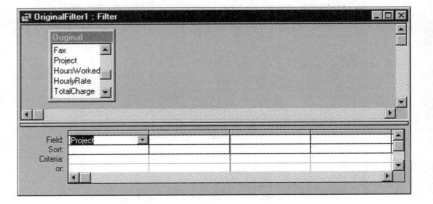

5 Now click in the Sort box underneath the Field box and select Ascending from the drop-down list.

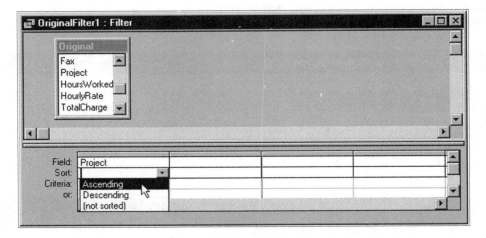

6 Drag the CustName field into the second Field box and set its Sort order to Ascending. This will sort the records by project type then by customer name.

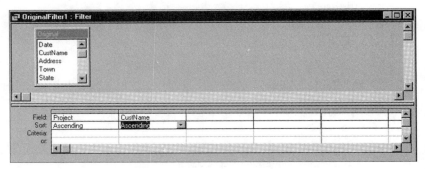

7 Finally, apply the filter by clicking the Apply Filter button on the toolbar, or by selecting Apply Filter/Sort from the Filter menu.

CustName	Address	Town	State	ZipCode	Phone	Fax	Project
Aardvark Ltd.	All Saints Street	Athens	OH	39812	216-376-1298	216-376-8811	Accounts System
James Builders	2131 New Street	Phoenix	AZ	78034	602-281-3318	602-281-7318	Accounts System
Miracle Supplies	18th Avenue	Oakland	CA	10593	415-671-6633	415-671-8833	Accounts System
Pedro Mana	Calle Sebastione	St. Paul	MN	65109	612-401-1350	612-401-1388	Accounts System
Major Records	Third Avenue	Stocksville	FL	10015	305-711-7851	305-711-8531	Catalogue System
Union Records	712 Main Street	Tampa	FL	51267	813-167-3520	813-167-3521	Catalogue System
Le Bistro	Rue Francais	Vancouver	WA	41322	206-133-8294	206-133-8295	Menu Generator
Martha's Bar	Top Street	Clarksville	NY	54876			Menu Generator
Jonahs Boats	The Quay	Stocksville	FL	16734	305-711-8855		Navigation System
J.R.Higgins	The Market	Green Bay	WI	61733	414-831-8812	414-831-7293	PC Upgrades
Cummings Intl.	124th Street West	Pittsburgh	PA	17265	412-455-6104	412-455-1399	Robotics Installation
Education Dept.	The Offices, City Square	Chicago	IL	10745	312-712-8567		Schools Support
Education Dept.	The Offices, City Square	Chicago	IL	10745	312-712-8567		Schools Support
Burger Queen	Constants Avenue	Houston	TX	30517	713-771-6727	713-771-6728	System Development
Miracle Supplies	18th Avenue	Oakland	CA	10593	415-671-6633	415-671-8833	Warehouse System
Miracle Supplies	18th Avenue	Oakland	CA	10593	415-671-6633	415-671-8833	Warehouse System

Record: I◄ ◄ 1 ► ►I ►* of 16 (Filtered)

Note that Access lets you enter up to ten fields in the grid when sorting records, rather than limiting you to three like Excel does.

Changing the Sort Preferences

When you sort records using the Filter grid, Access first sorts on the leftmost field, then the next one, moving from left to right. You can change which field is sorted first by clicking on the gray selector button at the top of the grid to highlight that column, then dragging it to another position. As you drag it, a thick black line shows where the field column you've selected will be placed. Also, the mouse pointer will change shape when you drag a column.

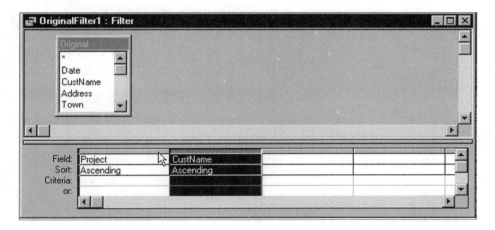

To delete a column from the grid, you just click on the gray selector button and press *Delete*.

Customizing the Toolbar

As it stands, using Advanced Filter/Sort is a bit more hassle than the other methods we've seen because we have to use the menu command rather than a toolbar button to open the window and edit the filter. The existing toolbar buttons only work for the simple filter and sort methods. However, Access allows us to customize the toolbars, so before we go any further we'll add a new button to the Table Datasheet toolbar to make working with advanced filters a bit easier.

Try It Out - Customizing the Table Datasheet Toolbar

1 Select Toolbars from the View menu. Access opens the Toolbars dialog showing which toolbar(s) are currently visible. Make sure you have Table Datasheet ticked, then click the Customize... button.

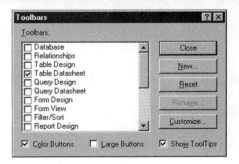

2 The Customize Toolbars dialog appears showing a list of different 'task types', called Categories. Select the Records category. The list of available buttons changes to show those for tasks connected with manipulating records.

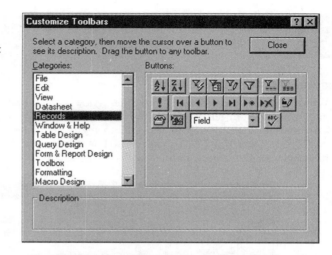

3 The one we want is Advanced Filter/ Sort. Click on it and drag it onto the existing toolbar at the top of the window, dropping it next to the Apply Filter button.

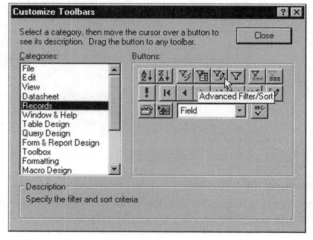

4 You can move the buttons about, and create spaces between them, while the Customize Toolbars window is open. Once you're happy with the layout, select Close.

5 Our new button will now carry out the Records | Filter | Advanced Filter/Sort menu command automatically.

So then, we've got the toolbar set up - let's try out an advanced filter.

Advanced Filtering

So far we've only used Advanced Filter/Sort to sort the records. As you'll no doubt have guessed, though, you use the same dialog to filter the records. All you need to do is enter the criteria into the grid in a similar way to the Advanced Filter we used in Excel. And, of course, you can sort the records that match the criteria as well.

Try It Out - Advanced Record Filters

1 Remove all filters and then open the Advanced Filter/Sort window using our new toolbar button.

2 Enter criteria into the grid on the Filter window as shown below:

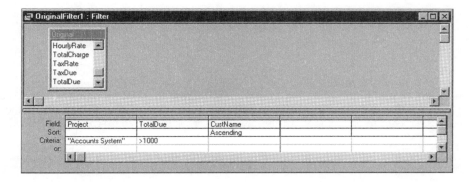

3 Click on the Apply Filter button. Access will display a list of the records that match the criteria. Since we specified Ascending sort order for the customers name, the records appear in that order.

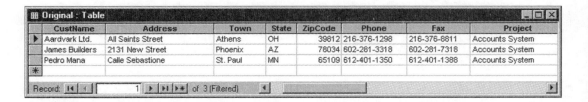

CustName	Address	Town	State	ZipCode	Phone	Fax	Project
Aardvark Ltd.	All Saints Street	Athens	OH	39812	216-376-1298	216-376-8811	Accounts System
James Builders	2131 New Street	Phoenix	AZ	78034	602-281-3318	602-281-7318	Accounts System
Pedro Mana	Calle Sebastione	St. Paul	MN	65109	612-401-1350	612-401-1388	Accounts System

Record: 1 of 3 (Filtered)

FYI You'll notice that the Access filter dialog behaves differently to Excel when entering text values for **Criteria**. In Access you must enclose text in quotation marks, though it will normally recognize that you're entering text and add them for you. If you enter a date, you'll see that Access encloses it in # (hash) symbols. Both quotes and hash symbols are required to meet the more stringent syntax rules of Access - we'll see more of this later. In the meantime, it's good practice to get used to entering the quotation marks and hash symbols as you type the values - it'll save confusion as we deal with more complex criteria values in later chapters. If you're not in the USA, you should check that your computer is using European date formats. If in doubt, you can type **#13/6/95#** or **#13 june#** and Access will recognize either as a date.

Using AND and OR with Advanced Filters

It's also possible to use advanced filters in conjunction with the Boolean operators **AND** and **OR**. This allows you to specify quite complex criteria.

Try It Out - Advanced Filters with Boolean Operators

Access makes even complicated criteria easy to deal with, as you will see here. We are going to look for Accounts System projects worth more than 1000 or Warehouse Systems worth more than 500 or any work we did in Stocksville, and then sort the results by date. Sounds complicated? Not at all!

1 Start off by removing all filters.

2 Click on our new Advanced Filter/Sort button on the Toolbar to open the Filter window.

3 Change the criteria in the grid to that shown below. Criteria on the same row must all be matched by a record if it is to be displayed. If you place criteria on different rows, only one of them has to be true for the record to be included. (If the or: line isn't visible on your screen, just extend the window).

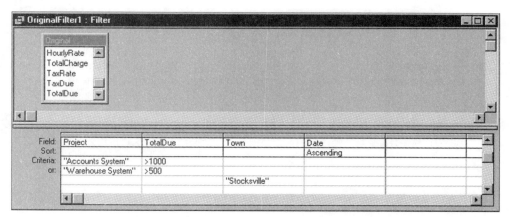

4 Click on the Apply Filter button. Again Access will display a list of the matching records only. This time we have specified Ascending sort order for the Date field, so the records appear in that order.

	Date	CustName	Address	Town	Project	TotalDue
	6/12/95	Aardvark Ltd.	All Saints Street	Athens	Accounts System	$2,128.00
	6/16/95	James Builders	2131 New Street	Phoenix	Accounts System	$1,176.00
	6/18/95	Miracle Supplies	18th Avenue	Oakland	Warehouse System	$1,010.10
	6/26/95	Miracle Supplies	18th Avenue	Oakland	Warehouse System	$854.70
	6/28/95	Pedro Mana	Calle Sebastione	St. Paul	Accounts System	$2,128.00
	6/30/95	Major Records	Third Avenue	Stocksville	Catalogue System	$1,536.80
▶	7/23/95	Jonahs Boats	The Quay	Stocksville	Navigation System	$693.00

Record: ◄ ◄ 7 ► ►I ►* of 7 (Filtered)

How It Works

In this case you can see that a record must have Accounts System for the Project **AND** a TotalDue greater than 1000 to pass the test in the first (Criteria) row. Similarly it must have Warehouse System for the Project **AND** a TotalDue greater than 500 to pass the test in the second (Or) row. In the third row it only needs to have Stocksville as the Town to pass.

A record will, therefore, be included if it passes the tests in the first row **OR** the second row **OR** the third row, giving us the result we need.

When you select **Remove Filter/Sort**, or click the **Remove Filter** button, the current filter is removed from the records, but Access remembers it. You can re-apply the same filter by clicking the **Apply Filter** button again, or change it by clicking our new **Advanced Filter/Sort** button.

So Access provides a very powerful tool for both sorting and filtering records. You'd need to break down the operation into several steps to achieve the same effect in Excel - creating an Advanced Filter and using the Sort functions separately.

Viewing Data in a Form

This seems like a good point to sneak a quick preview of an Access **form**. After all, Excel created one for us, so it's only fair to give Access a chance as well. We'll be covering forms in much more depth in Chapter 7, so we'll skip through this part fairly quickly.

Try It Out - Creating a Form

In this example we'll be creating a new object (the form) which helps you to manipulate the information contained within the table. This object is actually based on the table - Access uses the table's field names to create the various boxes on the form.

1 Start off in the usual way by removing all filters from the table. The table must be open before you can create a form. If you have made any changes to the table, you will be prompted to save the changes when you create the new form.

2 In the toolbar, click the down arrow button part of the New Object selector button. The list that appears shows the objects that you can create - click on AutoForm.

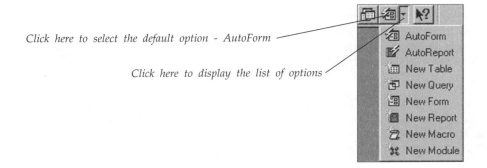

Click here to select the default option - AutoForm

Click here to display the list of options

FYI   AutoForm is the default option, so you could actually click on the button directly to
select it.

3   Access asks you whether
you want to save the
table. Click Yes.

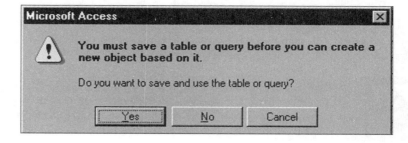

Microsoft Access

⚠ **You must save a table or query before you can create a
new object based on it.**

Do you want to save and use the table or query?

[Yes]   [No]   [Cancel]

4   Access now goes away and creates the new form. Although the layout of the fields is a little
different, it's really just like the one we used in Excel.

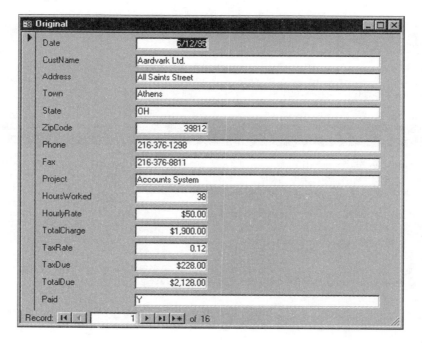

5   You can save the new form by clicking the Save button on the toolbar - you will be
prompted for a name. You needn't bother saving the form at the moment, though.

FYI   You'll notice that the fields that were calculated in Excel (and not shown as text boxes
there) are shown as text boxes in Access. This is because, when we imported the data,
Access converted the Excel formulas to their respective answers. This is one problem
we're going to have to fix later on, as we might actually want the formulas rather than
the answers.

56

Manipulating Data in a Form

The Access form doesn't have the selection of buttons that Excel has, but that doesn't mean it's any less powerful. At the bottom of the window are the now-familiar record navigation controls that enable us to move from record to record. (You can also use menu commands to move between records - select Go To from the Records menu, then select from First, Last, Next, Previous and New.)

Also, the toolbar still has the Sort and Filter buttons - you can sort the records by clicking on a field in the form and clicking the Sort Ascending or Sort Descending buttons on the toolbar. You can also filter the records using the Advanced Filter/Sort dialog just as you did in Table view. The form will then only display matching records and will show them in the order you specify.

Editing Records in a Form

You can, of course, edit records in a form simply by changing the contents of the text boxes (as you did with Excel's data form).

To add a new record, you would just click on the New Record button on the toolbar. You would then be transported to the new blank record that Access always makes available at the end of the table, where you can type in values. You move between fields using the mouse, arrow keys or the *Tab* key. Play around with the form so that you feel comfortable with it, but we recommend you don't save any changes for the moment so that we continue to work with the same data. Access will ask whether you want to save the form when you close it down - just click No.

You've now seen that you can transfer a spreadsheet quickly and efficiently over to Access and perform all the functions on the Access database version of the spreadsheet that you could with Excel. You may recall that when we imported the Excel spreadsheet into Access at the beginning of this chapter, the very first thing we did was to create a blank database file. There was another option, however, that allowed you to create a database from scratch. This was the Database Wizard. Close any forms you have open, then close the database itself by clicking the Close button in the top right of the Database window. We'll go back to where we started in this chapter, and give Database Wizard a try...

Using the Database Wizard

Access contains many **wizards** which are small programs designed to help you achieve complicated or repetitive tasks more easily. Amongst these is Database Wizard. This appears as an option in the New Database window when you first start Access. We'll try it out briefly now so that you have an idea of what it can accomplish.

Try It Out - Creating a New Database with Database Wizard

1 Select New Database from the File menu. If you were just starting up Access, you would select Database Wizard in the first window that appears and click OK.

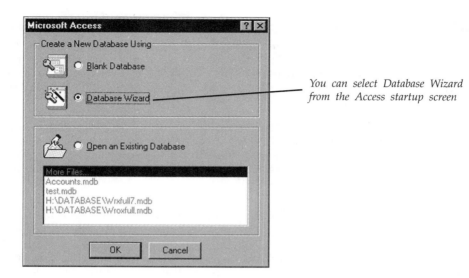

You can select Database Wizard from the Access startup screen

2 Access displays a window with two tabs. The General page contains the **Blank Database** option (which we used earlier), and any templates you may have created. Click on the **Databases** tab to see the different types of database that Database Wizard can create for you. Select the **Book Collection** database.

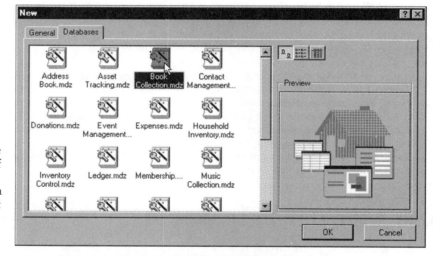

3 Click OK. Next you have to specify a name and folder for the database. Database Wizard suggests **Book Collection1** - leave this as it is, but change the folder if you want.

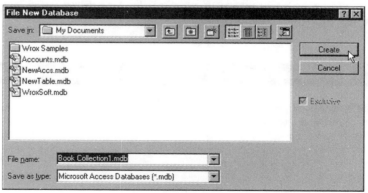

4 Click the **Create** button. The
Database Wizard creates the new
database on disk, opens an empty
Database window, and then
shows you the types of
information it will store.

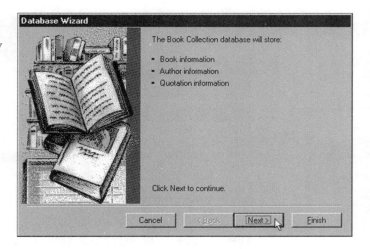

5 Click Next and you get
a list of the fields in
each table, plus the
opportunity to add
extra ones. You can also
include sample data -
make sure the **Yes,
include sample data**
checkbox is ticked.

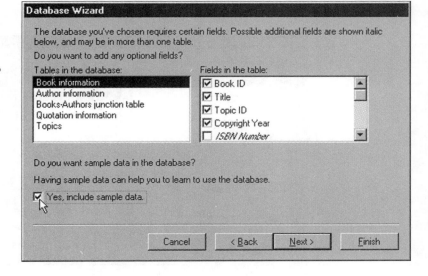

6 Click Next again. You can now tell Access which style you want for the screen displays. Pick one
that you like the look of.

7 Click Next again and you will get the chance to select the style for the printed reports.

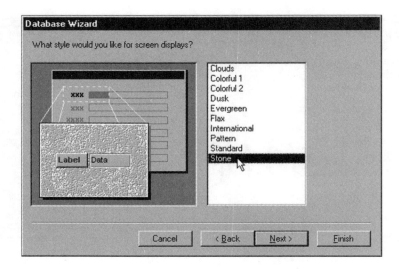

Again, select one you like the look of.

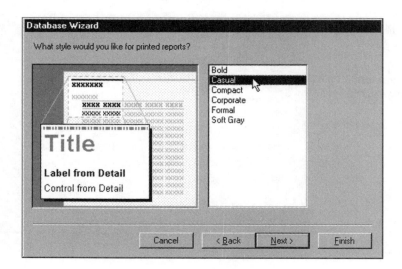

8 Move to the next window. This allows you to change the title of the database, and put a picture on the reports. Tick the Yes, I'd like to include a picture option, and click the Picture... button.

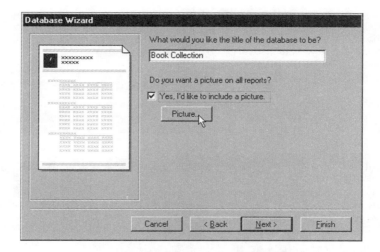

9 The Insert Picture dialog appears. Use this to go to your Access program folder, then change to the BitMaps folder, then to the Dbwiz folder. There you'll find some pictures you can use. Select one.

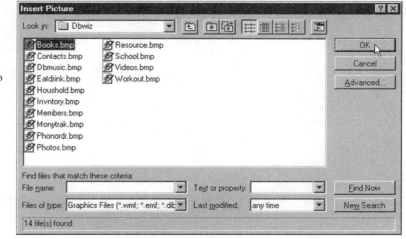

10 Click OK and you'll see the picture appear in the Database Wizard window. Click Next and in the final window make sure Yes, start the database is ticked. Don't tick the Display Help option.

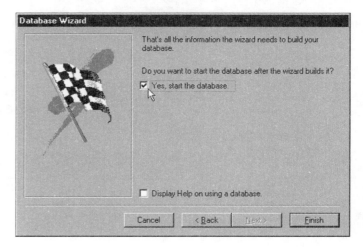

11 Finally, click the <u>F</u>inish button and Access will start to create the new database for you. You'll see a display of the progress - it can take some time.

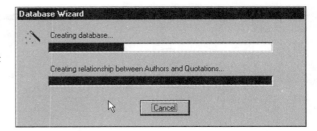

12 Once it's complete, the database starts running automatically. The Database Wizard has produced a very attractive front-end to our new database where we can select to view and edit data on books, quotations etc. We can also preview a report, or customize the switchboard (the term used to describe the front-end main screen where you navigate the database).

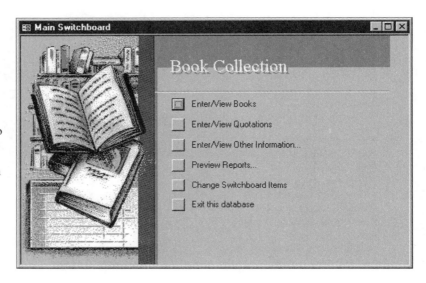

13 Select the first option on the list and you'll be greeted with a screen similar to the one below where you can enter and update information about the books. Access has placed some sample data in the database for us, as we asked it to. The background and styles were defined by you on earlier screens, so they might be different depending on which options you selected.

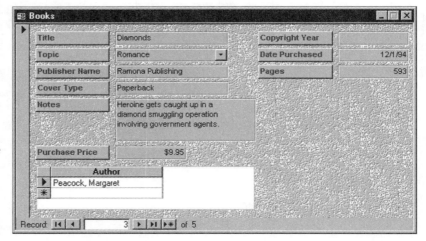

14 Close this view by clicking on the close button in the top right corner. You'll be taken back to the main switchboard screen. Click on the Preview Reports button, and in the next screen, select Preview the Titles by Topic Report.

Topic	Title	Author Name	Publisher Name
Titles by Topic			
Business			
	Planning Your Career	Fuller, Andrew	Jean-Paul Deloria
Health			
	Techniques of Tai Chi	Callahan, Laura	Ramona Publishing
Fiction			
	Dirk Luchte	Davolio, Nancy	GGG&G Publishing
	My Family	Leverling, Janet	GGG&G Publishing
Romance			
	Diamonds	Peacock, Margaret	Ramona Publishing

15 You can close the report and return to the main switchboard by clicking the Close button.

So this database allows you to enter and edit details of the books and print all manner of reports. All in all, it's quite a comprehensive application, and gives you a good idea of the kind of things that Access can do. And, of course, you can always modify it to meet your needs more closely. However, to do that you have to know how Access works. By the time you've worked through this book, you'll understand how these attractive applications are created, and be able to fine tune them or create new ones yourself.

Saving and Printing Out the Database

We discovered at the beginning of this chapter that Access behaves rather differently to most other applications when you create a new database. Instead of starting with an empty one called Untitled, as you would when using a word processor or spreadsheet, you have to specify straight away where you want the database to be stored on your disk, and what it's to be called. Access then creates the empty database for you.

As it runs, Access is continually saving the contents of your tables to disk. It's only when you create a new table or other object that Access prompts you to save the new item before you close down. So when you've finished, you don't have to explicitly save the database - it's already there on your disk.

You can't rename or copy a database just by selecting Save As - Access uses this option to copy and export individual parts of the database. If you want to copy a whole database, you must close it first and then use My Computer or Explorer to create a new copy, or move it to another directory.

Printing the Contents of your Table

You can print out the contents of your Access tables just as you would with Excel. Access contains the same standard menu commands and toolbar buttons, and uses the same standard Print and Print Setup dialog boxes as most other Windows programs.

Try It Out - Printing the Accounts Table

1 Open the Accounts database again by selecting it from the list of most recently opened files on the File menu. Then open the Original table by double-clicking on it in the Database window, or selecting it and clicking the Open button.

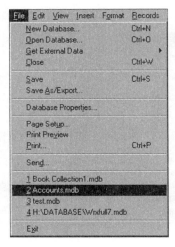

2 Select Print from the File menu to open the Print dialog. (If you don't need to change the print options, you can print directly by clicking the Print button on the toolbar.)

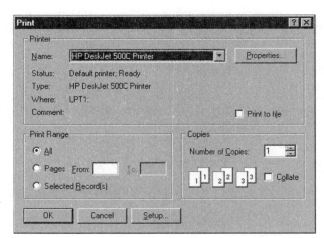

3 Select the print options you require and click OK. The options are similar to those in other Microsoft applications and you are no doubt familiar with them. You may want to specify Landscape mode in the Properties dialog to get the table on one page.

4 If you want to see a preview of the printed output, you can select Print Preview from the File menu, or click the Print Preview button on the toolbar.

Summary

Well, we've now got ourselves a shiny new database which can easily achieve all of the things that Excel (or a similar spreadsheet) could. You have converted the original set of data from the spreadsheet model to an Access table and performed almost all of the tasks that we carried out in Excel in Chapter 1, using the different Access methods of manipulating tables.

This chapter has shown you how you can obtain **information** from your data. We've still got a long way to go, as sorting and filtering records can hardly be considered as state of the art information retrieval methods, but the ground-work has been done and we're ready to see how Access can achieve a lot more.

We have covered:

- Importing data from Excel into Access.
- Updating and editing records.
- Sorting and filtering using both simple and more advanced methods.
- Customizing the toolbar.
- Viewing the records in a form.
- Saving and printing the records.

The one Excel task from Chapter 1 that we haven't implemented in Access yet is the subtotals function. This is because doing this in Access involves the use of **queries**, which is what we are going to look at in the next chapter.

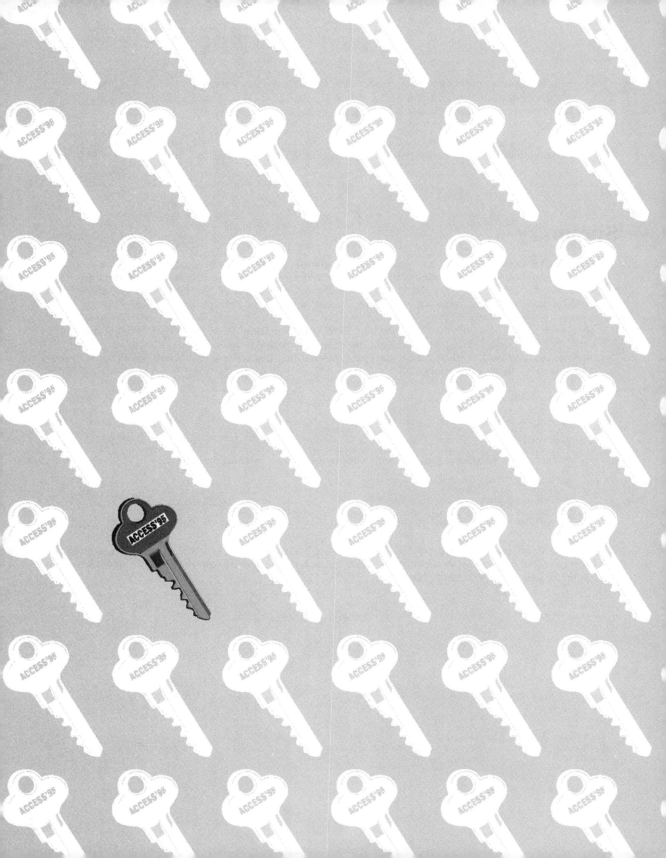

Beginning Your First Database Application

In this chapter we'll investigate further how to present the contents of your database in a way that allows you to obtain information from it rather than simply view data. We'll do this by using **queries** to select and display individual items of data (records and fields).

We'll also take a look at how we can modify existing tables, and learn the basics of creating new tables, before finally exploring how we can use **indexes** and **record keys** to further optimize our data storage. So this chapter basically breaks into three sections:

▶ Exploring how to retrieve information using Access queries.

▶ Looking at how tables are created and how we can select and modify field types.

▶ Understanding keys and indexes, and how we can use these to increase efficiency.

Obtaining Information Using Access Queries

We saw in Chapter 1 how Excel soon runs out of steam when asked to provide more than the most simple views of the data it stores. Access allows you far more flexibility when extracting data. For instance, even though Excel can display certain rows of data (by filtering them), and display the data in a form, it can only show the complete row. Also, it can sort rows into a different order, but it can't change the order of the fields - for instance, it couldn't display the name of the project in the first column. Access, on the other hand, gives you almost total control over what is displayed.

Introducing Queries

Access contains a tool called a **Graphical Query Generator** or the **QBE** (Query By Example) grid. You've already used this to create filters for sorting and selecting records, and we'll be using it again in this chapter to create queries. (A filter is just a special kind of query.)

 If you really want to sound as though you know what you're doing, you should talk about 'applying' a filter and 'running' a query.

What Is a Query?

A query is, in effect, an 'object' that takes one or more tables as its data source, and outputs a result which contains the fields and records we specify in the query.

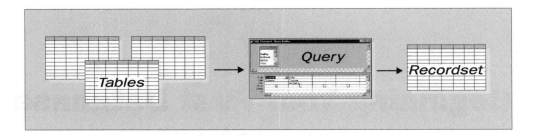

The result of applying a query to a table, or even several tables, is called a **recordset**. In its simplest form, a recordset is basically a subset of the records in the original table(s). We will be looking at recordsets in detail a bit later on, but for now we'll concentrate on queries.

Queries have their own list in the Database window - to see it you just click on the Queries tab. (This window is currently empty as we haven't created any queries so far). Whereas the filters we used earlier are only available while a table is open and are lost when you close the table, queries can be created and saved as independent objects. They can then be used for a variety of tasks, as you'll see as you work through this book. In fact, using Access to its full potential is based around different types of query. We'll start by creating some simple ones.

Simple Select Queries

There are many different types of query available in Access. The simplest is the **select query** which, as its name implies, selects records from one or more tables. To demonstrate how select queries work, we'll use one to select records from our Original table. First we'll select whole rows, just as we did with the filters we used with both Excel and in the previous chapter with Access, then we'll try selecting particular fields and rearranging the order they're displayed in.

We'll start by creating a query which displays the whole set of records. We'll then apply a filter which will sort the records by project name and then customer name. The results will then be displayed in the Datasheet view.

In the examples of this chapter we'll be using a copy of `Accounts.mdb`, which you should have created when you imported the Excel spreadsheet in the last chapter. In case you didn't do this, there's a copy of the database in the samples that were installed from the disk that accompanies this book. However, bear in mind the old saying - 'Doing is understanding....'.

Try It Out - Selecting Records with a Query

1 Open up **Accounts.mdb** and go to the Database window. Click on the Queries tab.

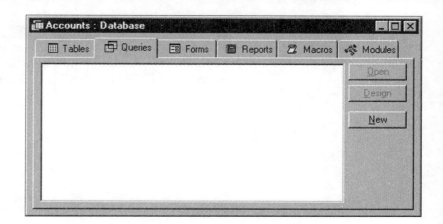

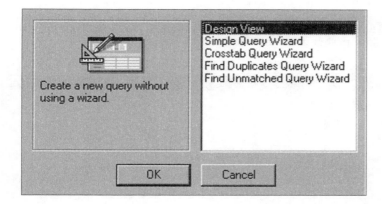

2 Click the <u>New</u> button and Access will display the New Query dialog.

3 We'll be using Query Wizards later in the book to create more complex queries, but, for the moment, just select Design View from the list and click the OK button. Access opens the Query Builder window. Note that the title bar of the background window reads Query1: Select Query - Access creates select queries (which just select items of data from the tables) by default (see the screenshot on the next page).

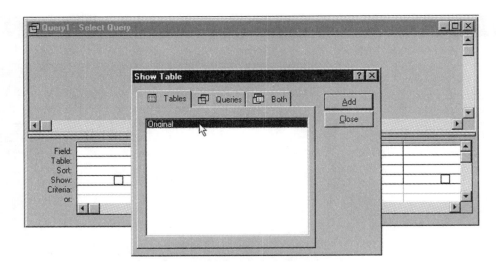

4 Here's the first difference between a filter and a query: Access displays a list of all the tables in the database and you have to tell Access which table you want the query to use (we only have one table in our database - Original). Select Original and click the **Add** button. Access will add this table to the query window. Click **Close** to shut down the **Show Table** window.

The Original table has been added to the query window

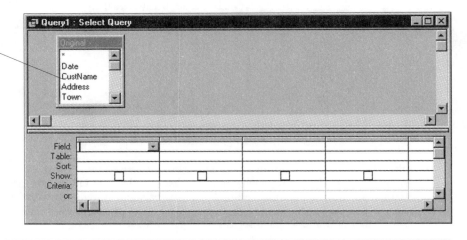

FYI The top entry in the list of fields in the **Original** table is an asterisk. If you enter this into the field box of the grid, it means 'All the fields'.

5 Click on the asterisk at the top of the Original table field list and drag it into the **Field:** row in the first column of the grid. The entry Original.* will appear in the Field box on the grid.

Field:	Original.*	▼		
Table:	Original			
Sort:				
Show:	☑		☐	☐
Criteria:				
or:				

6 Click on the down arrow beside this box. A list of all the fields in the table will appear.

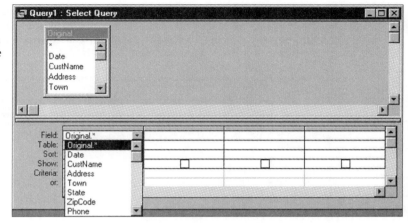

If you were to run the query now, all the fields in the table would be displayed. However, before we do that, let's just set a sort order for the records.

7 Click on the Project field in the list of fields of the Original table and drag it down to the Field: row in the second column of the grid. Alternatively, you can click in the second Field box, click the down arrow that appears and then select Project from the list of fields. The entry for the Table: row is automatically filled in by Access for you. Click on the Sort: row below it and select Ascending from the drop-down list. We'll sort the results by Project.

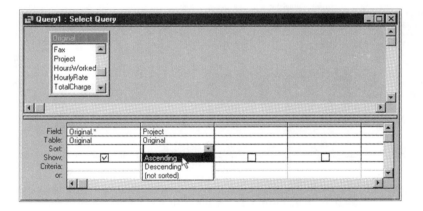

8 Click on the checkbox in the row labeled Show in the Project column of the grid to clear it. This simply indicates whether this field or column is to be displayed in the final results. We've already told Access to include all the fields so we don't want to include the Project field again.

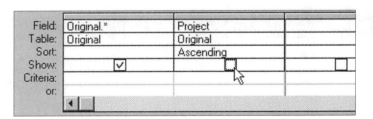

9 Now click on the CustName field in the list of fields from the Original table and drag it down to the Field: box on the third column of the grid. Click on the Sort: row below it and select Ascending from the drop-down list. This will sort the results by customer name for each project. In the same way as before, clear the Show checkbox for the CustName field.

Field:	Original.*	Project	CustName	
Table:	Original	Original	Original	
Sort:		Ascending	Ascending ▼	
Show:	☑			
Criteria:				
or:				

10 To see the results of the query, switch to Datasheet View.

- ☑ Design View
- SQL SQL View
- ▦ Datasheet View

Query1 : Select Query

	Date	CustName	Address	Town	State	ZipCode	Phone	Fax	Project	
▶	6/12/95	Aardvark Ltd.	All Saints Street	Athens	OH	39812	216-376-1298	216-376-8811	Accounts System	
	6/16/95	James Builders	2131 New Street	Phoenix	AZ	78034	602-281-3318	602-281-7318	Accounts System	
	7/13/95	Miracle Supplies	18th Avenue	Oakland	CA	10593	415-671-6633	415-671-8833	Accounts System	
	6/28/95	Pedro Mana	Calle Sebastione	St. Paul	MN	65109	612-401-1350	612-401-1388	Accounts System	
	6/30/95	Major Records	Third Avenue	Stocksville	FL	10015	305-711-7851	305-711-8531	Catalogue System	
	7/20/95	Union Records	712 Main Street	Tampa	FL	51267	813-167-3520	813-167-3521	Catalogue System	
	7/8/95	Le Bistro	Rue Francais	Vancouver	WA	41322	206-133-8294	206-133-8295	Menu Generator	
	7/18/95	Martha's Bar	Top Street	Clarksville	NY	54876			Menu Generator	
	7/23/95	Jonahs Boats	The Quay	Stocksville	FL	16734	305-711-8855		Navigation System	
	6/20/95	J.R.Higgins	The Market	Green Bay	WI	61733	414-831-8812	414-831-7293	PC Upgrades	
	7/3/95	Cummings Intl.	124th Street West	Pittsburgh	PA	17265	412-455-6104	412-455-1399	Robotics Installation	
	7/16/95	Education Dept.	The Offices, City Square	Chicago	IL	10745	312-712-8567		Schools Support	
	7/5/95	Education Dept.	The Offices, City Square	Chicago	IL	10745	312-712-8567		Schools Support	
	6/23/95	Burger Queen	Constants Avenue	Houston	TX	30517	713-771-6727	713-771-6728	System Development	
	6/18/95	Miracle Supplies	18th Avenue	Oakland	CA	10593	415-671-6633	415-671-8833	Warehouse System	
	6/26/95	Miracle Supplies	18th Avenue	Oakland	CA	10593	415-671-6633	415-671-8833	Warehouse System	
✱										

Record: ◄◄ ◄ 1 ► ►► ►✱ of 16

The table displayed is now the same as when you used a filter on the table directly. That's not all Access can do, though. By including the asterisk in the first column, you told Access to show all the fields in the table. Let's now be a bit more adventurous and display only selected fields.

Try It Out - Displaying Selected Fields

Let's have another look at the projects which have yet to be paid for. However, this time, we'll only display the fields that are relevant to our request. We only need to display the Project, CustName, TotalDue and Paid fields. We'll then display only those records with no value in the Paid field.

Note that unlike with a filter, when you run a query, Access only displays the fields you tell it to.

1 Following on then from the last Try It Out, click the Design View button on the toolbar, or use the Query Design command from the View menu to show the query design grid again.

2 Click the column selector (the narrow gray bar) above the Original column. (You can only do this when the cursor becomes a down arrow). When the column is highlighted, press *Delete* to remove it from the grid. Alternatively, you can just place the cursor somewhere in the column and select Delete Column from the Edit menu.

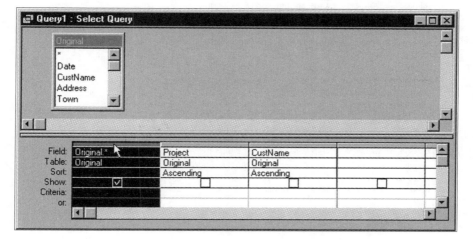

3 Turn on the Show checkboxes for the Project and CustName columns and then click the Datasheet View button on the toolbar to see the results. As you'd expect, you only get the two fields displayed, sorted by project then customer.

Project	CustName
Accounts System	Aardvark Ltd.
Accounts System	James Builders
Accounts System	Miracle Supplies
Accounts System	Pedro Mana
Catalogue System	Major Records
Catalogue System	Union Records
Menu Generator	Le Bistro
Menu Generator	Martha's Bar
Navigation System	Jonahs Boats
PC Upgrades	J.R.Higgins
Robotics Installation	Cummings Intl.
Schools Support	Education Dept.
Schools Support	Education Dept.
System Development	Burger Queen
Warehouse System	Miracle Supplies
Warehouse System	Miracle Supplies

FYI If the data in the columns doesn't actually fit into the columns, you can resize them by clicking on the black column divider in the gray header row and dragging until you can see the whole entry.

4 To display the amounts that the above customers owe and have paid, go back to design view and drag the TotalDue and Paid fields from the field list in the top section of the window into columns three and four of the grid. Click the Datasheet View button again and you will see the total value of each project, and whether it has been paid.

Project	CustName	TotalDue	Paid
Accounts System	Aardvark Ltd.	$2,128.00	Y
Accounts System	James Builders	$1,176.00	Y
Accounts System	Miracle Supplies	$616.00	Y
Accounts System	Pedro Mana	$2,128.00	Y
Catalogue System	Major Records	$1,536.80	
Catalogue System	Union Records	$2,260.00	
Menu Generator	Le Bistro	$276.00	Y
Menu Generator	Martha's Bar	$414.00	
Navigation System	Jonahs Boats	$693.00	Y
PC Upgrades	J.R.Higgins	$484.50	
Robotics Installation	Cummings Intl.	$648.00	Y
Schools Support	Education Dept.	$550.00	
Schools Support	Education Dept.	$1,950.00	
System Development	Burger Queen	$1,333.80	Y
Warehouse System	Miracle Supplies	$1,010.10	Y
Warehouse System	Miracle Supplies	$854.70	

Record: 1 of 16

5 To display only the projects which haven't been paid yet, you need to add a criteria to the grid. Back in design view, go to the Criteria row of the Paid column and enter Is Null. This tells Access to only include records which have **Null** (no value) in that field.

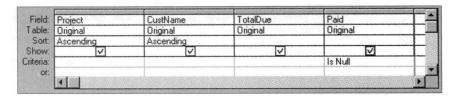

Field:	Project	CustName	TotalDue	Paid
Table:	Original	Original	Original	Original
Sort:	Ascending	Ascending		
Show:	☑	☑	☑	☑
Criteria:				Is Null
or:				

FYI Null is a special value in Access. If you have created records in a table, but have not yet placed values in the fields, Access stores Null in each one. This indicates that the field has not been given a value - it's not the same as just being empty. You can think of Null as meaning 'I don't know the value for this field'.

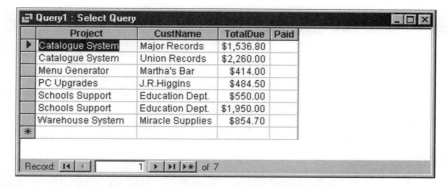

6 Switch back to datasheet view to see the results.

So Access queries can display almost any combination of records and fields from a table. You can:

◗ Display just the fields you require by selecting them from the list of fields in the table or by setting or clearing the Show check box.

◗ Choose which records you want to be included by putting conditions in the Criteria row of the grid.

◗ Set the sort order for one or more fields in the Sort row.

Reusing Queries

You still haven't seen the real power behind queries, though. When you applied a filter to the table in Chapter 2, Access simply changed the way the records were displayed in the table. When you closed the table and re-opened it, the records were displayed in their original order - the filter had gone.

However, just now when you used a query on the table, what you saw was not the original table, but a **recordset** created from it - if you look at the title bar in the previous figures you'll see that it still says 'Query1: Select Query' when the records are displayed. What you're looking at is a separate view of the records in the table, rather than the original table itself.

Try It Out - Saving a Query

If you want to use a query you have created regularly, you can save it as part of the database.

1 Click the Close box at the top right of the Query window. Access will ask whether you want to save the query.

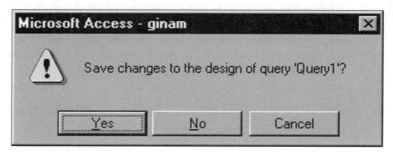

2 Click <u>Y</u>es and enter a name for the
query in the Save As dialog.

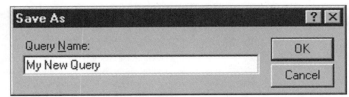

3 Click OK and Access will add the query to the Database window, where you can open it again
whenever you want to use it.

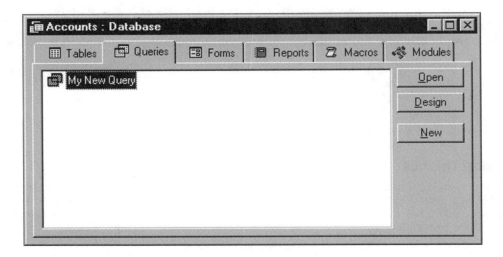

The Query Recordset

Now we can consider recordsets in more detail. If you remember, we defined a recordset as the
subset of records that result when you apply a query to a table. However, a recordset is not
actually a physical table in its own right, but a view of the original table. So, if the records you
see as the result of a query are only a view of the original table, you are probably wondering
what happens when you edit them. If you switch into datasheet view with any of the queries
you've used above, you can click on any field and change the contents of it. We'll explore this
further now.

Try It Out - Updating the Results of a Query

1 Create a new query by selecting the Queries tab in the Database window and clicking the <u>N</u>ew
button. Then select Design View and click OK. Add the Original table and <u>C</u>lose the Show Table
dialog.

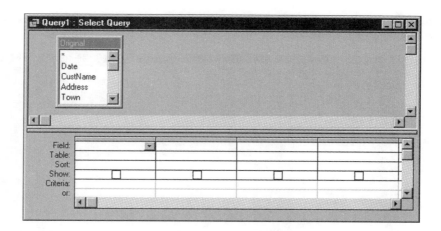

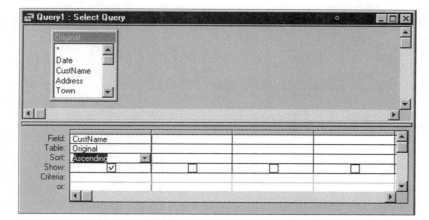

2 Drag the CustName field from the Original table field list into the first column of the grid. Select Ascending for the sort order.

3 Click the Query View button.

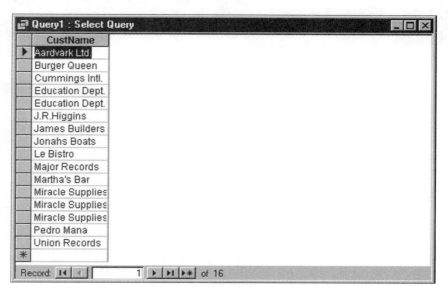

4 Size the window so that you just can see the customer name column and move it to one side of the screen by dragging the title bar in the usual way.

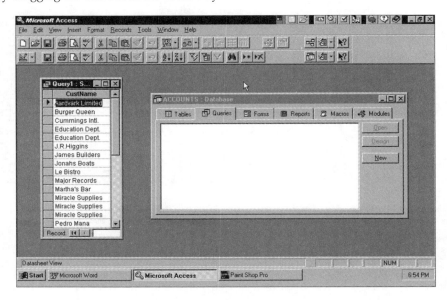

5 Now you need to open the Original table directly. Go back to the Database window and click on the Table tab. Select the Original table and click the Open button.

Once you have several windows open at once, especially if you have maximized them so that they occupy all the screen, it can be difficult to find the **Database** window. Because this window is the nerve-center of all the tasks we carry out, Access supplies a short-cut method of going directly to it. On most toolbars there is a **Database Window** button. This automatically restores any windows that are maximized back to their normal size and brings the **Database** window to the front. Of course, you can always use the **Window** menu to bring it to the front, but the toolbar button is far easier to use.

6 Move and size the Original table window so that you can see both the CustName field and the select query at the same time.

CustName
Aardvark Ltd.
Burger Queen
Cummings Intl.
Education Dept.
Education Dept.
J.R.Higgins
James Builders
Jonahs Boats
Le Bistro
Major Records
Martha's Bar
Miracle Supplies
Miracle Supplies
Miracle Supplies
Pedro Mana
Union Records

Date	CustName	Address	Town	State	ZipCode
6/30/95	Major Records	Third Avenue	Stocksville	FL	1001
6/18/95	Miracle Supplies	18th Avenue	Oakland	CA	1059
6/26/95	Miracle Supplies	18th Avenue	Oakland	CA	1059
7/13/95	Miracle Supplies	18th Avenue	Oakland	CA	1059
7/5/95	Education Dept.	The Offices, City Square	Chicago	IL	1074
7/16/95	Education Dept.	The Offices, City Square	Chicago	IL	1074
7/23/95	Jonahs Boats	The Quay	Stocksville	FL	1673
7/3/95	Cummings Intl.	124th Street West	Pittsburgh	PA	1726
6/23/95	Burger Queen	Constants Avenue	Houston	TX	3051
6/12/95	Aardvark Ltd.	All Saints Street	Athens	OH	3981
7/8/95	Le Bistro	Rue Francais	Vancouver	WA	4132
7/20/95	Union Records	712 Main Street	Tampa	FL	5126
7/18/95	Martha's Bar	Top Street	Clarksville	NY	5487
6/20/95	J.R.Higgins	The Market	Green Bay	WI	6173
6/28/95	Pedro Mana	Calle Sebastione	St. Paul	MN	6510
6/16/95	James Builders	2131 New Street	Phoenix	AZ	7803

78

7 Now click on any of the names in the Query window and change the contents of that field. Access displays the pencil marker on the record selector to show it is being edited. In the figure, we have edited the first row, changing 'Ltd.' to 'Limited'.

8 Now click on another record, or press the *Tab* or the down arrow key to move to another record. When you do this the changes to the record are saved automatically. At the same time, keep your eye on the equivalent record in the Original table. As the changes to the CustName field in the query are saved, the record in the Original table changes as well.

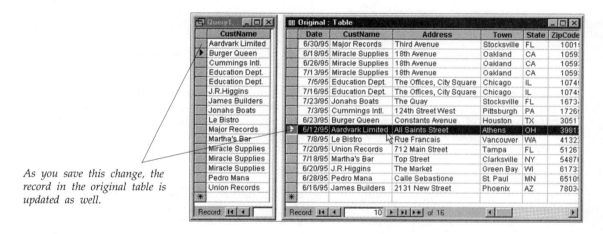

As you save this change, the record in the original table is updated as well.

Although this may not seem like earth-shattering stuff, it is highly significant to the way that Access works. Think about it like this - you have created a set of records that appear to be copies of those in your Original table. Yet, when you change one of the 'copies', the data in the original table changes as well. Surely this is not what you would have expected.

If you have followed any of the discussions about Windows 95 and the new developments in both applications and operating systems, you'll have heard talk about **objects**. What you've just seen is **object variables** in action - even though you may not have realized it. So what are objects then? And while we're about it, what are variables? Without going into too much depth, we'll take this chance to give you some background information as to what is happening in the example you've just seen.

Recordsets and Object Variables

In the previous example, the behavior of our query and the original data is totally foreign to the way we normally think about the way other applications work. If you copy part of a spreadsheet to a new sheet, or a document in a word processor to another document, the original and the copy become independent of each other. When you change the copy, the original document remains the same.

In our example, however, we created what seemed to be a copy of part of a table, but when we made changes to the copy, the original table changed as well.

To understand how this works, we need to look at the way that data is stored in a computer.

Storing Data in Variables

When you enter a value in a spreadsheet cell, say 42 in cell B2, it is stored in memory in such a way that the spreadsheet application can retrieve it again when required. You can also refer to the value yourself - if you enter =B2+10 in another cell, you see 52 appear. If you then change the value in cell B2 to 17, the new value 27 replaces the original one in the other cell.

If you have used a programming language before, you will recognize this as assigning values to **variables**. A variable is just a label or **identifier** of a stored value; you can refer to that value using the identifier. So we can assign the value 42 to a variable called A, then use the value

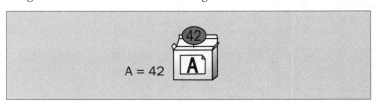

later through the identifier - for instance A * 2 would be 84. And, of course, we can use another variable to hold the result. B = A * 2 would mean that the variable B would then hold 84.

The good thing about variables is that they can hold different values. If B = A * 2 and we changed A to 14, then B would automatically become 28 - just as in our spreadsheet example. You can think of a variable as a pigeon-hole that holds a value, just like a cell in a spreadsheet or a particular location in memory. Any time we want to retrieve the value, we just use the identifier (or variable name) to refer to it.

Copying Variables

When we make a copy of a document, we copy all the variables as well - whether they are numbers, formulae, words, or even pictures, they are all stored in various memory locations. All we do is make a complete copy of all the contents in new locations. They then become independent. The cell B2 in the original spreadsheet and the cell B2 in the copy may now contain the same value, but in fact they are separate locations (or variables) which just happen to store the same value at the time. If you change one of them the other stays the same.

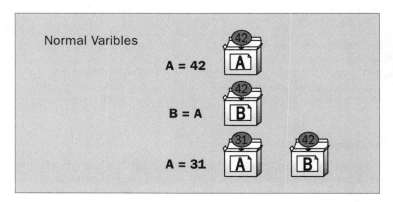

For instance, in the figure on the left, we set variable A to 42, then copy it to variable B. Then when we change A to 31, B is still 42, as you would expect.

When we run an Access query, however, we're not actually creating a **copy** of the original data. As you know, in most cases the result of a query is a set of records which contain data from the original table. This is called a **recordset**. However, what Access is doing behind the scenes is assembling a set of **links** to the original data, not a whole new set of locations. It creates a set of references to the original table's locations. So when the data in the query is edited, the changes are passed back to the original records through these references. What you are actually doing is changing the original data through these links; the changes are then reflected back into the results of the query.

Object Variables

A **recordset**, like many of the other things you'll meet in Access, is an **object**. An object is part of an application which has its own special way of behaving, and can carry out tasks using its own built-in information. We say that an object has its own **properties** and **methods**. For example, a screen form in Access is an **interface object** - it is something that is used to build the front-end that the users see when they work with a database. It has properties such as color, size, type of border, etc., and can carry out some operations itself. For instance, we can tell it to close itself using its own Close method. So it should come as no surprise to find that Access contains a new type of variable, called **object variables**. These are links to, or views, of variables, rather than the traditional variables you are used to. The values in a recordset are stored in object variables, and it is these that hold the special link, or reference, to the original table.

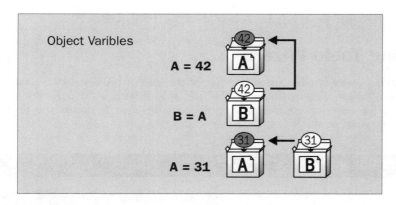

With object variables, when you assign a value to **A**, then set **B** equal to **A**, you are not storing the actual value but a link to the original memory location where **A** is stored. So if the original value in **A** changes and you then look to see the value in **B**, you are actually looking at **A** through this link. The figure will perhaps make it clearer. It shows how Access stores and refers to object variables such as our recordset.

Why You Should Use Recordsets

So perhaps now you can see the power that queries offer. Instead of manipulating the original data directly, you can create a new recordset that only contains the records and fields you are interested in, then manipulate the original records through the new recordset. To change just one customer's phone number in a table, you can create a recordset containing only the relevant phone number and edit it there. This may not seem like much of an advantage - but remember that the original table may contain thousands of records and to edit one record in the original table without creating a recordset, you would have to load in the whole table. You would also have to find the record you wanted. Using a query and its recordset is often far quicker.

We are now light years away from any task that Excel could have accomplished. Access is already proving far more powerful when manipulating the data we need to store. The two main reasons for this are:

▶ A recordset can contain almost any mix of records, sorted in any order, and containing only the fields you want to see.

▶ Recordsets can be **updatable** - you can edit and save changes to the original records by changing its contents. (If you have used earlier versions of Access, you will recognize this type of recordset as a **dynaset**).

FYI We say "can be updatable" because, although our select query created an updatable recordset, some types of query create non-updatable recordsets. In this case, you cannot edit the records. We'll learn more about these in future chapters. (Earlier versions of Access referred to this type of recordset as a **snapshot**).

Creating and Modifying Fields and Tables

One of the fundamental things you need to know when setting up a new database is how to create the tables that will hold your data. You can, as we've already seen, import data from other sources, but you may well want to set up an Access database from scratch.

Creating Tables Using Table Wizard

We'll start by looking at how to create a table using another of the built-in Access tools - **Table Wizard**. We'll see how you can create tables without the aid of Table Wizard a bit later, but for now you might as well make life easy for yourself - after all, you can always modify the results afterwards to fine-tune them to your needs.

Try It Out - Using the Table Wizard

1 Close the table and query from the last Try It Out if you still have them open (you needn't bother saving the query). Select the Table tab in the Database window and click the **New** button.

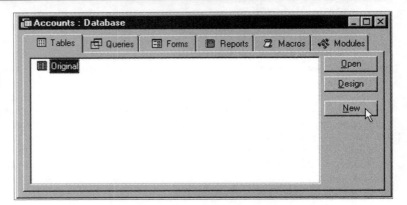

2 In the New Table dialog select Table Wizard and click OK.

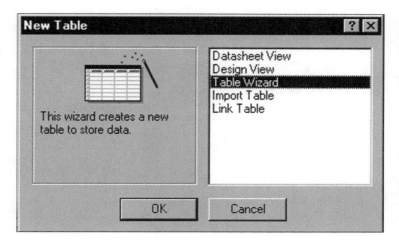

FYI If you did not install the wizards when you set up Access on your machine, or have un-installed them since, you will get an error message. Most of the Access wizards are 'Add-ins' that are loaded separately from the main Access program. If the wizards are not installed, select **Add-ins** from the **Access Tools** menu and then click **Add-in Manager**. Access displays a list of available **Add-ins**. You should see an entry '**Wizards**'. Select it and click the **Install** button, then **Close**. If you can't see **Wizards** in the list you will have to run the Access setup program again and install them from your program disks.

3 After much whirring from the hard disk, the first Table Wizard screen appears. This contains a list of sample tables and a corresponding list of sample fields. Select the business table list by clicking the Business option button under the list of sample tables.

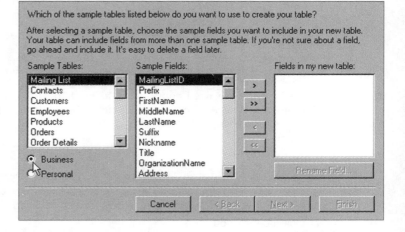

FYI You can select from two different types of sample table: **Business** and **Personal**. The business tables cover everything from customers and contacts to fixed assets, invoices and timesheets. The personal tables include recipes, plants, video collections and even rolls of film - certainly one of Microsoft's programmers was working overtime on this project! And for each table there is a corresponding long list of available fields you can choose to include in your new table.

4 We are going to create a table that resembles our Original table. Scroll down the Sample Tables list and select the Orders table and then the OrderDate field. Then click the top button marked '>' to place the field in the list for our new table. (Access automatically scrolls down to the next field in the middle window as you do this.)

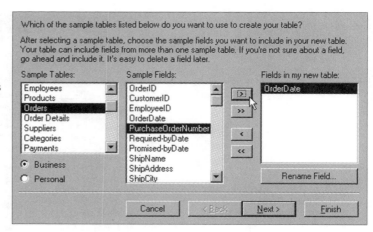

5 Now, from the list of sample tables, select the Customers table and add CompanyName, BillingAddress, City, StateOrProvince, PostalCode, PhoneNumber and FaxNumber. Next, from the sample table list, select the Projects table and add ProjectName and finally from the Time Billed table, add BillableHours and HourlyRate.

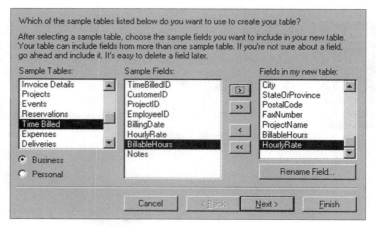

To complete the table we need some fields to hold the total cost before tax, the tax rate, and the total including tax. We'll also need a Paid field. These don't exist in the selection on offer, so we'll have to accept some fields whose names are not quite what we want, but whose field type is likely to be correct.

6 From the Order Details table select UnitPrice, Discount, SalesTax and SalePrice. The Discount field should give us a percentage-type field, and the rest currency-type fields. We'll sort out the Paid field later on.

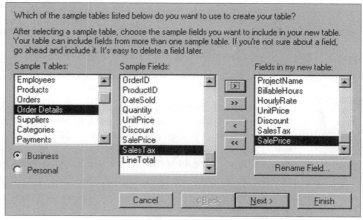

7 Now click the <u>N</u>ext button. In the next window, change the name of the table to TestTable, and leave the default setting so that Access sets the primary key for you (we'll come back to primary keys later in the chapter - don't worry about this for the moment).

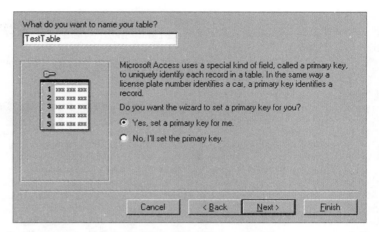

8 Click <u>N</u>ext again. We now have to tell Access whether our new table needs to be related to any others in the database. This is a subject for later chapters - for now, leave it set to not related to 'Original' (the only other table in the database).

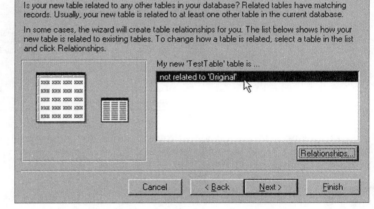

9 Click <u>N</u>ext again. In the final window select the first option - Modify the table design. We need to do this because the table design does not match our final criteria yet (if you remember, some of the table names weren't exactly what we wanted) and needs to be modified before we can start adding any data to it.

10 Finally, click the Finish button. Access then goes off and creates the new table for you. The result is a list of the fields you selected showing the field names and field types. You'll see that Access has added a field that you didn't specify at the top of the list - TestTableID. This is the primary key that we told Access to create for us. We'll come back to this when we look at keys and indexes a little later in this chapter.

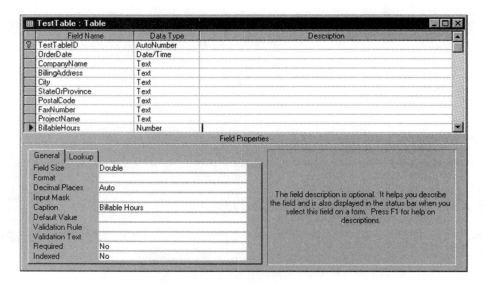

You are now in design view. You can alter any information about the table that does not suit your needs, from the table name right down to the data types and rules which enforce what data can and cannot be added to the table.

If you move your cursor over the leftmost button on the toolbar without clicking, you will see that despite the fact that the icon hasn't changed, the button is now known as the Table View button. This is because we're working with tables now, and although, like queries, tables have both datasheet and design view, they require a different format for their design and data entry. If you're very observant, you might also notice that when you click on the down arrow, the SQL view is missing - but we don't want to talk about that now.

Modifying Field Names in the New Table

Now that you have the basis for your new table, you can start to modify it so that it matches your needs more closely. You can change the field names by simply editing the entries in the left-hand column, for instance you could change Discount to TaxRate or OrderDate to ProjectDate. (For the purpose of the following examples, we are assuming that these have not been changed). Access has been quite clever in creating the table - you'll see that the second column contains the correct data type for each of the new fields: Text for the name and address, Number for the number of hours and Currency for the tax and price fields.

Field Properties

Access has also set up properties for each field - if you look at the lower half of the window, you'll see a short table. This is the Field Properties section and it's here that the fine details of each field are specified.

The PostalCode field is selected.

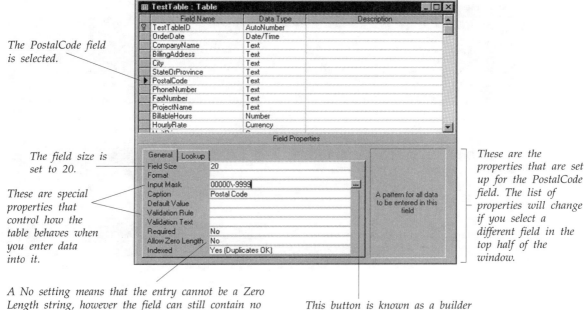

The field size is set to 20.

These are special properties that control how the table behaves when you enter data into it.

These are the properties that are set up for the PostalCode field. The list of properties will change if you select a different field in the top half of the window.

A No setting means that the entry cannot be a Zero Length string, however the field can still contain no data, i.e. Null. A Yes setting forces a value to be in the field before a record is added to the table.

This button is known as a builder button. Here it allows you to set a predefined input mask. We'll be looking at this later.

We'll be working with the different properties in this chapter as we see how we can modify the design and use the table. In the meantime just explore - you'll begin to get a feel for just how much built-in control Access has over the storage of data.

Viewing the New Table

Before we start modifying the existing fields, let's have a quick look at the new table we've created.

Try It Out - Viewing the New Table and Entering Data

1 Click the Datasheet View button to show the table in datasheet view. This is the same as selecting it in the Database window and clicking the Open button.

2 Have a look at the new table. As you can see it is empty, but that's to be expected seeing as you've only just created it and haven't yet entered any data. The table is similar to the one we imported from Excel, though it has a strange entry '(AutoNumber)' in the first field.

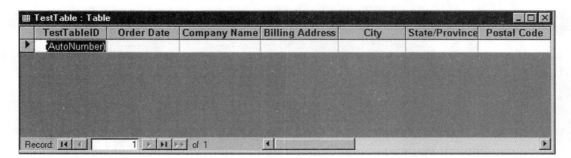

3 Click on the OrderDate field. You'll see that Access displays a blank **date pattern** for you to fill in. This is an example of an **input mask**.

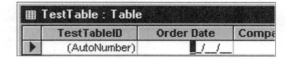

4 Now enter a date. Access adds a new blank record at the end and fills in the TestTableID field with a number. This is the **primary key** that you told Access to create.

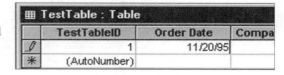

There is obviously more to this table than the one we imported from Excel. The differences are due to the **field properties** that Access added to the fields when it created the table. Don't worry about all the new terms for the moment; we will be covering them all in good time.

Modifying the Table

There are two stages to modifying existing tables - working with the field properties, and adding new fields or deleting existing ones.

Try It Out - Adding Fields

If you remember, we didn't include a Paid field when we used the Table Wizard to create our new table. We'll add this field now.

1 Click the Design View button on the toolbar, or select Table Design from the View menu to switch the table into design view.

2 Type Paid - the name of the field we want to add - in the Field Name column on the first blank row.

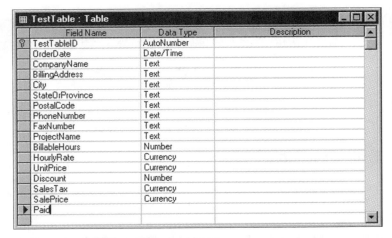

3 Press the *Tab* key to move to the Data Type column. Access inserts Text by default and displays a drop-down list button at the end of the field.

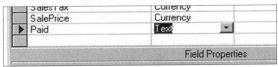

4 Open the drop-down list by clicking the down arrow. Select the Yes/No type field.

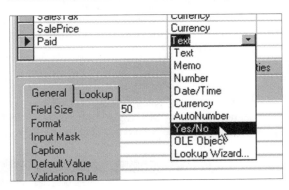

FYI A Boolean data type is a special type that can only be assigned one of two values, true or false. In Access these are often shown as **Yes/No** rather than **True/False**, but it will accept either when you come to place values in a table - even though it always displays them as **Yes** or **No**. This data type is useful because it allows you to limit what can be entered in the table to these values only.

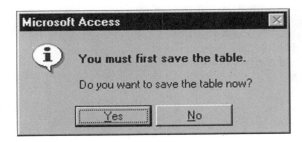

5 Change to datasheet view by clicking the Datasheet View button on the toolbar, or selecting Datasheet from the View menu. Access prompts you to save the changes to the design of the table. Click Yes.

6 Scroll (horizontally) through the field names and you will see the new field has been added to the end of the record. The Yes/No option in the Paid field is displayed as a box, and you can click it to switch between the Yes (ticked) and No (unticked) values.

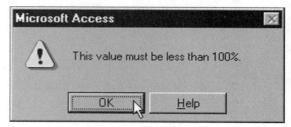

We have now set up the Paid field. Leave the table in this view for the moment, though, as we will be using it in the next Try It Out.

Error Checking

There is one other feature that the Table Wizard added to our table that we haven't yet investigated, and that is the ability to check for errors. To understand this facility, you must first see what happens when you try to enter erroneous information.

Try it Out - Error Checking

1 Scroll horizontally back along the field until you come to the Discount entry. It should read 0.00%. Try entering a number greater than 1 in this field. If you press return, then Access tells you that the data you've entered is not appropriate for that field.

2 This message is something that Access has done automatically without your bidding (we'll look at how it knows this in just a moment). Click OK to close the message box. Now enter 0.1. Press return again - Access changes the display in the Discount field to 10%, and accepts the new record.

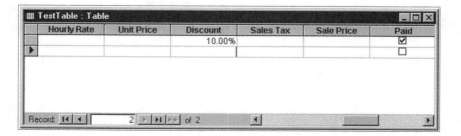

How It Works

To understand how Access spots the above error, you need to look at the properties for the Discount field. Go back to design view and click on the Discount field. You will see the following properties listed in the bottom half of the window:

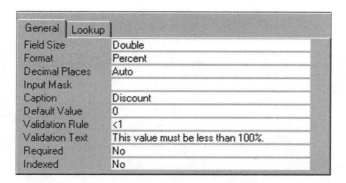

These properties were set up by the Table Wizard. As you can see, the Validation Rule is set as <1. This means that the value entered must be lower than 100%. So that explains the error message you just saw. The Validation Text is the message that is displayed when the Validation Rule is broken.

Input Masks

So, Access will perform error checking on the data that you enter into a table. There is, however, another way that Access limits possible input. Try entering different values into the PhoneNumber and FaxNumber fields. Here, Access is using the **input mask** that we saw earlier in the list of field properties to control what you can enter. An input mask only allows the user to enter information in a very controlled manner. It specifies which, and how many, characters can be entered.

Input masks are useful when you know the format of the data that you want the user to enter. For example, if you know that the phone number they will be entering will have a 3 digit area code, followed by 7 other digits, then you can set an input mask up for this format. Then, if the user doesn't enter 10 digits into the field, they will get an error message.

Let's have a closer look at this.

Try It Out - Creating an Input Mask

You can create and modify input masks by clicking the **builder** button (the button with the three dots or 'ellipsis') that appears when you click on the Input Mask field property.

1 Make sure you are back in Design View and select the PhoneNumber field. Place the cursor in the Input Mask field property and click on the builder button. If the design of the table has been changed, Access will prompt you to save it. Otherwise, simply proceed to step 2.

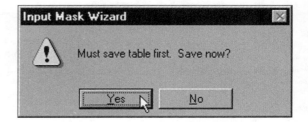

2 The Input Mask Wizard now opens, showing a list of the available pre-built input masks ready for use.

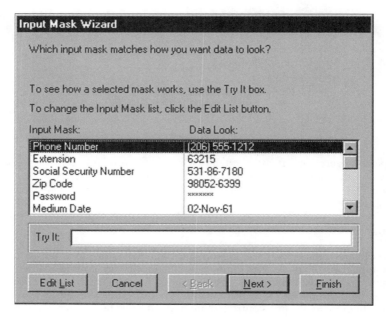

 FYI Note that the values that the Table Wizard uses to create the input mask will be appropriate for the country settings of your computer. If your machine is not set to **English (United States)**, you may find that the input masks are different.

3 Scroll down the list to see the other types - they range from Phone Number to Password and different Date and Time formats.

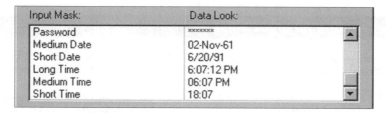

4 You can add new input masks to the list or change the mask that the pre-defined ones produce. Click the Edit List button to open the Customize dialog.

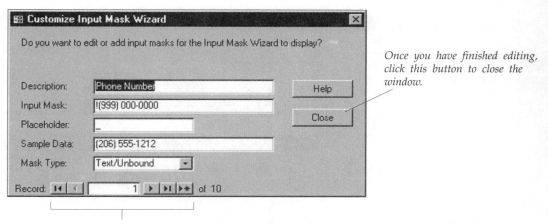

Once you have finished editing, click this button to close the window.

Use these buttons to scroll through the available types of input mask - they cover all kinds of unusual field types.

You can use the navigation controls at the bottom of the window to select the mask you want and then amend it as necessary. When you close the Customize Input Mask Wizard dialog box, the changes you have made are automatically saved. Don't change anything for the moment though - just close the window down.

5 Select the Phone Number mask in the top window and then click in the Try It: box. You can now test it out. Try entering just part of a number:

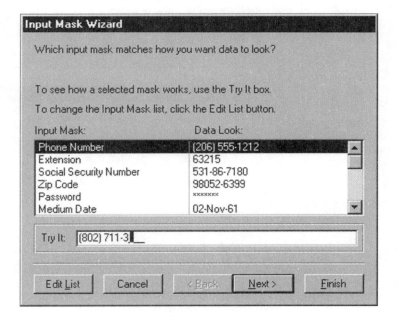

6 Click the Next button. The
Input Mask Wizard will
inform you that the value
you've entered is not
appropriate - it doesn't 'fit' the
mask.

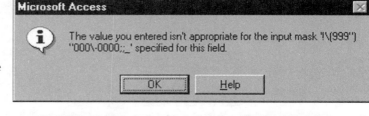

7 Click OK, then click in the Try
It: box and complete the
number. Then click Next. The
next window allows you to
change the input mask to suit
your needs if you want.
Change the **place-holder** (the
character that is displayed to
indicate where the numbers
are to be entered) from the
drop-down list to a hash sign.
If you now click in the Try It:
box, it will display hash signs
rather than blanks.

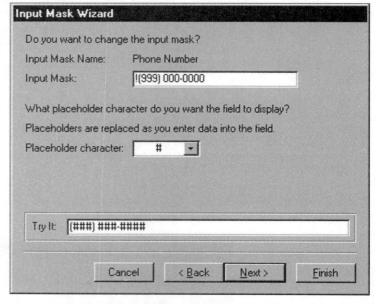

8 Now click Next again. The
next window allows you to
store the data into the table in
a different form to the way it
appears on screen. Leave the
second option selected so that
the symbols in the input mask
are not included in the table.

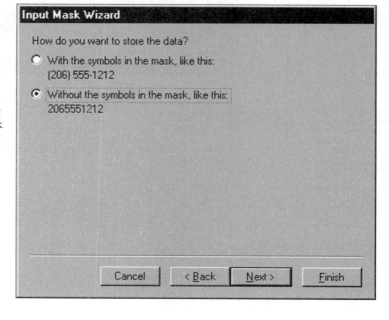

9 Click <u>N</u>ext again. That's all there is to it.

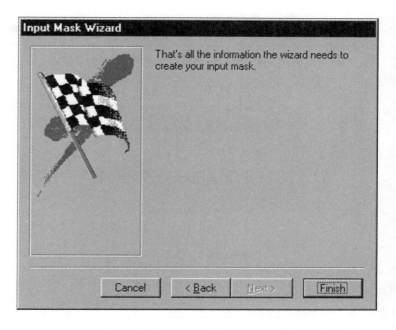

10 Just click the <u>F</u>inish button to enter the input mask into your table.

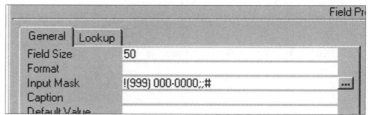

Creating Your Own Input Masks

When editing the list of input masks in the Input Mask Wizard, you need to know what the different characters in the masks mean. Once you are familiar with them, you can also enter your own input masks directly into the input mask property of the table. The following table lists the characters that you can use to specify how the mask works:

Character	Function of Character
0	Digits (0 to 9) are permitted, but plus and minus signs are not permitted.
9	Digits or space characters are permitted, but plus and minus signs are not permitted.
#	Digits or space characters are permitted, plus and minus signs permitted, spaces are displayed as blanks while in edit mode, but the blanks disappear once data is saved.
L	A letter (A to Z) must be entered.

Table Continued on Following Page

Character	Function of Character
?	A letter (A to Z) is permitted, but not obligatory.
A	A letter or digit must be entered.
a	A letter or digit is permitted, but not obligatory.
&	Any character or a space must be entered.
C	Any character or a space is permitted, but not obligatory.
. , : ; - /	Decimal point, thousands separator, date and time separators.
<	Converts all characters to lower case.
>	Converts all characters to upper case.
!	This character changes the input mask display from left to right to right to left. This only happens when characters on the left side of the input mask are optional. The exclamation point can be included anywhere in the input mask.
\	This means that the character that follows the \ is shown as a literal character.

If you look at the input mask we inserted into the table in the above example, you'll see that it is made up of three sections, separated by semi-colons:

Section 1   Section Section
                    2   3

The sections are used as follows:

 Section 1 is the input mask itself (for example, (999) 00-000!).

 Section 2 can be 0, 1 or blank. The section is used to tell Access how to store display characters in the table when you enter data. If you use 0, all symbols are stored with the value, e.g. if you typed (99) then (99) would be stored. If you enter 1 or leave this section blank, then only the characters that are typed in are stored, e.g. (99) would only store 99.

 Section 3 is used to define the character that appears before you type any characters into the input mask. You can use any character to indicate that something should be typed in e.g. ### ### ####.

Deleting Fields

So, we have now had a good look at how to add fields to a table and set up means for checking input. Before we look in a bit more detail at field properties, we'll just make sure you know how to delete fields. There's not a lot to this - in fact there is actually nothing new involved.

FYI We need all the fields we've just added to our new table, so unless you want to redo the table, you should just take our word for it that the following steps work.

Don't Try It Out - Deleting Fields

1 Select the whole field (in design view) by clicking the gray row selector button at the left of the row.

2 Press *Delete* or select Delete from the Edit menu. Alternatively, you can click anywhere in the row and select the Delete Row command from the Edit menu, or right-click and select Delete Row from the short-cut menu that appears.

3 Access displays a message asking you to confirm that you really do want to delete the field. If you answer Yes, you will, of course, lose all the data stored in that field.

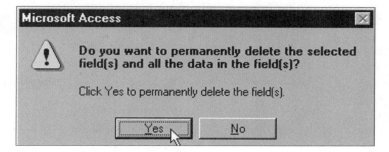

Working with Field Properties

The clever tricks we've seen Access do with the fields in our TestTable table are due to the field properties it set while the Table Wizard was creating the table. Once you have set (or changed) the Data Type for a field, the list of properties changes to reflect those appropriate for that type of field. Therefore, you should set the Data Type *before* you enter values for any properties. If you change it afterwards, some of the properties will not longer exist, and the ones that do may be cleared of their existing values, although the input masks won't be cleared.

For example, changing a Number type field to Text, removes the value that had been assigned to the Default Value.

You must be careful when changing the **Data Type** of fields when there is existing data in the table. If Access cannot convert the existing data into the new type, it will be lost. Say you wanted to change the **Data Type** of the **Paid** field to **Date/Time** so that you could store data about when the customer paid you. Access cannot convert a **Yes/No** entry into a real date. However, a Boolean (Yes/No) value is actually stored in Access as a number. Zero represents No (or False), and any other number is Yes (or True). Access doesn't change the actual Boolean value that is stored (either 0 or 1), because the Date field still holds a number. However, this number is just stored in Date format and is therefore meaningless.

Field Property Meanings

Once you have set the required Data Type for a field, you can go on to change the field properties to suit the data you will be entering in that field.

There are different properties available for different field types.

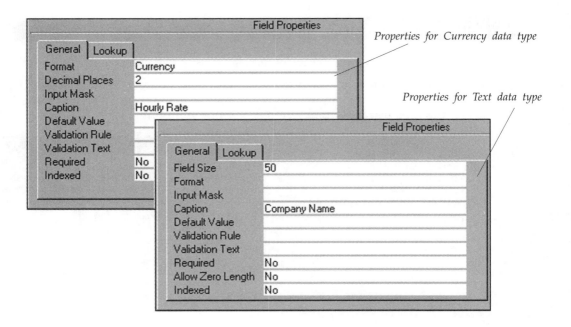

Properties for Currency data type

Properties for Text data type

The following table explains the different properties:

Property	Description
Format	Allows you to select how the data is to be displayed in the table. A drop-down list provides different options depending on the field type. For instance, you can display **Number** fields as General Number, Currency, Fixed, Standard, Percent or Scientific format. **Date/Time** fields can have a range of different layouts and **Yes/No** fields can be set to True/False, Yes/No or On/Off.
Decimal Places	If the field's data type is set to **Number** or **Currency**, Access also shows the Decimal Places property. The drop-down list allows you to either select Auto (which displays the actual number of places required for the value stored in the field) or set the number of places you require.
Field Size	If the data type is **Text** or **Number**, Access shows the Field Size property. This allows you to specify either a maximum number of characters for the field, or the size and type of number you want to store. The most usual are Integer or Long Integer for whole numbers, and Single or Double for numbers with fractional parts.
Allow Zero Length	Shown if the data type is **Text**. If Allow Zero Length is Yes and the user presses return without entering a value, the field will store an empty string. If it is No, Access replaces empty strings with a Null (no value) entry.
Input Mask	This is the property that allows you to specify exactly how actual values are entered and displays a series of guide characters in the field so that you just 'fill in the blanks'. For example an input mask of 99/99/00 displays __/__/__ in the field, and only accepts numbers in the correct positions.

Table Continued on Following Page

Property	Description
Caption	Allows you to change the text that is used in the column headings of the table in datasheet view. If it is blank, Access uses the field name.
Default Value	This is the value that will be stored in a new record when it is first created. Remember, Access always places a new blank record at the end of a table ready for data to be entered. So if, for example, you wanted a State field to default to FL in new records, you would place "FL" in the Default Value property.
Validation Rule	If you want a field to only contain certain values, you can place a condition in this property. After a record has been edited, and before it is saved, Access checks to see that any conditions here are met. To only allow values below, say, 100 for a Unit Price field, you would enter <100 for the Validation Rule. Access will not allow a record which breaks this rule to be saved.
Validation Text	If you use a Validation Rule in a field, you can enter the text of the message you want to be displayed when a record fails the test. The text you enter is shown as a message box when you try to save the record.
Required	This is a Yes/No property which allows you to specify whether all records must have a value for this field. Access will not save a record where a field that is marked as required is blank.
Indexed	Has three possible values: No, Yes (Duplicates OK) and Yes (No Duplicates), which you select from a drop-down list. We'll be considering what indexes are, and how we use them, at the end of this chapter.

 If you place a **Validation Rule** in a table that already contains data, Access can test the existing data against the rules to check that it all conforms. To do this you just select **Test Validation Rules** from the **Edit** menu.

The Properties Lookup Tab

You will have noticed the tab marked Lookup in the field properties part of the table. The tab is different for each field depending on which field is selected and which data type it is required for.

When the currently selected field in a table's design view is of the data type Text, Number or Yes/No, then the Display Control property on the Lookup tab shows the type of **control** that will be used to display the data. We'll be looking at controls in Chapter 6, as they are most concerned with **forms** and **reports**. All you need to know for the time being is that a control is an object that is used to carry out an action, display data or to enhance a form or report. The Lookup property determines what type of control will be used to display the data from the field on a form or report.

However, the property is also effective when we view a table - you saw earlier that the Paid field we added to our TestTable table was a checkbox. When you add fields to a table, Access sets the Display Control property to a default value. For Text and Number fields it is Text Box, and for Yes/No fields, it's Check Box.

Try It Out - Changing the Display Control

If you wanted to display the contents of your Paid field as Yes/No, or True/False, the check box would not be much help. You would have to change the control that is displayed when the table is viewed. This is exactly what we're going to do now...

1 Click on the Lookup tab to view the Display Control.

2 Change the entry from Check Box to Text Box using the drop-down list on the Display Control property.

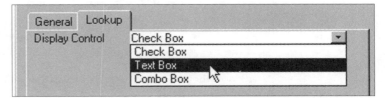

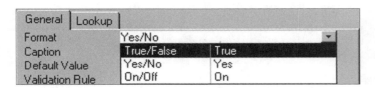

3 Go to the General tab and select the Format box. Click the down arrow to display the list of options and then select the True/False option.

4 Now view the table by selecting Table View. You will have to save the changes to the table first. The Paid field is now displayed as True or False in text form, rather than as a check box. Easy, huh!

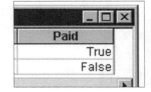

 FYI There is also a **Lookup Wizard...** option for the field types, available from the drop-down **Data Type** list. This is a little different to what we've seen above, and is used when you want to display a list of values in a field that the user can choose from. However, we're ahead of ourselves here - all these techniques, and the way they are used, will be covered as we look at other parts of Access a bit later. I'm afraid you're just going to have to be a bit patient.

Creating a New Table without Table Wizard

We said earlier that we would look at how to create a table without using the Table Wizard. Now that you've seen how data types and properties are set, and the effects they produce, you shouldn't find this too hard. In many cases, where the tables are relatively simple, you can often create them more quickly without the Table Wizard. Let's try this now.

Try It Out - Creating a Table from Scratch

1 Close any tables you have open and go to the Database window. Select the Tables tab and then click the <u>N</u>ew button. Access opens the New Table dialog.

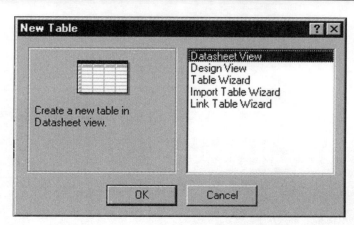

2 Select Design View and click OK. Access displays a new, empty table.

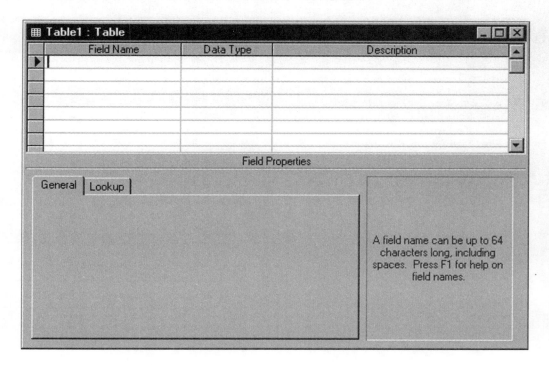

3 Enter the name for the first field - CustName, then press *Tab*. Access assumes we want the Text data type, which is correct.

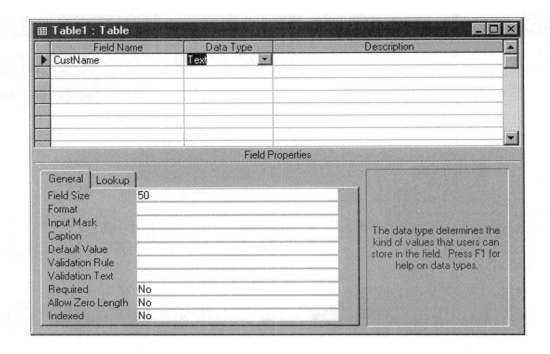

4 If you look at the Field Properties section, you can see that Access has set the default properties. It has set the Field Size (number of characters) to 50 and the Required, Allow Zero Length and Indexed properties to No. Change the Required property to Yes - we won't accept a new record without a customer's name.

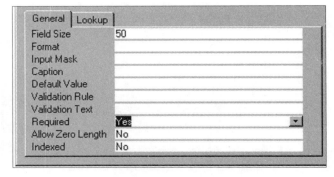

5 Now add some more fields as follows:

Field Name	Data Type	Field Size
Address	Text	100
City	Text	30
State	Text	2

6 Type in an input mask for the State field to force it to be upper case, and always contain two letters.

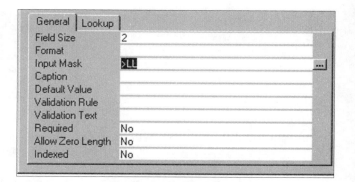

7 Add a CreditLimit field, setting the data type to Currency. Change the properties of the field so that Decimal Places is 0, the Default Value is 1000, and the Validation Rule is <10000, and add a Validation Text message along the lines of Credit limit must be less than $10,000.

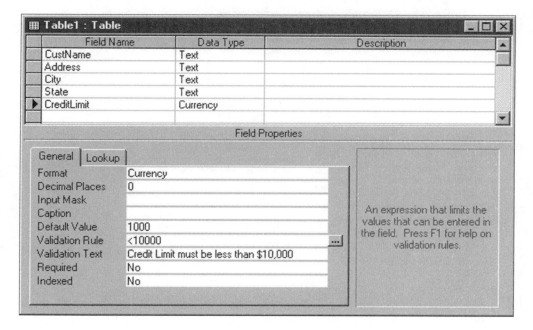

8 Switch to table datasheet view using the button on the toolbar (shown below). Access prompts you to save the design of the table (right).

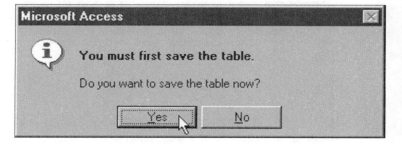

9 Click <u>Y</u>es. Access asks for the name of the new table. Enter New Customers and click OK.

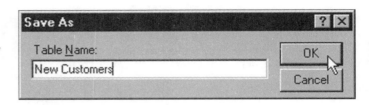

10 You will then be asked whether you want to create a primary key for this table. We will look at primary keys shortly, so just ignore this for the moment and click <u>N</u>o.

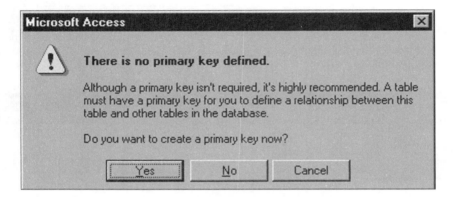

11 Now the new table appears. Type in some values. Remember to watch for the effects of the input mask in the State field - it automatically converts your text to upper case and only accepts two letters. If you only enter one and *Tab* to the next field you'll get an error message.

12 You'll see the default value of $1,000 shown in the CreditLimit field. Try changing this to a value greater than $10,000.

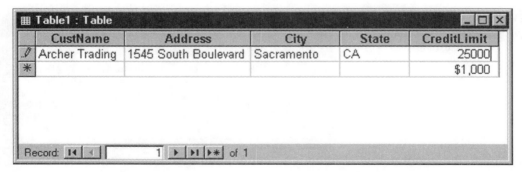

13 Now press *Tab*. Access displays the Validation Text message because the value we've entered breaks the Validation Rule for the field.

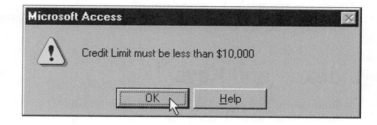

14 Correct the credit limit and then close the table. If you've changed the width of the columns you will be prompted to save these changes. Doing so ensures that next time the table will open with the same column widths, etc.

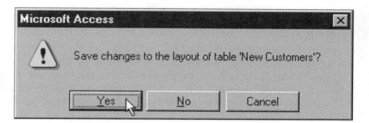

Altering the Look of the Table

You can change other aspects of the way that a table is displayed in table view. The options are available from the Format menu in table datasheet view. You can change the font and the size of the characters, turn off the gridlines, change the background colors and the way the grid is displayed. You can also change the row height and column width, and re-name, hide and freeze columns.

 If there are three dots after a menu option, it means that when you select it, you will be offered yet more options.

Try the different options out - it's quite surprising how different the table can be made to appear...

When you create a new table, or make any changes to the design of an existing one, Access prompts you to save the changes when you close it or switch to table view.

 All objects (tables, forms, reports, etc.) that you create in your database must be named, and these names appear in the relevant lists in the Database window. You can rename any of the objects by clicking on the name twice (slowly) just as you would in your Windows 95 desktop or file list windows.

You've now looked in depth at how to design tables, but discussion of a couple of aspects has been avoided until now. So, without further ado...

Indexes and Keys

Indexes are the method that Access uses to find a specific record quickly while keys are used to uniquely identify records. Both are intended to improve performance and keys also help to protect information within the database. We will look at indexes first.

Indexes

When you pick up a reference book to look for a particular item of information, the first thing you often do is to look in the **index** for the relevant page number. This makes a lot more sense than starting at page one and leafing through until you find what you're looking for. When you work with tables in your database, you often need to find a particular record. If you do a normal search, Access will start at the first record that you entered and search through until it finds the one you want - not the most efficient use of your computer's processing time. If there are a large number of records in the table, you will see the delay in the form of the hourglass cursor.

Access can, however, create **indexes** for the records in a table. If you regularly sort the records on one field, or search for records by specifying the value in a particular field, you can speed up the operation considerably by telling Access to create an index on that field. Like the index in a book, this is a list of all the contents of the field to which it applies, with a link that allows Access to go to the record you want - rather like a page number. If you index the customer name field and then tell Access to find the value "Miracle Supplies" in this field, Access finds it in the index and then uses the link to fetch the correct record.

Access has to maintain indexes each time you add, edit and delete records in the table. So if you specify a lot of fields to be indexed, you can slow down data entry. The trick is to be selective and only index the fields you know will be used regularly for sorting or searching in for information.

Creating an Index

If you want to create an index for a field in your database, you simply set the Indexed property of that field in table design view, as we saw in the previous section when modifying table properties. You can select from three values for this property - No, Yes (Duplicates OK) and Yes (No Duplicates). Selecting No tells Access that the field is not indexed. If you select Yes (Duplicates OK) or Yes (No Duplicates), Access will automatically create and maintain an index on that field and use it in your queries.

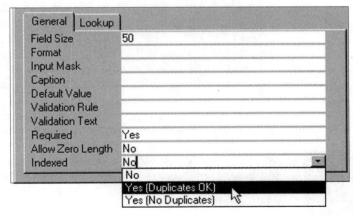

If you select the Yes (Duplicates OK) option, Access will allow you to enter more than one record in the table with the same value in this field. Suppose you had a table that you used to store a list of your customers. The Yes (Duplicates OK) value makes sense for a field that is used to store their surnames - it's likely that you will have more than one Smith amongst your clientele. If you had selected Yes (No Duplicates), Access would not allow you to enter two records with the same value in that field.

However, if you gave all your clients a unique Customer Number, it would be more sensible to use the Yes (No Duplicates) index type for this field. All the entries in the field would then have to be different and this will prevent you from accidentally allocating the same number to two customers.

Single- and Multiple-Field Indexes

The above types of index are called **single-field indexes**, as they only apply to a single field. The index contains an entry for each different value and links to whichever record contains that value. If there is more than one that contains the same value, then there is a link to each one. In a book, this type of index would be as follows:

Name	Page
Aronsen	10, 29
Burghart	17
Smith	14, 22, 28

Forename	Surname	Page
Mike	Aronsen	10
Pierre	Aronsen	29
Curt	Burghart	17
Aamon	Smith	14
Jack	Smith	22
Toni	Smith	28

Multiple-field indexes, on the other hand, are based on the values in two or more fields. For instance, if you have a Forename and Surname field in a table, you can create an index which combines both of these.

Now, when you use a query to search for Forename="Toni" AND Lastname="Smith", Access will use the multiple-field index to go directly to the correct entry, rather than having to search through three records.

Although you can set an index in the properties section of the table design window, Access also provides a dialog where all the indexes for a table are shown and can be modified. We'll use this now to view and modify the indexes that Access created in our TestTable table.

Try It Out - Creating and Modifying Indexes

1 Open the TestTable table in design view by selecting it from the Database window and clicking the Design button - or, if it is already open, by clicking the Design View button on the toolbar.

2 Click the Indexes button on the toolbar, or select Indexes from the View menu, to open the Indexes dialog.

Index Name	Field Name	Sort Order	
▶ CompanyName	CompanyName	Ascending	▲
OrderDate	OrderDate	Ascending	
PostalCode	PostalCode	Ascending	
⚐ PrimaryKey	TestTableID	Ascending	
ProjectName	ProjectName	Ascending	
			▼

Index Properties		
Primary	No	
Unique	No	The name for this index. Each index can use
Ignore Nulls	No	up to 10 fields.

3 There are indexes on several fields which we need to delete. Start with the CompanyName index - click on the gray selector button at the left of the row to highlight it, then press *Delete*. Repeat the process for OrderDate, PostalCode and ProjectName.

⚡ Indexes: TestTable ✕

Index Name	Field Name	Sort Order	
▶ CompanyName	CompanyName	Ascending	▲
OrderDate	OrderDate	Ascending	
PostalCode	PostalCode	Ascending	
⚐ PrimaryKey	TestTableID	Ascending	
ProjectName	ProjectName	Ascending	

4 To create a multiple-field index which combines the StateOrProvince and PostalCode fields, enter StateAndCode as a new index name on the first blank row of the Indexes dialog.

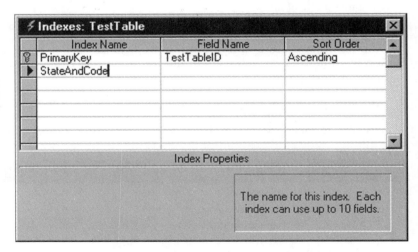

⚡ Indexes: TestTable ✕

Index Name	Field Name	Sort Order	
⚐ PrimaryKey	TestTableID	Ascending	▲
▶ StateAndCode			
			▼

Index Properties	
	The name for this index. Each index can use up to 10 fields.

5 Press the *Tab* key to
move to the **Field Name**
column. From the
drop-down list select
the **StateOrProvince**
field. You can leave the
sort order set to
Ascending.

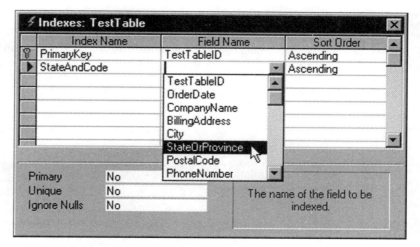

6 You have now created a
single-field index on
the **StateOrProvince**
field. To change it to a
multiple-field index,
move the cursor to the
next row of the **Field
Name** column and
select the **PostalCode**
field from the drop-
down list in this box.
When you have
finished, click on the
box in the right-hand
corner to close the
dialog down.

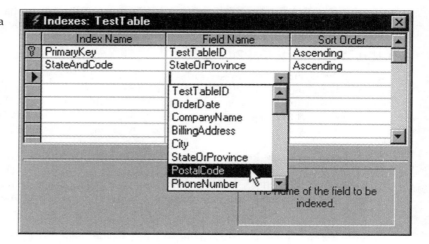

FYI Access treats all the fields it finds in the **Field Name** column as part of the same index
until it meets a new entry in the **Index Name** column. So to add another field to the
index, just select it in the next row.

You now know how to set up indexes. You might be wondering how you can see this index
working, but unfortunately, you can't. Access needs the index to be able to search efficiently
through the records, but in a small table like ours, the improvements in performance aren't
noticeable. However, in a 'real' database with thousands of records, an index makes all the
difference. Common sense should tell you that if you picked up a book, you'd get to a specific
subject quicker by using an index, than by going through the pages one at a time. However, if
the book was only 5 pages, then that might not be the case!

Using Primary Keys

As we said earlier, when you use an index where you have specified Yes (No Duplicates), you force Access to limit the values that can be stored in that field so that each is **unique** - no two records in the field can have the same value. This is useful if you have a field in each record which acts as an **identifier** for that record, e.g. a unique Customer Number.

When you used the Table Wizard to create the TestTable, you allowed the wizard to add a **primary key** - this is the TestTableID field at the top of the fields listed in design view.

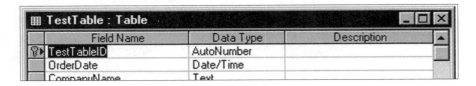

As you can see, its data type is set to AutoNumber. This means that when you enter records into the table in datasheet view, Access will automatically insert unique numbers into this field.

What is a Primary Key?

Generally you should try to set indexes on fields which are unique. This makes the index more efficient, reducing the search time for a query. However, it can be very difficult to find a field in which all the values are always unique - there could well be two Pierre Aronsens amongst your customers, in which case, not only does the index become less efficient, but there is no way of referring directly to just one of the records by using the name.

The aim of a **primary key** is to provide a field which contains values that are guaranteed to be unique for each record. As a result, searches using the primary key field are far more efficient than with any other field, and you can also refer to a particular record using the unique number. To ensure that the values remain unique, it must always be indexed with the Yes (No Duplicates) option.

As with normal indexes, you can have primary keys that are based on more than one field. You create a **multiple-field primary key** in the same way as a multiple-field index.

The AutoNumber primary key that Access created for us in TestTable is of data type Number and its Field Size is Long Integer.

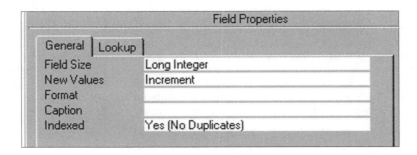

You can use a data type other than Number for the primary key if you like. For example, if we had a table containing parts for building computers, we could give them all different part identifiers such as DISC_7051 or TOWER_CASE and use these for the primary key.

Although the primary key seems to have no effect in our existing tables, when we come to redesign the structure of our database in the next chapter, this feature of Access be very useful.

Try It Out - Creating and Modifying a Table's Primary Key

You can create and change a primary key directly in table design view or by using the Indexes dialog. We'll look at both options now.

1 Make sure that the TestTable table is in design view. You'll see that the first row, TestTableID, has a 'key' marker on the row selector. This indicates that this field is the primary key for the table.

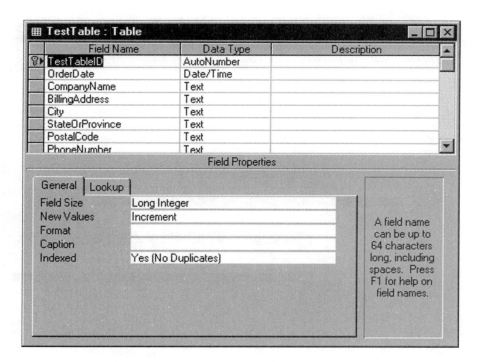

2 Select the OrderDate field (by clicking on the row selector) and then click the Primary Key button on the toolbar. The primary key marker moves to the selected field.

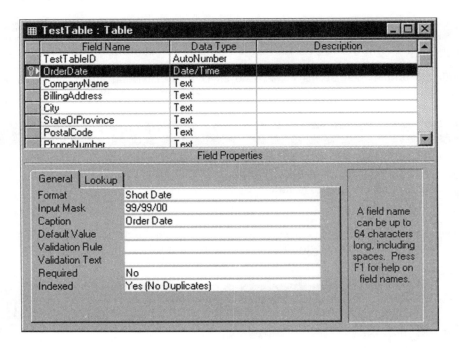

3 Now click the Indexes button on the toolbar to open the Indexes dialog. You'll see that the last row is our new primary key, OrderDate. When you click on it, the bottom part of the window shows that the index is the primary key, and that it is unique. This is equivalent to selecting the Yes (No Duplicates) option in table design view.

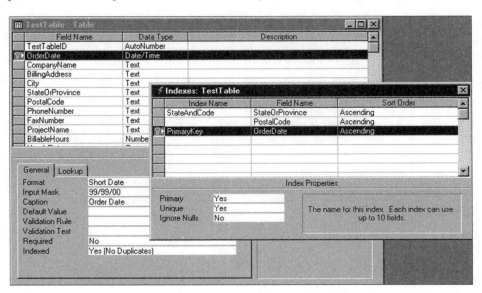

4 Close the Indexes dialog by clicking the Close box at the top right-hand corner of the window. Next we'll create a multiple-field primary key.

Note that although we will look at how a multiple-field primary key is set up, there are only limited situations where this type of primary key is acceptable. You'll see more discussion of the theory behind table design in Part 2 of the book.

5 In table design view, select both the TestTableID and OrderDate fields by clicking on the TestTableID row selector and then dragging the mouse onto the OrderDate row, so that they are both highlighted.

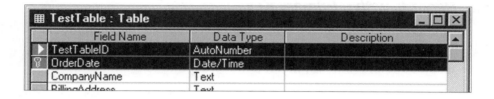

 If the two (or more) fields you want to use for the key are not adjacent, you can move them around in the grid by clicking on the gray row selector at the left of the field then clicking and dragging them up or down to the new position.

6 Now click the Primary Key button on the toolbar. Access marks both rows with the primary key symbol. This is our new multiple-field primary key.

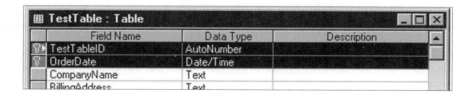

7 Open the Indexes dialog again by clicking the Indexes button on the toolbar. You can see the new primary key defined in the last two rows of the dialog.

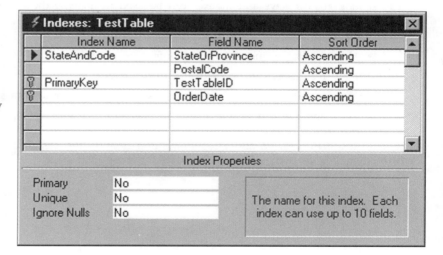

8 We won't be using the TestTable table again, so you can close it and remove it from your database. Close the Indexes and Table Design windows, then click the Table tab in the Database window. Select the TestTable table and press *Delete*.

Again you might wonder why we haven't demonstrated how Access uses the primary key. We've created a key to ensure there is no record duplication, but this is not the only purpose of a primary key. We have to consider why else we need a primary key before we can see how we might use it. This we will do in the next chapter.

Ordering Records with a Primary Key

One final thing to note about primary keys, is that when you first open a table and display the records, they are initially sorted in the order of the primary key. So if the primary key is a Number, the records appear sorted in numerical order. If you use a Text type field as the primary key, the records will, of course, appear sorted in alphabetical order of that field.

You can, therefore, use a primary key to make sure that the records appear in the required order when you view a table, without having to change the sort order. Remember that if you do change the order, and then close and reopen the table, the records will revert to the primary key order.

Summary

We have covered a lot in this chapter. The concepts are all important ones and ones that we will be meeting again before long, so it's worth just spending a couple of minutes making sure you are happy with them.

We started off by looking at what queries are and how simple ones are created. We will continue to spend time on queries in the next chapter as they are the real power-house behind how Access works and there is a lot more to learn.

We also looked at how tables are created and modified. You are now familiar with the different field properties and have seen how they can be used to prevent errors. By setting up input masks, for example, you can control the data that the user enters into your database. We also had a brief look at how keys and indexes can be used to increase the efficiency of a system.

In summary, you have learned:

- How to display just selected records from a table.
- How recordsets can be used to update tables.
- How to create tables - both using the Table Wizard and from scratch.
- What indexes and primary keys are and how they are set up.

In later chapters we'll go about redefining and refining the design of the database. What we've learned in this chapter will form the basis for these next stages.

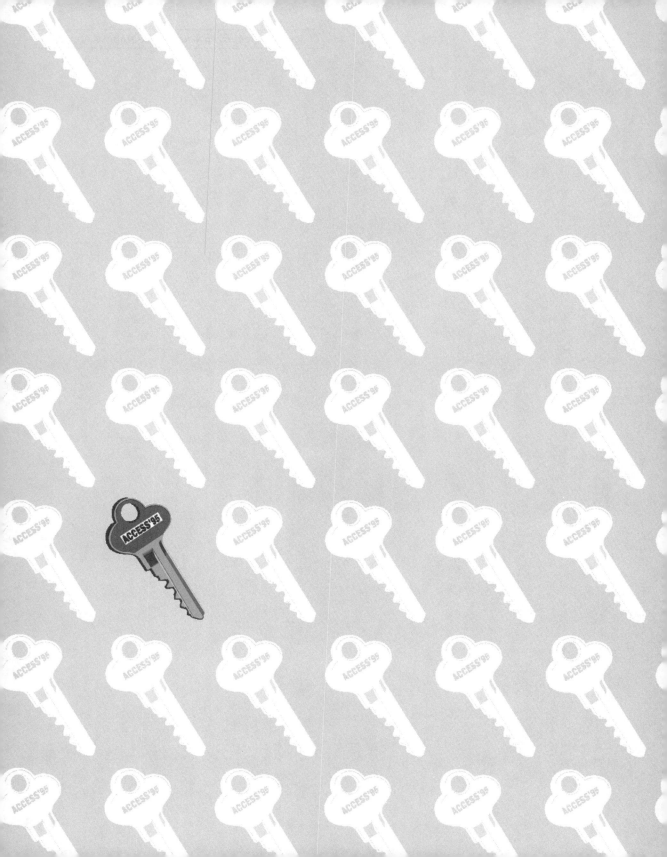

Refining Your Tables

We have now covered all the techniques we need to begin refining the design of our database. We want to make it easier to update repeated information and, at the same time, improve the efficiency of the system by using smaller tables. Ted Codd has laid down some mathematical rules for database design, but in this chapter we will concentrate more on applying common sense to the design, adding in a little background theory where appropriate.

In this chapter, we'll cover the following:

▶ Breaking the database into multiple tables.

▶ Relating the tables to each other.

▶ Using queries on related tables.

Redesigning Our Database

In Chapter 1 we looked briefly at some of the problems that the design of our original spreadsheet caused when we tried to store and analyze the information it contained. Our Access table still isn't particularly efficient - not because Access is deficient in any way, but because our design is. We'll now consider in greater depth the current design of our database, why it's inefficient and what can be done to improve it.

Splitting Accounts.mdb into Multiple Tables

We currently have just one single table in our database. Each record holds data about a particular project that we've worked on and the structure is as follows:

⊞ Original : Table			▲
Field Name	Data Type	Description	
▶ Date	Date/Time		
CustName	Text		
Address	Text		
Town	Text		
State	Text		
ZipCode	Number		
Phone	Text		
Fax	Text		
Project	Text		
HoursWorked	Number		
HourlyRate	Currency		
TotalCharge	Currency		
TaxRate	Number		
TaxDue	Currency		
TotalDue	Currency		
Paid	Yes/No		
			▼

Consider how you would add extra information to the table. You may want to store more details about each customer and project - for instance, the customer's e-mail address or credit rating, or the contact you deal with on a particular project. You may also want to store the names of all the people you talk to at that client's premises - for example, the managing director, IT manager and the systems engineer. How do you get all this data into the table? The most obvious way is to just add extra fields, so that the design of the table would look like this:

⊞ Original : Table			▲
Field Name	Data Type	Description	
▶ Date	Date/Time		
CustName	Text		
Address	Text		
Town	Text		
State	Text		
ZipCode	Number		
Phone	Text		
Fax	Text		
E-Mail	Text		
CreditRating	Number		
Contact1Name	Text		
Contact1Position	Text		
Contact1Phone	Text		
Contact1E-Mail	Text		
Contact2Name	Text		
Contact2Position	Text		
Contact2Phone	Text		
Contact2E-Mail	Text		
Contact3Name	Text		
Contact3Position	Text		
Contact3Phone	Text		
Contact3E-Mail	Text		
Project	Text		
HoursWorked	Number		
HourlyRate	Currency		
TotalCharge	Currency		
TaxRate	Number		
TaxDue	Currency		
TotalDue	Currency		
Paid	Yes/No		
			▼

What you've effectively got is a long record for each project with different sets of fields holding data for different aspects of that project.

118

This type of structure is called a **flat file** database, and is common in the less powerful database applications. As we saw in Chapter 1, though, the problem with this type of database is that the structure is inflexible. If a company changed address, for example, every time a record appeared in our database with that address, the entry would have to be changed. In the last chapter we designed a system using recordsets which would automatically update the corresponding table entry when we changed one entry in the recordset. However, this doesn't solve this particular problem - we'd still have to change each individual entry in the table or recordset. This isn't only a pain, but it also increases the likelihood of errors - all you have to do is accidentally miss one of the records and leave it with the old address and you'd end up with an incorrect database. With our small database, redesigning the whole thing might seem a bit excessive when we could change our entries by hand in five minutes and be relatively sure that we weren't creating any errors. However, if you were faced with changing a customer's address in a database with thousands of entries, you'd soon understand the problem. So what can we do about it?

Relational Databases

You'll recall that in Chapter 1 we considered how we could store information more efficiently in Excel by splitting the design of our database into several tables. We suggested using three - one each for our projects, customers, and contacts.

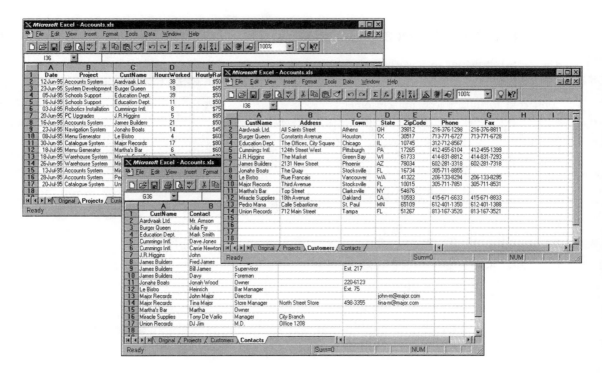

The problem was that Excel had no way of 'connecting' the different records from the separate tables or pages in the spreadsheet. You had to include the customer's name in each table so that you could tell which customer was connected to which project or contact and then, to retrieve information, you had to switch from one page to another each time you wanted to check out a particular project's details.

Access and other **relational** database programs, however, get round this by allowing you to link or **join** tables together, so that records in each table can **relate** to records in the others. The link between two records which hold data about the same item, such as the data about a project record and the customer for that project, is called a **relation**. The term **relation** covers all aspects of the way the join is handled by the database application. We'll be looking in depth at the theory of relations throughout this book.

The ability to form joins between tables is what differentiates a relational database from a flat file database and is the technique on which relational databases operate. Some database systems implement a half-way house solution to the problems of flat file databases. For instance, those based on the xBase format can form links in a limited way, but don't implement all the features required to be fully relational. Access, however, has been designed from the ground up to include all the functionality of a true relational database.

Let's go back our **Accounts** database then. We could just try using the structure we considered in Chapter 1 to see how this improves things, but perhaps we should be a little more scientific about it. We'll consider the 'rules' in a later chapter, but for the moment let's try applying some lateral thinking to the problem.

Designing the Different Tables

The record structure that we have is based around one record for each project. This record stores all the data connected to the project, the customer and to our contacts at that customer's premises. If you think of the different groups of data in a record, you'll see that we have a block of fields which contains the project data, a block that contains the customer data, and a block that contains the contacts data.

We're storing a record for each project we carry out, so you might consider the main focus of each record to be the project itself. Each project has a customer connected with it - you've got to be paid by someone after all - and each customer has one or more contacts connected with them for that project.

Details about the Customer

Details of our Contacts

Details of the Project

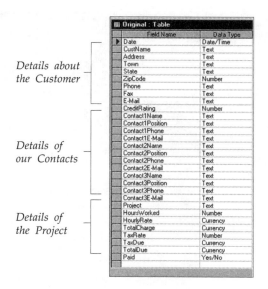

You could, therefore, divide the database up into three tables, using the type of project as the common field to link them, as illustrated:

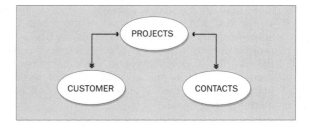

However, you can carry out more than one project for a customer, and the people you deal with may not be the same for each project. So already you're faced with a number of problems:

- You have to enter a lot of customer information which is duplicated for every project you carry out for them - for instance their address, phone number, fax number, etc.

- If a customer changes their phone number and you want to update your records, you have to edit every record which contains that customer's details.

- You cannot store information about a customer or your contacts until there is a project underway.

Entities

The solution to these problems is to step back from the detail of the current design, and consider the information you have to store as individual **entities**. An entity is database-speak for any of the individual things that you are storing information about. For example, if you had a list of every part that made up a motor car, you could break it down into entities such as the engine, body shell, dashboard, etc. So the Piston, Flywheel, Alternator and Radiator would be parts of the engine entity, and the Headlight, Door, Hood and Wing Mirror would be parts of the body shell entity.

We have already identified three entities amongst our data - **projects**, **customers** and **contacts**. If you think about it, though, you'll see that it's actually not the project but the customer that's the base of our data. The customer is the root of all the projects. You can carry out more than one project for a customer, and it's the projects that differ, not the

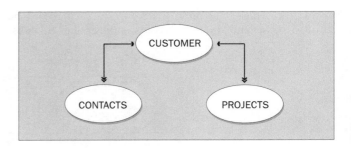

customer. The same applies to your contacts at each customer's premises - there may be different contacts for different projects, but they're all connected with the same customer. So our structure should be based around the customers, rather than the projects that we carry out for them.

One-To-Many Relationships

So we have three distinct entities: **customers** (including their name, address, phone and fax numbers etc.), **projects** (including the date, description and cost), and **contacts** (including their name, position, phone and e-mail address).

121

Note that, in the above figure, the entities are connected with an arrow which has a single head at one end and a double head at the other. This is a common way to show that the relationship between them is **one-to-many**. This means is that there can be several individual contacts or projects for each customer. For example, the database shows that we have three contacts at James Builders. If we only have one **customer** record stored in our database for James Builders, we need to be able to link all three **contact** records to it. So the link is **one** (customer record) **-to-many** (contact records). How the actual mechanics of this work will become clear as we look at relations in general.

Avoiding Repetition

One of the main problems that we identified earlier was the repetition of data in our table. When considering the design of a database, you want to look at which data is repeated and try and remove it. You do this by looking for **dependencies**. For instance, the value stored in the address field of a record is directly dependent on the customer and only the customer. The address is said to be **functionally dependent** on the customer. In the single table design, you will store an address several times if you carry out more than one project for the same customer. In database terms, this duplication of data is referred to as **redundancy**. If you duplicate information for each customer, you're obviously making life more difficult for yourself when it comes to updating a phone number or address.

There is also a problem of repeated fields in the contacts part of the record. You have to include room in the record to store details of more than one contact, but how many contacts should you allow for? If you plan for three, then, wherever there is only one contact at that customer, the records will have blank fields. And what happens when you're working for a major client who expects you to liaise with five people?

So we need to look for two types of repeating fields:

▶ Fields that are repeated in the same record and hold different values for the same entity, such the Contact details.

▶ Those that only occur once in each record but hold the same value for an entity in several different records, such as the Address details.

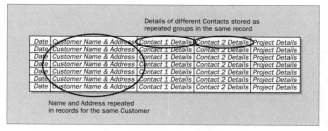

A good structural design will not have any groups of repeated fields. For example, we should only store a customer's phone number once in the database. It will then be easy to change the number when we need to.

If groups of similar fields containing different values are repeated in one record, such as the contact details in our **Original** table, it causes extreme difficulties when you come to analyze your data. This type of structure often occurs in a flat-file database system where there's no other option, but in Access it must be avoided at all costs. We do this by designing our tables so that as much of the repeated information as possible is removed from the database.

Our database will, therefore, consist of three entities and be based around the Customer table. This will remove the redundant repeating groups of fields and, therefore, make updating the data much easier. It will also solve the third problem we identified - we will be able to store details of a customer even if we haven't yet done any work for them. This has to be useful, because we'll be dealing with our contacts while we negotiate for the project, and we need to be able to store and retrieve their details.

Archiving Information in a Relational Database

If we look forward a little, there's another aspect of our database that we should consider. At some time in the future we'll probably want to clear out all the information about completed projects and archive it. Otherwise the table will just grow and grow until we run out of space to store it.

In the single table design, this would mean deleting the oldest records and effectively losing access to all the information they contain. If we had done some work for a customer five years ago, and they then called to say they wanted to implement a new project, we'd have lost all the information we had about them. We would also have lost information that could have been used for advertising purposes.

In the new design, we can store details about a customer without having to have a project record. A one-to-many relationship can be 'one-to-none' if there's no record linked to it in the other table. In this design we can delete the out-of-date project information, while keeping the details such as the customer address, phone number and other useful information in a separate table.

The Design So Far

So there are more and more reasons why we should consider breaking our tables down so that each one stores information that's only dependent on the entity it is concerned with. Here, then, is the design so far:

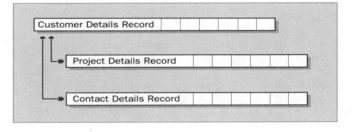

Parent and Child Records

Creating several tables does, however, cause a problem. In a one-to-many relationship, the table on the 'one' side is the **master** or **parent** table, and the table on the 'many' side is the **sub-** or **child** table. This type of relationship allows a parent record to exist which has no child records, but doesn't allow a child record without a parent. A child record which isn't related to a parent record (because the parent record has been deleted or lost for some reason) is called an **orphan** record.

Once an orphan record appears in your database, it's effectively lost - there's no link between it and the other tables, so you can't tell which record is the parent. For instance, the data in an orphan contact record is useless because you don't know which customer the contact details belong to.

As a simple example, imagine a table of customers and a table of invoices. To link an invoice to the correct customer we have a number in each table. But someone has deleted customer number 1655, so who are we going to send the bill for over $1000 to now?

Customers			**Invoices**		
CustKey	Customer		CustKey	Customer	*Value*
1651	Aarkvark Supplies		1651	Accounts System	*$4,178.67*
1652	Cummings Intl.	→	1655	Menu Generator	*$1,227.78*
1653	Miracle Supplies		1652	Navigation Generator	*$7,741.00*
1654	Union Records		1651	Menu Generator	*$2,659.95*
1656	Jonah's Boats		1654	Schools System	*$9,556.00*

If you're thinking that it would have been easier to stick with our original flat file system, then don't worry - Access contains methods for preventing orphan records appearing, as you'll see later on.

Relating the Tables Via a Primary Key

The only other thing we need to consider at this stage is how we're going to link the tables together. When we broke up the Excel table, we used the customer name to relate each record to its matching records in the other tables. This would be fine if we could be sure that all the customers we may deal with will have different names, but this is unlikely in the long term. There's just as likely to be an **Acme Trading Company** in Florida as there is in Alaska, so then we'd have to differentiate them on the address. All in all, it could become very confusing.

Instead, we'll use a technique that we met in the previous chapter - adding a **primary key** to the table. A primary key will automatically provide a code number for each customer which is guaranteed to be unique. We can then use this number in the linked records to identify which records belong to which customer. Although not strictly necessary, we'll also add an automatic primary key number to the Contact and Project tables. You'll see why we do this in a moment.

So we need to add the primary key fields to our tables. Here's the design in more detail:

We've added a Customer Key field which will be the primary key for the Customer table. Each customer will then have a unique customer number. In both the Project and Contact tables we've included two new fields. The first is a field that links the record back to the correct customer by holding the customer's unique number - the customer key. However, each customer can have more than one record in the Project or Contact

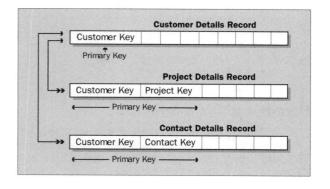

table. Therefore, we can't use the Customer Key field in the Project table as the primary key for that table - there may be more than one record with the same values in this field. And, of course, the same applies to the Contact table.

The way round this is to make the primary key for the Project and Contact tables a multiple-field key - and include a unique ProjectKey or ContactKey with the CustomerKey. You can probably now see why we elected to include a key field in the Project and Contact tables. While it's unlikely that our contacts at any one customer would be two people with the same name, it's quite likely that we could work on two projects with the same name for the same customer. The combination of CustomerKey and ProjectKey (or CustomerKey and ContactKey) is guaranteed to be unique.

So now our design is complete, and we are ready to consider how we implement it in Access.

Implementing the Multiple-Table Design

Although we won't be starting to build the Wrox Consultancy database application in earnest until Part 2, splitting up the tables is the first major step in the process. The finished application is called **Wroxsoft**, and we'll use the next few chapters to lay some foundations for this.

Try It Out - Creating the New Customer Table

The first thing we need to do is create the new database. For this, you'll need the single-table **Accounts.mdb** database we built in the previous chapters. In case you haven't been following the examples so far, we've supplied the database on the disk that accompanies this book. It will have been placed on your hard disk in the folder **BegAcc95** when you installed the sample files.

1 Create a new blank database and call it **Wroxsoft.mdb**.

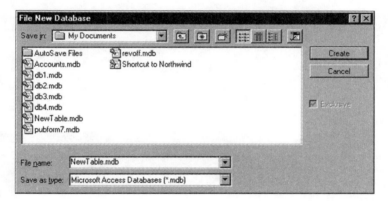

2 We are going to copy the Original table from **Accounts.mdb** into our new database and modify it there. Select Get External Data from the File menu, and click Import to open the Import dialog. Find your **Accounts.mdb** database (make sure the Files of Type: at the bottom of the window is set to Microsoft Access), select it and click Import.

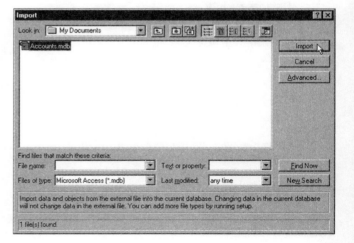

3 Access now displays the Import Objects dialog. Here we select which items in the **Accounts** database we want to import. The tabs allow you to select the type of object - just like in the normal Database window. You can import anything from one Access database into another. Select the Tables tab and click on the Original table.

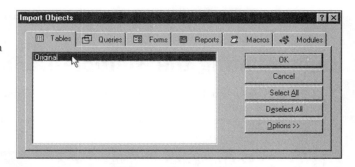

4 Now click the Options>> button. The window expands to show the options you can select when importing different objects. The only one of interest to us as the moment is Import Tables - make sure that Definition and Data (the default) is selected so that we import the existing data in the Original table as well as the design (definition) of it.

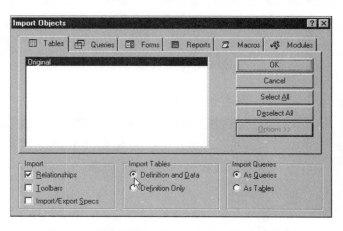

5 Click OK and Access imports the table. You'll see an entry for the Original table appear in the Database window.

6 We can now create the new tables. With the Tables tab selected in the Database window, click the New button. The New Table dialog appears.

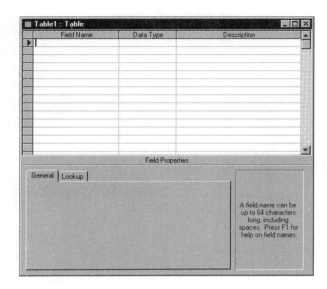

7 Select Design View in the list, and click OK. Access displays a blank table design grid. This will be the new Customer table.

We've now got a blank table set up, so the next job is to fill in the fields we need.

8 First we need to create the key field. In the first row type CustKey for the Field Name, and in the Data Type column select AutoNumber from the drop-down list.

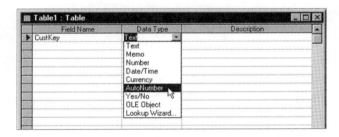

9 It's worth entering a description for the field in the third column. While not strictly necessary, a description is used to identify the field and is useful when creating a form or query based on the table. It's good to get in the habit of always adding a description - enter one now.

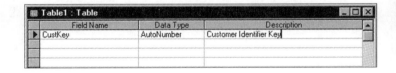

10 Now we'll tell Access that this field is the primary key for the table. With the cursor anywhere in the CustKey row, click the Primary Key button on the toolbar.

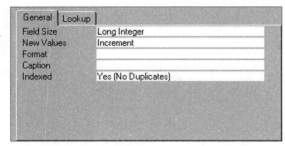

Access marks the field with the key symbol and sets its Indexed property to Yes (No Duplicates) - the value required for a primary key.

11 We can copy the rest of the fields from the Original table we imported. Select this table in the Database window (this will be behind the current window) and click the Design button to open it in design view. Move the windows around so that you can see both of them. You can minimize the Database window to make more room.

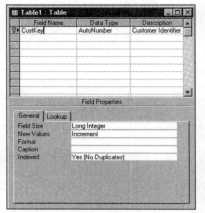

12 In the Original table click on the CustName field record selector and drag the mouse so that all the fields down to and including the Fax field are highlighted. Then press *Ctrl-C*, or select Copy from the Edit or short-cut menu, to copy the fields to the clipboard.

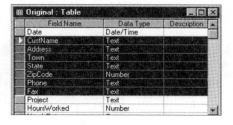

13 To copy the fields into the new table, go to the new table and click in the Field Name column of the first blank row under the CustKey field. Press *Ctrl-V*, or select Paste from the Edit or short-cut menu.

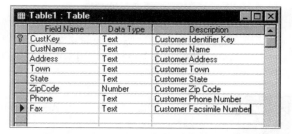

14 The final stages are to complete all the field descriptions and set the properties for the fields that we need. First go through the fields entering the descriptions:

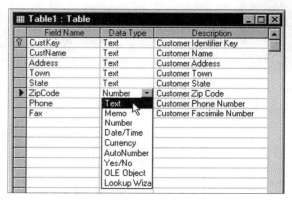

15 The only data type that you need to change is the one for the **ZipCode**. Access set it to a **Number** field, but it is probably best as a **Text** field - if we deal with customers outside the US we may need to include letters as well as numbers in this field. Change it now.

16 We also need to change some of the field properties. Change the Field Size settings for the **CustName** and **Address** to 60, for **Town** to 30, **State** to 2, **ZipCode** to 6, and **Phone** and **Fax** to 20.

17 We should also set any other indexes that we may need. Set the **Indexed** property for **CustName** to **Yes (Duplicates OK)**. This will be fine for our purposes.

18 The only other property that we need to change is the Required property for the CustName field. Change this to Yes to prevent records being created with no customer name.

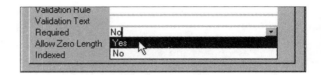

 You'll see that, by default, Access sets the **Required, Allow Zero Length,** and **Indexed** properties to **No**. Depending on how you intend to use your tables, you may wish to change these. You can also set up input masks for the **ZipCode, Phone** and **Fax** fields. Beware, though, of making the conditions for data entry too restrictive. For instance, you may at some stage want to enter the name and phone number of a prospective customer, but not know their full address. If you have set the **Required** property for the **Town, State** and **ZipCode** to **Yes**, you'll be prevented from entering the record into the table.

19 Finally, when you have set all the properties you need, close the table by clicking on the Close button at the top right of the window. Access asks whether you want to save the design of the table.

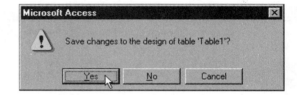

20 Select Yes and in the next dialog type Customer for the name of the table, then click OK.

That completes the design of the Customer table for the time being. In future chapters we'll come back and improve it. First, though, we need to complete the other two tables. These involve a similar process to the one you've just used. However, we'll need to adjust some of the fields as we go along.

The Project and Contact Tables

The first consideration when creating the Project and Contact tables must be the fields that form the primary key and link the record back to the correct customer. Our Customer table has an AutoNumber type field as the CustKey primary key. You'll recall that an AutoNumber field automatically generates a unique number (assigned by Access and based on the last autonumber value used in that table) each time a new record is added to the table.

We've already decided that we will use the same system to generate our ProjectKey field values for new records in the Project table, and that this will combine with the CustKey field to form the primary key to this table. But while the ProjectKey is a unique number, the CustKey must be set to the same value as the CustKey field in the Customer table to form this link. If this seems confusing, have another look at the diagram we used earlier. We'll flesh it out with some values to see how the links actually work:

CustKey Customer

147 Major Records			

CustKey ProjKey Project Details

147	365	Accounts System
147	357	Warehouse System

CustKey ContactKey Contact Details

147	791	Mark Cave
147	792	Lee Mitumisyo

Now you can see that we can't use an AutoNumber field for the CustKey in the Project table. Instead, it has to be a standard Number-type field which can hold the same values as an AutoNumber field. Access specifies this as a field of type **long integer**.

 A long integer is a whole number that is four bytes in size. Normal integers are just two bytes. As a result, long integers can store much larger numbers.

Because there can be several Project records linked to one Customer, the CustKey field may contain the same value in several records. Therefore, it *can't* be indexed as Yes (No Duplicates). So does this break the rule that a primary key field must contain unique values? No - remember that the primary key of the Project table is a combination of the CustKey and ProjectKey. Together, they will always be unique, even if alone, the CustKey isn't. So the design of the Project tables becomes:

	Field Name	Data Type	Description
🔑	CustKey	Number	Customer ID Key
🔑	ProjectKey	AutoNumber	Project ID Key
	Date	Date/Time	Date of Project
	Project	Text	Name of Project
	HoursWorked	Number	Number of hours worked
	HourlyRate	Currency	Rate charged per hour
	TotalCharge	Currency	Total before tax
	TaxRate	Number	Tax Rate (percent)
	TaxDue	Currency	Tax Due
	TotalDue	Currency	Total including tax
	Paid	Date/Time	Date Project paid

Project : Table

 You're not forced to use an **AutoNumber**-type field, or even a number, as a primary key. For instance, you could set the **CustKey** field to **Text** and use your own values, such as **MAJREC** or **MAJ01** instead of the **147** that we used above. The values could be created by the user when records are entered into the tables, and Access would automatically prevent the use of duplicates. Alternatively, you could set up the data entry form so that it created primary key values based on the customer's name. This type of key often makes finding a customer record quicker and easier, but it requires more work to set up. In this book we'll be sticking to **AutoNumber** types.

Try It Out - Creating the Project Table

We now understand the design of the Project table and have some ideas of how to implement it. All that remains is to put these ideas into practice.

1 Create a new table, go to design view and add a Number type field called CustKey. Set its Field Size property to Long Integer.

2 Add an AutoNumber type field called ProjectKey.

3 Now go to the design view of the Original table and copy all the fields we need into the new table: Date, Project, HoursWorked, HourlyRate, TotalCharge, TaxRate, TaxDue, TotalDue, and Paid. Change the Paid field so that it is of type Date/Time - we'll use it to store the date that we were paid, rather than just a Yes/No value. Then change the field properties to those shown below (any entries that are blank in the table below can be left set to their default value):

	Field Size	Format	Required
CustKey	Long Integer		
ProjectKey			
Date		Medium Date	Yes
Project	50		Yes
HoursWorked			
HourlyRate		Currency	
TotalCharge		Currency	
TaxRate		Percent	
TaxDue		Currency	
TotalDue		Currency	
Paid		MediumDate	

4 Set the primary key for the table by highlighting the top two rows, and clicking the **Primary Key** button on the toolbar.

Field Name	Data Type	Description
CustKey	Number	Customer ID Key
ProjectKey	AutoNumber	Project ID Key
Date	Date/Time	Date of Project
Project	Text	Name of Project
HoursWorked	Number	Number of hours worked
HourlyRate	Currency	Rate charged per hour
TotalCharge	Currency	Total before tax
TaxRate	Number	Tax Rate (percent)
TaxDue	Currency	Tax Due
TotalDue	Currency	Total including tax
Paid	Date/Time	Date Project paid

5 Finally, select the File menu and choose the **Save As/Export** option. Save the table as **Project** and close it.

So that's the **Project** table. Now all that's left is to create the **Contact** table. Moving straight on then...

Try It Out - Creating the Contact Table

We'll use a multiple-field primary key for this table as we did for the **Project** table. There are no contact fields in the **Original** table, so this time we'll have to create the whole table from scratch. We'll include a field to store the contact's position in the company, plus their address, phone number and e-mail address.

1 Create a new table. Go to the design view and add fields for the CustKey, ContactKey, ContactName, ContactPosition, ContactAddress, ContactPhone and ContactE-Mail as shown.

Field Name	Data Type	Description
CustKey	Number	Customer ID Key
ContactKey	AutoNumber	Contact ID Key
ContactName	Text	Contact's name
ContactPosition	Text	Contact's position/rank/etc
ContactAddress	Text	Contact's address/branch/etc
ContactPhone	Text	Contact's phone number
ContactE-Mail	Text	Contact's E-mail address

2 Then change the properties shown in the list below, leaving the rest set to their defaults.

	Field Size	Required	Indexed
CustKey	Long Integer		
ContactKey			
ContactName	50	Yes	Yes (Duplicates OK)
ContactPosition	50		
ContactAddress	255		
ContactPhone	20		
ContactE-Mail			

3 Set the multiple-field primary key by dragging over the first two rows and clicking the Primary Key button on the toolbar.

Field Name	Data Type	Description
CustKey	Number	Customer ID Key
ContactKey	AutoNumber	Contact ID Key
ContactName	Text	Contact's name
ContactPosition	Text	Contact's position/rank/etc

4 Save the table as Contact and close it.

We now have our three tables set up. Before we leave the table design, though, we need to add some data.

Adding Data to the New Tables

We already have most of the data we require in our Original table. Therefore, rather than typing all the entries in from scratch, we can just do a straight copy. This sounds easy enough, so let's have a go at it now. The obvious way is to copy the data from one table to another using the clipboard.

Try It Out - Copying Data into the Customer and Project Tables

1 Open the Original table and the Customer table you created earlier on. Move them around till you can see the columns we will be copying - you don't need to be able to see all of the records.

2 Select the columns in the Original table which contain the data to be copied by clicking on the column selector for CustName and dragging across until all the fields up to and including Fax are highlighted. Press *Ctrl-C* to copy the data to the clipboard.

3 Go to the Customer table and highlight the same fields as in the Original table. Then press *Ctrl-V* to paste the contents. Access asks you to confirm your action.

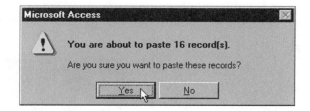

4 Click Yes and the records will be added to the new table.

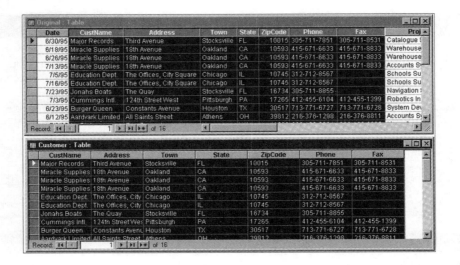

5 Now have a look at the CustKey field in the Customer table. Access has filled in a unique number for each record. (You may not get the same numbers as the figure below - don't worry about this. Access remembers the last Autonumber value you used and defaults to the next one).

If you look at the table, you'll see that there's more than one record for some customers. This is because the Original table contained **redundant** repeated data. We can remove this redundancy now because the records for the same customer are identical. We haven't included the data about each project in our records and this is what made the records different in the Original table.

6 Select the records that are repeated by clicking on their record selector at the left of the record and press the *Delete* key. You can select more than one record by clicking on the first and dragging the cursor over the next ones in the table.

7 Access removes the record(s) and asks you to confirm that you really want to do this - select <u>Y</u>es.

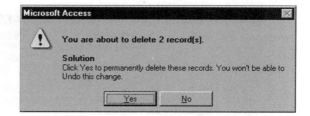

8 Repeat this for any other duplicated records (record 6 should be the only other one that needs deleting) then close the Customer table, saving the changes as you do so.

9 We must now copy the projects data into our new Project table. Open it in datasheet view.

We now hit a problem. The fields we need from the Original table are split up by the address fields, so you can't select them as one block like you did with the customer's name and address fields, and Access won't let you select non-contiguous blocks of fields. If you try to copy and paste the data one column at a time, you'll meet another problem. Remember that we set the Required property for the Date and Project fields to Yes. If we try to paste just the data from the Date field, Access stops us because the Project fields in the new records would be empty, and if we try to copy data from the Project field, we can't do anything because of the empty Date field. To get round this, we need to copy the entire record in one go - this means changing the order of the fields in the window.

10 In the open Original table, select the Date field and then click again on the field selector and drag it so that the dark vertical line is directly before the Project field. When you release the mouse button, the field is moved to the new location.

Date	CustName	Address	Town	State	ZipCode	Phone	Fax	Project	Hour
6/30/95	Major Records	Third Avenue	Stocksville	FL	10015	305-711-7851	305-711-8531	Catalogue System	
6/18/95	Miracle Supplies	18th Avenue	Oakland	CA	10593	415-671-6633	415-671-8833	Warehouse System	
6/26/95	Miracle Supplies	18th Avenue	Oakland	CA	10593	415-671-6633	415-671-8833	Warehouse System	
7/13/95	Miracle Supplies	18th Avenue	Oakland	CA	10593	415-671-6633	415-671-8833	Accounts System	
7/5/95	Education Dept.	The Offices, City Square	Chicago	IL	10745	312-712-8567		Schools Support	
7/16/95	Education Dept.	The Offices, City Square	Chicago	IL	10745	312-712-8567		Schools Support	
7/23/95	Jonahs Boats	The Quay	Stocksville	FL	16734	305-711-8855		Navigation System	
7/3/95	Cummings Intl.	124th Street West	Pittsburgh	PA	17265	412-455-6104	412-455-1399	Robotics Installation	
6/23/95	Burger Queen	Constants Avenue	Houston	TX	30517	713-771-6727	713-771-6728	System Development	
6/12/95	Aardvark Limited	All Saints Street	Athens	OH	39812	216-376-1298	216-376-8811	Accounts System	

Record: 1 of 16

FYI These changes only affect the view of the data - they don't alter the order of the fields in the original design. However, Access will ask whether you want to save the new datasheet view layout when you close the table.

11 We can now select the fields we need - select the Date field by clicking the gray column selector and dragging across to include the TotalDue field, but don't include the Paid field. This is of the wrong data type for our new field, and while Access will accept the records if you paste them, it will assign meaningless random date values to the fields.

12 Press *Ctrl-C* to copy the fields. Next, you must move to the Project table and then select all of the fields from the Date field across to the TotalDue field. Then press *Ctrl-V* to paste the records and click <u>Y</u>es to accept the change. If you make a mistake and select one too many or one too few fields, then the paste won't work and you'll have to try it again.

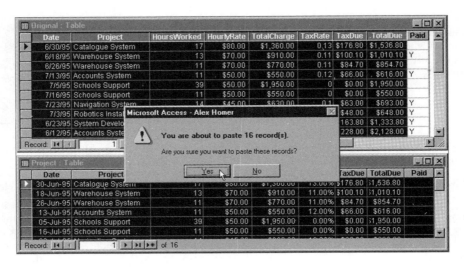

13 As you can see, Access again inserts unique AutoNumber values in the ProjectKey fields. However, the CustKey fields still contain zero. To add the correct CustKey value, you would have to find each record's customer key in the Customer table, by matching the project details in the Project table to the appropriate customer in the Customer table, using the Original table as the link between the two. To save you time, use the next screenshot to add the correct CustKey values into the Project table. You'll also need to go through adding dates to the Paid field for those projects that have been paid for. Close the table down when you have finished, saving the changes as you do so.

CustKey	ProjectKey	Date	Project	HoursWorked	HourlyRate	TotalCharge	TaxRate	TaxDue	TotalDue	Paid
1	1	30-Jun-95	Catalogue System	17	$80.00	$1,360.00	13.00%	$176.80	$1,536.80	
2	2	18-Jun-95	Warehouse System	13	$70.00	$910.00	11.00%	$100.10	$1,010.10	08-Mar-95
2	3	26-Jun-95	Warehouse System	11	$70.00	$770.00	11.00%	$84.70	$854.70	
2	4	13-Jul-95	Accounts System	11	$50.00	$550.00	12.00%	$66.00	$616.00	18-Sep-95
5	5	05-Jul-95	Schools Support	39	$50.00	$1,950.00	0.00%	$0.00	$1,950.00	
5	6	16-Jul-95	Schools Support	11	$50.00	$550.00	0.00%	$0.00	$550.00	
7	7	23-Jul-95	Navigation System	14	$45.00	$630.00	10.00%	$63.00	$693.00	26-Aug-95
8	8	03-Jul-95	Robotics Installation	8	$75.00	$600.00	8.00%	$48.00	$648.00	17-Jul-95
9	9	23-Jun-95	System Development	18	$65.00	$1,170.00	14.00%	$163.80	$1,333.80	27-Jul-95
10	10	12-Jun-95	Accounts System	38	$50.00	$1,900.00	12.00%	$228.00	$2,128.00	26-Jul-95
11	11	08-Jul-95	Menu Generator	4	$60.00	$240.00	15.00%	$36.00	$276.00	24-Aug-95
12	12	20-Jul-95	Catalogue System	25	$80.00	$2,000.00	13.00%	$260.00	$2,260.00	
13	13	18-Jul-95	Menu Generator	6	$60.00	$360.00	15.00%	$54.00	$414.00	
14	14	20-Jun-95	PC Upgrades	5	$85.00	$425.00	14.00%	$59.50	$484.50	
15	15	28-Jun-95	Accounts System	38	$50.00	$1,900.00	12.00%	$228.00	$2,128.00	29-Aug-95
16	16	16-Jun-95	Accounts System	21	$50.00	$1,050.00	12.00%	$126.00	$1,176.00	19-Aug-95
0	0									

FYI It's not difficult to move data from one table to another, but you will probably have realized that you can make things a lot easier for yourself by getting the design right in the first place. Just imagine the problems you would have with 20 tables, each containing 30 fields and with a few thousand records in each!

Filling the Contacts Table with Data

We now have data in both the customer and project tables; what remains is to add data to the Contact table.

Try It Out - Adding Data to the Contact Table

The Original table does not contain all the data we need. However, rather than type all the information in, we can go back to the Excel spreadsheet we used in Chapter 1 (**Accounts.xls**) and copy some of the columns from there.

1 Open the Excel spreadsheet and select the Contacts page. Highlight all of the cells which contain data, from the Contact column to the E-mail column (not the row that contains the column headings, though). Then press *Ctrl-C* to copy them to the clipboard.

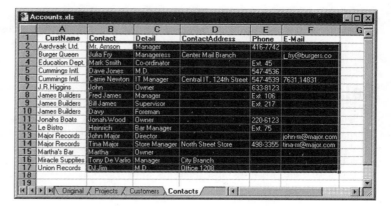

2 Switch to Access and open the Contact table in datasheet view. Select the five columns (ContactName to ContactE-Mail) to paste into. Press *Ctrl-V* and the data from Excel is pasted directly into the table. Access prompts you to accept the new records.

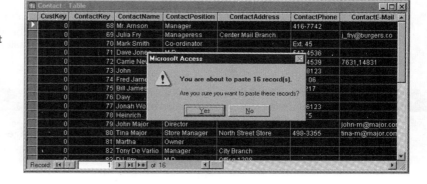

3 Click <u>Y</u>es to accept the new records. Then fill in the CustKey field by typing in the numbers shown here (these are taken from the relevant records in the Customer table).

CustKey	ContactKey	ContactName	ContactPosition	ContactAddress	ContactPhone	ContactE-Mail
10	68	Mr. Arnson	Manager		416-7742	
9	69	Julia Fry	Manageress	Center Mail Branch		j_fry@burgers.co
5	70	Mark Smith	Co-ordinator		Ext. 45	
8	71	Dave Jones	M.D.		547-4536	
8	72	Carrie Newton	IT Manager	Central IT, 124th Street	547-4539	7631,14831
14	73	John	Owner		633-8123	
16	74	Fred James	Manager		Ext. 106	
16	75	Bill James	Supervisor		Ext. 217	
16	76	Davy	Foreman			
7	77	Jonah Wood	Owner		220-6123	
11	78	Heinrich	Bar Manager		Ext. 75	
1	79	John Major	Director			john-m@major.com
1	80	Tina Major	Store Manager	North Street Store	498-3355	tina-m@major.com
13	81	Martha	Owner			
2	82	Tony De Varlio	Manager	City Branch		
12	83	DJ Jim	M.D.	Office 1208		
0	(AutoNumber)					

139

Notice how the values in the CustKey field appear in what seems like a random order. Remember that this is the only thing that links our contacts to the correct customer. The same applies with projects - each Project record contains a CustKey number as well, but no customer name. To find out the name of the contact for a particular project, we now need to look up the CustKey value in the Project table for that project, then look in the Contact table for the same CustKey value. And to find the customer's address, we need to find the same value in the Customer table.

As we discussed earlier in this chapter, Access makes life easy for us by allowing us to set up **relationships** that link the tables together and thus easily access data across the tables. We'll do this next.

Relationships

Although we now have a 'relational database' in that we have split up the tables so that we get maximum flexibility and efficiency, while removing redundant information, Access is still unaware that we have any **relations** in our database. (Relations is the term given to the links between different tables that enable Access to interpret the data they contain). We've set up the correct types of field to allow the relations to work, but now we need to tell Access which fields are related in which tables.

Relating the Tables to Each Other

To do this, we use the Relationships window. This is a desktop-style window where we can place the tables in our database, and manipulate them while forging the links between their fields. Access displays the relations in a graphical way that makes it easier to see what's going on. In this particular example, we will be linking the CustKey fields in the different tables to each other.

Try It Out - Using the Relationships Window

1 Make sure you have closed the Contact table and saved the changes. Then open the Relationships window by clicking the Relationships button on the toolbar, or if this button isn't visible, by selecting Relationships from the Tools menu.

2 Access displays the Show Table dialog and an empty window - we need to add our tables.

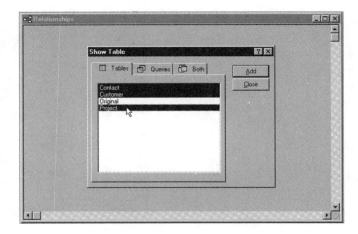

3 We can add tables easily. Select the Contact, Customer and Project tables by clicking on the first one and then holding down the *Ctrl* key while you click on the others. Then click the **A**dd button, then **C**lose. You can now see the three tables laid out, and by stretching their windows you can view all the fields. Note that the fields that make up the primary key of each table are shown in bold letters.

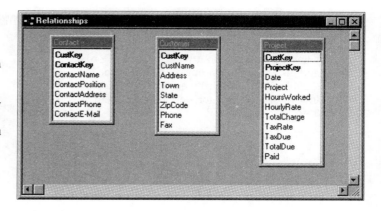

4 The easiest way to create a relationship is to drag a field from one table to another. Click on the CustKey field in the Customer table and drag it onto the CustKey field in the Contact table.

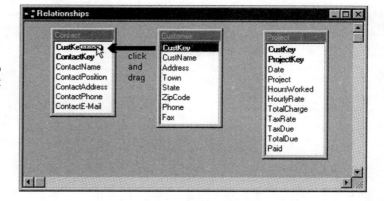

5 You now see another dialog showing the fields for the relationship in two lists marked Table/ Query and Related Table/Query. We dragged from the Customer table to the Contact table, so the Customer table is shown on the left. This will be the 'main' or 'parent' table and will be at the 'one' end of our new one-to-many relationship. The Contact table will be the 'sub' or 'child' table at the 'many' end of the relationship. Underneath the lists is a checkbox marked **E**nforce Referential Integrity. Turn this on - Access will enable the controls at the bottom of the window.

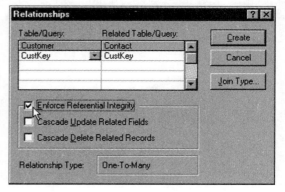

6 The Cascade <u>U</u>pdate Related Fields and
Cascade <u>D</u>elete Related Records options
allow us more freedom while editing records
and also help protect our data from damage.
We'll look at what this means in more detail
in a while. For the moment, just turn them
both on.

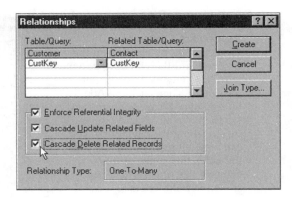

7 Click <u>C</u>reate to create the new
relationship. You'll see the
relationship shown as a line
between the fields, with the
one and many ends marked.
Note that ∞ (infinity) sign is
used to denote the 'many' end
of a relationship.

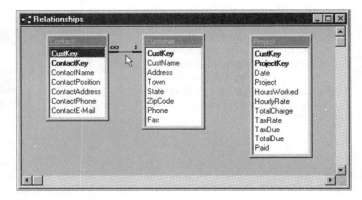

FYI If this doesn't happen and you get an error message, then that's because you've mistyped
or omitted one or more of the property entries for the **CustKey** field. If this is the case,
go back and check them thoroughly.

8 Now create a relationship between
the Customer and Project tables by
dragging the CustKey field in the
Customer table onto the CustKey
field in Project table.

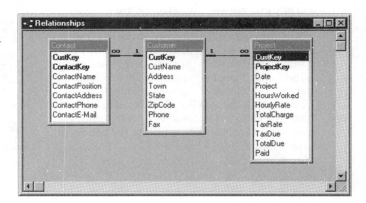

9 Close the Relationships window by clicking the Close box at the top right of the window. You'll be prompted to save the layout - select Yes.

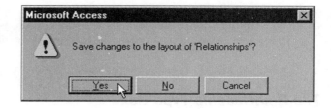

That's it. We now have a 'real' relational database, with the tables linked together enabling us to get information back out of them. We'll look at how we do this in a minute, but first we'll take a closer look at the Enforce Referential Integrity options that we rather glossed over in the example.

Understanding Referential Integrity

Referential integrity is one of the more prickly terms in the database canon, however, it sounds much worse than it actually is. Once you've put data into a database, you can use the Enforce Referential Integrity options that Access offers to ensure that records aren't lost. Earlier in this Chapter we saw how an invoice could remain unpaid because it had become 'detached' from its customer. This is a prime example of the way loss of integrity can affect the information you store.

In this chapter, we have created three separate tables from one table. We used the CustKey to indicate that data in one table was linked to data in another table. If two CustKeys matched, the records in the two tables were about the same project.

Imagine if you changed one of the CustKey entries to 9999. There are no other records with this key, so Access would have no way of 'knowing' which table this was linked to.

When we create a relationship between two tables, the child records are linked to their parent only by the values stored in the fields that form the relationship. If we change any of these values, the child record becomes linked either to the wrong parent record, in which case your database will give incorrect results, or it will no longer be linked to any parent at all, in which case it becomes an 'orphan', and the data it contains becomes inaccessible.

In database terms, this breaking of links is referred to as 'losing the integrity' of your data. Access can prevent this happening by automatically stopping a user from altering any of the linking field values in such a way that causes integrity to be lost. The user can still alter data, but not in a way that would cause problems. This is the meaning of the Enforce Referential Integrity option.

The Cascade Update and Cascade Delete Options

This still doesn't explain the other two options, though. Cascade Update Related Fields and Cascade Delete Related Records allow you to use a feature of Access that is not available in most other database systems. The word *cascade* gives a clue as to their function. Effectively, they create a domino toppling effect of changes.

If you check both options, Access will allow you to edit the values in the linked fields under certain circumstances, while still maintaining referential integrity. Look at each one separately:

> Cascade Update Related Fields - instead of preventing you from changing the value of the linking field in the parent record, if you check this option, Access will automatically update the linking field values in all the related child records so that integrity is maintained.

▶ Cascade Delete Related Records - if this option is selected and you delete the parent record, Access deletes all the child records as well (don't worry, it will check with you first), preventing orphans appearing in the database.

It's a good idea to consider using these options in all your own databases.

The Relationship Type Box

The other part of the dialog that we haven't discussed is the Relationship Type box. In order to enforce integrity checking, Access has to know which type of relationship you'll be using. The default is a one-to-many relationship and this is the one we saw earlier. We'll look at why you might want a one-to-one relationship in Chapter 9.

If you feel we've slightly glossed over these terms, then don't worry - we'll go back and look at them all in greater detail in Chapter 9. As yet they don't affect what we're doing, but when we come to design our sample application, they'll become much more important.

Using Queries on the Related Tables

To prove that we can retrieve the information that we've scattered across the tables in our database, we'll try using some simple queries to view the data in different ways. You'll recall that a query takes the data from a table and displays it by creating a recordset based on the fields we select and the criteria we apply. Only now we haven't got just one table to choose from, we've got three...

Try It Out - Retrieving Information from the New Tables

1 In the Database window click on the Queries tab, and select **N**ew. In the New Query dialog select Design View and click OK. The blank query grid appears, with the Show Table dialog open as well.

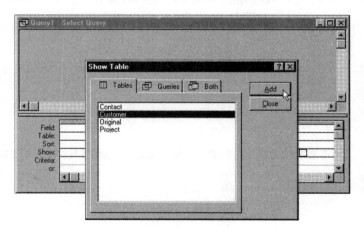

2 Select the Customer table and click **A**dd, then select the Project table and click **A**dd again. Finally click **C**lose to close the dialog. You'll see that Access has linked the two tables for us. It uses the relationships we set up in the previous section, and assumes that this is what we want to use in our query.

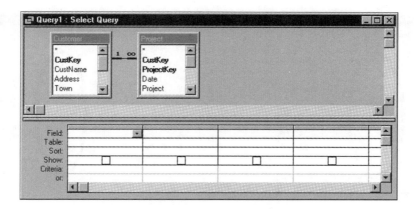

3 Drag the asterisk from the Customer table into the first column of the grid, and the asterisk from the Project table into the second column. (Remember that the asterisk means 'include all fields'.) You'll see that Access includes the table name in the Field row - it needs to know which table to take the fields from.

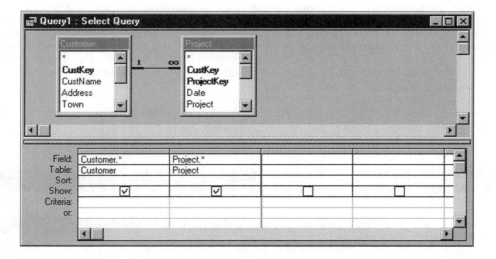

FYI When a query contains two tables which have fields with the same name, Access automatically adds the table name and a period to the field name so that you can tell which is which. Hence **Project.*** is all the fields in the **Project** table, and **Customer.CustKey** would be the value from the **CustKey** field of the **Customer** table.

4 Click the Datasheet View button on the toolbar to see the results. It looks very similar to our original table, except that it now includes the new CustKey and ProjectKey fields with their unique values. Access has linked the two tables together to form the original long records. You'll also see the linked field values at work - the Customer.CustKey and Project.CustKey fields in the same record contain the same values. It's these that link the records together.

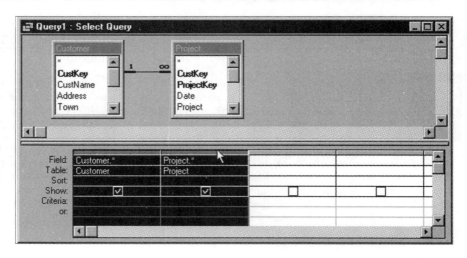

Customer.CustKey	CustName	Address	Town	State	ZipCode	Phone	Fax	Project.CustKey	ProjectKey	Date
1	Major Record	Third Aven	Stocksvill	FL	10015	305-711-7	305-711-	1	1	30-Jun-95
2	Miracle Suppl	18th Avenu	Oakland	CA	10593	415-671-6	415-671-	2	2	18-Jun-95
2	Miracle Suppl	18th Avenu	Oakland	CA	10593	415-671-6	415-671-	2	3	26-Jun-95
2	Miracle Suppl	18th Avenu	Oakland	CA	10593	415-671-6	415-671-	2	4	13-Jul-95
5	Education De	The Offices	Chicago	IL	10745	312-712-8		5	5	05-Jul-95
5	Education De	The Offices	Chicago	IL	10745	312-712-8		5	6	16-Jul-95
7	Jonas Boats	The Quay	Stocksvill	FL	16734	305-711-8		7	7	23-Jul-95
8	Cummings In	124th Stre	Pittsburgh	PA	17265	412-455-6	412-455-	8	8	03-Jul-95
9	Burger Queer	Constants	Houston	TX	30517	713-771-6	713-771-	9	9	23-Jun-95
10	Aardvark Limi	All Saints S	Athens	OH	39812	216-376-1	216-376-	10	10	12-Jun-95
11	Le Bistro	Rue Franc	Vancouve	WA	41322	206-133-8	206-133-	11	11	08-Jul-95
12	Union Record	712 Main S	Tampa	FL	51267	813-167-3	813-167-	12	12	20-Jul-95
13	Martha's Bar	Top Street	Clarksvill	NY	54876			13	13	18-Jul-95
14	R.Higgins	The Marke	Green Ba	WI	61733	414-831-8	414-831-	14	14	20-Jun-95
16	Pedro Mana	Calle Seba	St. Paul	MN	65109	612-401-1	612-401-	16	15	28-Jun-95

Record: 1 of 16

How It Works

What we've effectively done is tell Access to link each customer record to the project record that contains the same CustKey value - this is how we set up the relations.

One thing you should also have noticed is that Access has re-created the duplication of the customers' names and addresses. To join the two tables together, it creates a new record for each possible match between the existing records. If there are two project records which link to the same customer, it creates two records in the new recordset, and fills in the same customer details for both of them. If you think about it, there's no other option that makes sense, other than leaving blank fields in the second record. The fields have to be there because our query is instructing Access to create them.

Now we'll try something more adventurous. Let's suppose we've found a bug (sorry, 'unplanned feature') in our **Accounts** package. We need to talk to every customer to whom we've supplied this.

Try It Out - More Complicated Queries

1 Click the Design View button on the toolbar to go back to design view. Select the two fields in the grid by clicking on the column selector above the field and then delete them by pressing the *Delete* key.

2 Drag the CustName and Phone fields from the Customer table into the grid, then the Date and Project fields from the Project table. In the Sort row under CustName select Ascending, and in the Criteria row of the Project field enter "Accounts System".

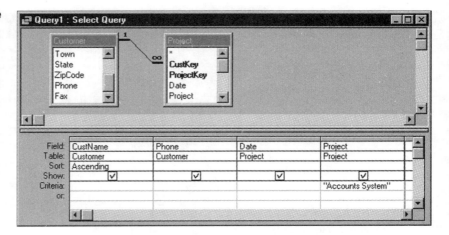

3 Click the Datasheet View button to see the results. Access shows four records. These are the four Accounts System projects we've worked on, sorted by customer name. We've pulled out two fields from each table, and limited them to projects for Accounts Systems. Access has done all the work of finding the linked data and building the new recordset.

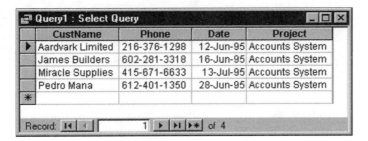

4 So let's see the name of the contact that we dealt with as well. Go back to design view and click the Show Table button on the toolbar. Select the Contact table, then Add and Close.

5 Access adds the table to our query, and shows the relationship it proposes to use. You'll see it better if you move the Customer table into the middle, between the other two.

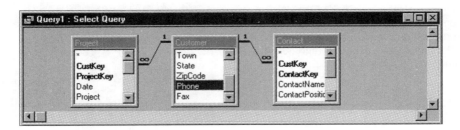

147

6 Drag the ContactName field from the Contact table into the grid, and drop it on the existing CustName field. Access moves everything along and inserts the ContactName field at the left of the grid.

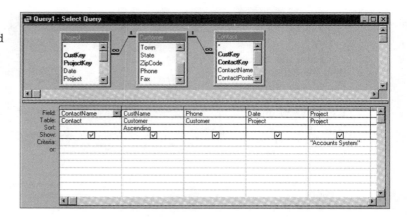

7 Click the Datasheet View button to see the results - now we've got five records. But look a bit closer. There are three for James Builders (we have three contacts there, so Access creates extra records), but what's happened to the Pedro Mana company? They appeared last time as having purchased our accounts package, but they don't show up in the new recordset.

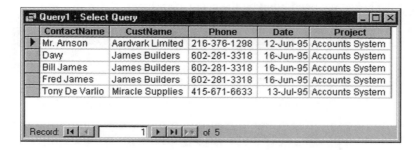

The reason for this is very simple. We've told Access to build new records by linking together the tables and including the particular fields we've asked for. But if you check out the Contact table, there's no record for Pedro Mana, even though they exist in the other two. So Access can't include them in the recordset. To understand how this comes about, we need to look at the relationship in a little more detail.

8 Go back to design view and double-click on the join line between the Customer and Contact tables. Access opens the Join Properties dialog. (If you get the Query Properties dialog, you missed the line. Try clicking once on the line to highlight it, then double-click on it.)

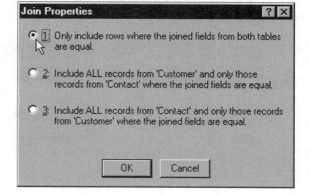

148

You'll see the problem straight away - the join is specified as 'Only include rows where the joined fields from both tables are equal.' Hence we don't get a row if there's no record on one side of the join. We can solve the problem quite easily.

9 Select option 2 - 'Include ALL records from 'Customer' and only those records from 'Contact' where the joined fields are equal.' Then click the OK button to close the dialog.

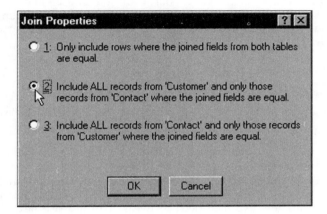

10 Click the Datasheet View button again, and now we have **Pedro Mana** back. And, of course, the ContactName field is blank - just what we wanted. Finally, click on the Close button. You needn't bother saving the query.

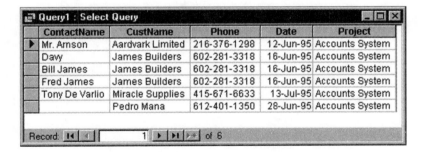

ContactName	CustName	Phone	Date	Project
Mr. Arnson	Aardvark Limited	216-376-1298	12-Jun-95	Accounts System
Davy	James Builders	602-281-3318	16-Jun-95	Accounts System
Bill James	James Builders	602-281-3318	16-Jun-95	Accounts System
Fred James	James Builders	602-281-3318	16-Jun-95	Accounts System
Tony De Varlio	Miracle Supplies	415-671-6633	13-Jul-95	Accounts System
	Pedro Mana	612-401-1350	28-Jun-95	Accounts System

So, now we can recover the data that we spread around in the three new tables almost as easily as we could from the single table. The structure seems to be working well and the effort of creating it was worthwhile. In the next two chapters you'll see how we can use the data in many more powerful ways now that we have a properly structured database to work with.

149

Summary

In this chapter we've introduced some basic concepts of relational database design because we discovered that our original single-table model was both inefficient and limiting. The flexibility of a database is almost exclusively based on the design of the tables which support it, though Access has many powerful features which can overcome minor design inelegance. However, there's nothing better to improve performance and make future maintenance easier than getting the design right at the early stages. Once we've built a full interface around our data, changing the layout of the tables becomes more and more difficult. For the time being, though, we've reached a situation where the design is perfectly acceptable for our requirements, and does not impose limits on either the storage or retrieval of the data it contains.

In this chapter, you've learnt:

▶ What a relational database is.

▶ How to create a multi-table database and relate the individual tables.

▶ The importance of referential integrity.

▶ How to retrieve information from related tables.

In future chapters we'll continue to consider design aspects, in fact, in Part 3, we'll review our design again by coming at it from a different angle - that of the mathematical rules we mentioned earlier. Perhaps then we may need to tweak it to increase flexibility even further.

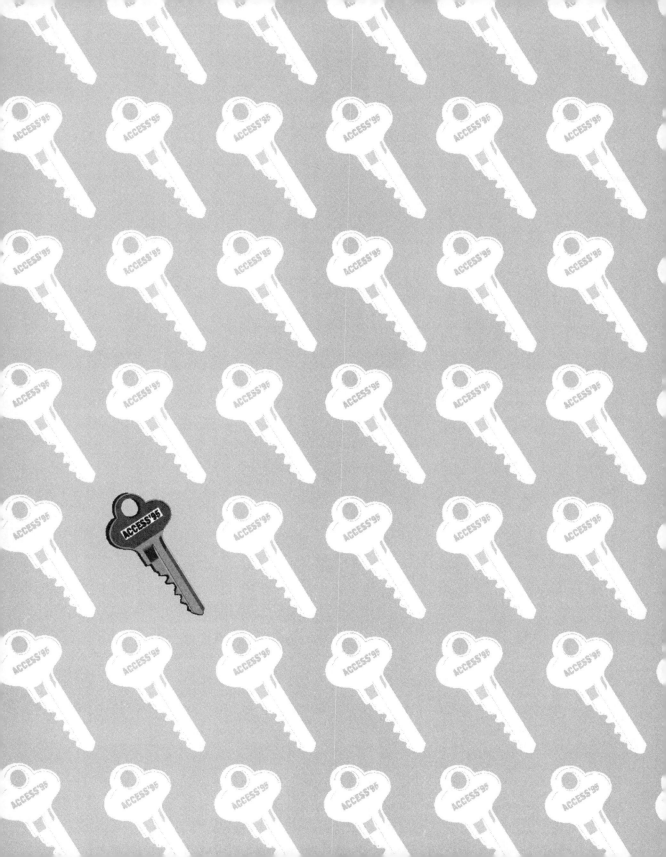

Extracting Information
From Your Database

In the last chapter we created a relational database and started to look at how we can extract information from multiple tables. This chapter is going to take you further down the same path. We will look in more detail at queries, examining how you can use them to make your database more flexible and, therefore, more useful.

You will see how to construct more complex queries using expressions and parameters and we'll look at the Expression Builder tool which Access provides to allow you to more easily piece together these complex queries.

So, to whet your appetite, you will very soon be familiar with:

- The language behind queries.
- How to use expressions to create new fields.
- How you can get input from users.

Coding Your Database

If the phrase **SQL** is new to you, or else conjures up images of incredibly complicated database systems, don't panic. It's not half as difficult as it is made out to be. SQL is the secret behind Access queries. Never mind 'It's all done with mirrors', in the case of Access, 'It's all done with SQL'. In Part 3 we'll focus more closely on what SQL really is, but in this chapter we'll provide a glimpse of how it works.

Under the Query Hood

You've been using simple queries quite happily up to now, but before we go much further, it's important to understand the basis on which queries work, as well as the different types of query available to you.

Whether you're filtering records from a single table, or retrieving selected data from a relational database, you are using queries to perform the task.

Remember the diagram from Chapter 3 which mapped out the relationship between tables, queries and recordsets? Here it is again:

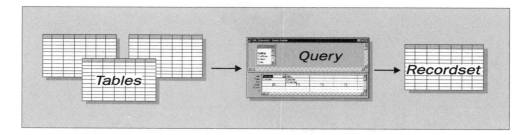

This is a very simplistic view of what is an incredibly powerful tool. As we saw in Chapter 4, we can select any combination of fields from one or more tables, then select the records we want, and finally display them sorted in the order we specify. Take a look at the next figure - it shows the process in more detail:

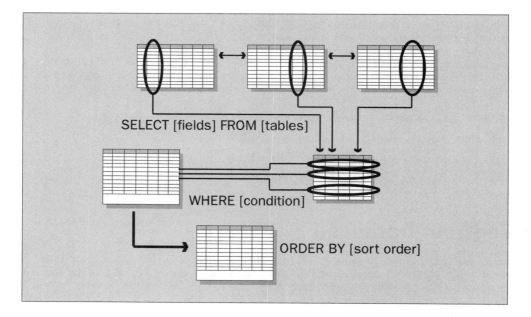

What Is SQL?

As you may have guessed, the above diagram is labeled as it is for a reason. It is, in fact, your first real taste of SQL. SQL (Structured Query Language) is the language that Access uses to create and manipulate databases. It is the standard database language, used not only in Access, but in every database program. Information passed between the tables and the parts of Access that actually carry out the query is communicated using SQL. When you use the QBE grid, for example, all of the things you do are translated into SQL. In fact, every query you create is represented in Access by an SQL statement. You can see the SQL equivalent of something you've done using the option on the Query View drop-down list that we've ignored so far: the SQL View.

Though we won't be considering SQL to any great extent until later chapters, we'll just see what it looks like. You'll need to be able to find and use the SQL window when we come to creating forms in Chapter 7.

FYI All the examples in this chapter and the following one make use of `NewTable.mdb` from the sample databases included on the disk. Make four copies of this database and name them `NewTab1.mdb`, `NewTab2.mdb`, `NewTab3.mdb` and `NewTab4.mdb`. We'll then refer to these copies in the examples throughout the chapters. You have to do this as some of the Try It Outs make changes to the data contained in the database.

Try It Out - A Quick View of SQL

We'll create a simple query that shows the name and phone number of our customers in Florida and then see how Access maintains a 'behind-the-scenes' version of it in SQL.

1 Open up **NewTab1.mdb** and in the Database window click the Queries tab. Click the New button, then select Design View and click OK to create a new blank query grid. Access opens the Show Table dialog.

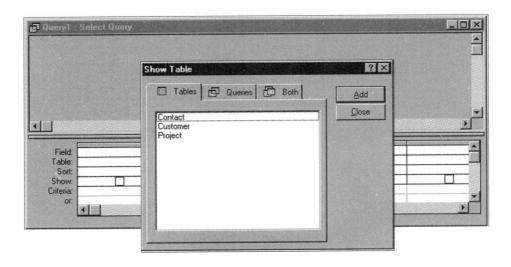

2 Select the Customer table and click <u>A</u>dd to add it to the query, then close the Show Table dialog.

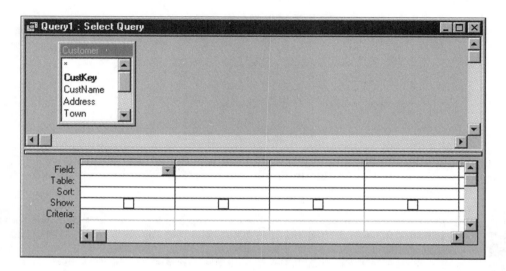

3 Drag the CustName, State and Phone fields to the grid and select Ascending for the Sort row under the CustName field.

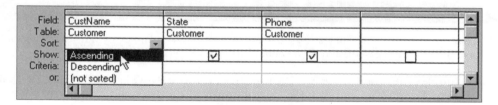

4 Enter "FL" in the Criteria row under the State field to limit the records to customers in Florida. (Access adds the quotation marks automatically if you forget.)

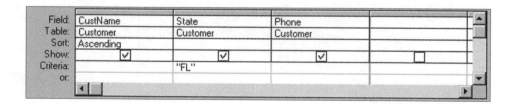

156

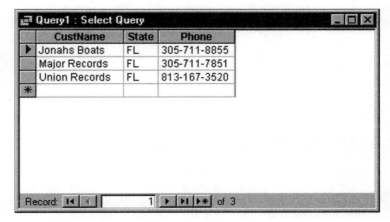

5 To display the results, switch to datasheet view by clicking the Query View button on the toolbar.

6 Now click the down arrow next to the Query View button to open the Query View list and select SQL View - Access opens a window showing the SQL statement that produces the recordset. This is the equivalent of the selections we made in the query grid.

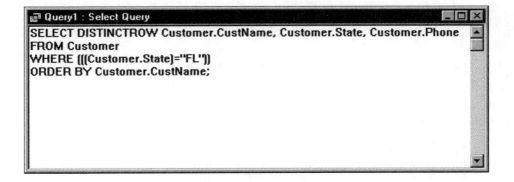

You can see how the SQL statement follows the diagram we saw earlier. The process is a series of steps which select the fields and records we want and then display the results sorted in the order we specify.

 In an SQL statement, the references to each field are preceded by the table name - **Customer.CustName** refers to the **CustName** field of the **Customer** table.

So there's a direct relationship between a query in the query grid and the SQL statement that supports it. Access actually uses the SQL statement, rather than the query grid itself, to obtain the data from the tables. The grid is just an easy way of creating the statement and saves you typing it in, as you have to in some database programs.

157

This ability to use and modify the SQL statement behind a query gives us access to the full power of a modern database system. It also means that we can use the actual statement in situations where we can't use the query grid itself - there are some kinds of query which can only be created directly in the SQL window and not in the Query Builder grid. However, this really only concerns the more unusual query types and you should generally have no reason to directly edit the SQL statement. In Part 2 we will look in detail at these types of query and you'll see more about using the SQL window.

More Complex Types of Query

If you look back at the diagram of how a query works, and at the SQL statement we saw in the Try It Out, you'll see there are four sections where we exercise control over the final recordset. We select the fields we want, specify the source tables, apply criteria, then sort the results. The following table summarizes what you can do with complex queries.

This query section:	allows you to specify:
SELECT [*FIELDS*]	Entire fields from a table
	Parts of a field from a table
	Values calculated from fields in a table
FROM [*TABLES*]	An existing table in the database
	An external table in another database or other application
	A recordset created by another query
WHERE [*CRITERIA*]	A simple match of field contents to a fixed value
	A partial match against the field contents using wildcards
	A logical or mathematical operation on the field contents
ORDER BY	Ascending or Descending, based on the values in the fields

So far, for each of these operations we've only used the simplest methods. However, there are a great many ways in which we can tailor queries to our needs.

Using Expressions in a Query

To be able to exploit the full potential of queries, or indeed any other part of Access, we use **expressions** to manipulate and modify the items that are stored in the database. An expression is simply a statement made up of **operators** and **functions** which produces a **result**. Don't panic - you've already used a function (**IsNull**) and operators will be more than familiar to you. In fact, they couldn't be easier.

Operators

The first thing you will have ever learned in arithmetic at school is how to use operators - the simple adding, subtracting, multiplying and dividing of numbers. These operators are applied to two numbers to produce the result, for example 3 + 8 = 11. There are other less common operators as well and some that only use one number to produce a result, e.g. the **Not** operator. Here's a quick summary of the ones we use most often. You have come across several of them already.

Operator	Example	What it does
Common Arithmetical Operators		
+	3 + 8 = 11	Adds two numbers together.
-	7 - 2 = 5	Subtracts one number from another.
*	2 * 4 = 8	Multiplies two numbers together.
/	9 / 2 = 4.5	Divides one number by another and gives a result which includes the fractional part.
\	9 \ 2 = 4	Divides one number by another and gives a result which includes only whole numbers (integers).
^	3 ^ 2 = 9	Gives the result of one number to the power of another, usually called exponentiation.
Comparison Operators		
<	3 < 8 = True	Returns true if the first number is less than the s second, otherwise returns false.
<=	5 <= 4 = False	Returns true if the first number is less than or equal to the second, otherwise returns false.
>	7 > 10 = False	Returns true if the first number is greater than the second, otherwise returns false.
>=	7 >= 7 = True	Returns true if the first number is greater than or equal to the second, otherwise returns false.
=	6 = 7 = False	Returns true if the first number is equal to the second, otherwise returns false.
<>	5 <> 8 = True	Returns true if the first number is not equal to the second, otherwise returns false.
Common Logical Operators		
And	(2 = 2) And (6 = 7) = False	Returns true only if both of the expressions are true, otherwise returns false.
Or	(2 = 2) Or (6 = 7) = True	Returns true if either of the expressions is true, otherwise returns false.
Not	Not (6 = 7) = True	Reverses the true or false result of the expression.

Table Continued on Following Page

Operator	Example	What it does
String Concatenation Operator		
&	"Mon" & "day" = "Monday"	Joins two strings together.

While all the other operators you've seen here operate on different data types such as numbers, currency, etc., the last one operates only on **strings**. A string is simply the way we refer to the text that is stored in a table, such as a customer's name, and is written with inverted commas (quotation marks) around it, for example "James Builders". You'll see examples of string manipulation as you work through this chapter.

Try It Out - Using Operators in a Query

One of the most common string operators is the concatenation operator which, as the name suggests, is used to join two strings together. We'll use it in the next example to produce a list of customer's names and addresses in a single field. Use the **NewTab1** database that you have open (just close down the SQL window - you needn't save the changes).

1 Start by creating a new blank query grid and add the Customer table to it.

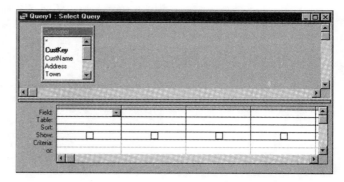

2 We're going to use an expression in our query. To create this, place the cursor in the Field row of the first column in the empty grid and press *Shift-F2*. This will open up the Zoom window.

 FYI The Zoom window is available in many places in Access and makes it a lot easier to enter and edit large expressions and statements. You can use it in most of the places where you enter text - in a query and in the **Properties** parts of other windows. Just place the cursor in a text box or cell and press *Shift-F2*. If the Zoom window is available, it will open automatically. You can also right-click and select **Zoom** from the shortcut menu.

3 Enter the expression shown (don't press *Enter* at the end of the line - if the window were wide enough, it would be all one line). Note that Access requires us to identify which parts of an expression are field names by enclosing them in square brackets.

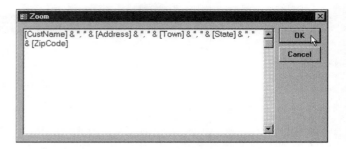

4 Click OK and Access copies the contents of the Zoom window into the query grid for you. Press *Tab* or the down arrow key to move off the cell and the syntax of the expression you've entered is checked - if there's an error it'll be highlighted. (You can make the column wider by placing the cursor between the column selectors and dragging it to the width you want).

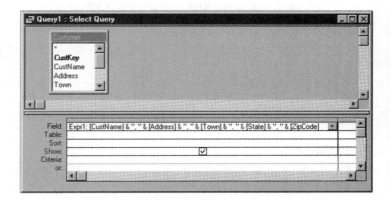

5 Once the expression has been accepted, you'll see that Access has added Expr1: at the beginning. Because the entry doesn't match any of the fields in the table, Access assumes it's a **calculated field** and names the field Expr1.

 A calculated field is simply a column in a query whose values are created by an expression, rather than being taken directly from the table that the query is based on. It provides a field in the resulting recordset that does not exist in the source records.

6 Change the field name by replacing Expr1 with FullAddress. Leave the colon after the field name in place - this is how Access knows where the field name ends and the expression begins.

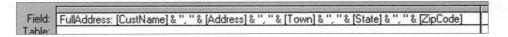

7 Now view the results of the query by clicking the Datasheet / Query View button on the toolbar. Access displays the new field with the customers' name and address. Again you can make the column wider by placing the cursor between the field name selectors and dragging it to the width you want.

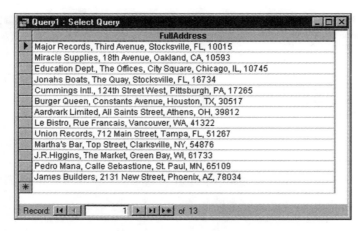

So, as you can see, the & operator has joined the values from several fields to create a new field. We'll look at the other operators you can use in later examples. However, first we need to be able to carry out more complex tasks than are possible using only the operators we've seen so far. To do this we use **functions**.

Functions

There are only so many things that you can do by adding numbers together or checking if they are equal. To achieve the complicated data manipulation that is necessary to get information out of your data, you need to use Access functions.

A function takes one or more **arguments** which it uses to produce a result. When you use a function, you will generally write the name of the function followed by a list of arguments in brackets. In Chapter 3, we used the **IsNull** function to display the records for projects that had been paid for. We used:

```
IsNull([Paid])
```

The function name is, of course, **IsNull** and the only **argument** is the name of the field which we want to examine. The function looks at the **Paid** field and returns **False** if there is a value stored in it, or **True** if not.

You may also see the arguments for a function described as parameters in other situations. However, in Access, parameters have a special meaning - so we'll stick to using the term argument.

There's a huge range of functions built into Access, from the simple **Date** function (which just returns the current date) to complex financial functions such as **FV** (which calculates the future value of an investment). There's a short list of some of the more common functions you will be using below, though for more detail you should look at Appendix A. You can also use the Access Help file to find lists of functions displayed by category by searching on functions: reference topics.

Function syntax	Example	What it does
Date$()	Date$() = "7-21-1995"	Returns the date set in your computer's operating system.
InStr (source, target)	InStr ("Today", "day") = 3	Finds the position of one string within another.
Int (number)	Int (7.31) = 7	Returns the integer part of a number.
Left$ (string, chars)	Left$ ("Today", 3) = "Tod"	Returns characters from the left-hand end of a string.
Now ()	Now() = 7-21-95 10:36:16	Returns the current date and time, using a special numeric format rather than a string.
Right$ (string, chars)	Right$("Today", 3) = "day"	Returns characters from the right-hand end of a string.
Sqr (number)	Sqr (16) = 4	Returns the square root of a number.
UCase$ (string)	UCase$ ("abc") = "ABC"	Converts a string into upper case.
Val (string)	Val ("123.4") = 123.4	Returns a number (data type) from a string which contains numbers as text.

Try It Out - The IIf Function

Our last Try It Out produced a list of names and addresses. Imagine, though, if you didn't know the address of a particular customer. You'd end up with a blank field, which isn't very helpful - how do you know whether the address is missing because it's not in the database or because you did something wrong when creating the query? It is far better to have Access recognize that a customer address is not known and to mark it accordingly. We can do this easily enough using the **IIf** function.

The **IIf** function allows us to select one of two values for a field based on a particular condition being met. The syntax is as follows:

IIf ({condition to test}, {value if true}, {value if false})

We'll use **IIf** to display *Address Unknown* for records where there's no address.

1 Go back into design view and open the Zoom window again by clicking on the Field box in the grid and pressing *Shift-F2*. Add code to the original expression so that you end up with the expression shown below. (We've shown the original expression in italics to help you. Don't forget the extra bracket at the end).

FullAddress: IIf(IsNull([Address]),[CustName] & " *Address Unknown*",*[CustName] & "; "
& [Address] & "; " & [Town] & "; " & [State] & "; " & [ZipCode]*)

163

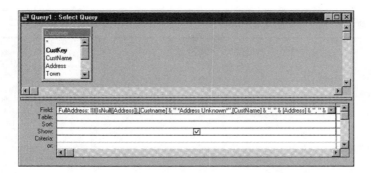

 FYI You can read this expression as follows: "If the address field is null (contains no value), then display the name and ***Address Unknown***, otherwise return the name and full address.

2 So that you can see the effect of the query, you'll have to delete the contents of one or more of the address fields in the **Customer** table. Go to the **Database** window, open the table, highlight the contents of some of the address fields and press *Delete*.

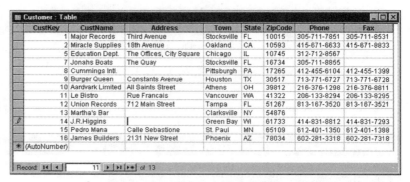

3 Close the table and switch back to the query grid. Click the **Datasheet / Query View** button to see the results of your query.

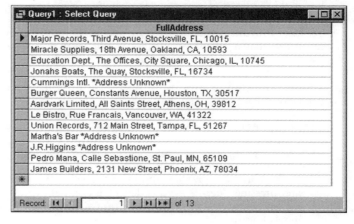

As you can see, the empty address fields are now marked as ***Address Unknown***.

Expression Builder

In the last two examples you've typed in long and rather convoluted expressions. You're probably wondering whether there's an easier method to build these expressions up.

Well, Microsoft again come to your rescue - this time with a tool known as Expression Builder. You can use this tool not only to create expressions, but also to explore the functions that are available. Expression Builder can be used in many different places in Access.

Expression Builder lists all the options available to you, so all you have to do is pick which ones you want. It will also remind you of the syntax of the different functions.

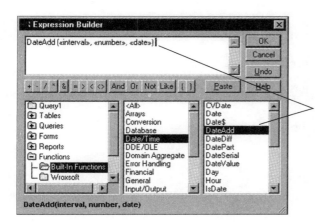

The DateAdd function calculates the date in x number of days. You'll see how it is used in the next example. Notice, though, how Expression Builder reminds you of its syntax - all you have to do is replace the markers with actual values.

Although, at first glance, it may look complicated with its multiple windows and selection of buttons, Expression Builder is really quite easy to use. In the figure above you can see it in use. The top window shows the expression you are building and allows you to modify it directly. Under this are buttons for all the operators that Access includes, such as +, -, & and <>. There are also buttons for the less common operators such as And, Or, Not, Like, etc.

Under the set of buttons are three windows. The one on the left shows the 'objects' in our database, arranged in a collapsible tree fashion. Here you can see we've opened the Functions part of the list and selected Built-In Functions. The middle window shows the different groups of functions and the right-hand list shows the individual function names for the group we've selected. To get more information on any function, just click on it and press *F1*.

The next example shows how Expression Builder is used to select functions and build up their arguments.

Try It Out - Using Expression Builder

Suppose we give our customers 28 days to pay from the date we finish the work. It would be useful to add a new field to the recordset to show when payment is due. We can use Expression Builder to build an expression that adds 28 days to the date that is contained in the Project table.

1 Close down the database from the previous example (you needn't save changes) and open up **NewTab2.mdb**, your second copy of **NewTable.mdb**. Create a new query and add the Project table to the grid. Drag the Date, Project and TotalDue fields into the query grid.

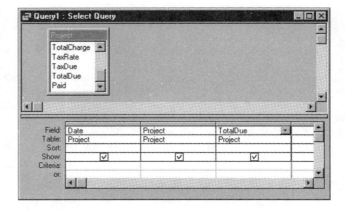

Now we're ready to call up Expression Builder to create the extra column.

2 Place the cursor in the Field row of the next empty column and click the Build button on the toolbar - Access opens the Expression Builder window.

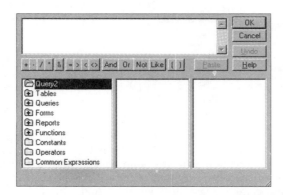

3 Double-click on the Functions entry in the left window to expand the tree and then select the Built-In Functions entry below it. In the middle window single-click on the Date/Time category to show just the date and time functions in the right-hand window.

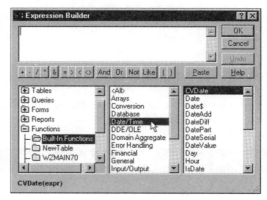

4 To get the day payment is due, we need to add 28 days to the date that the work was finished. Therefore, the function we want is DateAdd. Double-click on it to copy it into the top window, together with markers or place-holders, for its **arguments** (the information we have to supply for it to produce a result).

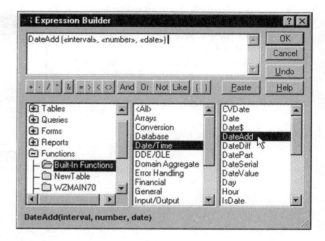

 The syntax for the **DateAdd** function is **DateAdd(interval, number, date)** where **interval** is one or more characters which represent the type of interval to be added, e.g. **"d"** to add days. The second argument is the number of intervals and the third is the date that the number of intervals should be added to.

5 Click on the first argument in the top window of Expression Builder, «interval» and you'll see Access highlights it for you - type "d" (you *must* include the quotes) to replace this. We're going to add days. Click on the second argument «number» and type 28 - the number of days we want to add.

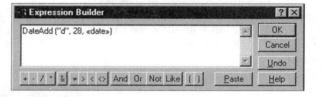

 If you forget the quotes round the **d**, you will get an error when you run the query - Access will assume that it is the name of a field. To cure this, just click on the expression in the grid and re-open **Expression Builder.** Double-click on the argument to highlight it and enter the correct value.

6 Click on the third argument «date». The date that we want to add the 28 days to is contained in our Project table, so we can get Access to add this value for us. In the lower left-hand window, double-click the entry for Tables to expand the tree and display all the tables in the database.

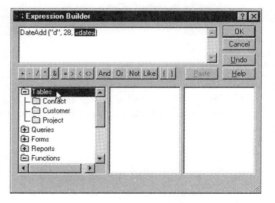

7 Select the Project table. The middle window will then display all the fields in this table. Click on the Date field and the right-hand window will show the properties of the field that we can use - in this case <Value>.

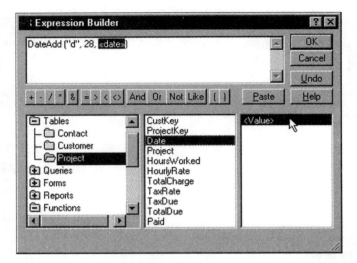

8 Double-click on the <Value> entry in the right-hand window. The marker in the top window will be replaced with [Project]![Date]. (Access uses the full description of objects in Expression Builder to avoid confusion - there may be instances with the same name, such as a Date field in two different tables.)

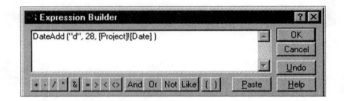

9 So now we've got our expression. Click OK to copy it back into the query grid. Make sure that the Show box is ticked, then press *Tab* or the down arrow key so that Access checks it. You'll see Expr1: added to the beginning again.

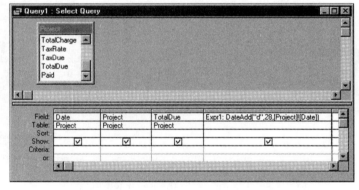

10 Change Expr1: to DateDue: and click the Datasheet View button on the toolbar. Access adds the new field with the payment date to the end of our recordset.

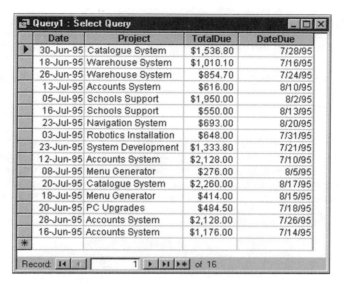

This is undeniably an easier way of building expressions than writing them yourself. It's also very flexible. Suppose that, after creating this query, we wanted to add another field. This time we want to offer 5% discount on the total due if the customer pays us on time. Let's add a field which shows the amount due after discount.

Try It Out - Adding a Discount Field with Expression Builder

The expression we need here is quite simple and you might think that it makes sense to type it straight into the grid:

1 Go back to design view and, in the Field column of the next empty field in the grid, type Discounted: [TotalDue]*0.95 to name the new field

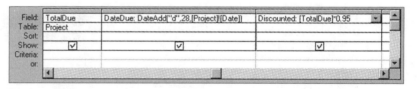

Discounted and set the value for each record to 95% of the value in the TotalDue field.

2 Click the Datasheet / Query View button to see the recordset.

Date	Project	TotalDue	DateDue	Discounted
30-Jun-95	Catalogue System	$1,536.80	7/28/95	1459.96
18-Jun-95	Warehouse System	$1,010.10	7/16/95	959.595
26-Jun-95	Warehouse System	$854.70	7/24/95	811.965
13-Jul-95	Accounts System	$616.00	8/10/95	585.2
05-Jul-95	Schools Support	$1,950.00	8/2/95	1852.5
16-Jul-95	Schools Support	$550.00	8/13/95	522.5
23-Jul-95	Navigation System	$693.00	8/20/95	658.35
03-Jul-95	Robotics Installation	$648.00	7/31/95	615.6
23-Jun-95	System Development	$1,333.80	7/21/95	1267.11
12-Jun-95	Accounts System	$2,128.00	7/10/95	2021.6
08-Jul-95	Menu Generator	$276.00	8/5/95	262.2

Record: 1 of 16

Well, it's not bad. We've got the right values. However, what we haven't got is a currency format. All Access has done is use the value in the TotalDue field and placed 95% of it in our new field. We'll use Expression Builder to specify the format we need and solve this problem.

3 Back in design view, delete the contents of the Discounted field in the grid and leave the cursor there. Click the Build button on the toolbar to open Expression Builder. We want to use the **CCur** function which converts the contents of a field into a currency value.

The **CCur** function is used to convert data from one type to another. Its syntax is **CCur (number)** where **number** is the value you want to convert. There are occasions when you have a number which is stored in ordinary numeric form, such as in a **Number** field in a table, and you want to change it to a currency data type - like that in a field which has its data type set to **Currency**. There are conversion functions like this for most data types, allowing you to convert between them as you need.

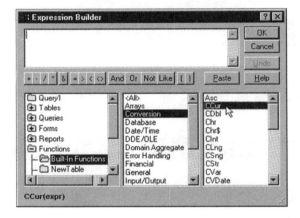

4 Double-click on Functions in the first window and select Built-In Functions. Then select Conversion from the middle window and double-click on CCur in the right-hand window to copy it to the top window. The single argument is «expr», the expression that we wish to convert. Click on it so that it's highlighted.

5 The expression we want to convert is the value from the Total Due field in our Project table, so double-click the Tables entry in the left-hand window and select the Project table. Then select the TotalDue field from the middle window and double-click on <Value> in the right-hand window.

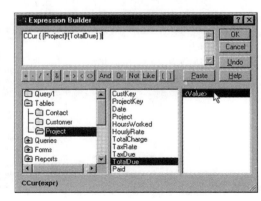

6 To calculate the discount, we need to multiply the value by 0.95. Access has left the cursor in the right place ready for us. Click the * button below the top window to insert the multiplication operator. Access then adds another «expr» for us. Click on «expr» and type 0.95 to complete the expression.

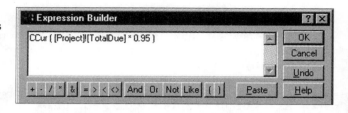

7 Click **OK** to copy the expression back into the query grid. Press the *Home* key to go to the start of the expression and type **Discounted:** as the field name.

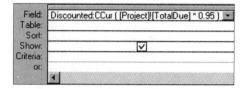

8 Click the **Datasheet View** button to see the result - nicely formatted currency values in our new field.

Date	Project	TotalDue	DateDue	Discounted
30-Jun-95	Catalogue System	$1,536.80	7/28/95	$1,459.96
18-Jun-95	Warehouse System	$1,010.10	7/16/95	$959.60
26-Jun-95	Warehouse System	$854.70	7/24/95	$811.97
13-Jul-95	Accounts System	$616.00	8/10/95	$585.20
05-Jul-95	Schools Support	$1,950.00	8/2/95	$1,852.50
16-Jul-95	Schools Support	$550.00	8/13/95	$522.50
23-Jul-95	Navigation System	$693.00	8/20/95	$658.35
03-Jul-95	Robotics Installation	$648.00	7/31/95	$615.60
23-Jun-95	System Development	$1,333.80	7/21/95	$1,267.11
12-Jun-95	Accounts System	$2,128.00	7/10/95	$2,021.60
08-Jul-95	Menu Generator	$276.00	8/5/95	$262.20
20-Jul-95	Catalogue System	$2,260.00	8/17/95	$2,147.00
18-Jul-95	Menu Generator	$414.00	8/15/95	$393.30
20-Jun-95	PC Upgrades	$484.50	7/18/95	$460.28
28-Jun-95	Accounts System	$2,128.00	7/26/95	$2,021.60
16-Jun-95	Accounts System	$1,176.00	7/14/95	$1,117.20

Record: 1 of 16

So we've found another way that we can exert more control over a query and tailor the results to meet our needs. We can create new fields from existing ones, or even add extra fields that don't exist in the original tables - just by using an expression to generate calculated fields.

While this may seem only an interesting exercise, don't underestimate it. Consider, instead, that now we're almost completely independent from the original design of our data tables. We can rebuild the complete structure of our data in any way we like and we have total control over the way the data is presented.

There's one important point that you should note here. In Chapter 3, we edited the results of a query (the recordset) to update the original table. However, if you try to edit the contents of the new fields we've added to the recordset above, you'll find Access won't allow it. This is because these new fields are **calculated fields** and not direct references to original fields. The changes cannot be reflected back into the original table. You'll find that most of the complex queries we use, where we're manipulating the data from the table before we display it, do not allow the resulting records to be updated.

Expressions as Query Criteria

You have now seen how to use expressions to create new fields. The next step is to apply criteria to select just the ones you want to include in the final recordset. It will come as no surprise to learn that you can use expressions as criteria...

Try It Out - Using Expressions to Display Selected Records

In this example, we'll use the **Like** operator to display selected customers' names.

1 Close down the last query (again, there's no need to save it) and create a new one. Add the Customer table to it, then drag the CustName field to the first column of the grid.

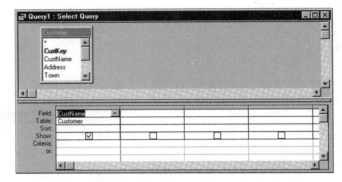

2 Click in the Criteria box and enter Like("M*").

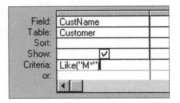

3 Switch to datasheet view. The result is only the customer names that match the pattern we've placed in the parentheses of the **Like** operator.

> **FYI**
>
> The **Like** operator compares the value in the field with the pattern we place in brackets following the word **Like**. The pattern can be any string of characters enclosed in quotation marks. The operator's power lies in the fact that you can include wildcards in the string, in the same way you can with file names in DOS. You can use an asterisk (*) to mean 'any number of characters' and a question mark (?) to mean 'any single character'. This technique allows you to search for a match in any part of a field.

172

4 Now switch back to design view and change the Criteria to Like("*Records*"). This will only match a customer name which contains the word Records somewhere in the field. Then change to Datasheet View to see the results.

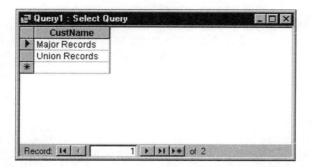

5 Edit the Criteria for the CustName field so that it reads Not(Like("*Records*")). Then switch to datasheet view to see the results. Access only displays those which do *not* have Records in that field.

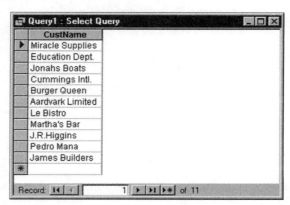

FYI The Not operator simply reverses the 'truth' of its argument. A record is only included in the results of a query if the criteria we apply returns True for that record.

The above examples may seem slightly trivial so, as a final example, we'll take a more complicated criteria and build it with Expression Builder. Suppose we want to know whether we did any work over a weekend (so that we can apply our overtime rate to it).

Try It Out - Building a Complex Expression with Expression Builder

In this Try It Out, we will work out which dates fell on weekends and which customers we worked for on a weekend. Then we will display a summary of this information.

1 Back in design view, delete the Criteria you've entered for the CustName field. Click the Show Table button on the toolbar and add the Project table to the query. Access links them together automatically.

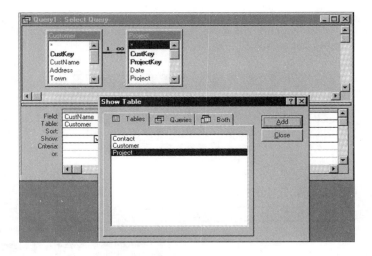

2 Drag the Date and Project fields from the Project table to the grid. This will display the customer name, the date and the project name.

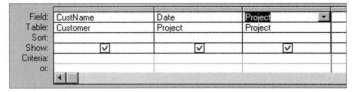

3 Now we need to build the new criteria. Click in the Criteria box under the Date field and click the Build button on the toolbar. Expression Builder appears. We will use the **Weekday** function to determine what day of the week a particular date was. This function takes a date as its argument and returns a number between **1** and **7** corresponding to the day of the week (**1** is Sunday, **2** is Monday, etc.). All we need to do then is check for Saturday and Sunday.

4 Open the Functions list in the left-hand window by double-clicking on it and select Built-In Functions. In the middle window select Date/Time. Scroll down the list in the right-hand window to find Weekday and double-click on it. Access places the Weekday function and its argument place-holder in the top window.

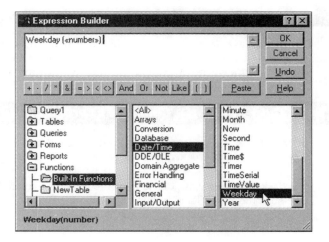

5 We need to check for two values of
Weekday - 1 (Sunday) or 7 (Saturday).
Click the = button underneath the top
window to add it to the expression.
Then type 1 to check for Sunday.

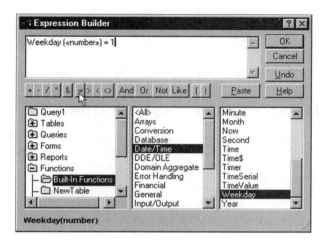

6 Now click the **Or** button, then double-
click the **Weekday** function in the right-
hand window again. Click = and type 7
to check for Saturday.

7 Now we just need to replace the
«number» place-holders with our **Date**
field. Highlight the first <<number>>
placeholder, select **Date** from the **Project**
table and double-click on <Value> in the
right-hand window to enter it into the
expression. Then click on the second
«number» place-holder and double-click
the <Value> entry again. The expression
is now complete.

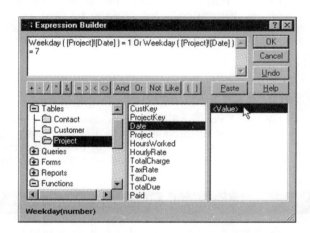

8 Click **OK** to copy the
expression into the query
grid, and switch to datasheet
view to see the results.

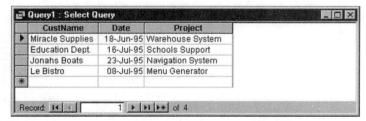

So Access operators and functions can be used to increase the control we have over the way a query works. We've seen how they can be used to create new fields (in the **SELECT [fields] FROM [tables]** part of the query), as well as control which of the new records are included in the resulting recordset (in the **WHERE [criteria]** part). Used in both parts of the process, they give us almost total control over the **information** we retrieve from our **data**.

Using Parameters in a Query

Up to now, when we've been designing queries, we've used either fixed values or expressions for the criteria which select the records we want. So, to select all the records whose Project is Accounts System, we placed Accounts System in the Criteria row. Access compared the Project field of every record to it and displayed only those that match. When we used an expression, Access only included the record if the expression evaluated to **True** for that particular record.

However, there are occasions when we, as developers of the database, can't know in advance exactly what the criteria will be. For instance, we may want to provide a query for our users which enables them to select the records which have a value in the Date field which is earlier or later than a date that they themselves specify. In this case, we obviously don't know what that date will be when building the query. Therefore, we can't include it in the Criteria row of the grid.

The way round this problem is to use a **parameter**. If we do this, then when the user runs the query, Access will display a dialog box asking them to enter the value to be used as the criteria. The user can enter any valid date and Access will use that date as the criteria.

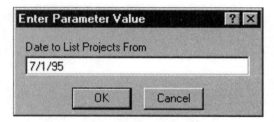

Setting Up a Parameter

We tell Access to display the dialog box by placing the text that forms the prompt in the Criteria row of the query grid. Access displays the dialog with this text and waits for the user to enter a value and click the OK button. It then uses the value that has been entered as the criteria of the query. Let's see how this works in practice.

Try It Out - A Simple Parameter Query

We'll build a simple parameter query which selects records dated on or after a date specified by the user when the query is run.

1 Create a new query (close the last one down without saving it) and add the Project table to it. Drag the Date and Project fields to the query grid. In the Sort: row for the Date field select Ascending - this will make it easier to see the results of the query. We want to display dates that are later than or equal to the date the user enters, so type >=[Date to List Projects From] in the Criteria row of the Date field.

Field:	Date	Project
Table:	Project	Project
Sort:	Ascending	
Show:	✓	✓
Criteria:	>=[Date to List Projects From]	
or:		

2 Click the Datasheet button to run the query. Access displays the Enter Parameter dialog with the prompt we placed in the Criteria row.

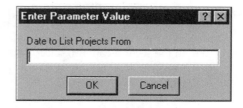

3 Enter the date 7/1/95 (or 1/7/95 if your computer is not set to US date format) and click OK. Access shows all the projects that were completed on or after 1st July 1995.

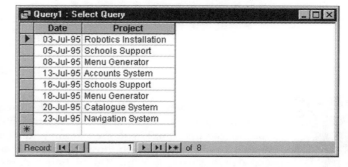

Well, that was easy enough, but let's have a look at one of the problems that can arise.

4 Go back into design view, then click the Datasheet button to run the query again. This time type 1st July 1995 in the Enter Parameter dialog.

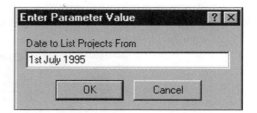

 You can enter a date into a dialog box like this in several different formats, depending on the settings of your operating system. However 1st July is not a format catered for by Access and will therefore be rejected by the system - Access is expecting a number for the day, not text. Access can accept 1 July 1995, but not 1st July 1995.

5 Access can't evaluate the parameter against the field, so the query doesn't run.

Rather than just letting Access give up when the user enters a value it can't deal with, it would be better to let the user know that they entered an inappropriate value. We can do this by setting a data type for the parameter.

6 In design view, select Para<u>m</u>eters from the <u>Q</u>uery menu - the Query Parameters dialog opens. In the first column, copy the text we used for the criteria parameter, which was Date to List Projects From. In the second column, select Date/Time from the drop-down list. Then click OK.

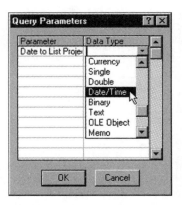

FYI The first column must match the text of the prompt exactly otherwise Access can't connect the two together. If it differs in any way, two **Enter Parameter** dialogs will appear when you run the query, one with each prompt. Remember that Access uses square brackets to denote a field name, so you must include them in the **Criteria** row of the query grid, but you don't need them in the **Query Parameters** dialog.

7 Run the query again and enter the same text again. This time Access recognizes that it's inappropriate for the data type we specified and prompts you to try again.

When you run a query, Access first prompts for the parameters you list in the Parameters window (you can use more than one in a query). It then checks the query for any other parameters that are required. If it finds any it hasn't already gathered a value for, it prompts for these next. This is why you get two prompts for a parameter if the entries in the query and Parameters window don't match exactly.

Sometimes, when you run an ordinary query and haven't specified any parameters in either the query or the Parameters window, you may see the Enter Parameter dialog appear. Recall that we used square brackets around the parameter in the query grid just as we had to when we used field names in a expression. Access treats anything it finds in square brackets firstly as a field name. If it can't find a field with this name, it then assumes it must be a parameter and prompts for the value. So if you have misspelled a field name in a query, or deleted the field from the underlying table, Access will consider it to be a parameter and prompt you to enter the value.

Summary

This chapter has given you a real taste of what you can achieve with queries. Although we've been using the Access query tool, remember that behind this it's SQL that's doing all the real work. We took our first glimpse at this language which underpins Access and indeed all main-line database systems. In particular we looked at the different parts of an SQL statement - **SELECT** information **FROM** a table **WHERE** a certain condition holds. We'll take a more detailed look at SQL later in the book.

This chapter has also introduced you to operators and functions, which can be used to build more complex queries. Access provides a tool to help you with this - Expression Builder makes your life easy by reminding you of the syntax of the different Access functions. We will be using Expression Builder in examples throughout the rest of the book.

This chapter has covered:

- Using operators and functions to build real queries.
- Using the Expression Builder to help build expressions.
- Getting input from the user by using parameters in your queries.

In the next chapter we'll continue looking at queries, covering the various types of query which are available in Access.

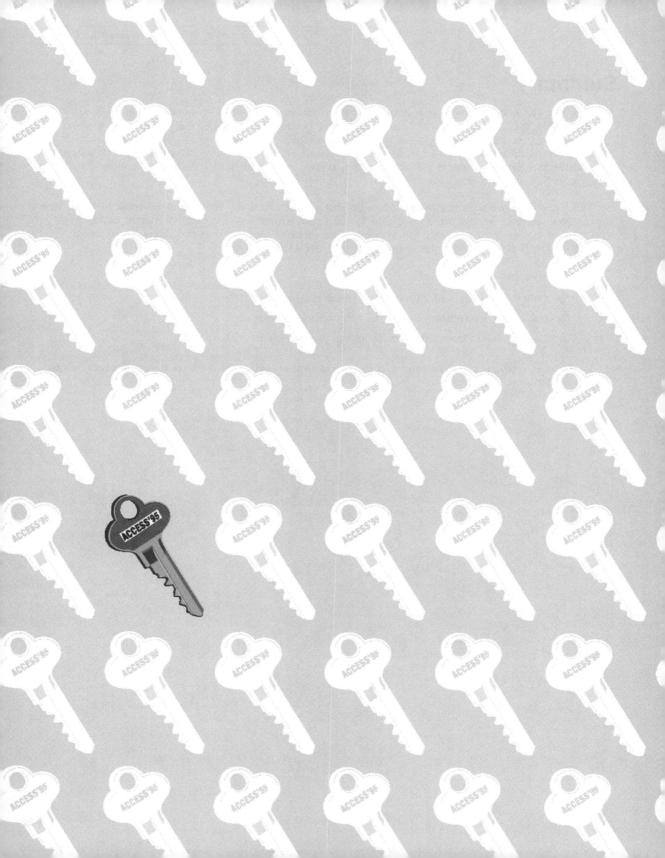

Further Types Of Access Query

You've done a fair amount of work with queries in the past few chapters. All the queries that you have used, however, have been what are known as select queries. While these are the most common type, Access does offer a range of different types of query.

In this chapter you will see how you can use queries to calculate summaries, create new tables and update existing tables. We will also use queries to finally carry out the task we set ourselves in Chapter 1 - summing data in a table.

This chapter will cover:

- Creating subtotals and performing other summary tasks.
- How to update records in a table.
- Archiving records.
- Deleting selected records using a query.
- How to join tables in a query.

The Different Types of Access Query

All the queries you have been working with up to now have been what are known as select queries. As the name suggests, these select fields and records from a table and display them as a recordset. There are, however, several different kinds of query in Access. Which one you use naturally depends on what you want to do. The following table summarizes the different kinds of query.

Type of query	Description
Select query	Selects and sorts fields and records to produce a new recordset.
Summary query	This is a special kind of select query which summarizes values from a set of records.
Crosstab query	This breaks records down into categories and displays summary information by category.
Action queries:	This performs the same operations as a select query, but instead of producing a recordset, the results act directly on the table. There are four kinds of action query.
Append query	Adds records to an existing table.
Update query	Updates records in an existing table.
Delete query	Deletes records from an existing table.
Make table query	Creates a new table and inserts records into it.

We'll look at each type of query in turn.

Summary Queries

Summary queries make it possible to perform different calculations on the values in records. For example, you can produce subtotals, find the average value in a field, find the minimum or maximum value, etc.

In other respects, summary queries are very similar to the select queries we've been using. You can include calculated fields and use criteria to display selected records. We'll start by summing values, then go on to look at the other summary functions that we can apply.

Try It Out - Creating Subtotals

In this example we will use a summary query to work out the details for each type of project we've carried out. We will show the number of hours worked on that type of project, the total charge, tax due and the amount we are owed for that type of project.

1 Open **NewTab3.mdb** and create a new query. Add the Customer and Project tables to it. The link between them appears automatically. Then drag the Project, HoursWorked, TotalCharge, TaxDue and TotalDue fields from the Project table into the query grid.

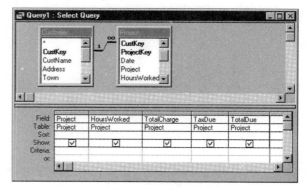

2 On the toolbar, find the Totals button and click on it. Access adds the Total: row to the grid and enters Group By for all the fields.

Field:	Project	HoursWorked	TotalCharge	TaxDue	TotalDue
Table:	Project	Project	Project	Project	Project
Total:	Group By	Group By	Group By	Group By	Group By
Sort:					
Show:	☑	☑	☑	☑	☑
Criteria:					
or:					

FYI The **Total:** row of the query grid is where we tell Access which summary function to carry out on the contents of the field. For example, we can add them all together, average them, or find the largest or smallest value. However, setting the value in the **Total:** row to **Group By**, tells Access that we just want the records to be divided into groups according to the values in that particular field.

3 Before we run this query, we have to specify which fields we want to be totaled. Under all except the Project field, select Sum from the drop-down list that appears when you click in the Total: row of the grid.

Field:	Project	HoursWorked	TotalCharge	TaxDue	TotalDue	
Table:	Project	Project	Project	Project	Project	
Total:	Group By	Sum	Sum	Sum	Group By	▼
Sort:						Group By
Show:	☑	☑	☑	☑		Sum
Criteria:						Avg
or:						Min
						Max
						Count
						StDev
						Var

4 Switch to datasheet view to see the results. Access displays the fields with new names - SumOfHoursWorked, SumOfTotalCharge, etc. and displays the total for each type of project. We left the Project field set to Group By, so Access adds up all the values for records which have the same value in the Project field.

Query1 : Select Query

Project	SumOfHoursWorked	SumOfTotalCharge	SumOfTaxDue	SumOfTotalDue
Accounts System	108	$5,400.00	$648.00	$6,048.00
Catalogue System	42	$3,360.00	$436.80	$3,796.80
Menu Generator	10	$600.00	$90.00	$690.00
Navigation System	14	$630.00	$63.00	$693.00
PC Upgrades	5	$425.00	$59.50	$484.50
Robotics Installation	8	$600.00	$48.00	$648.00
Schools Support	50	$2,500.00	$0.00	$2,500.00
System Development	18	$1,170.00	$163.80	$1,333.80
Warehouse System	24	$1,680.00	$184.80	$1,864.80

Record: 1 of 9

5 To explore grouping a little further, go back into design view and drag the CustName field from the Customer table into the first column of the grid - the others move to make room for it.

Field:	CustName ▼	Project	HoursWorked	TotalCharge	TaxDue
Table:	Customer	Project	Project	Project	Project
Total:	Group By	Group By	Sum	Sum	Sum
Sort:					
Show:	☑	☑	☑	☑	
Criteria:					
or:					

6 Leave the Total: entry for CustName set to **Group By** and click the **Datasheet View** button. Now Access displays a record for each project for each of the customers.

	CustName	Project	SumOfHoursWorked	SumOfTotalCharge	SumOfTaxDue	SumOfTotalDue
▶	Aardvark Limited	Accounts System	38	$1,900.00	$228.00	$2,128.00
	Burger Queen	System Development	18	$1,170.00	$163.80	$1,333.80
	Cummings Intl.	Robotics Installation	8	$600.00	$48.00	$648.00
	Education Dept.	Schools Support	50	$2,500.00	$0.00	$2,500.00
	J.R.Higgins	PC Upgrades	5	$425.00	$59.50	$484.50
	James Builders	Accounts System	21	$1,050.00	$126.00	$1,176.00
	Jonahs Boats	Navigation System	14	$630.00	$63.00	$693.00
	Le Bistro	Menu Generator	4	$240.00	$36.00	$276.00
	Major Records	Catalogue System	17	$1,360.00	$176.80	$1,536.80
	Martha's Bar	Menu Generator	6	$360.00	$54.00	$414.00
	Miracle Supplies	Accounts System	11	$550.00	$66.00	$616.00
	Miracle Supplies	Warehouse System	24	$1,680.00	$184.80	$1,864.80
	Pedro Mana	Accounts System	38	$1,900.00	$228.00	$2,128.00
	Union Records	Catalogue System	25	$2,000.00	$260.00	$2,260.00

Record: 1 of 14

Take a look at the results - you can open the Customer and Project tables from the Database window and compare them. Access has created one record for each type of project for each customer. So, in the case of the Education Dept. and Miracle Supplies, where we've worked on two projects with the same name, it has added together the values for the hours worked, the total charge and the tax due.

We can obtain totals down to any level of grouping we require - here we've seen them applied to just the project names, then to each project by customer. We can also go the other way - for instance, we can work out the number of hours spent working, regardless of project.

Try It Out - Summarizing Values in a Table

As well as producing totals, summary queries also enable us to calculate average values, display particular values, etc. In this next example, we will calculate the average amount of time worked on each project and average charge for each project. Just to make it hard, we will only display these details for Accounts System projects.

1 Go back into design view and delete the CustName field from the grid. Under the Project field change the Total: entry from Group By to Count. This will simply tell us how many records there are in the recordset.

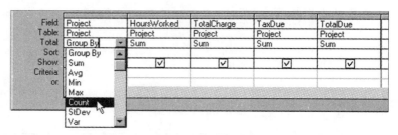

2 Switch to datasheet view. We now get just one record. This shows a count of the number of projects we've done, and the overall totals for the other fields.

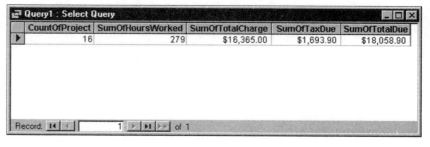

184

3 So now we can really get some information from the table. Back in design view, delete the TotalCharge and TaxDue fields from the grid, and add the

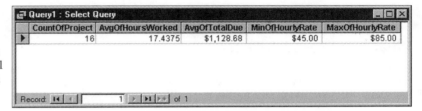

HourlyRate field twice. Then set the Total row to Avg for HoursWorked and TotalDue, Min for the first HourlyRate field and Max for the second one.

4 Switch to datasheet view - we now get the values for the number of projects, the average hours worked and total due, and the minimum and maximum hourly rates.

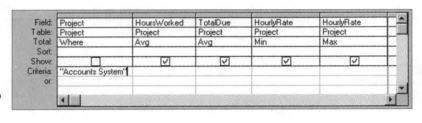

5 Finally, back in design view again, change the Total: entry for Project to Where and enter "Accounts System" in the Criteria row. This will limit the records to those for Accounts System projects only.

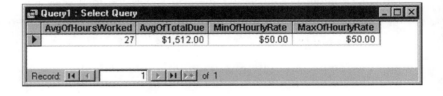

You'll see that Access clears the Show box automatically when the Total: row is set to Where.

6 Now switch to datasheet view. This time we get the average hours worked and total due, and the minimum and maximum hourly

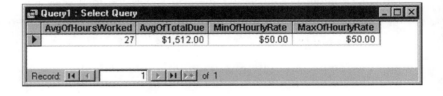

rates for Accounts Systems only. What more could you ask for in information retrieval?

We deliberately have not gone into a lot of explanation on summary queries. You'll no doubt agree that they are pretty intuitive. However, it's worth just spending a couple of minutes playing around so that you are familiar with the different options they offer.

Crosstab Queries

Just when you thought you'd found the ultimate in information retrieval, here's a type of query that will give you even more options for viewing information. Crosstab queries take the contents of a table and transform it (in the same way as you may have done with a spreadsheet) so that the information is summarized in columns rather than rows.

185

The Query Type Button

So far we have been using select queries. These are the default type of query and, therefore, we have not had to explicitly specify the type. When we want to use a crosstab query, however, we need to let Access know.

You can select the type of query you want to use from the Query menu, or from the toolbar. When you have a query open, there is a Query Type button available. This has a drop-down list button next to it, which shows the different query types.

What is a Crosstab Query?

Crosstab queries are best explained by way of an example. Suppose you have a table of sales from four grocery stores and each record contains the store name, the date, and the total sales value for that date - for instance:

Store	Date	Amount
City Square	24th March	$ 241.88
City Square	13th April	$ 188.50
King Street	6th February	$ 75.93
East Road	24th June	$ 167.31

What you'd like to do is compare the total monthly sales of each store. A crosstab query allows you to transpose the data into a grid where the store names form the row headings, the months form the column headings, and the grid shows the total sales for each store for each month.

Store	Jan	Feb	Mar	Apr	May	Jun
City Square	$1,520.06	$833.78	$3,032.55	$1,209.59	$1,472.88	$1,520.44
East Road	$2,160.47	$1,586.34	$1,822.96	$1,270.40	$997.33	$1,586.34
King Street	$997.33	$833.78	$755.20	$1,822.96	$755.20	$1,290.46
Queens Avenue	$2,815.76	$755.20	$1,270.40	$1,520.06	$892.10	$941.49

Try It Out - Using Query Wizard to Create a Crosstab Query

To demonstrate a crosstab query in action, we'll use one to show the total value for each project in the Project table. You're probably thinking that you could do this easily with a summary query - but in this example we're going to display the amount spent in each month, as well as the annual total.

Crosstab queries are more difficult to construct than the other types - you can use the Query Builder grid, but it is usually easier to use the Query Wizard. We'll use the wizard for this example and then have a look at the result in the Query Builder grid. This will give you a clearer picture of how each part of the query controls the way the data is displayed in the resulting recordset.

1 Close down the last query and, in the Queries tab in the **Database** window, click **New**. In the **New Query** dialog select **Crosstab Query Wizard**. Click **OK**. In the wizard's first window, select the **Project** table.

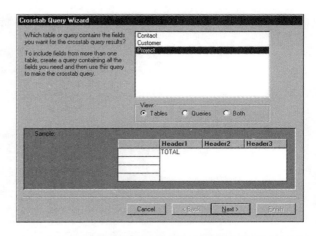

2 Click the **Next** button. Now we specify the headings for the rows. Select the **Project** field and click the **>** button. Access moves it to the right-hand list and places **Project1**, **Project2**, etc. in the diagram at the bottom of the window, to show how this will affect the final datasheet.

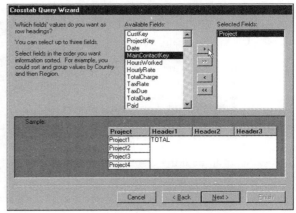

3 Click **Next**. Here we select the field for the column headings - select **Date** and you'll see it appear as the column headings at the bottom of the window.

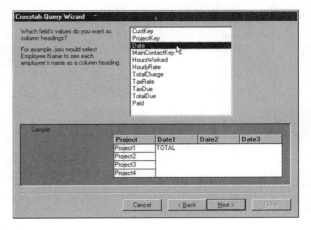

4 Click **Next** again. Because we have chosen a **Date/Time** field, Access asks how we want to break it into columns. Select **Month** and the preview will update to show the month names.

187

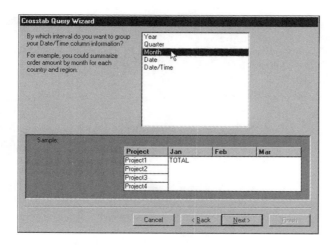

5 Click **Next** again. Now we have to specify which field we want to take the values to fill the crosstab grid from. We have got the project name down the left side of the recordset and want to work out the amount due in each month for each project. Therefore, select the **TotalDue** field from the left-hand list and **Sum** from the right-hand list. We also want to total the amounts due for each project, so tick the checkbox to include a summary for each row.

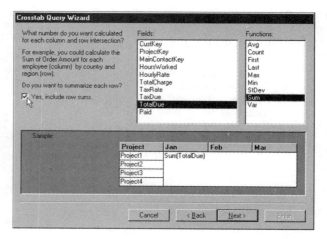

6 Click **Next** again. Enter a name for the new query and select the **View the query** option.

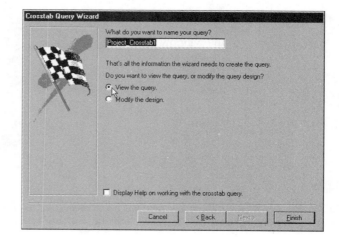

7 Click Finish and after some disk-whirring the final query appears, showing our projects down the left, the month names across the top, and the totals for each month in the grid, with a summary row before them. The Project table doesn't contain many months of data so a lot of the columns are empty. However, you can see the principle well enough.

Project	Total Of TotalDue	Jan	Feb	Mar	Apr	May	Jun	Jul	Aug	Sep	Oct	Nov	Dec
Accounts System	$6,048.00						$5,432.00	$616.00					
Catalogue System	$3,796.80						$1,536.80	$2,260.00					
Menu Generator	$690.00							$690.00					
Navigation System	$693.00							$693.00					
PC Upgrades	$484.50					$484.50							
Robotics Installation	$648.00							$648.00					
Schools Support	$2,500.00							$2,500.00					
System Development	$1,333.80						$1,333.80						
Warehouse System	$1,864.80						$1,864.80						

Record: 1 of 9

How It Works

Switch to design view and have a look at the grid. You'll see that there is a new row called **Crosstab:**. This controls how the fields are used to display the data. There are two fields which are **Row Headings**, one which is a **Column Heading** and one which is the **Value**. Access uses the settings in this row to decide how to analyze the data in the table when it builds the recordset.

Field:	Project	Expr1: Format([Date],"mmm")	The Value: TotalDue	Total Of TotalDue: TotalDue
Table:	Project		Project	Project
Total:	Group By	Group By	Sum	Sum
Crosstab:	Row Heading	Column Heading	Value	Row Heading
Sort:				
Criteria:				
or:				

As the names suggest, the **Row Headings** are used to identify each row and the single **Column Heading** breaks the data into the different columns. The data in the **Value** field is then allocated to 'cells', depending on the values in the **Row Headings** and **Column Heading** fields. Because we specified the **Sum** function, Access adds all the data that falls into each 'cell' together.

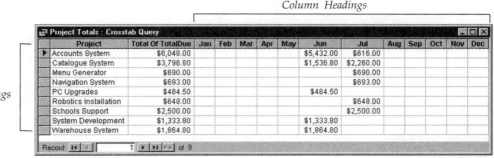

Column Headings

Row Headings

You may find it strange that the setting of the **Total of TotalDue** column is **Row Heading**. This just means it will occur once for each row, as you can see in the view of the resulting recordset, and contain the sum of the values from this row.

One other point to notice is the use of the **Format** function here to create the column headings for each month. The records contain actual dates, such as 21st July, so we need to create a column heading which only contains the three-letter month abbreviation for each one. The **Format** function requires two arguments - the value to be formatted and a 'format string' which specifies the format we require.

```
Format (value, format string)
```

The **value** is the entry in the Date field, so we use the field name - Date - for the first argument. The second is "mmm" which tells the **Format** function to return the three-letter month abbreviation only. This means that each value is reduced to just its month - the day part is lost. So records which have the same month fall into the same column irrespective of the day part of the Date field and they are added together to give the final value Expr1 which you can see in the query grid.

Now we've examined how a crosstab query works, we can modify it to improve the display somewhat. We'll display the project totals by week instead of by month and only display the weeks when some work was actually done. We'll make the modifications directly in the Query Builder grid.

Try It Out - Modifying a Crosstab Query

1 Click on the Expr1: field and press *Shift-F2* to open the Zoom window. The expression is Expr1:Format([Date],"mmm"). This takes the value in the Date field and converts it into a string containing the month abbreviation, such as Jan, Feb etc. We want to split the sales up by week number - the format argument

for this is ww. Therefore, change the entry in the Zoom box to Expr1: "Week " & Format([Date],"ww") and click OK.

2 Switch to datasheet view to see the results.

We've got a Total.. row summary, but no values in the rest of the columns. This is because Access has preset the column headings and the new values created for Expr1 by the query don't match these headings, so they cannot be placed in the columns of the grid. The columns still expect month names, but we are creating week numbers now.

3 To sort this out, go back to design view and double-click on a blank area in the top section of the query window, near the Project table. This opens the Query Properties dialog.

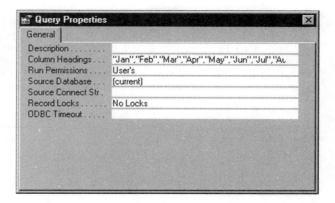

4 You can now see what is causing the problem - the Column Headings are set to Jan, Feb, Mar, etc. Delete the entire contents of this property and close the dialog. Then switch back to datasheet view and you'll get the result we want. Access just displays the amount due for each week and only shows columns for the weeks where we have data in the table.

Project	Total Of TotalDue	Week 24	Week 25	Week 26	Week 27	Week 28	Week 29	Week 30
Accounts System	$6,048.00	$3,304.00		$2,128.00		$616.00		
Catalogue System	$3,796.80			$1,536.80			$2,260.00	
Menu Generator	$690.00				$276.00		$414.00	
Navigation System	$693.00							$693.00
PC Upgrades	$484.50		$484.50					
Robotics Installation	$648.00				$648.00			
Schools Support	$2,500.00				$1,950.00		$550.00	
System Development	$1,333.80		$1,333.80					
Warehouse System	$1,864.80		$1,010.10	$854.70				

Record: 1 of 9

How the Query Properties Dialog Works

If you create data for the columns in the query and it doesn't match the column headings in the Query Properties dialog, it won't be shown in the resulting recordset - as we saw in the example above. If you leave the Column Headings property blank, however, Access creates columns for any data that's present.

The Column Headings entry in the Query Properties dialog is useful if you want a query to always use the same column headings irrespective of the data in the table. We saw this in the previous example where Query Wizard set it to months - even though there was no data for ten of the twelve months, it still displayed columns for them.

So here's another useful way to summarize information from our data. As well as summing the values, we could just as easily select Avg, Max, Min, etc. while using the Crosstab Query Wizard. We can also modify the query once the wizard has created it.

Note that crosstab queries are really only useful when you have numbers in the table to analyze. However, you could use the `Count` function to count the number of entries if they were text values.

Action Queries

We've now seen how we can get information out of the data in our database. The other major task for queries is to actually change the contents of tables, rather than produce recordsets based on them. This is where action queries come into play - and you'll be pleased to hear that, compared to the other information retrieval queries we've covered so far, they are relatively simple to use.

One of the major applications of action queries is archiving data from tables. For instance, the Project table will soon grow in size as we enter data for all the projects we carry out. At some point we'll need to move the older records to another table.

We have already mentioned that there are four types of action query:

Action query type	What it does
Append query	Adds new records to an existing table.
Update query	Updates existing records in an existing table.
Delete query	Removes existing records from an existing table.
Make table query	Creates a new table and places in it the records that the query produces.

We'll look at each of these in turn.

When using any action query, bear in mind that they'll change the data stored in the table on which they act. Instead of showing the results in a window, they carry out the modifications to the table. You may, therefore, wish to back up your database before you use them, in case anything goes wrong.

Action queries are basically select queries that perform an action instead of displaying records. Therefore, a second, useful safety measure is to create the action query as a select query first and then view the recordset it creates. You can check that only the records you want to modify or delete are included, before changing the query to the action you want and running it.

Update Queries

For our first Try It Out, we'll assume that the exchange code for Stocksville has changed from 711 to 738. We need to update all the records that contain the old value.

Try It Out - Using an Update Query on the Customer Table

1 Create a new query and add the Customer table to it. Drag the Town, Phone and Fax fields into the grid.

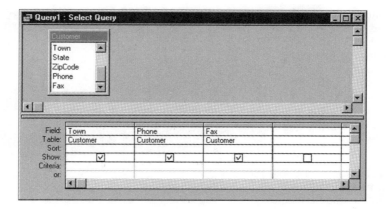

2 To limit the update to only the customers in Stocksville, enter "Stocksville" in the Criteria row of the grid under Town.

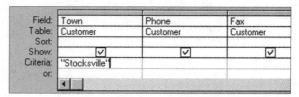

3 Switch to datasheet view to check that we only have the records we want to update.

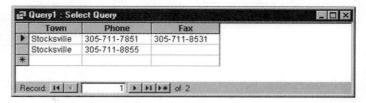

4 Now go back into design view and open the Query Type list on the toolbar. Select the Update query option. The grid changes to show a row Update To:. This is where we tell the query what value to place in that field.

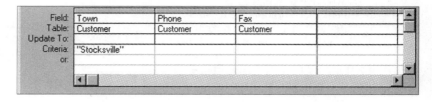

We need to create an expression that inserts the new area code and removes the old one. To do this we can use one of Access' string-handling functions that we mentioned in the last chapter. We'll insert the new code, then use the **Right$** function to split off the last 4 digits of the number (the part we want to keep) and add this to the new code using the **&** operator. We'll use Expression Builder to create the new expression.

The **Right$** function has the syntax **Right$(string, chars)**. It returns the first **x** (a number indicated by **chars**) characters from the right-hand end of the **string**.

5 Click in the Update To: row of the Phone field and then click the Build button on the toolbar to open Expression Builder.

6 The area dialing code hasn't changed, and we know the new exchange code, so enter "305-738" in the top window of Expression Builder. Now click the **&** button - we will add the last 4 digits of the number from the old Phone field.

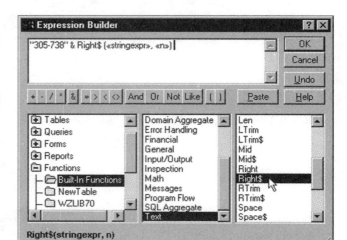

7 Double-click Functions in the lower left window and select Built-In Functions. In the middle window select Text from the end of the list and in the right-hand window double-click on Right$. Access adds it to the top window.

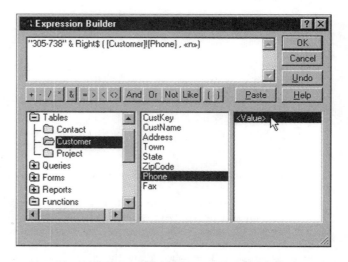

8 Now we have to replace the argument place-holders with values. The first argument is «stringexpr» - this is the value we want to work on. Click on it once to highlight it, then insert the <Value> from the Phone field of the Customer table.

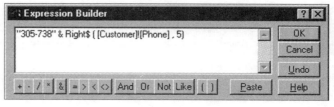

9 The other argument is the number of characters we want, counting from the right-hand end of the string. We need the last five - the four numbers and the preceding hyphen. So click on the «n» argument placeholder to highlight it and type 5.

10 Click OK to place the expression back in the Query Builder grid. Now we need to perform the same operation on the Fax field. Either use Expression Builder again, or just copy the expression in the Update To: row from the Phone field to the Fax field and edit the field name so that it reads "305-738" & Right$([Customer]![Fax],5)

Field:	Town	Phone	Fax
Table:	Customer	Customer	Customer
Update To:		"305-738" & Right$([Customer]![Phone],5)	"305-738" & Right$([Customer]![Fax],5)
Criteria:	"Stocksville"		
or:			

 Remember you can use *Shift-F2* to open the Zoom box. This makes editing the entry in the **Expression Builder** grid much easier.

11 To run an action query, you must click the Run Query button on the toolbar, or select Run from the Query menu. Instead of a datasheet, you will get a message telling you that two records will be updated. Accept the updates by clicking Yes.

Microsoft Access

ⓘ You are about to update 2 row(s). Once you click Yes, you can't use the Undo command to reverse the changes.

Are you sure you want to update these records?

[Yes] [No]

12 Now open the Customer table from the Database window. The records for our customers in Stocksville show the new exchange code.

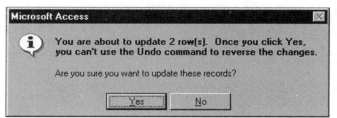

Customer : Table

	CustKey	CustName	Address	Town	State	ZipCode	Phone	Fax
	1	Major Records	Third Avenue	Stocksville	FL	10015	305-738-7851	305-738-8531
	2	Miracle Supplies	18th Avenue	Oakland	CA	10593	415-671-6633	415-671-8833
	5	Education Dept.	The Offices, City Square	Chicago	IL	10745	312-712-8567	
▶	7	Jonahs Boats	The Quay	Stocksville	FL	16734	305-738-8855	305-738
	8	Cummings Intl.	124th Street West	Pittsburgh	PA	17265	412-455-6104	412-455-1399
	9	Burger Queen	Constants Avenue	Houston	TX	30517	713-771-6727	713-771-6728
	10	Aardvark Limited	All Saints Street	Athens	OH	39812	216-376-1298	216-376-8811
	11	Le Bistro	Rue Francais	Vancouver	WA	41322	206-133-8294	206-133-8295
	12	Union Records	712 Main Street	Tampa	FL	51267	813-167-3520	813-167-3521
	13	Martha's Bar	Top Street	Clarksville	NY	54876		
	14	J.R.Higgins	The Market	Green Bay	WI	61733	414-831-8812	414-831-7293
	15	Pedro Mana	Calle Sebastione	St. Paul	MN	65109	612-401-1350	612-401-1388
	16	James Builders	2131 New Street	Phoenix	AZ	78034	602-281-3318	602-281-7318
*	(AutoNumber)							

Record: ◄◄ ◄ 4 ► ►► ►* of 13

It seems as though everything has gone well, but take another look. We've changed the Fax entry for Jonah's Boats, even though we didn't have a number in the first place. We blindly updated the contents of the fields without checking whether there was anything in them first.

We need to amend the Update To: expressions so that they're a little more selective - they need to check out the contents of the field first and only update it if it's not empty. An even better idea would be to check whether they contain the old code, and only change the ones that do.

Then we wouldn't need a criteria to select Stocksville - we could apply the update to all the records and it would then pick up all those with the code 711. This is what the next Try It Out will do.

Try It Out - Modifying the Update Query on the Customer Table

To check out the value in a field and take one of two different actions depending on that value, we need the **IIf** function. Remember that this takes the following form:

```
IIf(condition to test, value if true, value if false).
```

Our **condition to test** is the value in the Phone (or Fax) field - we will test whether it starts with 305-711. The **value if true** is the new number - "305-738" & Right$([Phone],5) and the **value if false** is the original value - we won't change it.

To test whether a value starts with a particular string of characters, we can use the **Left$** function. This is similar to the **Right$** function we used earlier, but operates on the left-most characters rather than the right-most.

So the expression we need for the Phone field is:

IIf (Left$([Phone],7) = "305-711", "305-738" & Right$([Phone],5), [Phone])

And similarly for the Fax field we need:

IIf (Left$([Fax],7) = "305-711", "305-738" & Right$([Fax],5), [Fax])

1 Start by editing the records in the table manually so that the they contain the old code - 305-711. Also remove the partial Fax entry for Jonah's Boats. Then close the Customer table.

Phone	Fax
305-738-1851	305-738-9531
415-071-6633	415-071-8833
312-712-8567	
305-738-8855	305-738
412-455-6104	412-455-1399
713-771-6727	713-771-6728
216-376-1298	216-376-8811
206-133-8294	206-133-8295
813-167-3520	813-167-3521
414-831-8812	414-831-7293
612-401-1350	612-401-1388
602-281-3318	602-281-7318

2 In query design view, click on the Update To: entry for the Phone field and then open Expression Builder. You'll see the current expression in the top window.

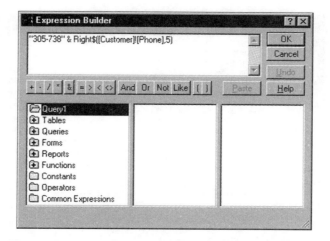

3 You could just modify the existing expression, but it's probably easier to delete it and start again. You'll find **IIf** in the Built-In Functions 'Program Flow' list and **Left$** in the 'Text' list. Try building this expression in the top window. If you get lost, you can simply edit it there so that it reads as shown below. (Note that Expression Builder will insert the tables' names in front of each of the field names).

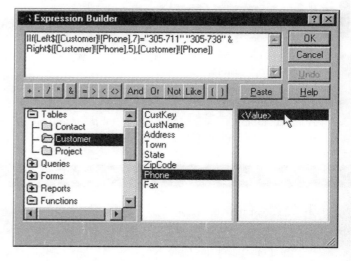

4 Repeat the operation with the Fax field, entering the expression:

IIf (Left$([Fax],7) = "305-711", "305-738" & Right$([Fax],5), [Fax])

5 Delete the Criteria in the Town column, then run the query by clicking the Run Query button on the toolbar. You'll see that this time Access reports it will update 13 records - there is no criteria to limit it this time, but our selective function will only make changes to the ones we actually want to update.

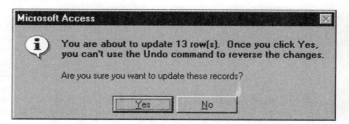

6 Click <u>Y</u>es and
then view the
results by
opening the
Customer
table from the
Database
window. We
have the
results we
want for the
fields with the
old numbers
in and the

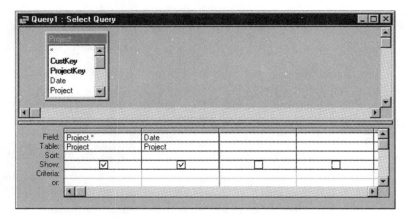

	CustKey	CustName	Address	Town	State	ZipCode	Phone	Fax
▶	1	Major Records	Third Avenue	Stocksville	FL	10015	305-738-7851	305-738-8531
	2	Miracle Supplies	18th Avenue	Oakland	CA	10593	415-671-6633	415-671-8833
	5	Education Dept.	The Offices, City Square	Chicago	IL	10745	312-712-8567	
	7	Jonahs Boats	The Quay	Stocksville	FL	16734	305-738-8855	
	8	Cummings Intl.	124th Street West	Pittsburgh	PA	17265	412-455-6104	412-455-1399
	9	Burger Queen	Constants Avenue	Houston	TX	30517	713-771-6727	713-771-6728
	10	Aardvark Limited	All Saints Street	Athens	OH	39812	216-376-1298	216-376-8811
	11	Le Bistro	Rue Francais	Vancouver	WA	41322	206-133-8294	206-133-8295
	12	Union Records	712 Main Street	Tampa	FL	51267	813-167-3520	813-167-3521
	13	Martha's Bar	Top Street	Clarksville	NY	54876		
	14	J.R.Higgins	The Market	Green Bay	WI	61733	414-831-8812	414-831-7293
	15	Pedro Mana	Calle Sebastione	St. Paul	MN	65109	612-401-1350	612-401-1388
	16	James Builders	2131 New Street	Phoenix	AZ	78034	602-281-3318	602-281-7318
✳	(AutoNumber)							

Record: |◄| ◄| 1 |►| ►| ►✳| of 13

blank field has not been changed.

FYI We could also have used the `Like` operator to check whether the existing value in the
field started with **305-711** instead of using `Left$`. Such is the variety of Access functions
that there are many ways of achieving the same result.

So that's how we use an update query. We can update several fields in one go and perform
different operations on each.

Make Table Queries

A make table query creates a new table based on the results of a query. We'll have a look at
how this type of query works now.

Try It Out - Using a Make Table Query

1 Create a new query, add
the Project table to it, and
drag the asterisk (i.e. all
the fields) and the Date
field into the grid. We'll
build a query that uses a
parameter for the date.

2 In the Criteria row under the Date field, type <[Archive Project records earlier than]. This is the
prompt for our Date parameter. Clear the Show checkbox for the Date field, otherwise it will be
included twice (because we have used the asterisk to include all fields).

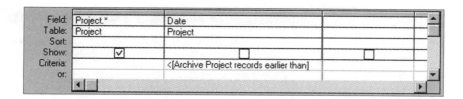

3 Open the Parameters window by selecting Parameters from the Query menu, enter Archive Project records earlier than in the first column and select Date/Time in the second column. Click OK to close the Parameters window.

4 Now we need to convert the query to a make table query. We want to create a new table containing the records which match our criteria. Click the Query Type button on the toolbar to open the list of query types and select Make Table. Access opens the Make Table dialog. Here we can specify the name of the new table and tell Access if it's in the current database or another one. Enter Archived for the name of the new table and make sure Current Database is selected.

5 Click OK to close the Make Table dialog - the title bar of the query now reads Query1: Make Table Query, but the grid remains unchanged. A make table query behaves much like a select query - you can even switch to datasheet view to see the results as a set of records. But when you run it the records are used to build a new table.

6 Click the Run Query button on the toolbar. Access opens the Enter Parameter Value dialog. Enter 7/1/95 for the date parameter (or 1/7/95 if you're not using US date formats).

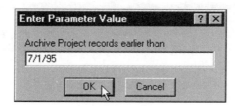

7 Click OK and Access displays a message showing the number of records that will be copied to the new table.

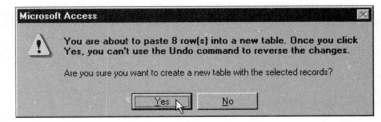

8 Click <u>Y</u>es to accept the changes and go back to the Database window. You'll see the new Archived table listed. <u>O</u>pen it and you'll see the records we've copied from the Project table.

	CustKey	ProjectKey	Date	Project	HoursWorked	HourlyRate	TotalCharge	TaxRate	TaxDue	TotalDue	Paid
▶	1	44	6/30/95	Catalogue System	17	$80.00	$1,360.00	0.13	$176.80	$1,536.80	
	2	37	6/18/95	Warehouse System	13	$70.00	$910.00	0.11	$100.10	$1,010.10	
	2	46	6/26/95	Warehouse System	11	$70.00	$770.00	0.11	$84.70	$854.70	
	9	49	6/23/95	System Development	18	$65.00	$1,170.00	0.14	$163.80	$1,333.80	
	10	40	6/12/95	Accounts System	38	$50.00	$1,900.00	0.12	$228.00	$2,128.00	
	14	52	6/20/95	PC Upgrades	5	$85.00	$425.00	0.14	$59.50	$484.50	
	15	53	6/28/95	Accounts System	38	$50.00	$1,900.00	0.12	$228.00	$2,128.00	
	16	43	6/16/95	Accounts System	21	$50.00	$1,050.00	0.12	$126.00	$1,176.00	
✱		.utoNumber)									

FYI Remember that the **ProjectKey** values are assigned automatically by Access according to the last autonumber value that was used. Therefore, the values you get may be different.

We've now created a new table. What happens, though, if we run the same query again?

9 Close the Archived table and click the Run Query button again. When you enter a date, Access prompts you that the table Archived already exists and prevents you from going any further.

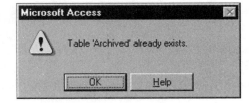

Append Queries

To add records to a table, we can use an append query. In the next Try It Out we will convert our existing make table query to an append query.

Try It Out - Creating an Append Query

1 Click the Query Type button on the toolbar and select Append. Access displays an Append dialog and suggests we append to the Archived table - the one we set up the original Make Table query to create. This is just what we want.

2 Click OK to close the dialog. The grid has now changed - we've got a new row called **Append To:** and the **Show:** row

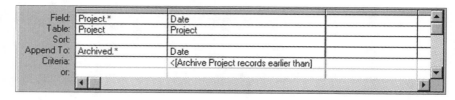

has gone. We have to tell Access which fields in the **Project** table are to be appended to which in the **Archived** table. We do this using the field names. It's suggested **Project.*** for the first field and put **Archived.*** in the **Append To:** row. This will append each field from the **Project** table to the one with the same name in the **Archived** table. This is what we want.

 The append query can handle tables with different structures by appending data to a field with a different name. You must then ensure that the data types, etc. are compatible between the fields.

Access has suggested how it thinks we want the fields appended to the **Archived** table. The only problem is the **Date** field - we included it in the grid so that we could use it with a criteria. However, we don't want it appended twice in the new table.

3 In the **Date** column, delete just the field name (Date) from the **Append To:** row so that it's not included twice. Now click the **Run Query** button on the toolbar and enter **7/12/95** for the date parameter (or **12/7/95** if you're not using US settings on your machine).

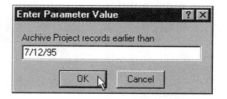

 Note that Access automatically assumes that the entry in the **Criteria** field is a parameter. This is because it does not recognize it as a table field name.

4 Click OK and Access displays a message showing the number of records that will be appended to the new table.

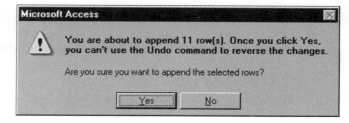

5 Click Yes and then open the Archived table from the Database window. You'll see the new records we've appended to the table.

	CustKey	ProjectKey	Date	Project	HoursWorked	HourlyRate	TotalCharge	TaxRate	TaxDue	TotalDue	Paid
	1	1	6/30/95	Catalogue System	17	$80.00	$1,360.00	0.13	$176.80	$1,536.80	
	2	2	6/18/95	Warehouse System	13	$70.00	$910.00	0.11	$100.10	$1,010.10	
	2	3	6/26/95	Warehouse System	11	$70.00	$770.00	0.11	$84.70	$854.70	
	9	9	6/23/95	System Development	18	$65.00	$1,170.00	0.14	$163.80	$1,333.80	
	10	10	6/12/95	Accounts System	38	$50.00	$1,900.00	0.12	$228.00	$2,128.00	
	14	14	6/20/95	PC Upgrades	5	$85.00	$425.00	0.14	$59.50	$484.50	
	15	15	6/28/95	Accounts System	38	$50.00	$1,900.00	0.12	$228.00	$2,128.00	
	16	16	6/16/95	Accounts System	21	$50.00	$1,050.00	0.12	$126.00	$1,176.00	
	1	1	6/30/95	Catalogue System	17	$80.00	$1,360.00	0.13	$176.80	$1,536.80	
	2	2	6/18/95	Warehouse System	13	$70.00	$910.00	0.11	$100.10	$1,010.10	
	2	3	6/26/95	Warehouse System	11	$70.00	$770.00	0.11	$84.70	$854.70	
	5	5	7/5/95	Schools Support	39	$50.00	$1,950.00	0	$0.00	$1,950.00	
	8	8	7/3/95	Robotics Installation	8	$75.00	$600.00	0.08	$48.00	$648.00	
	9	9	6/23/95	System Development	18	$65.00	$1,170.00	0.14	$163.80	$1,333.80	
	10	10	6/12/95	Accounts System	38	$50.00	$1,900.00	0.12	$228.00	$2,128.00	
	11	11	7/8/95	Menu Generator	4	$60.00	$240.00	0.15	$36.00	$276.00	
	14	14	6/20/95	PC Upgrades	5	$85.00	$425.00	0.14	$59.50	$484.50	
	15	15	6/28/95	Accounts System	38	$50.00	$1,900.00	0.12	$228.00	$2,128.00	
	16	16	6/16/95	Accounts System	21	$50.00	$1,050.00	0.12	$126.00	$1,176.00	
*		(AutoNumber)									

Record: 1 of 19

Delete Queries

OK, so we've got our old records into the Archived table by using a make table query to create the table, then an append query to add more records to it. The next problem is how do we remove the archived records from the original Project table? You've guessed it - we use a delete query.

Try It Out - Using a Delete Query

1 Close the table from the last Try It Out and go back to the query. Then click the Query Type button on the toolbar and select

Field:	Project.*	Date	
Table:	Project	Project	
Delete:	From	Where	
Criteria:		<[Archive Project records earlier than]	
or:			

Delete to convert the query into a delete query. Access changes the rows in the query grid. The Append To: row is removed and it now has a row named Delete:. It places From in the first column of this row and Where in the second column. This means Access will delete all the fields from the Project table where the criteria for the Date field (our parameter) is true.

2 Change the parameter for the Date field in the Criteria row of the query grid so that it reads <[Delete Project records earlier than] and change the entry in the Parameter dialog accordingly.

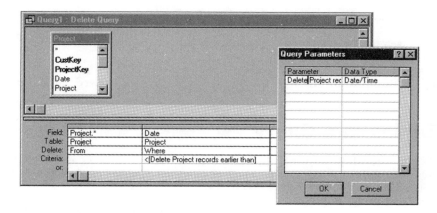

3 Before we run the query to delete the records from the Project table, we'll check it works properly - a good idea when using a delete query. Click the Datasheet / Query View button on the toolbar and enter 7/12/95 for the parameter. Access shows the records that would be deleted if we had clicked the Run Query button.

4 All is OK, so we can now run it as a delete query. Go back to design view and click the Run Query button on the toolbar. Enter 7/12/95 for the date parameter again.

5 Click OK and Access displays a message showing the number of rows that will be deleted.

> **Microsoft Access**
>
> ⚠ You are about to delete 11 row(s) from the specified table. Once you click Yes, you can't use the Undo command to reverse the changes.
>
> Are you sure you want to delete the selected records?
>
> [Yes]   [No]

6 Click Yes to accept the deletion, then open the Project table from the Database window to see the results. There are only the most recent five left.

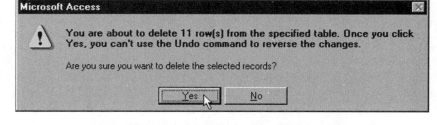

Well, you've now had a brief tour round all the different types of query that Access offers and you should be able to see the many ways that you can manipulate data. We'll be using most of these types of query in the **Wroxsoft** application we build in Part 2.

There's just one more thing about using queries that we should consider before we leave this chapter - how we can control the way that the tables we use in a query are joined together.

Joining Tables in a Query

In previous examples, when we used a query with more than one table as the source for the records, Access joined the tables together automatically according to the links (or **relationships**) that were defined earlier.

So, for example, when we added the Customer and Project tables, Access linked them together on the CustKey field, in accordance with the relationship we set up using the Relationships window.

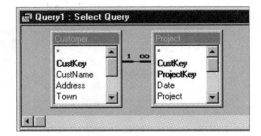

However, we are not confined to using this 'default' relationship. We can set up our own joins between tables in a query so that we get the results we want. To see this in action, we need to make a small modification to the Project table. We'll add a field called MainContactKey to each Project record and use it to store a reference to one of the contacts in our Contact table. This will be the person with whom we liaise for the project.

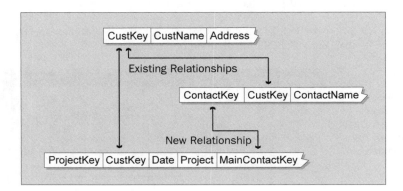

Now when we're entering records into the Project table, we can specify which of the contacts we have at that customer's premises is the main one for that particular project. Of course, we could just have made the new field a Text field and entered their name, but this way we can use the Contact table to store their address and phone number, etc. as well. This not only helps to keep down the redundancy of data, but it also means that we can select a contact from the ones we have at that customer - we don't have to enter the name and details directly.

So let's try it out. We need to modify the original Project table first, then we'll use the new field to include the main contact's details in a query.

Try It Out - Adding and Using a Main Contact Field in the Project Table

1 Close down the last database and open **NewTab4**. Again, this is just a clean version of the **NewTab1**. Open the Project table in design view and insert a row under the existing Project field by highlighting the HoursWorked row and pressing the *Insert* key.

2 Type in the field name - MainContactKey - and set its data type to Number. In the Properties section check that the Field Size is Long Integer and the Indexed property is Yes (Duplicates OK) - this will speed up our queries. Leave the rest of the settings at their defaults.

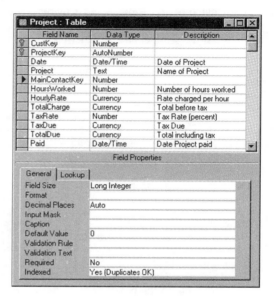

3 Switch to datasheet view by clicking the Datasheet button on the toolbar. (You'll be prompted to save the new table design). Now open the Contact table and enter some values from the ContactKey field in the Contact table into the MainContactKey field of the Project table. Leave the MainContactKey field blank in some records, though. (You should, of course, check that the contacts you enter for a project for a particular company actually belong to that company, but we'll let you get away with it this time.)

Project : Table

CustKey	ProjectKey	Date	Project	MainContactKey	HoursWor	HourlyRate	TotalCharge	TaxRate	TaxDue	TotalDue	Paid
1	44	30-Jun-95	Catalogue Sys	12	17	$80.00	$1,360.00	13.00%	$176.80	$1,536.80	
2	37	18-Jun-95	Warehouse Sy	15	13	$70.00	$910.00	11.00%	$100.10	$1,010.10	
2	46	26-Jun-95	Warehouse Sy	3	11	$70.00	$770.00	11.00%	$84.70	$854.70	
2	56	13-Jul-95	Accounts Syst	10	11	$50.00	$550.00	12.00%	$66.00	$616.00	
5	47	05-Jul-95	Schools Supp	5	39	$50.00	$1,950.00	0.00%	$0.00	$1,950.00	
5	57	16-Jul-95	Schools Supp	4	11	$50.00	$550.00	0.00%	$0.00	$550.00	
7	60	23-Jul-95	Navigation Sys		14	$45.00	$630.00	10.00%	$63.00	$693.00	
8	48	03-Jul-95	Robotics Insta	2	8	$75.00	$600.00	8.00%	$48.00	$648.00	
9	49	23-Jun-95	System Devel		18	$65.00	$1,170.00	14.00%	$163.80	$1,333.80	
10	40	12-Jun-95	Accounts Syst		38	$50.00	$1,900.00	12.00%	$228.00	$2,128.00	
11	51	08-Jul-95	Menu Generat	1	4	$60.00	$240.00	15.00%	$36.00	$276.00	
12	59	20-Jul-95	Catalogue Sys	11	25	$80.00	$2,000.00	13.00%	$260.00	$2,260.00	
13	58	18-Jul-95	Menu Generat	12	6	$60.00	$360.00	15.00%	$54.00	$414.00	
14	52	20-Jun-95	PC Upgrades	16	5	$85.00	$425.00	14.00%	$59.50	$484.50	
15	53	28-Jun-95	Accounts Syst	2	38	$50.00	$1,900.00	12.00%	$228.00	$2,128.00	
16	43	16-Jun-95	Accounts Syst	10	21	$50.00	$1,050.00	12.00%	$126.00	$1,176.00	
*	0	Number)		0							

Record: |◄| ◄ | 1 | ► | ►I | ►* | of 16

205

4 Now close the Project and Contact tables and create a new query by clicking **N**ew in the Database window Queries list. Add the Project and Contact tables to it. You'll see that there is no join between them in the query - remember that originally we only created relationships between the Customer and Project, and Customer and Contact tables. There is no direct relationship between the Project and Contact tables.

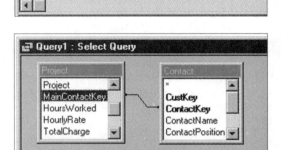

5 We can now create a new join. Click on the MainContactKey field in the Project table and drag it to the ContactKey field in the Contact table. This method is similar to the one we used to create relationships in Chapter 4. A join line appears linking the two fields.

6 Drag the Date, Project and MainContactKey fields from the Project table to the grid. Then drag the ContactKey and ContactName fields from the Contact table to the next columns of the grid.

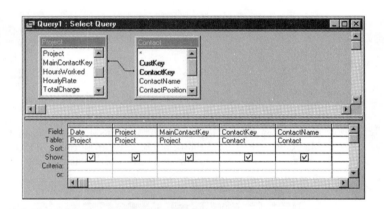

7 Switch to datasheet view. You'll see that each project now has the details of the contact added to it. However, look a bit closer - some of the projects are missing. There are 16 project records, but not all of them are shown. If we don't have a contact specified in the MainContactKey field, the projects don't appear in the resulting recordset.

Date	Project	MainContactKey	ContactKey	ContactName
08-Jul-95	Menu Generator	1	1	Mr. Arnson
03-Jul-95	Robotics Installation	2	2	Julia Fry
28-Jun-95	Accounts System	2	2	Julia Fry
26-Jun-95	Warehouse System	3	3	Mark Smith
16-Jul-95	Schools Support	4	4	Dave Jones
05-Jul-95	Schools Support	5	5	Carrie Newton
16-Jun-95	Accounts System	10	10	Jonah Wood
13-Jul-95	Accounts System	10	10	Jonah Wood
20-Jul-95	Catalogue System	11	11	Heinrich
30-Jun-95	Catalogue System	12	12	John Major
18-Jul-95	Menu Generator	12	12	John Major
18-Jun-95	Warehouse System	15	15	Tony De Varlio
20-Jun-95	PC Upgrades	16	16	DJ Jim

Record: |◄| ◄ | 1 | ► | ►| | ►* | of 13

8 We need to look at the type of join we've created to see why. Go back into design view and click on the join line between the tables. Then double-click to open the Join Properties dialog.

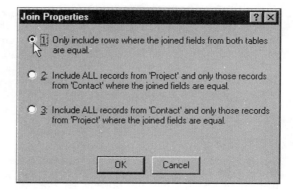

9 The reason we have lost some records is that the join that Access has created only includes rows where there are matching values in both tables. Where there is no MainContactKey, we get no record. Select Option 2 - 'Include ALL records from Project and only those records from Contact where the joined fields are equal.'

10 Click OK to close the Join Properties dialog and switch to datasheet view again. Now we can see all the Project records and those with no MainContactKey have blank fields for the contact details.

Date	Project	MainContactKey	ContactKey	ContactName
23-Jun-95	System Development			
12-Jun-95	Accounts System			
23-Jul-95	Navigation System			
08-Jul-95	Menu Generator	1	1	Mr. Arnson
03-Jul-95	Robotics Installation	2	2	Julia Fry
28-Jun-95	Accounts System	2	2	Julia Fry
26-Jun-95	Warehouse System	3	3	Mark Smith
16-Jul-95	Schools Support	4	4	Dave Jones
05-Jul-95	Schools Support	5	5	Carrie Newton
16-Jun-95	Accounts System	10	10	Jonah Wood
13-Jul-95	Accounts System	10	10	Jonah Wood
20-Jul-95	Catalogue System	11	11	Heinrich
30-Jun-95	Catalogue System	12	12	John Major
18-Jul-95	Menu Generator	12	12	John Major
18-Jun-95	Warehouse System	15	15	Tony De Varlio
20-Jun-95	PC Upgrades	16	16	DJ Jim

Record: 1 of 16

The first join we created (in Step 5) was an **inner join**. When we changed the join properties in Step 9, we specified a **left join** - identified by the arrow head that appeared on the join line in the query. Option 3 would have given us a **right join**. You'll come across these joins again when we look at SQL (Structured Query Language) in more depth later on.

The join we've created in our query is temporary - unlike the relationships we defined for the tables in Chapter 4 which always apply, this join only takes effect within the query itself.

Summary

We've come a long way in the last few chapters from our spreadsheet data retrieval methods. Instead of just finding and sorting records, we've been able to burrow down into the data and retrieve real information.

In this chapter we have started discussing more complex type of queries, including those with which you can amend records within the database (collectively known as action queries).

You are now familiar with all the different types of query that Access offers:

- Select queries
- Summary queries
- Crosstab queries
- Action queries - update, append, make table, and delete queries

With queries we have a very powerful way of getting data out of our database, but it's now time for us to move on to the other aspect of our database system. In the next chapters we'll be considering more elegant ways of getting data in and information out of our database tables.

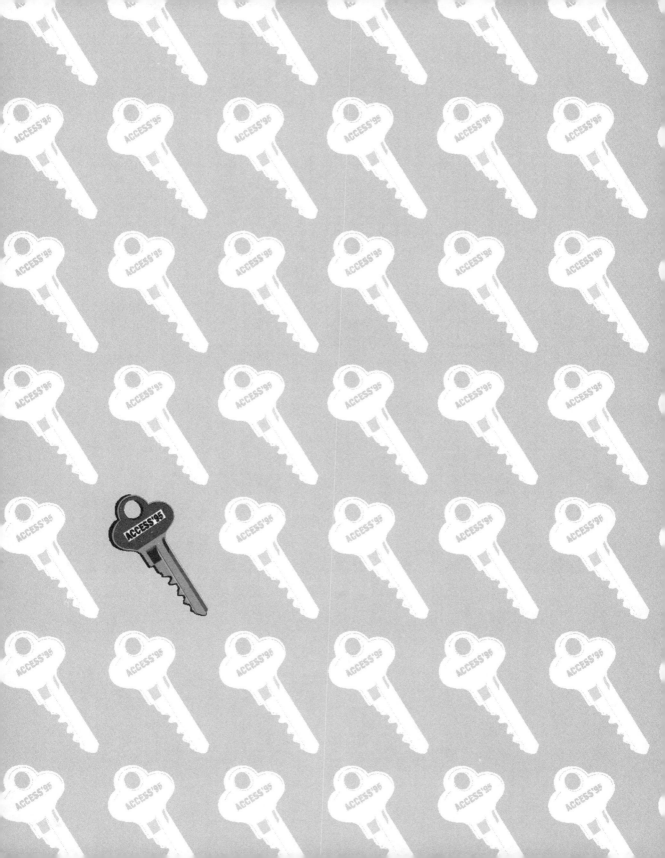

Getting Data Into Your Database

Up to now, we've been looking at how the working parts of Access are used to form a data storage and retrieval system. These 'behind the scenes' objects - tables and queries - are what do all the real work. An Access database is rather like an expensive sports car - everything looks smooth and elegant on the outside, but there is a mass of whirling gears, shafts and intricate moving parts underneath that do all the work.

When using a database, you wouldn't expect to have to enter data directly into a table or create queries yourself - you'd expect a modern application to have all the glamour and elegance of that sports car. Users want an intuitive user interface where they can just click buttons or select options to carry out their tasks. In this chapter, we will start to look at how this can be achieved.

In this chapter, we'll look at:

- How to present information to the user.
- How to add text boxes and other controls to a form.
- How to produce attractive user interfaces.
- How to get information from your users.

Creating Simple Forms

Forms are basically screen windows that sit on top of your tables and provide an easy way for users to view and alter the information contained in one or more tables. Instead of having to decipher row upon row of confusing data, users can fill in boxes on the screen to add or alter a record. With forms, you can provide information in an attractive and intuitive format that is easy to read and understand.

Forms also add a distinct layer of extra functionality to a database, in that you can use them to control how the user interacts with the underlying table. You'll see some of these techniques in the next few sections, as we first build a simple form from scratch and then create a more complicated one using the Form Wizard. We'll finish up by building a form that can be used to get information from a user, but which isn't actually linked to a table or query.

The forms in our first few examples are based directly on a table, but remember that we generally base a form on a query - we'll see how and why later. So let's start with a simple form based on our Project table.

Try It Out - Exploring the Form Window

1 Open up **NewTable.mdb** (this will be pretty familiar to you by now). Select the Forms tab in the Database window and click the New button. Access displays the New Form dialog. This contains a list of the different wizards that are available and a drop-down list where we select the table that we want to base the form on. Make sure that Design View is selected in the upper list and select the Project table from the drop-down list at the bottom.

2 Click OK and Access opens a new blank form in design view. The form is displayed in its own window, with several floating windows on top. These are the Toolbox, Field List and Form Properties windows.

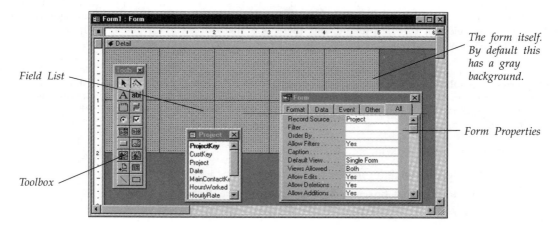

Field List

Toolbox

The form itself. By default this has a gray background.

Form Properties

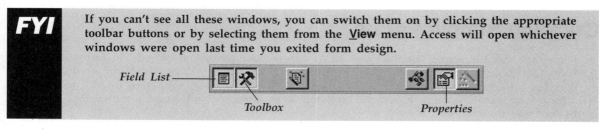

FYI

If you can't see all these windows, you can switch them on by clicking the appropriate toolbar buttons or by selecting them from the View menu. Access will open whichever windows were open last time you exited form design.

Field List

Toolbox

Properties

3 Have a look at the Form Properties window. This shows the various settings for the properties of the form itself. The second entry on the Format page, Default View, tells Access whether to display just one copy of the form or as many as will fit on the screen. Make sure the entry for Default View is set to Single Form.

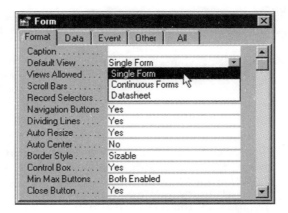

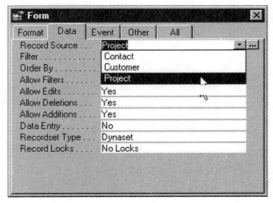

4 Click the Data tab and you'll see that the first property - Record Source - is set to the name of the table where the data to fill the form will come from. In our case it's the Project table, which is what we selected in the New Form dialog. You could change it to a different table (or query) using the drop-down list, but leave it set to Project for this example.

5 Move to the main Form1:Form window and click in the Detail section in the middle of the form in the main window. The Form Properties window changes to the Section: Detail window. (A form can contain different sections including a header and footer; we'll look at these later). In the main form window you can see that the Detail section selector (the narrow gray bar at the top of the form) is depressed, showing that this is the section to which the Section: Detail properties window refers.

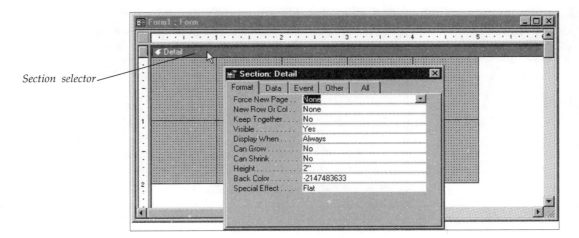

Section selector

6 Click on the square at the top left of the form window where the rulers meet. A black square appears indicating that the properties display has changed back to the Form Properties window.

Spend a couple of minutes familiarizing yourself with these windows - they will be used throughout the chapter. Next we'll add some functionality to our blank form by adding some controls to it.

Controls

When we look at the contents of a table in datasheet view, Access displays the data like a spreadsheet, in a series of rows and columns. However it's rare that we would use this method to show information or to edit and update it. In general, we make use of a form which displays the different items of data from each record in a more attractive and intuitive way. It does this by linking the fields in the records with **controls** on the form.

Controls are the text boxes, labels, list boxes, checkboxes, etc., that can display the information from a table. They can be positioned anywhere on a form. You should note that controls do not actually hold the data - it is still stored in the underlying table. What you see is a copy of the data from the table, and you can edit this copy in the control. It's only when you save the record that the new values in the controls are copied back into the table to update it. You can also use controls to display information that isn't contained in a table, such as a heading or the date - we'll look at these later in this chapter.

Access contains a range of control types which mirror those you see in other Windows applications. They broadly fall into two groups - **data-aware controls** that can display data from the table and allow it to be edited, and those which do not hold data from the table but are simply used to display fixed information, initiate an occurrence of an action within the database, such as closing the form (this is known as an **event**), or just decorate the form. These are often called **static controls**.

The following table outlines the main controls that you will be using:

Data controls	What they do
Text Box	Displays text that the user can edit. Can show one or more lines and is used to display numbers and currency values as well as ordinary text.
Option Group	A frame that holds two or more option or toggle buttons from which the user can select only one. Used to select one when there are several choices for an option.
Option Button	An on/off control which displays as a circle. When it is on (selected) it displays a dot and when off (unselected) it is empty.
Toggle Button	A button which toggles on and off. It remains depressed when clicked the first time, then rises when clicked again.
Check Box	An on/off control which displays as a square. When it is on (selected) it displays a tick or check mark and when off (unselected) it is empty.
List Box	Displays a list of values from which the user can select one.

Table Continued on Following Page

Data controls	What they do
Combo Box	A list box and text box combined. It allows the user to either select an item from a list supplied or else to enter their own value.
Object Frame	Holds an object which is not normal text or a number value from a table. Often used to hold a chart or picture but can also hold other objects such as sounds or a document from another application. Generally, the object can be edited within the application that created it.

Other controls	What they do
Label	Holds text which is entered at design-time and cannot be edited while the form is in use. Used to display titles and information or identify other controls. A label can be attached to most types of data control so that it moves when the control is moved.
Command Button	The normal push-button used in all Windows applications. It appears to be depressed only while the mouse button is held, rising again when the button is released. It is generally used to start another event, such as closing a form or opening another one.
Image	Used to display a static picture or graphic that cannot be edited while the form is in use.
Page Break	Causes the form or report to start a new page - either on screen or on a printer.
Line	Displays a line - used for decoration or illustration.
Shape	Displays a circle, oval or rectangle on the form or report. Used for decoration or illustration.

Try It Out - Adding Controls to a Form

We'll add some text boxes to the form to display the contents of the Project table.

1 Go to the Field List window and click on the Date field. Hold the mouse button down and drag it onto the middle of the from. When you release the button, Access automatically creates a text box and label for the date field.

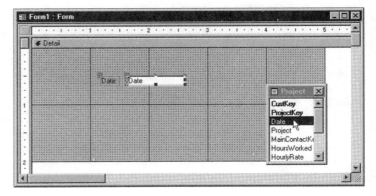

2 We can also add more than one field at a time. Click on **Project** in the **Field List**, scroll down to the last field and hold down the *Shift* key while you click on it. Access selects all these fields. Drag them onto the form and place them under the **Date** text box. Access creates text boxes for all of them, enlarging the form as necessary.

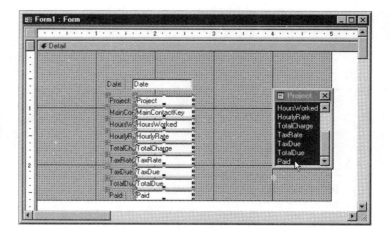

3 At the moment you are in design view. Click the **Form View** button on the toolbar. The text boxes now display the data from the first record in the **Project** table. You can move to other records using the record navigation controls at the bottom of the window. You can also edit the contents of the table in the new form, but as before, you should take care when editing, as any changes you make will be saved permanently in the database.

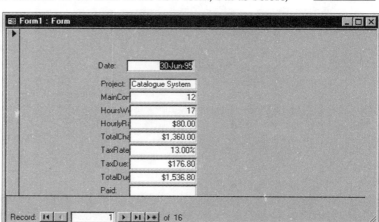

Working with Controls

You can see in the previous example how different a form is to the datasheet view of a table. You place on it individual controls which correspond to the fields in the table, but you only need to add the ones you want and you can place them in any arrangement. Forms are the basic ingredient to building an interface between the data in the tables and the user.

Selecting and Moving Controls

To work with a control you first have to select it. You normally do this in one of two ways. Clicking on a control with the mouse selects it and adds black selection boxes at the corners and along the edges. You can select more than one control by holding down the *Shift* key while you click on them. Each one that is selected displays the squares around the perimeter.

Alternatively you can select controls by dragging a 'selection rectangle' over them. If you click on a blank area of the form and hold the mouse button down while you drag over the controls, Access displays a rectangle from the point where you started dragging to the present cursor position. When you release the mouse button, any controls which are wholly or partially enclosed in the rectangle are selected.

FYI You can change the default behavior of this selection method by selecting **Options** from the **Tools** menu and clicking the **Forms/Reports** tab. There are two **Selection Behavior** options - **Partially Enclosed** and **Fully Enclosed**. When **Fully Enclosed** is chosen, only controls which are wholly enclosed in the rectangle will be selected.

Once you have selected one or more controls, you can move them. If you move the cursor over a label, it changes from an arrow to an 'open hand'. You can then click and drag the selected label to move it.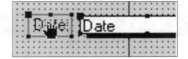

If you try moving one of the labels you just placed on the form, you will notice that Access moves the text box as well - it's treated as being the same object. When Access created the text box control (when we dragged the field from the Field List onto the form), it also created the label control. This label is attached to the text box at the moment, so it will move when the text box is moved. If you delete the text box, the label is deleted as well, but you can delete the label without deleting the text box. If you only want a label, you should create one separately rather than as part of a text box. However, we're moving a bit too quickly here - you'll catch up with these techniques later in the chapter.

If you want to move just the label or just the text box, move the cursor over the larger square at the top left of the object until it turns from an open hand to a 'pointing finger'. Then you can drag each object individually.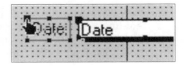

To change the size of a label or text box, you place the cursor over any one of the other corner selection boxes until it changes to a double-headed arrow. You can then drag it to the new size, just like you would with a normal screen window.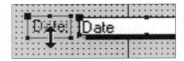

The Grid

The rows of dots that make up the grid on the form are not visible in form view (when the form is in use displaying data), but only when you are working on the form in design view. The grid is used to help you align all the controls so that they look right. Otherwise it would be very difficult trying to get them all in straight lines across and down the form. You can change the distance between the dots on the grid by altering the Grid X and Grid Y properties in the form Properties window. Fewer dots make it easier to line the controls up.

By default, Access will 'snap' all the controls to the grid, aligning the top left of the control to the nearest grid point. If you re-size a control using the mouse, the other corners will snap to the grid as well. However, you can switch off this behavior if you wish - either permanently or just for one operation. Holding the *Ctrl* key down while you move or re-size a control will allow you to place it between the grid points. You can also turn the snap to grid feature on and off using the Snap to Grid command in the Format menu.

Positioning Controls

When you come to design forms, you often find that after experimenting with the layout the controls don't quite line up properly. You can change the size and position of several controls at once by selecting them and using the commands in the F_ormat menu (A_lign, S_ize, Horizontal Spacing and V_ertical Spacing).

If you place controls on top of each other, you can use the Bring to F_ront and Send to B_ack commands to show one control on top of others. For example, if you add a filled rectangle shape to the form, it will hide any other controls underneath that were already there. By using the Send to B_ack command, you force Access to display the other controls on top of the rectangle so that they become visible again.

Try It Out - Adding Drop-Down List Boxes to a Form

Let's make the form more user-friendly by adding a drop-down list box for the Project field. Then, when a user wants to add new records, they can simply pick the project type from the list provided.

1 Click the Design View button on the toolbar to return to design view and click once on the background of the form to ensure none of the controls are selected. Then click on the Project text box on the form (not the label next to it) and press the *Delete* key. This removes both the label and the text box from the form.

2 Now go to the toolbox and check that the Control Wizards button is depressed. This tells Access to start the relevant wizard when we place a new control on the form. These wizards help you to create a control by guiding you through all the decisions on how the control is to behave. We'll see this by using Combo Box Wizard to help us add a combo box (a drop-down list box) to the form.

3 Click on the Combo Box button in the toolbox. Note that it remains depressed. When you move the cursor over the form window, it changes to a miniature combo box showing that the next control we place will be a combo box. (But don't click on the form yet.)

4 Go to the Field List, click on the Project field and drag it onto the form where the original Project field text box was. Because the wizard button is 'on', Access starts the Combo Box Wizard. In the first window, select the second option - 'I will type in the values that I want'.

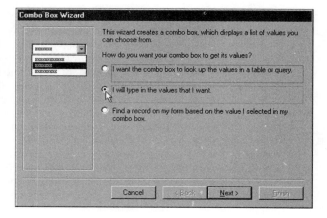

5 Click the <u>N</u>ext button. Now we can define what we want in the list. First, make sure the number of columns is set to 1 - we only want to display a list of project names. We can type the values we want to see in the list into the mini-table under the **Number of columns** box. Enter **Accounts System, Warehouse System** and **Menu Generator**, pressing *Tab* between each one.

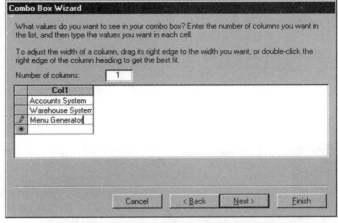

6 Click the <u>N</u>ext button. In this window, we tell Access what to do with the value we select from the list. We want it stored in the **Project** field, as Access suggests. Make sure you have these options set.

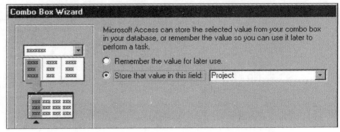

7 Click <u>N</u>ext again. Make sure the label for the combo box is **Project**, and make sure the **Display Help** option is not checked. Then press <u>F</u>inish. Access places the combo box on the form. If you look at the **Data** page of the **Properties** window, which now shows the properties for our new combo box, you'll see that Access has set the **Row Source Type** to **Value List** and the **Row Source** to the list we entered in the wizard. Remember that you can see the entries more clearly by clicking on them and pressing *Shift-F2* to open the **Zoom** window.

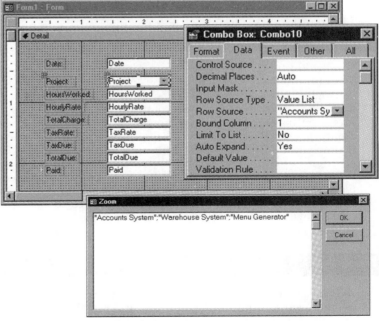

219

8 Switch to form view by clicking the Form View button on the toolbar. You can now set the value of the Project field by either selecting it from the list or by typing in a new one (we only included 3 types of project in our list). If you change a record, the changes will be saved permanently as soon as you move to another record.

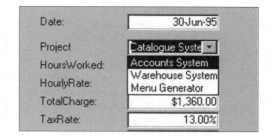

Date:	30-Jun-95
Project	Catalogue System
	Accounts System
HoursWorked:	Warehouse System
HourlyRate:	Menu Generator
TotalCharge:	$1,360.00
TaxRate:	13.00%

FYI When we looked at the properties of the form, the **Record Source** was set to **Project**, the name of the table that supplies the records for the form. In the properties for the new combo box we have a **Row Source** entry which performs a similar task. It tells the combo box what to display in its list. The **Row Source Type** entry above it - **Value List** - simply indicates the type of list we're using - you'll see more of this later.

9 Switch back to design view, click on the combo box and look at the Limit To List entry on the Data page of the combo box's Properties window. It's set to No at the moment which is why we can enter values that aren't in the list. Change it to Yes and go back to form view. Try entering values that are not in the list - Access won't accept them. This is a useful way to control the entries that can be placed in the tables. When you've finished experimenting go back to design view and set the property back to No.

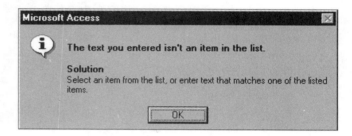

Microsoft Access

ⓘ The text you entered isn't an item in the list.

Solution
Select an item from the list, or enter text that matches one of the listed items.

OK

Changing a Control to Another Type

You don't actually have to remove a control to replace it by a different type, as we did in the previous example. Access allows you to directly change a control from one type to another. If you right-click on the control and select Change To from the short-cut menu that appears, Access displays a list of the compatible control types and you can simply select the one you want. This saves you having to change the properties that you have already set up for a control when you change it to another type. This method does not invoke the control wizards that we used above - it simply places the new control.

When you change a control to another type, Access only offers you the choice of **compatible** types. For example, you can change a text box to a list box or a combo box, but not to a toggle button - the type of data that a text box holds could not be displayed with a toggle button. You could, however, change a checkbox (for example) into a toggle button or an option button - each of these control types can display Yes/No or True/False values.

Try It Out - Basing the Combo Box on a Query

As we have mentioned, forms are often based on queries rather than directly on tables. In this example, we'll change the combo box we created in the previous example so that it retrieves the values for its list from a query, rather than from a list that we type in. We'll also extend the list to include all of the project types.

1 Click on the Project
combo box you created
in the previous example
and open the Properties
window. Change the
Row Source Type
property to Table/Query
by selecting this from
the drop-down list.
Click in the Row Source
box and delete the
contents, then click the
builder button (the
button on right with
three dots on it). Access
opens the Query Builder
window, which looks
very much like the QBE
grid we used to create
queries in previous chapters. This time the window title shows SQL Statement. This is because we
are creating an SQL statement as a query. The Show Table window is also opened automatically.

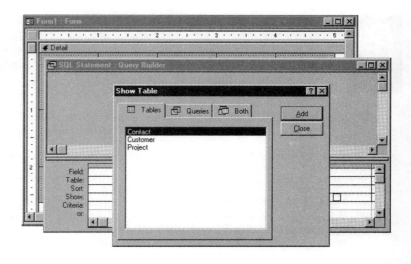

2 Add the Project table to the grid and close the Show Table dialog. Drag the Project field to the grid
and set its Sort order to Ascending.

3 Click the Query View button on the
toolbar to see the results. We have a list
of all the project names in the table.
Unfortunately, though, as there are
some records with the same project
type, some project names are listed
more than once.

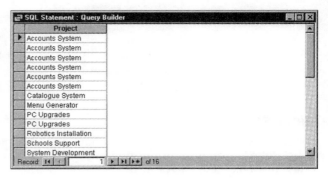

4 To prevent this happening we
need to tell Access not to
include duplicate values.
Switch back to design view
and double-click on the gray
background at the top of the
query window. This opens the
Query Properties dialog. The
entry for Unique Records is set
to Yes, while the one for
Unique Values is set to No.
Change Unique Values to Yes.

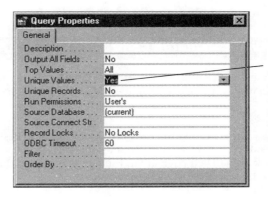

*You can double-
click on No to
change it to Yes.
Double-clicking is
an easy way of
cycling through the
available values.*

221

FYI When it runs a query, Access first selects the records, then the fields. So, in our example, it included every record in the first pass because **Unique Records** was set to **Yes**. When it selects the fields it only limits these to unique values if the **Unique Values** entry is set to **Yes**. Obviously, you cannot specify **Yes** for both **Unique Records** *and* **Unique Values**, though you can specify **No** for them both.

5 Close the **Query Properties** dialog and switch to query view. Now we have the list we want. Close the query, saving the update to the combo box property when prompted.

6 Back in the main form window, you'll see Access has placed the SQL statement

SELECT DISTINCT Project.Project FROM Project ORDER BY Project.Project;

in the **Row Source** property. This is the equivalent of the query we created in the **Query Builder** grid. Switch to form view to see the results - we get a list of all the project names in the combo box, created each time the form is opened by the SQL statement in the **Row Source** property.

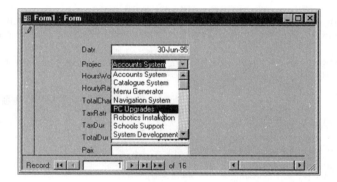

Calculated Controls

Remember in Excel how we used formulae to calculate the values for the TotalCharge, TaxDue and TotalDue columns of our original table? When we moved the data into an Access table we lost this link - the values in the fields became just numbers and were no longer calculated from the other values. Using a form, we can solve this problem. Access allows us to use **calculated controls** on a form, which are automatically updated when the other fields are edited.

Try It Out - Adding Calculated Controls

We'll change the TotalCharge, TaxDue, and TotalDue fields to formulae. These three fields will then be automatically recalculated if the values in the HoursWorked, HourlyRate or TaxRate fields change.

1 Switch the form we created in the previous example to design view and click on the TotalCharge control. (Make sure you do not click the label next to it because this has it's own set of properties.) Have a look at the Data page in the Properties window. The Control Source is TotalCharge - the field in the table where the value comes from.

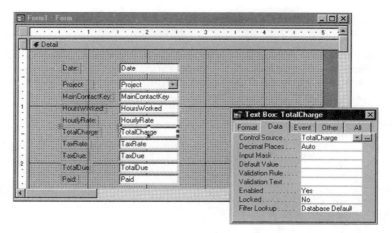

2 Click on the control source property entry and click the builder button. This opens Expression Builder, where we can create an expression which calculates the value in the control. It shows the current Control Source property - TotalCharge. Delete the current expression.

3 In the left-hand window of Expression Builder is our form, Form1. In the middle window is a list of the controls on the form. In the right-hand window are the properties for the form and its controls. To calculate the total charge, we need the expression HoursWorked * HourlyRate. Select HoursWorked in the middle window and double-click on the <Value> entry in the right-hand window. Click the * (multiply) button under the expression window, then select HourlyRate and double-click the <Value> entry for this control. Access builds our expression in the top window, including the square brackets which identify the items as field names.

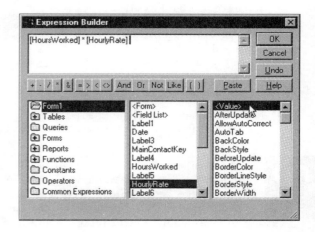

4 Click OK to close Expression Builder and press *Return* to accept the expression in the Properties window. You'll see that Access adds an equals sign at the beginning, and the control on the form now contains the expression we've created.

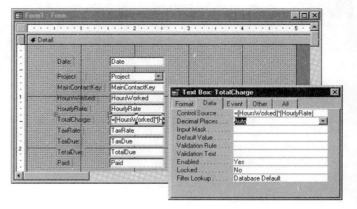

5 Repeat this process with the TaxDue and TotalDue controls using the expressions [TotalCharge] * [TaxRate] and [TotalCharge] + [TaxDue] respectively.

6 Now switch to form view and try editing the values in the HoursWorked, HourlyRate and TaxRate controls. For example, change the TaxRate to 20.00%. You'll see the values in the calculated controls change as soon you move the cursor off each field. Try editing one of the calculated fields - you'll find that Access prevents you and displays a message in the status bar at the bottom of the main window. Once you have completed this step, change the values you edited back to what they were originally.

> Control can't be edited; it's bound to the expression '[TotalCharge]+[TaxDue]'.

7 Go back to design view and select TotalCharge, TaxDue and TotalDue by clicking on TotalCharge first, then holding the *Shift* key down while you click the other two. Access selects them all, displaying small squares at the corners. You'll see that the Properties window is now titled Multiple selection - any changes we make will be reflected in the properties for all the selected fields.

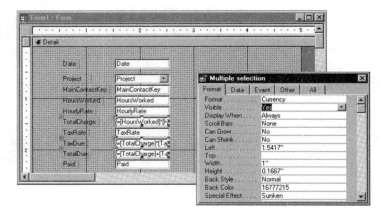

8 In the Data page, change the Enabled property to No. The contents of the controls on the form are grayed out (disabled). Then change the Locked property to Yes. We get them back again in black.

FYI The **Enabled** and **Locked** properties determine whether or not that control can be used to edit the data in the underlying table or query. They are used to control access to the form. If the **Locked** property is set to **Yes,** Access will allow the user to place the cursor in the control, but not to change the data in it. This can be confusing, so you would normally set the **Enabled** property to **No** as well - this prevents the user from placing the cursor in the control at all. If both the **Enabled** property and the **Locked** property are set to **No,** the contents of the control are grayed out

9 Switch to form view and try editing the contents of any of the TotalDue, TaxDue and TotalCharge fields. Now you can't actually place the cursor in them at all. This way of preventing a user from editing a field is a lot more intuitive than depending on the error message created when you tried to change the contents at step 6. To make it even easier for the user to see what is happening, you could make these 'fixed' controls stand out by changing their color.

So we *can* automatically calculate the totals. The only problem here is that we have 'disconnected' the three calculated fields from the original table by changing the Control Source property. The contents of the controls no longer show the contents of the fields in the table and, when the contents of the control change, the fields in the table will not be updated. If you were to open the Project table alongside your form and then change some values on the form, you would find that when you move to another record, the other fields in the table are updated to the new values in the normal controls. The fields used for calculated controls, however, don't change.

When a control is linked to a field in a table (or query), it's called a **bound** control. Our calculated controls are **unbound**, so they no longer reflect the contents of the underlying records. This is something we'll have to keep in mind when we come to refine our tables in the next part of the book, where we build our application.

Creating Professional Looking Forms

At the moment, your form doesn't really look like it belongs to a professional database. Presentation is all important when you're creating applications for distribution. You want your users to like what they see and, more importantly, to find the interface intuitive and easy to understand.

You'll find that the light gray background and sunken appearance of the controls is the default for Windows 95. Access produces this type of form by default. You may, however, want to customize your forms and create something a bit more exciting. Let's have a look at how you'd go about doing this.

Try It Out - Changing the Appearance of a Form

1   Switch to design view and make sure you have the formatting toolbar visible. If you have used other Microsoft applications, you will find this toolbar pretty familiar.

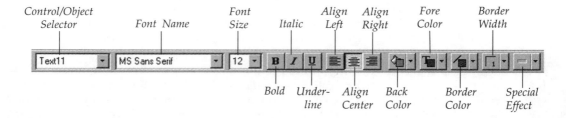

FYI   Remember you can select which toolbars are visible using the **Toolbars** command from the **View** menu.

2   We'll start by changing the color of the form. Click on the background of the form, then click the down arrow next to the **Back Color** button on the toolbar and select a color from the palette by clicking on it. We'll pick bright yellow.

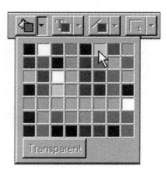

225

3 Go down the column of labels re-sizing them, so that you can see all of the captions. Just click on each one in turn and place the cursor over the top left selection box, then drag to the left. Now select all the text boxes by clicking with the mouse on the main form just above the controls and dragging down so that the rectangle you are drawing encloses part or all of each text box (don't include the labels). When you release the mouse button, Access selects

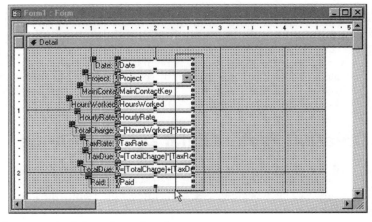

the text boxes by adding square boxes around the edges of each one.

4 Click the down arrow next to the **Special Effect** button on the toolbar and select **Shadowed**. Access adds a shadow to all the selected controls.

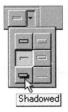

5 Now select just the labels. Open the **Back Color** list and click the **Transparent** button so that the labels have a clear background. You can also use the **Fore Color** list to set the color of the text - we've left ours set to the default black. Click the **Align Right** button on the toolbar so that the captions are aligned with the right-hand end of the labels. Then select the **Format** menu and click on **Align** and then **Right**. This aligns the actual labels, as opposed to the text within the label.

FYI You can alter the defaults for Access's controls, so that when you create new controls in future, they have different colors, text alignments and special effects. If you find that your controls have different default settings to ours, then they have probably been altered. To set the defaults for a control, change the colors, alignment, effects, etc., to the ones you want, then select **Set Control Defaults** from the **Format** menu while that control is selected. From then on (until you change them again), all new controls *of that type* will have the new default settings. You have to set the defaults for each type of control (text box, combo box, radio button, etc.) separately.

6 Change the size of the text boxes so that they show their contents comfortably. You can also change the size of the form. Then switch to form view to admire your work.

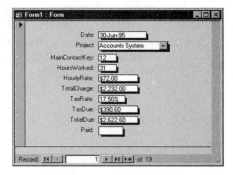

7 If you want to jazz up your form still further, you can display a picture for the background, instead of just changing the color. You do this by altering the Picture property. Switch to design view and click in the box at the top left-hand corner of the form window where the rulers meet to select the form itself. Then open the Format page of the Properties window and scroll down until you get to the Picture property. This is currently set to (none).

8 Click in the Picture property and click the builder button. This opens Picture Builder. Select your Access program folder, then BitMaps, Styles and finally select one of these pictures that are supplied with Access. We've chosen Clouds.wmf.

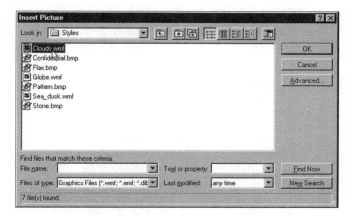

9 Click OK. Access places the file name in the Properties window. The Picture Type property under this is set to Embedded because the picture is now stored in the form itself. Set the Picture Size Mode to Stretch so that the picture is stretched to completely fill the form and leave Picture Tiling set to No.

It is possible to display a picture, or other object, on a form while keeping it stored on disk in a separate file - rather than within your Access database. You'll meet this technique in Part 2 where we deal with Object Linking and Embedding (OLE). Here, though, we are embedding the picture, i.e. storing it inside our database, rather than as a separate file.

10 Finally switch to form view to see the result.

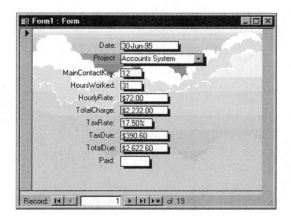

How the Picture Properties Work

The Picture, Picture Type, Picture Size Mode and Picture Tiling properties of a form are used to control exactly how a picture is used for the background of a form. The Picture property is set to the full path and name of the picture file we want to use. If we are storing the picture within the form itself, we set the Picture Type to Embedded; if we just want to link the form to a picture file on disk, we set it to Linked.

The Picture Size Mode can be set to Clip, Stretch or Zoom. Clip just shows as much of the picture as will fit on the form without changing the scale or proportions of the picture. Setting it to Zoom will allow the picture to grow or shrink to fit the form, but keep the proportions of the picture the same - so there may be a blank area at the top and bottom or at the sides. The Stretch setting, on the other hand, allows the picture to be adjusted both ways so that it fills the form and the proportions are changed accordingly.

Finally, if the picture is smaller than the form, we can get Access to display more than one copy of it. Setting Picture Tiling to Yes means that Access completely covers the form with full copies or parts of the picture.

It's not hard to produce attractive and interesting effects on forms. However, you should bear in mind that the more effects you introduce, the slower your form operates. If you have pictures and a lot of special effects on your forms, Access has to do a lot more work each time you update the screen.

Using AutoFormat to Change the Appearance of a Form

The formatting methods we have looked at so far allow you to customize your own forms - you choose how the form will look. However, Access also offers you an AutoFormat option, which allows you to change the format and appearance of an existing form using a pre-set list of formats. The appearance of the form we created using the Clouds picture is actually one of the looks you can create using AutoFormat. The screenshot here shows the Dusk format:

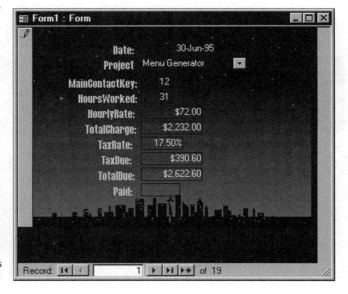

You may want to create your own AutoFormats - for instance, if you have a particular house-style that you want all your forms to follow. This is easy enough - you just set up the look you want for your forms, then run AutoFormat. All you need to do then is select the Customize button and Access allows you to select the current form as a new AutoFormat template.

More Complex Forms and the Form Wizard

Now that we know the basics of form construction, we'll have a go at using the Form Wizard to create one. Our database contains two tables with data about our customers and the contacts we have at each place. Because these two things are likely to be viewed and edited together, we should consider placing them both on the same form. However, there can be more than one contact for each customer so we can't use the simple form design we saw above - this would be OK for the customer's details, but how would it display details about more than one contact?

The answer is a main form to display the customer data, with another form nested inside it to display the contact data. That way we can scroll from one contact to the next in the subform, while the main form continues to display the customer information. All we have to do is make sure we link them together in such a way that the contact's part of the form only shows the contacts who work for the customer currently showing in the main (customer) part.

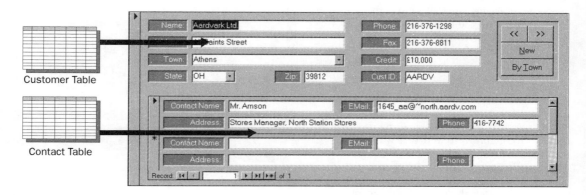

Customer Table

Contact Table

It's not difficult to create this type of form from scratch, but we'll let Form Wizard do it for us and then examine the results.

Try It Out - Creating a Customer and Contacts Form with Form Wizard

1 Close the present form. In the Database window, select the Forms tab and click New. Then, in the New Table dialog, select Form Wizard from the top list and select the Customer table as the source of the form's records in the drop-down list below this. Click OK and Access starts the Form Wizard. The first screen shows the table we selected - Customer - and a list of the available fields in that table.

2 Select the fields that we want to include in the main (customer) part of the form. We want all of them except CustKey - this is an automatic counter field so there's no need to show it. The quick way to select all the fields is to click the >> button to copy them all to the right-hand list, then to remove the CustKey field, select it and click the < button.

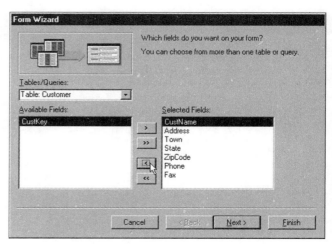

3 The next step is to select the fields we want for the subform (contacts) part. We do this in the same window - the two tables are related together, so the Form Wizard will be able to make sense of the link and produce the form/subform we want. Select the Contact table in the Tables/Queries drop-down list (replacing Customer) and then select all the fields except the two key fields, CustKey and ContactKey.

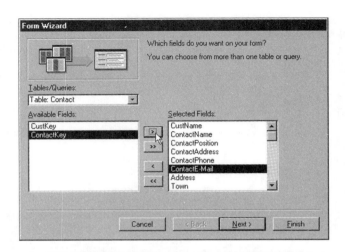

4 Click Next. We now have to tell Access which table is to be used for the main form and which for the subform. For example, if we view the data by Customer, then the main form will contain the Customer data and the subform will show the related Contacts. If, on the other hand, we view the data by Contact, then we'll get the opposite result. Click on each in turn and the Form Wizard will show you the options. We want to have the customer details in the main form, so the first option is correct. Don't click on Next> for the moment though.

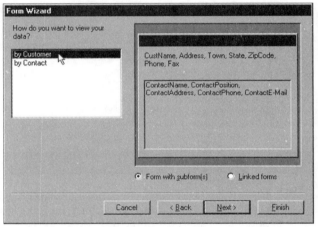

5 We can also use the Form Wizard to create linked forms rather than a form and subform. To see what this means select the Linked forms option - instead of placing the subform inside the main form, it creates a separate form which is opened by a button on the main form and shows the related records from the other table.

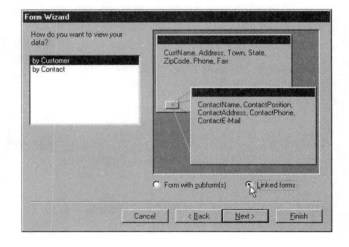

6 Make sure you select the Form with subforms(s) option and click Next. Now we can select the layout of the subform - either tabular using text boxes and other controls or in datasheet view like a table. Select Tabular.

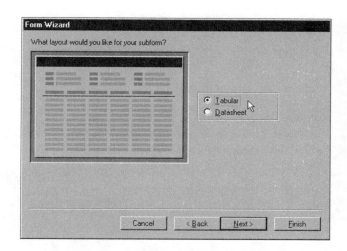

7 Click Next again. Now we can select the style we want for our form. Pick one you like.

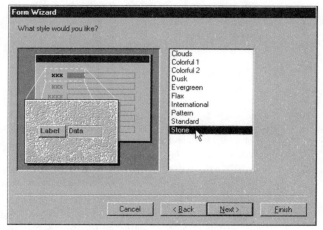

8 Now click Next again. Access suggests names for the forms - leave these as they are and tell Access to Open the form to view or enter information. Make sure the Display Help checkbox is 'off' and then click Finish. Access creates a main Customer form and Contacts subform and opens them showing the data from our tables.

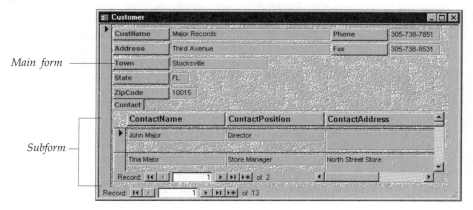

Main form

Subform

Exploring the Form

Form Wizard produces a form where we can enter and edit data in the Customer and Contact tables together. There are two sets of record selectors, one on each form, so we can scroll and select records for each independently. Let's just spend a couple of minutes looking at the different features that the form includes.

Headers and Footers

If you switch to design view, you'll see that Access has added two new sections to the form: a Form Header and Form Footer. These are empty.

Form header —

Form footer (you may have to enlarge the window or scroll down to see this)

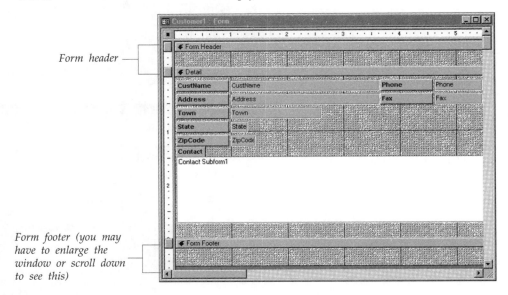

You should note that these sections are always visible in form view. In design view, when you scroll up and down, the sections disappear, but in form view they stay put. They can, therefore, be used to add a title or other information if required. You can extend the header by placing the cursor over the top of the Detail section selector (the gray bar) until it turns into a north/south arrow. Then you can drag the Detail section selector downwards.

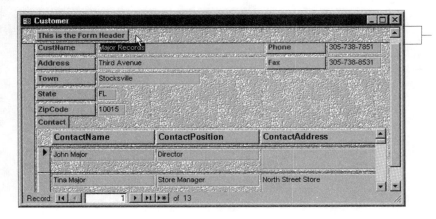

As you scroll down, the header stays in view.

The display of the form header and footer is controlled by the Form Header/Footer option on the View menu. There's also a Page Header/Footer option. Select this so that it is ticked (you must be in design view). Access will then add page header and page footer sections to the form.

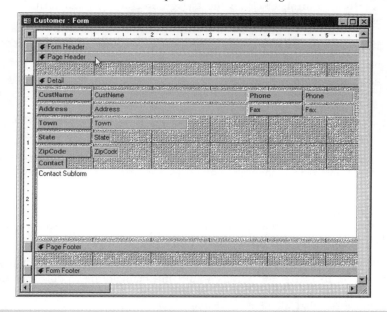

 When you view a form on screen, the form header and footer always appear on the screen. When you print the form, the form header prints at the top of the first page while the form footer prints at the bottom of the last page. The page header and footer *never* appear on the screen, but they print at the top and bottom of each page (except on Page 1, where the page header prints after any form header). If you want either a header *or* a footer, not both, you must make sure you re-size the one that's empty, so that it doesn't show as a blank area in form view or when printed.

How the Forms Are Linked

If you look at the Data tab in the Properties window when the subform is selected, you'll see the entries Link Child Fields and Link Master Fields. They're both set to the name of our 'linking field' - CustKey. This is how Access links the two forms together so that they display the correct records. When you display a customer in the main form the subform shows only the contact records for that customer - as you would expect.

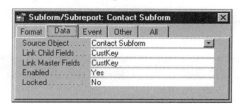

Access uses the relationships we set up between the tables (in the Relationships window) to link the two forms. It will usually set the Link Child Fields and Link Master Fields properties automatically when you create a form with an embedded subform. If not, for instance if there is no relationship between the tables, you will have to enter the values for these fields yourself.

The Subform

The Contact subform is shown on the main form as a white rectangle. This is a control in its own right - a **subform control**. Click on the background of the main form, then double-click on the subform control. Access opens the Contact subform in a separate window.

The Contact subform looks just like the main form. That's because subforms are really just normal forms - the only reason they are known as subforms is because they are embedded in other forms.

The subform control on the main form acts as a window through which we can view the subform. So if the subform is wider than the control, we only get to see part of it and have to use the scrollbars that appear around it to see the other parts.

It is usually far more intuitive if all the whole width of the subform is visible in the main form - the user will expect to resize and scroll around the main form window, but may not appreciate that they have to scroll across the subform as well. One of the things we'll be doing is to redesign the subform so that all of it is visible.

Working with Headers and Footers

If you look at the Contact subform, you can see that the Form Wizard has placed the labels for the text boxes in the Form Header section of the form while the text box controls were in the Detail section. Our main form only displays the details of one customer at a time, but the subform has to be able to display several contacts at the same time. Its Default View property is, therefore, set to Continuous Forms so that it displays more than one copy of the form. If there are more than will fit, it will add scroll bars so that the user can scroll through them. By placing the labels in the Form Header section, they remain in view while the user scrolls down through the records.

This is quite a common arrangement on both forms and reports. If you look at the main form, both the text boxes and labels are in the Detail section. How do you get the labels into the header and leave the text boxes in the Detail section? If you try dragging either a label or a text box to the header section (by using the top left selector with the 'single finger' pointer), you'll see the problem - you can move them both together, but there's no way they're going anywhere on their own. Or is there....?

Try It Out - Rearranging the Text Boxes and Labels

1 Click on a label to select it and press *Ctrl-X* (cut).

2 Click in the header section and press *Ctrl-V* (paste). Access places the label in the header, where it is now independent from the text box.

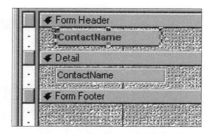

3 Change the appearance of the label using the various buttons on the formatting toolbar. For example, here we've set the font size to 16, selected **Bold** and **Italic**, set the **Text Alignment** to **Center**, the **Back Color** to **Dark Gray** and the **Fore Color** to **White** and finally selected the **Sunken Special Effect**.

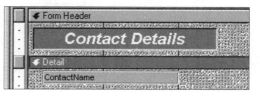

We'll now tidy up one or two of the features of the subform and then see how we save the changes back into the main form.

Try It Out - Redesigning the Subform

1 If you haven't already opened the subform in a separate window, do so now by clicking on the main form, then double-clicking on the subform. It is much wider than the main form which is why we couldn't see all of it in design view.

2 Change the labels as shown in the screenshot. Then go to the form header section of the subform and select all of the labels. Choose a font that you like, change the size and make it bold. Then select <u>S</u>ize from the F<u>o</u>rmat menu and choose to <u>S</u>hortest and using the same menu, decrease the Hori<u>z</u>ontal Spacing.

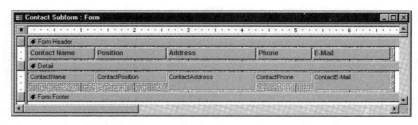

3 Resize the form, by dragging the right hand edge, so that the controls fit comfortably Now we've just got to insert the changed subform back into the main

form. Close it down, saving the changes when prompted to do so. Access takes us back to the main form and automatically inserts the new version of the subform into it.

4 Although we've reduced the width of the subform, it is still too wide to fit into the subform control on the main form and you'll have to resize it to fit. This will mean making the main form wider as well, otherwise you'll just see part of the subform surrounded with scroll bars.

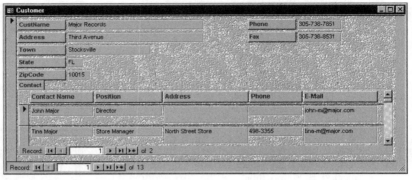

Experiment by switching to design view and back to form view, adjusting the size of the subform control on the main form until it looks right.

FYI

Remember that the **Contact** control on the main form (the white rectangle) is like a window through which the **Contact** subform is visible. Once you have set the size of the subform, you usually have to change the size of the control on the main form to get it to look right.

Forms and Queries

Up to now we've based our forms directly on tables by setting the Record Source property to the name of the table which supplied the records for the form. We'll look now, though, at how we can base a form on a query instead.

Why Base a Form on a Query?

In Chapter 2, we used a simple form to look at our Original table and found that we could change the order in which the records were displayed by using the Sort buttons and menu commands. We could also limit the records that were displayed using a filter. However, each time the form was opened, it displayed the records in the original (default) order.

So what controls the default order of the records? Obviously, the table that the form is based on. The order of the records in the table is controlled by the primary key if there is one, or by the order in which they were added to the table if there's no primary key. This is the order we see when we first open the form.

If we base the form on a query, the default order will be the order of the records in the recordset that the query produces. Remember that a query can sort the records into almost any order, so the form will display the records in the order we specify in the query. And queries can do more than that. We can select which records to include in the recordset using criteria. Therefore, a form based on this type of query will only display the records that meet the criteria we specify - we can effectively apply a default filter. You can still change the sort order when using a form, or further restrict the records displayed by using a filter on the form, but when the form is opened, the default sort order will always be that set by the query. And, of course, you can never see records which have been filtered out by the criteria in the query - you only get to work with the recordset that the query produces.

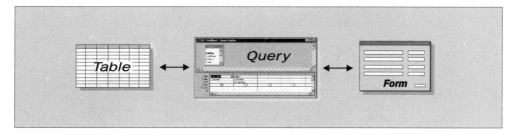

Queries have another property that makes them useful as the basis for forms. A query can select which fields to include in the resulting recordset and, if we join tables together in a query, we can include fields from more than one table. So a form can display selected fields from several tables. For example, in Chapter 6 we created a query that included the contact name, customer name and some details of each project. A form based on this query could display all these fields, even though they come from different tables.

Finally, we saw how a query can (in most cases) allow us to update the original table by changing the contents of the recordset the query produces. A form based on a recordset also allows us to update the original tables.

To summarize then, we would base a form on a query when:

▶ We want to change the default sort order of the records.

▶ We want to control which records are displayed in the form.

▶ We want to include fields from more than one table in a form.

Building a Form Based on a Query

When we create a new form, we can base it on an existing query as it's created. The New Form dialog allows us to select either a table or an existing query as the source for the form's records. If you had already created a query called An Existing Query, you'd see its name in the drop-down list.

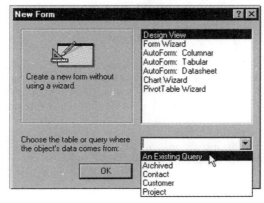

In design view, the fields in the query's recordset appear in the Field List window, just as the fields from the table did in our earlier examples. The only difference is in the Properties window. The Record Source property is now set to the name of the query rather than the table name.

237

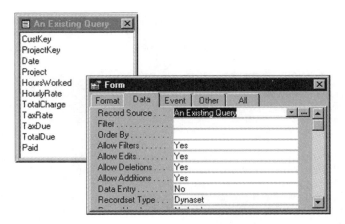

If you have an existing form based on a table and you want to base it on a query instead, you just need to change the Record Source. You just click on the property entry and then select an existing query from the drop-down list or else click the builder button to start Query Builder, where you can design the query you want. When you close Query Builder, the Record Source property is updated with the SQL statement that produces the recordset. However, you must ensure that you include in the query all the fields needed for the controls on the form. If you don't, Access will display #Name? in the control when you switch to form view, because it can't find the field that supplies the data for that control.

FYI We'll look at SQL (Structured Query Language) in more depth in a later chapter. Once you are familiar with this, you will be able to type an SQL statement directly into the **Properties** window as the **Record Source**.

Creating Unbound Forms and Dialogs

When we built our simple Projects form earlier on, we discovered that we could use calculated controls on a form. These controls are called **unbound** controls because they're not 'connected' or **bound** to a field in the underlying table or query. In the same way, we can use a form that's not based on a table or query at all - an **unbound form**.

The concept of an unbound form may seem a bit strange to you. However, there are occasions when we want to use a screen window, but don't need it to be linked to a specific set of records. For instance, if we want to use more than one subform within a main form, we can base each of these on the required tables, but insert them into an unbound main form.

A more common use of unbound forms is to create a dialog window which simply collects information, rather than modifying records in a table. For instance, you may have a report that prints a list of your customers broken down by state, but only want to print those from one particular state. By using a dialog form, you can allow the user to select which state they want, then just print those records.

In the next example, we will create a dialog form that allows us to select which Project and Sales records we want to archive. You can create this form in any existing database, or create a new one by selecting New Database from the Access File menu and choosing Blank Database.

Try It Out - Creating the Archive Records Form

1 In the Database window Forms list, click the **New** button. In the **New Form** dialog, select **Design View** and leave the Table/Query name blank. Click OK and Access displays a blank form. In the **Properties** windows the entry for **Record Source** is blank.

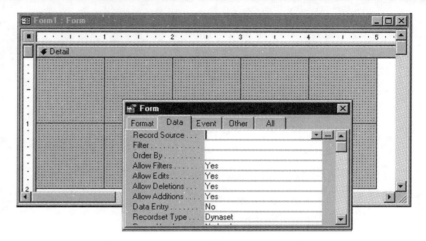

2 Place the cursor on the edge of the form and drag it to about a quarter of the screen size. Now we need to place some controls on the form. The first thing we need is a means to select the type of records we want to archive. The control we need here is an option group - a set of buttons where you can select the option you want. We'll use a wizard to help create this.

3 Make sure you have the **Control Wizards** button in the toolbox depressed, click on the **Option Group** control in the toolbox and then click in the top left of the form.

4 Access opens the Option Group Wizard, asking first for the captions we want for our option buttons. Enter **Archive Project Records** and **Archive Sales Records**, pressing *Tab* inbetween.

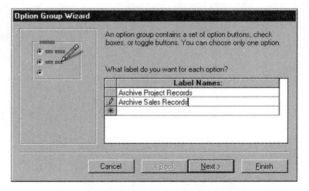

5 Click **Next**. We want the default to be project records, so select **Yes, the default choice is:** and make sure **Archive Project Records** is selected.

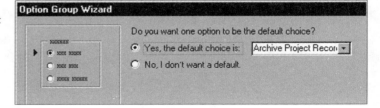

6 Click <u>N</u>ext. Now we are prompted for the option button values which allow us to identify which option a user has selected. We will be looking at how you carry out an action according to which button the user chooses in Part 2. Don't worry about this for the moment - just leave these values set to their defaults.

7 Click <u>N</u>ext again and then set the button type to Option Buttons and select Sunken for the Style. (If you want to see the various types, select them and check out the preview).

8 Click <u>N</u>ext. Enter 'Select Records' as the title for the group and make sure the Display Help option is 'off'.

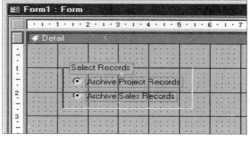

9 Now click <u>F</u>inish and Access creates the option group for us.

We've now got our option buttons set up. We'll add the rest of the controls we need and then think about tidying up the form at the end.

10 We need a text box to enter the date for the latest records that we want archived. Select the Text Box control in the toolbox and click in the middle of the form to place a text box control there. Click on the text box label, then double-click on it - Access highlights the caption. Type the new caption 'Date of latest records to archive:' and press *Return*. Then move the label and text box so that it's visible.

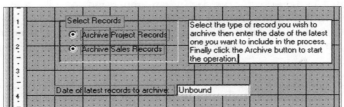

11 We should add some guidelines for the users so they know what they're expected to do. Select the Label control in the toolbox and click on the form on the right hand side, then type in the text shown in the screenshot and press *Return*.

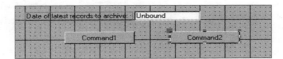

12 Finally, we need a button that the user can click to start archiving the records and another that cancels the operation. We won't use a wizard this time, so turn 'off' the Control Wizards in the toolbox by clicking on the button so it is *not* depressed. Then click on the Command Button control in the toolbox and click on the form to place a push button. Repeat the process to place another one next to it.

13 Now we need to set the names of the controls so that the user knows what they are all for. Access gives them names like Command3 and Text5, which aren't very intuitive and give no indication of their function. Select each of the controls in turn by clicking on them and change the properties in the Format and Other pages as in the table on the following page. You can check you have selected the right control by looking at the title bar of the Properties window.

Control	Property	Enter...
Select Records frame	Name	fraSelectRecords
Archive Projects option button	Name	optProjects
Archive Sales option button	Name	optSales
Date text box	Name	txtDate
First push button	Name	cmdArchive
	Caption	&Archive
	Default	Yes
Second push button	Name	cmdCancel
	Caption	&Cancel
	Cancel	Yes

FYI   Setting the **Default** property for a push button to **Yes** means that it will be activated when the user presses the *Return* key. Setting the **Cancel** property to **Yes** means it will be activated by the *Escape* key. Typing an ampersand (&) in a control's name sets up a 'hot key' for the button. The letter following the ampersand will be underlined on the form, indicating that when the user presses *Alt* plus that letter, the button will be activated. These are all standard methods for use in a dialog window or screen form.

14 Select all the controls on the form. Then select 10 from the Font Size drop-down list - this changes the size of the text in all the controls to 10 point.

15 Now move the controls to where you want them and select the <u>S</u>ize option from the F<u>o</u>rmat menu and then to <u>F</u>it to get them just the right size for the text they contain. Remember, you can select more than one item either by dragging a selection rectangle over them, or by holding the *Shift* key while clicking on each one.

Move the controls like this ———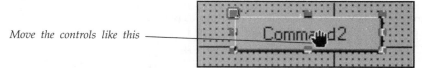

16 Click on the background of the form and use the formatting toolbar to set it to blue/green. Click on the Select Records label, open the Special Effects list on the toolbar and click the Raised button. Set its foreground color to dark red using the control on the formatting toolbar.

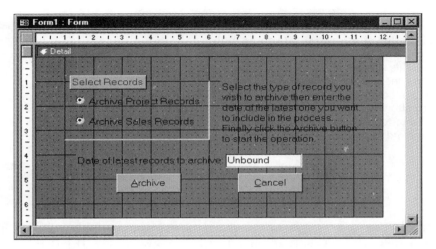

17 Now, for the final flourish, click on the **Rectangle** control in the toolbox. Click near the top left of the form and drag down to near to the bottom right. A rectangle appears around all the controls. Using the formatting toolbar, change the background color to light gray and, in the **Special Effects** list, click the **Raised** button. The rectangle now covers all the other controls.

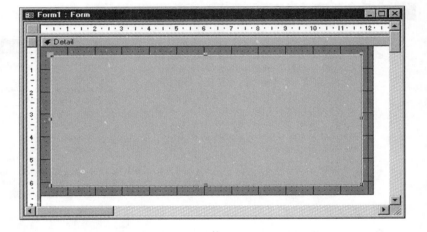

18 Select **Send to Back** from the **Format** menu and the controls re-appear, together with a raised platform behind them. Switch to form view to see the form in all its glory.

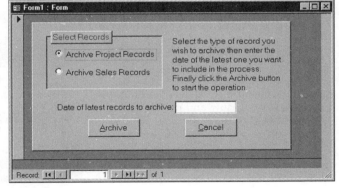

We've still got a few things to do. One of these is to set up the tab order. This determines the sequence in which you move around the form, i.e. which control the focus moves to each time you press the *Tab* key.

19 Back in design view, select Tab Order from the View menu - Access displays the Tab Order dialog. This allows you to click on controls and drag them up or down until you are happy with the order. There's also an Auto Order button which automatically sets the order from top to bottom. Make sure you have the order set as shown here.

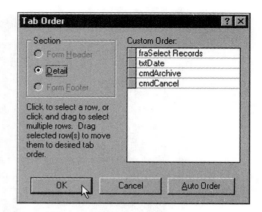

20 Another nice touch would be to display a suggested date in the Date box when the form appears. We can use the Default Value property of the text box to do this. Click on the text box and, in the Data page of the Properties window, click on the entry for Default Value. A builder button appears.

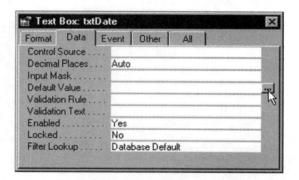

21 Click the builder button to open Expression Builder. We will set a default date of six months before the current date and we'll use the **DateAdd** function to do this. Double-click Functions in the left-hand window and select Built-In Functions. Select Date/Time in the middle window and double-click on DateAdd in the right-hand window to place it in the top window.

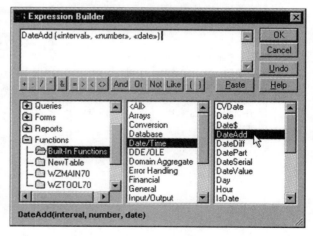

22 The «interval» we want is months, so click on the place-holder and type "m". The number to add is -6, so click on the «number» place-holder and enter -6. For the «date» we want to use today's date. Access can supply this with another function - Date. Click on the place-holder and then double-click the entry for Date in the right-hand list. Access places it in our expression.

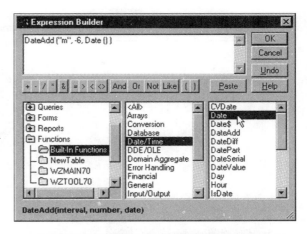

23 Click OK and Access updates the Default Value property. We also need to set the display format for the date. Click on the Format tab in the Properties window, select the Format property and then select Medium Date from the drop-down list.

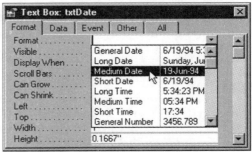

24 Before we try the form out, there are some other properties that we must set to ensure the form is displayed like a dialog window, rather than a data entry form. Click on the form selector (the square at the top left of the form window where the rulers meet) so that it contains a black square and the Properties window shows the properties for our form. Then set the properties in this list as shown in the table below.

Property	Value	Explanation
Caption	Select Records to Archive	The text shown in the title bar of the form.
Default View	Single Form	We want to show one single form rather than several copies.
Views Allowed	Form	Only allow form view.
Scroll Bars	Neither	No scroll bars on the window.
Record Selectors	No	No record selectors at the bottom of the window.
Navigation Buttons	No	No record navigation buttons at the bottom of the window.

Table Continued on Following Page

Property	Value	Explanation
Dividing Lines	No	No lines between the records on screen.
Auto Resize	Yes	Determines whether the form window is re-sized to fit a complete record.
Auto Center	Yes	Places the form in the middle of the application window. (It doesn't center the form on the form background though.)
Border Style	Thin	Single width non-sizable border.
Control Box	No	No control menu on the form.
Max Min Buttons	None	No maximize or minimize buttons.
Close Button	No	No Close button on the form.
Modal *in the 'Other' page of the Properties Window*	Yes	The user has to close the form by pushing a button before they can use another form (like a message box).

FYI These properties will make our form behave like a dialog, but you'll only see the full effects of **Auto Center** and **Auto Resize** when the form is opened from the **Database** window. If you switch to form view now, it is still displayed like a normal form. However, you'll find that the **Close** button has disappeared, so to close the form you have to use the **Close** option on the **File** menu or switch back to design view using the toolbar button.

25 Close the form and save it - call it Archive Selector. Now go to the Database window and select it in the Forms list, then click **Open**. The form is displayed as a dialog in the center of the screen and shows our suggested archive date.

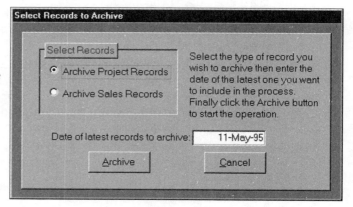

26 Click the Archive and Cancel buttons - nothing happens. We haven't told Access what to do when they're pressed. We'll look at how we set up **macros** to control a form and perform other database actions in Part 2. In the meantime, just close the form using the **Close** option on the **File** menu or by switching back to design view and clicking the Close button.

Summary

So we've seen how we can create forms which serve different purposes. We can use them to manipulate the data stored in tables, or as a dialog to get information from our users. The application that we will build in Part 2 will use a selection of forms of both types. We've also seen some different types of controls and improved the look of our forms so that they appear like those in a professional application. We looked at how a control and a form can be bound to a table or field and explored the use of unbound controls and forms. We've also seen calculated controls at work.

Form design is as much an art as it is a science and you should set out to try to achieve an attractive appearance while retaining a standard, intuitive layout. Windows defines standards for the design of screen forms so that a user will automatically understand how they work. For instance, it's usual to have the 'action' and 'cancel' buttons at the bottom or down the right side of the window. You should aim to follow the layouts you are used to seeing in other applications.

This chapter has covered:

- What forms are.
- How to add controls to a form.
- How to alter the appearance of a form.
- Main and subforms.
- How to create unbound dialog forms.

Designing Reports

In the previous chapter, we considered what a form is and how we design and build one. In this chapter, we'll move on to a task which is, in some ways, very similar - creating reports. We covered a lot of ground in the chapter about forms and you'll be pleased to know that designing and building reports uses many of the same basic techniques for placing controls and manipulating properties. We won't, therefore, cover these again in depth - if you've worked through the previous examples you'll have no problems following the Try It Outs in this chapter. The areas we will look at are:

- Creating a simple report.
- Producing different layouts on a report.
- More complex reports and Report Wizard.
- Creating a report using fields from different tables.
- Using calculated fields on a report.

What Is a Report?

Whereas **forms** are generally used to interact with a user on screen, displaying the contents of a recordset or table and allowing them to be edited, **reports** are used to present the contents of the database in a meaningful and structured way - normally by printing them out as hard copy. And while forms allow the two-way passage of data between user and tables, reports are intrinsically one-way.

For example, a form allows us to enter details about a new customer, or scroll through the details of existing customers, modifying them as we need to. We tend to view one customer at a time and work with all the data for that customer.

However, a report will tend to be a listing (on screen or via a printer, but usually the latter) of all the customers, or at least a preset selection. It may not need to contain all the information about each customer and can summarize the details in different ways to give an overall picture of our data.

Customer List   23-Oct-95

Aardvark Ltd.   *Phone:* 216-376-1298
All Saints Street   *Fax:* 216-376-8811
Green Bay   *Credit:* $10,000
WI   39812   *Alpha:* AARDV

   Mr. Arnson   *EMail:* 1645_aa@~north.aardv.com
   Phone: 416-7742   *Addr:* Stores Manager, North Station Stores

---

Burger Queen   *Phone:* 713-771-6727
Constants Avenue   *Fax:* 713-771-6728
Houston   *Credit:* $5,000
TX   30517   *Alpha:* BURGE

   Julia Fry   *EMail:*
   Phone: *Addr:* Manageress

Cummings Intl.   *Phone:* 412-455-6104
124th Street West   *Fax:* 412-455-1399
Pittsburg   *Credit:* $25,000
PA   17265   *Alpha:* CUMMI

   Carrie Newton   *EMail:* carrien@cummings.intl.com
   Phone: 547-4539   *Addr:* IT Manager

   Dave Jones   *EMail:* davej@cummings.intl.com
   Phone: 547-4536   *Addr:* M.D.

Creating a Simple Report

The basis behind a report is that a single section is repeated, once for each record that is to be included. When we create a form, we have a Default View property which allows us to choose whether we want to display either one copy or multiple copies of the form.

When we create a report, we don't have a Default View property - the sections automatically repeat for each record. So, if we base a report on the Customer table and place controls for the name and address fields, the report will print out the name and address for each customer in the table. However, we do have a lot of control over how the sections appear, including the order in which they are sorted and whether there is a break in the report at the beginning or end of each one.

Let's build a simple Customer report, using just the Customer table for the time being. We'll take it in three distinct stages: creating the outline for the report, adding controls to the report and finally, sorting and grouping the records. Later, we'll add other tables and build a report which displays a lot more information.

Try It Out - Creating a Customer Report Outline

1 Open the **NewTable** database, click the
Reports tab in the Database window and
click New. In the New Report dialog, make
sure Design View is selected in the top list
and select the Customer table in the drop-
down list below it.

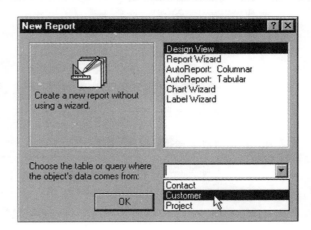

2 Click OK and Access displays a blank
report in design view. Re-size it to about
three quarters of the screen width. Note
that it looks very similar to a form, with
Page Header and Page Footer sections.
Open the View menu - you'll see a Report
Header/Footer option. Turn this on and
Access will add these sections to the
report.

3 The report header and
footer are only printed
once - at the beginning
and end of the report,
while the page header
and footer are printed
once for each page.
Therefore, we should
put a title in the report header - click
on the Label control in the toolbox
and click in the Report Header
section. Type Customer List and
press *Return*, then use the controls
on the formatting toolbar to choose
the Impact font and enlarge it to 26.
You'll also have to re-size the label.

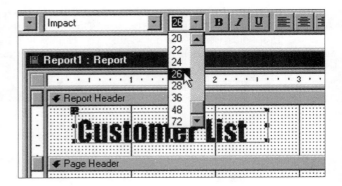

251

4   Select the Line control in the toolbox, click in the **Report Header** and, holding the mouse button down, drag a line under the label. Set its thickness by clicking the down arrow part of the **Border Width** button on the toolbar and selecting 2-pt Border Width.

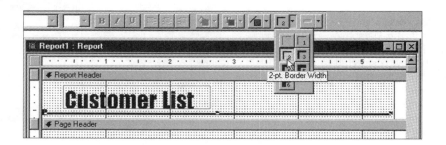

5   We won't be using a page header, so drag the top of the Detail section header upwards until it meets the **Page Header** section. Remove the report footer by dragging the bottom of the report 'page' upwards to meet the **Report Footer** selector. Re-sizing the sections like this means they don't leave a blank area on the printed page.

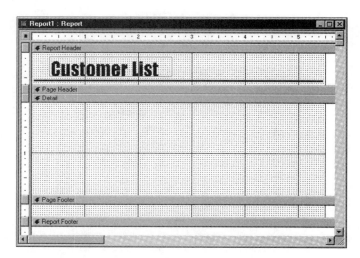

6   Select the **Text Box** control in the toolbox and click in the **Page Footer** to place a text box in this section. Then delete the label part. We'll use this text box, which will be printed at the bottom of each page, to show the page number. Click on the text box to select it and click in the **Control Source** property in the **Data** page of the **Properties** window. (If the Properties window is not visible, you can show it by clicking the **Properties** button on the toolbar, or by selecting **P**roperties from the **V**iew menu.)

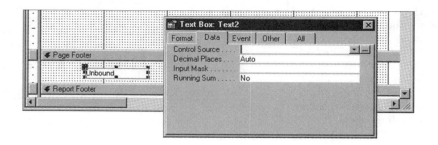

7 Click the builder to open Expression Builder. Select Common Expressions from the list in the left-hand window, Page N of M in the middle window and double-click on the entry in the right-hand window to copy it into the top part of Expression Builder. This expression will return the page number and total number of pages.

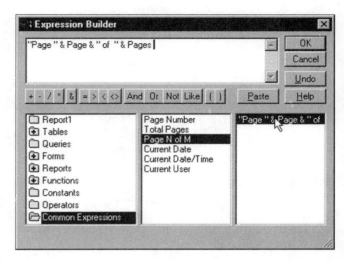

8 Click OK to update the Control Source property. Now we'll add another text box to show when the report was printed. Place a new text box in the Page Footer to the right of the last text box, delete its label and select the Control Source property as before. Click the builder button to open Expression Builder and select Common Expressions in the left-hand window again, Current Date/Time in the middle window and double-click on the entry in the right-hand window. The expression **Now()** returns the current time and date.

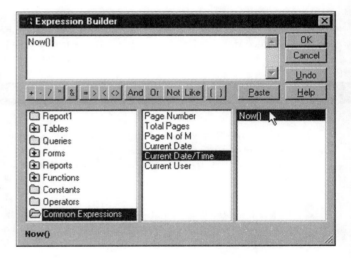

9 Click OK to update the Control Source property. We also need to change the Format property. Click the Format tab in the Properties window and select General Date from the drop-down list in the Format property.

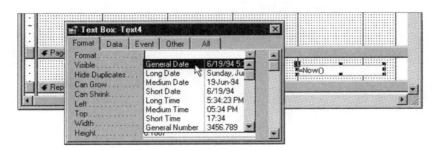

10 Click on the line that we created in the **Report Header** section and press *Ctrl-C* to copy it. Then click in the **Page Footer** section and press *Ctrl-V* to paste it there. Access pastes it right at the top of the section - you can move it down slightly by clicking on it and dragging it to another position.

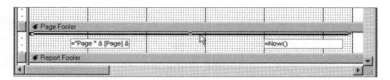

Adding Controls

So the basic format of the report has been created - all we need now is to add the information that we want to display. To do this, we place controls in the **Detail** section which will show the contents of the records. The whole of the **Detail** section of the report is repeated once for each record, so we design it as though it was just going to hold one copy of the information. This means we need to size it so that it's just large enough for the controls we're going to include.

We create controls on a report in the same way that we did when building a form. In this particular Try It Out, we're going to add the customer's name, address, phone and fax number to each record. We're also going to add a function which checks to see whether or not there is a customer address and prints "Address Unknown" on the report if there is no entry in this field.

Try It Out - Adding Controls to Our Customer Report

1 Click on the **CustName** field in the **Field List** window and drag it into the middle of the Detail section to create the **CustName** control. (If the **Field List** window is not visible, you can show it by clicking the **Field List** button on the toolbar, or by selecting **Field List** from the **View** menu.)

2 Delete the **CustName** label - we don't need it. Make the **CustName** text box bold and re-size it so that it's large enough to hold the customer's name. Then drag the **Phone** and **Fax** fields onto the report below **CustName**. You can leave the labels for these to show which is which.

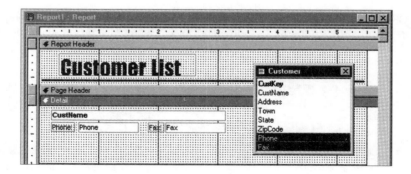

Now we need to include the address details. Instead of using different text boxes for each part, we'll combine them all into one and print the address as a single line. The expression we'll use is already familiar to you. It concatenates all the fields of the address into one line of text and uses an **IIf** statement to give the result *Address Unknown* if there's no address information available.

3 Place another text box under the Phone control by clicking the Text Box button in the toolbox and clicking in the Detail section of the report. Delete the label part and extend the box so that it is big enough to hold the address details. Then click twice on the text box - the cursor appears in it. Enter the expression:

=IIf(IsNull([Address]), "* Address Unknown *", [Address] & ", " & [Town] & ", " & [State] & ", " & [ZipCode])

and press *Return*. Typing into a text box control is the same as typing in the Control Source property of the Properties window. When you press *Return* or select another control, Access automatically updates the Control Source property.

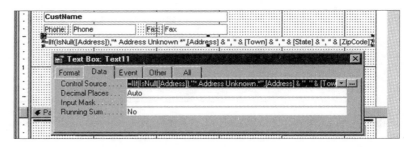

4 Re-size the Detail section by dragging the top of the Page Footer selector bar upwards. Then drag a selection rectangle around all the controls in the Detail section and Page Footer (so that they're all selected) and set the font size to 10 using the selector on the toolbar. To re-size the controls to the new font size, select Size from the Format menu and click 'to Fit'.

5 Now let's see what the report looks like. There is a Report View button on the toolbar. This allows you to select one of two different preview modes. One shows the report in Print Preview using the real data from the underlying records and the other - Layout Preview - shows it with sample data. This sample data is taken from the table in such a way as to reduce the time it takes to display the preview and is useful for getting the layout right. Try each one out to see the report we've created. Here we've used the Print Preview method.

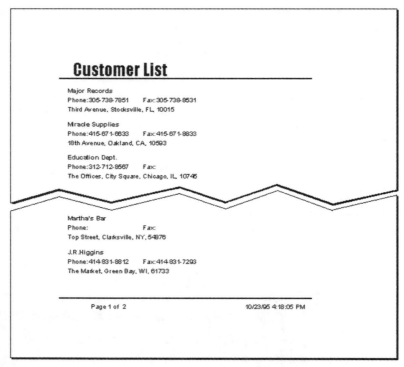

Customer List

Major Records
Phone: 305-738-7851   Fax: 305-738-8531
Third Avenue, Stocksville, FL, 10015

Miracle Supplies
Phone: 415-671-6633   Fax: 415-671-8833
18th Avenue, Oakland, CA, 10593

Education Dept.
Phone: 312-712-8567   Fax:
The Offices, City Square, Chicago, IL, 10745

Martha's Bar
Phone: Fax:
Top Street, Clarksville, NY, 54876

J.R.Higgins
Phone: 414-831-8812   Fax: 414-831-7293
The Market, Green Bay, WI, 61733

Page 1 of 2   10/23/95 4:18:05 PM

6 Click the Close button on the toolbar to close the preview and return to design view.

Displaying the Records in the Required Order

One problem with the report we've just created is that the records are displayed in the same order as in the table - the order of the table's primary key. We saw the same thing with forms earlier. We can, however, control the sort order directly in a report and also **group** the records to break the report into sections. For instance, we can sort the records by State, then set up the report so that it breaks each time the State changes. We can display sub-headings to break the report up into sections and even print the customers from each State on separate pages. Let's try this out. First we'll group the customers by state and display the states in alphabetical order; then we'll get rid of this ordering and sort the customers in plain alphabetical order, in the style of an index.

Try It Out - Sorting and Grouping Records on the Customer Report

1 Click the Sorting and Grouping button on the toolbar. Access opens the Sorting and Grouping dialog which contains two columns. We place a field name or expression in the first and select the sort order in the second. Select the State field from the drop-down list in the first column. Access automatically sets the sort order to Ascending.

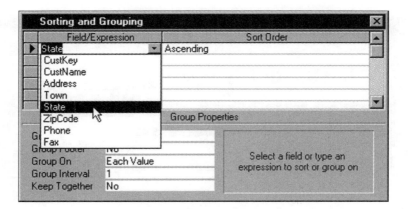

2 Five Group Properties appear in the bottom dialog. Set **Group Header** and **Group Footer** to Yes. As you do so, Access adds these sections to the report.

State header

State footer

> The new sections are a header and a footer which are printed each time the value in the **State** field changes. The **Group On** property in the **Sorting and Grouping** dialog is set to **Each Value**, so the header and footer will be displayed for each different value of the **State** field. Notice the 'group' symbol in the row selector for the **State** field - this indicates which field the report is grouped on. There's also a **Keep Together** property. If we set this to **Yes**, Access will automatically start a new page if the information for a group will not all fit on the current page.

3 Drag the State field from the Field List window into the State Header section of the report, set it to 12pt bold text and re-size it to fit. Now the state will be printed each time it changes, before the records for that state.

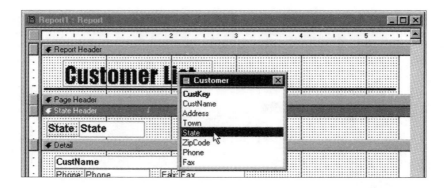

4 Preview the results. The customers are broken down by state and the states are listed in ascending order, as we specified in the Sorting and Grouping dialog.

5 You might have noticed that the customers are not in any particular order within each state. To fix this, switch back to design view, go to the Sorting and Grouping dialog and select the CustName field in the row below State. Leave the Group Properties at their defaults, though. This sorts the records by customer name within each state, but doesn't place headers and footers for CustName on the report. Preview the report to see the effect - now the customers in each state appear in alphabetical order.

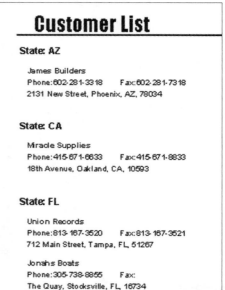

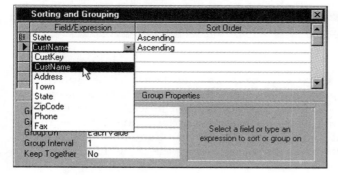

6 To print each state on a separate page, we need to add a Page Break control to the state footer. This will cause a page break each time the state changes, after the records for that state. Click on the Page Break control in the toolbox and click on the State Footer section to place it. It is displayed as a small dotted line. Preview the report again to see it working.

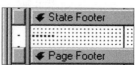

7 Now let's try breaking the report up in a different way. Go back to design view and select the State row in the Sorting and Grouping dialog by clicking on its row selector. Press *Delete* to remove it - Access prompts you to confirm this before removing the sections and their contents from the report.

8 Click in the CustName row and set the Group Header property to Yes, Group On to Prefix Characters and leave the Group Interval set to 1.

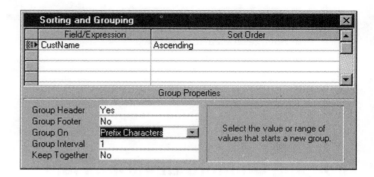

9 Place a text box in the CustName header section of the report and delete its label. Set the font to 24pt bold and re-size it to fit. Now click twice on it and enter the expression
`=Left$([CustName],1)`.

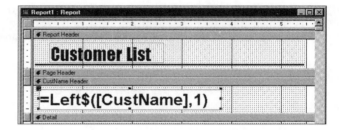

FYI Remember that the `Left$` function simply returns a number of characters from the left of the string. `Left$([CustName]),1)` takes one character from the value in the CustName field. So, if the string in the CustName field was **Alpha**, then the function would return **A**. If the function was `Left$([CustName],2)`, then **Al** would be returned. `Right$` has the same syntax, but it takes characters from the right of the string.

10 We've told Access to sort the records by the customer's name and then group them each time the first character of the customer name changes. So the CustName header will only be printed when the first letter of the name changes. Switch to Report View to see the result. Now we get the records broken down by their first letter.

11 If you look at the entries for J or M, you'll see that we've lost the alphabetical order within the groups again. Access only sorts the groups themselves, not the contents within them. We need to add another line to the Sorting and Grouping dialog to do this. Press the Close button and go back to design view. In the Field/Expression column, below the existing CustName

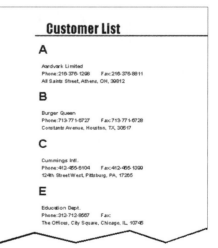

group row, select CustName again. Leave the sort order as Ascending and the Group Properties at their defaults. Notice that the row selector only displays the grouping symbol for rows which have a group header or footer.

12 Preview the report to see the results. We now get the customers listed alphabetically within each group.

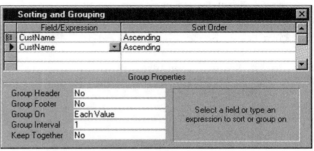

Grouping On More than One Field

Of course, we're not limited to just one level of grouping. For instance, we can group our customers first by state, then by town. All we have to do is select the Town field in the next available row in the Sorting and Grouping dialog and set the Group Header and Group Footer properties to Yes.

Access then adds sections for these groups to the report, placing them inside the state header and footer and around the Detail section. Of course, we have to use some common sense when selecting the group order - remember that Access sorts the records in the order we specify in the Sorting and Grouping dialog, starting with the first field we select. It would be pointless to group by town then by state because for each town group, there is only going to be one state (unless, of course, there were several towns with the same name but in different states!).

So now the State Header is printed first, followed by the Town Header, then the Detail section for each record which has a matching state and town. After this the Town Footer prints, followed by the Town Headers and corresponding Footers for other records with towns in that state. Then comes the State Footer. The process is then repeated again for the next state.

It's often useful to open the table or query that's the basis for your report and look at the records themselves. You can only group on fields (or parts of a field) that are actually in the recordset you're using. You may have to create a query, or modify the existing one, to include the field you want to group on.

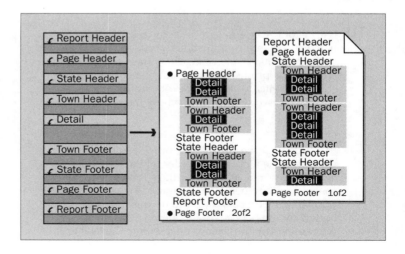

More Complex Reports and Report Wizard

We've seen how to create a simple report based on one table. We can sort the records in any order, break the display up into sections with sub-headings and even create a phone-book style report using the first letter of each customers name.

So, having learned the basic techniques, we can now explore how we create more complex reports. There are two main things to look at here - summarizing the data in a table and combining fields from different tables.

In Part 2, we'll look at another aspect of reports - using sub-reports within a main report to display information from linked tables. This is very similar to the technique we used in the customer and contacts form in Chapter 7.

We'll use a Report Wizard and let it create a complex report based on our Project table. This report will contain several numerical fields and summarize the data in different ways. We'll group the report by project type and sort the projects in each group in order of date, with the most recent first.

The report will calculate the sum of all the hours worked, the total charge for all projects of a particular type (e.g. all Accounts System projects) and also the total tax due and the total amount due. It will calculate the average hours worked on each project type, the average hourly rate and the average total due. We will also calculate maximum and minimum values for the hours worked, the hourly rate, the tax rate and the total due. Finally, we will calculate the percentage of hours worked on one project type out of all projects and the percentage of the total charge, the tax due and the total due of one project type out of all projects. Once it's finished we'll have a look at the results and see how it works. Again, we'll use the **NewTable** database supplied with the sample files.

Try It Out - Creating the Project Summary Report

1 Select the Reports tab in the Database window and click <u>N</u>ew. Access opens the New Report window. Select Report Wizard in the top list and the Project table in the drop-down list below this.

2 Click OK and Report Wizard opens. The <u>T</u>ables/Queries entry is set to Project - as we specified in the New Report window. We need to select the fields we want to include in the new report. Select all except the CustKey and ProjectKey fields.

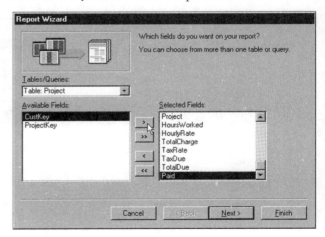

3 Click <u>N</u>ext. Now we can select which fields we want to group by. We want to summarize the data by project, so select just the Project field and click the > button. Report Wizard shows it as a group header.

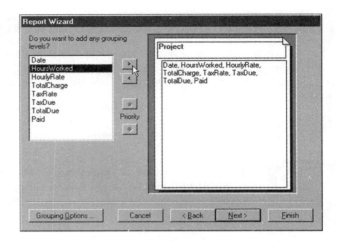

There is also a button marked **Grouping Options...** at the bottom of the window. This allows us to set the other group properties we saw in the previous example, for instance grouping on the first one or more characters of the field, or by different time intervals if it is a **Date** type field.

4 Click <u>N</u>ext again. Now we can set the sort order of the Detail section of the report - in other words the order of the records within each project group. Select Date in the first sort box and click the A-Z button next to the field to change it to read Z-A. This will sort our records in descending date order.

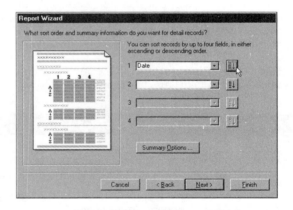

5 Now we must set the summary options. Click the Summary <u>O</u>ptions.. button to open the Summary Options window. This shows all the numeric fields together with their available summary functions. We can also opt to show the <u>S</u>ummary Only rather than the <u>D</u>etail and Summary. Leave the <u>D</u>etail and Summary option selected and set the field summary options as in the screenshot below. Make sure you also select the Calculate <u>p</u>ercent of total for sums option.

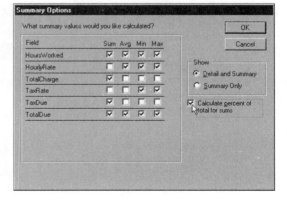

6 Click OK to close the Summary Options window and click Next. In the next window we set the layout options for the report. Select the Outline 1 layout and Landscape orientation. Also make sure that the Adjust the field width so all fields fit on a page option is set.

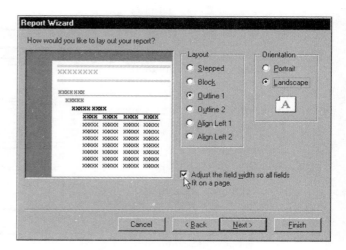

7 Click Next again and select a style you like for the report. We've selected the Bold style.

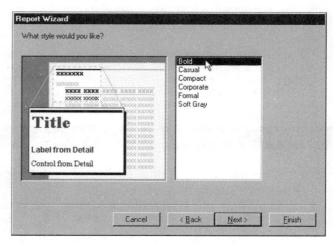

8 Finally click Next and enter a name for the report - call it Project Summary. Make sure that Preview the report is selected and that the Display Help... option is not checked. Click Finish.

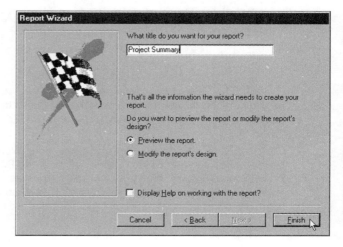

9 Access then creates the report. There is a section for each type of project with rows containing the details of each individual project. Under that is a summary section. For our HoursWorked field, for instance, Access shows the total number of hours worked on Accounts System projects, the average number of hours for a project and the minimum and maximum number of hours. Then below that is the percentage this represents of the total number of hours worked on all projects. If you go to the last page you'll find Access has also created a row containing the Grand Totals. Click the Print button on the toolbar if you want to see the results printed out as hard copy.

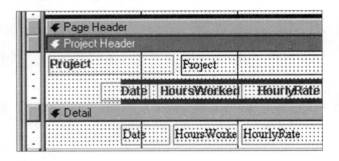

Report Wizard has done everything almost exactly as promised. Before we delve into exactly how it's done this, though, we should first deal with a couple of minor problems that have arisen. You'll find that the column labels don't quite line up correctly and that the format of some of the fields a little confusing.

Try It Out - Tidying Up the Project Report

1 Switch to design view and move the Date label in the Project Header so that it no longer overlaps the HoursWorked label and lines up correctly with the text box in the Detail section. Move the HoursWorked label so that it lines up with the column beneath.

2 Carefully drag a selection rectangle so that it only includes the text boxes in the summary section of the HoursWorked column. Click the Align Right button on the toolbar to make them all line up correctly.

3 Click on the text box in the Avg row of the HoursWorked column (not the Avg label at the extreme left of the row) - you can see in the title bar of the Properties window that it's named Avg Of HoursWorked. In the Format page of the Properties window, change its Format property to Fixed and, in the Data page, change its Decimal Places property from Auto to 2. This will prevent any recurring decimal places, such as .333333, from occurring and ruining our layout.

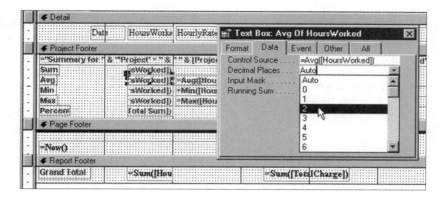

4 Add a page break to the bottom of the Project footer by selecting a page break control from the toolbox and placing it. To see the effect of these changes, click the Report View button on the toolbar. Once you're happy with the results, switch back to design view again.

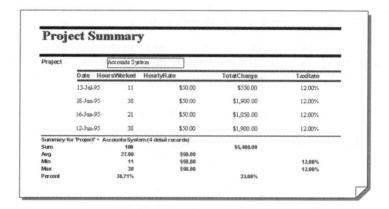

How the Report Works

Click on the HoursWorked text box in the Detail section and look at the Data page of the Properties window. Access has created a normal text box control named HoursWorked and bound it to the HoursWorked field. So, for each record it displays the value stored in the HoursWorked field.

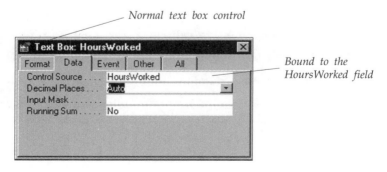

Normal text box control

Bound to the HoursWorked field

Click on the text box in the Sum row of the Project Footer section. Access has named this Sum Of HoursWorked and inserted the expression `=Sum([HoursWorked])` which produces the total for the HoursWorked field from all the records in that section. This is a calculated control.

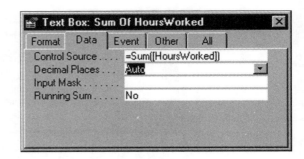

In the HoursWorked column of the Report Footer is another calculated control named HoursWorked Grand Total Sum. This contains the same expression. However, here it calculates the total for *all the records*, whereas the Sum Of HoursWorked control in the Project Footer only uses the records that actually appear *in that section*. The Report Footer section only occurs at the end of the report, so you can think of it as containing all the records.

Other calculated controls in the Project Footer section show the Average, Minimum and Maximum values. These are similar to the Sum control, but use other **SQL aggregate functions** to calculate their results. We'll look in more depth at these functions later in this chapter.

Finally, there is the Percent calculated control in the Project Footer section. This shows the percentage that the records for each project represent of the total for all projects. Access has named this control Percent Of HoursWorked and placed in its Control Source property the expression:

=Sum([HoursWorked])/([HoursWorked Grand Total Sum])

This simply divides the total of the HoursWorked for that project by the grand total for all projects. The Format property is set to Percent, so the result is displayed as a percentage.

One other item worth noting is that Access's Report Generator is **two-pass**. This basically means that when you include summary fields, Access goes through the records in the table twice. This means it can calculate the totals and grand totals in the first pass, then use this information to calculate the values for other calculated controls in the second pass.

SQL Aggregate Functions

We used several aggregate functions in the last example to summarize information in our table. Here's a summary of what each of the functions does.

Function	Description
`=Sum` ([*field*])	Total of the values in the group.
`=Count` ([*field*])	The number of records in the group.
`=Avg` ([*field*])	Average of the values in the group.
`=Max` ([*field*])	Maximum of the values in the group.
`=Min` ([*field*])	Minimum of the values in the group.

Creating a Report from Several Tables

So we've seen how easy it is to build a complex report using a Report Wizard. This is often the best way to tackle report creation, rather than starting from scratch. You can experiment with the other Report Wizards to see what they do. Then, once the wizard has done the hard work, you can tidy up the finished report and make additions or change it to suit your needs more exactly, as we did in the last example.

Reports are generally most useful, though, when you use data from several tables, rather than just one. Next we'll look at how you can create a report which uses fields from different tables to show the different customers we've worked for and groups the information by project. We'll also add a simple summary field to show the total value for each project.

Try It Out - Creating a Customer by Project Report

1 Create a new report by clicking <u>N</u>ew in the Database window Reports list. In the New Report dialog make sure that Design View is selected and leave the Choose the table or query... entry blank.

2 Click OK and Access creates a new blank report. In the <u>V</u>iew menu, turn on the P<u>ag</u>e Header/Footer and Report <u>H</u>eader/Footer options. Re-size the Report Header and Page Footer sections so that they don't print.

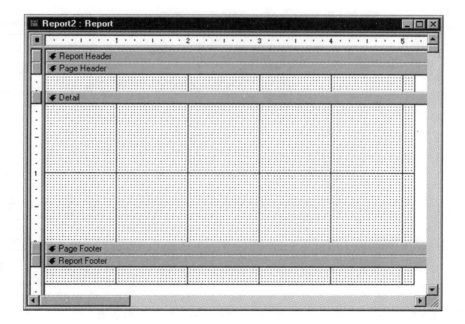

3 Click the square in the left-hand corner of the report window where the rulers meet, so that a small black box appears. In the Data page of the Properties window, click on the Record Source property - this is empty because we did not choose a table or query in the New Report dialog.

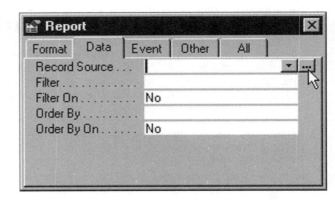

4 Click the builder button to open Query Builder. Add the Customer and Project tables to the grid and close the Show Table dialog. Access automatically joins the tables together using the relationships we created in Chapter 3.

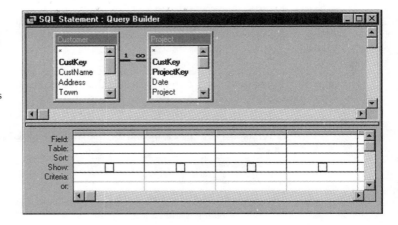

5 Drag the Project, Date, HoursWorked and TotalDue fields from the Project table to the grid and the CustName field from the Customer table.

Field:	Project	Date	HoursWorked	TotalDue	CustName
Table:	Project	Project	Project	Project	Customer
Sort:					
Show:	☑	☑	☑	☑	☑
Criteria:					
or:					

6 Click the Datasheet View button on the toolbar to see the results of the query. We have a record for each project and Access has added the customer name from the linked Customer table to each record.

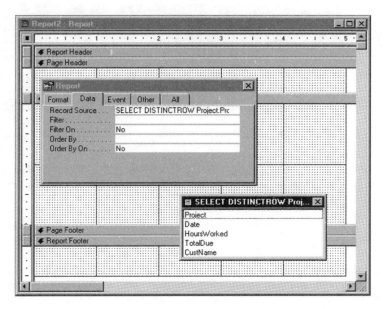

7 Close the query by clicking the Close box in the top right of the window. Access asks whether we want to update the SQL property - click Yes. You can see that the SQL statement that creates the recordset is now placed in the Record Source property of our report. Open the Field List window and you'll see that it contains the fields in our query; these come from the two linked tables.

8 Now that we have the records, we just need to build the report. We want it to group on the project name, so open the Sorting and Grouping window and select Project for the Field/Expression column. Access sets the sort order to Ascending. Select Yes for the Group Header and Group Footer properties for this field, so that you create Project Header and Project Footer sections on your report.

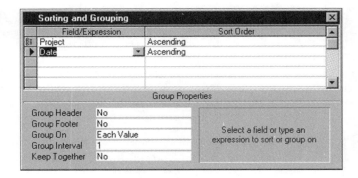

9 In the next row of the Sorting and Grouping dialog, select the Date field. We'll sort the entries for each project by date.

10 Now we can place the controls. Drag the Date, CustName, HoursWorked and TotalDue fields into the Detail section. Cut the labels from the Date, HoursWorked and TotalDue controls and paste them into the Page Header section. Delete the CustName label completely.

11 Drag the Project field into the Project Header section. Change the font size to 14 and make it bold. Then re-size the Project text box so that the text fits. Add a line control to the top of the Project Header and Report Footer sections and adjust the text alignment, font, size and position of the other controls to give a neat layout.

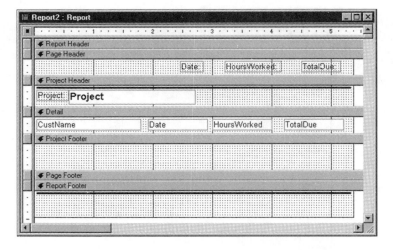

12 Now create two unbound text box controls by clicking on the Text Box control in the toolbox and clicking in the Project Footer section of the form. Change one of the labels to read 'Totals:' and delete the other label. Align them with the HoursWorked and TotalDue controls in the Detail section and set the Format property of the one under TotalDue to Currency.

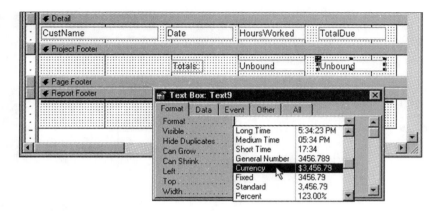

13 Now we need to create the expressions that calculate the totals for our records. Click on the unbound control in the **Project Footer** under **HoursWorked** and in the **Data** page of the **Properties** window click on the **Control Source** property. Click the builder button to open **Expression Builder**.

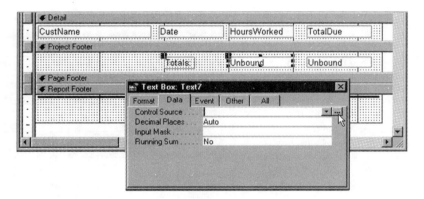

14 Double-click **Functions** in the left-hand list and select **Built-In Functions**. Select **SQL Aggregate** in the middle list and double-click on **Sum** in the right-hand list. Access places it in the top window. Click on the «**expr**» place-holder and select our report in the left-hand list - it will be the first entry at the top of the list (because we haven't saved and named it yet, it will be called **Report2** or something similar). In the middle list, select the **HoursWorked** control and double-click on the <Value> entry in the right-hand list. This completes the expression for us.

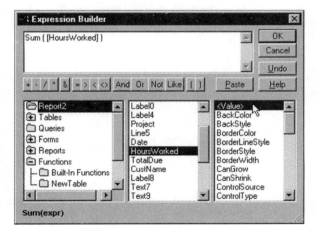

271

15 Click OK to update the Control Source property. Now repeat step 14 with the other unbound text box using the TotalDue control as the «expr». Click OK to complete this step. These controls will calculate the total values for each project.

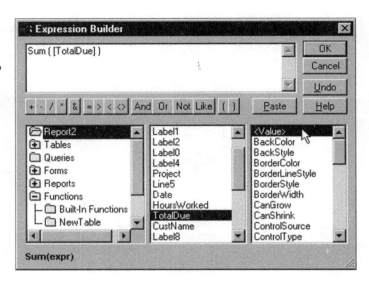

16 Now we can create the Grand Total controls. These use the same expressions as those in the Project Footer section, but are placed in the Report Footer so that they total up all the records. Drag a selection rectangle over the Totals: label and the two calculated controls and copy and paste them into the Report Footer section. Move them into position and change the label to read Grand Totals:.

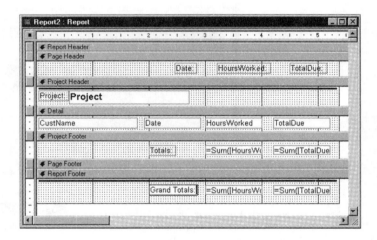

17 Place a label control in the Page Header section and type a name for the report - Projects by Customer will do. Set the font and size to suit.

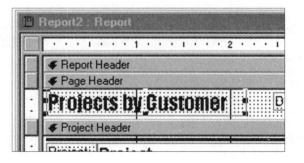

18 Preview the report to see the results. Each project is listed by type, with the dates and customer names, plus the hours we worked and the total due for that project. The report also summarizes the number of hours worked and the total due for each project type and gives the overall totals at the end. Don't worry if your final report doesn't look quite like this. Go back and re-size the different sections and move the labels and text boxes around until it does. Then you can close and save your report.

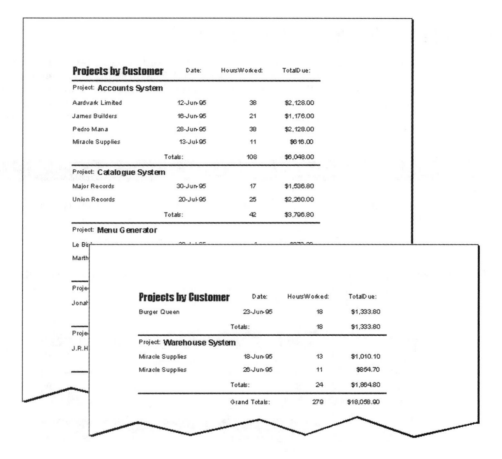

FYI You may find that the records and totals for one of the projects are split over two pages, because they will not all fit on one. You can use the **Keep Together** property in the **Sorting and Grouping** window to solve this problem. Setting it to **With First Detail** prevents the **Project Header** appearing at the bottom of a page without any records from the **Detail** section, while **Whole Group** moves the whole section, including the header and footer, onto the next page if it will not fit on the current one.

How It Works

Basically, we've done nothing new. We've simply queried two tables and then created a report from the results. We've combined two of the concepts that we learnt earlier to give us more information. This is what we're going to do when we start building our sample application in Part 2. However, before we move on to this, there's one last trick that reports can provide for you; we'll look at it now.

Creating Running Sums for Records

You can provide a **running sum** of the values in each record using a text box in the Detail section of the report. Set its Running Sum property and it will display the 'total so far' for each record. You can select whether the running total returns to zero at the end of each group or whether it continues to increment throughout the whole report - set it to Over Group to zero it each time the group changes, or to Over All to display a running total for all records. If you want to do both, simply place two text boxes and set one to Over Group and one to Over All.

Try It Out - SQL Aggregates and Running Sums

1 Create a new report, selecting Design View in the top list of the New Report dialog and the Project table as the basis for the report.

2 In the View menu, turn Page Header/Footer off and Report Header/Footer on.

3 In the Sorting and Grouping dialog, select the Project field in the first row. Check that its sort order is Ascending and set the Group Header and Footer properties to Yes. Access inserts the Project Header and Footer sections in the report.

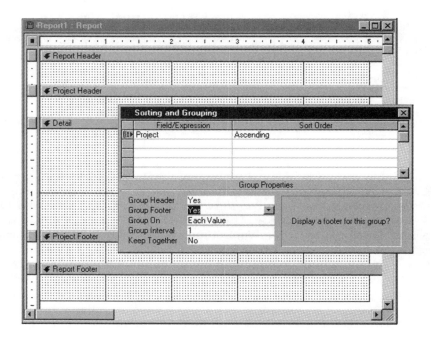

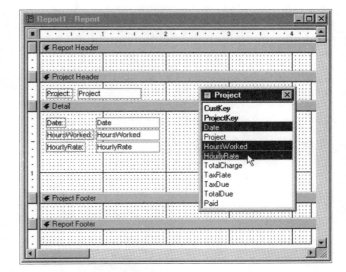

4 Drag the Project field from the Field List window into the Project Header, then select the Date, HoursWorked and HourlyRate fields and drag them into the Detail section of the report.

5 Create two unbound text box controls by clicking the Text Box button in the toolbox and clicking in the Details section of the report. In the Other page of the Properties window, set the Name of the first to RunSum_Project and the second to RunSum_All.

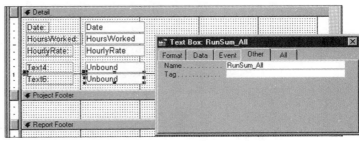

6 In the Data page for both of them, change the Control Source property to HoursWorked.

At the moment, these controls will just show the value of the **HoursWorked** field for each record. We need to tell Access to show the running sums instead. We do this using the **Running Sum** property of the controls.

7 Click on the first text box and, in the Data page of the Properties window, find the Running Sum property. Set it to Over Group. Repeat for the second text box, but set its Running Sum property to Over All.

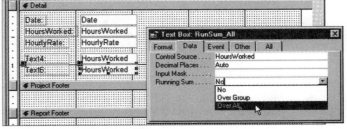

8 Select all the labels from the text boxes in the Details and cut and paste them into the Project Header section. Then re-arrange the controls and labels so they run horizontally to give a neat display. You'll also want to change the Captions of Text4 and Text6 in the Properties window to Group RunSum and Over All RunSum.

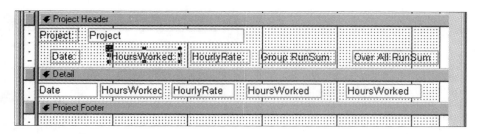

9 Now we need to create the summary calculated controls in the Project Footer section. Create five unbound text box controls in the Project Footer section, under the HoursWorked column, and edit the labels to show the summary information we will be displaying - as in the screenshot below:

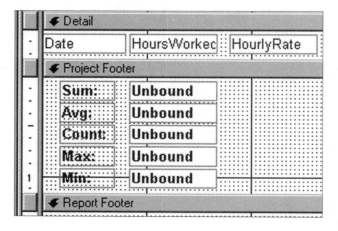

10 Select them all and, using *Ctrl-C* and *Ctrl-V*, make a copy of all five under the HourlyRate column. Delete the labels so the report looks like this:

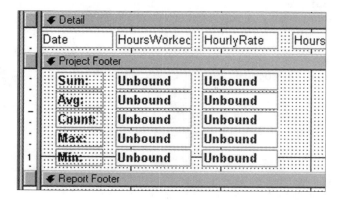

11 Now we need to make sure that the controls display their information correctly and neatly. Drag a selection rectangle around all the text boxes and labels in the Project Footer and click the Align Right toolbar button. Then select just the text boxes under the HourlyRate control and set their Format property to Currency.

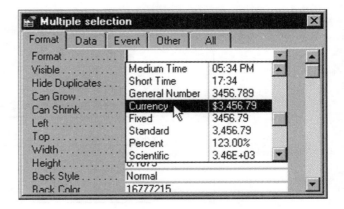

12 Now we need to place a function in each that calculates the values from the records. We'll just use the more common ones for now - if you're feeling mathematical you can include variances and standard deviations later! You can either create the functions using Expression Builder or type them in directly.

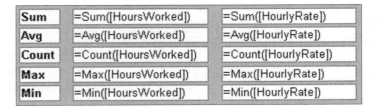

Sum	=Sum([HoursWorked])	=Sum([HourlyRate])
Avg	=Avg([HoursWorked])	=Avg([HourlyRate])
Count	=Count([HoursWorked])	=Count([HourlyRate])
Max	=Max([HoursWorked])	=Max([HourlyRate])
Min	=Min([HoursWorked])	=Min([HourlyRate])

FYI These will display the summary for each project, because they're in the **Project Footer** section. We just need to repeat the same controls in the **Report Footer** section to display a summary for all projects.

13 Select all the controls in the Project Footer section and copy them into the Report Footer using *Ctrl-C* and *Ctrl-V*. Then add a few Line controls to break up the sections and give the report a title in the Report Header section.

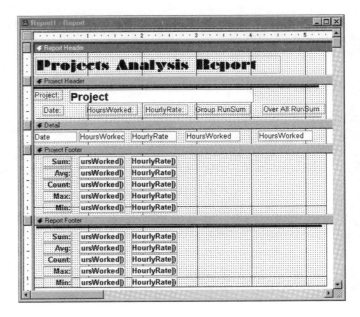

14 Click the Report View button on the toolbar to view the results.

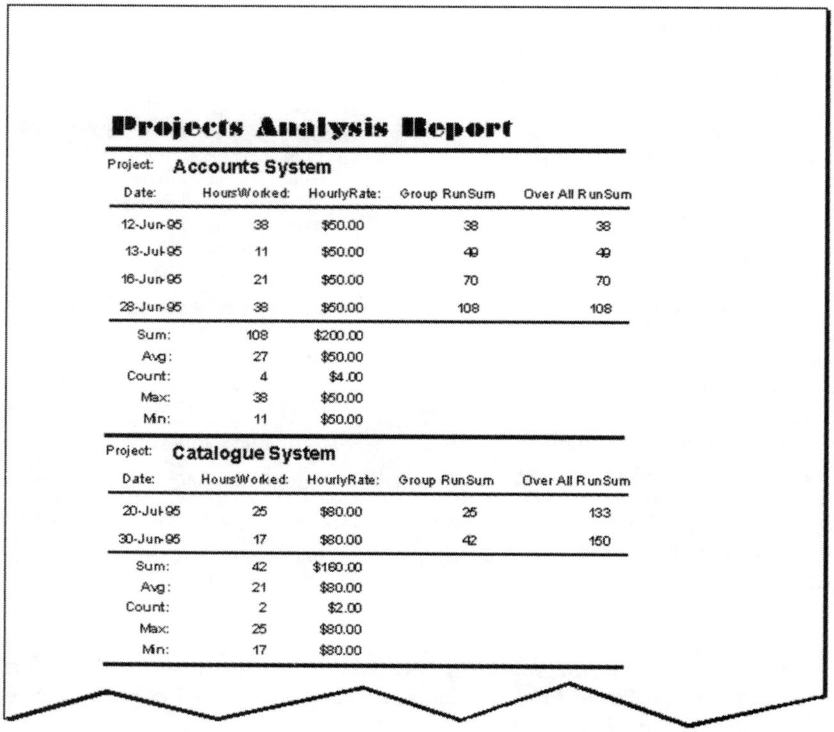

Projects Analysis Report

Project: Accounts System

Date:	HoursWorked:	HourlyRate:	Group RunSum	Over All RunSum
12-Jun-95	38	$50.00	38	38
13-Jul-95	11	$50.00	49	49
16-Jun-95	21	$50.00	70	70
28-Jun-95	38	$50.00	108	108
Sum:	108	$200.00		
Avg:	27	$50.00		
Count:	4	$4.00		
Max:	38	$50.00		
Min:	11	$50.00		

Project: Catalogue System

Date:	HoursWorked:	HourlyRate:	Group RunSum	Over All RunSum
20-Jul-95	25	$80.00	25	133
30-Jun-95	17	$80.00	42	150
Sum:	42	$160.00		
Avg:	21	$80.00		
Count:	2	$2.00		
Max:	25	$80.00		
Min:	17	$80.00		

You can see that we now have a running sum for each individual project, as well as one that shows the running total for all projects. This is a useful little feature that can be added without much effort.

Summary

While we have by no means covered all the different aspects of creating reports, you should now have mastered all the general techniques that you'll need. There's almost no limit to the ways that Access can provide information - you'll see more examples in Part 2 of this book.

The important things to remember when generating reports are:

▶ How to work with controls on reports.

▶ How to sort and group records.

▶ How to create reports using Report Wizard.

▶ How the SQL aggregate functions can help you produce summaries.

▶ How to calculate running sums.

With this chapter we have reached the end of Part 1, 'Understanding What Access Does'. By now, you should have a grasp of all the basic techniques required for building a database. Of course, we're still only scratching at the edge of what Access can achieve. Remember the sneak preview of our Wrox Consultants database system you saw in the Introduction? It uses all the basic methods we've learned here. You will see how in Part 2.

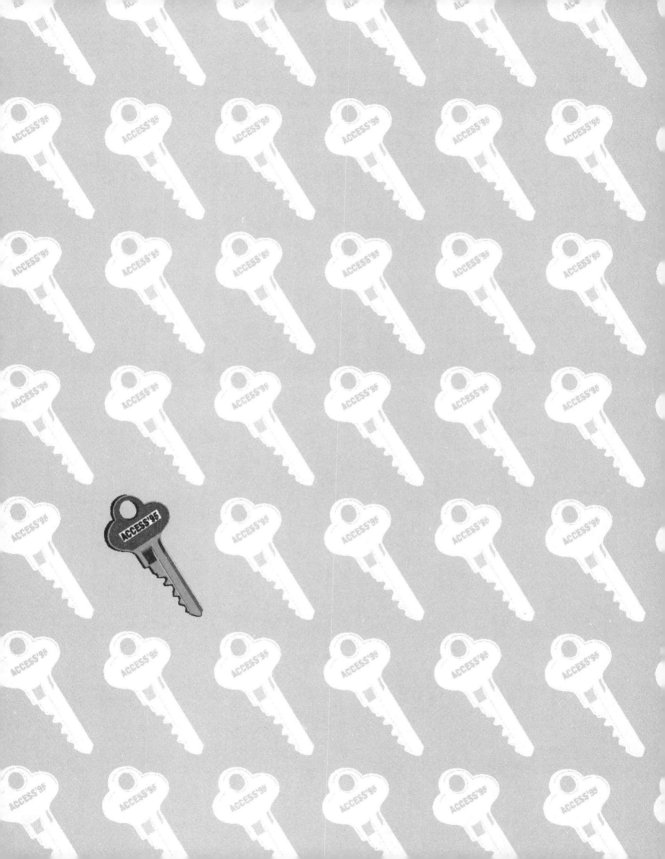

part 2

Creating Desktop Applications

Part 2 of this book marks a change in both style and emphasis. We've spent the past eight chapters concentrating on the basic techniques of building and manipulating objects, such as tables, queries, forms and reports. Over the next five chapters we'll be moving on at a somewhat quicker pace. In this part we will be looking at the design and build of the **Wroxsoft** *application. This is the database that keeps track of all the business carried out by Wrox Consultancy.*

Providing you've worked through the previous chapters and feel reasonably confident with the basic concepts of Access, you will have no problems following this part. There are no significant new objects to master - we'll just be refining the objects we've already introduced (tables, queries, forms and reports) and developing the techniques for using them. We'll also spend quite a bit of time looking at how to add functionality to the interface to enable the user to interact with the database, and achieve the results they want.

So this part is where our work gets interesting - up to now we've been building the **database***, here we start the process of turning it into an* **application***.*

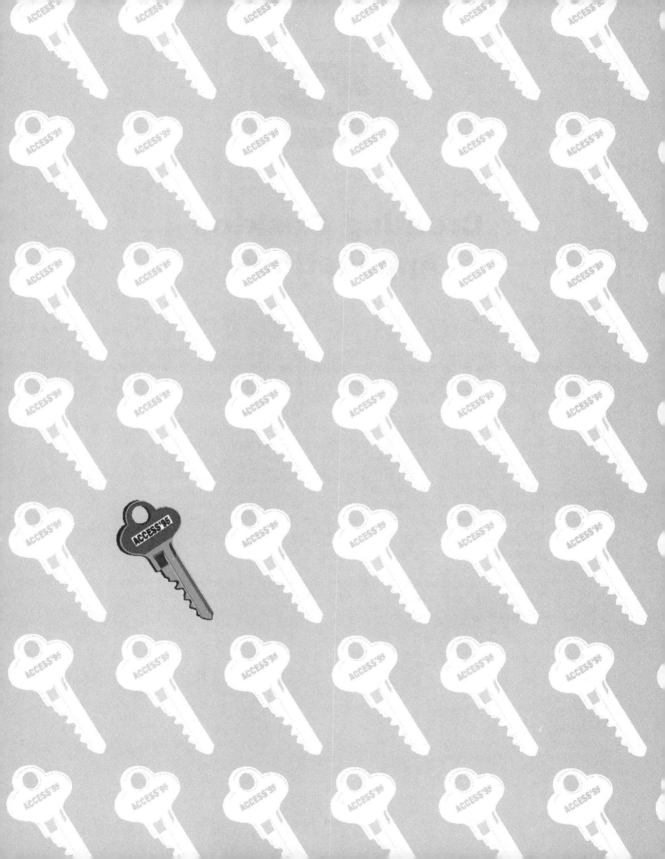

The Big Picture

In this chapter, we start the process of designing and building our **WroxSoft** application by looking at how, and why, we should plan the structure and layout of a database. We'll then move on to actually develop the basic structure of our application using these design outlines. Once we've formulated the outline plan, we'll look in detail at how we are going to store the data and discuss the tables that form the basis of the application. By the end of the chapter we'll have got the table design right and will be in a position to move on to building the interface itself, as well as the queries that will bridge the two.

We will cover:

- The specification of our application.
- The structure of the interface.
- Designing the tables and relationships.
- Adapting our old design for new requirements.
- Building the tables.
- Relating the tables together.

An Introduction to Database Design

It's often said that a software project doesn't start to go wrong until you ask the end-user what they actually want it to do - and from there on it's all down-hill. This is a rather pessimistic attitude to software design, but unfortunately it has a distinct ring of truth. Trying to tie down the final specification of a database system is often compared to the proverbial task of nailing jelly to the ceiling. Just as soon as you think you've got it right, the goal posts move and it's back to the drawing board.

In any situation the requirements for information change. We live in a high-tech world where almost anything is possible and the expectations of your users have been tuned by modern business software that does everything they could possibly want and three times as many things they ever dreamt of.

We cannot attempt to satisfy every expectation, so we *must* decide what we want our system to do and be aware of the demands that will be placed on it. When designing a database for your own personal use, this is not too difficult. But when faced with designing a system for a whole department, then you have to get everyone to agree on the basic requirements. And this can be the hardest part of the whole project.

There are several stages of design that we'll work through to develop and modify the structure of our database. These stages are:

- Analyze the requirements.
- Design the structure and interface.
- Design and build the data store.
- Build the queries to bridge the gap between the two.
- Build the forms and reports.
- Link the objects together.

Analyzing the Requirements

In the previous chapters, we've moved our data from an Excel spreadsheet to a set of tables within Access and looked at many aspects of how we can view the data to get useful information from it. However, a project actually starts at a far more basic level: the first step is to get the user to communicate to the analyst/designer exactly what they want their system to do. Our situation is a little artificial in that we're taking the role of both designer and end-user, but this doesn't mean the job is any less important - we still need to draw up a **requirements definition**.

The Requirements Definition

The requirements definition is simply an English language description of exactly what the business does and what the system is expected to do. We can't start to design the application until we're sure of what our aim is. We'll start with the requirements definition for Wrox Consultancy.

What the Business Does

Back in Chapter 1, we were using a spreadsheet that, up till then, had supported our business functions - at that time all we were doing was carrying out development work on various computer projects for a range of customers. We were designing, building and installing a range of software products from accounts systems to menu generator programs and performing PC support work and network maintenance.

Being astute business people, however, we have realized that working on projects for our customers inevitably means that we are recommending software for them to buy. A series of discussions has led us to consider selling software as well as providing consultancy services. By stocking the software we recommend, we can increase profits. We need a database that is able to handle this aspect of the business as well.

The spreadsheet we've been using had evolved - as so many systems do - from just being used in the real world. So its structure, based around a row of data for each project we carried out, really came about more by accident than design. This structure made perfect sense at the time and it was only as we examined it more closely in Access that we discovered the flaws. In particular, there was duplication of data and a general lack of facilities for storing information on each of our customers. If you want to review the reasons behind the design modifications we have made so far, look back at Chapter 3.

What Our System Should Do

We need a system that will store details of our customers and contacts, the projects we carry out, the software we sell and the stock of software we hold. We also need to be able to produce invoices and statements, customer and stock lists and provide ways of monitoring and analyzing information about our sales and profits. And, of course, we must be able to maintain the data by archiving old project and sales records.

Normally, if the designer and end-user were two separate people, the designer would then write down what he thinks that the user thinks the system should do. Needless to say, this rarely corresponds to what the user thinks the system should do! This stage of consultation is generally very lengthy and leads to many drafts and redrafts of the requirements definition and even the building of prototypes. However, we don't have this problem, as we're designing a system that we intend to use ourselves.

Specification

The next stage is to translate this rather vague definition into a more solid **specification**. This involves defining the objects that we will be using. As you know, each table, query, form and report is an individual object and can be thought of as operating separately from the other objects (though, of course, each depends on others in the chain for its data - for example, a form uses the recordset that is created by a query or the records in a table).

We can identify the different objects that we will need in our database by examining the actions or tasks that we need to perform. To achieve a good design, we should ensure that the definitions of the objects in the database don't overlap; this means we should aim to create separate objects for each different task. However, if we have two (or more) tasks that are very similar, we may be able to use the same object for both.

At this stage, we need to sit back and break the requirements definition down into a list of all the tasks we will need. We also need to examine any existing system that we plan to replace. Does it contain tasks that we need to include in our specification or are they just there as a legacy from the original poor design? How should we replace the existing tasks? Is there a better way to do it? At the end of the day, you often find that the end-user knows full well what the system should achieve. After all, they are the ones who have to use it every day.

Having made a list, we can then gather the different tasks into functionally similar groups. This will mean we can assign the same type of object to each task in the group. For example, we can break the tasks that we need to achieve with our database into three groups:

- Entering, editing and updating records
- Producing reports
- Database maintenance

We then need to decide on the type of object that will accomplish the task.

Task	Objects which will achieve the task
Enter, edit and update records.	Form to edit customer details
	Form to edit contact details
	Form to enter and edit project work
	Form to enter and edit software sales
	Form to edit software stock

As you can see, we have assumed that selling software will require a form where we can enter sales and another where we can enter and maintain details of the stock range we keep. This will also mean storing the information in tables - you'll see more of this later in the chapter.

Task	Objects which will achieve the task	
Produce reports	General reports	Report to produce invoices
		Report to produce statements
		Report to produce customer lists
		Report to produce stock lists
	Sales information	Report software sold and profits
		Report projects completed
		Report sales performance

Inevitably, the final details of how these reports will appear can't be decided yet - we need to perform a far more detailed analysis to find out exactly what information is required to appear on each one. And, of course, there could be others that we've missed, or that future needs will dictate. However, as long as we have the basic plan laid out ready and the information is available in the underlying tables, we know that we can modify the actual reports as needed.

Task	Objects which will achieve the task
Database maintenance	Query and table to archive project work records
	Query and table to archive software sales records

These database maintenance tasks are the most obvious ones that we'll need to accommodate - as new project work is carried out and software sales are made, the number of records in the database will grow. Unlike the customer records which we need to refer to on a regular basis, once a project or sale is paid for we can generally remove it from the database to some form of back-up storage.

Structuring the Interface

Next, we must decide how our users will manipulate all these objects. Do we let them just select each one from the Database window, as we've been doing up to now? Or should we have a screen with a button for each one so that they can choose from there? If you examine almost any modern application, you'll see that they often aim for a simple opening screen - one that eases the user into the program without frightening them with a mass of choices.

We'll aim to do the same, using the functional groups we've identified so far. In our case, we will use a main opening screen which is both simple and attractive to give the application that polished look and make starting to use it as intuitive as possible. This way we can hide some of the complexity under a system of sub-menu screens.

We also need to think about how the user will switch from one task to another. Will some tasks be carried out automatically when a certain event occurs, such as printing an invoice when we enter a software sale? Which tasks are used most often and which can be hidden away as they are only used infrequently? Are there any objects where we should worry about security and be selective about the users who can access them? We'll consider these questions as we further refine the design throughout this chapter.

The Main Menu

The first step is to lay out a plan for the basic structure of the interface. We'll use the groups of tasks we identified earlier to create an opening main menu selection screen. The main screen will, therefore, be divided into sections, each containing the tasks from one group. This top-level main menu will then give easy access to the features we need for everyday use.

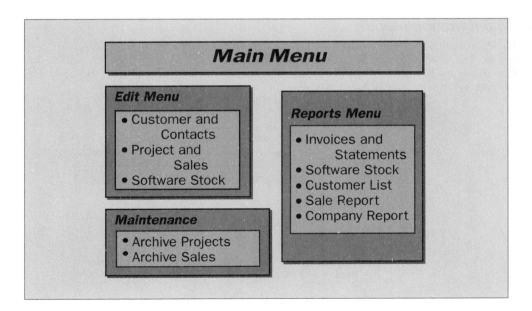

We then need to define each of the sub-menus which can be accessed from the main menu. The most common tasks are on the Edit section of the opening screen, so let's start there.

The Edit Menu

We will constantly want to be adding and updating records in the main tables. So we must be able to select these tasks from the main menu and open a screen form which allows us direct access to the records we want to work with.

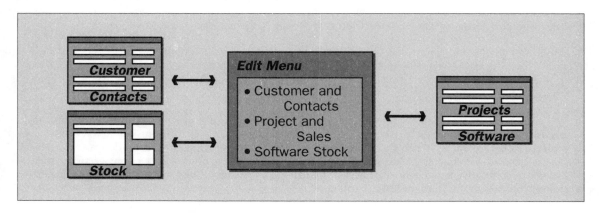

You can see that we've elected to use a customer editing form which contains a section for our contacts. This makes sense, as these entities are closely associated with each other. When we select a customer, we can then work with the contacts information for that customer. A similar argument applies to the projects and sales entry form. Here we'll be able to select a customer and work with either the projects or software sales (or both) for that particular customer. That just about completes the Edit menu, so we'll move on to the Maintenance section next.

The Maintenance Menu

The Maintenance section is used to run the archive procedure for either the project or the sales records. The user needs to be able to enter the date of the newest records to move to the archives, so each option opens another screen where this can be entered. The archive procedure can then be run for the relevant records.

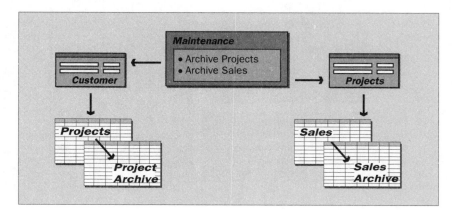

That's all the Maintenance menu needs to do, so we'll move on to the third and last menu.

The Reports Menu

The Reports section of the opening screen contains the invoicing task which we'll need regularly, but most of the others are used less often, probably monthly. For invoicing and statements, we'll need to be able to select the customer, so this again must offer a sub-menu screen to enter the details. The sales report menu can be used to offer a range of different reports such as sales by month, sales by customer, project analysis, etc. In fact, many of the options will produce a sub-menu where we select exactly which task we need. Our design for the reports section is therefore multi-level and a lot more complicated than the other sections.

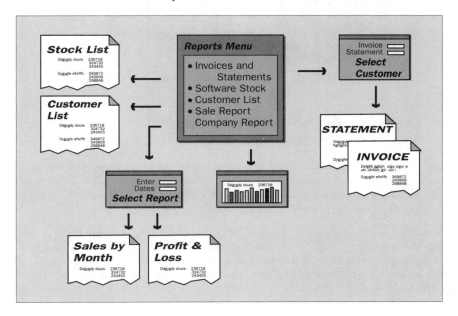

Handling Interaction between Objects

So we now have a basic plan of the interface objects we need to build and how they relate together. Of course, there will be interaction between them. For instance, it would be nice to be able to open a software stock details screen while we are entering a software sales record. And having entered a new project or sale, we should be able to generate an invoice directly, instead of going back to the main menu and into the invoicing section that way. It's likely that we'll want to print an invoice when we enter details of a completed project or software sale, so we might as well do it at that point. Therefore, we should include a path to the invoicing task directly from the Projects and Sales form. We'll consider how we achieve this in more detail as we come to design the forms. Because we've specified them as separate individual objects, we should easily be able to switch between them without disturbing the underlying structure of the design. So we'll just define the paths that the user should be able to take through the forms.

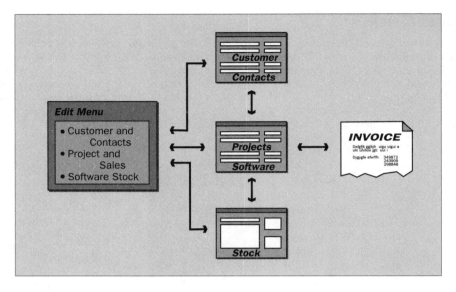

This leads to the next question. How are we actually going to carry out the invoicing? If we were designing a true 'accounts package', we would need to maintain sales ledgers and invoice tables. However, we can manage with a simpler system. We'll look for ways to manage the creation of invoices and recording of payments as we design the tables.

Even in a relatively simple application such as this, there are a multitude of possible ways of designing the interface. Then, when it all appears finished, someone will suggest an improvement that is blindingly obvious - yet no-one considered it in the design stage. And, of course, as soon you start to use an application like this, you very quickly find out where the weak points of the design are!

So don't expect to get it right first time. Just remember that if you design in a structured and objective manner, with clearly defined purposes for each form and report, the objects can be modified and re-used as you go along. If you simply throw all the parts together, with the path through them resembling spaghetti, you may never be able to change it without the whole structure collapsing round your ears.

Designing Our Tables and Relationships

In Part 1, we developed the tables that we imported from Excel using a 'common sense' approach. We divided the single table up into three in an attempt to increase the efficiency of the way data was stored and allow increased flexibility when retrieving it. As we suggested then, there are rules which we can apply to check that we have an optimal structure. In this section we'll go back to the original single table and briefly walk through the steps of developing the design - but this time following more scientific methods.

Normalization of Database Tables

The technical term for optimizing the structure of tables in a database is **normalization**. This term often scares people off, but it is really nothing to worry about. All we mean by normalizing a database is that we're going to eliminate redundant or duplicated information from our tables. We've actually carried out the first stage of this in Part 1 without even mentioning the word, so let's see how our current design compares. Along the way, we'll look out for opportunities for improvements we can make, bearing in mind the new requirement to store software stock and sales information.

Summary of Our 'Common Sense' Approach

Our original table came from an Excel spreadsheet which was used to store details of the various projects carried out by us. It was really just a list of all the projects, with all the relevant information included on each row. Basically, the design was a group of fields which contained details about the customer, then another group containing the project information.

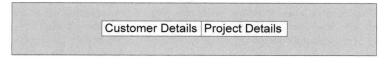

We thought it would be useful to include details of the people we dealt with on each project, but came up against the problem of deciding how many contacts we were likely to deal with. We could include extra fields for each contact, say their name, e-mail address and home or mobile number. But, if we had to allow for three or four contacts, we would be adding a lot of extra fields, many of which may be empty. Besides, these fields would form a duplicated group for each project, producing an untidy structure.

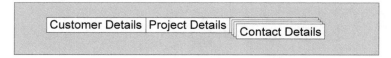

We also discovered that we were repeating the customer's details in many records. If we carried out more than one project for a customer, we stored their address, phone and fax numbers in each record, leading to more duplication.

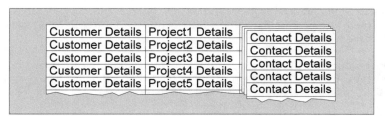

We, therefore, had to remove redundant or duplicated information from individual records and from different records. This, as we mentioned, is the first stage of normalizing our database. We could certainly see that our contact detail fields produced redundancy - there could have been many of them that were empty. And, of course, if we dealt with the same contact over several projects their details were repeated each time we entered a project record. While the customer's details were not repeated in any one record, they may well have been repeated in the table by occurring more than once in different records. So we had to remove both these areas of duplication.

The solution we came to, using just pure common sense, was to split the information into three tables. Each table would then store only one occurrence of a particular entity - each customer, contact or project would only be stored once. As we examined this further, we discovered that the root of all our data was the customer. A customer could have more than one contact and more than one project, so we constructed the three tables with the customer as the 'root'.

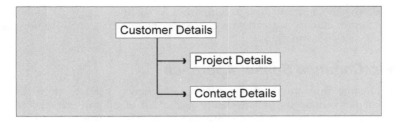

Using a Primary Key in Our 'Common Sense' Approach

To allow us to link each customer record with the correct contact and project records, we inserted a special 'key' field into each table. In the customer details table, this was implemented using the special Access **AutoNumber** field type, which automatically produces a unique value for each record. Next we arranged for the key value for each customer to be stored in the key field of their matching records.

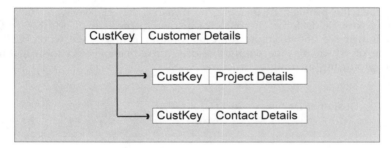

We then looked at how we could provide a **primary key** for each table. This is a unique value which identifies each record and acts as the main index, setting the order of the records in the table. In the Customer Details table, the CustKey field became the primary key because we knew it would always be a unique value. However, in the contacts and projects tables, the CustKey field could contain several instances of the same value, because a customer could have more than one contact or project associated with them.

To enable us to produce an identifier key for the contact and project tables, we gave them their own unique key, again using an AutoNumber type field. We combined their key fields with the customer key field to produce the primary key for these two tables.

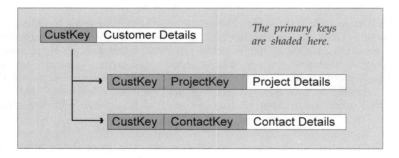

The primary keys are shaded here.

This is where we left the design in Part 1. We have been using it successfully, so are we safe to assume it's correct? Well if we apply the rules to it, there are some problems - as we'll see.

The Stages of Refining Your Tables

We've seen the first stage in refining tables. However, there are several stages that we must go through to perfect the design. Just removing the extraneous information from our database isn't enough, as you will see. The four stages are:

 Removing duplicated or redundant data.

Providing a minimum unique identification key in each table.

Solving all cases of functional dependency in records.

Taking into account stability and security in table design.

So we need to check that our tables conform at each stage. Don't worry if you don't understand these terms yet, we'll explain them and discuss why you need to carry out each stage in just a moment.

Each stage helps the database attain a **normal** form. After the first stage, the database is said to have attained **first normal form**. After the second stage the database attains **second normal form**. For our database to be considered normalized, we need it to have attained **third normal form** which is achieved after we've solved all cases of functional dependency This isn't as bad as it sounds - all it means is that we must check that the fields in each record are actually required to be in their table and not in another table. The fourth and final stage just involves the tidying up of our database design.

FYI If you study the traditional rules for normalization of databases you will see that we have simplified the process a little. Normalization can be achieved using a purely mathematical-type approach and can consist of more, and different, stages to the process we will be using. However, you'll find that our methods provide a far more intuitive view of the process and ultimately produce as good a result.

To design and normalize any database successfully you must have a fairly good knowledge of what the data actually represents. Many of the stages involve judging what values will be stored (how large they're likely to be, in what format they need to be stored) and how they relate to one another. While you can apply rules broadly across a database design and check if it conforms, you may find that some of the questions involve a real appreciation of how the data will be used. This is another case where, if you were creating a design for a third person end-user, only they would be able to provide the answers.

Removing Duplicated or Redundant Data

We should already have accomplished first normal form by splitting the original table up into three separate tables. In each table there are no obvious fields which form repeating groups that could be removed - either in the same record or in different records. Those that do contain repeating data, such as the project name, cannot be removed without losing information. So we must accept that many of the records may contain the value 'Accounts System' for instance - this information is not **redundant**.

In general, we remove duplicated or redundant data by moving the fields concerned into a new table and providing a link between it and the original table. The records in the new table can then be referenced to the correct ones in the original table. This link is maintained by adding a key field to both tables and placing in these fields the same value for records each side of the link.

1st Normal Form: The Rule.

No records should contain information that is redundant - i.e. repeated in a single record or in several records in the same table. Removing unnecessary duplication and redundancy satisfies the conditions for the table to be considered in 1st Normal Form

Providing a Minimum Unique Identification Key in Each Table

We've also already provided a unique identifier for each table. We added AutoNumber type fields to each table which Access will maintain for us by storing a unique number in each one. This unique identifier is called the primary key and must contain different values for every record in the table. We used the CustKey field in the Customer table for this and combined the CustKey, ProjectKey, CustKey and ContactKey in the other two tables.

However, here is our first problem. The rules insist that the primary key must be the **minimum** required to uniquely identify a record - no element (or attribute) of the key can be removed without losing this uniqueness. We implemented the ContactKey and ProjectKey fields as AutoNumber types, so these alone will produce a unique value in each table. Therefore, our multiple-field primary key is wrong. The primary key for each table only needs to contain the actual record key, rather than a combination of the customer and record key. Our design then looks like this.

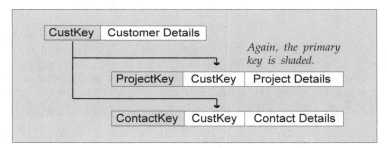

Again, the primary key is shaded.

In general, we provide a minimum unique identification key by using an AutoNumber type field, or by specifying one field to be indexed with no duplicates allowed and telling Access that this is the primary key for the table. When we create a new table without creating a primary key, Access can automatically add an AutoNumber field and make it the primary key for that table. Once a field has been marked as the primary key, Access will not allow us to store duplicate values in it.

2nd Normal Form: The Rule.

It must not be possible to remove any attribute of the primary key of the table without losing the uniqueness of this key. Achieving a minimum unique key for the records in a table satisfies the conditions for it to be considered in 2nd Normal Form

Solving All Cases of Functional Dependency in Records

This rather complicated phrase really means that we must check that the data we are storing in each record actually needs to be in the table or can it be put in another separate table. In fact, there are two parts to the process - we must ensure that all the attributes (fields) in a record are functionally dependent on the record key and that none are functionally dependent on other values in the record. Think of it in terms of if the value in our primary key changes, will the data contained in the fields also change? This sounds more than a little complicated, but can easily be explained by looking at our present table design.

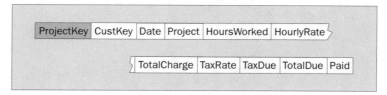

The primary key, we've now decided, is just ProjectKey. And we have to include the CustKey field because it forms the link with the correct customer record. So, are all the other fields necessary? The way to think about it is to look for **functional dependency** - are all of the other fields fully dependent on the value stored in the primary key?

The value in the primary key defines which particular project the record is for, so obviously the date, project name and hours worked are specifically dependent on the project and therefore are dependent on the primary key. The same applies to the Paid field - it tells us if we've been paid for that particular project. But what about the others? Does the hourly rate depend on the type of project, for instance do we always charge the same rate for Accounts Systems? Here we have to have direct knowledge of how the data is going to be used. If we set up the system in such a way that it always charges the same, we could end up severely limiting the user's options. We will, instead, assume that the contract for each project is negotiated and so the rates depend on the actual project itself (and hence the ProjectKey) and not the type of system.

This is a fine example of how an attribute, or field, could have been functionally dependent on another attribute in the record and not on the primary key. And our table contains several others. For instance, what is the tax rate dependent on? It could be that we apply a standard rate for all projects, in which case the tax rate is not dependent on *any* of the other fields and should not be included in the table at all. Or perhaps it's dependent on the type of project and so again, must be removed from the table. We could do this by creating a **look-up table** which stores the different tax rates for each type of project (a look-up table is simply a separate reference table). When we want to know the tax rate, we just look up the project type in one column and read off the tax rate from the other. So we would use a table like the following.

Project	TaxRate
Accounts System	10%
PC Support	12%
Menu Generator	6%

This gives us another advantage: if the tax rate for Accounts Systems is changed to 12%, we simply alter the value in our look-up table and all the existing records would automatically use the new value. If we stored the tax rate in every record we would have to change them all - a much bigger job. So the logic behind normalization can produce a more efficient system.

But what if the tax rate was different for each state we worked in? It may then be dependent on two factors, project and state. No problem - we add another field to the look-up table for the states. Then, when we want to look up a tax rate, we just match the values in both the Project and State fields.

Project	State	TaxRate
Accounts System	FL	10%
Accounts System	WA	12%
PC Support	FL	6%
PC Support	WA	0%
PC Support	NY	8%

The table will contain values for all the types of projects for all the states we work in.

Notice that this table has no single field which contains unique values. To provide a primary key for it will mean including both the Project and State fields - a multiple-field primary key. This is one of the few occasions where this type of primary key is actually required. It is a safe bet because we know that any one combination of Project and State in this table will not be repeated in any other record in the table. If you're confused, think of it this way - it doesn't matter how many Accounts systems there are in Florida, they're all going to have the same tax rate of 10%.

So we can safely use the look-up table for our tax rate. But what actually does happen when the government changes the tax rate in California, or for Warehouse Systems. If we allow the change to be reflected through all our completed projects, we are changing history. When we invoice a customer for work we've done, we charge tax at the rate ruling at that time. Unless we actually store the rate we applied, we can never be sure that our data reflects the truth. We are endangering the **integrity** of our database, because we will lose an item of data that cannot be reconstructed from those that remain. This means that the tax rate actually does depend on the particular project and so we do need to store it in our table.

Of course, you could argue that the tax rate is actually dependent on the date. We could set up a table that stores the rates applicable over different periods of time for each type of project in each state and reconstruct the tax rate for any project that way. However, once the dependency becomes this strained, it is generally best to abandon attempts to remove it. If you're not careful, you can make the structure of your design so complex that it becomes impossible to work with. Remember, we are supposed to be looking for attributes that are functionally dependent.

Are there any other dependencies we should examine? The answer is yes, we have three - TotalCharge, TaxDue and TotalDue. These fields were originally calculated columns in our Excel spreadsheet and got moved into our database table as values rather than formulae. And, to make matters worse, they no longer actually reflect the values from which they were calculated. If we change the value in the HoursWorked field, the totals don't change to match. So they are obviously redundant - in fact, we only left them in at first because we had found no other way of storing the information. But recall queries and calculated controls on forms? They can quite successfully re-create these values, as we demonstrated in Part 1.

If we're right, normalization should remove these fields. Look at the dependencies - obviously these three fields have no functional dependence on the actual project and hence on the primary key. They are entirely dependent on another field (or fields), so they should be removed. We can *always* reconstruct the information they contain from the values in the other fields.

Before we finish, we must check out the Customer and Contact tables. If you look back at these, you'll see that they are much simpler in form. Each stores only the details relevant to that particular customer or contact, such as the name, address, phone number, e-mail address, etc. Each of these is functionally dependent on the primary key of the table and not directly dependent on any other field. While we could possibly argue that the state depends on the town and the zip code depends on the address, trying to replace these with look-up tables is likely to be a pointless exercise. And in any case, they are not functionally dependent in the full sense of the word. There will always be at least two towns with the same name in different states and to find a zip code from an address would mean a look-up table containing every possible address. So we can accept the current design.

3rd Normal Form: The Rule.

Every field in a record must be functionally dependent on the primary key of the record and no field should be entirely dependent on any field (or fields) other than the primary key. Solving all cases of functional dependency for the records in a table satisfies the conditions for it to be considered 3rd Normal Form

Taking into Account Stability and Security in Table Design

Finally, we must consider the practical side of the design. At this stage of normalization, the database has reached **third normal form**. All redundant data has been removed, functional dependencies investigated and the correct primary key assigned. In theory, we have the most efficient design. Now we take into account other factors which may affect it.

A prime example is when we store a lot of data about one entity. For instance, in a factory we may have an inventory of component parts for our products. We give each a unique part number which becomes the primary key, then include all the relevant details that are functionally dependent on the part itself. We could store everything from the price and supplier code to the technical specification and test results. The outcome can be a very long record with a lot of fields.

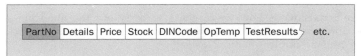

It's likely that the majority of times a user accesses this record, it will be to get information from the Price, Stock and Details fields. We won't often need to access the other fields. By including them all in one table, we're forcing Access to load the whole record each time it wants a value from any field. The way round this is to split the table into two parts, linked with a 'one-to-one' relationship. One table holds all the everyday information and the other the less used data. We'll include the part number as the primary key in each, so that we can always relate the two parts of the record together and so we can rebuild the complete record at any time using a query. The one to one relationship means that when you join the tables, for each record in the first table, there is only one record that relates to it in the second. So you'll only get information on the record you want when you run a query on the tables.

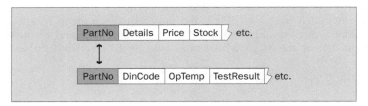

Another case we should consider is security. If we store data about our employees, for instance, the records in the table will include a mixture of information. Obviously, we'll include their name and address, department, position, etc. and these details will need to be quite freely available to many users. However, we're also likely to store confidential information such as their salary and tax details. To prevent unauthorized users gaining access to this, we'd need to implement some clever security around the queries that have access to the table.

An easier solution is to split the table into two, as we did for the parts records. We can then implement different security levels on each table, so that only the appropriate users can access the confidential details.

In general, we should consider how the data in a table will be used and whether we need to implement different security levels on different parts of a table. Then we can split them up to make it easier to control access to data and to make changes to the table structure, and the application parts that use them, less likely to generate errors. We also improve data handling efficiency by limiting frequent accesses to relevant fields only.

Having followed all these steps, we should have restructured the tables and relationships so as to achieve an optimal structure and design.

Adapting Our Design to the New Requirements

Having proved that the basic three-table design is sound, we will now look at the changes we've got to make to incorporate the new requirements - i.e. selling software products as well as carrying out work on different projects. Along the way we'll modify the tables to make them more appropriate to our needs.

Final Modifications to Our Existing Tables

The first thing we'll consider is how we're going to carry out the invoicing process. We've already decided that we don't need a full ledger-based system with tables of invoices and payments and that we'll aim to find a simpler method instead.

The three stages of handling a sale (or project) are:

> Actually making the sale.

> Invoicing the customer for the amount due.

> Getting paid.

These are the only things we're really interested in. So, as long as we can record these three events, we can control the invoicing and payments side of our business. We already know when we've made a sale because a project record will be created at this point. It contains the date, so we also know the date of the sale. Our project record also contains a Paid field which started out as a simple flag ("Y" or empty), but has since been changed into a Date field, so we know when we got paid. All that's left is the invoicing; the most obvious way to handle this is to add an Invoiced field to the project records and insert in it the date we send an invoice out. With these three dates we can tell at any stage which sales have still to be invoiced and what payments are due.

The Customer Table

So let's look at the issues that affect each table, starting with the Customer table.
If a customer doesn't pay us, it's probably wise to stop giving them credit. So we need to know if they're credit-worthy when we attempt to enter a sale and we should plan to store this information. Because it's information about the customer and not dependent on any particular project, we should store it in the Customer table. That way there will be only one occurrence of it per customer and it will conform to our rules of normalization. What we actually put in this field depends on how we intend to monitor 'credit-worthiness'. We could store a maximum credit limit and use a calculated field on the form to show if they are over their limit, or we could just store their total unpaid amount. We could even use it as a simple flag - 'Yes' if we can trust them to pay us and 'No' if we want payment up front.

Ordering of Records

One pertinent point is how we're going to control the order in which records are displayed in our customer forms and reports. At the moment, the primary key will reflect the order that they were entered into the table, because it's an AutoNumber data type. Although we can sort the records by the customer's name, this doesn't always produce the best ordering. For instance, Mr. Jackson will come with the M's instead of the J's and W.S.Arkwright Farming will be next to Williams Supplies instead of next to Aardvark Corporation.

A common solution is to add an extra field to the records and use it to store a text identifier for each customer, so that Mr. Jackson will have the identifier JACKS and W.S.Arkwright Farming becomes ARKWR or similar. A popular type of identifier uses a number as well, so that we could have JACK01, JACK02, etc. It's well within the power of Access to create these automatically, though learning to do this is a bit beyond the scope of this book. What we'll do is to create a 'halfway-house' solution which proposes a value and allows the user to edit it.

So we'll include this type of identifier field in the table and set its indexed property to Yes (No Duplicates) to ensure each one is unique. We could actually use this as the primary key for the table because it meets the requirements of being a minimum unique identifier for each record. And, of course, the table will then always be sorted by alphabetical order of customer.

The only problem we have now is that we can't easily import existing data into the table, because Access can't create this key automatically like it does with an AutoNumber type. So for our application, we'll stick with the AutoNumber primary key and add an Alpha field to store this identifier. We can then sort the table alphabetically by customer when required.

The Project Table

So that's sorted out our Customer table. In the Project table, we've already introduced an Invoiced field and removed the redundant totals fields. The only other changes are the introduction of the MainContactKey (which we discussed in Chapter 6) to link a project to the main contact from that customer and a ProjectMemo field which we'll use to store notes about the projects.

The Contact Table

We don't need to make any structural changes to our Contact table. We'll just change the field layout around to give us a more logical field sequence. It's generally a cosmetic change rather than a necessary one.

Diagrammatic Representation of Our Design

So, the final design for our three tables is complete. Unless you've been taking this down on paper, you'll probably have some difficulty visualizing what the final design actually looks like. Here's a diagram to help you:

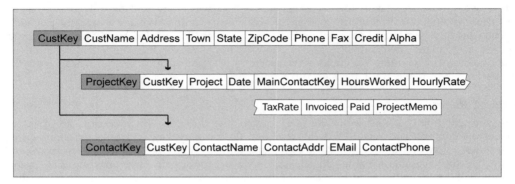

Designing the Software Sales Tables

Now it's time to decide what new tables we need to be able to document our software sales. The first step is to look for any new **entities** that will appear. We identified our original three entities as customers, contacts and projects. Obviously we will also need to store data about each sale, so we can assume that sales is an entity. It could be similar to a project - with values for the date, item, quantity, price, discount, etc. So a software sale record may look like this:

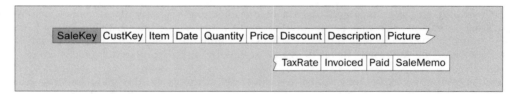

We've got all the information we need for a sale in one record. But remember the rules of normalization. We've used a minimum unique identifier, SaleKey, as the primary key, but some of the fields are not functionally dependent on this key. The description and picture of the item are dependent on the item itself, not the actual sale, so they must be removed.

 Note that Access is able to store pictures (and other objects) in a table. We'll talk more about this in Chapter 12.

We can raise the same arguments about the price and tax rate fields that we did with project records. However, as we found out there, to prevent loss of integrity in our data we have to store the values for each sale. Increases in the price of our software or changes to the discount structure must not affect any existing records in the table. So we cannot use look-up tables for these fields.

We need to place the fields we remove in a separate table. This becomes the Software Stock table and is another entity. In it we can store all kinds of information about our products. It will include a primary key which uniquely identifies each product, rather like a part number, so we can use this key to link a sale to the relevant software item.

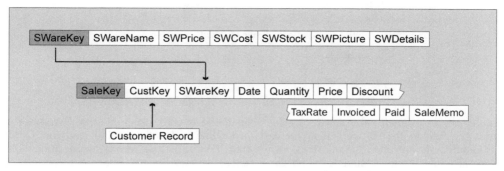

Our sale record then only contains the data that is relevant (and functionally dependent) on the sale itself. And because it contains a CustKey field, we can link it to any customer. The CustKey and SWareKey fields are not the primary key and so can contain duplicated values. Therefore, each customer can have more than one sale and each software stock record can refer to several sale records - both these links are one-to-many.

Now consider what happens when a customer places an order for some software. We add a new record to the Sale table and put the customer key in the CustKey field to link the sale to them. Next we find the item in our stock table and copy the price into the new record, then fill in the rest of the details. But if the customer wants to buy two different items, we've got a problem. The only way round this is to add a new record for each different item - not ideal. And if we add extra fields to the sale record to include more than one item, we're back to the same situation that we had with our contacts in the Customer table. How many items should we allow for? No matter how many we allow for, we'll get repeating groups of fields in each record, several of which may be empty.

Designing the Orders Tables

So we need another table to hold the details of each different product in an order. This is a standard situation when we use a database to store sales of any products. We need to create two tables - one to hold the details about the order itself and the other to hold details of each product line we sell. And again, we link them together with key fields.

One table will be the Order table and the other the OrderLine table. We need to bear our normalization rules in mind as we select the fields for each table. Which attributes of an order are functionally dependent on the order itself and which are dependent on the particular line of the order? Well, we can place the Date, Invoiced, Paid and SaleMemo fields in the Order table because they are constant for the whole order, while the other fields change depending on the software item.

An obvious choice for the primary key in the Order table is the order number; this can be implemented as an AutoNumber data type. We should place a key field in the OrderLine table to hold this value and link it to the correct order. We still need a primary key for the OrderLine table - we'll use an AutoNumber here as well. Notice that we don't need to link the OrderLine table back to the customer by including a CustKey field- it's already linked indirectly through the Order table.

This gives us a design for the software sales side of the overall structure. The **SWareKey** field provides the link to the software item for each order line and both this link and the **OrderNo** link to the **Order** table are one-to-many. This means that if there is one record in our first table, there could be several records related to it. So there can be several lines to one order and each product in the **Software Stock** table can refer to several order lines.

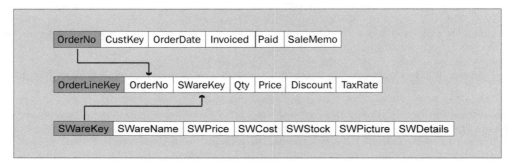

FYI

One interesting point here is that we don't actually need to use a separate **OrderLineKey**. In theory, the combination of the **OrderNo** and **SWareKey** are unique for any record, because no item of software should be repeated on any one order. We could, therefore, use a multiple-field primary key which comprised the **OrderNo** and **SWareKey** fields.

Before we can do this, though, we need to ask the question - will there ever be an occasion when the same item of software appears twice on one order? If we wanted to charge a different rate for two copies of a product (say we gave one half-price for any two purchased) then it would. Again, you have to know exactly how the system will be used before you can make this kind of decision. In our case, we'll stay with the **OrderLineKey** as the primary key for our table.

Our Final Database Design

So now we can put the whole thing together. The final design incorporates all the new tables we've designed and the figure shows the links between them. As usual, we've placed an arrow head at one end of the links to show which is the 'many' end of each one-to-many relationship.

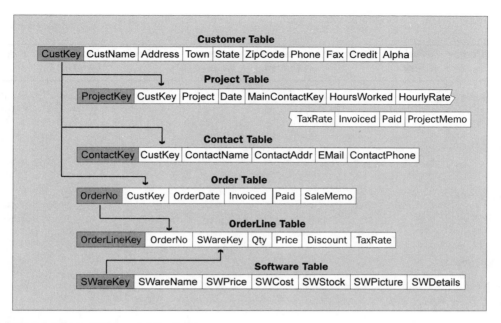

Building the Final Tables

Having decided on the final design for our tables, we can now go ahead and create them.

To save you having to modify the existing Customer, Contact and Project tables and create all the new ones from scratch, we've supplied the finished versions for you. They are in a database called **Part2.mdb** that will have been installed with the other sample files. We described how tables are created in Chapter 4, so we don't need to cover this in depth again. Instead, we'll look at the aspects of the tables that are new to us, including some new types of field.

The Customer Table

Our main table is the Customer table and all the others revolve around it. The field types are shown in the screen-shot here (you can check these in **Part2.mdb**). The table on the following page shows the particular properties we have set for each field. The others are left set to their default, which may just be blank.

The properties in the General tab of each field should look like this:

Customer	Field Size	Format	Decimal Places	Default Value	Required	Allow Zero Length	Indexed
CustKey	Long Integer						Yes (No Duplicates)
CustName	50				Yes	No	Yes (Duplicates OK)
Address	100				No	No	No
Town	30				No	No	No
State	2	!>			No	No	No
ZipCode	10				No	No	No
Phone	20				No	No	No
Fax	20				No	No	No
Credit		Currency	0	0	No		No
Alpha	5	!>			Yes	No	Yes (No Duplicates)

The primary key is CustKey and this is indexed as Yes (No Duplicates). We've indexed the Alpha field in the same way so that the user is forced to enter a unique text identifier for each record.

To decide which other fields to index, we must consider how we will be using the table. We use an index where a field is regularly sorted or searched - either from the toolbar and menu commands, or by a query. This speeds up the operations, but can slow down the entry and editing of records in a table, as Access then has to maintain all the indexes as we work. So we trade off query speed against data entry speed. If a query is used as the basis for a form, it is run each time the form is opened. So if it sorts the records into the correct order for that form, we should index the sorted field to make the form appear more quickly. This is the case with our Alpha field - we'll generally display the records in the order of the Alpha field contents to place the customers in alphabetical order. There's no point in indexing a field which contains the same value in many of the records, such as the State field, and we are unlikely to search or sort on the Phone and Fax fields often. However, it is worth indexing the customer name, as we may need to search for values in this field.

The only items that are Required are the customer name and Alpha identifier - all the others are optional so that we can enter partial details about a customer, then complete them as the rest of the information becomes available.

Notice the entry for the Format property for the State and Alpha fields. This controls how the value is presented on screen, but does not affect the actual stored value. We've used an exclamation mark to force the entry to be left-aligned and a 'greater-than' symbol to force all text into upper case. So if we enter 'james' for the Alpha field, it will appear as JAMES and our states are capitalized as well. You can find a list of available format characters in the Access Help file - search for Format Property.

When we specify a **Format** property in a table and base a form or report on that table, the control that displays the data inherits the same **Format** property. So we don't need to specify it again in the **Properties** window of the control. If we change it in the table, it will automatically change in all the controls based on it. However, we can over-ride the property setting inherited from the table by specifying a new value in the control's **Properties** window.

The Contact Table

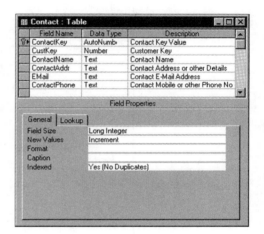

Next, the Contact table. Here the primary key is ContactKey. We've also indexed the ContactName, but allowed duplicates in this field. The CustKey field must have a Field Size property of Long Integer to allow it to be related to the AutoNumber type CustKey field in the Customer table. The only fields that we've specified as Required are the CustKey (to maintain the link with the Customer table) and the ContactName. All the others are optional. Again, you should put in only the fields shown in this screenshot, noting that we are removing the ContactPosition field.

The properties of the General tab of each field look like this:

Contact	Field Size	Decimal Places	Default Value	Required	Allow Zero Length	Indexed
ContactKey						Yes (No Duplicates)
CustKey	Long Integer	Auto	0	Yes		No
ContactName	50			Yes	No	Yes (Duplicates OK)
ContactAddr	100			No	No	No
Email	50			No	No	No
ContactPhone	20			No	No	No

The Project Table

The Project table is a little more complicated. The primary key is ProjectKey and you'll see we've set the Format property to "P "0000.

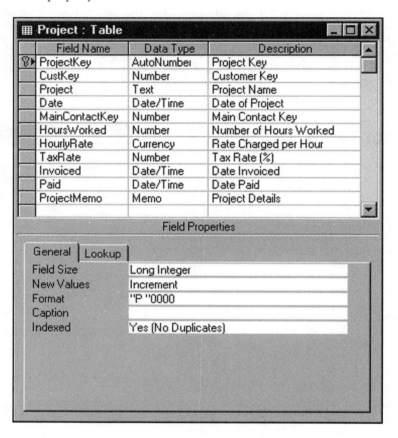

The **Format** property displays the part of the string in quotation marks actually as part of the string. The four zeros just denote the amount of digits in the key. For example, a key with this format would read **P 0123**.

This displays the value from the field as though it were a project number - P 0156, for instance. This will be useful when we come to produce invoices. It doesn't affect the value stored in the table.

The field properties on the General tab look like those shown opposite:

Project	Field Size	Format	Decimal Places	Default Value	Required	Allow Zero Length	Indexed
Project Key		"P "0000					Yes (No Duplicates)
CustKey	Long Integer		Auto	0	Yes		No
Project	25				Yes	No	No
Date		Medium Date		Date()	Yes		No
Main Contact Key	Long Integer		Auto	0	No		Yes (Duplicates OK)
Hours Worked	Double Number	General	Auto		Yes		No
Hourly Rate		Currency	2	50	Yes		No
TaxRate	Single	Fixed	2	10	Yes		No
Invoiced		Medium Date			No		No
Paid		Medium Date			No		No
Project Memo					No		No

The CustKey link field is again Required and a Long Integer. The other Required fields are Project, Date, HoursWorked, HourlyRate and TaxRate. We've also used a Long Integer field of Number type to provide the link to the main contact for each project.

You'll see we've set the Default property for the Date field to Date(). This is the Access function that returns the current date and so it will automatically enter the date set in the computer's operating system when we enter details of a new project. The Default for the HourlyRate field is 50 and for the TaxRate field we've used 10. The user will be able to change the values as they enter a record.

FYI

The **Default** property sets the value for the field when a new record is added, but does not affect modifications to existing records. Default values are very useful if you know what the likely value of a field is. For instance, if most of our customers are likely to be in New York we can use "NY" as the default for the **State** field. If the customer is elsewhere, the user can still change the value as they wish.

You'll notice that we haven't used the Percent format for the TaxRate field. Whether you wish to do so depends on how you expect your users to enter the values. For example, if you enter 10 into a percent-formatted field, Access displays the value as 1000%. To get 10% you have to enter 0.1 (which is, after all, 10 percent).

Most users are likely to type in the percentage as a normal number rather than a value less than one, so by using a Fixed format we can store and display the number in a more intuitive way. It just means we've got to keep this in mind when we perform any calculations with the value.

Fixed Format Numbers and Memo Fields

When we set the Format property for a field to Fixed we are instructing Access to always display the value it contains as a number and, where appropriate, include a decimal point and any required digits after it. We can also control the number of digits after the decimal place, by setting the Decimal Places property. The default is Auto, so Access would display values such as:

3.2154   4   71.4

If we set the Decimal Places property to 2, however, they would be displayed as:

3.22   4.00   71.40

The only unfamiliar field type is the Memo field. This is simply a text-type field which can hold up to 1.2Gb of information and is useful for storing unstructured information, such as notes about a project, or other details. We'll see it in use as we develop the application.

The Software Stock Table

This table will hold details of all our software stock. Notice it contains an OLE Object type field to hold the picture of the software. This type of field can be used to hold any object from an application that supports **OLE** (Object Linking and Embedding), or an **OLE Package** created with Object Packager. We'll discuss OLE in detail in Part 3 of this book.

Here the primary key is SWareKey and we've used the Format property so that it displays as WS 016 or similar. We've specified that the software name is indexed and that it, plus the price, cost and stock values are Required. The picture and details (another Memo field) are optional.

Software	Field Size	Format	Decimal Places	Default Value	Required	Indexed
SWareKey		"WS "000				Yes (No Duplicates)
SWareName	50				Yes	Yes (Duplicates OK)
SWPrice		Currency	2	0	Yes	No
SWCost		Currency	2	0	Yes	No
SWStock	Integer		0	0	Yes	No
SWPicture					No	
SWDetails					No	No

The Order Table

The Order table holds the global details of an order and the individual order items are stored in the OrderLine table. They are linked by the OrderNo field.

Order	Field Size	Format	Decimal Places	Default Value	Required	Indexed
OrderNo		"S "0000				Yes (No Duplicates)
CustKey	Long Integer		Auto	0	Yes	No
OrderDate		Medium Date		Date()	Yes	No

Table Continued on Following Page

Order	Field Size	Format	Decimal Places	Default Value	Required	Indexed
Invoiced		Medium Date			No	No
Paid		Medium Date			No	No
SaleMemo					No	No

The Order table has the primary key field OrderNo and, again, we've used the Format property to give a letter and number format such as S 0415 for the order number. It uses a Long Integer field of Number type - CustKey - to link it with the correct customer and this and the order date are Required. The Default property automatically sets the OrderDate to today's date for new records, though it can be changed by the user afterwards.

The OrderLine Table

Finally, the OrderLine table. This has the OrderLineKey as the primary key and two Long Integer fields to link it to the correct order and software item.

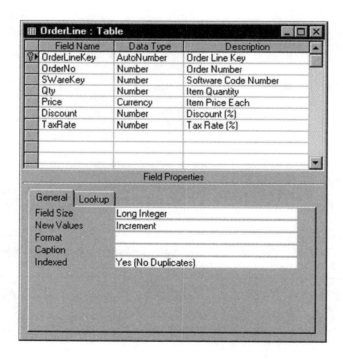

OrderLine	Field Size	Format	Decimal Places	Default Value	Required	Indexed
OrderLineKey						Yes (No Duplicates)
OrderNo	Long Integer		Auto	0	Yes	No
SWareKey	Long Integer	"WS "000	0	0	Yes	No
Qty	Integer		0	1	Yes	No
Price		Currency	2	0	Yes	No
Discount	Single	Fixed	2	0	No	No
TaxRate	Single	Fixed	2	10	Yes	No

We've used the Default property to set the quantity in new records to 1 and the tax rate to 10. Again, we've used Fixed format fields for the percent values to make entering data easier and more intuitive. All the fields except Discount are Required in this table.

Relating the Tables

Having built all the tables, we just have to link them together to complete our data store. All of the relationships we've used are one-to-many and we'll take advantage of Access's ability to Enforce Referential Integrity and Cascade Updates and Deletes. We created the relationships between the Customer and Contact and Customer and Project tables in Chapter 4, so now we just need to create the new ones for the Software, Order and OrderLine tables.

Try It Out - Relating the Software, Order and OrderLine Tables

1 If it's not already open, load **Part2.mdb** and then open the Relationships window with the Relationships command on the Tools menu. Then open the Show Table dialog by clicking the Show Table button on the toolbar, or right-clicking on the Relationships window and selecting Show Table.. from the short-cut menu that appears.

2 Select the Order, OrderLine and Software tables by holding down the *Ctrl* key while you select them with the mouse. Click Add, then click Close to close the window.

3 Link the Customer table to the Order table by dragging the CustKey field from the Customer table and dropping it on the CustKey field in the Order table. Set the options for Enforce Referential Integrity, Cascade Update Related Fields and Cascade Delete Related Records so that they are ticked. Then click Create.

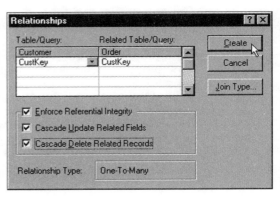

4 Link the Order table to the OrderLine table by dragging the OrderNo field from the Order table and dropping it on the OrderNo field in the OrderLine table. Set the options Enforce Referential Integrity, Cascade Update Related Fields and Cascade Delete Related Records to 'on'.

5 Link the Software table to the OrderLine table by dragging the SWareKey field from the Software table and dropping it on the SWareKey field in the OrderLine table. Set the options Enforce Referential Integrity, Cascade Update related Fields and Cascade Delete Related Records to 'on'. That completes the linking of the tables.

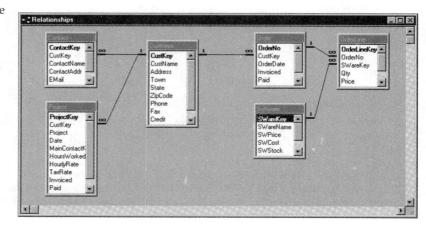

Now the Relationships window should look similar to the screenshot, although your table might be in a different position to ours. Once you're happy that the relationships are right, close the window down and save the relationships.

Using the Table and Lookup Properties

You've seen that each field in a table has separate properties, but Access also provides properties for each table as a whole. If you have a table open, you can select Properties form the View menu and Access will display the Table Properties dialog.

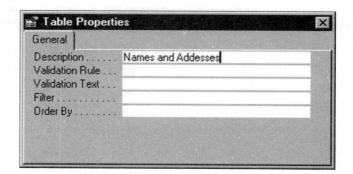

The Description property is used to identify the table in the Database window. If you turn on Details view by right-clicking the Database window Tables list and selecting View then Details (or by selecting Details from the View menu), Access shows the description along with the other details of the table. We've provided descriptions with our tables so that you can see them in the Database window. You should get into the habit of writing your own in this property each time you create a new table.

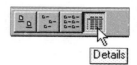

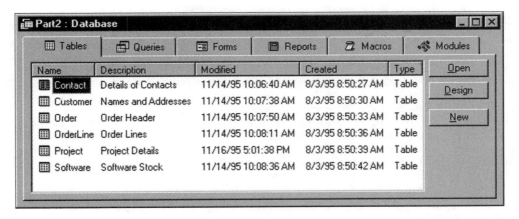

The Table Properties dialog also contains a Validation Rule property and the corresponding Validation Text property. The validation rule for an individual field, which you set in the Field Properties section of the table design window, applies only to the value of that field. However, the validation rule for the table can be used to ensure, for example, that a particular combination of fields meets the required criteria.

Let's say you have two fields in a record where only one is actually required, but it could be either - in other words, as long as the user fills in *one* of them you can accept the record. You can't check this in the Validation Rule of the fields, because this only applies to each one individually. And you can't set the Required property, because you don't know which one will be filled in. The solution is to place an expression in the Validation Rule of the whole table which checks that one or the other is completed.

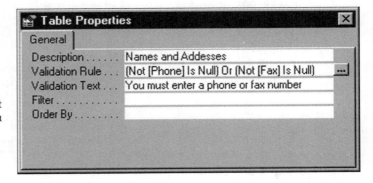

We've entered the expression:

(Not [Phone] Is Null) Or (Not [Fax] Is Null)

for the Validation Rule in the properties of the Customer table. If we now try and enter a record in the table which has neither a Phone nor a Fax number, Access displays the Validation Text message and will not save the record. You can create the validation rule using Expression Builder - just click the builder button that appears when you place the cursor in the property.

The other two properties allow you to control how the records are displayed when the table is opened in table view. You can specify the name of a Filter to limit the records which are included and the name of a field in the Order By property to determine the order in which the records are sorted.

The Lookup Properties Tab

When we looked at table design in general, way back in Chapter 4, we briefly mentioned the properties on the Lookup tab of a table's fields. We'll examine these a little closer now and create a look-up field for our Customer table. A look-up field provides a list of values that the user can select from, displayed as a drop-down list - like a combo box on a form.

You can create a look-up field in two ways, either by setting the properties by hand or by using the Lookup Wizard. In Chapter 8, we saw how to create a combo box which displayed a list of values from the table, such as a list of customers, and allowed the user to select one of the existing customers or enter a new one. By setting the Lookup properties, you can achieve the same effect in the design of a table. This control will then be used automatically when you place the field on a form, including all the property settings from the Lookup tab.

We'll set the properties for a look-up field using Lookup Wizard, then see what it has done in the Lookup tab properties afterwards.

Try It Out - Creating a Lookup Field

1 In **Part2.mdb**, open the Project table in design view. Select Lookup Wizard.. from the drop-down list in the Data Type column for the CustKey field.

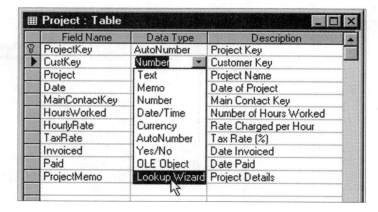

2 Access starts Lookup Wizard and the first window asks if we want to use a table or query for the values in the look-up list, or type them in ourselves. Select the option which reads 'I want the lookup column to look up values in a table or query'.

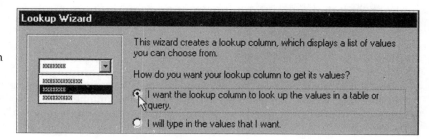

314

3 Click <u>N</u>ext. We must now tell the wizard which table to take the values from. Select Customer - we want to display a list of existing customers from the Customer table so that the user can select the one they want for a project.

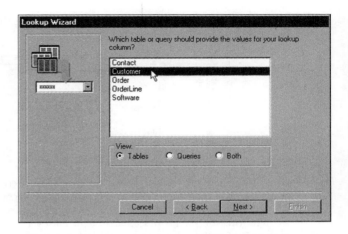

4 Click <u>N</u>ext. Here we can select the fields we want to include in the list - select CustKey, CustName and State.

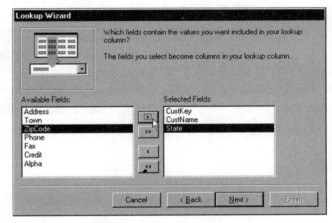

5 Click <u>N</u>ext again. Now we get to see how the list will look. However, the CustKey column is not visible straight away because Access has suggested hiding it. Turn off the Hide Key Column checkbox and the column comes back into view.

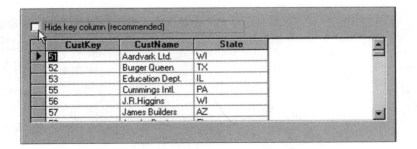

6 Change the columns to the correct width by placing the cursor on the divider between the fields in the title bar and clicking and dragging.

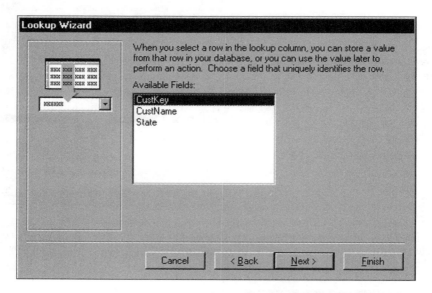

7 Click Next and we've just about finished. We need to tell Access which column from the three contains the value we want to store in our Lookup field. In other words, when we select one of the rows from this drop-down list of values from the Customer table, which of the values in that row should be placed in the CustKey field of the Project table? The one we want is obviously CustKey, so make sure that the field name is set to this.

8 Click Next again and we just have to set the name for the Lookup column. Access suggests the current name as the default - just accept this and make sure that the Display Help option is not ticked.

9 Click <u>F</u>inish. Access prompts you to save the changes to the design of the table. Click <u>Y</u>es, then change to datasheet view and click in the CustKey column of the table. The drop-down list appears showing all the customer key numbers together with a reminder of which customer they refer to. You can then select any of the values from the table.

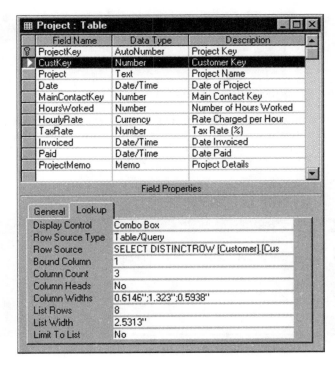

How It Works

Switch back to design view, click on the CustKey field row and open the Lookup tab in the Field Properties.

Lookup Wizard has set the Display Control to Combo Box and the Row Source Type to Table/Query - just what we would have expected. The Row Source is an SQL statement which selects the customer key, name and state from the Customer table. Click the builder button at the right-hand end of the property entry to see the QBE grid. The query selects the three fields, but it doesn't sort them. So select Ascending in the Sort row for the CustName column, then close the query and save the changes.

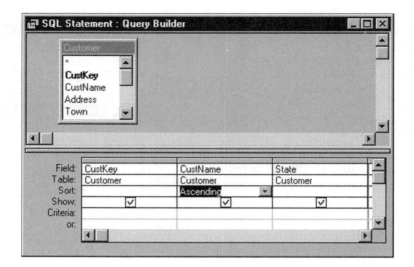

The Bound Column property of the CustKey field is 1, which tells Access that the value from column 1 of the drop-down list is to be placed in the field when we make a selection.

 Note that **Bound Column** does not define which value is shown in the list on screen - the first value in the list is always shown by default. **Bound Column** specifies which value is placed in the control - this will become clearer in the next chapter.

The Column Count is 3, which tells Access to display three columns in the list (the three returned by our query) and the Column Heads is No, so there are no column headings in the list.

For the Column Widths property the wizard has entered 0.6146";1.323";0.5938" which, of course, are the widths we made each of the three columns. (If your machine is set up to use other than US measurements, they will be shown in cm instead.) The List Width is set to the total width of the actual list. You can change the settings for Column Widths and List Width to suit your data.

The other two properties allow you to specify the number of rows that are displayed in the list - set List Rows to 20 to make it easier to select a customer - and whether new values can be entered or only ones that are already in the list. If you set Limit To List to Yes and enter a value that's not already in the table, Access displays an error message and prevents the value being entered in the table.

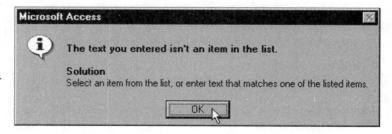

As well as displaying a choice of values in table datasheet view, look-up fields have another use. When you are creating a form and drag a field from the Field List onto it to create a control, Access uses the Lookup property to decide what type of control to use. If it's set to Combo Box, Access creates the complete combo box including the query and other settings that you place in the Lookup tab of the table. If you always intend to use a particular type of control for a field, this can save a great deal of time when you're building forms. As well as Combo Box and the default Text Box, you can create Lookup properties for List Boxes and Checkboxes - depending on the data type of the field.

Now your design is complete and your database is full of information. In the next chapter we'll make it start to resemble a full application.

Summary

In this chapter, we started with a look at the overall concepts required for a successful database design. We identified six main stages:

- Analyze the requirements.
- Design the structure and interface.
- Design and build the data store.
- Build the queries to bridge the gap.
- Build the forms and reports.
- Link the objects together.

We've covered the first three in this chapter - basing it on the tables we've already been using in Part 1, which, after all, seemed to work fine. Along the way we developed them to store data in a more suitable fashion and found a simple way to control the invoicing task.

We also added extra parts to the basic structure and designed tables so that we can use our database to manage the sale of software products as well as for carrying out work on particular projects for our customers.

Having stabilized the design, we then went on to build the tables we'll need. We now have the data store ready and can start constructing an interface round it. This is the subject that the next few chapters will address.

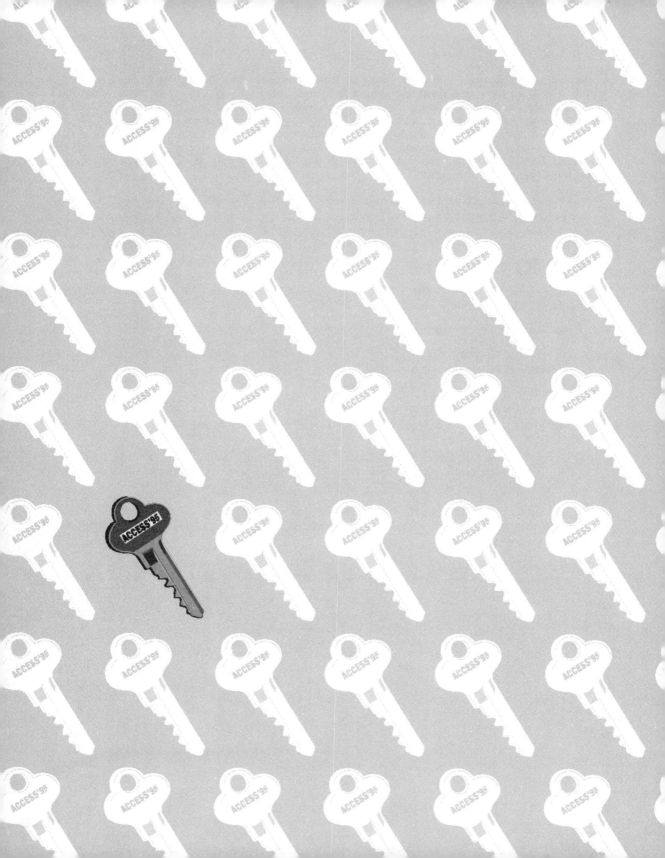

Constructing The Interface

The next step in our design process is to construct the objects that make up the interface between the tables and the user. This involves, as you saw in Chapter 7, the use of **forms**, which allow us to build attractive screen windows and add extra functionality to the process of entering and viewing data. For instance, we can control which fields are available for editing, calculate values from the data, and make the whole thing a lot more intuitive than editing a table directly.

The aim of this part of the book is to turn our existing **database** into an **application**. When designing the interface, we must bear in mind that the user probably has no knowledge of how Access works. It is our job to offer an intuitive and highly controlled environment, which requires no special knowledge to navigate. It must appear as a program specifically designed for the task in hand. This is what we mean by 'turning a database into an application'.

During this chapter, we will cover:

> An introduction to macros.

> Opening and closing forms with buttons.

> Using multiple subforms.

> Basing forms on queries.

> Handling Record Updates in subforms.

> Error trapping.

Automating the Interface

You'll recall that the main tasks we identified in the previous chapter were based around three forms:

> The Customer and Contacts form is used for viewing and editing details of each customer and the people we work with there.

> The Projects and Sales form is where we enter, edit and view the details of each project we carry out and each software sale we make.

> The Software Stock (or Catalog) form is used to view and edit information about the different items of software that we stock and sell.

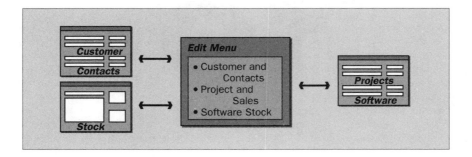

We are going to look at the first two forms in this chapter, then move on the software form in Chapter 11. We don't intend to go into detail on the methods of creating forms and queries, as we covered this in Part 1, but we still have a few things to learn about the objects used in the construction of an application's interface.

Well, we promised a change of style in this part. Rather than getting you to create the whole application by hand, we are going to give you the almost complete application (**WroxSoft.mdb**), and then go back and analyze the methods used to create each of its sections. You'll find that the application is just a natural extension of the concepts you have learned in the first part of the book. Before you think life is getting too easy, though, note that you'll still have to modify and tweak parts of the application yourself, as well as learn how to program the interface!

The Sample WroxSoft Application

Load up **WroxSoft.mdb** and play around with it a bit to see how it works.

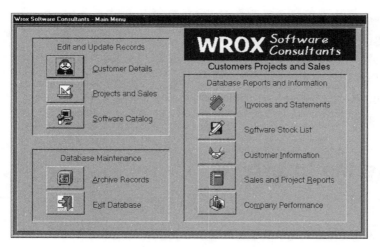

The **WroxSoft** application is designed for use in SVGA screen mode or better, i.e. at least 800 x 600 resolution. If your system is set up for VGA (640 x 480), you will find that the screen forms overlap the edges of the screen. However, Access will add scroll bars to the main window so that you can see all the forms by scrolling them.

The Special Toolbar

Once you start the application, you'll find that the menu bar changes. The menu commands are all for actions specifically designed for the user of the application. We've also included a special toolbar so that you can 'get inside' the application to view and edit the objects. This includes the Design View and Database Window buttons. Once you switch to design view, the usual Access menus reappear and you can use Access in the normal way.

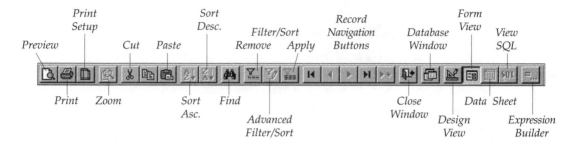

Bear in mind that we've included these buttons for the purposes of this book - to allow you to examine the way the application is built up. In a normal application, you will most likely want to 'lock' the application by omitting these buttons. There will then be no way to switch to design view - your users will only be able to open and close the objects that you allow them access to.

FYI

If you hold down the *Shift* key while an Access database is loading, it will not start running automatically, as our sample does. You will find yourself instead at the database window. If you find you have locked yourself out by changing or hiding the toolbar, you can use this method to get access again. Just exit the application, then reload it while holding down *Shift*. You can also show the **Database** window by pressing *F11*, though it is possible to prevent this, as you'll see in Chapter 13.

Introducing Macros

The application looks very different from our initial attempts at forms and reports. However, there are not as many new things involved as you might think. The magic that we have used to automate the interface and make it more user-friendly is all based on the use of **macros**. It is macros that make the buttons work when you click them, enabling you to switch from one form to another, open reports and generally navigate through the application. Macros are small portions of code which usually correspond directly to actions that the user could perform. You can, therefore, use macros to automate the repetitive tasks within an application. You'll see what we mean if we take a look at some simple ones within our database.

Macros in Action

Go into the Customer Details form. You'll see that we've used a combo box for the Town and State fields. This means the user can select these entries from a list, which not only saves them a bit of typing, but also ensures (as far as possible) that spelling mistakes are avoided - which is useful if the user is likely to sort the records in a report by town or state. If you go to a new record (click the **New** button) and select a town from the drop-down list, you'll see that the state is filled in automatically. You can still change it if the application gets it wrong, but is another technique that helps speed up data entry.

323

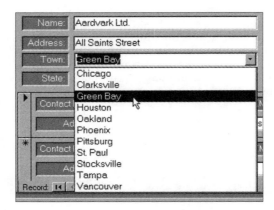

While you've got a new record open, enter a name for the customer and press *Tab*. As soon as you move to the next field, the customer ID (the **Alpha** field) is filled in with a suggested customer identifier, which you can then edit if you wish. This is all done with macros.

The Difference between Code and Macros

There are two ways of automating the interface in Access. As in many other applications, you can use either code or macros. These are important terms and it is vital that you understand the distinction between them.

Macros are list of commands that are executed at the click of a button. They mimic the user's movements within the database and perform actions that the user could carry out. Hence they are useful for simple and repetitive tasks, though they can be used for a lot more.

Code can be broken down into two types:

> **Visual Basic for Applications** (VBA) - Access contains an implementation of Microsoft's new standard Visual Basic language. Unlike a macro, this can be used to control almost every aspect of your application.

> **Structured Query Language** (SQL). We've already talked about how you can manipulate data using SQL. This is the language that controls the interaction between Access and the database tables.

To give you an idea of what the different methods can accomplish, have a look at the following table. It shows some common tasks and specifies which of the three methods you would normally use to carry them out.

Task	Macros	VBA	SQL
Open and close forms and reports	✓	✓	✗
Change the appearance of the interface	✓	✓	✗
Change the values in form and report controls	✓	✓	✗
Change the values in fields of a table	✓	Via SQL	✓
Add or delete records in a table	✗	Via SQL	✓

As you can see, Visual Basic for Applications is a very powerful way to control your application. We do not intend to go into detail about VBA in this book - the learning curve can be steep and no doubt you'll agree that you have enough on your plate for the moment. However, we should point out that VBA does have many advantages over macros and, once you've mastered the basics of using Access, you should plan to move on to learning VBA. Look out for our sister publication *'The Beginner's Guide to Access 95 Programming with VBA'*.

The advantages of VBA include the fact that it:

> Provides greater functionality than a macro.

> Can help trap errors.

> Is easier to read and makes the database easier to maintain.

> Is faster to execute than macros.

> Is common to many Microsoft Office applications.

Structured Query Language is basically a way of manipulating the information stored in tables or recordsets created from tables, and is not designed for manipulating the user interface. As we've seen already, it is the base upon which Access queries are built.

We do not use VBA at all in our application. There is actually very little complex processing to be done - mainly switching between forms and reports, and looking up values, and this can be done with macros. Indeed, macros are often used because they are both quicker and simpler to build than writing VBA code. We can also use macros to execute SQL statements and this provides a means of achieving the only thing that macros can't cope with on their own - adding and deleting records.

A More Detailed Definition of a Macro

A macro is a set of instructions, such as OpenForm or SetValue, each of which cause Access to carry out a specific task. The individual instructions are referred to as **macro actions**, though the term 'macro' is often used to refer to both the single lines of a macro, as well as the whole thing. You build a macro by selecting the macro actions that you require from the set provided by Access. In most cases, you also supply **arguments** with a macro action to tell Access which objects or values to use. Arguments can be constructed using Expression Builder. Macros are written and stored on **macro sheets** and these can be seen and manipulated using the Macros tab in the Database window.

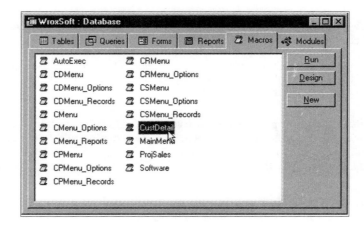

In general, we place several macros on one sheet, and use different sheets for different objects. So, for example, the CustDetails macro sheet contains all the macros for the Customer Details form. This way, if we want to copy a form from one database to another, we can be sure that all the necessary macros go with it by just copying the relevant macro sheet.

You have seen the macro that suggests a customer ID at work. We'll start by creating a macro similar to this one.

Try It Out - Using a Macro to Propose the Customer Identifier

When a user enters a name of a customer in the Customer Details form, and then moves to the next field, the customer's identifier is filled in automatically. The user can, however, still edit the suggestion. We will build a macro similar to this one, creating an identifier that uses the first five characters of the customer's name, converted to upper case.

1 From the main menu of **Wroxsoft.mdb**, click the Close Window button on the toolbar to close the main menu. (If you entered a town and customer name as prompted above, you may get a message saying that you cannot save the record at this time. Don't worry about this - you don't want to save it anyway.)

2 Click the Database Window button to show the Database window, and open the Forms list. Create a new blank form by clicking the **New** button. In the New Form dialog, select Design View in the top window and the Customer table in the drop-down list below. Click OK.

3 Drag the CustName and Alpha fields from the Field List window to the form to create the two text box controls. Re-size the CustName text box to make room for the customer's name.

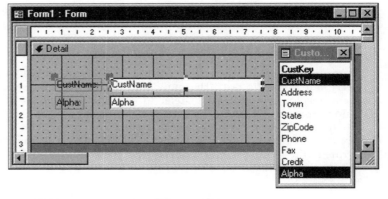

4 Save the new form by clicking the Save button on the toolbar. In the Save As dialog, enter the name TestForm and click OK.

We want to create a macro that supplies the customer ID when the user moves to another control, *after* changing the value in the CustName control. To do this, we can use the CustName control's After Update property.

> **FYI**
>
> The **After Update** property is on the **Event** tab of the **Properties** window. As previously mentioned, an event is simply an occurrence of an action within the database. If you put the name of a macro in this property, Access will run that macro after the user has updated the value in the control.

5 Open the Properties window for the CustName control and select the Event tab. Click in the After Update property. Access shows two buttons: a drop-down list and a builder button.

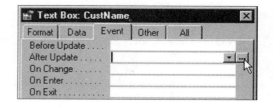

6 Click the builder button and select Macro Builder from the Choose Builder dialog. Then click OK. In the Save As dialog, change the name to TestMacro and save the new macro sheet by clicking OK.

7 Access creates a new blank macro sheet with two columns - Action and Comment. You can use the Comment column to enter any text - it allows you to document the macro so that you can understand it when you come back to it again. Note that wherever you click on the macro sheet, Access displays a hint in the bottom right-hand corner telling you what it expects you to enter. Add a comment to the first line so that we know what the macro does.

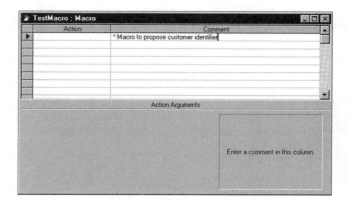

 Macro sheets contain two more columns which are hidden by default. If you turn these on now, they will be displayed for every new macro you create. Select **Options** from the **Tools** menu and click the **View** tab. Make sure that both the checkboxes in the **Show in Macro Design** section are ticked, and click **OK**.

8 Now we can actually start to build our macro. We want it to change the value of the Alpha control (the customer ID), so click in the Action column and select SetValue from the list of macro actions.

 The **SetValue** action requires two arguments which you can see in the bottom of the window. Item is the thing we want to set - in this case the **Alpha** control on our form, and **Expression** is where we tell Access what value to set it to. We can use **Expression Builder** to create both these arguments.

9 Click on the Item argument at the bottom of the macro window, and click the builder button that appears. Access opens Expression Builder.

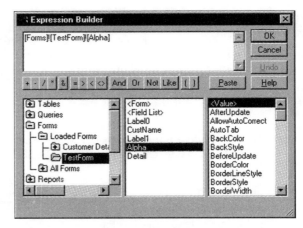

10 Double-click on Forms in the left-hand list, then double-click Loaded Forms and select TestForm - our new form. In the middle window select the Alpha control, and in the right-hand list double-click the <Value> entry. Access places the text Forms![TestForm]![Alpha] in the top window. This tells Access to use the Alpha control on the TestForm.

11 Click OK and the expression is placed in the Item argument on the macro sheet.

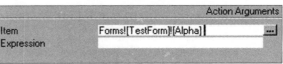

Now we can create the expression that calculates the suggested customer ID. We need to extract the first five characters from the contents of the CustName control, and convert them to upper case. To do this we use two of Access' built-in functions - UCase$ and Left$.

12 Click in the Expression argument and click the builder button to re-open Expression Builder. In the left-hand list, double-click Functions and select Built-In Functions. In the middle list select Text and in the right-hand list double-click on UCase$. In the top window Access places the text:

    UCase$(<stringexpr>)

13 Click on the <stringexpr> argument so that it is highlighted, and double-click on Left$ in the right-hand list. Access replaces «stringexpr» with the Left$ function so that the expression reads:

    UCase$(Left$(<stringexpr>, <n>))

FYI **You might notice that the list of functions also include Left and UCase.** Don't use these - they serve the same purpose but use a different data type and you should be careful not to confuse the two.

14 Click on the new <stringexpr> argument so that it is highlighted. Double-click on Forms in the left-hand list, then double-click Loaded Forms and select TestForm. In the middle window select the CustName control, and in the right-hand list double-click the <Value> entry. Access replaces the <stringexpr> place-holder with the name of the field. Our expression then reads:

    UCase$(Left$(Forms![TestForm]![CustName],<n>))

15 Finally, click on the «n» argument place-holder and type 5 - the number of characters we want. Click OK and Access fills in the Expression argument in the macro sheet. The final expression is:

    UCase$(Left$(Forms![TestForm]![CustName],5))

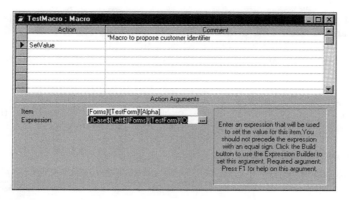

16 Close the macro window by clicking the Close button at the top right of the window, and select Yes to save the changes. Access displays our TestForm with the name of the macro sheet - TestMacro - in the After Update property of the CustName control's Properties window. Now, when the event occurs, i.e. when the value in the CustName control is changed and the user moves to another control on the form, Access will execute our new macro.

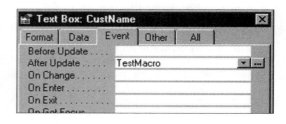

17 Let's try it out. Switch to form view. Access displays the form showing the first record in our **WroxSoft** database.

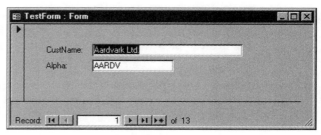

18 So that we don't change any existing customers' details, click the New Record button at the bottom of the form window to go to a new blank record.

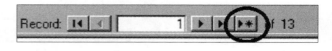

19 Enter a customer's name and press *Tab* to move to the next control. The Alpha control is filled in automatically, using the first five characters of the name you enter.

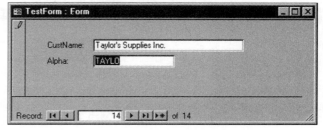

20 Once you've finished experimenting, delete the records you've added to the customer table, then close the form and delete it and the TestMacro macro from your **WroxSoft** application by selecting them in the Database window and pressing *Delete*.

We have calculated a suggested value for the Alpha field and placed it on the form using a single SetValue macro action. This is a very simple example, but it does show you how using Expression Builder can save time and effort when you need to use expressions in arguments for a macro. We even used it to enter just the name of a control for the Item argument - you can use it in most places like this.

Now we'll take a general look at how a macro sheet is used. In the last example we used a macro sheet containing just one macro. If you open the CustDetail macro in the **WroxSoft** application, however, you'll find it contains several macros on one sheet.

Identifying a Macro by Name

If you only place one macro on a sheet, and leave the Macro Name column blank, you can just enter the macro's name in the Event tab. However, if there is more than one macro on a sheet, you cannot do this. Scroll down the sheet to find the macro called SetAlpha (you'll need to turn on the Macro Names column if you haven't already done so).

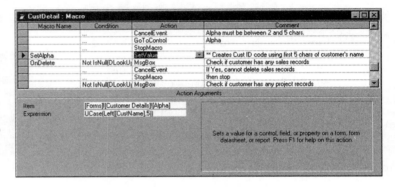

This macro is the same as the one we created for our TestForm, but to identify it when there are several macros on one sheet, we need to give it a name which is unique for that sheet. This means that we can store more than one macro on each sheet, and avoid filling the Macros window with hundreds of individual sheet names. Access starts executing the macro from the first line (where the macro name is) and stops only when it reaches a blank line or a different macro name. To use this macro in an event property, we have to supply the name of the macro, as well as the name of the sheet. So we would set the After Update property of the CustName control to CustDetail.SetAlpha - we place a full stop between the sheet name and macro name.

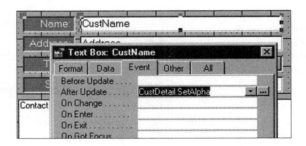

You have now seen how to create a simple macro. We are going to spend the rest of the chapter looking at the Customer Details form and the Project and Sales form, examining in particular how macros are used in them. We'll start with the Customer Details form.

The Customer Details Form

Among the forms we built in Part 1 was the Customer and Contact Details form. We used the Form Wizard to construct this for us, then modified the appearance afterwards. We have added several extra features to this form in our **WroxSoft** application. We've included a header with a title graphic, and a footer with buttons to move to other screens. There is also a combo box in the footer section where you can choose which customer's details you want to view. Then there are buttons to move back and forth through the records, insert a new record, and change the order in which the records are sorted.

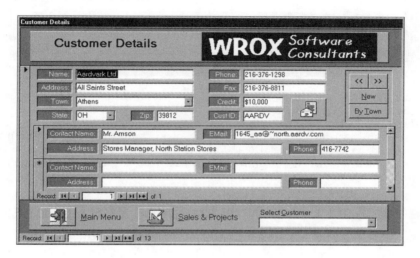

The underlying recordsets for the main and subforms are produced by queries, rather than being based directly on the Customer and Contact tables. We've done this so that the records appear sorted in alphabetical order by customer and contact respectively. You can see the query that does this by opening the Properties window for the form, and looking at the Record Source. It's set to the SQL statement:

```
SELECT DISTINCTROW Customer.* FROM Customer ORDER BY Customer.Alpha;
```

This selects all of the fields from the Customer table and sorts them by the Alpha field as opposed to the CustKey field. If you click the builder button in the Properties sheet, you'll see the query in Query Builder, and by clicking the Datasheet button on the toolbar, you can view the contents of the records.

The Contacts Subform

The Record Source for the Contacts subform, which displays the contact details for each customer, is set to

```
SELECT DISTINCTROW Contact.* FROM Contact ORDER BY Contact.ContactName;
```

so the contact records are displayed in order of the ContactName.

331

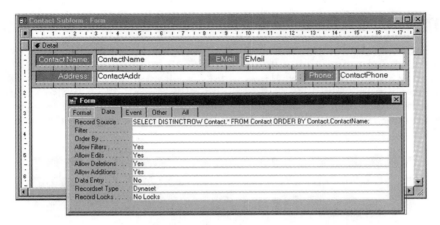

The main and sub-forms are linked together on the CustKey field. You can see this in the Properties sheet for the Contact subform - the Link Child Fields and Link Master Fields are set to CustKey. These two fields govern the way the form and subform interact. The purpose of linking the two is to ensure that the Contacts subform displays the correct contact information for the customer displayed on the Customer Detail form. For example, Mr Arnson should be the contact for Aardvark Limited and when you move to the next record, the contact subform should change to the information relevant to Burger Queen.

Changing the Sort Order with the Click of a Button

Now that we've had a look at how the form works, it's time to delve into some of the automated features. The macro we built in the first example consisted of just one action (SetValue). However, we often need to use several macro actions to achieve the result we want and, in the process, we need to make decisions about which ones to execute.

We use **conditions** to control which actions are performed. A condition is an expression that Access evaluates before it performs an action - if it evaluates to **True** the action is carried out, and if it is **False** the action is ignored. Conditions are entered into the Condition column of the macro grid.

So lets try a multi-action macro which will change the order in which the records in the form are displayed when a button is clicked. At the moment the records are ordered by customer name - the SQL query statement which selects all the fields from the table and sorts them by the Alpha field is as follows:

```
SELECT DISTINCTROW Customer.* FROM Customer ORDER BY Customer.Alpha;
```

To change the sort order we can just specify a different query for the Record Source. This could be the name of a query that we have already created, or an SQL statement with a different **ORDER BY** clause. We'll use the second method so that we don't have to create a separate query in the Database window as this may cause confusion about which query does what. It will also mean that the Customer Details form is more self-contained - if you copy it to another database you won't have to worry about copying the query as well. The SQL statement we need is:

```
SELECT DISTINCTROW Customer.* FROM Customer ORDER BY Customer.Town;
```

All our macro has to do is to set the Record Source property of the form to this statement when a button is clicked.

If you look on the form, you'll see a By Town button. This is what changes the sort order of the records. The By Town button is a special kind of button called a toggle button. It remains depressed when clicked the first time, only rising when you click it again. Therefore, in order to be able to sort the records in the right order, we need to know whether or not the button is pressed. We find this out by checking the **value** of the button, as you'll see in just a moment.

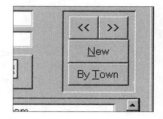

Sorting the Customer Records By Town

If it's not already open, open the Customer Details form in design view by selecting it in the Forms list of the Database window and clicking the Design button. Open the form Properties window. Then click the Data tab to show the data properties for the form. The Record Source is set to the SQL statement:

```
SELECT DISTINCTROW Customer.* FROM Customer ORDER BY Customer.Alpha;
```

This sorts the records by Alpha (i.e. by customer name) when the form is first opened. (Remember that you can use the Zoom window to see the whole statement).

Now select the By Town button on the Customer Details form. You can see from the title of the Properties window that it's named btnByTown. Click the Event tab, and look at the On Click event. It's set to CustDetail.SortByTown. This is the name of the macro that runs when By Town button is pressed. (The SortByTown macro is on the CustDetail macro sheet).

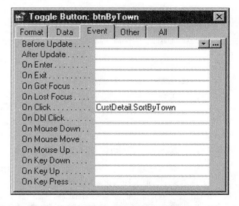

Go back to the Database window and select the Macros tab. Open the CustDetail macro in design view, and find the macro named SortByTown.

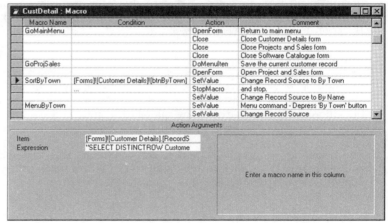

We're going be looking at several macros in this chapter. To make it easier for you to follow, we will to show them in the following format:

Column Name: [Macro Expression]

The Action column contains the name of the macro to be executed. It also takes a set of arguments which appear at the bottom of the macro sheet. We will show these arguments indented from the actual column, like this:

Action: [Macro Name]
   Item: [Macro Argument]

Access doesn't display macros like this, but hopefully it will make analyzing the listings easier.

The SortByTown macro uses three macro actions and a condition:

Condition: [Forms]![Customer Details]![btnByTown]
Action: SetValue
   Item: [Forms]![Customer Details].[RecordSource]
   Expression: "SELECT DISTINCTROW Customer.* FROM Customer ORDER BY
                   Customer.Town;"

Condition: ...
Action: StopMacro

Condition:
Action: SetValue
   Item: ·   [Forms]![Customer Details].[RecordSource]
   Expression: "SELECT DISTINCTROW Customer.* FROM Customer ORDER BY
                   Customer.Alpha;"

How the SortByTown Macro Works

The first action has the condition [Forms]![Customer Details]![btnByTown]. This refers to the <Value> property of the By Town button on the form - if we omit the name of the property the default property is assumed. For most controls, including push buttons and toggle buttons, the default property is its value, and the value of a toggle button is **True** if it's depressed and **False** if not. So the condition [Forms]![Customer Details]![btnByTown] will only be **True** if the By Town button has been pressed.

When you first click the button after opening the form, it will be depressed, so the condition is **True** and the first line is executed. This uses the SetValue action to set the Record Source property of the Customer Details form ([Forms]![Customer Details].[RecordSource]) to the new SQL statement that sorts by the Town field. Notice that we have to enclose the statement in quotation marks. If you omit the quotation marks, Access will assume this is an expression rather than a SQL statement and you will get an error.

The next line has an ellipsis (...) as the condition. This is a short-hand way of repeating the condition from the previous line, and saves Access having to re-evaluate it. So the result of this condition is also **True**. Therefore the StopMacro action is run, which, surprisingly enough, stops the macro. This means the last line of the macro is not run. The records are now sorted by town and the button remains depressed to show us that this is the case.

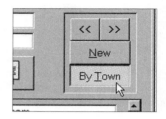

The By Town button is a toggle button, which means that each time you click it, the value changes. You click it to depress it, then click it again to return it to its initial (raised) state. The second time the button is clicked, its value changes from **True** (depressed) to **False** (not depressed) and it initiates another On Click event. This causes the macro to be run again. This time, the condition in the first line ([Forms]![Customer Details]![btnByTown]) is false and so the first macro action is skipped. We move on to the second line, but the condition is still false and this line is skipped as well. There is no condition on the third line of the macro, which means that this action is executed, no matter what the value of the button is. The action uses the SetValue action to set the Record Source property of the Customer Details form ([Forms]![Customer Details].[RecordSource]) back to the SQL statement that sorts by the Alpha field.

Looking Up the State Value

Now that you've seen how **conditions** can be used in a macro, we'll move on to a more complex example. You have seen how our application automatically proposes a State each time you enter or change the name of the town in a customer's record. It does this by looking in the existing records for the value of the town you enter on the form, and returning the value from the State field of the first one it finds. It also disregards records where the State field is empty - remember we have allowed the user to enter customers in the database even if they don't know their full address.

Domain Aggregate Functions

To find the value, we want we use the **DLookup** function. This is one of the **domain aggregate functions**. In Chapter 8 we used SQL aggregate functions to calculate totals and averages on a report. Domain aggregate functions are similar, but we can use them in expressions instead of just in SQL statements and calculated controls. Here are some of the more common functions, and the results they produce:

Function	Result
DLookup	The value in a particular field.
DSum	The total of the values in a field.
DCount	The number of records in the domain.
DAvg	The average of the values in a field.
DMax	The maximum of the values in a field.
DMin	The minimum of the values in a field.

All these have the same syntax as **DLookup** - they use two required arguments and a criteria that is optional. The arguments are:

```
DLookup («expr», «domain», [«criteria»])
```

where:

«expr»	is the name of the field we want to return the value from.
«domain»	is the name of the table we want to look in.
«criteria»	defines the records we want included in the search. If it is omitted, all records from the table are included.

Domain aggregate functions are processed in a different way from other Access functions, and require the arguments to be enclosed in inverted commas. So, to find the value in the State field of the Customer table where the Alpha field contains the value AARDV, we would use the expression:

DLookup ("[State]", "Customer", "[Alpha] = 'AARDV'")

Notice that we enclose the field name in square brackets and each whole argument in double inverted commas. We also have to use single inverted commas to define any parts of the argument that are themselves strings. This isn't necessary if we are looking for a value rather than a string. For example, to include only records where the Credit field is greater that 10000, we would use:

DLookup ("[State]", "Customer", "[Credit] > 10000")

If there is more than one record that meets the criteria when you use **DLookup**, Access chooses the first one. However, the other domain aggregate functions use all the records that meet the criteria to provide the sum, average, count etc.

The power offered by these functions is well worth the extra effort required to use them, and they can be created quite easily using Expression Builder.

Try It Out - Using DLookup to Suggest a State

We are going to set up a macro to automatically supply the state when the user specifies a town. For instance, if the town supplied was San Francisco, the macro would automatically fill in the state as California or CA.

1 Close down any forms that are open and, in the Forms list of the Database window, click New to create a new form. Select Design View in the top window of the New Form dialog and the Customer table as the source of the records for the new form. Click OK.

2 Open the Field List window and drag the Town and State fields to the form to create two text box controls.

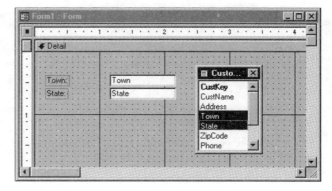

3 Click the Save button on the toolbar to save the form. Enter the name SuggestState and click OK.

4 We want the macro to run when the value in the Town control changes. Therefore, click on this control and open the Properties window. Select the Event tab and click in the After Update property.

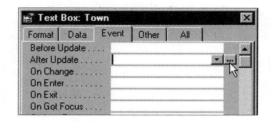

5 Click the builder button and select Macro Builder in the Choose Builder dialog. Enter SuggestState when prompted for the name of the macro, and click OK.

We only need one macro action to actually set the State for our form, but there are other things we must consider. We've allowed the Customer table to contain blank Town fields where we don't yet have the customer's full address. If the user went to change the Town on the form, but then deleted the entry and so left it blank, we will be looking for a Town entry of null in the table, and could find any record that has a blank Town field. So we must first check for a blank in the Town control on the form. Also, after we've filled in the State, we need to ensure that the focus moves to this control, ready for the user to accept it, or change it if we get it wrong - there could be towns with the same name in different states. So our macro is a little more complex than we first thought.

6 In the first row of the new macro we need a condition to check whether the Town control contains null - and if it does we need to stop the macro. The action is simple - StopMacro. Select this from the drop-down list in the Action column.

7 We can create the condition with Expression Builder, even though there is no builder button when you click in the Condition column. Place the cursor in the Condition column of the first row and click the Build button on the toolbar to open Expression Builder.

8 To check for a null value we use the **IsNull** function. In the left-hand list double-click Functions, select Built-In Functions, and in the middle list select Inspection. In the right-hand list double-click on IsNull.

9 We then replace the «varexpr» place-holder with the name of our Town control. Click on «varexpr» so it's highlighted. Double-click Forms in the left-hand list, and then double-click Loaded Forms. Select SuggestState, and in the middle list select Town. Then double-click <Value> in the right-hand list. The complete expression is shown on the next page.

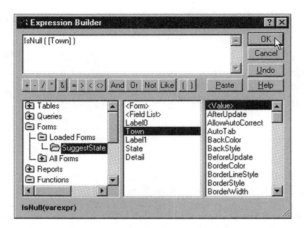

10 Click OK to place it in the Condition column. The macro will now stop if this condition is **True**, i.e. the Town control is blank.

11 If it's not blank, execution moves on to the next line where we need the set the value of the State field. Select SetValue for the Action, and click in the Item argument at the bottom of the macro window. Enter [State] for the argument.

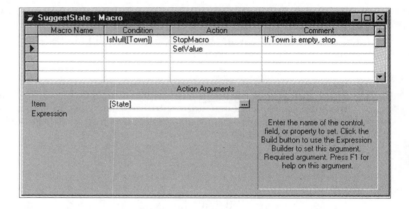

 If the macro is always going to be run from one particular form, we can use this shorthand syntax to refer to the controls on that form. If we just use the control name and omit the form name, Access will assume we are referring to a control on the form that currently has the focus. You need to be a little careful when using this method if you are likely to use the same macro in different places. However, we are quite safe here because it is only executed in the **After Update** event of the **Town** control.

12 Now we need the Expression to calculate the value for the State field. Click in the Expression argument and click the builder button to open Expression Builder. Double-click Functions and select Built-In Functions, then select Domain Aggregate and double-click on DLookup. Access places the function and argument place-holders in the top window.

13 Click on «expr» and type "[State]", which is the field we want to return the value from. Remember to enclose it in inverted commas. Then click on «domain» and type "Customer", which is the table name. Again, remember the inverted commas.

14 Finally, we need to enter the «criteria». Click on it and type:

338

"[Town]=Forms![SuggestState]![Town]"

This limits the records that are included to those where the Town *field* in the table ([Town]) is equal to the Town *control* on the form ([Forms]![SuggestState]![Town]).

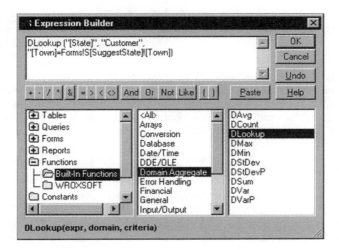

In the **Criteria** argument of a function, Access assumes all the entries refer to the underlying table, not the controls on the form. Hence we have to specify the **Town** control using the full syntax.

15 Click OK to place the criteria in the Expression argument on the macro sheet. Finally, we need to move the focus to the State control. In the third line select the GoToControl macro action and, for the Control Name argument at the bottom of the window, enter State. This is one of the places we cannot use Expression Builder - we just enter the name of the control on the form, omitting the square brackets.

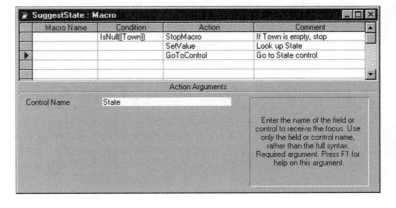

16 Close the macro window by clicking the Close button at the top right of the window and select Yes to save the changes. We can see our SuggestState form with the name of the macro sheet. SuggestState is in the After Update event of the Town control's Properties window. Our macro will run when the event occurs, i.e. when the value in the Town control is changed and the user moves to another control on the form.

17 Now we can try it out. Switch to form view and click the New Record button at the bottom of the form window to go to a new blank record.

18 Enter a value for the town and press *Tab* to move to the next control. The State control is automatically filled in from the Customer table.

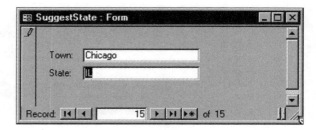

You'll find that you get an error when you try to move to another record or save the current one because, when we created the table, we specified that all new records must have a value for the CustName field and we aren't entering one here. Therefore, you won't be able to enter any *new* records in the table, though you can change existing ones. (When you get the error message, you'll have to press *Esc* twice to clear the values you entered before you can do anything else.)

If you look in the CustDetail macro sheet, you'll find a similar macro named TownChange. The difference is that we've used a slightly more complex criteria:

"Customer.[Town]=[Forms]![Customer Detail]![Town] AND Not IsNull(Customer.[State])"

This is simply to ensure that we only include in the domain (the records that we are taking the value from) those records which actually have a value for the State field.

The Select Customer Combo Box

Now lets move on to another part of our Customer Details form. When you use a form to display information about one entity at a time, such as our Customer Details form, it can be exasperating for the user to have to scroll through all the records to find individual customers. We have allowed them to change the sort order so that they can scroll through the customers by town instead of by name, but even though Access includes various find and filter methods, it can still take time to display a particular customer's record. If they are on the phone at the time, you won't create a very good impression by keeping them waiting.

The easiest way to select a customer, or any other entity, is from a scrollable list of names in a drop-down list. You'll see that we have provided for this with the Select Customer combo box at the foot of the form. When you select a customer from this list, you call a macro which finds and displays the corresponding customer details. The list itself displays all the customers sorted by name, and scrolls automatically to the next matching entry as you type the first characters of the name. To show the names in alphabetical order, it uses the customer ID values from the Alpha field in the records, but it displays the full name in the control. We saw how to build a combo box in Part 1 using the Combo Box Wizard. We'll now look at how this combo box, and the macro behind it, works.

How the Combo Box Works

In form view, select a customer from the Select Customer combo box to see how it works. The form displays the details for the customer you select. Notice that the list contains two columns when you open it - the customer's name and ID (the Alpha field).

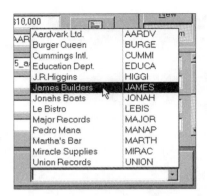

Switch to design view and click on the Select Customer combo box in the form. Open the Properties window and look at the title - the name of the control is cboCustFind. Click the Data tab and you'll see the settings for the combo box's list. The Row Source Type is set to Table/Query - we are supplying the values to fill the list from a query. The Row Source is an SQL statement which creates the list using the records in the Customer table. It selects the CustName and Alpha fields, and sorts them by Alpha. The statement we've used is:

```
SELECT DISTINCTROW Customer.CustName, Customer.Alpha FROM Customer ORDER BY Alpha;
```

The next on the list is the Bound Column property. Here we tell Access what the value of the control will be when the user makes a selection. The number corresponds directly to a field in the table or query that forms the combo box's Row Source. We've set it to 2, as we want to set the value of the combo box to the Alpha field of the record that is selected, and Alpha is the second field in the Row Source query. We've also set the Limit To List property to Yes, so that even if the user types directly in the combo box, they can still only select existing customers.

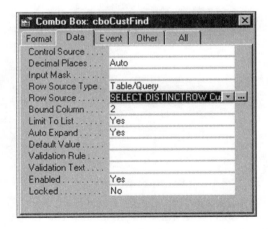

Next click the Format tab. Here we've set the Columns Widths to suit our data, and changed the List Rows to 20 to display more than the default 8 lines.

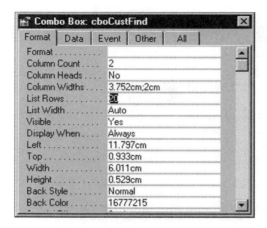

Now click the Event tab and look at the After Update property. It's set to CustDetail.FindCust - the FindCust macro on the CustDetail macro sheet. This macro runs each time we update the combo box contents by selecting a customer from the drop-down list, or by typing into the combo box directly.

Selecting a Customer from a Combo Box List with a Macro

So let's look at the macro itself. In the Database window select the Macros tab, click on the CustDetail macro sheet and open it in design view. Scroll down to the FindCust macro. It looks more complex than the ones we've used before, but don't worry, we'll look at each line in turn.

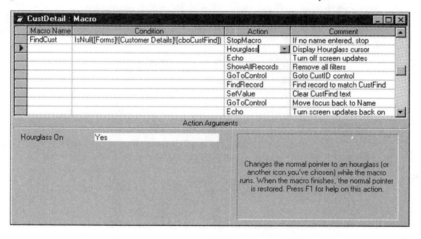

When an After Update event occurs for the Select Customer combo box and FindCust is called, Access locates it in the macro sheet and runs the first line. The first line simply stops the macro if cboCustFind (the combo box) is blank. This may seem strange, as we are selecting from a list of customers, but there is a reason for it. At the end of the macro, we will clear the combo box. This could, in theory, generate another After Update event, in which case, the macro would loop back to the beginning. The macro displays the fields in the record whose CustName value matches that in the combo box (i.e. it displays the details of the customer we select), and so, if the box was blank, we would obviously want to stop the macro there and then. This is what the StopMacro action does.

342

However, using a SetValue action to update a control does not actually trigger the After Update event, so we are safe. But it's a good idea to put this safeguard in the macro, just in case of unforeseen problems. So the first line of the macro is:

Condition: IsNull([Forms]![Customer Details]![cboCustFind])
Action: StopMacro

The next line then starts the macro proper. First we turn on the Hourglass cursor while the macro runs. This just lets the user know that something is actually happening.

Action: Hourglass
 Hourglass On: Yes

Next we turn off screen updating using the Echo action. This speeds up the operation and also allows us to display text in the status bar so that the user knows what is happening while the screen is 'frozen'.

Action: Echo
 Echo On: No
 Status Bar Text: Please Wait..

We want to move to the record for the customer that has been selected in the combo box. To move to a different record, we must first remove any existing filters that may be applied, so that we can 'see' all the records and start the search from the first one. The ShowAllRecords action takes care of this.

Action: ShowAllRecords

The next thing to do is search for the customer name, which we do using the FindRecord action. FindRecord simply finds the next record which meets the specified criteria. In our case, we want it to look in the Alpha field of the table to match the value in the cboCustFind combo box (remember the Bound Column property of the combo box means its value is set to the Alpha field of the selected customer).

In order to find a record, though, we first have to place the current insertion point (the text cursor) in the control of the field we want to look in. FindRecord does not have an argument for the name of the field where we want to search - instead it assumes that the field which supplies the values for the current control on the form is the one we require. So the next stage is to place the cursor in the Alpha control. To do this, we use a GoToControl action.

Action: GoToControl
 Control Name: Alpha

Once we have placed the cursor on the Alpha control, we can search for the next record that meets the criteria. FindRecord takes the criteria as a Find What argument. This argument takes an expression, text, number or a date and looks for a record that matches it. We use =cboCustFind to match the value selected in the Select Customer combo box, i.e. the customer that you want to find details for. The = sign simply indicates that we're using an expression.

Action: FindRecord
 Find What: =cboCustFind
 Match: Whole Field
 Match Case: No
 Search: Down

343

Search As Formatted: No
Only Current Field: Yes
Find First: Yes

The Match argument indicates that we're looking to match the whole of the value in the combo box, not just part of it. We're not interested in matching case so that is set to No. The setting for the Search argument means we'll search down from the current record and specifying No for Search As Formatted means we're not looking for something in the same format as our criteria. We only need to search one field in each record so Only Current Field is set to Yes and we want to start from the beginning of our list of records, not at the current record, so we set the last argument to Yes as well.

Now we can tidy up. We clear the combo box by using SetValue.

Action: SetValue
  Item: [cboCustFind]
  Expression: Null

We move the focus to the customer name on the main form.

Action: GoToControl
  Control Name: CustName

Finally we turn screen updating back on, which completes the FindCust macro.

Action: Echo
  Echo On: Yes
  Status Bar Text:

The ValidRecord Macro

Before we leave the Customer Details form, we'll look briefly at one more macro. When your users make changes to a record and save it, or else create a new one, we should check that all the information we need has been entered. We are already doing this to some extent through the properties we specified for the Customer and Contact tables. Access won't save a record if a field that is the primary key of the table, or is marked as Required, is empty. The same applies if the values in a field which is Indexed (No Duplicates) are not unique. However, the error message is rather cryptic - it may offer 'Customer.Alpha contains Null' or warnings about 'Violating Referential Integrity'.

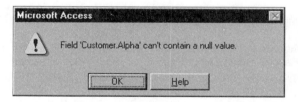

To display a more meaningful message, we can use a form event property to run a macro that checks the values the user has entered and displays a message of our choice. The macro we use in **WroxSoft** is fairly simple - it just checks that the fields we need have enough characters entered in the controls on the form. The macro is called ValidRecord and we have placed the name in the Before Update event of the form, so that it is executed *before* the record is saved. Look at the Properties sheet to see it. You can, of course, make the checks as comprehensive as you like.

Let's take a look at the sequence of actions on our macro sheet:

Macro Name	Condition	Action	Comment
ValidRecord	Len([CustName])<5	MsgBox	Check customer name length
	...	CancelEvent	Customer name must be at least 5 chars.
	...	GoToControl	CustName
	...	StopMacro	
	Len([Alpha])>5 Or Len([Alpha])<2	MsgBox	Check Cust ID length
	...	CancelEvent	Alpha must be between 2 and 5 chars.
	...	GoToControl	Alpha
	...	StopMacro	

Action Arguments

Message	Customer name must be at least five
Beep	No
Type	Warning!
Title	Invalid Customer Code

Enter a macro name in this column.

In our ValidRecord macro we conduct two separate checks using conditions. The first condition checks that the value entered for the customer name is at least 5 characters. The second checks that the Alpha (customer ID) code is at least 2, and not more than 5, characters. If either is **True**, the macro cycles through the following:

▶ The MsgBox action which displays a meaningful message, which is held in the Message argument of MsgBox.

▶ The CancelEvent action which cancels the update to the underlying record.

▶ The GotoControl action which moves the insertion point back to the control where the problem occurred.

▶ The StopMacro action which simply stops the macro from executing further.

FYI

When a record is edited in a form, Access copies the values from the table or query into an edit buffer. As you change the values in the controls on the form, it is this buffer that is updated and not the original values. This is why you can press *Escape* and cancel the updating of a record while the 'pencil' is shown on the record selector.

You can simulate the pressing of *Escape* using the macro action **CancelEvent**. This abandons any edited values in the controls on the form and leaves the original record unchanged.

Now, when the user accidentally puts in incorrect information, a meaningful error message will be displayed and the user can then correct the problem, and save the record.

Push Buttons

Macros aren't only used to perform error checking and create better selection boxes. They are actually used in a far more fundamental part of the application. As you use the application, you'll see that many of the actions you carry out are controlled by push-buttons, or **command**

buttons, of various types. For instance, you can change the order in which the records are displayed using the By Town **toggle** button. There are also 'normal' buttons with just a caption - like you find in every Windows application - and picture buttons with a caption next to them.

We're going to look now at how these buttons are created, and then see how we make them do something useful using macros. Access provides a short cut for creating buttons called Command Button Wizard. However this is a rather specialized and we need to know a little about the theory, so we'll create them by hand instead..

Creating and Using Standard Command Buttons

Standard command buttons are the type originally included in Windows applications, before the advent of toolbars and other graphical buttons. They just display a text caption and appear to be depressed when you click on them, returning to the 'raised' position when you release the mouse button. They can often be activated by pressing *Alt* and the letter that is underlined on the button's caption (the hot-key).

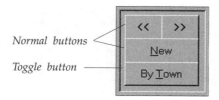

Creating Picture Buttons and Captions

Most modern applications make use of buttons which display a graphic instead of, or as well as, the text caption. Access allows us to create buttons with either, but not both. However, we can attach a label to a button in the same way that we do to a text box control, and use a hot-key in the label to activate the button instead of clicking on it with the mouse.

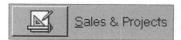

Let's start by creating a button with a picture on it.

Try It Out - Creating a Picture Button

Before we start we need to create a form to test out the different types of button on.

1 Select the Forms tab in the Database window and click New. In the New Form dialog select Design View in the top list and leave the combo box empty. Click OK to create a new blank form which is Unbound i.e. not based on a table or query. Click the Save button on the toolbar and enter ButtonTest for the name; then click OK.

2 Make sure that the Control Wizards button is off (not depressed) and then press the Command button in the toolbox and put it anywhere on the blank form.

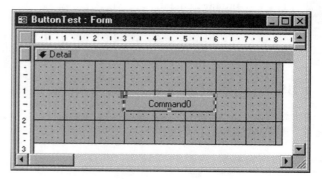

3 To turn this normal command button into a picture button, go to the Properties window and select the Format tab.

Access just requires the full path and file name of the graphic to be used in the **Picture** property. Access will then load the picture and display **[bitmap]** in the **Properties** sheet. Ordinary **.bmp** Windows files or **.ico** icon files are the two permitted types of graphic. (In the **WroxSoft** application all the graphics on the buttons are icon files.)

4 Click the builder button in the Picture property. Picture Builder opens and you can select a picture from the standard types included with Access. As you select each one, the result is shown in the left-hand window.

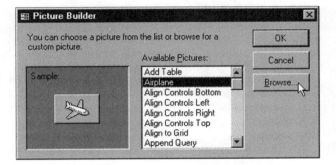

5 If you can't find a suitable graphic here, you can click Browse.. to open a normal file selector window, where you can select any other **.BMP** or **.ICO** type file. We've supplied a few icons for you to experiment with. They will have been installed with the other sample files from the disk that accompanies this book. Choose one and then click OK.

The original caption of the button is no longer shown - but you can create a label with a hot-key for the button. Click the Label control in the toolbox and then click next to the button. Type the caption, including an ampersand (&) before the letter you want to be the hot-key. Then click on the label to select it, press *Ctrl-X* (cut), click on the push button, and press *Ctrl-V* (paste). Access attaches the label to the button, and now it moves when the button does, just like a label caption for a text box.

Making a Button Do Something Useful

Of course, there's no point having buttons on a form unless they actually do something. We have to connect them to a macro (or a VBA code routine) which carries out some action when they are pressed - just like we did with the toggle button when we wanted to change the sort order of the records.

As you'll no doubt expect by now, we connect an object with a macro using the Event tab in the Properties sheet of the object. We'll build a macro that closes the form when the button we've just created is clicked.

Try It Out - Closing a Form with a Push Button

1 Still using the ButtonTest form, select the Events tab of the Properties sheet, and click in the On Click event box. Click the builder button that appears, select Macro Builder and click OK. Then type CloseFormButton as the name of the new macro and click OK again. Access creates a new macro sheet.

2 In the Action column select Close, and for the arguments at the bottom of the window select Form as the Object Type, and ButtonTest as the Object Name. Leave the Save argument as Prompt.

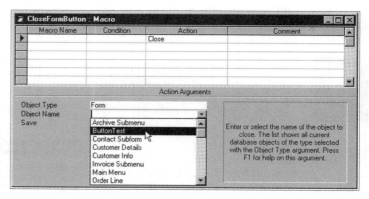

3 Close the macro sheet with the Close button at the top right of the window and save the macro when prompted. Now switch to form view and click the button you created. The form closes and Access prompts you to save it. You can select No - we don't need to save the changes.

We've created a simple picture button that, when clicked, closes the form. It works by running the macro CloseFormButton. This macro consists of one action - Close, which simply closes what it is told to via three arguments:

▶ Object Type - in this case the form.

▶ Object Name - in this case ButtonTest.

▶ Save - we left this blank so the macro prompts the user for a response.

Opening Forms with a Button

You can create buttons which open forms in the same way using the same methods as above, replacing the CloseForm action with OpenForm. The main arguments to specify are the name of the form to be opened and the view that the user is permitted (e.g. Form). We'll look at this in more detail in just a moment. You can also use the OpenReport and OpenQuery macro actions. You'll see more of these later in the book. The OpenReport action is very similar to OpenForm - it uses arguments which specify the name of the report, and control how it is displayed.

Using Buttons to Open Forms and Reports

You'll recall that during the design of the interface, we identified a need to move between the Customer Details, Projects and Sales and Software Catalog forms without going back to the main menu each time.

As well as having a button which closes each of these forms, we've added push buttons which open the form we want to move to. All these buttons use the OpenForm and CloseForm macro actions you've seen here to show the correct form to the user when the buttons are pressed.

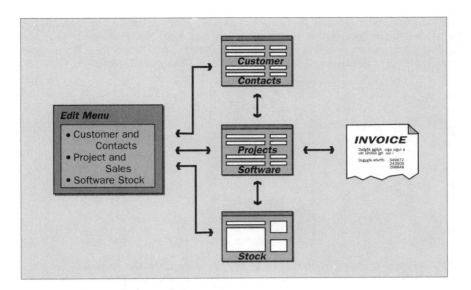

Opening a Form with a Particular Record Displayed

In the Customer Details form, the Sales and Projects button at the bottom of the form opens the Projects and Sales form. It is likely that the user, having been looking at the details for one particular customer, will use this button when they want to enter details of a project or software order for that customer. So, when they open the Projects and Sales form, they will expect it to already be set to that customer.

Have a look at the On Click property of the Sales and Projects button. It is set to CustDetail.GoProjSales, i.e. it will run the GoProjSales macro when clicked. Open the CustDetail macro sheet in design view and look at the GoProjSales macro. This consists of two macro actions. The first of these - DoMenuItem - simply carries out a normal Access menu command.

Action   DoMenuItem
    Menu Bar: Form
    Menu Name: Records
    Command: Save Record
    Subcommand:

We need to save the current record before we move to the Projects and Sales form because it shows information from the Customer table in the top part of the form. If we don't save any changes to the Customer record first, they will not appear in the Projets and Sales form. Even worse, if we enter details for a new customer, we won't see anything in the Projects and Sales form at all because the new record will not yet be placed in the Customer table.

We can then open the Projects and Sales form with an OpenForm action. The Where Condition argument is an expression:

[CustKey]=[Forms]![Customer Details].[CustKey]

Now look at the Customer Details form in design view. In the top left corner, there is a text control which is bound to the CustKey field (its Control Source is CustKey). It, therefore, contains the value of the customer key (the primary key of the table) for that customer. This is not visible in form view because its Visible property is set to No. However, we can still use the value it holds in our macro. We want to open the Project and Sales form at the record whose CustKey field matches the current CustKey field in the Customer Details form.

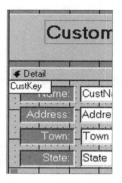

The Where Condition argument requires us to specify a field in the recordset which is the Record Source of the form we are opening. Therefore, [CustKey]=[Forms]![Customer Details]![CustKey] means that the form will open at the record whose CustKey value matches the CustKey value of the record currently displayed in the Customer Details form.

So the macro action and its arguments are:

Action: OpenForm
  Form Name: Projects and Sales
  View: Form
  Filter Name:
  Where Condition: [CustKey]=[Forms]![Customer Details]![CustKey]
  Data Mode: Edit
  Window Mode: Normal

Of course, there could be several records that match a condition - if we had used [Town]=[Forms]![Customer Details]![Town], we would see the records that have the same town as that currently displayed in the Customer Details form. We have effectively applied a filter to the form which limits the records that are displayed to those which match the Where Condition.

To see the other records in the Projects and Sales form, you have to use the Show All Records command. We met this earlier when we created the macro which allows us to select customers using the combo box at the bottom of the form.

We can also use the technique that we've just explained with an OpenReport macro action - this would limit the records that are included in a report to those which match the Where Condition in the OpenReport macro action. You'll see this used in the next chapter.

The Projects and Sales Form

We've spent quite a bit of time examining the different features of the Customer Details form. A lot of these are also used in the second of our main forms - the Projects and Sales form. Open this up in form view and spend a couple of minutes familiarizing yourself with how the form operates.

Using the Form

Here the user can edit details of each project or software sale, and enter new ones. The form shows relevant details about the selected customer and, like the Customer Details form, contains a Select Customer combo box so that they can select a different customer. However, the user cannot edit the customer details in this form - instead they must use the button at the bottom of the screen to open the Customer Details form, and make any changes there.

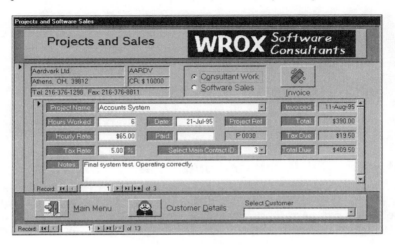

Next to the customer name are two option buttons (sometimes called radio buttons because they operate like the waveband selectors on old radios!). These allow you to select whether you wish to edit the project records or sales records and display the records relevant to the selection. If you select Software Sales, a button appears allowing you to move to the Software Catalog form and view the products on offer. There is also an Invoice button so that you can produce an invoice immediately after entering a project or sale, and buttons at the bottom of the screen to take you back to the main menu or Customer Details form.

Preventing Access to Certain Fields

You should always aim to make it clear to users just what they can do on each form. On this form there are several fields that cannot be edited - we have set the background color of these fields to the same as the main form, while those that can be edited are white.

To see how we prevent users editing data in a control, switch to design view and click on the CustName text box. In the Properties sheet you'll see that the Enabled property is set to No, and the Locked property to Yes. You may remember this combination from Chapter 7 - it allows Access to display the text as normal, but won't allow the user to enter the field to change the contents. If you just set the Enabled property to No, Access displays the values 'grayed out'.

Using Multiple Sub-forms

The Projects and Sales form is a little unusual as it uses a series of different sub-forms within the main form, and allows the user to edit either project details or software sales records by making the relevant subform visible, and hiding the other. The Software Sales subform also contains another subform. If you remember, our sales are recorded using two tables - the Order table which contains details of the order itself, and the OrderLine table which contains details of each line of the order i.e. which products make up the order. We, therefore, need a subform for the OrderLine table within the form that is linked to the Order table.

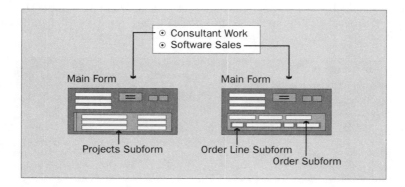

Showing and Hiding Sub-Forms and Buttons with a Macro

Click on the option buttons in design view. If you look at their Option Value properties on the Data sheet of the Properties window, you will see that the first one is set to 0 and the second is 1. As the application runs, Access sets the Value property of the option group frame (fraSaleType) to the Value of the option button currently selected. Because we set the Default Value property of the frame to 0, the first option will be selected when the form is first opened. The Project subform should, therefore, be the one that is visible at the start. To ensure this, we set the Visible property of the Project subform to True, and make the same property of the Order subform False.

When the user changes the type of sale (from consultant work to software sales or vice versa), an On Click event is generated for the frame. We use this to make the right subform(s) and buttons visible by setting their Visible properties with a macro. To see how this is done, click on the frame round the options buttons and check the Properties sheet. In the Events tab, the On Click property is set to the name of a macro - ProjSales.TypeChange. Click the builder button next to the name and Access opens the ProjSales macro sheet. Scroll down to the TypeChange macro.

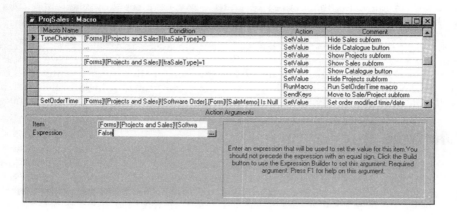

The TypeChange Macro

The first thing we have to do is check the Value of the frame (fraSaleType). If it's 0, the consultant work (projects) option is selected and so the Software Order form is made invisible.

Condition: [Forms]![Projects and Sales]![fraSaleType]=0
Action: SetValue
  Item: [Forms]![Projects and Sales]![Software Order].[Visible]
  Expression: False

We work through the SetValue actions, changing the Visible property of each object to suit. To repeat the condition from one line to the next, we can use the shorthand syntax of an ellipsis in the Condition column. First the Catalogue button (btnSoftware) is made invisible. (Note that the objects are referred to by the Name specified in the Other sheet of the Properties window, not by their Caption - which is what appears on screen.)

Condition: ...
Action: SetValue
  Item: [Forms]![Projects and Sales]![btnSoftware].[Visible]
  Expression: False

Then the Projects subform is made visible:

Condition: ...
Action: SetValue
  Item: [Forms]![Projects and Sales]![Projects Subform].[Visible]
  Expression: True

If, on the other hand, the value of fraSaleType is 1, not 0, it is the Software Sales option that is set, so we change the Visible properties of the forms and Catalogue button accordingly:

Condition: [Forms]![Projects and Sales]![fraSaleType]=1
Action: SetValue
  Item: [Forms]![Projects and Sales]![Software Order].[Visible]
  Expression: True

Condition: ...
Action: SetValue
  Item: [Forms]![Projects and Sales]![btnSoftware].[Visible]
  Expression: True

Condition: ...
Action: SetValue
  Item: [Forms]![Projects and Sales]![Projects Subform].[Visible]
  Expression: False

If it's a software sale, then a RunMacro action is executed.

Condition: ...
Action: RunMacro
  Macro Name: ProjSales.SetOrderTime

This runs the SetOrderTime macro, which inserts the current time and date into the Notes: control of the Order subform. Finally, irrespective of the setting of fraSaleType, we use SendKeys to send a *Tab* keypress which moves us to the first field in the subform. The Wait argument simply tells Access whether to hold execution of the macro until the *Tab* key movement (and any other macros this sets off) is completed or continue with the macro while the *Tab* key movement is processed.

Condition:
Action: SendKeys
  Keystrokes: {TAB}
  Wait: No

Basing Forms on Queries - the Projects and Sales Form

As with the Customer Details form, the values to fill the main form and the three sub-forms are supplied by queries. This allows us not only to control the order in which the records are displayed, but also to create new fields for our forms. We'll look at the queries that are the basis for each form.

The Projects and Sales Form Query

The main form is based on values selected from the Customer table because we want to look at project and order records for one customer at a time. This query selects the customers name, together with their credit limit, identifier, and the value of the primary key (CustKey). There are also several calculated fields in the query. You'll recall that when we use calculated fields in a query, we cannot update the fields in the original table. However, we don't need to allow updates to the Customer table in this form, so the query doesn't have to produce an updatable recordset.

Check out the query by going to the main form's Properties window, selecting Record Source and clicking the builder button.

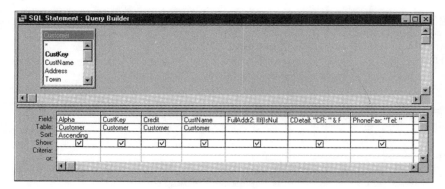

The calculated fields we use are FullAddr2, CDetail and PhoneFax - each of which combines information from fields in the original table to produce text values for our form. These look much neater than individual controls.

The fields are calculated as follows:

    FullAddr2: IIf(IsNull([Town]),Null,[Town] & ", " & [State] & ", " & [ZipCode])

    CDetail: "CR: " & Format([Credit],"$ 0")

PhoneFax: "Tel: " & [Phone] & "   Fax: " & [Fax]

The calculated fields just supply extra text to the form to make it more informative, and in the case of FullAddr2, just provide punctuation between the town, state and zip code in the address. The following diagram shows how the fields look on the actual form.

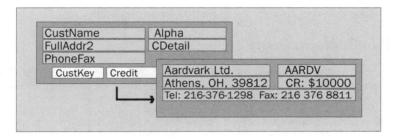

The Projects Subform Query

The query for the Projects subform takes all the values from the Project table and adds several calculated fields to give the totals for each project. It sorts the records using the Date field. The Show: checkbox for this field is cleared because the Date field is automatically included in the recordset when the asterisk is used.

As before, to view the query, open the Project form from the Database window, go to the Properties window, select Record Source and click on the builder button.

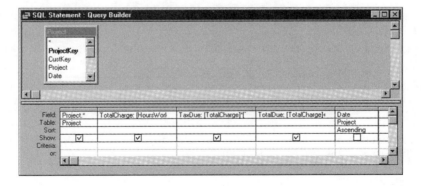

The calculated fields are displayed on the subform, but cannot be edited - just what you would expect when using the form. However, the query constantly updates these using the values from the other controls as we enter information about a project. The three calculated fields are

355

TotalCharge: [HoursWorked]*[HourlyRate]

TaxDue: [TotalCharge]*[TaxRate]/100

TotalDue: [TotalCharge]+[TaxDue]

We saw how these calculated fields were created back in Chapter 7.

The Order Main Subform Query

This uses a simple query which selects all the fields from the Order table, and just sorts them by OrderDate. This form displays the values from the Order table, and acts as the 'container' for the Order Line subform.

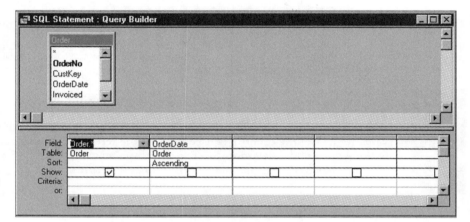

The Order Line Subform Query

This query is similar to the one used in the Projects subform. It selects all the values from the OrderLine table, and adds calculated fields for the individual line totals. Because the primary key for the

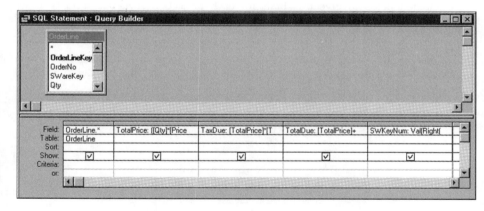

table is OrderLineKey, the records will automatically appear in the order that they were entered into the table, so we don't need to sort them.

The three calculated fields for the totals are

TotalPrice: ([Qty]*[Price])-([Qty]*[Price]*[Discount]/100)

TaxDue: [TotalPrice]*[TaxRate]/100

TotalDue: [TotalPrice]+[TaxDue]

We also need to be able to refer to the value in the SWareKey field which stores the link to the item of software for each line of the order. The control on the form displays it as WS 001 etc., because that's how we set the Format property in the table. To look up values using a macro, we need just the number part of the value, so we've also calculated this in the query, and we store it on the form in a hidden text box which is found in Form Footer, just visible in design view - then we can refer to it easily at any time. So the final calculated field in the query is:

SWKeyNum: Val(Right([SWareKey],3))

Handling Record Updates in Sub-forms

One problem you may encounter when using sub-forms is that the user may enter values in the subform of a new record without entering any in the main form. To see this, open the Customer Details form in form view, and click New to move to a new record. Enter a name in the Contact Name control in the subform, then press *Shift-Enter* (the shortcut for saving a record to the database) or move back to an existing record, to save the new record. Access tells you that there is an error, and the record is not saved.

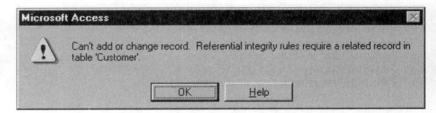

The reason is quite simple - because we haven't typed anything in the main customer part of the form, Access has not inserted a new customer record. We can't save a new contact record because there is no value in the linking field (CustKey) of that record. Therefore, as you can't delete entries, you will have to undo the amendments you've just tried to make and abandon the new record. Press the *Esc* key to do this.

This is unlikely to happen in the Customer Details form because the user is almost bound to enter some details for the customer first, and so Access will insert a new record. Then, when they start typing in the Contacts subform, a Contact new record can be created - there will be a value in the linking CustKey field.

However, the same is not true of the Order subform in the Projects and Sales form. There is no reason to expect that the user will edit any controls in the main Order form before editing the Order Line subform - the Default Value of the OrderDate field is set to the current date and the Invoiced and Paid fields will not be touched when entering a new order. Therefore, the Order No: control, which displays the primary key of the table formatted to display as an order number will not contain a value and no new record will have been created. If the user enters values straight into the Order Line subform, there will be no matching Order record for the new records to link to, and an error will be displayed.

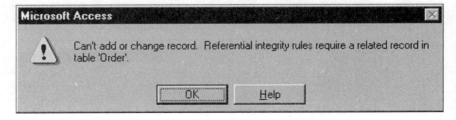

One way round this is to leave the OrderDate control empty so the user has to type it in, and create a new record that way. However, we don't want to sacrifice usability - instead we cheat a little. When we looked at the macro that made the sub-forms visible (TypeChange), we saw that an extra action was performed for a software sale. It should now be clear to you why we used the RunMacro action to execute the SetOrderTime macro. This inserts the current time and date into the Notes: control of the Order subform if it is empty. As this is inserted, Access creates a new Order record automatically, so then the user can add details to the Order Line subform without problem.

If the user doesn't enter anything in the Order Line subform, we get an Order record with no order lines. This doesn't cause a problem because the queries that process the order data will automatically filter out these orders - they won't appear on invoices and statements. However, they still waste space in our table, and we need to remove them. We'll see how to do this when we look at the **action queries** in **WroxSoft** in Chapter 13.

Looking Up the Main Contact for a Project

To end this discussion of the two main forms in our application, we'll look at another example of how simple macros are used to make entering data more user friendly. In the Projects subform, the user can set the value for the main contact by looking at a list of the existing contacts for that customer in a drop-down combo box list.

The control is a normal combo box like we've seen used before, and is bound to the MainContactKey field. To fill the combo box we use a **SELECT** query which takes the ContactKey and ContactName values from the Contact table, and uses a criteria to limit them to the contacts for the currently displayed customer. To see the query, open the Properties window for the MainContactKey combo box and click the builder button in the Row Source property.

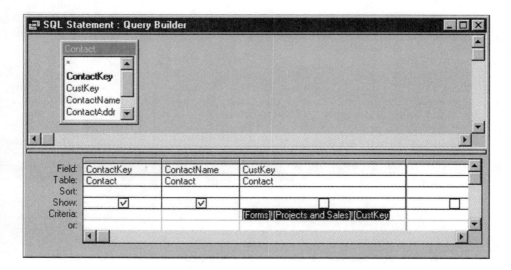

The criteria for the CustKey field uses the non-visible CustKey control on the Project and Sales form which contains the customer key value for the customer currently displayed. The recordset produced by the query will only contain the contact records which have the same value for the CustKey field as the current record on the Project and Sales form - in other words the contacts for the current customer. To show both the ContactKey and ContactName, we've set the Column Count to 2 and specified the widths for the columns. We've also set the Limit To List property to Yes, so that the user can only select an existing contact, and the Bound Column to 1, so that the value for the first column (ContactKey) is placed in the MainContactKey control.

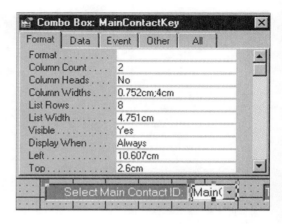

Selecting a Software Item for the Order Line

When it comes to entering an order line, the user will want to select the item of software from the range we have, and get some indication of whether it is in stock at the present time. They can do this by clicking the Catalogue button on the main form, and viewing the records in the Software Catalogue form. However, a neater way is to implement a drop-down combo box which displays this information - in the same way as they would select the customer that they want. This is the Product combo box.

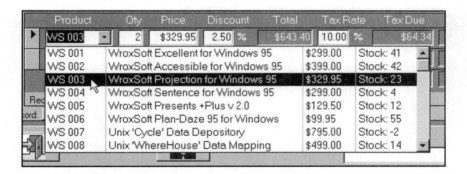

The combo box is implemented in a similar way to the MainContactKey combo we've just seen. However, the query that drives it is a little more complicated. It returns five fields: SWareKey, SWareName and SWPrice are taken directly from the Software table, but the other two are calculated fields. Available is made up of the word "Stock" and the actual value in the SWStock field, and SWKeyNum is the value in the SWareKey field with the leading "S" stripped off and converted to a number. You'll see why in a moment.

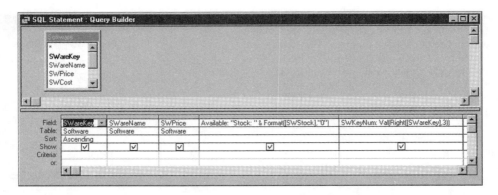

The list in the combo box only contains four columns - the last one (SWKeyNum) is hidden because its width is set to zero in the Column Widths property. We only include it in order to retrieve the key number of the chosen item so that we can look up the other details. The user sees the actual product number (SWareKey) in the first column.

Looking Up the Price in the Software Table

If you look at the Column Count and Bound Column properties, you'll see that the value placed in the field is actually the value from the hidden fifth column - SWKeyNum. When the user selects a product from the list, the new product code is inserted in the Product control on the form. Because the control is formatted to show it as a product number, we get WS008 or similar. Once the value is inserted, an On Click event occurs. The On Click event property is set to ProjSales.ProductChange - the ProductChange macro on the ProjSales macro sheet.

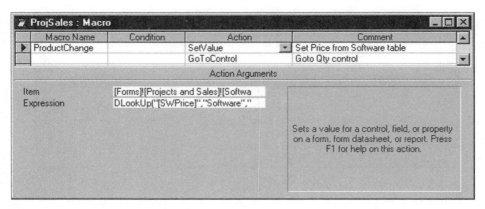

This two line macro first fills in the Price control on the form with a SetValue action. This uses the **DLookup** function to fetch the value from the SWPrice field in the Software table where the key (SWareKey) is equal to the value placed in our combo box. To work correctly this requires the value in the combo box to be a *number* - the data type of the SWareKey field in the Software table is of type AutoNumber - this is why our query generated a number type instead of just placing the product number (SWareKey) there.

   Action: SetValue
     Item: [Forms]![Projects and Sales]![Software Order].[Form]![Order Line].[Form]![Price]
  Expression: DLookUp("[SWPrice]","Software","[SWareKey]=Forms![Projects and Sales]![Software
                 Order].Form![Order Line].Form![Product]")

360

The macro then moves the focus to the Qty control so that the user can enter the required quantity.

Action: GoToControl
Control Name: Qty

The user can still change the price by editing the contents of the Price field - remember we had to allow for the 'buy two and get one for half price' situation.

In the **ProductChange** macro, we used **Expression Builder** to create the **Item** and **Expression** arguments - and it produces rather wordy syntax. While you can shorten this to just the control names, if the macro runs from this form, you may find all kind of error messages appear which can be difficult to trace. It's probably easier to let **Expression Builder** ensure you have the correct and full syntax.

Identifying Controls on Forms and Sub-forms

The long control identifiers used to describe the full path to a control can seem intimidating until you get used to them. Every object in Access belongs to a collection, and the first part of the identifier is the name of the collection e.g. Forms. So

Forms![Projects and Sales]

is simply the Projects and Sales form. (The square brackets are required because the name contains spaces).

Forms![Projects and Sales]![Software Order]

is then the Software Order subform on the Project and Sales form.

When you come to refer to **controls** on a subform which have the same name as a field in the underlying table, you must prefix them with the word 'Form' so that Access knows you mean the control, not the field. (Notice that the prefix is 'Form', not 'Forms' - which is the name of the collection). The Order Line subform is actually a control on the Software Order form, so the path to it is:

Forms![Projects and Sales]![Software Order].Form![Order Line]

Therefore, the Product control on the Order Line subform is

Forms![Projects and Sales]![Software Order].Form![Order Line].Form![Product]

361

Remember, you can always use Expression Builder to avoid having to create these long identifiers by hand. Just click the builder button in a property, macro argument, or on the main toolbar to open Expression Builder.

Finding Errors

Before we finish this chapter, we'll have a quick look at what you can do should you find that your macros aren't working properly. If you make a mistake when entering the arguments for a macro or use the wrong action, you may get an error message when you run the macro telling you that it has failed. For example, if you mistype the name of a field, Access will tell you it can't find it on the form:

Once you acknowledge the error by clicking OK, Access displays the Macro Failed dialog, showing you the action that it was trying to execute when the error occurred.

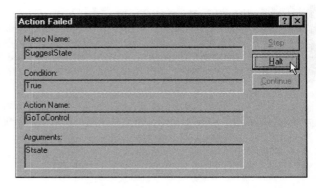

You can see it was running GoToControl and looking for Stsate. In this case you would then know what the problem was and could edit the macro to cure it. However, sometimes Access does not display a message, but doesn't provide the result you expect either. If this happens, you can ask Access to take you through the actions it has performed step-by-step, so you can check the results at each stage. This involves switching to **single-step** mode.

Single-Stepping Through a Macro

Open the SuggestState macro that we created earlier and click the Single Step button on the toolbar (you can only see this when a macro sheet has the focus). When you click it, it remains depressed to show that you are in single-step mode.

If you click the Continue button, access turns off single-step mode and all the macros run as normal. To go back to single-stepping, you have to click the toolbar Single Step button again.

Now go back to your SuggestState form - open it from the Database window if it has been closed. Move to a new record and enter a town - Green Bay will do. Press *Tab* and you'll see each macro action being carried out, with the condition and its arguments listed. Access even tells you if a condition is **True** - it displays **True** or **False** before the condition itself. If there is no condition, it still displays **True** - the action will be carried out anyway. Each action is shown before it is carried out. When you click the Step button, Access executes the action, then stops and displays the next one. This enables you to examine each step for whatever it is that is causing the error.

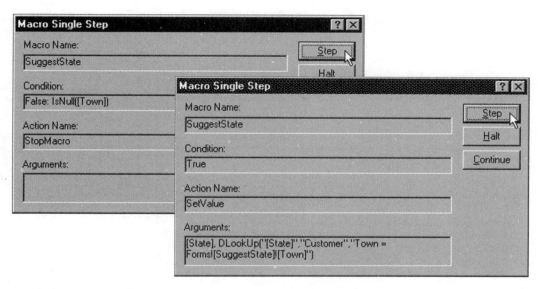

Remember to turn off single-stepping when you've finished - just click the button on the toolbar again.

Summary

In this chapter we've spent a lot of time on the two main forms that are the basis for our **WroxSoft** application. We've shown how you can make your forms far more attractive and user friendly. Many of the techniques we've used are duplicated elsewhere in the application, and you should experiment with it to see how it all fits together. Remember that you can find the macro for an event by opening the Event tab of the Properties window for that particular control, or the form itself, and clicking the builder button.

We have covered:

⯈ What macros are and how they are created.

⯈ How to open a form at the right record.

⯈ How to automatically show and hide forms and buttons.

⯈ How to find errors in a macro.

The only other data entry form is the Software Catalog form, and we'll look at this in the next chapter.

Manipulating And Outputting Information

In the last chapter we looked at the two forms that are the main base for entering data into our application - the Customer Details form and the Projects and Sales form. In this chapter, we're going to move on to look at the ways that information is output from our database.

Forms can be used for output - we'll start this chapter by looking at the Software Catalog form which is used both to enter and edit, and to output information on the screen. However, to produce a hard copy of the information you would generally use a report. You *can* print a form, but if it's been designed for use on screen, it's unlikely to be very useful when printed. On screen, the form is interactive - the user scrolls through the records while viewing the information. They can't do this using the resulting hard copy.

This chapter is, therefore, predominantly about reports. We'll examine the reports in **WroxSoft**, considering, in particular, invoices and statements. We rather left this subject in the air in Part 1.

More specifically, we'll cover:

▶ The different reports in the **WroxSoft** database.

▶ Using subreports.

▶ How to set up invoices and statements.

▶ Complex queries.

Getting Product Information

In Chapter 9, we discussed how we adapted the database design so that we could keep track of our software sales as well as consultancy work. We identified the need to be able to quickly locate details about each product as orders are entered.

To this end, we implemented the Software Catalog form, which we can access from a push button in the Projects and Sales form. It shows all the details about the items we sell, including the amount in stock, price, cost and even a picture of the package:

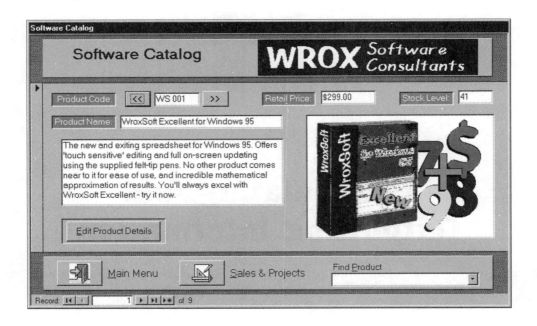

This gives you the information you need on the screen. However, if you're off-site, perhaps working at the customer's premises, you need the information in hard copy form. To do this, we use the Software Stock report - it contains the same information, but outputs it in a way more suited to hard copy.

The form and report are very similar in design and build. We'll have a look at them now.

The Software Catalog Form

When the user opens the Software Catalog form, they see a description, picture, and other details about each software product. The form is based on an SQL query which takes all the records from the Software table and sorts them by the SWareKey field.

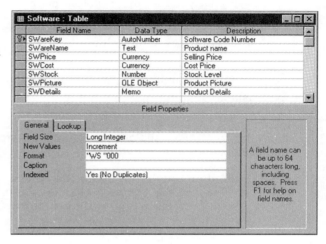

When we created the Software table, we set the data type for the product description field (SWDetails) to Memo, and the picture field (SWPicture) to OLE Object. The Memo field is similar to those used in the other forms, and allows the user to enter large quantities of text just like in a simple text editor. The OLE Object field is a little more complicated; we'll see how these types of fields are used in the next chapter.

We expect this form to be mainly used for browsing through the stock when a customer inquires about the products, rather than entering and updating information. We've designed the form so that when you first open it, all the details are 'read-only' - you can't edit the values in the controls. If you try clicking on each one, you'll find that you can't place the cursor in them. The Enabled property is set to No, and the Locked property set to Yes for each one. However, you can scroll through the records using the '<<' and '>>' buttons or the normal record navigation buttons at the bottom of the window.

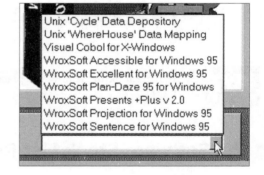

We've also provided a Find Product combo box, similar to the Find Customer ones you saw in the other forms, so that you can go directly to any item or just see a list of them. This uses the same methods as the Find Customer combo on the Projects and Sales form to display the details of the record you select.

The remaining button on the form allows you to edit the product's details. If you need to change an existing record, or add or delete records, click this button. The text boxes are then enabled and can be used to edit the values in each record.

Clicking this button also causes another control to appear - the Cost Price. This was hidden when the form was first opened - its Visible property was set to No. When you click the Edit Product Details button, a macro runs which sets the Visible property of the Cost Price control to Yes, and changes the Enabled and Locked properties of the other controls to allow them to be edited.

Have a look at the On Click event of this button. It's set to Software.EditStock - the EditStock macro on the Software macro sheet. Open the macro sheet by clicking the builder button and scroll down until you find the EditStock macro.

This macro simply contains a list of SetValue actions. Each one changes something to do with the form - for instance, the first two:

Action:	SetValue
Item:	[Forms]![Software Catalog]![SWareKey].[Enabled]
Expression:	True

Action:	SetValue
Item:	[Forms]![Software Catalog]![SWareKey].[Locked]
Expression:	False

set the Enabled property of the SWareKey control, which holds the software key such as 'WS001', to True and the Locked property to False. These settings mean that the contents can then be edited in the normal way. The rest of the SetValue actions repeat these settings for the other controls, until we reach the final entry:

Action:	SetValue
Item:	[Forms]![Software Catalog]![SWareKey].[Locked]
Expression:	False

which makes the Cost Price control visible by setting its Visible property to True.

Action:	SetValue
Item:	[Forms]![Software Catalog]![SWCost].[Visible]
Expression:	True

At the top of the form, in the form header section, is the company logo. This is displayed as a graphic in an OLE control.

 We'll be looking at how we place graphics and pictures in forms and reports in the next chapter.

The Software Stock List Report

The Software Stock List report is very similar to the Software Catalog form - it displays the contents of the Software table, only as hard copy rather than on screen. To see how the report is designed, select the Reports tab in the Database window, select Software List and click the Design button.

The report is based directly on the Software table as we want all the records from the table, and the primary key's sort order is sufficient. We also don't need to take advantage of the report's sorting and grouping facilities. There is a **Page Header** which contains an unbound OLE control for the logo and text boxes and labels to hold the address, and a **Page Footer** which contains the date and a page number - created using calculated controls.

The **Detail** section contains standard text box and label controls which display the information from our **Software** table, plus a bound OLE control for the product's picture.

By carefully sizing the **Detail** section, we have arranged for each page to contain two records - we know what size the section should be because there are no repeating groups which might vary with each record. The result is a neat display, designed to resemble a printed catalog, which contains current information such as the price and stock levels of each product:

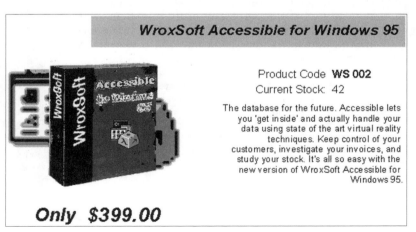

Database Information Reports

The Database Reports and Information section of the main menu gives the user access to the various reports that are available. These are divided into categories:

▶ Invoices and Statements, which we'll be looking at later in this chapter.

▶ The Software Stock List, which we saw in the previous section.

▶ Customer Information, which allows us to select different reports about our customers (sorted by customer).

▶ Sales and Projects reports, which categorize and sort the information according to the type of transaction, both for project work and software sales.

▶ The Company Performance report, which displays graphs of the main aspects of our company and its sales.

We'll have a look at each of these reports to see how we can put what we have learned to use to create informative and attractive reports, while also introducing some new techniques to keep the pot boiling.

The Customer Information Reports

Click on the Customer Information button and you'll be taken to another form and offered a selection of four reports. With the exception of the Sales By Customer report, these are fairly simple reports which retrieve information from our tables and present it in a useful manner, sorted by customer.

The Sales By Customer report displays a chart of total sales by month for each customer. We'll look at this when we come to using charts in reports in the next chapter.

Listing Customers by Name and by Town

If you click the Customer Listings button, a dialog pops up, allowing you to decide the order in which the customer records are printed, or whether to just print the customers from one particular state.

This dialog is similar to the Archive Records form we built in Chapter 7. It uses an option group with option buttons to select the order in which the records are printed, and a **list box** to display all the states.

The list box is a control we haven't used before, but it's like a combo box in many respects: it displays a list of values from which the user can select. In our case, it displays a list of states, generated by a query from the information held in our tables.

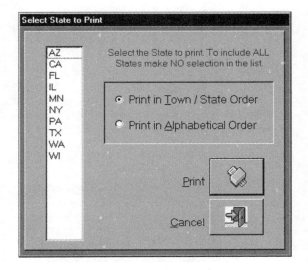

You should also notice that we have set this form's properties so that it behaves like a dialog box. It has no record source property entry (it's unbound), and the other display characteristics - such as the use of scroll bars and navigation buttons - are set to emulate a normal Windows dialog box.

If you open the Customer List and Customer By Town reports side by side in design view, you'll immediately see the similarities. Both reports include a header with the report name and date, and a footer with the page number. And both are based directly on the Customer table - their Record Source property is set to Customer:

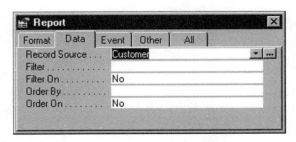

Select the Customer List report and open the Sorting and Grouping dialog (use the toolbar button or select Sorting and Grouping from the View menu). The only field in the dialog is the Alpha field, set to sort Ascending, so in this report the records are displayed alphabetically by customer name.

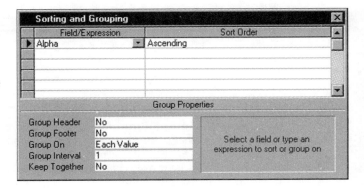

Now switch to the Customer By Town report. Here, we have set up grouping on the State and Town fields, and specified the sort order of the records in each to Ascending. There's a group header and footer set up for the State field, and a header for the Town field. We've also set the sort order for the records in the Detail section to Ascending on the Alpha field, by selecting this in the last line of the dialog.

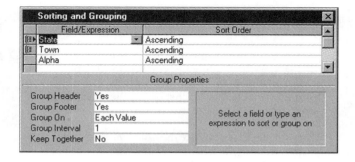

The result of these settings is that the State and Town are printed in their respective headers:

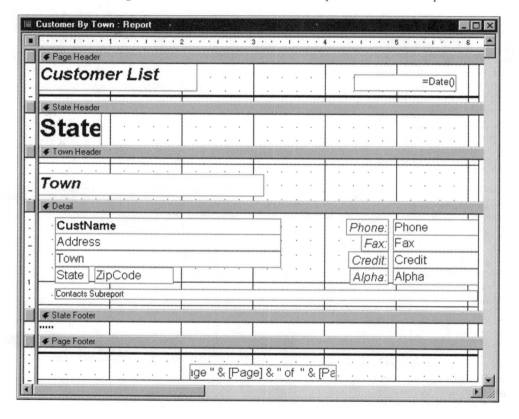

Using Subreports in a Main Report

In both the Customer List and Customer by Town reports, there is another control in the Detail section below the customer address fields - the Contacts Subreport. We can embed one or more subreports into a main report in the same way that we embed subforms into a main form. These are viewed in the same way as a subform - just double-click on the control and Access opens the report in a separate window.

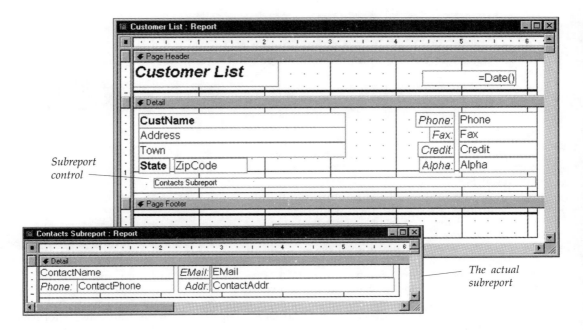

The Contacts subreport is a simple report with no headers or footers; its Record Source is the Contact table. If you open the Sorting and Grouping dialog, you'll see that we're just sorting the records by ContactName.

Go back to the main Customer List report and look in the Properties window. The Link Child Fields and Link Master Fields are both set to CustKey - this is the field that forms the link between the Customer and Contact tables. So, as it prints, the subreport only displays the Contact records for the customer currently being printed.

373

The Can Grow/Can Shrink Properties

You may have noticed that the size of the Contact subreport control on the main report isn't large enough to show even one contact's record, never mind several. Yet the printed report quite happily includes them all. What's more, if there's a customer where there are no contacts at all, you don't get a blank space on the report - the gap where the contact details would have been is closed up. This effect is controlled by two more properties of the form - the Can Grow and Can Shrink properties. By default, Access sets the Can Grow property for a report to Yes and Can Shrink to No. The result is that the control can grow in size down the page so that all the records are printed. The following lines are just pushed down as well. We've changed the Can Shrink property of the subreport to Yes as well, so that empty subreports don't take up space on the printed page.

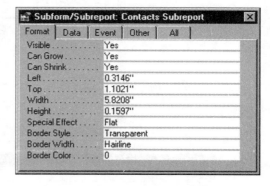

The sections on a report have their own Can Grow and Can Shrink properties - Access sets these to match the settings of the control's properties, but you can change them separately. However, you should bear in mind that setting a section's Can Grow property to No when a subreport control in that section has its Can Grow property set to Yes can cause information to be lost - it won't fit in the available space. You need to experiment with the properties before changing them from the default.

Inserting a Subreport into a Main Report

You can insert a subreport into a main report (or a subform into a main form) simply by dragging it from the Database window into the report in design view, and dropping it into the section where you want it displayed. You should take advantage of this wherever possible as it means you can use the same subreport in more than one main report and, therefore, speed up development.

If you have previously created a relationship between the tables, Access will also automatically fill in the values in the Link Child Fields and Link Master Fields properties of the subreport. If Access cannot automatically set these properties, you will have to do this yourself. You need to identify which field in each table or query is to be used to link them together, just as you would if you were creating a permanent relationship between them. Bear in mind that the fields may not have the same name.

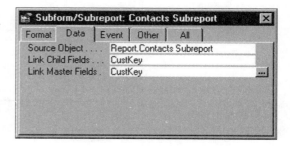

The Customer History Report

The other customer report worth a look is Customer History. This displays the customers in alphabetical order showing all the project work and software sales for each one. The report looks a lot more complicated than any we've seen so far, but it is, in fact, quite similar to the other customer lists.

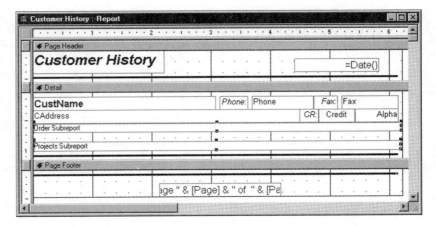

Customer History   13-Sep-95

Aardvark Ltd.   *Phone:* 216-376-1298   *Fax:* 216-376-8811
All Saints Street, Athens,OH,39812   *CR:* £10,000   AARDV

OrderNo	Date	Invoiced	Paid	Goods	Discount	Total	Tax Due	Order Total
S 0005	2/19/95	2/21/95	4/3/95	$959.75	$16.50	$943.25	$94.33	$1,037.58
S 0006	7/5/95	7/8/95	8/3/95	$659.90	$0.00	$659.90	$65.99	$725.89
			Totals:	$1,619.65	$16.50	$1,603.15	$160.32	$1,763.47

Ref	Date	Invoiced	Paid	Project	Hours	Total	Tax Due	FinalTotal
P 0029	8/7/95	8/7/95		Accounts System	17	$1,105.00	$55.25	$1,160.25
P 0030	7/21/95	8/11/95		Accounts System	6	$390.00	$19.50	$409.50
P 0031	8/8/95			Accounts System	3	$195.00	$9.75	$204.75
			Totals:		26	$1,690.00	$84.50	$1,774.50

Burger Queen   *Phone:* 713-771-6727   *Fax:* 713-771-6728
Constants Avenue, Houston, TX, 30517   *CR:* £5,000   BURGE

OrderNo	Date	Invoiced	Paid	Goods	Discount	Total	Tax Due	Order Total
S 0007	6/13/95	7/15/95	7/28/95	$499.00	$0.00	$499.00	$62.38	$561.38
			Totals:	$499.00	$0.00	$499.00	$62.38	$561.38

Ref	Date	Invoiced	Paid	Project	Hours	Total	Tax Due	FinalTotal
P 0032	6/14/95			Menu Generator	12	$660.00	$82.50	$742.50
			Totals:		12	$660.00	$82.50	$742.50

The first point of interest is the report's Record Source property. We've used a query in the form of an SQL statement which selects the Alpha, CustKey, CustName, Phone, Fax and Credit fields, plus a calculated field which builds the customer's address into one line of text:

CAddress: [Address] & ", " & [Town] & ", " & [State] & ", " & [ZipCode]

This gives us the information for the Detail section of the report describing each customer. Underneath this are two subreports - the Order Subreport and Projects Subreport.

Open these two - you'll see that they're similar. Both are based on a query that produces a record for each project or software sale, including the totals before and after tax, and the tax due. We'll be discussing these queries in the next section covering Invoices and Statements.

In the Sorting and Grouping dialog associated with the main report, you'll see that the Order and Projects subreports are sorted by order number and project number respectively, and each has a header containing the field names, and a footer which has calculated controls to display the totals for the appropriate subreport.

Invoices and Statements

In Chapter 9, we designed our tables so that we could store dates for each project or sale - when it took place, when it was invoiced and when we got paid. However, we never really considered how we were going to carry out the actual task of creating invoices and statements. As it stands, the Projects and Sales form will look after inserting the date that the transaction took place - the Date field is specified as Required in the design properties of both the Order and Project tables. There's also a text box control where the date we get paid can be entered. However, we've implemented the Invoiced control as Disabled and Locked - it can't be edited in this form.

We want the Invoiced field to be automatically updated in the records when we send an invoice. This is desirable because we may not send the invoice on the same day that the sale is made, and also, if we do it automatically, it saves having to remember to update each record when we send out a batch of invoices.

If we do this, we'll also be able to find out which transactions haven't yet been invoiced (as the Invoiced field will be empty), and which have been invoiced, but not paid for (the Invoiced field will contain a date, but the Paid field will be empty). It will also allow us to print customer invoices and end of month statements at the click of a button.

 As we pointed out earlier, this is a simple system and is not designed to replace a full accounting package. However, it does provide a quantum leap from the capabilities we had when we were using the original spreadsheet.

The Invoice Reports

As the structures of the Project and Order tables are different, we'll implement two types of invoice - one for project work and one for software sales. They look similar, but the body of each is different.

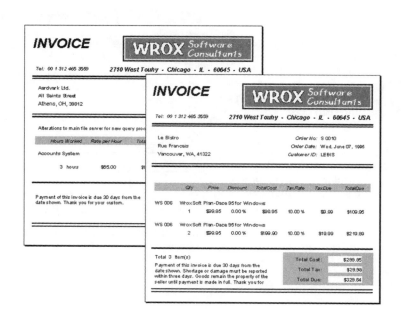

The Project Invoice Report

The query that the Project Invoice report is based on draws information from the Customer and Project tables, outputting the customer's name, address and a calculated field made up of the town and state. It adds to this most of the fields from the matching Project records, including three calculated fields: the total cost before and after tax and the total tax due.

The recordset it produces contains a record for each project for each customer. However, we only want to include projects that haven't yet been invoiced, so the query contains a criteria on the Invoiced field. We've included the Invoiced field in the grid and set its Criteria: to Is Null, clearing its Show: box so that it doesn't appear in the recordset.

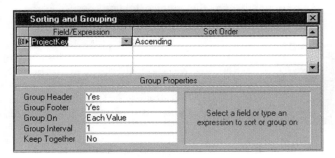

We've made use of the report's internal sorting and grouping facility to sort and group the records by Project Key, so that we can 'break' the report for each different project - we'll print a separate invoice for each project.

The design of the report is relatively simple: the Page Header contains our logo in an unbound object frame, and our address. The ProjectKey Header contains the customer's details and the ProjectMemo field. This is sized very small but has its Can Grow property set to Yes, so it only takes up as much room on the report as required to accommodate any text in it. We've also put the column labels in this section.

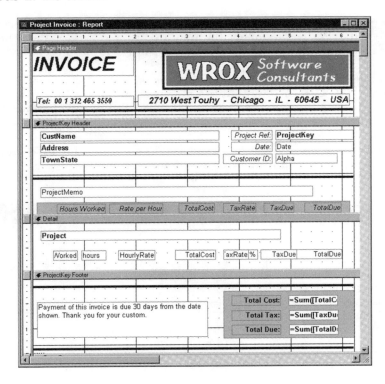

377

The Detail section has the project name and the various values for that project including the calculated fields for the totals that we created in the query. Finally, the ProjectKey Footer contains a series of calculated controls which sum the total cost before and after tax, and the tax amount, to give the invoice totals. These use the SQL aggregate functions we saw in Chapter 8.

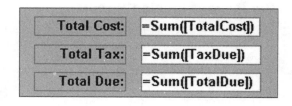

FYI

You will have noticed that we've summed the records to provide the totals in the **Footer** section, yet we know there will only be one record in the **Detail** section - each project is invoiced separately. We've done this for two reasons: it keeps the two invoice reports (**Project** and **Software Sales**) as similar as possible, and allows future development where there may be more than one project on each invoice.

At the bottom of the ProjectKey Footer there's a page break control which forces a new page for each project, and hence a new invoice. The shaded backgrounds are just there to make the report more attractive - they're rectangles with their Back Color set to light gray.

The Sales Invoice Report

This report produces an invoice for sales of software. While the structure of this report is quite different from that of the Project Invoice report, it contains many of the same unbound controls such as the header logo, company address, and the customer's details. We copied these them from the Project Invoice report, rather than creating them from scratch.

FYI

To copy a control from one report to another (or from one form to another), just open both reports, click on the control you want to copy and press *Ctrl-C*. Then click on the other report, in the section you want the control to be placed, and press *Ctrl-V*.

If you want to copy a whole report (or any other object), select it in the **Database** window and press *Ctrl-C*, then *Ctrl-V*. Access prompts you for a name for the new copy and places it back in the **Database** window. You can also use this method to copy objects between databases.

Remember, you can also get the **Copy** and **Paste** commands by right-clicking on an object in the **Database** window or on a form or report.

The Record Source for the Sales Invoice report is a complex SQL statement. In fact, this query is considerably more complicated than the one we used for the Project Invoice. It uses the Customer, Order, OrderLine and Software

OrderNo	OrderDate	CustName	Alpha	Address	TownState	SaleM	SWareKey	SWareNam	Qty
S 0010	07-Jun-95	Le Bistro	LEBIS	Rue Francai	Vancouver,		WS 006	WroxSoft Pl	1
S 0010	07-Jun-95	Le Bistro	LEBIS	Rue Francai	Vancouver,		WS 006	WroxSoft Pl	2
S 0016	21-Jul-95	Cummings I	CUMMI	124th Street	Pittsburg, P		WS 007	Unix 'Cycle'	3
S 0016	21-Jul-95	Cummings I	CUMMI	124th Street	Pittsburg, P		WS 008	Unix 'Where	2
S 0017	04-Aug-95	Cummings I	CUMMI	124th Street	Pittsburg, P		WS 009	Visual Cobo	1
S 0019	07-Jul-95	Pedro Mana	MANAP	Calle Sebas	St. Paul, Mi		WS 002	WroxSoft Ai	4
S 0023	17-Jun-95	Miracle Sup	MIRAC	18th Avenue	Oakland, C/		WS 001	WroxSoft E:	2
S 0026	19-Jul-95	Major Recor	MAJOR	Third Avenue	Stocksville,		WS 008	Unix 'Where	3
⊙utoNumber)									

Record: 9 of 9

tables to produce a recordset which contains a record for each line of each order for each customer.

We need to include every line of every
order because we will be printing these
on the invoice. We've also included
Criteria which limits the records to
those not yet invoiced, just as we did
in the Project Invoice report.

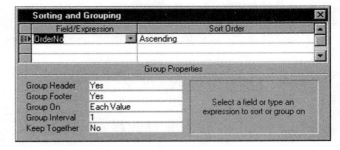

Even though the query is complex, the
report itself is again quite
straightforward. Sorting and Grouping
is set to 'break' the report each time
the order number changes, so that each order appears on a separate invoice:

The Page Header and OrderNo Header are identical to those on the Project Invoice report,
except that the SaleMemo field is used instead of the ProjectMemo and the column labels are
slightly different. The OrderNo Footer is also very similar, but now includes an additional count
of items to make customer's goods inwards easier.

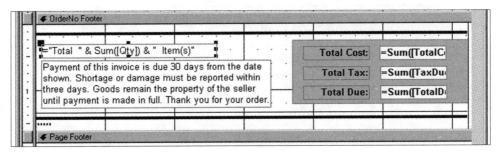

The Detail section contains all the basic information about the software plus the calculated fields
which hold the totals before and after tax, and the total tax due. However, you should
remember that there can be more than one record for each order number now, so the Detail
section will repeat for each order line on that order. Once all the lines for an order are printed,
the OrderNo Footer prints, and the Page Break control at the bottom of this forces a new page
- and hence a new invoice.

The Statement Report

Now that we've solved the problem of producing invoices, we can turn our attention to creating
a **statement**. This will show all the payments that are still due. This is a somewhat simplified
approach as you would normally expect to show all the transactions for the month, plus those
still outstanding from previous months and any payments made - giving a final total. As we
aren't using ledger tables to store this kind of information, the task becomes rather complex and
so, for clarity, we've chosen to stick with a simpler structure and method.

While we used two different invoice reports, one for each type of transaction, we can't really do
this with our statements. Our customers will not appreciate two different statements from us
each month, so we need to combine the projects and software sales information into one
document - the Statement report.

The obvious difficulty is how do we deal with the two quite different record structures? One
way would be to use separate subreports inside the main Statement report body - one for

projects and one for sales. But, in fact, we don't need as much information to produce a statement as we do to produce an invoice. We just need the order ref/invoice number, a brief note of the invoice details, the totals before and after tax, and the tax rate and tax amount.

Ideally, we want to output these on the report in Date order, so here's what we're aiming at:

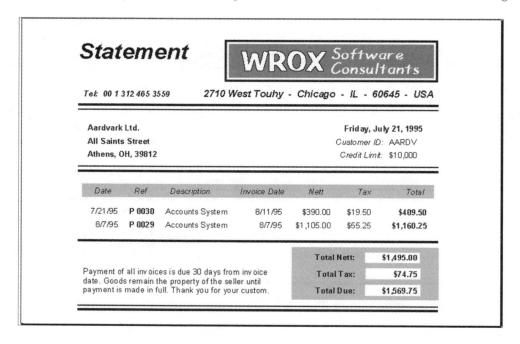

To achieve this, we need a recordset that contains a record for each invoice. We'll look at the query in a moment, but for now have a look at the recordset it produces:

The Sorting and Grouping dialog uses the Alpha field from this recordset to 'break' the report for each customer, before sorting the records in Date order.

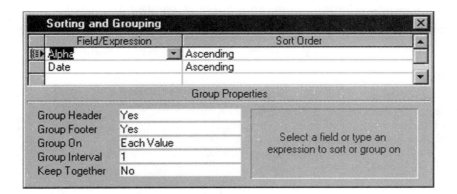

In design view you can see that the report is very similar to the two Invoice reports. It has a Page Header with the company logo and address, and a Detail section containing the values for each invoice. The Alpha Header contains the same customer information as the invoice reports, as well as the column headings for our statement. The Alpha Footer contains the same calculated controls to sum the values before and after tax, and for the total tax due. There's also a label with a terse warning Payments due exceed your credit limit - we'll come to this later as well.

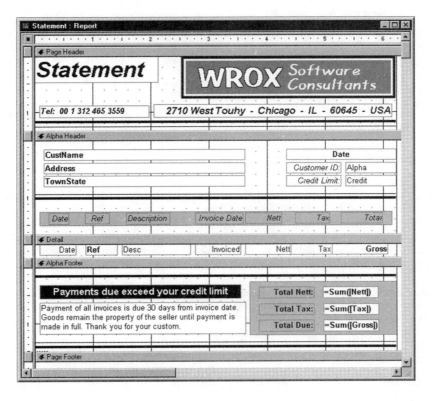

OK, so we've kept you waiting long enough. It's time to look at the query that combines the records from the two different tables to produce the recordset for the report. We'll work through this now to show you how it can be done.

Union Queries

When we use a select query, we can combine the records from different tables, but the result is extra fields, not more records. For example, if we use a select query to combine the Order and Project tables, we get a new table containing a field for each of the fields in both original tables.

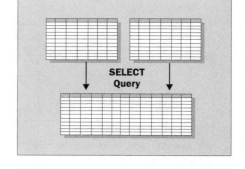

We need a recordset that includes both the project and sales records. Therefore, we need to combine them the other way, so that we have the same number of fields but more records. This is similar to **appending** the records from one table to another:

However, to use an **append query** we have to create new tables - we can't use this method to create a recordset. A more efficient way is to use a **union query**. This takes the two source tables (or recordsets) and appends one to the other.

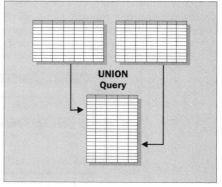

The Statement Report Union Query

To produce the complex recordset that we require for the Statement report, we need to create a **chain** of queries. This means we create each query from the results of other queries.

To actually create the necessary recordset for the Statement report, the first step is the Project Totals query. Take a look at the QBE version of the query in the database (select Project Totals in the Queries page of the Database window and click Design) or review the equivalent SQL statement shown below:

```
SELECT DISTINCTROW Project.CustKey, Project.ProjectKey, Project.Project,
Project.Date, Project.Invoiced, Project.Paid, Contact.ContactName,
Project.HoursWorked, [HoursWorked]*[HourlyRate] AS PCharge, [PCharge]*[TaxRate]/100
AS PTax, [PCharge]+[PTax] AS PTotal
FROM Project LEFT JOIN Contact ON Project.MainContactKey = Contact.ContactKey;
```

FYI We will cover SQL in more detail in Chapter 14, so don't worry if you are confused by the above statement. Remember that you can always view the query in the more familiar Query grid.

This query uses the Project and Contact tables, and links them so that all Project records are included and only those Contact records where the ContactKey value matches the value in the MainContactKey field of the Project table. So, if there's no main contact for a project, we still get a record. As you can see, we also use three calculated fields to create the necessary information for our recordset, providing us with ledger totals for each project.

It's worth taking a look at the resulting recordset at this stage, to familiarize yourself with the content and to check that the query as a whole is functioning as you would expect:

Project Totals : Select Query

CustKey	ProjectKey	Project	Date	Invoiced	Paid	ContactNam	HoursWor	PCharge	PTax	PTotal
51	P 0029	Accounts	7-Aug-95	7-Aug-95		Mr. Arnson	17	1105	55.25	1160.25
51	P 0030	Accounts	21-Jul-95	1-Aug-95		Mr. Arnson	6	390	19.5	409.5
51	P 0031	Accounts	8-Aug-95			Mr. Arnson	3	195	9.75	204.75
52	P 0032	Menu Gen	14-Jun-95			Julia Fry	12	660	82.5	742.5
55	P 0033	Sales Trac	3-Apr-95	4-Apr-95		Carrie Newto	51	2473.5	185.5125	2659.0125
55	P 0034	Sales Trac	0-Apr-95			Carrie Newto	7	339.5	25.4625	364.9625
55	P 0035	Sales Trac	5-May-95	0-May-95	3-Jul-95	Carrie Newto	33	1600.5	120.0375	1720.5375
53	P 0036	School Infc	17-Jun-95	19-Jun-95		Mark Smith	63	4725	0	4725
53	P 0037	School Infc	21-Jul-95			Mark Smith	14	1050	0	1050
57	P 0038	PC Suppor	3-Feb-95	6-Aug-95	3-Apr-95	Bill James	4	160	20	180
57	P 0039	PC Suppor	8-Aug-95			Bill James	9	360	45	405
57	P 0040	PC Suppor	8-Aug-95	0-Aug-95		Bill James	7	280	35	315
58	P 0041	Navigation	14-Apr-95	14-Apr-95		Jonah Wood	19	1615	129.2	1744.2

Record: 1 of 24

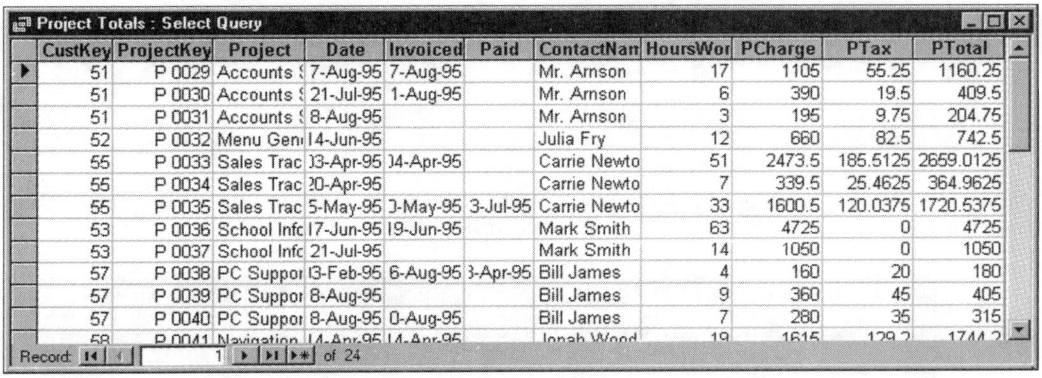

Now, we need the same information about our software sales from the Order table, but unfortunately it's not that easy. There are several OrderLine records for each Order record, so we have to sum the values from them to give the totals for each order using a **totals query** (one of the summary queries).

To complicate matters, we can't use calculated fields in a totals query, so to get the calculated values for each order line (the total before and after tax and the total tax due), we have to first create a query to achieve this using the Order and OrderLine tables.

For this task, we have used the Order Analysis query:

```
SELECT DISTINCTROW Order.CustKey, OrderLine.OrderNo, [Qty]*[Price] AS OPrice,
[Qty]*[Price]*[Discount]/100 AS ODiscount, [OPrice]-[ODiscount] AS OCharge,
[OCharge]*[TaxRate]/100 AS OTax, [OCharge]+[OTax] AS OTotal
FROM [Order] INNER JOIN OrderLine ON Order.OrderNo = OrderLine.OrderNo
ORDER BY Order.CustKey, OrderLine.OrderNo;
```

This query links the Order and OrderLine tables and creates the various totals we need for each order line, including the customer key and the order number. Again, it's worth looking at the resulting recordset. Notice that there is a record for each line of each order.

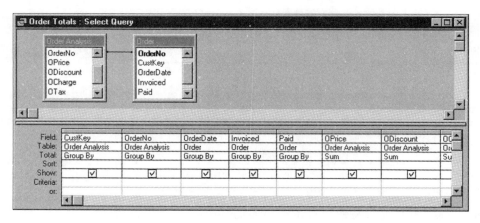

CustKey	OrderNo	OPrice	ODiscount	OCharge	OTax	OTotal
51	5	$299.85	0	$299.85	29.985	$329.84
51	5	$659.90	16.4975	$643.40	64.34025	$707.74
51	6	$659.90	0	$659.90	65.99	$725.89
52	7	$499.00	0	$499.00	62.375	$561.38
55	8	$6,986.00	1397.2	$5,588.80	558.88	$6,147.68
55	8	$1,399.30	279.86	$1,119.44	111.944	$1,231.38
55	16	$2,385.00	0	$2,385.00	238.5	$2,623.50
55	16	$998.00	0	$998.00	99.8	$1,097.80
55	17	$599.00	0	$599.00	59.9	$658.90
55	27	$3,588.00	358.8	$3,229.20	403.65	$3,632.85
55	28	$0.00	0	$0.00	0	$0.00
55	28	$9,540.00	1431	$8,109.00	810.9	$8,919.90
56	9	$399.00	0	$399.00	39.9	$438.90

Record: 8 of 41

Now we can add together the records for each order to give the Order totals, rather than the OrderLine totals we have here. To do this we use a totals query:

The source for this query, called Order Totals, is the Order table and the recordset we created in the Order Analysis query, linked on the OrderNo field.

As you saw in Chapter 6, when we select the Totals button Access adds the Total: row to the grid, allowing us to perform a variety of mathematical functions on the data.

The CustKey, OrderNo, OrderDate, Invoiced and Paid fields are set to Group By so they appear in the recordset as normal, but the calculated fields from our Order Analysis query have Sum in the Total: row. These settings cause the query to return one record for each order, adding together the calculated field entries for any orders with multiple order lines.

Totals button

Running this query should present you with the following recordset:

	CustKey	OrderNo	OrderDate	Invoiced	Paid	SumOfOPric	SumOfODisc	SumOfOCha	SumOfOTax	SumOfOTota
	51	5	19-Feb-95	21-Feb-95	3-Apr-95	$959.75	16.4975	$943.25	94.32525	$1,037.58
	51	6	05-Jul-95	08-Jul-95	-Aug-95	$659.90	0	$659.90	65.99	$725.89
	52	7	13-Jun-95	15-Jul-95	8-Jul-95	$499.00	0	$499.00	62.375	$561.38
	55	8	15-May-95	0-May-95	4-Jul-95	$8,385.30	1677.06	$6,708.24	670.824	$7,379.06
	55	16	21-Jul-95			$3,383.00	0	$3,383.00	338.3	$3,721.30
	55	17	04-Aug-95			$599.00	0	$599.00	59.9	$658.90
	55	27	24-Aug-95	24-Aug-95		$3,588.00	358.8	$3,229.20	403.65	$3,632.85
	55	28	24-Aug-95	24-Aug-95		$9,540.00	1431	$8,109.00	810.9	$8,919.90
	56	9	13-Mar-95	15-Mar-95		$1,556.40	0	$1,556.40	155.64	$1,712.04
	56	14	21-May-95	26-Jul-95		$989.85	0	$989.85	98.985	$1,088.84
	59	10	07-Jun-95			$299.85	0	$299.85	29.985	$329.84
	60	11	04-Mar-95	04-Mar-95	-Mar-95	$798.00	0	$798.00	79.8	$877.80
	60	26	19-Jul-95			$1,497.00	149.7	$1,347.30	134.73	$1,482.03
▶	62	20	03-Feb-95	03-Feb-95		$6,275.35	1568.8375	$4,706.51	470.65125	$5,177.16

Record: 14 of 21

So now we have two queries, Order Totals and Project Totals, both of which are good starting points for our complex Statement report record source. However, one thing you should notice is that although the two queries produce recordsets which are similar, the field names don't match, and they're not similar enough to be combined directly. We need to fine-tune each recordset first using another query.

We know what the final recordset needs to look like so we can modify the results of the Project Totals and Order Totals queries to suit. We need a recordset containing the CustKey, Date, a Description and Reference for each item, plus the Nett, Tax, and Gross values for each, as well as the appropriate Invoiced date:

	CustKey	Date	Desc	Ref	Nett	Tax	Gross	Invoiced
	51	7/21/95	Accounts S	P 0030	390	19.5	409.5	8/11/95
	51	8/7/95	Accounts S	P 0029	1105	55.25	1160.25	8/7/95
	53	6/17/95	School Info	P 0036	4725	0	4725	6/19/95
	55	4/3/95	Sales Track	P 0033	2473.5	185.5125	2659.0125	4/4/95
	55	8/24/95	Software	S 0027	3229.2	403.65	3632.85	8/24/95
	55	8/24/95	Software	S 0028	8109	810.9	8919.9	8/24/95
	56	3/13/95	Software	S 0009	1556.4	155.64	1712.04	3/15/95
	56	5/21/95	Software	S 0014	989.85	98.985	1088.835	7/26/95
	57	8/8/95	PC Support	P 0040	280	35	315	8/10/95
	58	4/14/95	Navigation S	P 0041	1615	129.2	1744.2	4/14/95
	60	6/19/95	Warehouse	P 0047	350	35	385	6/19/95
▶	62	2/3/95	Software	S 0020	4706.5125	470.65125	5177.1638	2/3/95
	62	7/19/95	Software	S 0024	1236.4875	123.64875	1360.1363	7/21/95
	66	7/9/95	Software	S 0025	474.05	47.405	521.455	7/11/95

Record: 12 of 14

We'll create the new query based on the Project Totals query. Basically, all this has to do is select the fields we want and change the names to suit. We can also take the opportunity to format the ProjectKey field so that it appears like a project number (such as 'P 0047') and, because we're only using it for Statements, we need only include records where the Paid field is empty and the Invoiced field is not:

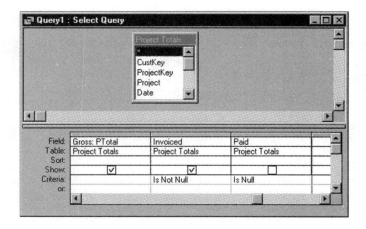

The recordset this produces is exactly what we want. To see it, switch to datasheet view:

CustKey	Date	Desc	Ref	Nett	Tax	Gross	Invoiced
51	07-Aug-95	Accounts System	P 0029	1105	55.25	1160.25	07-Aug-95
51	21-Jul-95	Accounts System	P 0030	390	19.5	409.5	11-Aug-95
55	03-Apr-95	Sales Tracking	P 0033	2473.5	185.5125	2659.0125	04-Apr-95
53	17-Jun-95	School Info System	P 0036	4725	0	4725	19-Jun-95
57	08-Aug-95	PC Support	P 0040	280	35	315	10-Aug-95
58	14-Apr-95	Navigation System	P 0041	1615	129.2	1744.2	14-Apr-95
60	19-Jun-95	Warehouse System	P 0047	350	35	385	19-Jun-95

Record: 8 of 8

We now need to repeat the process using the Order Totals query. We simply select and rename the appropriate fields, reformat OrderNo (e.g. 'S 0164') and restrict the selection to records where the Paid field is empty and the Invoiced field is not.

The only major difference between the two queries is the Desc field. As we can have more than one software product on each order, we can't place the name of the product in the new Desc field as we did with the project name. Instead, we use a calculated field which is just filled with the value 'Software'.

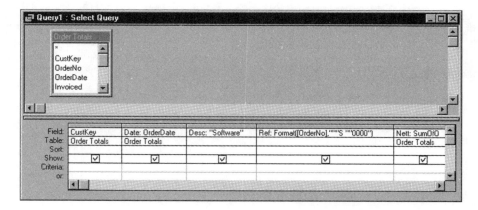

386

Again we've limited the records to those that have been invoiced but not yet paid. To see the results of this query switch to datasheet view. The structure is the same as the previous one and the target recordset.

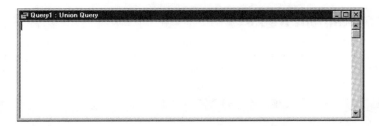

	CustKey	Date	Desc	Ref	Nett	Tax	Gross	Invoiced
	55	24-Aug-95	Software	S 0027	$3,229.20	403.65	$3,632.85	24-Aug-95
	55	24-Aug-95	Software	S 0028	$8,109.00	810.9	$8,919.90	24-Aug-95
	56	13-Mar-95	Software	S 0009	$1,556.40	155.64	$1,712.04	15-Mar-95
	56	21-May-95	Software	S 0014	$989.85	98.985	$1,088.84	26-Jul-95
	62	03-Feb-95	Software	S 0020	$4,706.51	470.65125	$5,177.16	03-Feb-95
	62	19-Jul-95	Software	S 0024	$1,236.49	123.64875	$1,360.14	21-Jul-95
▶	66	09-Jul-95	Software	S 0025	$474.05	47.405	$521.46	7/11/95

Record: ◄◄ ◄ 7 ► ►► ►* of 7

So, we're now ready to combine these two queries together using a union query. We can't do this with the Query Builder as it doesn't support union queries. Instead, we have to build it in a different manner.

We create a new blank query without adding any tables, then select SQL Specific from the Query menu, and click Union. Access opens an empty window:

Query1 : Union Query

To create a union query, we must enter an SQL **UNION** statement. This is just the two SQL statements that create the recordsets we want to join, separated by the **UNION** keyword. We've already got the two queries that produce our recordsets, so we switch these to SQL View and copy the SQL statements from each.

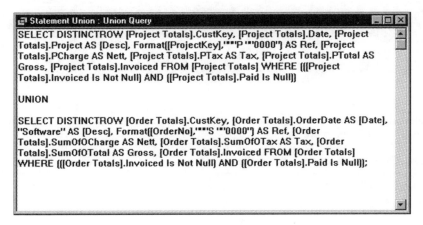

```
Statement Union : Union Query

SELECT DISTINCTROW [Project Totals].CustKey, [Project Totals].Date, [Project
Totals].Project AS [Desc], Format([ProjectKey],'""P '"0000") AS Ref, [Project
Totals].PCharge AS Nett, [Project Totals].PTax AS Tax, [Project Totals].PTotal AS
Gross, [Project Totals].Invoiced FROM [Project Totals] WHERE (([Project
Totals].Invoiced Is Not Null] AND [[Project Totals].Paid Is Null])

UNION

SELECT DISTINCTROW [Order Totals].CustKey, [Order Totals].OrderDate AS [Date],
"Software" AS [Desc], Format([OrderNo],'""S '"0000") AS Ref, [Order
Totals].SumOfOCharge AS Nett, [Order Totals].SumOfOTax AS Tax, [Order
Totals].SumOfOTotal AS Gross, [Order Totals].Invoiced FROM [Order Totals]
WHERE (([Order Totals].Invoiced Is Not Null] AND [[Order Totals].Paid Is Null]);
```

387

This rather intimidating statement will produce a recordset which combines the summaries of all our invoiced but unpaid projects and software sales. We've saved this query as Statement Union. Running this query produces the following results:

	CustKey	Date	Desc	Ref	Nett	Tax	Gross	Invoiced
▶	51	7/21/95	Accounts System	P 0030	390	19.5	409.5	8/11/95
	51	8/7/95	Accounts System	P 0029	1105	55.25	1160.25	8/7/95
	53	6/17/95	School Info System	P 0036	4725	0	4725	6/19/95
	55	4/3/95	Sales Tracking	P 0033	2473.5	185.5125	2659.0125	4/4/95
	55	8/24/95	Software	S 0027	3229.2	403.65	3632.85	8/24/95
	55	8/24/95	Software	S 0028	8109	810.9	8919.9	8/24/95
	56	3/13/95	Software	S 0009	1556.4	155.64	1712.04	3/15/95
	56	5/21/95	Software	S 0014	989.85	98.985	1088.835	7/26/95
	57	8/8/95	PC Support	P 0040	280	35	315	8/10/95
	58	4/14/95	Navigation System	P 0041	1615	129.2	1744.2	4/14/95
	60	6/19/95	Warehouse System	P 0047	350	35	385	6/19/95
	62	2/3/95	Software	S 0020	)6.5125	470.65125	5177.1638	2/3/95
	62	7/19/95	Software	S 0024	36.4875	123.64875	1360.1363	7/21/95
	66	7/9/95	Software	S 0025	474.05	47.405	521.455	7/11/95

Record: 1 of 14

Back to the Statement Report

Now that we've done the hard work, let's return to the report itself to see where to go from here. Take a look at the record source that the report is based upon. Notice that it doesn't use the Statement Union query directly - it's just one of the sources of the final query:

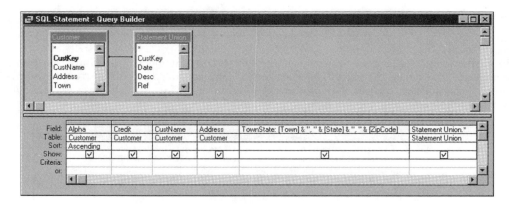

By linking the Statement union query we've just created to the Customer table, we can provide all the details we need for our Statement report and only include records for projects and sales which haven't yet been paid.

You can see now what we meant earlier when we said that you could do almost anything with queries. We've used the output of one query as the input to another so that we have a recordset which exactly matches our needs. Union queries add another level to our ability to manipulate data.

388

The disadvantages of chaining queries is that each query in the chain has to be executed again if the source records change. So it obviously takes a lot longer to run than a simple query. And, of course, in our union query there are actually two chains providing source records.

A union query demands that the two recordsets are of the same format, i.e. have the same number of fields. Strange results can occur if you don't get the fields in the same order. Access will still integrate the records, but the fields from the second query will appear in the wrong fields in the resulting recordset. Access uses the format of the first query as the basis of the results set.

Using 'On Format' to Show Information

You'll recall we found a rather terse message on the Statement report in design view, yet you may not have seen it when you ran the report in the normal way. The message only appears on the statement if the total exceeds the customer's credit limit - if you check the Format tab in the Properties window for this label (it's named lblOverCredit), you'll see that the Visible property is set to No. When the report is printed, a macro checks the total of the statement and compares it to the customer's credit limit. If it is exceeded, the macro sets the label's Visible property to Yes for that record only.

Event	Description
On Format	Occurs before the section is formatted, but after the values that will be used in it are known.
On Print	Occurs after the section has been formatted, and before printing starts.
On Retreat	Assuming the Keep Together propety is set, this occurs if the end of a page is reached and the section will not fit. Access then has to go back to the beginning of the section and move it to the next page.

Each section of a report has events which occur at various stages of the printing process. Click on the section header - the gray bar with the section name on it - then click the Events tab in the Properties window to see them.

If we place the name of a macro in the On Format event, we can examine the values in the controls on the report - Access will know what they contain at that point. We've placed MainMenu.StatementFormat in the On Format event of the Alpha Footer section. This will run the StatementFormat macro on the MainMenu macro sheet:

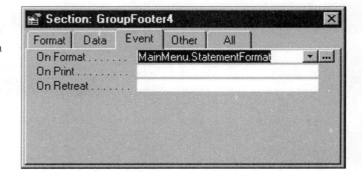

Open the macro sheet, and scroll down to the StatementFormat macro. It consists of just one action:

Condition: [Reports]![Statement]![Grand_TotalDue] > [Reports]![Statement]![Credit]
Action: SetValue
 Item: [Reports]![Statement]![lblOverCredit].[Visible]
 Expression: Yes

The condition compares the value in the Grand_TotalDue control on the report (which holds the statement total) with the value in the Credit control. If the first is greater, it sets the Visible property of the lblOverCredit (our message) to Yes.

So, now we have the three reports we need - two for invoicing each type of transaction and one to produce monthly statements. The way that we've constructed them means that they include all the records from our tables which haven't yet been invoiced or, in the case of statements, have been invoiced but not paid.

This is OK for batch invoicing, say once a week, and monthly statements, but it's not terribly useful if we just want a particular invoice or statement. We need to be able to select which ones we want to print - either by customer or by individual project or sale, so that we can print the invoice for a transaction that we've just entered in the Projects and Sales form.

The Invoice Selector Form

When you select the Invoices and Statements option in the main menu, the application displays a separate form where you can select what to print. You can select Invoices or Statements, and then specify if you want them for all customers or just one particular customer.

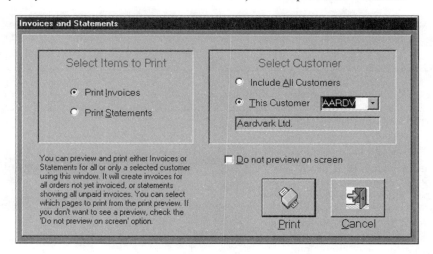

By investigating this form and its associated properties, you will soon be able to deduce that it's being used as a dialog, with all the normal settings for such a form. As for the actual contents of the form, we're already familiar with most of the controls. However, the extra combo box in the Select Customer frame makes this one more interesting.

The combo box is disabled (grayed out) when you open the form, but is enabled when you select the This Customer option button. When you select a customer from the list, their name is placed in the text box below. But look at the list in the combo box - there are only a few of the customers there. Now select the Print Statements option and open the combo again. This time the list is different.

Developing the Combo

Check out the combo box's Row Source property; it's set to the name of a query – Customers for Invoice. This query supplies the list of customers for the combo box. You can examine it by clicking the builder button in the Row Source property:

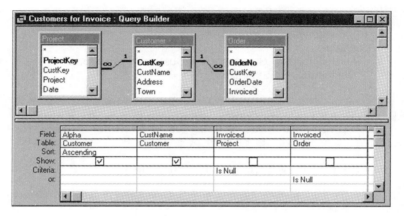

The query takes the customer's name and Alpha code from the Customer table, but only for those customers where there is a null (empty) Invoiced field in a Project or Order record. In other words, it only includes customers who have a project or sale which hasn't been invoiced.

If you now look at the query called Customers for Statement, you'll see that it is pretty similar, except that now the Null is in the Paid field. This query produces a list of customers who have been invoiced for something and haven't yet paid us.

So, to get the required effect, all we have to do is make sure the Record Source of the combo box is set to the correct query when the user selects Print Invoices or Print Statements - a simple task for a macro. The macro in question is attached to the On Click event of the option group frame, and is called MainMenu.SelItemChange. Take a look at it:

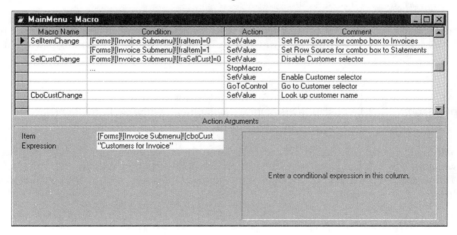

This macro checks the value of the option group fraItem. If the first option is selected, it will be 0; if the second option is selected, it will be 1. A SetValue action is used to set the Row Source of the combo box to the name of the correct query:

Condition: [Forms]![Invoice Submenu]![fraItem]=0
Action: SetValue
 Item: [Forms]![Invoice Submenu]![cboCustomer].[RowSource]
 Expression: "Customers for Invoice"

or Print Statements:

Condition: [Forms]![Invoice Submenu]![fraItem]=1
Action: SetValue
 Item: [Forms]![Invoice Submenu]![cboCustomer].[RowSource]
 Expression: "Customers for Statement"

Underneath this, you'll see the other two macros that the form uses. SelCustChange runs when the user clicks the Select Customer option buttons, checking to see if the selected option is Include All Customers, i.e. if the Value of fraSelCust is 0. If this is true, it disables the combo box by using SetValue to change its Enabled property to False, then stops.

Condition: [Forms]![Invoice Submenu]![fraSelCust]=0
Action: SetValue
 Item: [Forms]![Invoice Submenu]![cboCustomer].[Enabled]
 Expression: False

Condition: ...
Action: StopMacro

If the macro is still running, the selected option must be This customer (the Value of fraSelCust is 1), so we need to enable the combo box and move to it.

Action: SetValue
 Item: [Forms]![Invoice Submenu]![cboCustomer].[Enabled]
 Expression: True

Action: GoToControl
 Control Name: cboCustomer

The cboCustChange macro runs when the user selects a name in the combo box, and it uses a SetValue action with the **DLookup** function to find the customer's name, placing it in the text box underneath.

Action: SetValue
 Item: [Forms]![Invoice Submenu]![txtCustomer]
 Expression: DLookUp("[CustName]","Customer","Alpha = Forms![Invoice Submenu]![cboCustomer]")

The expression part searches the Customer table for a record where the Alpha field is equal to the value in the cboCustomer combo box on the form. It then returns the value from the CustName field of that record and the SetValue action places this in the txtCustomer text box on the form.

So we've seen how we can implement invoicing and creating statements. We've built forms and reports which offer our users the flexibility and ease-of-use that they're now beginning to expect from our application.

Complex Queries as a Basis for Reports

With the exception of the Statement report, all the reports we've seen so far are based on relatively simple queries or directly on the tables in our application. While this can show useful information, it's only directly applicable if you want to know about one particular customer, project or sale. In a business environment much of the data that any company processes every day is effectively lost. It's still stored in the tables of the database, but there's no real method of accessing it in a way that provides information about trends and changes in the business.

This has always been one of the complaints leveled against the main-frame computer and centralized data processing system. In Part 3 of this book we'll be looking at a relatively new subject called **data warehousing**, where the useful parts of this daily stream of data are captured and stored so that they can provide a real commercial advantage to the business.

However, there's a lot we can still do with our existing tables. In fact, with Access you are only limited by your own ability to construct ever more complex queries. In theory, you can extract almost any data and use it as the basis for another query, before repeating the process to get exactly the result you need - just like we did with the chain of queries that supply the records for our Statement report.

The Four Sales and Projects Reports

Our application presents the user with two report submenus - Customer Information and Sales and Projects Reports. The Customer Information reports, as we saw earlier, are primarily aimed at displaying information broken down by customer. However, the Sales and Projects Reports option on the main menu opens a list showing four other reports where the focus is more on information about the business as a whole. These retrieve information sorted by the project type or software sale, and show trends that are useful in planning for the future.

393

To show how versatile Access is at creating different types of reports, we've chosen four quite different ones:

▶ The Projects and Sales report summarizes all the project work done and software sales made, by type, giving an overall listing and providing the total values. It's an easy way to see how the company is performing.

▶ The Payments Outstanding report simply lists each type of project or sale that hasn't yet been paid for. It's similar to the Customer History report, but sorts the information in a different way.

▶ The Software Sales Income report provides a list of software sales by product, showing the profit made on each one. This helps pick out poor selling lines, or those that we have to sell at low margins. It includes the order number so that we can track where the sale was made.

▶ The Projects Analysis report is basically the one we created in Part 1. It breaks down the projects by type, and shows useful information about the rates we charge and the amount of time we spend on each one.

We'll take a brief look at just the first three of these - we created and studied the Projects Analysis report in Part 1. While we won't go into great depth, we'll try and point out the basis on which they work. Actually creating them is simple once you've got the sorting and grouping right, and you're working on a recordset that contains the values you need. Remember that you can always experiment by creating the queries first from the Database window, and viewing the resulting recordset. Once you're satisfied with the information, it's a relatively easy task to build the report around it.

The Projects and Sales Report

This is a little unusual as the main report isn't based on any records - the Record Source property of the report is blank. This is an unbound report, and is used in a similar way to the unbound form we used as a selector dialog window. It's simply a container for the subreports:

There are two subreports in the Detail section - one that provides the information about projects and the other for sales. As the main report is unbound, it only displays one Detail section when you print it.

Sales and Projects Summary

13-Sep-95

Projects Summary

Ref	Date	Invoiced	Paid	Project	Hours	Total	Tax Due	FinalTotal
P 0029	8/7/95	8/7/95		Accounts System	17	$1,105.00	$55.25	$1,160.25
P 0030	7/21/95	8/11/95		Accounts System	6	$390.00	$19.50	$409.50
P 0031	8/8/95			Accounts System	3	$195.00	$9.75	$204.75
P 0032	6/14/95			Menu Generator	12	$660.00	$82.50	$742.50
P 0033	4/3/95	4/4/95		Sales Tracking	51	$2,473.50	$185.51	$2,659.01
P 0034	4/20/95			Sales Tracking	7	$339.50	$25.46	$364.96
P 0035	5/15/95	5/20/95	7/3/95	Sales Tracking	33	$1,600.50	$120.04	$1,720.54
P 0036	6/17/95	6/19/95		School Info System	63	$4,725.00	$0.00	$4,725.00
P 0037	7/21/95			School Info System	14	$1,050.00	$0.00	$1,050.00
P 0038	2/3/95	8/16/95	4/3/95	PC Support	4	$160.00	$20.00	$180.00
P 0039	8/8/95			PC Support	9	$360.00	$45.00	$405.00
P 0046	5/30/95	5/30/95	7/5/95	Warehouse Syste	19	$950.00	$95.00	$1,045.00
P 0047	6/19/95	6/19/95		Warehouse Syste	7	$350.00	$35.00	$385.00
P 0048	7/4/95	7/4/95	7/17/95	Warehouse Syste	3	$150.00	$15.00	$165.00
P 0049	2/15/95	2/17/95	6/28/95	Menu Generator	5	$425.00	$34.00	$459.00
P 0050	5/7/95	5/20/95	7/3/95	Warehouse Syste	27	$1,485.00	$133.65	$1,618.65
P 0051	6/28/95			Warehouse Syste	19	$1,045.00	$94.05	$1,139.05
P 0052	7/19/95			Sales Tracking	14	$980.00	$98.00	$1,078.00
				Totals:	427	24,858.50	1,683.91	$26,542.41

Software Sales Summary

OrderNo	Date	Invoiced	Paid	Goods	Discount	Total	Tax Due	Order Total
S 0005	2/19/95	2/21/95	4/3/95	$959.75	$16.50	$943.25	$94.33	$1,037.58
S 0006	7/5/95	7/8/95	8/3/95	$659.90	$0.00	$659.90	$65.99	$725.89
S 0007	6/13/95	7/15/95	7/28/95	$499.00	$0.00	$499.00	$62.38	$561.38
S 0008	5/15/95	5/20/95	7/4/95	$8,385.30	1,677.06	$6,708.24	$670.82	$7,379.06
S 0009	3/13/95	3/15/95		$1,556.40	$0.00	$1,556.40	$155.64	$1,712.04
S 0010	6/7/95			$299.85	$0.00	$299.85	$29.99	$329.84

Page 1 of 2

394

However, the subreports do have repeating Detail sections for each record and can grow down the page as required, as you saw when we looked at the Can Grow properties earlier on. So, the Detail section of the main report will grow in length, expanding to cover more than one page if necessary:

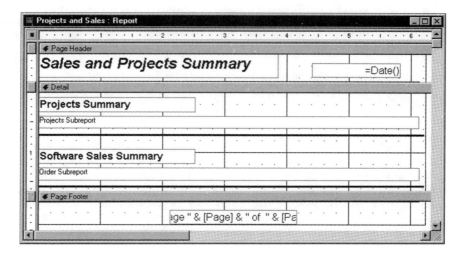

The records for the two subreports come from the two queries we've already created for our invoices and statements. The Projects Subreport is based on the Project Totals query, and the Order Subreport on the Order Totals query. The two subreports are similar, each using a header to display the field descriptions and a footer with the calculated totals controls.

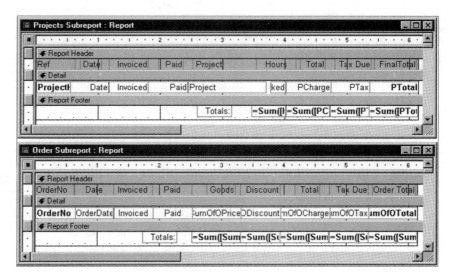

This is a good example of how you can re-use existing queries. If you look at the results of the Project Totals query, you'll see it actually contains fields that we don't use in our subreport. This isn't important, and it does mean we don't have to worry about creating a new query.

Project Totals : Select Query

	CustKey	ProjectKey	Project	Date	Invoiced	Paid	ContactNam	HoursWor	PCharge	PTax	PTotal
▶	51	P 0029	Accounts {	7-Aug-95	7-Aug-95		Mr. Arnson	17	1105	55.25	1160.25
	51	P 0030	Accounts {	21-Jul-95	1-Aug-95		Mr. Arnson	6	390	19.5	409.5
	51	P 0031	Accounts {	8-Aug-95			Mr. Arnson	3	195	9.75	204.75
	52	P 0032	Menu Gen	14-Jun-95			Julia Fry	12	660	82.5	742.5
	55	P 0033	Sales Trac	03-Apr-95	04-Apr-95		Carrie Newto	51	2473.5	185.5125	2659.0125
	55	P 0034	Sales Trac	20-Apr-95			Carrie Newto	7	339.5	25.4625	364.9625
	55	P 0035	Sales Trac	5-May-95	0-May-95	3-Jul-95	Carrie Newto	33	1600.5	120.0375	1720.5375
	53	P 0036	School Inf	17-Jun-95	19-Jun-95		Mark Smith	63	4725	0	4725
	53	P 0037	School Inf	21-Jul-95			Mark Smith	14	1050	0	1050
	57	P 0038	PC Suppor	3-Feb-95	6-Aug-95	3-Apr-95	Bill James	4	160	20	180
	57	P 0039	PC Suppor	8-Aug-95			Bill James	9	360	45	405
	57	P 0040	PC Suppor	8-Aug-95	0-Aug-95		Bill James	7	280	35	315
	58	P 0041	Navigation	14-Apr-95	14-Apr-95		Jonah Wood	19	1615	129.2	1744.2

Record: ◀◀ ◀ | 1 | ▶ ▶◀ ▶* | of 24

If you change a query that is used in more than one place, you must ensure that it performs correctly each time. If you remove any fields, for instance the ones we aren't using in the **Projects Subreport**, you'll 'break' any other forms or reports which require that field. You'll then get **#Name?** or **#Error?** displayed instead of the right field. You should also bear in mind that a query can be used as the basis for another one by nesting them, so you can cause other queries to fail as well.

The Payments Outstanding Report

The query for this report supplies all the information it needs - there are no subreports. The information is displayed by project or sale type, and each type is sorted by date.

Payments Outstanding by Type
Tuesday, September 13, 1995

Accounts System

			Date	Invoiced	Nett	Tax	Gross
P 0030	AARDV	Aardvark Ltd.	7/21/95	8/11/95	£390.00	£19.50	£409.50
P 0029	AARDV	Aardvark Ltd.	8/7/95	8/7/95	£1,105.00	£55.25	£1,160.25
				Totals:	£1,495.00	£74.75	£1,569.75

Navigation System

			Date	Invoiced	Nett	Tax	Gross
P 0041	JONAH	Jonahs Boats	4/14/95	4/14/95	£1,615.00	£129.20	£1,744.20
				Totals:	£1,615.00	£129.20	£1,744.20

PC Support

			Date	Invoiced	Nett	Tax	Gross
P 0040	JAMES	James Builders	8/8/95	8/10/95	£280.00	£35.00	£315.00
				Totals:	£280.00	£35.00	£315.00

Sales Tracking

			Date	Invoiced	Nett	Tax	Gross
P 0033	CUMMI	Cummings Intl.	4/3/95	4/4/95	£2,473.50	£185.51	£2,659.01
				Totals:	£2,473.50	£185.51	£2,659.01

So, we need a recordset which contains all the projects and sales that are currently unpaid, i.e. have a blank Paid field. As we're sorting them by project or sale type, we need them to be in one single recordset. We already have a query that does this - the Statement Union Query we used to print the customer's statements:

	CustKey	Date	Desc	Ref	Nett	Tax	Gross	Invoiced
▶	51	7/21/95	Accounts System	P 0030	390	19.5	409.5	8/11/95
	51	8/7/95	Accounts System	P 0029	1105	55.25	1160.25	8/7/95
	53	6/17/95	School Info System	P 0036	4725	0	4725	6/19/95
	55	4/3/95	Sales Tracking	P 0033	2473.5	185.5125	2659.0125	4/4/95
	55	8/24/95	Software	S 0027	3229.2	403.65	3632.85	8/24/95
	55	8/24/95	Software	S 0028	8109	810.9	8919.9	8/24/95
	56	3/13/95	Software	S 0009	1556.4	155.64	1712.04	3/15/95
	56	5/21/95	Software	S 0014	989.85	98.985	1088.835	7/26/95
	57	8/8/95	PC Support	P 0040	280	35	315	8/10/95
	58	4/14/95	Navigation System	P 0041	1615	129.2	1744.2	4/14/95
	60	6/19/95	Warehouse System	P 0047	350	35	385	6/19/95
	62	2/3/95	Software	S 0020	4706.5125	470.65125	5177.1638	2/3/95
	62	7/19/95	Software	S 0024	1236.4875	123.64875	1360.1363	7/21/95
	66	7/9/95	Software	S 0025	474.05	47.405	521.455	7/11/95

Record: 1 of 14

However, this only contains the customer key field, CustKey, while we need the customer's ID code and name. No problem - we just use the Statement Union query as the basis for a new query and link it to the Customer table. Then we can retrieve the customer details and create a new recordset that has all the information we need:

```
SELECT DISTINCTROW Customer.CustName, Customer.Alpha, [Statement Union].Date,
[Statement Union].Desc, [Statement Union].Ref, [Statement Union].Invoiced, [State-
ment Union].Nett, [Statement Union].Tax, [Statement Union].Gross
FROM [Statement Union] INNER JOIN Customer ON [Statement Union].CustKey =
Customer.CustKey;
```

If you run this query, you'll get the following recordset:

	CustName	Alpha	Date	Desc	Ref	Invoiced	Nett	Tax	Gross
▶	Aardvark Ltd.	AARDV	7/21/95	Accounts System	P 0030	8/11/95	390	19.5	409.5
	Aardvark Ltd.	AARDV	8/7/95	Accounts System	P 0029	8/7/95	1105	55.25	1160.25
	Education De	EDUCA	6/17/95	School Info System	P 0036	6/19/95	4725	0	4725
	Cummings Int	CUMMI	4/3/95	Sales Tracking	P 0033	4/4/95	2473.5	185.5125	2659.0125
	Cummings Int	CUMMI	8/24/95	Software	S 0027	8/24/95	3229.2	403.65	3632.85
	Cummings Int	CUMMI	8/24/95	Software	S 0028	8/24/95	8109	810.9	8919.9
	J.R.Higgins	HIGGI	3/13/95	Software	S 0009	3/15/95	1556.4	155.64	1712.04
	J.R.Higgins	HIGGI	5/21/95	Software	S 0014	7/26/95	989.85	98.985	1088.835
	James Builde	JAMES	8/8/95	PC Support	P 0040	8/10/95	280	35	315
	Jonahs Boats	JONAH	4/14/95	Navigation System	P 0041	4/14/95	1615	129.2	1744.2
	Major Record	MAJOR	6/19/95	Warehouse System	P 0047	6/19/95	350	35	385
	Miracle Suppl	MIRAC	2/3/95	Software	S 0020	2/3/95	4706.5125	470.65125	5177.1638
	Miracle Suppl	MIRAC	7/19/95	Software	S 0024	7/21/95	1236.4875	123.64875	1360.1363
	Union Record	UNION	7/9/95	Software	S 0025	7/11/95	474.05	47.405	521.455

Record: 1 of 14

Back in the report itself, the sorting and grouping is set to break on the Desc field - the project or sale description - and sort the records in each by Date. From there, it's a simple matter to build the final report.

The Software Sales Income Report

This report has the same simple structure as the Payments Outstanding report. There are no subreports - we simply break the report on software product type and summarize the data for each one. We also use calculated fields to show the percentage profit for each item, and the overall results.

Software Sales Income   9/13/95

WS 001   WroxSoft Excellent for Windows 95

OrderNo	Qty	Cost	TotalCost	Nett	Total Nett	Profit	Total Profit	Margin
S 0009	1	$188.33	$188.33	$299.00	$299.00	$110.67	**$110.67**	37.01%
S 0020	3	$188.33	$564.99	$224.25	$672.75	$35.92	**$107.76**	16.02%
S 0021	2	$188.33	$376.66	$224.25	$448.50	$35.92	**$71.84**	16.02%
S 0023	2	$188.33	$376.66	$224.25	$448.50	$35.92	**$71.84**	16.02%
Totals:	8		$1,506.64		$1,868.75		$362.11	19.38%

WS 002   WroxSoft Accessible for Windows 95

OrderNo	Qty	Cost	TotalCost	Nett	Total Nett	Profit	Total Profit	Margin
S 0009	1	$260.00	$260.00	$399.00	$399.00	$139.00	**$139.00**	34.84%
S 0011	2	$260.00	$520.00	$399.00	$798.00	$139.00	**$278.00**	34.84%
S 0019	4	$260.00	$1,040.00	$359.10	$1,436.40	$99.10	**$396.40**	27.60%
S 0020	3	$260.00	$780.00	$299.25	$897.75	$39.25	**$117.75**	13.12%
S 0022	2	$260.00	$520.00	$299.25	$598.50	$39.25	**$78.50**	13.12%
Totals:	12		$3,120.00		$4,129.65		$1,009.65	24.45%

The key to producing the report is a fairly complicated query called Software Profit which links two tables, OrderLine and Software. This query allows us to pull the necessary information from the database in order to fully describe the financial side of the software sales business:

```
SELECT DISTINCTROW OrderLine.SWareKey, OrderLine.OrderNo, Software.SWareName,
OrderLine.Qty, Software.SWCost, [Qty]*[SWCost] AS TotalCost, ([Price])-
([Price]*[Discount]/100) AS NettEach, [Qty]*[NettEach] AS TotalIncome, [NettEach]-
[SWCost] AS ProfitEach, [ProfitEach]*[Qty] AS TotalProfit, [ProfitEach]/[NettEach]
AS Margin
FROM Software INNER JOIN OrderLine ON Software.SWareKey = OrderLine.SWareKey
ORDER BY OrderLine.SWareKey;
```

We take the SWareKey, OrderNo and Qty fields from the OrderLine table, and the SWareName and SWCost fields from the Software table. Then we create the six other calculated fields to give us the rest of the values we need from the records.

TotalCost: [Qty]*[SWCost]
NettEach: ([Price])-([Price]*[Discount]/100)
TotalIncome: [Qty]*[NettEach]
ProfitEach: [NettEach]-[SWCost]
TotalProfit: [ProfitEach]*[Qty]
Margin: [ProfitEach]/[NettEach]

Now we've got the recordset we need, we use the report's sorting and grouping to break the report into sections for each product using the software key, and sort each section by order number:

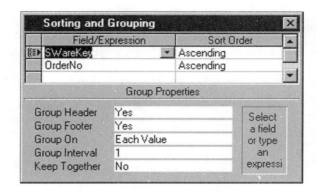

Notice that we can't sum or average the individual Margin for each record to get the overall Margin. Instead, the calculated control in the footer sections uses the values in the TotalProfit and TotalIncome controls of each record. We use the expression:

=Sum([TotalProfit])/Sum([TotalIncome])

which sums the values for each record, then divides the total profit by the total income to give us the correct result.

Making Objects Portable and Reusable

The holy grail of modern programming is that objects should be **portable** and **re-usable**.

An object is portable if it is fully self-contained, i.e. it doesn't rely on other objects. The ultimate aim is to be able to take a finished object, such as a form or report, and drop it into another application without having to modify it. This goal is still some way off with Access because each object is built upon others, but with careful consideration at the design stage, you can go some way to achieving portability. To this end, we've tried where possible to include SQL statements as the Record Source for our forms and reports, rather than relying on separate queries. We've also kept all the macros for a particular object together on one macro sheet.

Although our objects might not be as portable as we would like, because they depend on each other, we have had a lot of success with re-usability. Many of our forms, reports and queries use other queries as their base, while our subreports have often been used in several different main reports.

In the end, the extent to which you achieve the goals of portabililty and reusability depends on how well you design your application 'up front'. You'll always have to modify it as you go along, either under pressure from users or as you find better ways to accomplish a task, but as long as you can keep to a modular structure, and be aware of the dependencies between the objects, you can continue to develop an application without it all falling down around your ears.

Summary

In this chapter, we've taken a fairly brisk tour of the different reports, and some more of the forms, that our **WroxSoft** application uses. If you've worked through Part 1 of the book, you should have had no problem following the techniques that we've used.

We have, however, covered some quite complicated queries and have often concentrated on the SQL statement behind the query rather than the more familiar Query Grid. As we've mentioned, entering a query as an SQL statement in a Record Source property makes the object more self-contained and portable and is therefore worthwhile. We'll be taking a more in-depth look at SQL in Chapter 14.

We've covered:

- The implementation of the different **WroxSoft** reports.
- How you can create invoices and statements.
- How to print sections on a report with varying numbers of records and not waste space.
- Using union queries to tailor the resulting recordset to what you need.

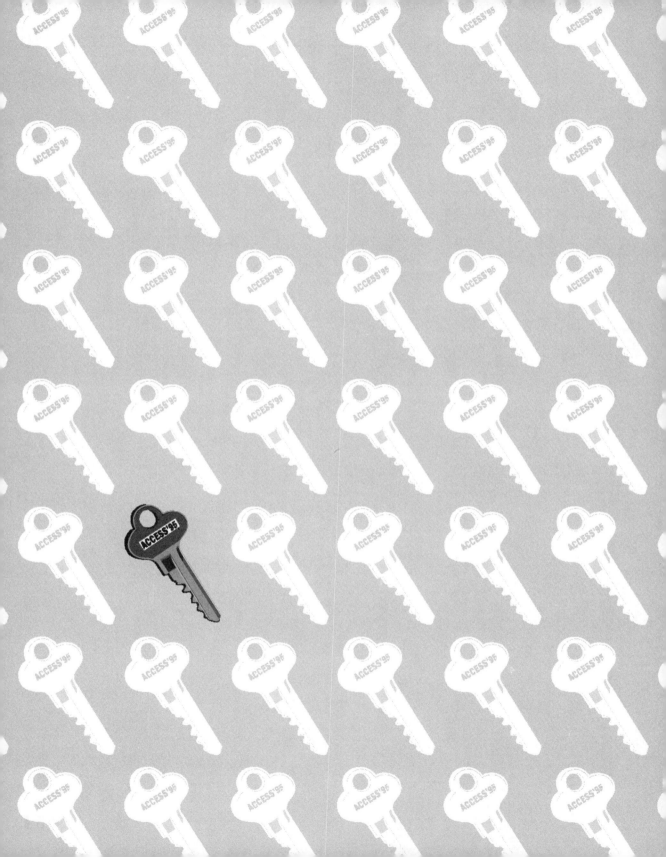

Graphics, Pictures, Charts And OLE

As you use the **WroxSoft** application, you cannot fail to see that we have included various graphics and pictures in the forms and reports it contains. These provide a visual guide for the user, as well as making the application more attractive and the reports more meaningful. In this chapter, we'll look at the different ways that you can display pictures in an application. We'll also examine how you can include other objects, such as charts, sounds and video clips.

We do all this with **OLE** (Object Linking and Embedding). OLE allows one application to use the functionality of another to carry out tasks that it cannot achieve itself and, as user's expectations become more and more sophisticated, is fast becoming the norm in modern PC applications. We will show you how you can extend the functionality of your applications through the use of this technique.

So, this chapter covers:

- Using image controls to display static graphics.
- What object linking and embedding is.
- Using bound and unbound OLE controls.
- Creating charts with Microsoft Graph

Using Image Controls on Forms and Reports

If we just want to display a picture or graphic on a form or report, such as the logo you can see throughout our application, we can use an **image** control. The control actually holds a copy of the picture inside it. We can use a variety of types of picture file in an image control: **bitmaps** such as `.bmp` and `.dib` files, **metafiles** such as `.wmf` and `.emf` files and Windows **icon** files (`.ico`).

FYI Bitmap picture files are those created by a paint-type program, such as Microsoft Paint. Metafiles are often referred to as vector files because they contain instructions on how the picture is to be drawn, rather than the picture itself. Metafiles are usually created by draw-type programs such as Corel Draw, and look better when scaled to different sizes.

We'll start off by looking at how a picture can be displayed on a form using an image control. The example will use another of the sample applications supplied with this book. It's called **BoundOLE.mdb** and will be installed in your **BegAcc95** folder with the other sample files.

Try It Out - Using an Image Control to Display a Picture

1 Open the **BoundOLE.mdb** sample database. Create a new blank form by selecting the Forms tab in the Database window and clicking New. Select Design View in the New Form dialog and leave the source combo box empty. Click OK and Access creates the new form.

2 Click on the Image button in the toolbox and then click on the form. Access opens the Insert Picture dialog.

3 Move to the **BegAcc95** sample folder, select the file **Sentence.bmp** and click OK. Access places the image on the form.

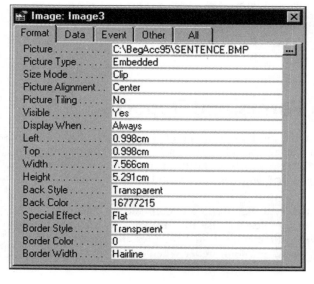

4 Open the image control's Properties window and select the Format tab. The Picture property is set to the full path and name of the image we've inserted.

5 Make the control narrower by dragging one of the selector boxes on the side of the control. Access displays only the central part of the picture because the Size Mode property is set to Clip. This means that the image is displayed in its original size and only the section which fits inside the control is shown. We see the central section because the Picture Alignment property is set to Center.

6 Experiment with the Picture Alignment property - this allows us to change the placing of the image, or the visible part of it, in the control. We can select Top-left, Top-right, Center, Bottom-left or Bottom-right.

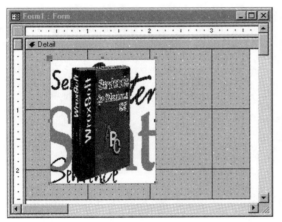

7 Now change the Size Mode property to Stretch and Access stretches or shrinks the picture so that it fills the control. You'll notice that the proportions of the picture change to match the proportions of the control.

8 Now change the Size Mode property to Zoom and Access re-sizes the image so that it all fits in the control, while maintaining the aspect ratio so that it looks correct. However, part of the control is now empty because the shape of the picture is different to the shape of the control.

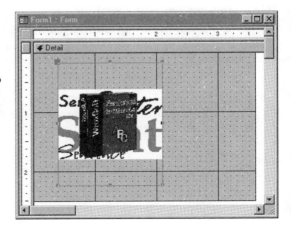

405

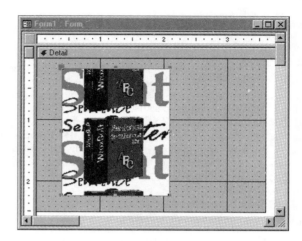

9 Set the Picture Tiling property to Yes. Now Access displays several copies of the image in the control.

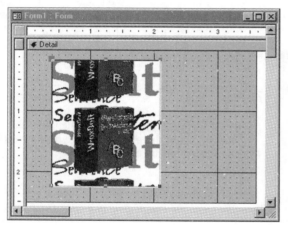

10 You can also define the type of border for the image by setting the Border Style to Solid or any of a variety of line types and selecting the Border Color and Border Width you require. Instead, we'll use the 3D appearance common in most applications - just set the Special Effect property to Sunken.

To change the picture that is displayed, we just select the Picture property and click the builder button. Access opens the Select Picture dialog where we can select a different picture file.

Why Use an Image Control

Image controls are useful if you want to provide a picture which the user can click on to perform an action - such as a graphical menu where each option is a picture on a form. To provide this functionality, Access allows you to use macros in the image control's On Click and On Dbl Click events, just as you would for a command button.

Access also provides the ControlTip Text property, which allows you to set tooltips for your image control. Any text that you type into this property will appear as a tooltip if the user holds the mouse over the control for a few seconds.

To see this working, enter some text in the ControlTip Text property of our new image control and switch to form view. Place the mouse pointer over the picture and after a couple of seconds the text appears.

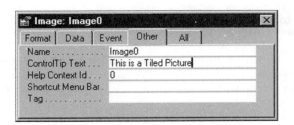

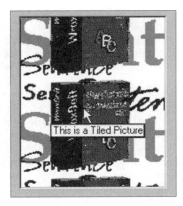

Using an OLE Control to Display Images

OLE stands for **Object Linking and Embedding**. This is a growing technology that allows one application to use the functions of another, so it does not have to implement the functions itself. For instance, Access doesn't offer any way to edit bitmap pictures, such as those we have used in our **WroxSoft** application. Instead, it uses OLE methods to allow you to alter the pictures using an external image editor such as Windows Paint.

Both the Software Catalog Form and Software Stock Report use OLE controls to display pictures of the software products. You'll have noticed that the main forms also use a graphic in the header - the company logo. You could, of course, use an image control for them, as we saw in the last section. The difference between an OLE control and an image control is that an OLE control allows you to edit the picture in place, whereas with an image control you are stuck with the image that you inserted. More on this later.

The picture that you see of each software product is also displayed in an OLE control. The only difference between the product pictures and the logo is the way they are inserted into the application - with the software pictures, the data comes from our tables and changes as you scroll through the Software records. We used the Windows Paint application to create and modify the original pictures.

Reviewing OLE Controls

Before we look at the actual process of inserting objects into OLE controls, it is useful to look at the properties of an already filled OLE control. Open the **Wroxsoft** application and check out the SWPicture OLE control on the Software Catalog form.

The Control Source is SWPicture - the name of the field in the Software table that contains our pictures. As you can see, for this basic use of an OLE control not many of the properties are used - this should start to indicate to you how powerful the OLE control can be.

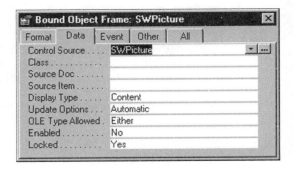

The other properties define how the control behaves when displaying an object (the picture) and what kinds of object we can place in the control. Don't worry, all this will become clear as you work through this chapter.

407

The Two Types of OLE Control

There are two different types of OLE control in the Access toolbox - **bound** and **unbound** OLE controls. To display objects which are stored in our tables, we use a bound control. An unbound control displays the same object no matter which record is current.

You can think of the difference between the two as being like that between a text box control on a form and its label. The text box shows a value from each record as you scroll through them, while the label displays the same text for every record. The text box is bound to the source table (or query), while the label control is unbound.

Our **Wroxsoft** application uses a bound OLE object control to display pictures of the software and an unbound OLE object control to display the logo in the form header.

Unbound Object  *Bound Object*

One of the features of an OLE control is that you can set its properties to allow the user to edit the pictures they contain using another application. We have disabled this feature in our **Wroxsoft** application, as it tends to make the application run more slowly. We are just using the OLE controls to display the pictures. However, we will look at how you can allow the picture that is displayed in an OLE control to be edited later in the chapter.

Object Linking and Embedding

OLE is a huge subject, large enough to fill a book on its own. However, in this chapter, we'll aim to give you a broad introduction so that you have a basis on which to explore further.

As Windows and its applications have developed over the years, they have offered more and more functionality - but often at the expense of valuable disk space. The more features an application contains, the greater the amount of disk space required.

Recent software releases are beginning to show signs of a change in direction. Instead of including every type of function in every application, the trend is to use the functions of one application from within another. OLE allows you to insert an **object** inside another application's document - be it a spreadsheet, DTP package, word-processor or a database.

The application you are using to create the main document is called the **container** or **client**, and the program whose functions you are borrowing is called the **server**. Therefore, Access becomes the client when we insert a picture into our database - and the picture editing program, such as Microsoft Paint, becomes the server. When we include a chart in a report, the server is the Microsoft Graph application.

As the container application does not include functions to modify the original object, it uses the functions of the server application. With most types of object, double-clicking it in the container application's document starts the server application and loads the object into it. When you close the server application, the newly updated object is placed back in the original document. If we were using a picture, for example, the process would be as shown on the next page:

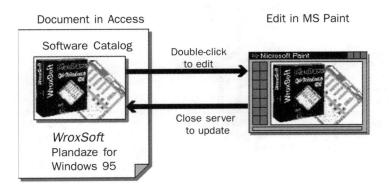

Document in Access   Edit in MS Paint

There are two ways that we can insert an object. We can either **embed** it in the container document (such as our database table) or we can **link** it to the container document. Hence the term Object Linking and Embedding.

When to Link and When to Embed

The difference between linking and embedding lies in how the object is stored. When it is **embedded**, the data that makes up the object is stored inside the document. When it is **linked**, the data is stored in a separate file in the format of the application that created it. The container document just holds a link to the file so that it can be loaded when required.

Each method has its own advantages. If you want to copy and move the container file about (for example, our **Wroxsoft** application), you should consider embedding the OLE object in it, as we have done with the pictures of the software. When you move or copy the file, you automatically include the pictures because they are contained within it.

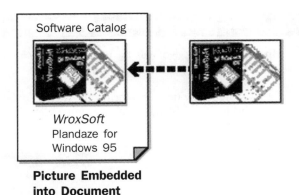

Picture Embedded into Document

However, depending on the size of your OLE objects, embedding can make the database very large as it has to accommodate the objects within its own file.

You also need to consider whether the object will be edited. If you edit an embedded object, you are only updating the embedded copy - not the original. If you link the object, it remains in a file on disk. Other applications can then update it and, when you open it up in Access again, you always see the latest version. This can be important in a multi-user environment or if you are using objects that are regularly changed.

409

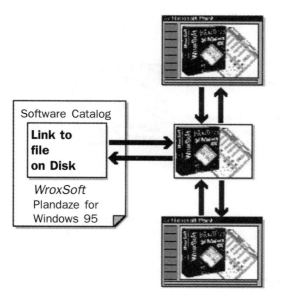

The only problem with linking is that, if you want to make a copy of the document, you also have to copy the object (picture) files. And, if they are moved to a different location, the links will be broken and Access will not be able to find the original files.

OLE is not just limited to pictures. You can use an increasing number of servers to place objects in your documents. Depending on your system setup, you will probably find servers which allow you to embed or link spreadsheets, sound and video clips, equations and many others. To see how OLE works, we'll try embedding and linking a picture into a new form.

Try It Out - Using an Unbound OLE Control to Display a Picture

In this example, we will be using one of Windows' own applications - Microsoft Paint - as the server application.

1 Create a new unbound form and place an unbound OLE control on it by clicking the Unbound Object Frame button in the toolbox and clicking on the form.

2 Access opens the Insert Object dialog allowing you to select the type of object you want for this control.

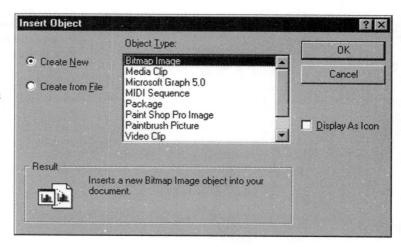

FYI

Here we can see a list of the types of object that we can insert - your list may differ depending on which other applications you have installed on your machine. The list will include the standard Windows object types, such as Bitmaps and Pictures, as well as MIDI clips and other sound objects.

3 We'll start with a picture. Make sure that the Create New option is selected and click on Bitmap Image. Check also that Display As Icon is not ticked - you'll see more of this later. Click OK and Access opens the Paint application with a blank picture. You'll see that the OLE control on the form is grayed to indicate that the object is being edited.

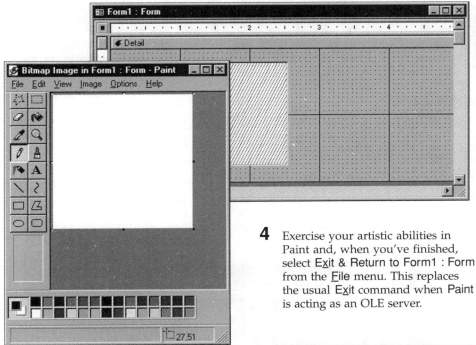

4 Exercise your artistic abilities in Paint and, when you've finished, select Exit & Return to Form1 : Form from the File menu. This replaces the usual Exit command when Paint is acting as an OLE server.

5 The new picture appears in the Access form. The property that determines how the picture is sized to fit the control is called Size Mode and is found on the Format tab. This property acts just like its image control counterpart, allowing you to stretch, clip or zoom onto the picture. The rest of the image control's display properties, such as the border properties, are also available here. Set these properties as you feel appropriate.

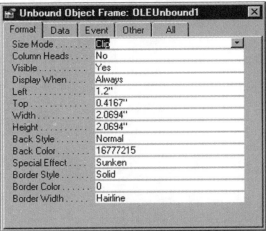

411

The Data tab is where Access stores all the properties that relate to the actual picture that is held in the control. The first is the OLE Class - it's set to Paint which is the object type created by the Paint application. The Display Type is Content - remember we did not select the Display As Icon option when we created the object. If we had, this would be set to Icon and instead of displaying the picture, the control would display just the Paint icon - or the icon of the application that created the file.

At the bottom of the list, the Enabled property is set to No and the Locked property to Yes. This is the default for this type of control, which means that by default you can't change the contents in form view.

 You should note that all of these properties can be altered except for Display Type. Once an object has been inserted into an OLE control, this property is set for the life of the object. If you wish to alter it, you will need to delete the contents of the control and re-insert the object selecting the appropriate setting for the Display as Icon option.

Editing An Object

If you want the user to be able to edit an object stored in one of your controls in form view, you must have the Enabled property set to Yes and the Locked property set to No. If you apply these settings to our example, then switch to form view and double-click on the control, Access re-opens Paint with the picture displayed, allowing you to use Paint's functions to edit the picture.

You'll notice that the display has changed somewhat. We are still working within Access rather than in a separate window, but the menu commands have changed to include those offered by Paint. And the toolbox and color selector from Paint have also become part of the Access environment.

Paint allows this form of **in-place activation** because the application supports the latest version of OLE, called **OLE 2.0**. Some applications only support OLE 1.0 and so have no support for in-place activation. In this case, the server will open in a separate window, just as Paint did when we first created the picture.

When you have finished editing an in-place activated object, simply click anywhere on the form outside the OLE control. Access regains control, saves any changes that you made and closes down the server.

So, as you have seen, if you add an **OLE control** to a form and place a picture in it, the picture can be updated while the form is in use - in form view. If you use an **image** control to display a picture, you can only update it in design view, not in form view.

Of course, you can also edit the picture in the OLE control in design view. However, when you do this, it opens the Paint application as a separate window again, just as it did when we first created the picture. In-place activation only happens when the form is being used in form view.

We've also seen OLE 2.0 in operation. When you edit the picture in form view, it appears as though the Paint program is actually part of Access rather than a separate application. This is one of the keys of OLE 2.0 - to allow an application to use the functions of another while appearing to include them itself. The user can be unaware that they are actually using a different program.

OLE Object Frame Properties

There are some properties that we didn't consider while we were using the form. For instance, the OLE Type property is set to Embedded. The picture is embedded within the form rather than being linked to it from a file on disk. We'll see how to link objects a little later on. There is also an OLE Type Allowed property which is set to Either. This controls how the user of the form can insert new objects. Again, we'll come to this shortly.

Have a look at the Other tab in the Properties window. Here there is the Auto Activate property. It's set to Double-Click - we had to double-click the object to 'activate' it. You can set this property to Manual, so that you have to handle the activation yourself using code or to GetFocus, where the control is automatically activated as soon as it gets the focus.

You can see now why whole books are written about OLE - there is a lot going on behind the simple example we've seen. To clear it up a little, we'll look at some of the properties that control the behavior of the object and see what they do.

Property	Options	Effect
Display Type	Content	Display the object as it normally appears.
	Icon	Display the object as an icon in the control.
Update Options	Automatic	Update the object when the original changes.
	Manual	Update only on command from the user.
OLE Type	Linked	The object is in a linked file on disk.
	Embedded	The object is embedded in the document.
	None	The control contains no object.

Table Continued on Following Page

Property	Options	Effect
OLE Type	Linked	Allow only linked objects to be inserted.
Allowed	Embedded	Allow only embedded objects to be inserted.
	Either	Allow both types of objects to be inserted.
Enabled	Yes	User can enter the control to edit the contents.
	No	User cannot enter the control.
Locked	Yes	User can change the data in the control.
	No	User cannot change the data in the control.
Auto Activate	Manual	Requires VBA code to activate the server.
	GetFocus	Server activates when the control gets the focus.
	Double-Click	Server activates when the control is double-clicked.

Using Existing Objects

In the previous example, we created the object, a bitmap picture, when we placed the OLE control on the form. However, we can also insert a new or existing object into the OLE control. We'll see the flexibility of the OLE control by using the same form we used for displaying and editing a bitmap to run a sound file. Note that, if your system is not set up to play sounds, you will not be able to hear the sound played and you may get an error message.

Try It Out - Running a Sound File

1 Make sure the form we used earlier is displayed in form view. Highlight the OLE control and right-click on it. Select Insert Object - Access opens the same Insert Object dialog we saw earlier.

2 Select the Create from File option and browse through your system for a sound file, such as a **.wav** file - try the file called **The Microsoft Sound.wav** that you should be able to find in your **Windows/Media** directory.

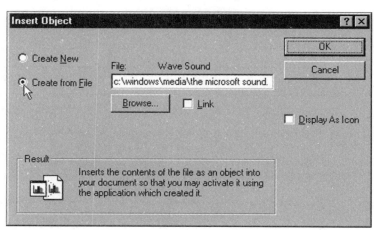

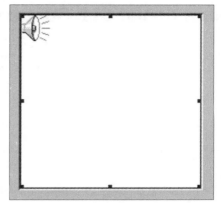

3 Click OK and Access places the sound object in the OLE control. Of course, it can't display it as a sound, so instead you'll see it is displayed as an icon.

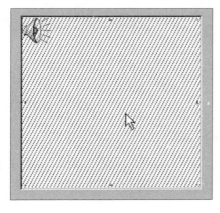

4 Now double-click on the object to activate it. Access plays the sound and the OLE control is grayed out while it does so. Access is, in fact, activating the Windows sound system and passing the embedded copy of the sound to it.

Forcing the User's OLE Choice

All this freedom is great for you, the developer, but there may be times when you want to restrict the user to just linking or just embedding. To this end, Access provides you with the OLE Type Allowed property on the Data tab. If you set the property to Linked (instead of the default Either), the user is presented with a slightly altered version of the Insert Object dialog when they attempt to place an object in the control.

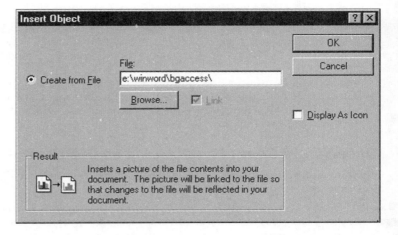

As we have specified that the object must be linked rather than embedded, there is only one option - Create From File - and the Link option is ticked and cannot be changed. So we can only link an existing object rather than creating and embedding a new one. However, we can still use the Display As Icon option if we want it displayed as an icon rather than in its normal format, though of course some files will always be displayed as an icon - as we saw with our sound file earlier on.

Using Bound OLE Controls

By now, you should have a feel for some of the different ways OLE can be used. We've only looked at an unbound object frame so far, so let's now have a look at a **bound object frame** or **bound OLE control**. Basically, this is the same as its unbound cousin but, like the other Access data controls, it has a Control Source property in the Data list. This defines which field in the underlying table or query contains the objects that are displayed.

You store OLE objects in a database table using an OLE Object field. The table can store a different object for each record - for example, each Software record in our **WroxSoft** application stores a picture of the software product. A bound OLE control will display the object from that field in the current record.

The content of an OLE control can take one of three formats:

▶ An embedded copy of the actual object.

▶ A link to the object in a file on disk.

▶ A converted copy of the object that can no longer be edited.

We'll have a look at each of these - how we can use them and what they mean to the end user. How you actually insert the object is broadly the same for all three formats. You can:

▶ Copy and paste them using the clipboard.

▶ Drag and drop them from My Computer or Explorer.

▶ Use the Insert Object menu command.

Bear in mind that you can insert objects into an **unbound** OLE control in much the same way. Once you've inserted the object, you can switch to design view and see *how* it was inserted by checking the OLE Type property in the Data tab of the Properties window.

Again, we'll be using the **BoundOLE.mdb** sample database. This database is very simple - it is made up of one table and a related form for user input and data display. The table is composed of three fields - a unique identifier, an OLE Object field and a description - and the form provides the user interface.

Embedding a Copy of an Object in an OLE Control

You can insert an object into a database using the clipboard - you just copy and paste it in the same way as you would with text.

Try It Out - Embedding Graphics Using the Clipboard

1 Open the Sample form in the **BoundOLE** database. This just has a bound OLE control and a text box on it.

2 Open the Windows Paint application from your Start menu (you will find it in the Programs/Accessories list) and open **Sentence.bmp** from the **BegAcc95** folder.

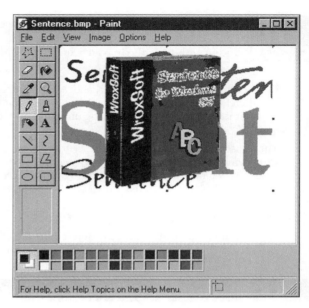

3 In the Edit menu, click Select All, then Copy to place the picture on the clipboard. Alternatively, you can right-click and select the commands from the shortcut menu that appears.

4 Now go back to Access. Click on the bound OLE control and open the Edit menu. There are two paste commands: Paste and Paste Special. Paste simply places an embedded copy of the graphic into the control. However, you have much more control over the process if you select Paste Special, so we'll use this option.

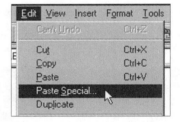

5 Select Paste Special - Access opens a dialog box which allows you to select the format in which to save the object. If you paste the graphic as a Bitmap Image, Access will allow you to edit it in-place using Paint. The other two options are Picture, which stores the object as a metafile (the instructions on how to draw the graphic as opposed to the actual pixels of the graphic itself) and Device Independent Bitmap, which stores the graphic as another type of bitmap. If you select either of these, you break the link between the graphic and Paint, and Access will not allow the user to edit the image at run-time.

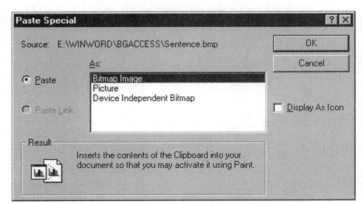

FYI

If we select **Bitmap Image**, we can choose to display it as an **Icon** rather than a **Picture**, but if you select a different option, such as **Picture**, this option is not available. There is no point displaying an icon if the object we insert cannot be edited again.

6 Select Bitmap Image, click OK and Access embeds the graphic into the bound OLE control and, therefore, into the underlying field in the BoundOLE table. We can double-click it in form view to edit it in Paint, just like with the unbound OLE control we used earlier.

The most important point to note is that using the clipboard in this way only allows the objects to be embedded. This is because we copied the *contents* of the picture to the clipboard and so, when we come to paste it into the control, Access cannot link it because it doesn't know where the original object is stored on disk.

Using Drag and Drop to Embed an Object

Another method of inserting an object into an OLE control involves using **drag and drop**. Essentially this is just a shortcut to the Copy and Paste commands.

Try It Out - Inserting an Object Using Drag and Drop

1 Go to a new record using the record navigation controls.

2 Open My Computer or Explorer and re-size the window so that you can see both Explorer and the Access form.

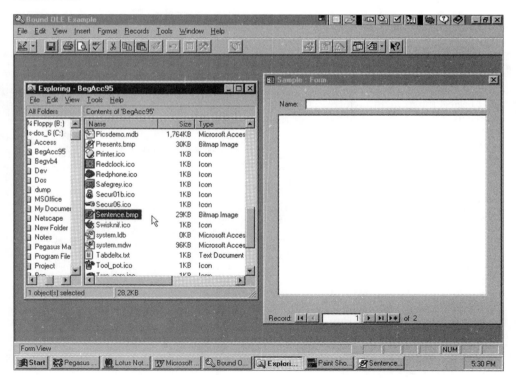

3 Click on **Sentence.bmp** in My Computer or Explorer, drag it into Access and drop it on the bound OLE control.

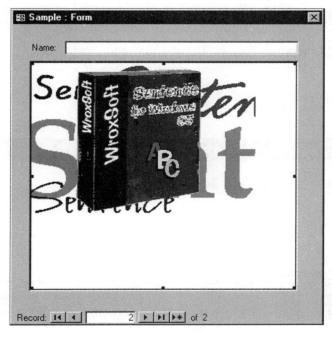

4 Access automatically inserts the object for you. It handles all the finer details and provides you with an embedded copy of the object that you selected.

Using the Insert Object Command

You can also embed an object in an OLE control using menu commands. With the form open in form view, right-click on the control and select Insert Object from the short-cut menu. Alternatively, you can select Object from the Insert menu when the OLE control is selected. We used this method earlier to insert an objet into an unbound OLE control.

Access opens the Insert Object window and here we can select the type of object. As long as the Create New option is selected, the new object will be embedded in the control on the form (there is no file on disk to link it to). We can also decide whether to display it as an icon. This method gives us the most control over how the object is embedded.

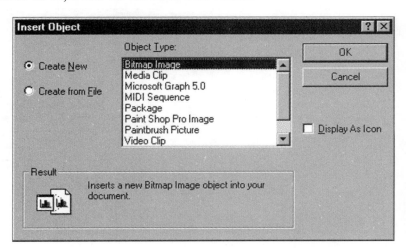

Creating a Link to an Object in a File on Disk

We can link an object in an OLE control to a file on disk using the same three methods as we did to embed it. However, there are certain limitations as you'll see.

Linking an Object Using Copy and Paste

When you copy an object and paste it to the clipboard, Access only allows you to embed it when you select Paste Special. However, if you copy the object itself to the clipboard, instead of selecting the *contents* of the object as we did before, Access will provide you with the option of linking the object to your database.

Try It Out - Copying and Linking an Object

1 Move to a new record in **BoundOLE.mdb**.

2 Open Explorer and select the sample video clip **RockClmb.avi**.

3 Copy the object using *Ctrl-C*, click on the bound OLE control and select Paste Special from the Edit menu.

 FYI You should note that the Paste Special option is not available from the right-click menu - only from the Edit menu. You can use Paste from the right-click menu, but this will automatically embed the object into the database.

4 Access throws up the usual Paste Special dialog, except that this time, we can choose to Paste Link.

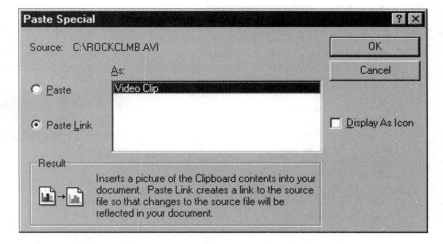

5 Access will then link the object into the database, and display the first frame of the video in the bound OLE control.

6 To run the video, simply double-click on the bound OLE control. Access will then run the server application and get it to load and play the file.

So what's the difference between this time and the last time we used Paste Special? Well it's not the Paste Special that is different, it's the *object* that we copied. If we open the object in its own application and select part or all of it, then Copy this selection to the clipboard, we get a copy of the contents. But if we select it in My Computer or Explorer and select Copy, we are actually copying the filename information. So when we Paste Special it into the OLE control we get the option of embedding the data (Access will copy the contents of the file from disk to the control) or linking, where Access will just insert the path and filename into the OLE control.

Linking an Object Using Drag and Drop

When you use drag and drop to insert an object, the default is to embed the object. However, if a **bound** OLE control's OLE Type Allowed property is set to Linked, the object cannot be embedded. So Access will link it instead. If you drag and drop onto an **unbound** OLE control, the object will always be embedded.

Linking an Object Using the Insert Object Command

To do this, simply click on the bound OLE control and select the Object from the Insert menu. Access opens the Insert Object dialog.

To link an object rather than embedding it, just choose Create from File and make sure that the Link checkbox is selected. When you attempt to edit a linked object, Access calls the server as normal, except that the server is opened in its own window, rather than in-place.

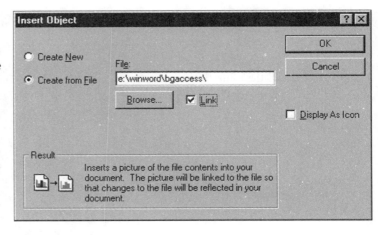

Linking to Part of an Object

In the case of Excel and some other major applications, the way that data is stored means that the files you see are really a collection of objects and you have direct access to each one. This means that you can place part of the contents of such a file into your database by linking to the original file.

Try It Out - Linking to Part of an Excel Spreadsheet

1 Open the **Accounts.xls** in Excel. (If you don't have Excel, you can use most other modern Windows spreadsheet applications. You can also use any spreadsheet file.)

2 Select the Projects sheet and highlight the first four cells of one row by clicking in the first column and dragging across to the fourth. Copy the cells to the clipboard using *Ctrl-C*.

	A	B	C	D	E	T
1	Date	Project	CustName	HoursWorked	HourlyRate	
2	12-Jun-95	Accounts System	Aardvaak Ltd.	14	$50.00	
3	23-Jun-95	System Development	Burger Queen	18	$65.00	
4	5-Jul-95	Schools Support	Education Dept.	39	$50.00	
5	16-Jul-95	Schools Support	Education Dept.	11	$50.00	
6	3-Jul-95	Robotics Installation	Cummings Intl.	8	$75.00	
7	20-Jun-95	PC Upgrades	J.R.Higgins	5	$85.00	
8	16-Jun-95	Accounts System	James Builders	21	$50.00	
9	23-Jul-95	Navigation System	Jonahs Boats	14	$45.00	
10	8-Jul-95	Menu Generator	Le Bistro	4	$60.00	
11	30-Jun-95	Catalogue System	Major Records	17	$80.00	
12	18-Jul-95	Menu Generator	Martha's Bar	6	$60.00	
13	18-Jun-95	Warehouse System	Miracle Supplies	13	$70.00	
14	26-Jun-95	Warehouse System	Miracle Supplies	11	$70.00	

Original \ **Projects** \ Customers \ Contacts

3 Switch back to Access, move to a new record in the **BoundOLE** database, click on the OLE control and select Paste Special from the Edit menu. Now Access offers the option to insert the cells as a Microsoft Excel Worksheet. Select this option and be sure to select the Paste Link option.

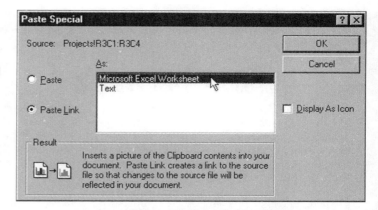

4 Click OK and Access will create a link to the spreadsheet file and display the current values in the control on the form. You may have to go back to design view and re-size the control so that you can see them all.

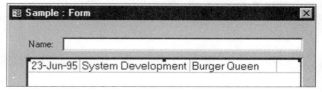

5 Now switch back to Excel and change the values in one of the cells you copied, then save the file to disk. In Access the contents of the OLE control are automatically updated.

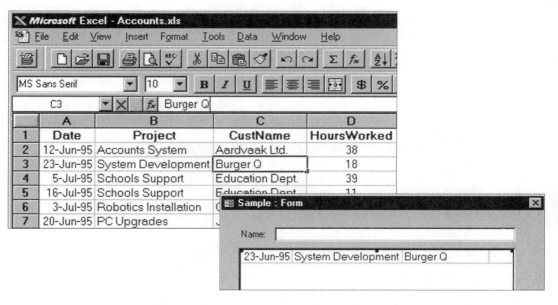

This is a very important technique with many obvious applications in the commercial environment. You can use it to display and store parts of very complex spreadsheets or other objects. It could even form the basis of your company's Executive Information System - providing summaries or consolidations of the information needed to make those everyday business decisions.

This method of linking a spreadsheet to a database also has one more advantage. If you activate the link to the spreadsheet, not only will Access cause Excel to run and load the appropriate file, it will also cause the information in the worksheet to be highlighted. This can be a very useful feature if you are working with large spreadsheets.

Converting an Object to Other Formats

As you saw in the previous examples, when you are inserting an object using Paste Special or the Insert command, Access provides a choice of formats in which you can save it. However, displaying objects in a control so that they can be edited in the server application can be expensive in terms of speed and memory overhead. Each time a bound OLE control has to display a different object it has to prepare the control for the in-place activation of the appropriate server.

To alleviate this problem, Access allows you convert the original objects to a simple graphical version. This means that the object can't be edited any more, but the load time is greatly reduced. This is the technique we used in our **WroxSoft** application with the graphic form header logos and the pictures in the Software Catalog form.

To convert a bitmap type object, you right-click on the OLE control and select Bitmap Image Object from the shortcut menu (or select Bitmap Image Object from the Edit menu) and click Convert. Access opens the Convert dialog and shows the different formats that the object can be converted to.

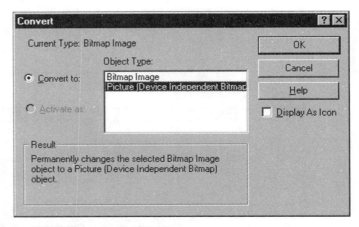

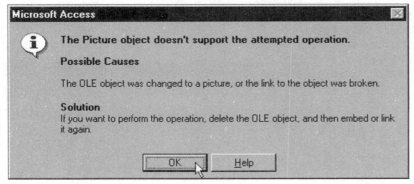

For example, here we can select the Picture option to convert the bitmap into a simple picture, embedded in the form. If the user then tries to edit the graphic, a message appears informing them that the picture cannot be edited.

 Note that this process only affects the current record in a bound OLE control. To convert all the bitmaps in a table in your database, you must repeat the process for each record.

Updating the Link to a File

If a linked object is moved to
another location on disk, or if
you want to review any of the
links that you have set up in
your database, you use the
OLE/DDE Lin<u>k</u>s option on the
<u>E</u>dit menu to display the Links
dialog. This option is only
available when you are focused
on a record that contains an
OLE control with a linked object
stored in it. Some types of
object may not support this
option, though the usual bitmap
(**.bmp**) file will.

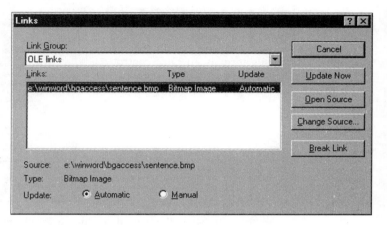

This is the 'control panel' where we can manipulate the links to the source files. We can change
the link type to Manual or Automatic (equivalent to setting the Update Options property), Update
the object now if the link is a manual, Open the source file in the appropriate application,
Change the source to a different file and Break the link between the source file and the
database.

If we choose to break the link, Access converts the object link to an embedded object without
server support - in other words, breaking a link to a graphic has the same effect as replacing
the link with an embedded version and converting it to a Picture.

Experiment with Picsdemo

There is a file on the disk called **Picsdemo.mdb**. This shows you some of the ways that OLE
can be used to brighten up your database applications. Load it up and take a look.

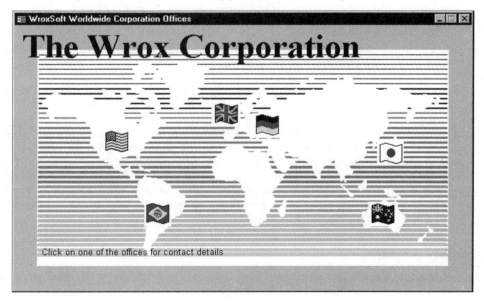

Click on a flag on the opening screen to open a window which contains the details of that branch of the company. In the top left of the details form is an OLE control which displays one of a variety of items - a sound file, icon or picture.

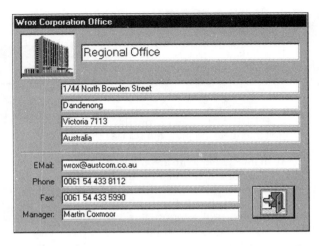

Double-click on these to open them in their source application and then try replacing them with your own objects. You can switch to design view to see and change the properties of the OLE control (press *F11* to show the Database window) and you can open the Offices table to see how the objects are stored.

	PKey	Office	Addr1	Addr2	Addr3	Addr4	Tel	Fax	EMail	Manager	Flag
►	1	Corporate Hea	Wrox Corporati	2710 Wes	Chicago, I	USA	001 312	001 312	100063.	Art Bertzel	Wave Sound
	2	Divisional Offic	Office 441		St Mary's	Rio de Jar	Brazil	0055 21	0055 21	pedr@w	Pedro Annistaz	Bitmap Image
	3	Production Offi	30 James Road	Tyseley	Birmingha	UK	0044 12	0044 12	anon@w	David Davis	Wave Sound
	4	Marketing Divis	Krietenhof 334	611341 Pf	Bissingen	Germany	0049 66.	0049 66.	wroxmkt	Hans Mueller	Bitmap Image
	5	Eastern Manuf	144 Eastern Hi	Shinajuzu	Tokyo	Japan	0081 3 5	0081 3 5	wrox.eas	Reiko Shimizu	Bitmap Image
	6	Regional Office	1/44 North Bow	Dandenon	Victoria 71	Australia	0061 54	0061 54	wrox@a	Martin Coxmoo	Bitmap Image
*	umber)										

Record: ◄ ◄ | 1 | ► ►I ►* | of 6

Using Charts in a Report

Our **WroxSoft** application contains two reports which display charts: the Sales By Customer Report and the Company Performance Report. The first of these displays a single chart (or graph) showing the total purchases for each customer by month. The second uses a selection of graphs and a table to show the overall performance of the company as a whole. The way they are designed, though, is substantially different and we'll take a look at each in turn.

FYI Whenever you use a graph in Access, either on a form or a report, you are using OLE to embed a graph object. This object is created and maintained by the Graph application that is part of the standard Access installation (it is also used by other applications). If you have moved any of the required files around on your machine or made changes to the setup in other ways, you may receive an error message when you try to use a form or report that contains a graph. To cure this, you will have to re-install Microsoft Graph from your original program disks.

The Company Report

This report provides real information about the data in the database. It has four pages and shows three graphs and a table of sales by month by product.

426

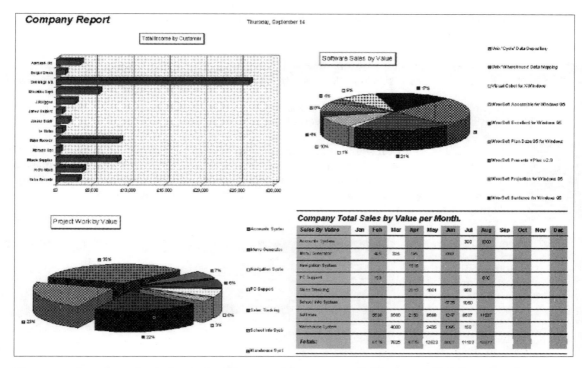

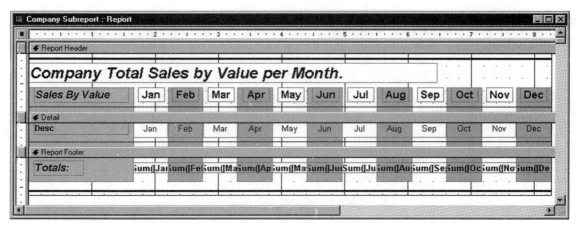

The report is unbound - it is not based on a table or query. It has just a Detail section, into which we've placed Unbound Object Frames for the graphs, and a Subreport for the table of monthly sales. As it is unbound, it only displays one Detail section when run, and we've carefully sized each graph and used Page Break controls to divide it into the four pages.

The subreport is based on a crosstab query which is itself based on a union query. The sources of the records for this union query are the Project Totals and Order Totals queries we created for our Statements report. They are combined in a similar way here, except that this time, the queries include all the records - not just those that haven't been paid. To examine the subreport, double-click on it while the main Company Report is open in design view.

The three graphs in the report are created by Microsoft Graph, using Chart Wizard. We'll see this in action next.

Try It Out - Creating a Graph in a Report

1 Create a new unbound report and add a chart control to the details section. Note that if you can't find the chart control in your toolbox, you can select it from the <u>I</u>nsert menu.

FYI You can add a chart control button to any toolbar or to the **Toolbox** itself. Select **Toolbars** from the <u>V</u>iew menu and select the toolbar you want to add it to so this is displayed. Then click **Customize** and select **Toolbox** in the **Categories** list. Click on the **Chart** button and drag it to the toolbar of your choice. Then click **Close** to close the **Customize** dialog.

2 When you place a chart control, Access automatically starts Chart Wizard. The Chart Wizard's first step is to select the table or query we want to use as the basis for the new graph. Note that this means that the chart can have a completely different record source to the other information displayed on the report. Click the Queries option button to show the queries in the application and then select the Project Totals query.

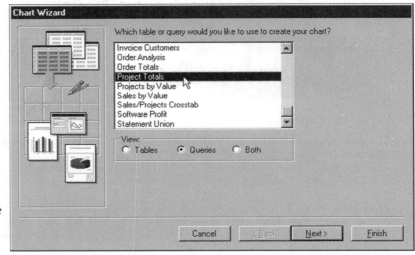

3 Click <u>N</u>ext and select the fields that contain the data we want to include in our graph. For this example, select the Project, Date and PTotal fields.

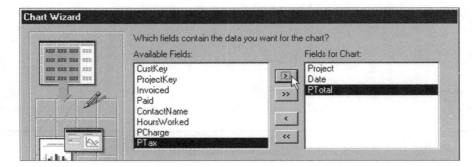

4   Click <u>N</u>ext again. Now we need to tell Chart Wizard what kind of chart we want. Select the 3D Column Chart.

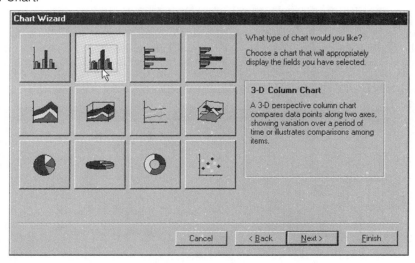

5   Click <u>N</u>ext and now we can see how it will look.

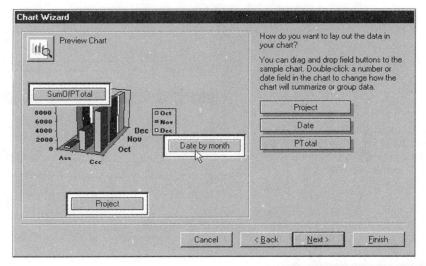

6   Access has suggested grouping the dates of the projects by month and this is what we want. However, we could change it using the Date by Month button next to the chart axis. Double-click this to open the Group dialog.

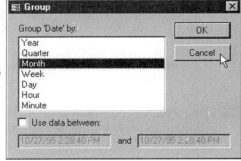

7 Here we can also select which records we want to include in the chart by clicking the Use date between: checkbox and entering the dates. However, we'll leave it set to include all the records from the query. Click the Cancel button to close the Group dialog.

8 Chart Wizard has placed the Dates on the left axis and the Projects at the front. In our case, it would be better if they were the other way round. Click on the Project button in the right part of the window and drag it onto the Date by Month button next to the chart. This changes the axis to show the projects on the right. Now drag the Date button from the right-hand side of the window onto the Project button at the bottom of the chart to place the dates across the front.

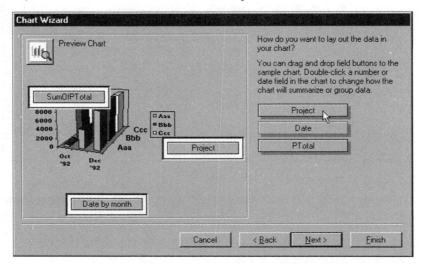

9 At this point, it would be a good idea to preview the chart - click the Preview Chart button at the top right of the Chart Wizard window.

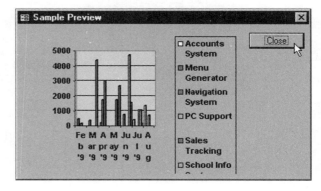

10 Well, it's not quite what we expected, but no doubt things will improve as we go along. Click Close to close the preview and then Next to move on.

11 Finally, we can tell the Chart Wizard what the Title of the chart is and whether we want to include Legends (the list which shows the color of each bar and tells you what it refers to). Enter Project Sales By Month for the chart title and make sure the No, don't display a legend option is selected. Also check that the Display Help option is not ticked.

12 Click Finish and the chart appears on our report. It may well look nothing like the one we've specified in Chart Wizard, because Access hasn't yet run the query which will build our new graph.

13 Click the Print Preview button on the toolbar to see the new graph. It looks a bit closer to what we wanted, but is not likely to win any prizes yet. There's still some work to do.

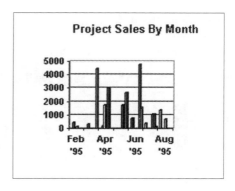

What Chart Wizard Has Done

To see what Chart Wizard has done, and how we can improve the graph, switch back to design view and click on the graph control. Open the Properties window and click the Data tab. Now you can see that the graph control is really an OLE control in disguise. It has the same properties as a normal OLE control - the OLE Class is set to Microsoft Graph 5.0 Chart and the OLE Type is Embedded.

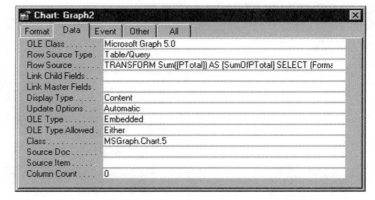

The graph takes its values from an SQL statement that the Chart Wizard has created from the original query we supplied. Open up the query in Query Builder for a more graphical representation of what it has done.

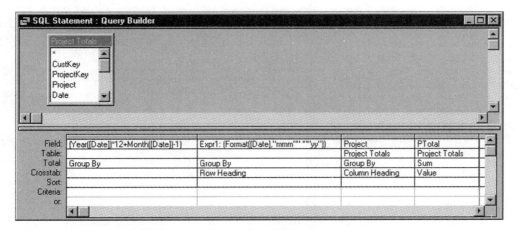

This is a crosstab query which takes the values from the Project Totals query and converts them to a table of values suitable for the graph. (You will learn more about how SQL is used to create crosstab queries like this in Chapter 14.)

Editing the Embedded Graph

We have embedded a Microsoft Graph object in the control. So to edit it we just double-click on it and the Graph application opens with the chart displayed. We can then modify it.

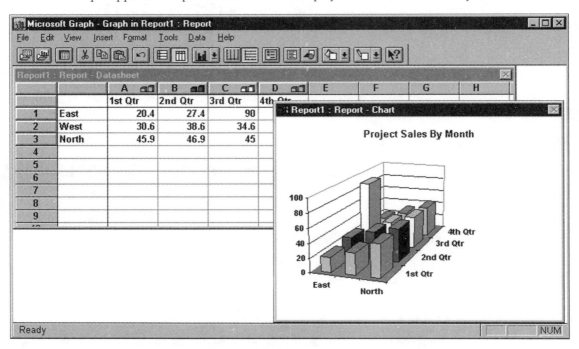

As you can see in the above screenshot, we've used the Graph application to make several changes to the chart. First, we selected Chart Type from the Format menu and Options... to open the Chart Subtype dialog. Here we selected the right-hand option to display the bars one behind the other, rather than all in a single row.

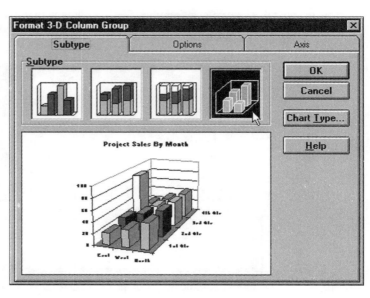

Next we selected 3-D View from the Format menu and turned off the Right Angle Axes option, before changing the angle of view using the various rotation controls.

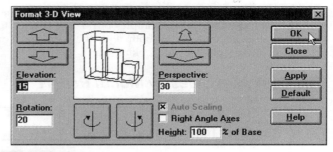

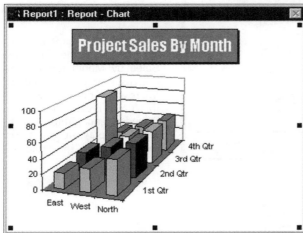

We have also changed the font, style and colors of the text on the axes and chart title, by selecting them and using the various options in the Format menu. And by clicking on the vertical axis and selecting the Number tab of the Format window, we've set the axis to show currency values rather than just plain numbers.

Finally, we need to re-size the chart to suit the final size on the report. Drag the chart window to the size you want, then close Graph to update the OLE control in the original report. Here's the finished thing, shown in print preview mode.

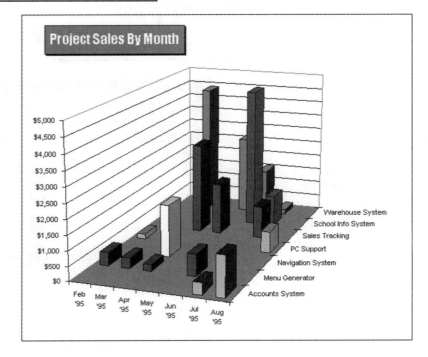

Microsoft Graph is very flexible, allowing you to change nearly every characteristic of the chart very quickly. This makes Graph both a very useful tool and a monster. You will probably have to experiment quite a lot, both with the data that you feed in and the formatting of that data, to get the graph you are looking for.

The Customer Sales by Month Report

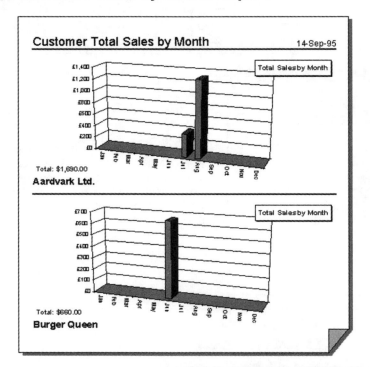

To finish this chapter, we'll look briefly at the Customer Sales by Month report. This also uses graphs created in Microsoft Graph. However, this time it uses them in a Bound Object Frame, so the report displays a graph for each record in the table.

Take a look at the Sales By Month Report in design view.

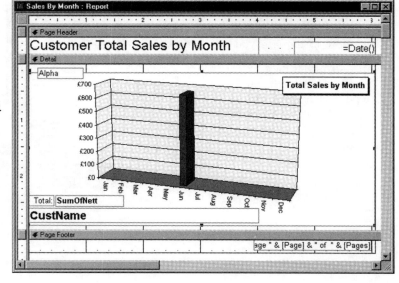

The Record Source is an SQL statement that uses a query called **Customer Total Sales**. This query uses the same union query as the **Company Report** to get the total sales by month for each customer. You will find that graphing your data is much simpler if you understand it, so taking a look at the data before you start off the Chart Wizard is a good idea.

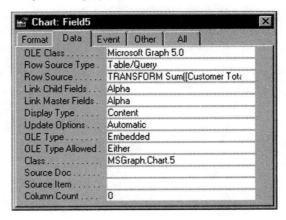

CustName	Alpha	SumOfNett
Aardvark Ltd.	AARDV	1690
Burger Queen	BURGE	660
Cummings Intl.	CUMMI	18133.2
Education Dept.	EDUCA	5775
J.R.Higgins	HIGGI	2546.25
James Builders	JAMES	640
Jonahs Boats	JONAH	1615
Le Bistro	LEBIS	299.85
Major Records	MAJOR	2677.3
Miracle Supplies	MIRAC	6391.5
Pedro Mana	MANAP	1436.4
Union Records	UNION	1519.05

In this case, you can see we have one record for each customer containing their name, customer ID and the total sales made to them.

In the report itself, we just use the **Sorting and Grouping** dialog to sort the records by the **Alpha** field, so we get a **Detail** section printed for each customer. To make the final printout clearer, we have also added controls to show their name and total sales.

We then used the Chart Wizard to create the graph for each customer, selecting the same query for the chart as for the report (**Customer Total Sales**). This time, however, Chart Wizard displays an extra screen. As we are using a bound OLE control to display the graphs, we need to tell Access how the graphs relate to the records that they are displaying.

This is a similar technique to the one we used with the main and subreport in Chapter 11. In this case, the linking field is **Alpha** - Access uses this field to link the graph to the record currently displayed in the report. You can see the linking fields in the **Link Master Fields** and **Link Child Fields** properties, in the **Data** page of the **Properties** window.

Chart: Field5	
OLE Class	Microsoft Graph 5.0
Row Source Type .	Table/Query
Row Source	TRANSFORM Sum([Customer Tot:
Link Child Fields . . .	Alpha
Link Master Fields .	Alpha
Display Type	Content
Update Options . . .	Automatic
OLE Type	Embedded
OLE Type Allowed .	Either
Class	MSGraph.Chart.5
Source Doc	
Source Item	
Column Count	0

In other respects, the chart is created exactly as before. Again, you will probably have to experiment with a few of the settings to get the graph that you are looking for, but with practice the results can be quite amazing.

Summary

This chapter has shown you how you can provide visual information in your applications using graphics and charts. We started off by looking at image controls and the different ways they can be used to present a picture or a graphic. The sample **WroxSoft** and **Picsdemo** applications both make wide use of graphics to present an attractive interface to the user.

However, much of what you have seen in this chapter is not actually Access-specific. OLE is a technology that is appearing in almost all modern PC applications and will soon be finding its way onto other platforms as well. It is part of a strategy which should give us smaller and more efficient applications in the future, together with the ability to construct our own custom applications using compact OLE-enabled components.

However, that's in the future and you shouldn't start holding your breath yet. Today, OLE is mainly used as a way for applications to gain functionality that they lack themselves. It also allows you to store objects from other applications in a data file, or create links to them on disk.

You'll no doubt have noticed that OLE is also very memory-hungry. On less than a 16MB machine these processes can be slow, but the benefits they offer are well worth the extra resources they require.

This chapter has covered:

- An introduction to OLE.
- The difference between image controls and OLE controls.
- How to link and embed objects in an OLE control.
- How to display information from your database in charts.

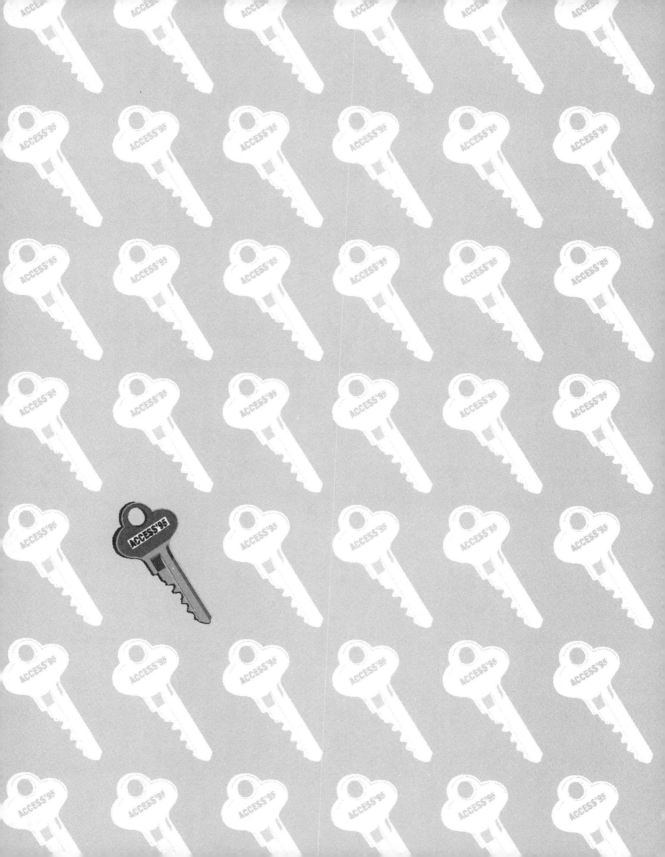

Customizing And Automating The Front End

This chapter is the final one of Part 2, and completes our tour of the sample **WroxSoft** application. In the previous chapters we've constructed all the main parts of our application: the forms and reports that the user sees and the tables and queries that support them. By following a logical design, we can build each object separately, and test and refine it as needed.

To make a usable and attractive application, we need to blend all the skills we've learned, and be able to link the objects in our application in a way that makes sense to our users. When they power-up the application, they won't expect to be greeted with the Database window. We must provide a series of screens and menus that guide them through the tasks they need to accomplish.

So, in this chapter, we'll be looking at wider aspects of Access, and the design of the application as a whole.

Amongst the topics are:

- Menu bars and toolbars.
- Navigating through the application.
- More on action queries.
- Archiving records.
- Creating invoices and statements.
- Mail merge.

The Main Menu Form

When we discussed our interface design in Chapter 9, we decided on a main menu screen (or switchboard) which would be at the heart of the application. Users would select the particular form or report they wanted from here, and return to it afterwards.

This broke the main tasks down into three groups: editing and updating records, producing reports from the database, and archiving old records. Our application mirrors the original design.

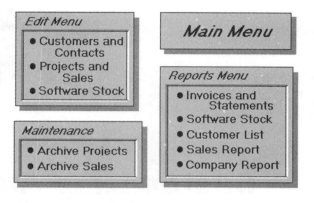

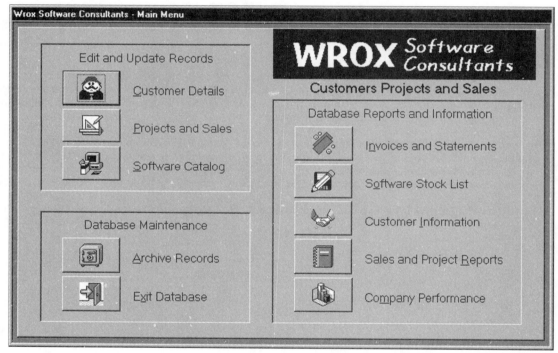

Open the main menu in design view to see how it works. If you look at the Properties window under the All tab, you'll see that the form is unbound (the Record Source property is blank), and we've turned off the Scroll Bars, Record Selectors, and Navigation Buttons. We've also set Auto Resize and Auto Center to Yes, Control Box to No, and Min Max Buttons to Max Enabled.

There are picture buttons to select each task, with a label that provides a caption and hot-key. And, of course, the logo has been added in an object frame. You're already familiar with many of the techniques employed in the main menu, but in this chapter we'll consider how to control the pull-down menus and toolbars, and how we allow the user to exit from the application. You'll recall that we looked at how hot-keys are created back in Part 1, by cutting and pasting a label onto a command button and adding an ampersand (&) to the label in the Caption property box activates the button.

Using Custom Menus

Access contains a series of menu bars which are displayed automatically - which menu you see depends on which object has the focus at the time. If we leave the default menus visible, the user will have full access to the application, just as we do when developing it.

We can remove the standard menu bars altogether, though this does make the application look a little odd. So, instead, we create our own custom menu bars, and display these. They only contain the options that we want to make available to the user. To create a custom menu bar, we can either copy an existing one and just modify it, or else create a new one from scratch. And, of course, we can create a different menu bar for each form.

In **WroxSoft**, there's a simple menu bar which contains just two top-level commands - Options and Reports. When you select these, you get a pull-down list with commands that basically duplicate the push buttons on the forms, enabling you to move between the forms and reports without using the mouse.

How much functionality you build into your custom menus depends on what use you expect to be made of them. The important point is that *you* control which ones are available. You can (and generally should) effectively lock users out of the design mode of Access - so that they can run the application, but not modify it.

To demonstrate how menus are created, we'll build the menu bar for the main opening screen. We'll build a simple Options menu which allows the user to open forms or exit the application. When it's finished it will look like this: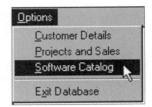

To create the menu we use another of Access' built-in tools, Menu Builder. The menu options that we create in Menu Builder can execute either an existing Access menu command, a macro, or a VBA code routine - so in effect, we can accomplish almost any task from a menu.

We already have the macros we need for our Options menu - they are the ones that are run when the user clicks one of the buttons on the main menu form. These are all in the MainMenu macro sheet, and accomplish the tasks of opening the other forms and exiting from the application. You'll see more about the macros themselves after we build the menu bar.

Try It Out - Creating a Menu Bar for the Opening Screen

1 In **WroxSoft**, open the Properties window of the main menu and select the Other tab.

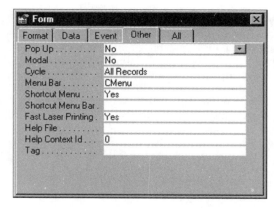

2 Place the cursor in the Menu Bar property and delete CMenu - this is the custom menu that normally appears on the main menu form. Then click the builder button at the end of the property entry.

3 Access opens a window where we can select either to use an existing menu as a template and modify it, or create a new one. Select the <Empty Menu Bar> entry to create a new one.

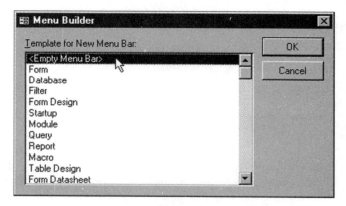

4 Click OK. Now we can see the new blank menu bar in Menu Builder. Enter &Options in the Caption box. This will be the first 'top level' menu entry. Next add the text that will be displayed on the status bar when we select the option.

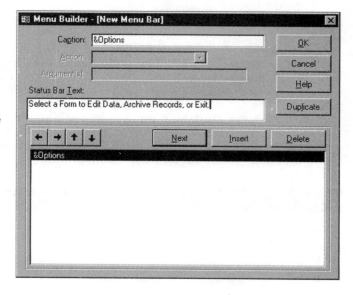

FYI Remember that the ampersand (&) denotes the 'hot-key' letter which can be pressed in conjunction with *Alt* to activate the menu command from the keyboard instead of using the mouse. For example, **&Options** can be activated by pressing *Alt-O*.

5 Click <u>N</u>ext. Now we enter the second level menu commands - the first of these is &Customer Details. Enter this and add the status bar text.

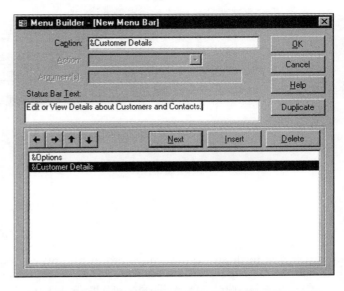

6 As it stands, the Customer Details option will appear next to Options as a top level command. To place it on the drop-down menu below Options, we need to indent it. Select the &Customer Details line in the lower window and click the right-facing arrow button. Access indents it and places three dots before it.

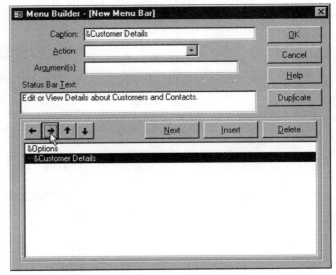

7 The Action and Argument(s) text boxes in the top half of the window are now enabled - before they were grayed out because we were working on a top-level menu command. Open the drop-down list in the Action box to see the options available.

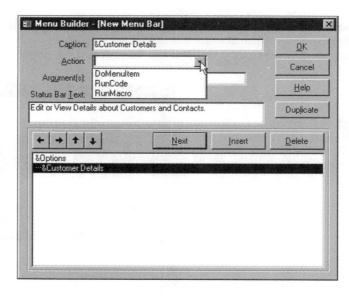

Here we can select from three options. DoMenuItem allows us to carry out any of the Access menu commands when the user selects this option on the new menu. For example, if the required task was to delete the current record in a form, we could select DoMenuItem for the action and specify the argument as Form,Edit,Delete Record - the Delete Record command on the normal Access Edit menu. The RunCode action means we can execute a VBA routine in response to a menu selection and RunMacro lets us use a macro to carry out the actions. We'll be using the RunMacro action.

8 Select RunMacro as the Action for the menu command, then enter MainMenu.DoEditCust for the Argument. This is the name of the macro that we want to run when this option is selected - the DoEditCust macro on the MainMenu macro sheet. This is the macro that runs when the user clicks the Customer Details button on the main menu form.

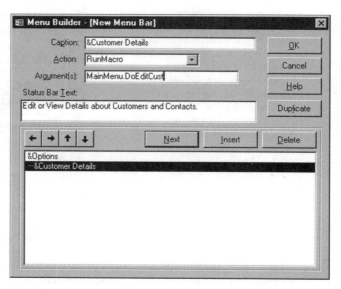

9 Click Next, and enter the remaining options, indenting them all under &Options.

Caption	Action	Argument	Status Bar Text
&Projects and Sales	RunMacro	MainMenu.Do EditProject	Edit and View Details of Projects and Sales
&Software Catalog	RunMacro	MainMenu.Do EditSWare	Edit and View Details of the Software Range
E&xit Database	RunMacro	MainMenu.Do ExitDB	Exits the WroxSoft application

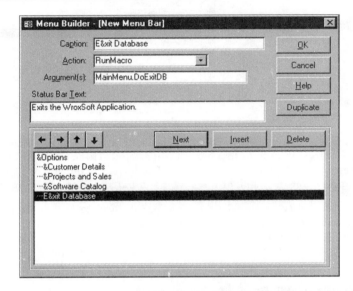

10 Menus often have separator bars to divide the entries into related groups. We'll separate the Exit option from the others. Select &Exit Database in the lower window, and click the Insert button. Access creates a blank row and automatically indents it.

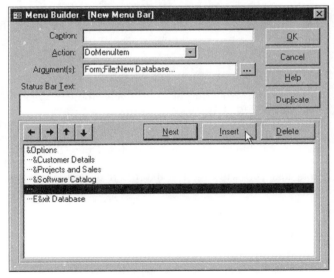

11 Enter a hyphen (-) for the Caption and press *Tab*. Access places it in the lower window. This entry will provide the bar between the Software Catalog and Exit Database menu options.

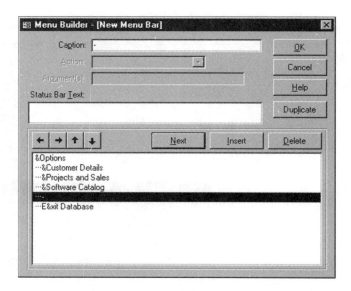

FYI The other buttons in the **Menu Builder** window allow you to duplicate an existing menu bar, delete entries from it, or just move them around. These are useful if you're modifying an existing menu bar template. Click the **Duplicate** button to copy an entire menu bar. Access prompts for the name of the new menu bar and places it in the **Database** window.

When you're modifying an existing menu bar, the **Delete** button removes the menu item currently selected in the bottom part of the window. The up and down arrow buttons move it up and down in the window, and hence to another place in the menu structure. The right and left buttons indent an item, or remove the indent if there's one already.

13 Click OK and Access prompts for the name for the new menu bar. Enter TestMenu and click OK.

14 Access closes Menu Builder and places the new menu TestMenu in the Menu Bar property of our form. This menu will now be displayed when the main menu is active in form view. Try it out.

How It Works

So what has Menu Builder done? Open the Database window and select the Macros tab. Menu Builder has added two new macros - TestMenu and TestMenu_Options. When a form becomes active, Access uses its Menu Bar property to decide which menu bar to show. If the property is blank, it displays the default menu - the Form View menu. However, if there's an entry, it looks for the matching macro and runs this. Open the TestMenu macro in design view.

Note that you will only see the Macro Name (and Condition) column if you have turned these on in the Access Options window.

This contains one action - AddMenu. The Menu Name argument is &Options and this is what's displayed on the menu bar. The Menu Macro Name argument is TestMenu_Options, which is the name of the other macro Menu Builder created in the Database window. Finally, the Status Bar Text argument is what we entered in

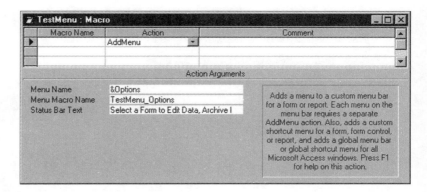

Menu Builder, and is shown when this option is selected on the menu bar. So, the macro will place the top level menu, then use the TestMenu_Options macro to create the lower level menu entries.

Open the TestMenu_Options macro in design view. Here we can see the entries that appear on the Options menu. Each one has an Action with its Macro Name argument set to the name of the macro we want it to run when selected - these are the names we entered in Menu Builder.

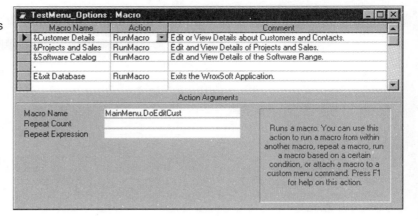

It's possible to edit the macros that Menu Builder creates directly, but it's better to use Menu Builder itself to change and update existing menus, and to create new ones. If you change the macro in the Macro window, you may find that Menu Builder is unable to read it when you next try to open it here. Instead, go back to design view of the main menu and, in the Properties window, place the cursor in the Menu Bar property of the form and click the builder button. Access opens Menu Builder and automatically reads in the existing menu. You can then edit as required, and when you click OK to close Menu Builder, all the macros are updated.

Of course, we can build much more complicated menus than the example we saw above. For instance, the following figure shows the Menu Builder window and the equivalent File menu that's displayed when the Access Database window is active. To see this, just delete the existing Menu Bar property in the main menu form and click the builder button. When Menu Builder prompts for a Template, select the Database entry and click OK.

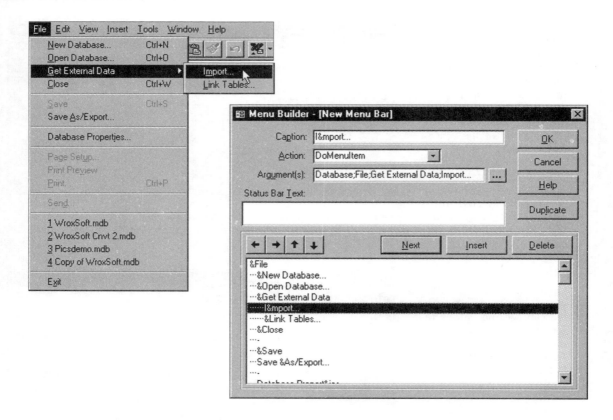

You can see that the top-level entry (the one that's always visible) is File, and under it are the ones that appear when the menu is opened or 'dropped down'. However, the Import command is indented twice, so it doesn't appear on this second-level menu but only appears when the Get External Data command is selected. This is a third-level entry. When one of these exists, Access automatically adds an arrow marker to the entry above it when you open the menu, to tell the user that there are more options below.

Remember that if a menu option opens a dialog box, the standard way of specifying this on the menu is to place three dots after the command. For example, in the screenshot, the New Database... command opens the file selector dialog, while the Close command simply closes the database directly.

Menu Bars for the Other Main Windows

As you've seen, using macros to create menu bars can soon fill up the Macro list in the Database window - it's important to use names which clearly identify each one, otherwise you can become lost when trying to work with them. Access' Menu Builder does name them in a sensible way for you, providing you use a meaningful name when you first create the menu.

Although you can base a menu bar on an existing template, the Template list doesn't include menus you build yourself, so copying one of your new menus and modifying it is a little more difficult. It's generally easier to just create them from scratch each time using Menu Builder.

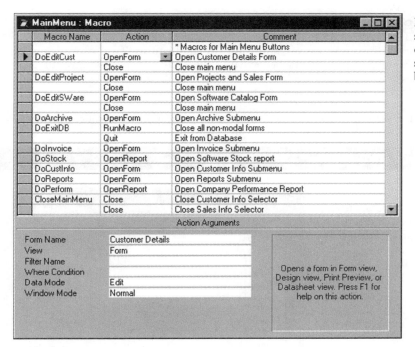

For example, as you have seen, the menu bar on our opening screen runs the same macros as the push-buttons on the forms.

When we create a new menu bar for the Projects and Sales form, we need to include commands to move to the Customer Details form and Software Catalog form, as well as back to the Main Menu form. The macros to do this are already on the ProjSales macro sheet - we created them when we placed the push-buttons there. So, it's no major task to get Menu Builder to create the menu, including the RunMacro statements, and select the names of these macros in the Argument(s) text box.

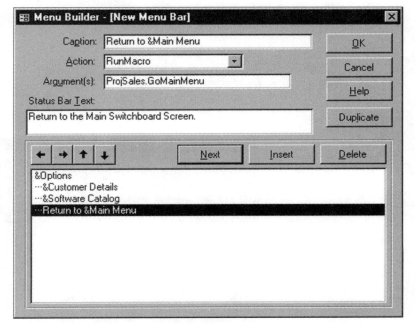

Creating, Showing and Hiding Toolbars

As well as menu bars, Access displays one or more standard **toolbars** as it runs, changing the ones that are shown according to the object that is active at the time. You'll most probably not want to let your users have access to the design view of your application, and will, therefore, have to replace the standard toolbars with your own customized ones.

The buttons you choose for your toolbars will depend on the application, and your users' needs.

Try It Out - Creating Your Own Toolbar

1 In design view, select Toolbars... from the View menu. This opens a dialog where you can select which toolbars you want displayed.

2 Click the New.. button. Access prompts for a name for the new toolbar. Enter TestToolbar and click OK.

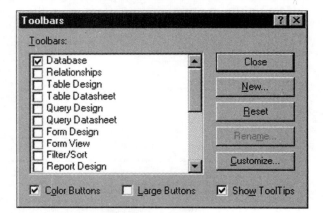

3 Access creates a new empty toolbar, just big enough for one button, and adds its name to the Toolbars window. You can see that it is ticked, showing that it is currently displayed.

The new toolbar

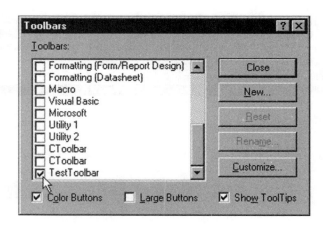

4 Click the Customize button. Access opens the Customize Toolbars dialog, showing a list of categories and their available buttons. If you place the mouse pointer over any button, you'll get a tooltip telling you what it does.

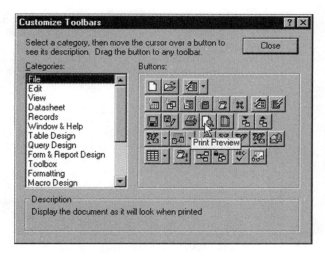

5 Place a few buttons on the new TestToolbar by dragging them from the display of buttons in the Customize Toolbars dialog onto the new toolbar. As you add each one, the toolbar expands to make room. Make sure you drop each button onto the bar - if you drop it too far away, Access creates a new toolbar and places the button on that instead.

6 You can order the buttons by dropping them where you want them, or by clicking on them and dragging them to a new position. To create a space between buttons, just drag one to the right and drop it again. You can also change the shape of the toolbar by dragging one of the edges, just as you do with a normal window.

7 Try scrolling through the different categories. Some buttons are duplicated, but there are many different ones. Then select the All Forms category from near the end of the list. Access displays a list of all the forms in the application. Drag one of these to the new toolbar. If you place the mouse pointer over the new button, the tooltip shows that it will automatically open that form for us.

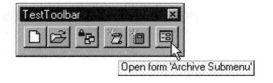

8 The same process works with tables, queries, reports and macros. Access can create toolbar buttons that will open each of these objects for us. Try dragging some onto the new toolbar.

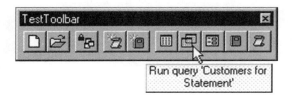

FYI Using toolbar buttons this way allows us to introduce extra functionality into our applications. Because a toolbar button can be used to run any macro, we can build macros to carry out any functions we need, then offer them to the user as standard toolbar buttons complete with tooltips.

9 Once you're happy with your new toolbar, click the Close button on the Customize Toolbar dialog. Now you can try out the toolbar buttons to see how they work. Notice that Access automatically disables those that aren't appropriate - depending on which is the current active window. For example, the Print button is 'grayed out' when the Database window is active, but is enabled when you click on a form.

You can edit a toolbar at any time in the Customize Toolbar dialog. To remove a button you just drag it off the toolbar. You can also modify the built-in toolbars by selecting them in the Toolbars dialog. In fact, once you have the Customize Toolbars dialog open, you can modify any toolbar that's visible, not just the one you've selected in the Toolbars dialog. If you modify an existing one then change your mind, you can select it in the Toolbars dialog and use the Reset button to set it back to its original (default) layout.

If you select a toolbar you've created yourself, however, the Reset option is replaced by a Delete button. This allows you to delete any custom toolbars that you've created. The three check boxes in the Toolbars dialog allow you to specify whether the toolbars display colored or large buttons instead of the standard ones, and whether tooltips are displayed.

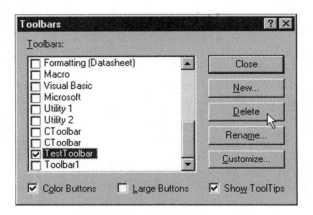

Displaying Toolbars

The Toolbars dialog shows which toolbars are currently displayed. As you click on the option box for each toolbar it is displayed or hidden immediately. When the option is ticked, that particular toolbar is displayed.

If you select a toolbar in this way, it will remain on view all the time, rather than appearing and disappearing according to which object is active. For example, if you select the Filter/Sort toolbar by clicking on it in the Toolbars dialog, it will be shown no matter which form or report is current.

You can also use the ShowToolbar macro action to show and hide toolbars. This takes two arguments - the Name of the toolbar, and a Show argument which is either Yes, No or Where Appropriate. The Name is that shown in the Toolbars dialog, or if it's a custom toolbar, the name you gave it when you created it. If you set the Show argument to No, that toolbar is permanently hidden; if you set it to Yes, the toolbar will be permanently displayed.

If you want a built-in toolbar to only be visible when certain forms or reports are active, you should use the Where Appropriate argument. This tells Access to only show the toolbar in situations where it would normally be used. For example, if you run the following macro:

> **Action:** ShowToolbar
> > **Toolbar Name:** Macro
> > **Show:** Where Appropriate

the Access built-in Macro toolbar will only appear when the current window is a macro window. When you switch to another window, it will be hidden. Note, though, that this technique only works with the Access built-in toolbars. This isn't really surprising - after all, with custom toolbars Access has no way of knowing which windows are appropriate. To show your own toolbars only when certain forms are active, you need to do some extra work.

Displaying a Toolbar only with a Specific Object

In this case, or indeed if you want to display a built-in toolbar with one form, but not with others, you can use a ShowToolbar macro action in the On Activate and On Deactivate properties of the relevant form. The toolbar will then only be visible when that form is the current one.

For example, you could set the On Activate property of the Main Menu form to MainMenu.ShowTBar, and the On Deactivate to MainMenu.HideTBar. You would then add these macros to the MainMenu macro sheet. An On Activate event occurs when the form becomes the active one by being opened or brought to the front of the other windows. The On Deactivate event occurs when another window becomes active.

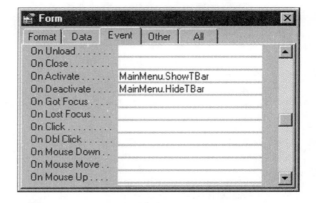

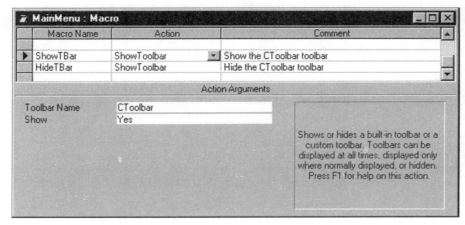

The first macro, ShowTBar, uses the ShowToolbar macro action to display the custom toolbar CToolbar by setting the Show argument to Yes. HideTBar just sets the Show argument to No. Hence, each time the form becomes the active one, the CToolbar toolbar is displayed, and when another form becomes active it is hidden again.

The Application Start-up Properties

When our application first starts up, the custom toolbar, CToolbar, and custom menu, CMenu, are displayed. We set this using the Startup dialog, which specifies how the application should appear when it first starts. To open this dialog, select Startup.. from the Tools menu.

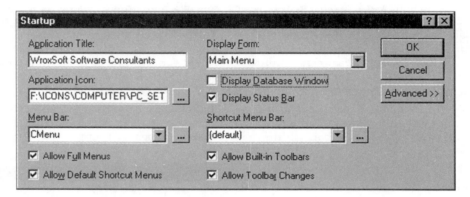

Here you can enter a title for the application. This will be shown in the main Access window title bar instead of 'Microsoft Access'. You can also select a different icon for the title bar - to select one either type in the name or use the builder button next to the text box to open another dialog where you can select the icon you want.

There are options to select the menu bar for the application, and here we have selected our custom one CToolbar. This is displayed all the time that the application is open. Then, below this we can tell Access whether we want it to display the normal full menus (the ones at the top of the screen) and the shortcut (right-click) menus. You should take care if you clear the Full Menus check box - you can find that you're unable to use the application at all if there are no menus displayed. It's wise to make a copy of your application before you start experimenting with the settings in the Startup dialog.

On the right-hand side of the dialog you can select which form you want to be displayed when the application starts. We've set this to Main Menu - the main 'switchboard' form in our application. Below that we've cleared the Display Database Window option so that the Database window isn't visible, but we've left the Display Status Bar option ticked. We haven't specified a shortcut menu bar - we have left the normal ones active. However, you can specify a particular one here by entering its name, or by clicking the builder button and creating it using Menu Builder. Finally, we can select whether to display the default built-in toolbars as the application runs, and whether to allow the user to change which toolbars are displayed with the Toolbars... command on the View menu.

Bypassing the Application Start-up Settings

You can force Access to ignore the settings in the Startup dialog by holding down the *Shift* key while the database is loading. (You can also press *F11* to show the Database window after it has loaded, providing no other dialog boxes are open). However, if you want to secure an application so that your users can't get access to the design, you can prevent these methods being used to bypass the Startup settings.

Clicking the Advanced button extends the window and shows extra options. If the Allow Use Of Special Access Keys checkbox is cleared, it prevents the users from bypassing the Startup settings or using *F11* to open the Database window. Again, take care when you use this - it's possible to lock yourself out of your own application this way!

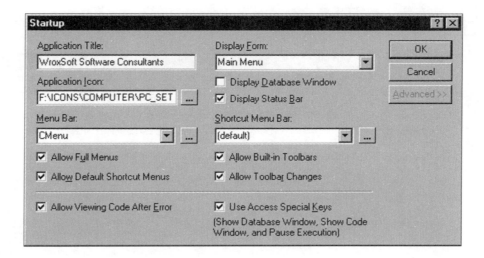

The other option in the extended part of the Startup dialog allows you to prevent users from stopping code in the database while it's running. If you press *Ctrl-Break* while a VBA code routine is running, Access stops it and opens the Code Editor window. To prevent this happening (and stop users from being able to edit the code), clear the Allow Viewing Code After Error checkbox.

Closing Down the Application

When your user has finished working with the application, they need to close it down. In the previous chapter we saw how we can close the different form windows using the Close macro action in response to a button click. We can close down a database by closing the Database window or selecting Close from the Access File menu while the Database window is the current window. However, the Close macro action can't be used to close the Database window directly.

It's likely, though, that what you'll actually want to do is close Microsoft Access itself - you want to hide the Access system from the users as far as possible. When our users have finished with the **WroxSoft** application, we return them to Windows desktop so that they can select another application to run. To close Access, we use the Quit macro action.

Open the MainMenu macro sheet by selecting it in the Database window and clicking the Design button. Scroll down to the DoExitDB macro. This runs when the user clicks the Exit Database button on the Main Menu form, or selects Exit Database from our custom Options menu. You'll see that it first runs another macro - called SubCloseAll - which closes all the open form windows.

Action: RunMacro
    Macro Name: SubCloseAll
    Repeat Count:
    Repeat Expression:

This macro is simply a set of Close actions which close the Customer Details, Projects and Sales, and Software Catalog forms. This isn't strictly necessary, as you'll see in a moment, but is included for tidiness and because it's good practice. It ensures that all changes to the records are saved.

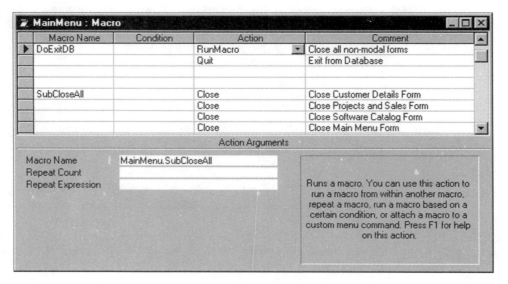

Next the macro uses the Quit action.

Action: Quit
    Options: Save All

This closes Microsoft Access altogether. The Options argument is Save All, which saves any changes to objects in the database before closing. You can also select Prompt to prompt the user to save the changes, or Exit which closes Access without saving the changes.

Moving between the Main Forms

When we were designing our application, we identified a need to be able to move between forms. If a customer calls to order a copy of *WroxSoft Accessible*, we need to be able to open the Customer Details form to see whether they have an account and to check their details, then move to the Projects and Sales form to enter the order. We may also want to open the Software Catalog to tell them about the product. Finally, we need to create an invoice so that we can dispatch the goods.

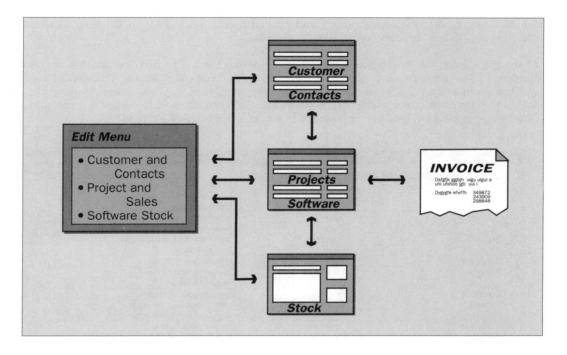

This process would be a lot more difficult if we first had to close the current form, then go back to the main menu and open the new form from there. Not only would it be slow and cumbersome, but we would also have to find the customer each time we opened the form again. We have two options to get round this - we can leave each form open, which would mean that the user has to close them when they're finished with, or we can provide a specific route through the forms for them to follow.

Many Windows applications use the first method. By using the maximize and minimize buttons, and dragging windows around, the user can have them all open and just switch between them. This can, however, cause problems. Leaving an unused window open may mean accidental key presses can alter the data unintentionally, and each open form uses memory and resources that can slow the system down. It also makes it difficult to synchronize the forms so that the same record is displayed in each - we would like each form to show the same customer as the user switches between them. And, if the user is only working in one form, we can cause delays by continually updating the other windows. So we've gone for the second method, as in our original plan.

Normally, when you open a form it just displays the first record. But if you're using the **Customer Details** form and then open the **Projects and Sales** form, you would expect it to show the same customer, not the first one. This is called synchronizing the forms and is a method that makes your application much easier to use.

Plotting a Route through the Application Using Macros

We've removed the control boxes and minimize buttons so that a user can't close a window except with the push-button on the form, and they navigate a route that we've planned, automatically closing unused windows and synchronizing the records in the new windows they open. Again, this is all done using simple macros.

To see them, open the MainMenu macro sheet in design view. The first few macros are used to open and close the various forms from the main menu. For example, the DoEditCust macro uses an OpenForm action to open the Customer Details form, then a Close action to close the main menu. The DoStock macro, which runs when the Software Stock List button is pressed, uses an OpenReport macro to open the Software List report in print preview mode.

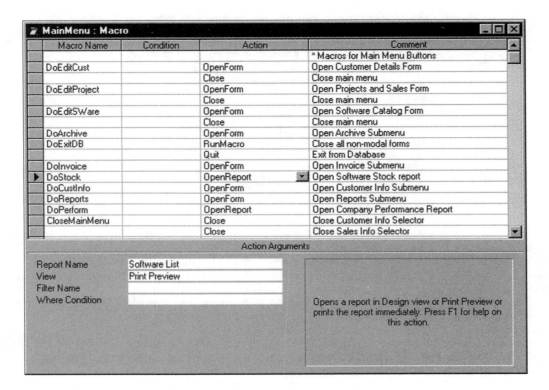

Similarly, the ProjSales macro sheet contains the macros that run when the user clicks the Main Menu, Customer Details or Software Catalog buttons in the Projects and Sales form. We saw how the records in the different forms are synchronized in Chapter 10.

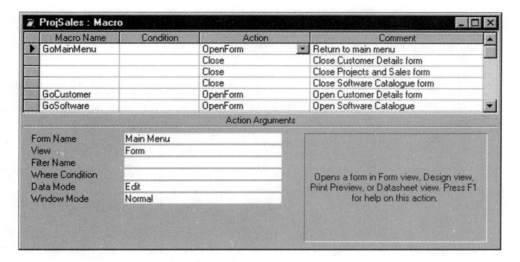

You'll see that we sometimes close a form when we move to another, and sometimes leave it open. It all depends on how you think the user will navigate through them. If you leave unused forms open, you can slow down the application by absorbing memory for the open forms. However, re-opening a form, rather than just switching back to it, takes longer - so if you expect the user to need it again you may decide to just leave it open, covered by the other form windows. If a form contains a lot of graphics and pictures, it will use considerably more memory so you should only have it open when absolutely necessary. You can limit the amount of memory required by using fewer colors in graphics, logos and pictures - try to limit them to 16 colors wherever possible.

We know that a user may switch between the Customer Details, Projects and Sales, and Software Catalog forms while entering an order, so we leave these open when they move from one to another. But as soon as they switch back to the main menu, we close any of these that may still be open.

 When you use an **OpenForm** action and specify a form that is already open, Access just brings that form to the front. It doesn't open another copy of the form.

The Report Selector Forms

Because there are several reports in our application, we've chosen to break them down into groups to make the main menu more usable. Rather than having thirteen buttons in the Reports and Information section, we've got just five. Two of these open the report selector forms which offer a further choice of reports. The two sub-menus are the Customer Information Selector and the Sales and Projects Reports Selector.

These are, of course, just smaller versions of the main menu, but with some important differences. You'll notice that when you open one of these from the main menu, you can't switch to another form or use any of the pull-down menu commands. The forms are displayed as dialogs and all other tasks stop until you choose a report, or close the selector with the Cancel button.

Using 'MouseMove' to Show Information

In the last chapter, we saw how you can use the ToolTip property of a control to display a short text message when the mouse pointer hovers over the control. However, Access detects events for a control whenever the mouse pointer is moved over it. You'll notice that, in the Report Selector forms, a description of each report is shown at the foot of the menu as you move the mouse pointer over the different buttons. This is done with the On Mouse Move event.

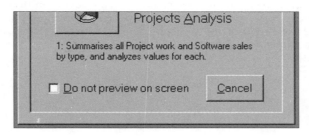

Open the Reports Selector form in design view from the Database window and highlight the Projects and Sales button. Open the Properties window for the button, and click the Events tab. The On Mouse Move property is set to MainMenu.ShowProjSaleInfo. Click the builder button at the end of the property to open the MainMenu macro sheet, and scroll down to the ShowProjSaleInfo macro. This macro is also placed in the On Mouse Move property of the label next to the button, so it runs each time the mouse pointer is moved over the button or its label. There are others which run for the other buttons, and one which is placed in the On Mouse Move property of the rectangle control behind the buttons, so it runs when the mouse pointer is moved away from a button or label.

Macro Name	Condition	Action	
ShowProjSaleInfo	Left([Forms]![Reports Selector]![txtReportInfo.Caption],1)<>"1"	SetValue	▼
ShowOutstandInfo	Left([Forms]![Reports Selector]![txtReportInfo.Caption],1)<>"2"	SetValue	
ShowIncomeInfo	Left([Forms]![Reports Selector]![txtReportInfo.Caption],1)<>"3"	SetValue	
ShowAnalysisInfo	Left([Forms]![Reports Selector]![txtReportInfo.Caption],1)<>"4"	SetValue	
ClearReportInfo	Left([Forms]![Reports Selector]![txtReportInfo.Caption],1)<>"S"	SetValue	▼

Action Arguments

Item   [Forms]![Reports Selector]![txtReport
Expression "1: Summarises all Project work and [...]

Sets a value for a control, field, or property on a form, form datasheet, or report. Press F1 for help on this action.

How the Macro Displays Information

This is all very well, but it doesn't explain how the event causes text to be displayed. In the bottom part of the form is a label control called txtReportInfo. This is empty when the form first opens, but each macro places text into it each time it runs. However, the macro runs for each mouse movement detected, so it will be executed many times while the pointer is over the same control. This causes the text to flash in an unpleasant manner, so we need to add a Condition to each macro action which prevents this. Basically, each macro sets the text only if it isn't already set to the correct thing - it knows this by checking the first character of the text that's already in the text box. If it differs, the macro will change the information to display the right information for that button. For example, the ShowProjSaleInfo macro is:

Condition: Left([Forms]![Reports Selector]![txtReportInfo].Caption,1)<>"1"
Action: SetValue
    Item: [Forms]![Reports Selector]![txtReportInfo].Caption
    Expression: "1: Summarizes all Project ..(etc).. shows values for each."

The macro is basically the same for each button on the form except that the numbers and information change. There is a condition which utilizes the **Left** function to determine the number of the text in the box. When the mouse pointer moves over the background rectangle, the ClearReportInfo macro sets the text back to the general help text.

The **Left** function is similar to the **Left$** function we met earlier. However, the value it returns isn't actually a string, but a variant - one of Access' internal data types.

Using a Dialog to Get Values from the User

You've seen how our Report Selector forms 'hold the focus' until you select a report or close it. If you open one of the forms in design view, you'll see that the Border Style has been changed to Thin, and the Min Max Buttons property set to None. This prevents the user re-sizing the form, or maximizing or minimizing it. But the Pop Up and Modal properties are both set to No. We can use these properties to make a dialog type form. Setting Pop Up to Yes makes the form remain on top of all other windows, but doesn't prevent you selecting another window or menu command. Setting the Modal property to Yes, however, means the form keeps the focus until it's closed. In other words, you can't select any other object while the form is open.

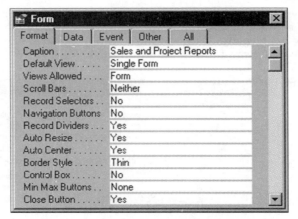

However, neither of these will achieve quite what we want. We'd like the form to hold the focus, so that it's not left open while the user does something else. But, if we set the Modal property to Yes, then we have to close the form to continue. In this case, we lose the values of any controls that are on it. Here, there's only the Print Preview checkbox, but in other forms, such as the Invoice Selector, there are many more.

The way round this is to hide the form rather than closing it. It will then remain in memory with all the controls set to the same values as when it was visible. As soon as we hide it, Access continues execution of any macros or code that were suspended while it was open, and we can still retrieve the values from the form when it's not visible. To hide a form, we set its Visible property to False (No). This can only be done via a macro or VBA.

So how do we make it modal in the first place? We could set the Modal property of the form to Yes, so that it always opens as a modal form. However, the OpenForm macro action has an argument - Window Mode - which controls how the form is displayed, and we'll use this method instead. To open the Select State form as a modal form we use the macro action:

```
Action:      OpenForm
    Form Name:       Select State
    View:            Form
    Filter Name:
    Where Condition:
    Data Mode:       Edit
    Window Mode:     Dialog
```

Selecting which Report to Open

When the user clicks a button on the Customer Information Selector or Sales and Projects Report Selector we have to open the required report. Of course, we can tell which report they want by the button they select. Like the Main Menu form, each button has a different macro in its On Click property. The macro opens the correct report. For example, the <u>S</u>ales by Customer button has its On Click property set to MainMenu.DoCustSales, which refers to the DoCustSales macro on the MainMenu macro sheet. This macro uses an OpenReport action to open the Sales By Month report.

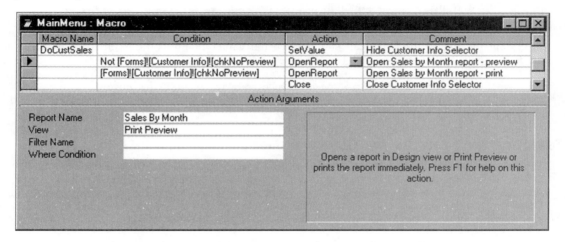

However, there's something else to consider - remember there are checkboxes on the Report Selector forms which allow the user to skip the print preview of the report and just print it directly. So, we need to look at the value of this checkbox, named chkNoPreview, before we know whether to open the report in print preview or print mode. We've used a macro with four actions. The macro first hides the Report Selector form by setting its Visible property to False:

Action: SetValue
> **Item:**   [Forms]![Customer Info].[Visible]
> **Expression:**   False

Then it uses two OpenReport actions, each with a condition. If the value of the chkNoPreview control (the Don't preview on screen.. checkbox) is False, then this first action will be executed, and the report will be opened in print preview mode.

Condition: Not [Forms]![Customer Info]![chkNoPreview]
Action: OpenReport
> **Report Name:**   Sales By Month
> **View:**   Print Preview
> **Filter Name:**
> **Where Condition:**

Otherwise, it's skipped and the second action is executed which opens the report in print mode.

Condition: [Forms]![Customer Info]![chkNoPreview]
Action: OpenReport
> **Report Name:**   Sales By Month
> **View:**   Print
> **Filter Name:**
> **Where Condition:**

463

Finally the macro closes and removes the hidden Customer Info form from memory.

Action: Close
    Object Type: Form
    Object Name: Customer Info

So, it's fairly easy to open the correct report from our selector forms using simple macros. And by hiding the dialog form, we can still retrieve the values of the controls on it to decide which mode to open it in. But there are two other Selector subforms in our application, and these are both more complicated than the Report Selectors. When we use the Customer Listings option, the Select State form allows us to specify which state we want to see customers from, and the Invoices And Statements selector allows us to choose a particular customer to print invoices or statements for.

Selecting the State for the Customer List

When a user selects the Customer Listings option from the Customer Information Selector, the Select State form opens. Here, they can elect to print just records from one state, and specify whether to print them in alphabetical order or by town. The Customer Listings button uses an OpenForm action, but sets the Window State to Dialog so that it becomes a modal form, as we saw earlier. The user can't use any other forms while this one is displayed.

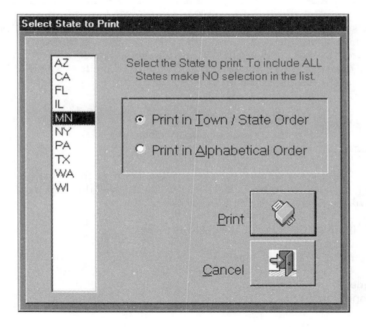

When the user clicks the Print button, we have some decisions to make before we know which report to open. We need to look at the way the customers are to be sorted, and decide whether we are meant to be displaying all records or just those from the one selected state. We then need to check whether the user wants to print the listing directly or preview it on screen. Summarized, this is a list of all the possible decisions that could be taken:

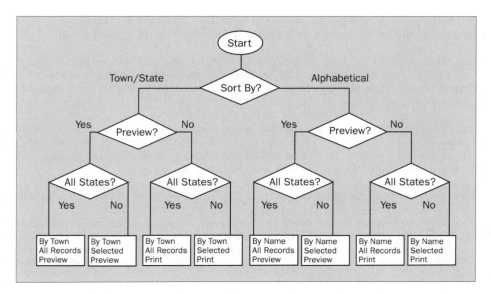

Clicking the <u>P</u>rint button runs the StateOK macro on the MainMenu macro sheet. This macro uses two SetValue actions to hide the Customer Information Selector and the State Selector forms - we can't close them because we need to refer to the controls in our macro. Next we decide how the records are to be sorted by retrieving the value of fraListBy, the option frame on the Select State form. If it is 0, we open the Customer By Town report, and if it's 1 we open the Customer List report. However, we can't open the reports directly yet - first we need to check the value of chkNoPreview (on the Customer Information Selector form) to see whether we should preview the report or print it directly. So, we use a RunMacro action to run another macro, either PrintByState or PrintByAlpha.

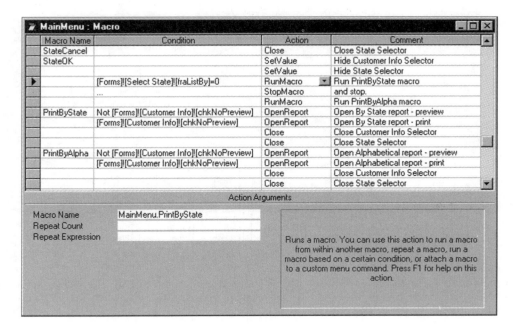

465

The PrintByState and PrintByAlpha macros are similar - they use a condition which retrieves the value of the chkNoPreview control and then run the report in the correct view.

The only other decision we have to make is whether to show all the records or just those from one state. This is done by using an **IIf** statement in the Where Condition argument of the OpenReport actions. (The decision to show records from all or one state isn't affected by whether we're in preview.)

You'll see that the StateList list box on the Select State form, like most other controls, has a Value property. If any of the entries in the list is selected, the Value of the control is the selected entry. If no entry is selected, the Value is Null. So we can check this and produce a Where Condition that will limit the records that are displayed as required.

=IIf([Forms]![Select State]![StateList] Is Null, "","[State] = Forms![Select State]![StateList]")

This expression returns an empty string (**""**) if there's no selection, or the Where Condition [State] = Forms![Select State]![StateList] if one is selected. The report then shows the records that match the condition - either matching the selected state, or showing all of them if the result is an empty string (which is equivalent to entering no condition). Finally, we close the State Selector and Customer Information Selector forms.

Selecting which Invoices or Statements to Print

If you thought that the choices involved in printing the right customer listing were complicated, brace yourself for this: on the Invoices and Statements Selector, the user can print either an Invoice or a Statement, all the customers or a selected customer, and on top of that, they can preview their choice on screen or print it directly. And, of course, there are two types of invoice - a Project Invoice and a Software Invoice. Here's an outline of the decision process:

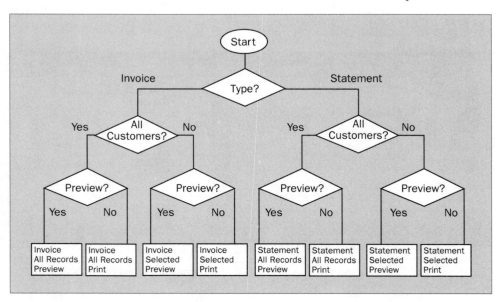

To handle all these choices, we again use RunMacro actions to split up the tasks. Open the MainMenu macro in design view find the InvoiceOK macro. This runs when the Print button is clicked.

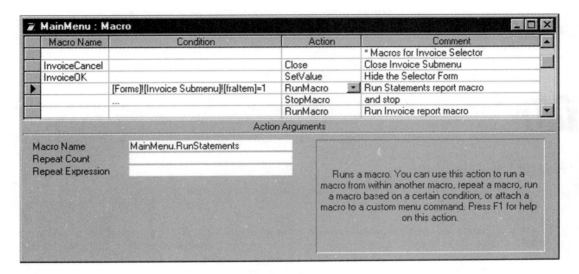

The first step is hide the selector form. Then the macro checks fraItem - the Invoice or Statement option frame - to see what the user has selected. If value of fraItem is 1, we execute the RunStatements macro, otherwise we execute the RunInvoices macro.

Printing the Statements

The RunStatements macro is the simplest. This checks the value of fraSelCust, the option frame where the user selects to print details of all customers or one particular customer. If the value is 0, we execute the All_Statements macro, otherwise we execute the Select_Statements macro.

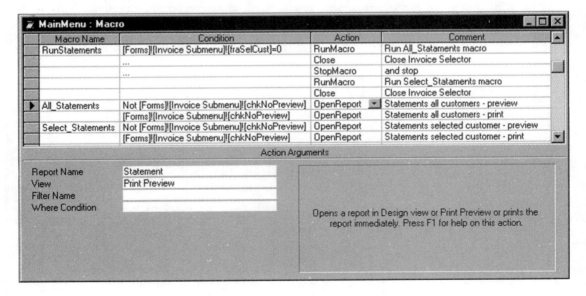

These macros then retrieve the value of the chkNoPreview control and either preview or print the statement. The All_Statements macro uses no Where Condition so that all customers are included, while the Select_Statements macro uses the value of the cboCustomer control on the Invoice

Selector form to limit the records to those with a matching value for the Alpha field. In other words, they only display the record of the selected customer. The expression used to limit the customers that are included is:

[Alpha]=[Forms]![Invoice Submenu]![cboCustomer]

 FYI Remember that the **Statement** report has its own criteria which limit the records that are included to those that have been invoiced but not paid.

Printing the Invoices

If the user selects Print Invoices, the task becomes a little more complicated. The theory is the same, but we have to use two different reports - the Sales Invoice and the Project Invoice reports. For simplicity, we just run both of these - they will only print invoices if the customer hasn't yet been invoiced because we used criteria in the design of the report to limit the records that are included. If there are no sales for one type of invoice (Projects or Software Sales), that report just produces a blank invoice. So the design of these macros is basically similar to the statement macros; they just include an extra OpenReport action.

However, we have another job to do. We have to set the Invoiced date field in the Project or Order table for the sales we're invoicing. We do this using action queries. You'll see the queries themselves later on - for now, just look at the actions in the macro sheet. We use a RunSQL statement action, and the SQL statement that forms the query is shown in the SQL Statement argument of each, at the bottom of the macro window. So the RunInvoices macro looks like this:

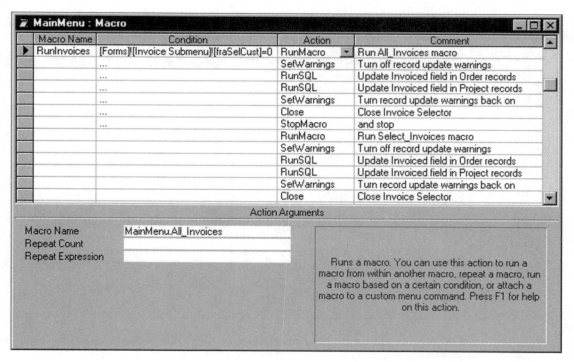

If fraSelCust is 0 (we're including all customers), the All_Invoices macro runs. This macro just checks the value of the chkNoPreview control and either previews or prints the two reports including all the customers. Then, we turn off the warning messages (which would normally be shown when the tables are updated), run the two action queries to update the Order and Project tables, turn the warnings back on, and then close the Invoice Selector form.

The **SetWarnings** macro action is used to suppress any warning messages and other message boxes while the macro is running. However, error messages are always displayed. It's equivalent to pressing *Enter* whenever a warning or message box is displayed to select the default choice - typically an **OK** or **Yes**. When the macro finishes Access automatically turns the display of messages back on, however it does no harm to include an action to do this yourself.

If fraSelCust is 1 (we are invoicing only the selected customer), the Select_Invoices macro is executed instead. This again checks chkNoPreview to determine the view for the two reports, and uses a condition to limit the records to those for the selected customer, just like when we printed statements. The Where Condition is:

   [Alpha]=[Forms]![Invoice Submenu]![cboCustomer]

Then, we again use two SQL action queries to update the Invoiced dates in the tables, but this time they only update the records for the selected customer. Again, we'll look at these queries in more detail in a while.

So we can open the correct Statement or Invoices report, and update the Invoiced fields in the Order and Project records when we do. And if the user opens the report in print preview mode, all they have to do is click the Print button on the toolbar once they're happy with the information it contains and it will be actually printed. However, there is one more aspect of invoicing that we have to consider.

Invoicing a Sale Directly

When the user is entering a sale or project (in the Projects and Sales form) they can invoice just that sale or project directly, by clicking the Invoice button on that form.

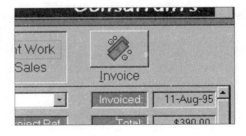

Here, the decisions we have to make are a little different. Instead of allowing the user to preview the invoice, we would normally print it directly. And because we can tell which type of sale it is, we only need to use one Invoice report, rather than printing both as we did in the Invoice Selector form. However, we need to check if it has already been invoiced - the user could be viewing a sale that was made (and invoiced) earlier and have hit the button in error. We should also check the customer's credit rating to see if the value of the sale exceeds it. So the plan is:

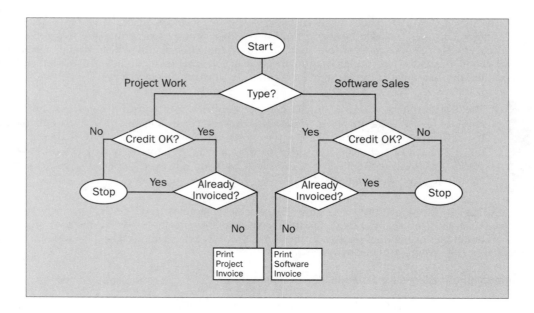

 So that you can see the system working even if you haven't got a printer attached, we've set up the sample application to default to **Print Preview** when you click the **I**nvoice button. To change this you just need to change the open report's **View** argument to **Print**.

The DoInvoice Macro

The **I**nvoice button runs the DoInvoice macro, this time on the ProjSales macro sheet. This macro simply checks the value of fraSaleType - the option frame where the user selects either **Co**nsultant Work (projects) or **S**oftware Sales. If it is 1, we know we are working on a software sale, otherwise it's a project. We then execute either the SalesInvoice or ProjectInvoice macro.

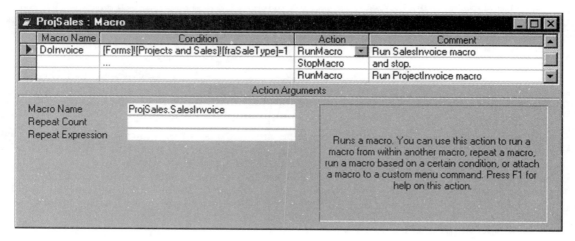

These macros are again similar. They check the customer's credit limit by comparing the value in the hidden text box VCredit (on the Projects and Sales form) with the total value of the sale - either the TotalDue control on the Projects subform or the Grand_TotalDue control on the Order subform. If the condition is **True**, meaning that the customer can't afford any more, then a MsgBox action displays a message telling the user this and the macro stops. The Condition for a project is:

[Forms]![Projects and Sales]![VCredit] < [Forms]![Projects and Sales]![Projects Subform].[Form]![TotalDue]

If the customer can afford the sale, then the macro checks to see whether the sale has already been invoiced. If it has, the Invoiced control on the relevant form won't be Null. Again, if this is the case, a message is displayed and the macro stops. The Condition used here is:

Not IsNull([Forms]![Projects and Sales]![Projects Subform].[Form]![Invoiced])

If all is well, and the macro is still running, we can open the Invoice report using a Condition to limit it just to the current project or software sale. For example, the ProjectInvoice macro uses:

[ProjectKey]=[Forms]![Projects and Sales]![Projects Subform].[Form]![ProjectKey]

as the Where Condition for the OpenReport action. As a result, we only print the correct invoice for that project or software sale.

Finally, we can turn off the update warnings, run the query which updates the Invoiced field for that record only, and turn the warnings back on. The invoice has been produced and the table updated with a simple click of the Invoice button.

 We've used macros to achieve our desired results, but you should note that in this situation, VBA could do the job more efficiently.

Updating Tables with Action Queries

We now have a working application and can move around the forms and open the reports from a series of menu and submenu screens. The forms allow the user to edit and update records, delete them, and add new ones. However, there are some record handling tasks that our application must achieve without user intervention.

For example, we've already identified that we'll automatically set the date in the Invoiced field of Project and Order records when an invoice is printed. And, of course, we also need to update the stock level in the Software table when we sell any products. Other tasks include archiving old Project and Sales records and deleting blank records - remember that in Chapter 10 we found that blank Order records could appear in our database because we ensured that Access inserted a new record in the form when the user entered a value in the Order Line table.

To change the contents of a table automatically, we use action queries - we examined these in Part 1 and used them to create a new table, append records to an existing table, and delete records. In our **WroxSoft** application we use them in several places.

Setting the Invoiced Date with Queries

When we produce an invoice, we need to set the Invoiced field of the records in the Project and Order tables that have been invoiced to today's date. The macros we saw earlier do this using the RunSQL macro action to execute an SQL action query. We'll be looking at SQL in depth in the next chapter, but here we'll show you how these queries look in the Query Builder grid.

Printing Invoices for All Customers

The simplest situation is when we're sending out invoices for all customers. We print a Project Invoice for every project that hasn't been invoiced, and a Sales Invoice for each order that hasn't been invoiced. So, to update the tables, we just need to set the Invoiced field for all records which don't have it set already - i.e. those that have not yet been invoiced. This is the query we use to update the Order table.

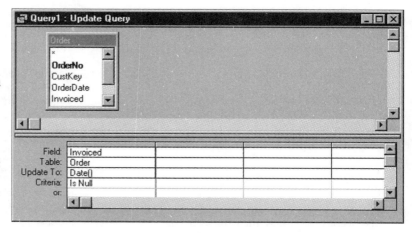

It contains just the Invoiced field, and sets the value in it to today's date using the Date() function. The Criteria for the Invoiced field is Is Null, so only records which have Null in that field will be updated. Similarly, the query for the Project table is:

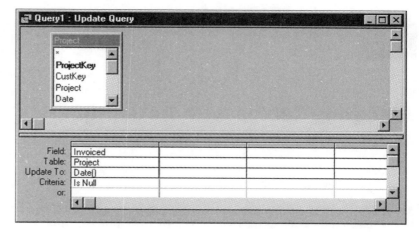

Printing the Invoice for a Selected Customer

When we invoice a selected customer using the Invoice Selector form, we must update only the records that haven't been invoiced for that customer. So we need to add an extra field to the grid, and use this in the Criteria for selecting the records. The extra field is the Alpha field which contains the ID of the customer selected on the Invoice Selector form. However, this doesn't appear in the Order or Project tables, so we need to add the Customer table to the grid as well. This is automatically linked to the Project or Order table because of the relationships we created when we built the tables.

To select only the customer currently shown on the Invoice Selector form we place the criteria: [Forms]![Invoice Submenu]![cboCustomer] in the Alpha column of the grid. Of course, we don't specify a value for the Update to: row as we don't want to change this in the original table - we're only using it to select the correct records. The query for the Project table is exactly the same, but updates the Project table rather than the Order table.

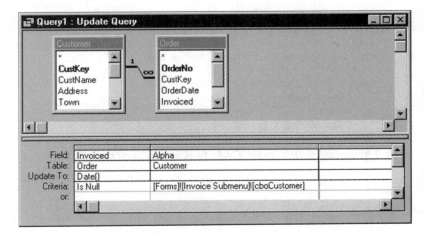

Printing an Invoice from the Projects and Sales Form

The other situation we met earlier is when we print an invoice directly from the Projects and Sales form. In this case, we know the OrderNo or ProjectKey value (it's displayed on the form), so the Criteria is just this. The Order and Project tables contain all the fields we need, so we only use one table in each query. The criteria limits the records that are updated to the one currently on display in the Projects and Sales form.

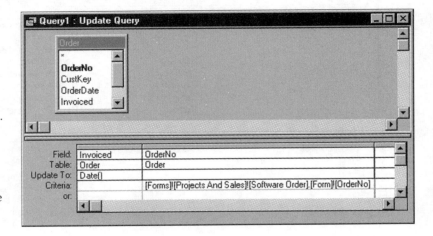

Updating the Software Stock Levels

When we sell items of software from our range, we must reduce the stock figure in the Software table to reflect the sale. We should also increase the figure if a sale is canceled. To keep the stock figure up to date, we use an action query which runs when a new software order is entered or an existing order is deleted. There are two queries, and this time we've stored them as individual objects in the Database window, rather than as SQL statements in a RunSQL macro action. This is mainly because the SQL statement that produces these queries is too long for the macro argument, which is limited to 255 characters.

The OpenQuery macro action is used to execute a query which is stored in the Database window. This can be used to open any kind of query, not just an action query. It takes three arguments. The Name of the query is self-explanatory. The other two determine how the data is displayed, and whether the results can be edited or not. The View argument can be Datasheet, Design or Print Preview, and the Data Mode can be Add, Edit or Read Only. However, as our queries are action queries, it doesn't matter what we use for these arguments. For example, to execute the Update Stock query we've used:

> **Action:**   OpenQuery
> **Query Name:**   Update Stock
> **View:**   Datasheet
> **Data Mode:**   Edit

The UpdateStock and DeleteSale Macros

The stock figure is kept up to date by two macros - UpdateStock and DeleteSale. These macros are placed in the After Insert and On Delete event properties of the Order Line subform and are therefore run when a record is inserted into or deleted from the subform. The UpdateStock macro runs the query that subtracts the number of items sold from the existing stock, and the DeleteSale macro executes the Delete Stock Record query which just adds them back again.

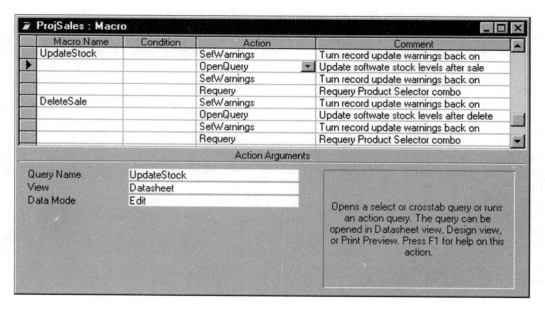

We'll look at these queries together, because they're almost identical. They link the OrderLine and Software tables so that we have access to all the fields we need. The criteria is that the OrderLineKey and OrderNo values of the Order Line *subform* match the OrderLineKey and OrderNo in the table, so that we only select the record for the current order line. Then we can update the SWStock field in the Software table - either subtracting the value of the Qty field from it, or adding it if the user is deleting a record.

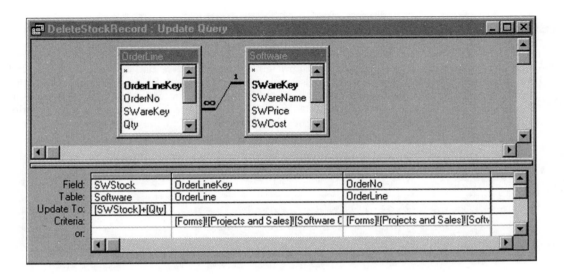

The Criteria for the OrderLineKey column in both queries is:

[Forms]![Projects and Sales]![Software Order].[Form]![Order Line].[Form]![OrderLineKey]

and for the OrderNo column it is:

[Forms]![Projects and Sales]![Software Order].[Form]![OrderNo]

Finally, notice that the two macros, UpdateStock and DeleteSale, end with a Requery action. These update (or re-query) the list in the Project combo box - where you select the product for the order. This ensures it always shows the current stock level. If we didn't do this, the list would only be updated when the form was closed and re-opened.

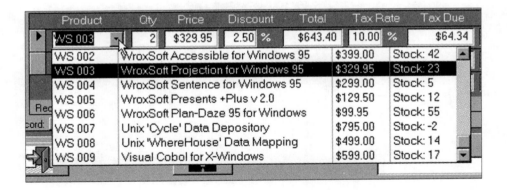

Removing Blank Sales Records

In Chapter 10, when we were creating the Projects and Sales form, we discovered a problem inherent with using a form that has a subform embedded in it. We had to force a new record to be inserted in the Order table when the user selected the Software Sale option to prevent them creating a new OrderLine record which had no matching Order record. We did this by entering the time and date in the new order's Detail field. However, now if the user closes the window without entering any lines for the order, the blank record is left in the Order table.

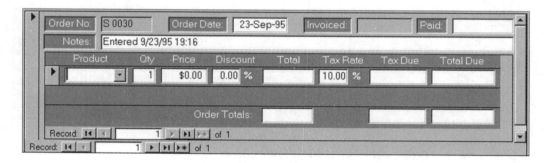

While these blank records don't affect the running of the application, we should, in the interests of efficiency and good practice, remove them. We do this when the Projects and Sales form is closed, by running an action query that deletes any Order records that have no matching OrderLine records.

The On Close event occurs when a form is closed. In the Projects and Sales form we've set the On Close property to ProjSales.OnClose. This macro just uses the RunSQL action to remove any blank records from the Order table. It turns the update warnings off first, and back on afterwards, so that the user is unaware that this is happening.

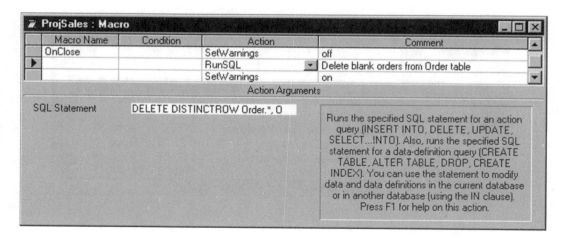

When viewed in Query Builder, the query itself looks complicated - it contains a join which selects all the records from the Order table and only those from the OrderLine table where the joined fields are equal. (To see this double-click on the join line to open the Join Properties dialog.)

If we used a normal join, any Order records which had no OrderLine records wouldn't be included. A normal join only produces a record where there are matching values in both tables and there are no OrderLine records which match the blank Order records - and these are the ones we need to delete.

When the query selects an Order record which has no matching OrderLine record, the fields which would normally come from the OrderLine record are set to Null. So, all we need to do is specify a criteria of Is Null for the OrderLineKey column. The query then removes all the Order records where this is **True** - these are the blank orders.

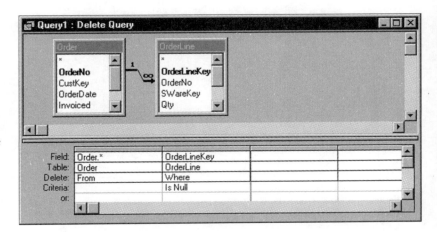

Controlling Deletion of Records

If the user makes an error when entering a record for a project, they may decide to delete the whole record and re-enter it. The Projects and Sales form allows them to delete the record by clicking on the record selector bar at the left of the window and pressing *Delete*.

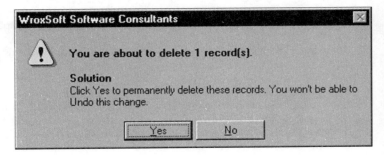

However, what happens if they accidentally select the main form record rather than the Project Subform record? Access will, after prompting, delete the customer record. When we set the relationships for our tables, we specified Enforce Referential Integrity and Cascade Deleted Records in the Relations window. Here, you can see the various tables in our application, and the way they are related to each other:

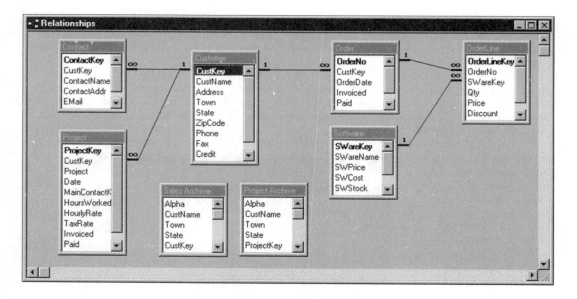

To enforce referential integrity when deleting a Customer record, Access is forced to do a cascaded delete. This is a delete where Access not only deletes the customer record, but also any linked records for this customer - all their contacts, projects, and software orders. It has to do this to protect the integrity of the database - removing a customer record means that the CustKey value in the linked records, which is the only way we can identify which customer they belong to, will have no meaning. So we need to take steps to protect our data from this happening.

Deleting Records in the Projects and Sales Form

Among a form's Event properties is the Allow Updating property. The default value for this is Default Tables, but on the Projects and Sales form we've set Allow Updating to No Tables. Remember that you can't edit the Customer record from this form, so we can use the No Tables setting to prevent *any* changes to the Customer table here.

The setting of the Allow Updating property only affects the main form. Each subform has its own Allow Updating property, and for the Projects, OrderMain, and OrderLine subforms, these are set to Default Tables. So the user can still edit and delete records in these. And because of the Enforce Referential Integrity setting we used in all the relationships we set between tables, deleting an Order record will - as you would expect - automatically delete all the linked OrderLine records.

Deleting Records in the Customer Details Form

We must allow our users to delete Customer records somewhere, otherwise the database will fill with unused accounts and details of companies who have gone out of business. There may be perfectly acceptable reasons for deleting a customer's details, and we would obviously expect to delete all the records in other tables that apply to that customer. The Customer Details form is the obvious place to allow this to happen.

In our application, we have decided that we still need to retain information about any project work or software sales we made to customers after they have been deleted - even if only for tax reasons. Obviously we can't keep these in the original tables because this would require a matching customer record, as we've seen. So instead we'll arrange for all the information we need to keep to be placed in the Archive table; then we no longer need to keep the matching Customer record.

So now we have the rule for deleting a customer record - it can only be done in the Customer Details form, and any existing Project or Order records must be archived before the Customer record is removed. We've already covered the first part by preventing updates to the Customer table from the only other form that contains the customer record.

To achieve the second part, we need to control deletions in the Customer Details form. We use the On Delete event which occurs when the user selects a record and presses *Delete*.

Checking for Project and Order Records

The On Delete property of the Customer Details form is set to CustDetail.OnDelete. Have a look at this macro:

	Macro Name	Condition	Action	Comment
▶	OnDelete	Not IsNull(DLookUp("[CustKey]", "Order","[CustKey] = Forms![Customer Details]![CustKey]"))	MsgBox	Check if customer has any sales records
		...	CancelEvent	If Yes, cannot delete sales records
		...	StopMacro	then stop
		Not IsNull(DLookUp("[CustKey]","Project","[CustKey] = Forms![Customer Details]![CustKey]"))	MsgBox	Check if customer has any project records
		...	CancelEvent	If Yes, cannot delete projects records

CustDetail : Macro

Action Arguments

Message	Unarchived Sales records exist for th
Beep	Yes
Type	Critical
Title	Cannot Delete

Enter a conditional expression in this column.

The macro checks for any existing Project or Order records for the customer currently shown in the Customer Details form, using the value of CustKey from the hidden CustKey control on the form. This control is bound to the CustKey field in the Customer table, so it contains the current customer key value.

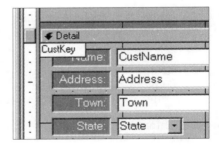

So all we need to do is look for any Project or Order records with this value in the CustKey field. To do this we use the **DLookup** function. We've met this function before - it requires three arguments: the **Field** we want to look in, the name of the **Table**, and the **Where Condition** that selects the record(s) we want.

```
DLookup ( Field, Table, Where Condition )
```

The function returns the value from the specified **Field** of any record in the specified **Table** which matches the **Where Condition** we've used. If no record matches the condition, the function returns Null. Therefore, we can get the function to return the value of the CustKey field in the Order table for any record that has the same CustKey value as the hidden CustKey control on the form. If there are no Order records with this value, we know that there are no orders for that customer. So our expression is:

Not IsNull(DLookUp("[CustKey]","Order","[CustKey] = Forms![Customer Details]![CustKey]"))

This will be **True** if there are any Order records and **False** if not, because we test the result of the **DLookup** function using Not IsNull(). We can now use this expression as the Condition in our macro. If it is **True**, we display the message "Unarchived Sales records exist for this customer" and cancel the deletion of the Customer record.

Condition: Not IsNull(DLookUp("[CustKey]","Order","[CustKey]= Forms![Customer Details]![CustKey]"))
Action: MsgBox
    Message: Unarchived Sales records exist for this customer.
    Beep: Yes
    Type: Critical
    Title: Cannot Delete

To cancel the deletion of the record we use the CancelEvent action, which is equivalent to pressing the Cancel button when Access prompts to confirm the deletion of a record. Then we stop the macro.

Condition: ...
Action: CancelEvent

Condition: ...
Action: StopMacro

If there are no Order records for this customer, we check for any Project records using the same technique.

Condition: Not IsNull(DLookUp("[CustKey]","Project","[CustKey]= Forms![Customer Details]![CustKey]"))
Action: MsgBox
    Message: Unarchived Sales records exist for this customer.
    Beep: Yes
    Type: Critical
    Title: Cannot Delete

Condition: ...
Action: CancelEvent

The Customer record will only be deleted if there are no matching Order or Project records. If any records are found, one of the CancelEvent actions will cancel the deletion of the customer's details from the database.

Deleting Records in the Software Catalogue Form

All the orders stored in our database use a **key** to refer to the item of software sold, they don't store the name of the package. Remember that each software sale is held in two tables - the Order table which has a record for each order, and the OrderLine table which holds the details of each line of that order.

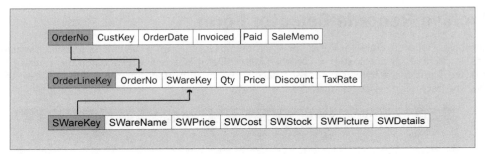

If we allow the user to delete a Software record, we will lose the connection between the SWareKey in any OrderLine records for that product and the SWareKey in the Software table. The value in the SWareKey field of the OrderLine records becomes meaningless if there's no record in the Software table with that value for SWareKey. So, before we can allow a user to delete a Software record, we need to make sure there are no matching OrderLine records. If there are, the user must archive them first to remove them from the 'active' tables. Archiving them, as we'll see in the next section, preserves the full details about the software for each order.

The situation, then, is very similar to deleting Customer records. We use a similar condition to check for matching records, and cancel the event if any are found. Our macro starts running when the user presses *Delete* - and, unless a CancelEvent instruction is executed in the macro, Access automatically deletes the record when the macro finishes. The macro itself doesn't delete the record, it just cancels the event, if the conditions are met.

In this case, if there are no records, the Condition in the OnDelete macro is **True**. The StopMacro action is then executed and, because we haven't issued a CancelEvent instruction, the deletion takes place.

> **Condition:** IsNull(DLookUp("[SWareKey]","OrderLine","[SWareKey]= Forms![Software
>   Catalogue]![SWareKey] "))
> **Action:**   StopMacro

If the macro is still running, we know that there are unarchived sales for this product, so we can warn the user with an appropriate error message and cancel the deletion of the Software record. We don't need to repeat the Condition this time.

> **Action:**   MsgBox
>   **Message:**   Unarchived orders exist for this product.
>   **Beep:**   Yes
>   **Type:**   Critical
>   **Title:**   Cannot Delete
>
> **Action:**   CancelEvent

Archiving Records

In Part 1 we looked at an Archive Records Selector form where the user can select which old records they want to move from the current Project and Order tables into the Archive tables. They do this by specifying the date of the latest record that they want to archive. In our **WroxSoft** application the form is similar, but now we've added pictures and functionality to the buttons. We also discussed how action queries can be used to move records from one table to another. We'll now look at how this has been implemented in practice in our sample application.

The Archive Records Selector Form

The Archive Records Selector form includes an option group (fraArchive) to select which type of records to archive, and a text box control (ArchiveDate) where we can enter the date of the last records we want to archive. We've also placed two push-buttons on the form to allow the user to Archive the records or Cancel and close the form.

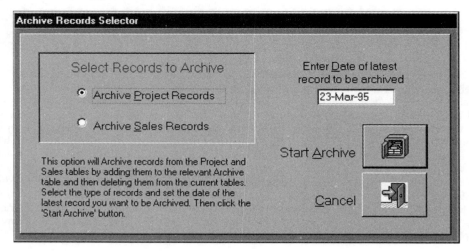

The Archive Tables

Before we can archive records, we have to have a table to append them to. In Part 1, we used a make table query to create a table, then showed how an append query could add records to it. However, as we discovered earlier in this chapter, we need to include some extra information in our Archive tables because if we only identify a project or sale using the CustKey customer key, then delete the original Customer record, we lose the link between the two tables. We also noted that, because we specified Enforce Referential Integrity and Cascade Record Deletes, when we delete a Customer record, any linked records are also deleted.

So our Archive table must not only be different in structure, it must also be unrelated to the Customer table so that records aren't deleted when a customer is removed. Because the structure of the Project and Order tables is different (remember the Order table has a linked OrderLine table as well), we will use two separate Archive tables, Project Archive and Sales Archive.

Go to the Database window and select Relationships from the Tools menu. You'll see our two Archive tables, with no link to the existing tables. You can also see that they contain several fields that aren't in the original Project and Order tables.

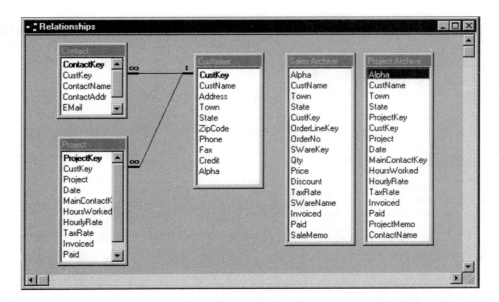

So that you can see the tables better, we have removed some of the other tables from the **Relationships** window in the screenshot.

In the Project Archive table we've included the Alpha, CustName, Town and State fields from the Customer record. Therefore, if the original customer is removed from the database we still have the details we need in this table. We've also included the name of the contact we dealt with - if the customer details are deleted we also lose the names of our contacts, so just keeping the MainContactKey is no use. And, of course, we include all the fields from the Project table. Here's the final design of the Project Archive table.

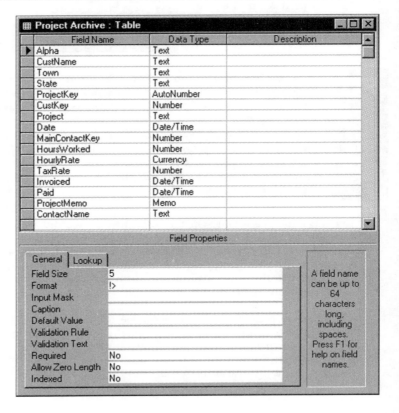

The Sales Archive table is actually based on the OrderLine table rather than the Order table. We've elected to store all the lines of each order, rather than just the summary, and so we add a record for each line of each order we archive. We take the same Alpha, CustName, Town and State fields from the Customer record, and all the fields from the OrderLine record. We also need the OrderDate, Invoiced and Paid fields from the Order table, and we might as well include the SaleMemo field from there as well. And what about the software name? If we only store the SWareKey value (the key to the Software table) and that item later becomes obsolete and is deleted, we lose the ability to see what product we sold. So we also need to include the SWareName field from the Software table.

Field Name	Data Type	Description
Alpha	Text	
CustName	Text	
Town	Text	
State	Text	
CustKey	Number	
OrderLineKey	AutoNumber	
OrderNo	Number	
SWareKey	Number	
Qty	Number	
Price	Currency	
Discount	Number	
TaxRate	Number	
SWareName	Text	
Invoiced	Date/Time	
Paid	Date/Time	
SaleMemo	Memo	

Sales Archive : Table

Field Properties

General | Lookup

Field Size	5
Format	!>
Input Mask	
Caption	
Default Value	
Validation Rule	
Validation Text	
Required	No
Allow Zero Length	No
Indexed	No

A field name can be up to 64 characters long, including spaces. Press F1 for help on field names.

FYI These tables break almost every rule of normalization we looked at in Chapter 8 - they contain enough duplicated and dependent values to make a seasoned database programmer despair. But they're not actually part of our database, and they're not related to any other tables. In fact, we would normally use the archive process to create them in another database, or export them directly in a different format - either to a central file store or perhaps to back-up tapes. So we don't need to be concerned about the niceties of the structure; we just need to make sure that we have all the data we need to reconstruct the contents should we have to refer to them in the future. We'll be looking at how we export data in Chapter 15.

You can build these tables in the same way as we did in Part 1, by creating a make table query and running it, then converting it to an append query to add records. Alternatively, you can just create a new table from the Database window, then open all the other tables that provide values for the new table and copy the fields across. This is probably the easiest way to do it, and it ensures that all the properties from each field, such as the Format and Decimal Places, are also copied to the new table.

Remember, to copy a field from one table to another you just click on the field selector (the gray box at the left of the window) to highlight the row. Then press *Ctrl-C* to copy it to the clipboard, move to the new table, highlight the row where you want to place the field, and press *Ctrl-V* to paste it in. You can select more than one field if they're next to each other by clicking on the field selector for the first one and dragging over the others.

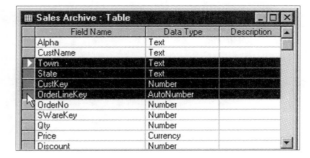

Using Append and Delete Queries to Archive Records

The action queries that we use in **WroxSoft** must transform the data to fit the new table format (as described above). There are two append queries - one for the Project Archive table and one for the Sales Archive table. The queries are Archive Projects and Archive Sales.

The Archive Projects Query

The Archive Projects query is the simpler of the two. It is an append query that uses fields from the Project, Customer and Contact tables.

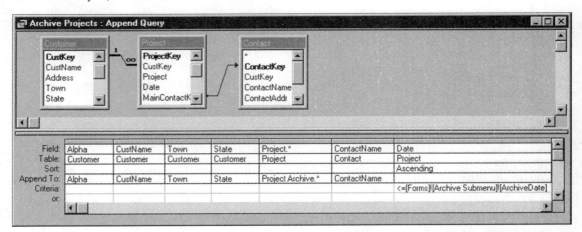

The last column in the query sorts the records by date, but doesn't place the value from this column in the table - the Append To: row is blank. (The Date field is already included because we have used Project.* to include all the fields from the Project table). Double-click on the background of the Query window, near the source tables, to open the Query Properties dialog. You'll see that the Destination Table is set to Project Archive, and the Destination DB property is set to (current) - the destination table is in the current database.

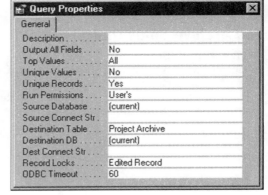

The other point to note is that we have specified a left join for the link between the MainContactKey field in the Project table and the ContactKey field in the Contacts table. Click on the link in the query and double-click to open the Join Properties dialog (or right-click on the join and select Join Properties). We have selected 'Include all records from Project and only those records from Contact where the joined fields are equal'.

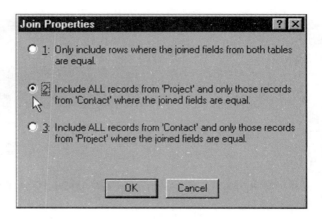

Because some projects may not have a main contact specified, the value in this field will be zero or null. If we used a normal inner join, 'Only include rows where the joined fields from both table are equal', we would find that these Project records wouldn't be included in the query result and, therefore, they wouldn't be appended to the Project Archive table.

The other point is that we have to tell the query which records to append to the new table. The Archive Submenu form contains a text box called ArchiveDate where we enter the date of the latest record to be archived. We use the value of this text box in the expression that forms the criteria for the query. We place

<=[Forms]![Archive Submenu]![ArchiveDate]

in the Criteria: row of the Date field, and Access then only includes records where the date is less than or equal to the value in the ArchiveDate control on the form. If the Archive Submenu form isn't open when the query runs, Access assumes the entry is a parameter and prompts for the value.

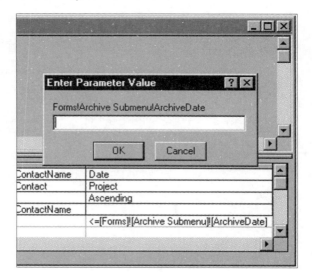

The Archive Sales Query

The Archive Sales query is a little more complicated. For this we need four source tables - the records we are archiving come from the OrderLine table, but we also need information from the Order, Customer and Software tables. However, all the joins are those that we specified in the Relationships window when we created the tables. We just need to make sure we select the correct fields to be appended to the Sales Archive table.

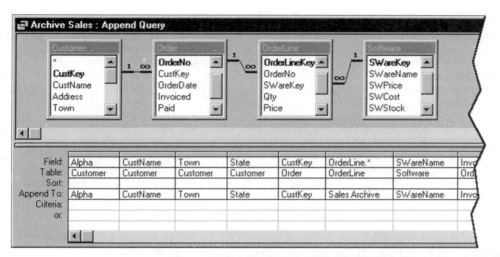

Once we've appended the records to the Archive table, we can delete them from the original Project or Order tables. And, of course, deleting the Order records will automatically delete the matching OrderLine records, because we specified Cascade Record Deletes when we originally created the relation between the tables. To delete the records we use a delete query.

We've implemented the deletes as SQL statements which are run directly from the macro that carries out the archiving - you'll see this in just a moment. The statements are:

```
DELETE DISTINCTROW * FROM [Project] WHERE ([Date] <= [Forms]![Archive
Submenu]![ArchiveDate]);
```

```
DELETE DISTINCTROW * FROM [Order] WHERE ([OrderDate] <= [Forms]![Archive
Submenu]![ArchiveDate]);
```

These will delete all records from the table where the date is less than or equal to the value in the ArchiveDate text box of the Archive Records form.

Testing for Success of a Query

So having created the tables and queries for archiving the records, all we need to do is add the macros that automate the Archive button. However, consider what happens when an action query runs. After it has identified the changes to be made to the tables, either appending or deleting records, it prompts you to confirm the action. If you click Cancel, no updates are made to the tables. If the user does this as our append query runs, the records won't be archived. However, the delete query will still delete the records from the original table, even though they haven't been archived. We, therefore, have to depend on the user also canceling the delete query as well to prevent this.

487

To avoid this, we can turn off the warning messages that are displayed when the query runs. The **SetWarnings** macro action causes Access to automatically respond with **OK** when the confirmation message appears. As long as the query doesn't produce an error (which would happen, for example, if an illegal date was entered in the **ArchiveDate** text box), the whole process runs without the user being able to cancel it. But this isn't the best way - the user receives no guidance as to how many records will be archived. If they've accidentally entered the wrong date, they may archive and delete more records than they planned.

Instead, we'll use a different method, and one which shows how you can control action queries using a macro. Once the append query has run successfully, but before the delete query runs, the Archive table contains records which still exist in the original tables. In the original tables, the records are identified by a **ProjectKey** or **OrderNo** and, because this is an **AutoNumber** field, the values increase as records are entered. So we can be fairly sure that the record with the highest **ProjectKey** or **OrderNo** in the **Archive** table will be the most recent, and have been added by the append query that has just run.

We then check that this record still exists in the original table. If not, there was a problem with the append query - either an error or the user canceled it. In this case we can display a warning and abort the delete query.

One other check that we can make is to see if there are any records in the original table that have not been paid - we don't want to archive these. So before we run the archive queries, we check there are no records in the specified range with a **Null** in the **Paid** field.

The macros that carry out the record archiving are on the **MainMenu** macro sheet - have a look at them:

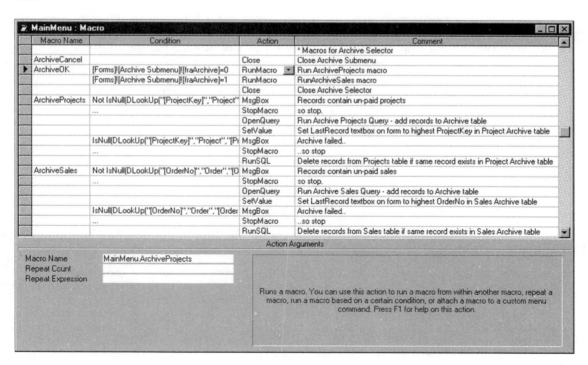

The ArchiveCancel macro uses the Close action to close the Archive Selector when the user presses the Cancel button - the On Click property of the Cancel button on the Archive Submenu form is set to MainMenu.ArchiveCancel.

> **Action:**   Close
> > **Object Type:**   Form
> > **Object Name:**   Archive Submenu

The ArchiveOK macro runs when the Archive button is pressed. It examines the value of fraArchive on the Archive Submenu form to see if the user has selected Project or Sales records. If the value is 0, we archive Project records, and if it's 1 we archive Sales records. In both cases the macro uses a RunMacro action to execute another macro - either ArchiveProjects or ArchiveSales.

> **Condition:** [Forms]![Archive Submenu]![fraArchive]=0
> **Action:**   RunMacro
> > **Macro Name:**   MainMenu.ArchiveProjects

> **Condition:** [Forms]![Archive Submenu]![fraArchive]=1
> **Action:**   RunMacro
> > **Macro Name:**   MainMenu.ArchiveSales

The ArchiveProjects and ArchiveSales macros are very similar - we'll look at ArchiveSales. The first step is to check that all the projects are paid. We use the DLookup function in the Condition to return the ProjectKey value of any record in the Project table where the Paid field is Null and the Date field is less than or equal to the value in the ArchiveDate control on the Archive Submenu form. If this returns Null, we know that no such records exist, in other words they are all paid. If it returns a value, the Condition is true and we can display a warning using the MsgBox action and stop the macro running, which cancels the archive process.

> **Condition:** Not IsNull(DLookUp("[ProjectKey]","Project",[Date] <= [Forms]![Archive
> > Submenu]![ArchiveDate] AND [Paid] Is Null"))
>
> **Action:**   MsgBox
> > **Message:**   Project records contain some that are still un-paid.
> > **Beep:**   Yes
> > **Type:**   Critical
> > **Title:**   Cannot Archive

followed by

> **Condition:** ...
> **Action:**   StopMacro

If the macro is still running at this point, we know we can now start the archive process. The first step is to execute the append query using the OpenQuery action.

> **Action:**   OpenQuery
> > **Query Name:**   ArchiveProjects
> > **View:**   Datasheet
> > **Data Mode:**   Edit

Next, we need to store the highest ProjectKey value so we can check whether it's still in the original Project table. We can't use variables in macros, so we'll store it on the Archive Submenu form using a hidden text box. If you open the form in design view you'll see this text box, named LastRecord, with its Visible property set to No. We use a SetValue macro to place the value we want to store in it.

> **Action:** SetValue
> > **Item:** [Forms]![Archive Submenu]![LastRecord]
> > **Expression:** DMax("[ProjectKey]","Project Archive","")

This uses the **DMax** domain aggregate function to find the highest value in the ProjectKey field of the Project Archive table. The final argument is an empty string because we don't need to specify a **WHERE** condition - we can look at all the records in the table. So now we just check if the same record is still in the Project table as we expect it to be, again using the **DLookup** function. If it's not, the function returns Null, and as something has gone wrong, we stop the macro.

> **Condition:** IsNull(DLookUp("[ProjectKey]", "Project", "[ProjectKey] = [Forms]![Archive Submenu]![LastRecord]"))
> **Action:** MsgBox
> > **Message:** Could not move records to Project Archive
> > **Beep:** Yes
> > **Type:** Critical
> > **Title:** Archive Failed

followed again by

> **Condition:** ...
> **Action:** StopMacro

Finally, if our macro is still running, we can delete the original records using the SQL statement we saw earlier.

> **Action:** RunSQL
> > **SQL Statement:** DELETE DISTINCTROW * FROM Project WHERE ([Date] <= [Forms]![Archive Submenu]![ArchiveDate]);

So the process is:

- Copy the records we want to archive into the Archive table.
- Get the highest ProjectKey (or OrderNo) in the Archive table. This will be the last one we added because the ProjectKey and OrderNo values increase as new records are added to the Project and Order tables.
- Look for this value in the original Project (or Order) table. If it is there, the append must have been successful - if it failed, the highest value in the Archive table will be less than any that are still in the original table.
- If the append query was successful, delete the same records from the original table. Once we've deleted them from the original table, the next time we run the archive process the whole cycle is repeated, and the highest value in the Archive table will be less than any in the original table when we start. We've protected our table against records being deleted without being appended to the Project Archive table first.

The ArchiveSales macro, which runs if the user has selected Sales records, is exactly the same, but of course uses the Sales and Sales Archive tables instead.

Mail Merging with Microsoft Word

There is one button on the Customer Details form which we haven't considered yet. It's used to start the mail merge facility. Mail merge is a common application in today's business climate. It allows you to use the information stored in your database to produce standard letters in a word processor - in this case Microsoft Word.

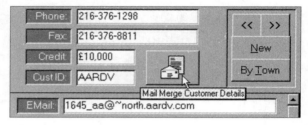

 If you haven't got Word, you'll find that clicking the Mail Merge button will produce an error message.

When you click the Mail Merge button, our **WroxSoft** application opens the Customer table and starts Mail Merge Wizard which guides you through the process of mail merging the customer details, either into an existing Word document or into a newly created one. We won't be covering mail merge in detail as it is a huge subject, but we'll show you how you can use it within our application and give you some indications of what is possible.

Try It Out - Mail Merging with the Customer Details

1 Open the Customer Details form in the **WroxSoft** application, and click the Mail Merge button on the form. Access opens Mail Merge Wizard.

2 Here we can either select an existing document (such as a standard letter) or create a new one. Select Create a new document....

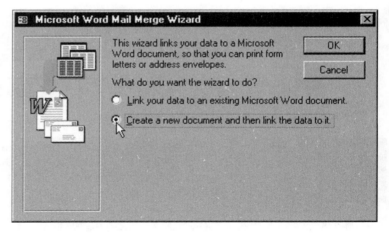

3 Click OK, and Microsoft Word opens. If you look at the Windows 95 taskbar, you'll see that Word has started another copy of our **WroxSoft** application. It will use this copy to manipulate the data without affecting the original one.

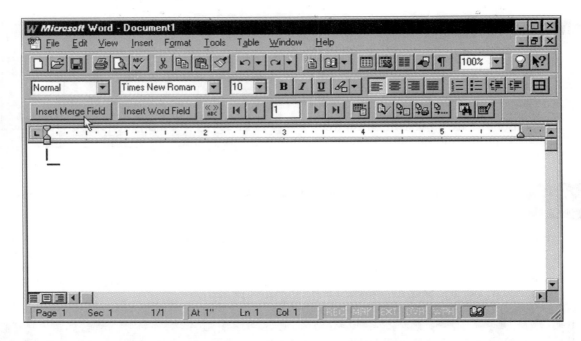

4 We'll create a standard letter to tell our customers what their credit limit is. First, we need the customer's name address at the top of the letter. To do this we insert **merge fields** from the Customer table. Click the Insert Merge Field button just above the document in Word.

5 Select CustName from the list of fields that Word has discovered in the Customer table. It places this field in the document surrounded with the 'double-arrow' field markers.

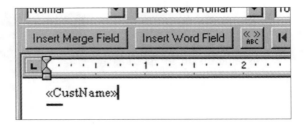

 FYI Note that if you get {MERGEFIELD CustName} instead of <<CustName>>, you are only viewing the link to Access and not the data itself. To change this, in Word select **Options** from the **Tools** menu. Click on the **View** tab and from the **Show:** list, click on the **Field Codes** option so that it isn't ticked.

6 Press *Return* to start a new line, and insert the Address field, then continue adding fields and typing the letter until it looks like our example below. As you can see, you can include merge fields anywhere in the document.

492

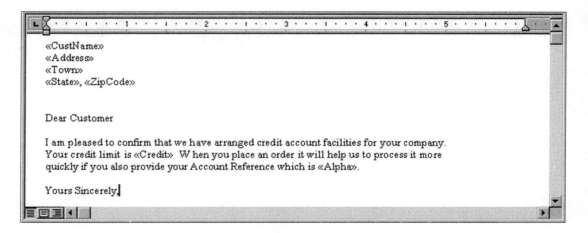

7 Now we'll see the results of merging the data from the Customer table. Click the View Merged Data button. Word shows the document with the values from the first Customer record filled in.

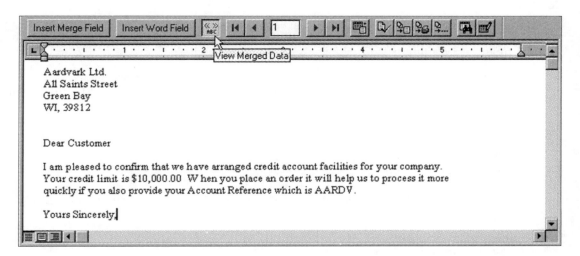

8 Click the Next Record button and Word fills in the values from the next Customer record. You can step through the records like this, or use the record navigation buttons to go to the last, previous, next or first record at any time.

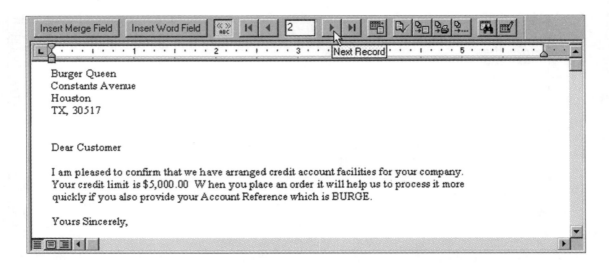

How It Works

So now you can see how organizations create those personalized letters and junk mail - when mail merge is done well it can seem like you are the only person in the town to have had a letter from them because it looks like it's been typed by hand!

The **WroxSoft** application starts mail merge by using a macro called MailMerge which runs when a button on the Customer Details form is clicked. This has two actions. The first simply opens the Customer table in datasheet view.

Action: OpenTable
    Table Name: Customer
    View: Datasheet
    Data Mode: Edit

The second is a DoMenuItem action which selects the Merge It option from the OfficeLinks section of the Tools menu.

Action: DoMenuItem
    Menu Bar: Form
    Menu Name: Tools
    Command: OfficeLinks
    Subcommand: Merge It

By default, when Mail Merge Wizard starts, it uses the table or query that is currently active, so this macro forces it to use the Customer table by opening it first. You could, of course, open a different table or a query using the same method to make it the subject of the mail merge.

Mail Merge Possibilities

We've only seen a simple example of mail merge here. You could create a query which combines data from several tables and use this as the basis for the mail merge. In fact, it's a remarkably powerful tool. If you save the letter you've just created in the previous example, you can use it over and over again. For example, you could send a copy to a new customer once you have set up their account without redoing the letter - just click the Mail Merge button in the Access Customer Details screen and select Link your data to an existing Microsoft Word document in Mail Merge Wizard.

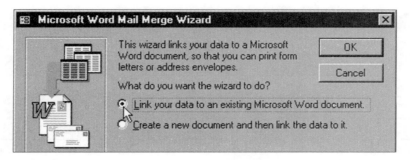

Access displays a file selector dialog where you can select which saved document you want to use. Once you open it, you just need to select which records you want to print. You do this using the other buttons on Word's Mail Merge toolbar.

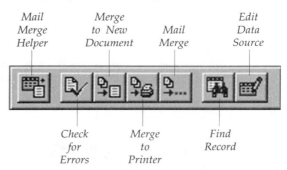

The most useful of these is Mail Merge Helper. This displays a graphical guide to setting up the mail merge, and shows the source of the records - you can see it's set to WroxSoft.mdb!Table Customer. You can even edit the contents of the table by clicking the Edit button.

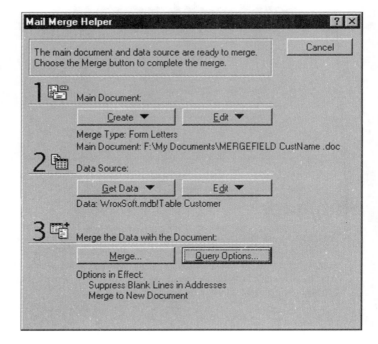

495

Under this are two buttons. Query Options opens a window where you can select which records you want to include in the merge process. Here we've specified just the record for Burger Queen. You can also specify the order that the records are sorted in.

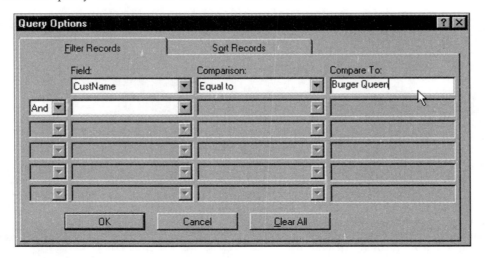

Click the Merge button and then you can start the mail merge process by selecting Printer in the Merge To: box, and specifying All or a range of Records to Be Merged.

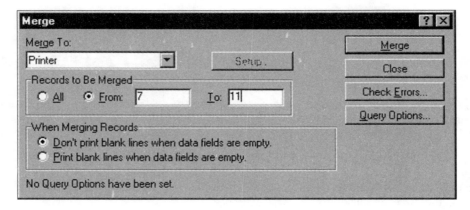

Summary

We've now reached the end of Part 2, where we've seen how our **WroxSoft** sample application is built up from a range of different objects linked together. When you first see an application like this, it appears to be a mass of complicated queries and macros - but we hope to have shown you how each part performs its own, generally simple, task. As a whole, though, the parts provide a great deal of power to the user.

All database applications work this way. When you build your own, you just have to remember to design it well first. You can then create each component separately to meet the design. Once you have them all working you can stitch the whole application together using macros, switchboards and submenus.

Alternatively, once you have the basic design complete on paper, you can create the main menu and submenus first, so that you actually have the outline of the application working early on. Then just build each of the different queries, forms and reports and add them to the application. Make sure that each component is tested as it is created. In this way, you keep adding working parts to a working database and you can keep checking with your users to ensure the application is meeting their needs and expectations.

The important thing is to make sure that each component is as independent of the others as possible, and make each one highly focused on just one task. For example, we noted at the design stage that there was a need to be able to move between the main editing forms and generate invoices, without having to keep going back to the main menu. Once we had built the forms and reports that were involved in this process, we were able to add push buttons that allowed our users to follow this route, without having to modify their structure.

In Part 3, we move on to some of the more advanced topics that you'll come up against as you improve your knowledge and expertise with Access. We've touched on some of them already, while others will be completely new. However, once you're familiar with the concepts we've used so far, you'll find that these allow you to add even more functionality to your applications.

497

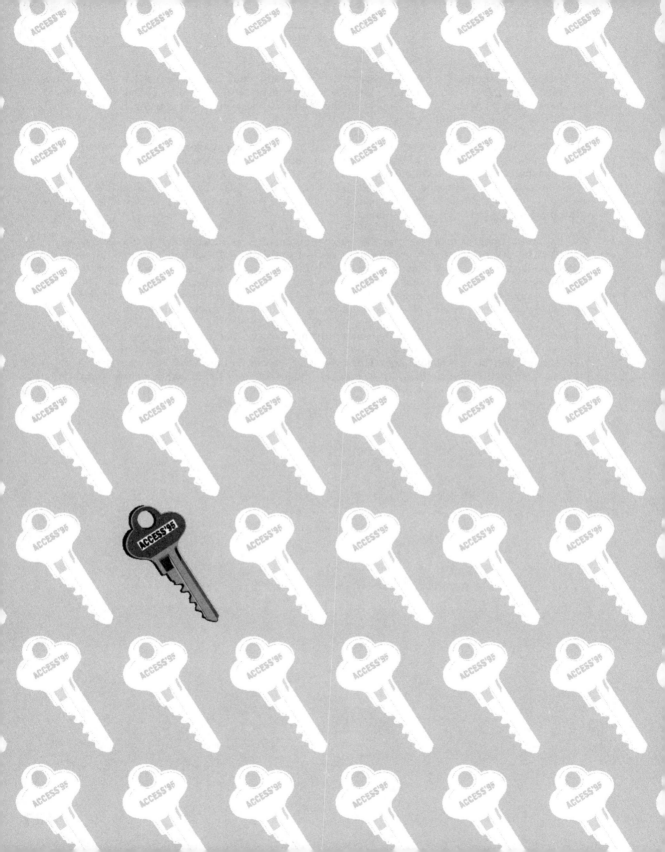

part

Creating Workgroup Applications

This part of the book marks another change in emphasis and style. In the first two parts of the book we looked at the techniques involved in designing and building a database, and at how these were applied in our sample **WroxSoft** *application.*

Now in Part 3 we move on again - this time to look at how a database system can be used in a wider context. The term **workgroup** *is much misused, and tends to hold a different meaning for different people. Generally speaking, a workgroup consists of several computers, usually linked together by a network of some type. Each user is working separately, but as part of the same team and towards a common goal, for instance the users could be the design team for a new office block or the accounts department of a large corporation.*

The idea is to allow work, in the form of data and documents, to be shared amongst the group - everyone has access to the information they need to carry out their part of the overall task. In this part of the book we'll consider the background to this and show you how you can configure Access to allow the data and objects within it to be shared amongst the members of a workgroup.

The first two chapters are about looking at how the data is stored and processed. We'll see how data is manipulated within Access, following on from the use of queries that you've seen in previous chapters. Then we'll move on to show you how Access can retrieve and work with data from other sources, and how the Access interface can be separated from the data in tables. Then, finally, we'll look at the tasks involved in administering a multi-user system. We'll look at aspects such as security, maintenance, and the integrity of the data when it is being used by several people.

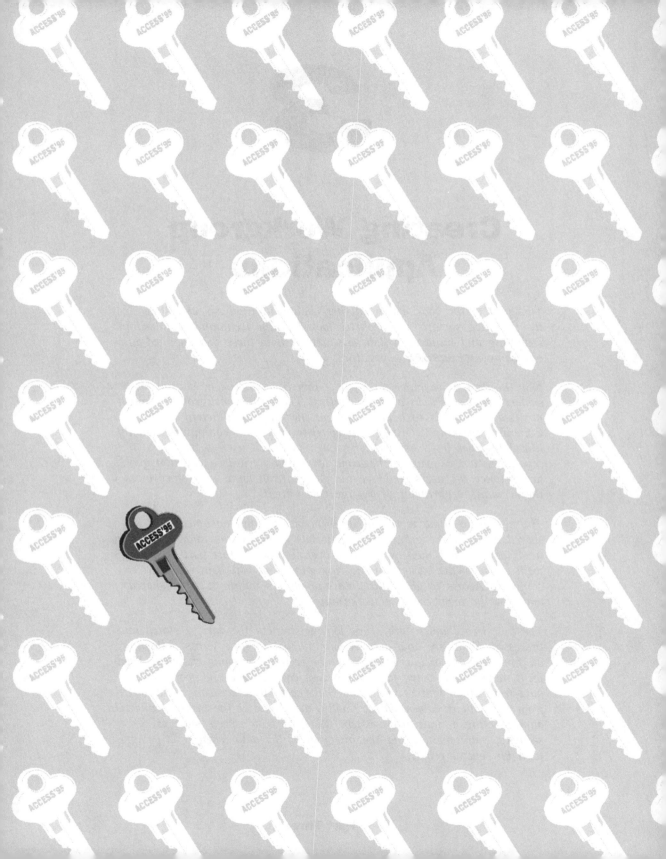

SQL And Advanced Queries

Whenever we've come across SQL before within our application, we've shied away from talking about it with the exception of union queries. Everything we've needed to do could be achieved within the confines of the Query Builder grid. However, now that we've created the application, we can delve deeper into how Access itself operates and look at SQL - the programming language that Access uses to pass the user's queries to and from the database.

In this chapter, we're going to learn SQL so that, when you see SQL statements, you'll be able to understand what they're doing and be able to modify them directly, without the aid of the grid. This will give you far greater power over queries and doesn't require that much extra effort. You'll find that SQL statements mirror all the queries we've learned so far anyway. We'll look at each statement in turn and cover:

- The **SELECT** statement.
- The **DELETE** statement.
- The **SELECT INTO** statement.
- The **INSERT** and **UPDATE** statements.
- Joins in SQL statements.
- Advanced queries.

What Is SQL?

Up until the early 1990s, most PC database systems included methods of finding, sorting and retrieving data which were proprietary to that system. In the main-frame world, though, a standardized language had been emerging for many years, its development monitored by the American National Standards Institute. This is a data querying language that is universal across different computer systems - SQL (Structured Query Language).

Vendors of database systems compete by including extensions proprietary to only one system, with the result that most systems offer a language that is broadly ANSI compatible, with some 'un-standard' features. Access is slightly different, though. It includes a broad implementation of SQL that is very similar to ANSI SQL, but not actually compliant. Instead, much to the chagrin of the SQL standards committee, it has evolved on a parallel path using different data types and offering extra features.

The Need for SQL

When we looked at the theory behind designing the structure of the tables in our databases, we saw that the most recurrent theme was splitting the tables down into smaller ones and using relations to link them together. We could always retrieve information about a particular entity using these links and, as the tables became smaller, the efficiency of the database improved and redundant (duplicated) information was removed.

However, the result is that the information we need to work with is broken up across several tables. We can't look at one record in a table to see all the information about, say, a project or software sale. Instead, we need to track from one table to another, looking for records that are linked - sometimes through intermediate tables.

By using queries, forms and reports, we have automated this process within our application. You just run the Customer Sales History report, or open the Projects and Sales form to find the answer. We have created recordsets without needing to know any SQL at all. But if we can't create the recordset that we need using the Query Builder grid alone, then it becomes clear that we need extra power.

Our Model of a Query

Back in Chapter 5, we broke down a query into its different components, resulting in this diagram:

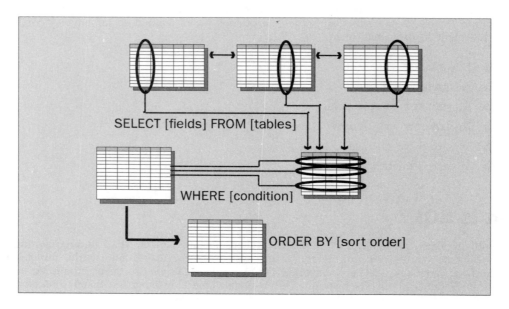

SELECT [fields] FROM [tables]

WHERE [condition]

ORDER BY [sort order]

Even when the data we need is split across different tables, we can recreate the original table, or create a whole new one, using a query. We just select which fields we want from the source tables, apply criteria to select which records are to be included and sort them as required. The result is a recordset containing the information we need and we can even turn this into a table.

This diagram shows how queries work, but it is also a model of how an SQL statement works. When we create a query, as we saw in Chapter 5, Access creates the equivalent of that query in SQL. This diagram is just a typical **SELECT** statement in SQL broken down into its components. The statement selects records from a table that meet a certain criteria and sorts them if required. The result is a recordset from the table.

 FYI While a table is a set of records stored on disk within a database system, the term recordset is used to refer to information which is stored dynamically in the memory of the computer. If we write the contents of a recordset (the results of a query) to disk using a make table query, it becomes a table.

So both SQL and queries are a way of creating new recordsets from existing ones. We can also use **nested queries** - remember that the source of a query can be a recordset produced by another query instead of a table, or even a mixture of tables and recordsets. By manipulating the original sources of data with SQL statements, we can join tables together in almost any way we like to arrive at the recordset we need.

In fact, SQL isn't just a type of query - an SQL statement actually *is* a query. Or to put it the other way round, queries are actually SQL statements. Once we appreciate this, we no longer need to worry about whether we use SQL or Query Builder, because they are both just a means to the same end - creating the recordsets that we need to access the information buried in our data.

Why Do We Use SQL?

Before we dive into the theory and practice of SQL, we need to answer the question most people ask - why should I learn SQL? Here are five good reasons:

▶ Because it is at the heart of almost all modern data-processing systems.

▶ Because it offers you more power than is available from the QBE grid.

▶ Because you've already used SQL repeatedly and managed quite well without 'learning' it, so it's not difficult to pick up.

▶ Because Access provides the Query Builder tool which can, in most cases, create an SQL statement automatically, so mastering the syntax is no problem.

▶ Because it makes our database tidier and more efficient.

There is only so much you can do by pointing and clicking. Some queries, such as union queries, pass-through queries and data definition queries, can be built only with some knowledge of SQL. There is also the special case of SQL sub-queries - where you use one or more SQL statements within another SQL statement to find or test for the existence of particular values. And if you need to run a query against many non-Access types of database, such as Oracle and DB2, you'll find that you cannot work with the tables in them in the same way as you would with Access tables. Instead, you have to use a special type of SQL statement to return the results or update the tables. We'll look at these types of query in this chapter as we examine SQL in more depth.

The Use of SQL in WroxSoft

SQL is the basis of all Access' built-in data manipulation operations. When you construct a query using Query Builder, Access creates an equivalent SQL statement behind the scenes and stores this rather than the settings you make in the Query Builder grid. When you re-open the query, Access re-creates the settings in the query grid using this statement. You can view the SQL statement at any time by selecting SQL View from the Query View drop-down list button, by selecting SQL from the View menu, or by right-clicking in the top section of the query grid and selecting SQL View from the short-cut menu that appears.

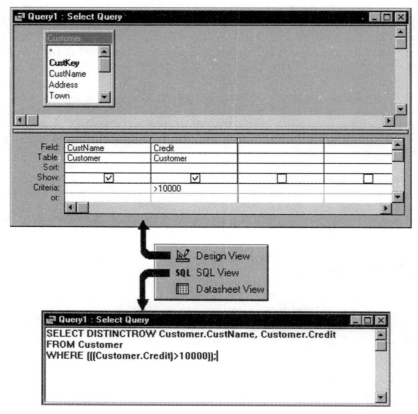

You can see why we use SQL - if we had to create every query we use and store it in the Database window Queries list, it would soon become impossible to remember what they all do and find the one we want. And if we wanted to use the same query for more than one task, say as the Record Source for three different reports, we'd have to be careful that any changes we made to it when modifying one report didn't stop it working in the others.

We've seen in the previous sections of the book how we use an SQL statement directly in the Record Source property of a form and report, or as the Row Source for a list or combo box control. These are only some of the places you can use SQL statements. Others include:

▶ In a form that displays information about the different projects, where you always want the records sorted by date. Instead, of creating a query Projects By Date and saving it so that it appears in the Database window, we can just use **SELECT * FROM Project ORDER BY Date** as the Record Source property of the form.

> In a combo box control that displays a list of customer codes. To save creating and storing the query Customers By IDCode, we can use

SELECT Alpha FROM Customer ORDER BY Alpha as the Row Source of the combo box.

> In a macro that archives data from the Project table. Instead, of using the OpenQuery action to run a query Delete Old Projects, we can use the SQL statement **DELETE * FROM Projects WHERE Date < Forms![Archive]![Date]** as the SQL Statement argument of a RunSQL macro action.

Using the Query Grid to Create SQL Statements

As a taster for how SQL works and before we consider the theory of the language, we'll take a look at the link between the Query Builder grid and the SQL statement it creates for us.

Try It Out - The SQL Statement in Query Builder

1 Open the **WroxSoft** application and close the main menu screen using the Close Window button on the toolbar, then click the Database Window button to show the Database window.

2 Select the Queries tab and create a new query by clicking the <u>N</u>ew button, selecting Design View and clicking OK. Add the Customer table to the query and close the Show Table dialog.

3 Drag the CustName field into the first column of the grid and the Credit field into the second column. Enter the Criteria >10000 for the Credit field and set the Sort Order to Ascending.

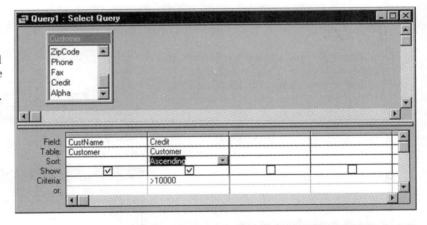

4 Click the Datasheet View button on the toolbar to view the results - Access displays the name and credit value of customers with a credit limit greater than 10000.

5 Now select SQL View from the Query View button on the toolbar - Access displays the SQL window showing the SQL statement that creates the recordset.

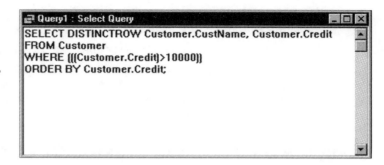

6 We'll edit this to see what difference it makes to the query. Delete DISTINCTROW, the Customer table names and period and remove the brackets. Delete the line-breaks so that we have a much simpler statement.

```
Query1 : Select Query                                          _ □ ×
SELECT CustName, Credit FROM Customer WHERE Credit>10000 ORDER BY Customer.Credit;
```

7 Now switch between design view, SQL view and datasheet view - nothing else has changed. We get the same results and the query grid is just the same as it was.

8 Go to SQL view and we'll edit the SQL statement again. This time change CustName to Town and 10000 to 5000. Then go to design view - the query grid has changed to show the new query.

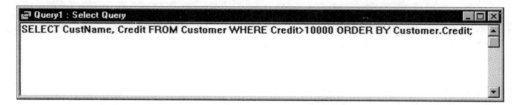

9 Click the Datasheet View button and Access displays the new recordset showing the towns and credit values for the new set of customers.

Town	Credit
St. Paul	$7,500
Phoenix	$7,500
Green Bay	$10,000
Tampa	$12,500
Chicago	$15,000
Oakland	$17,500
Stocksville	$18,000
Pittsburgh	$25,000
*	$0

Record: |◄ ◄ | 1 | ► ►| ►* | of 8

So we can translate an SQL statement into a set of entries on the query grid, as well as create the query using the grid and then convert it into an SQL statement.

You'll have noticed that our simpler version of the SQL statement worked the same as the original, more wordy version. However, as you may remember, we have to be a little careful when we omit all these 'extra' parts of the statement. We'll see why a bit later.

While we've got the query open we'll just see how much influence Access has over the SQL statement. Switch to design view to show the query grid and save the query as Query1 (click the Save button on the toolbar), then close it. Back in the Database window select the query and open it in design view, then switch to SQL view.

You'll see that Access has changed the statement back almost to its original form. However, notice that it's still left out the **DISTINCTROW** keyword.

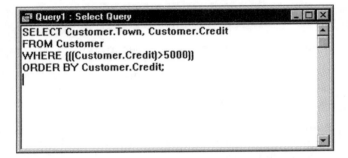

```
Query1 : Select Query
SELECT Customer.Town, Customer.Credit
FROM Customer
WHERE (((Customer.Credit)>5000))
ORDER BY Customer.Credit;
```

If you repeat the process, but save it while you are in SQL view rather than design view, the results are different again. This time Access makes no changes to the text of the statement, although it reinstates the line breaks.

Some types of query can't be shown in design view, such as the union query we used in Part 2, so Query Builder does not make any changes at all to these.

So what have we learned? Well, Access is capable of handling standard SQL statements without using the SQL grid, but it will make an attempt to translate them into the grid where possible. And while we can always use Query Builder to produce an SQL statement for us, it may create one that is a lot more wordy than we need and which fits into its own structure rather than following the standard SQL syntax.

The Types of SQL Statement

It's time to look at the theory of SQL, by examining the different types of statement that you can use. Each one corresponds to a type of Access query (the types you see on the Query menu when you have a query open). The basic types are:

SQL statement type	Equivalent Access query type
SELECT statement	Select query
DELETE statement	Delete query
INSERT statement	Append query
SELECT INTO statement	Make-table query
UPDATE statement	Update query

Table Continued on Following Page

SQL statement type	Equivalent Access query type
TRANSFORM statement	Crosstab query
UNION query	SQL specific query
Pass-through query	SQL specific query
Data definition query	SQL specific query

SQL statements have three parts:

[parameter declaration;] [manipulation statement] [option declaration];

When we use parameters with a query, we must declare these first. This section is optional because we don't always use parameters in a query. If a parameter declaration section is used, it is separated from the rest of the statement with a semi-colon.

Next comes the manipulation statement - the **SELECT** or **DELETE** part - which specifies the operation we want to carry out, the source and destination for the data and the conditions where it is to apply. This is the main body of the SQL statement. The final section declares the options for the query to run - it's optional but, when used in Access, it is always **WITH OWNERACCESS OPTION**. This option merely gives the user who runs the query the same permissions as the owner of the query. Obviously this can only be done within a secure environment (more of this in Chapter 16). We'll display the SQL statements in the following format and you can type them in directly in SQL view.

```
SELECT fields
FROM tables
```

You can type everything in on one line, but for clarity we'll display each clause of the statement on a different line.

Finally, the whole statement always ends with a semi-colon as well. We'll come back to parameters later. First we need to consider the manipulation part and we'll start by looking at the **SELECT** statement we've used regularly in the past.

The SELECT Statement

In the Try It Out earlier, you saw that the **SELECT** statement has distinct sections.

```
SELECT   fields
FROM   tables
WHERE   condition
ORDER  BY   field(s);
```

The statement we used was:

```
SELECT CustName, Credit
FROM Customer
WHERE Credit>10000
ORDER BY Credit;
```

In this statement we're just selecting the CustName and Credit fields from the Customer table. The condition is that the value in the Credit field is greater than 10000 and the resulting records are sorted by the value in the Credit field.

If we want to include *all* the fields from the Customer table, we substitute the short-hand syntax of an asterisk for the **SELECT** part. The asterisk functions in the same way as it does in the QBE grid.

```
SELECT *
FROM Customer
WHERE Credit>10000
ORDER BY Credit;
```

If we want to include all the records, rather than just those with a credit value greater than 10000, we omit the **WHERE** part:

```
SELECT *
FROM Customer
ORDER BY Credit;
```

If we want to sort the records in descending order, we just add the keyword **DESC** after the name of the field.

```
SELECT *
FROM Customer
ORDER BY Credit DESC;
```

And, of course, if we don't want the results to be sorted at all, we can omit the **ORDER BY** part as well:

```
SELECT *
FROM Customer;
```

This just provides a list of the customers in the database - in fact, a copy of the original Customer table, because we haven't specified any condition or sort order to limit the records.

So there's no mystery about the way SQL works - it follows the same methods as the Query Builder grid. When creating **SELECT** statements in Query Builder:

▶ We **SELECT** *fields* by dragging them into the columns of the grid, or by using an asterisk to include them all.

▶ We specify that the fields come **FROM** *tables* by adding the tables to the query so their names appear under the name of the field.

▶ We tell Access to only include the fields **WHERE** the *condition* we enter in the criteria row of the grid is satisfied.

▶ We set values in the Sort row to **ORDER BY** *fields*.

Joining Tables in an SQL Statement

This arrangement is fine as far as extracting data from one table is concerned, however we often need data from more than one table. We'll now try a more complicated **SELECT** statement and see what Query Builder makes of it. We'll **join** fields from more than one table to create the new recordset.

Try It Out - Showing a List of Projects

1 With **WroxSoft** still open, go to the Database window. Select the Queries tab and create a new query by clicking the <u>N</u>ew button, selecting Design View and clicking OK. Close the Show Table dialog without selecting any tables.

2 Click the SQL button to open the SQL window. Access displays the 'blank' query as:

```
SELECT DISTINCTROW;
```

3 Delete the existing text and type in the following SQL statement:

```
SELECT Date, CustName, Town, Phone, Project
FROM Customer
INNER JOIN Project ON Customer.CustKey=Project.CustKey
ORDER BY Date;
```

4 Switch to datasheet view to see the results - Access displays a list of projects sorted by date and shows the customer's name and town.

	Date	CustName	Town	Phone	Project
▶	03-Feb-95	James Builders	Phoenix	602-281-3318	PC Support
	15-Feb-95	Martha's Bar	Clarksville		Menu Generator
	03-Mar-95	Major Records	Stocksville	305-711-7851	Warehouse System
	11-Mar-95	Major Records	Stocksville	305-711-7851	Warehouse System
	22-Mar-95	Le Bistro	Vancouver	206-133-8294	Menu Generator
	03-Apr-95	Cummings Intl.	Pittsburgh	412-455-6104	Sales Tracking
	12-Apr-95	Le Bistro	Vancouver	206-133-8294	Menu Generator
	14-Apr-95	Jonahs Boats	Stocksville	305-711-8855	Navigation System
	20-Apr-95	Cummings Intl.	Pittsburgh	412-455-6104	Sales Tracking
	07-May-95	Union Records	Tampa	813-167-3520	Warehouse System
	15-May-95	Cummings Intl.	Pittsburgh	412-455-6104	Sales Tracking
	30-May-95	Major Records	Stocksville	305-711-7851	Warehouse System
	14-Jun-95	Burger Queen	Houston	713-771-6727	Menu Generator
	17-Jun-95	Education Dept.	Chicago	312-712-8567	School Info System
	19-Jun-95	Major Records	Stocksville	305-711-7851	Warehouse System
	28-Jun-95	Union Records	Tampa	813-167-3520	Warehouse System
	04-Jul-95	Major Records	Stocksville	305-711-7851	Warehouse System
	19-Jul-95	Major Records	Stocksville	305-711-7851	Sales Tracking

Record: 1 of 24

5 Now go to design view - Access displays the query grid showing how the SQL statement has been translated. It's exactly how we would have created it using the grid.

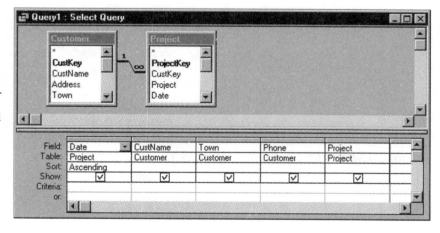

510

6 Close and save the query *while you're in design view*. Then open it again from the Database window and switch to SQL View. Access has added the name of the table and a period before each field name:

```
SELECT Project.Date, Customer.CustName, Customer.Town, Customer.Phone,
Project.Project
FROM Customer
INNER JOIN Project ON Customer.CustKey = Project.CustKey
ORDER BY Project.Date;
```

7 Switch to datasheet view - nothing else has changed. We get the same results as we did from the original SQL statement.

How It Works

So Access insists on including the field names in an SQL statement even though they're not necessary. But look back at our original statement. Our **FROM** section is:

```
FROM Customer
INNER JOIN Project ON Customer.CustKey=Project.CustKey
```

As with queries, we specify the table names here, because there are two fields with the same name, one in each table so that Access can uniquely identify each field. This is true not only in the **FROM** part of the statement, but elsewhere as well if the two tables have other fields with the same name.

The DELETE statement

Having seen how a **SELECT** statement duplicates the features of an Access select query, we'll move on to look at the other types of query that Access supports directly. (We'll leave the SQL specific queries until the end of the chapter, though.)

After the **SELECT** statement, the next simplest is the **DELETE** statement, equivalent to the Access delete query. This simply removes records from a table. The syntax of the statement is:

```
DELETE   [fields]
FROM   tables
WHERE   condition  ;
```

Notice that the **fields** part is optional - in SQL you don't need to identify any fields because the whole record is being deleted. However, Access allows you to display the results of a query in datasheet view so that you can see which records will be deleted when you run the query. To do this, it must have at least one 'output field' to display, so it includes at least one in the statement it produces. We'll see this next.

Try It Out - Deleting Records from the Project Table

1 Close the last query and then, in the Database window, open the Tables list and select the Project table. We'll make a copy to work with, to save deleting records from the original one. Press *Ctrl-C* and *Ctrl-V* to copy and paste the table. In the Paste Table As dialog, name the new table TestDelete. Ensure that the Structure and Data option is selected.

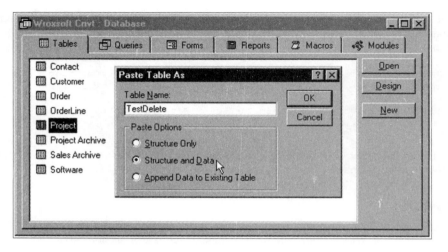

2 Select the Queries tab and create a new query by clicking the New button, selecting Design View and clicking OK. Close the Show Table dialog without selecting any tables.

3 Switch to SQL view and delete the 'blank' query text. Replace it with the following SQL statement:

```
DELETE
FROM TestDelete
WHERE Project="Menu Generator";
```

4 Switch to design view to see how this looks in the query grid.

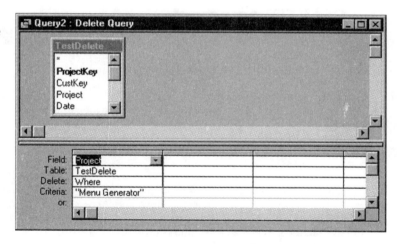

5 Now change to datasheet view - Access displays an error message saying that the query must have at least one output field.

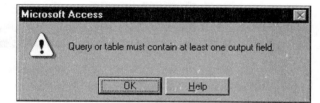

6 Close the message box by clicking OK and switch to SQL View - Access has altered the original SQL statement by adding **TestDelete.Project** between the **DELETE** and **FROM** keywords.

```
DELETE TestDelete.Project
FROM TestDelete
WHERE Project="Menu Generator";
```

7 Go to datasheet view again and this time you'll see a list of projects from the records that will be deleted when the query is run.

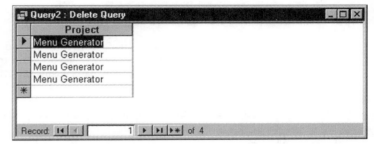

8 The query can actually work without the TestDelete.Project field name. Go to SQL view and delete it again, so we have the original statement. Then click the Run button on the toolbar to execute the query without displaying the records. We get a message telling us the records will be deleted.

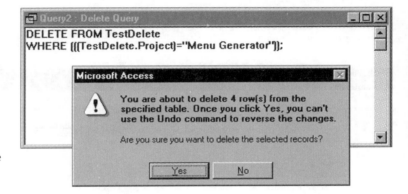

9 Click Yes and then open the TestDelete table to view the results. The menu generator projects have been deleted from the table.

How It Works

The more observant of you will have spotted that we cheated slightly here, in that we ran the SQL query in two different ways. The first time we ran the query in datasheet view, but the second time we actually executed the run option.

When we run the **DELETE** statement, we don't view the table beforehand. **DELETE** doesn't need to know which fields you're removing, it automatically assumes that you want to remove the whole record or records that meet that criteria. Indeed, **DELETE** can't remove part of records, it has to remove whole records.

So what can we learn from this? It's possible to run a **DELETE** query without specifying the names of fields, but if you want to check which records you are about to delete, you need a slightly amended query. When Access amended the SQL query, it only amended it so you could see one field of the record you were about to delete. To see the whole record beforehand, you can use an asterisk.

513

So, to delete all the Customer records where the town is New York, we could just use:

```
DELETE *
FROM Customer
WHERE Town="New York";
```

This will satisfy the demands of Query Builder, as well as doing the job we want.

The SELECT INTO Statement

In Part 1, we looked at how we can create a new table and then add records to it using queries. In Part 2, where we considered how to archive records in our **WroxSoft** sample application, we saw the same process. We can create a new table using a **SELECT INTO** statement, which is the equivalent of a make table query.

The syntax of a **SELECT INTO** statement is again very similar to the normal **SELECT** statement:

```
SELECT   fields
INTO   newtable
FROM   tables
WHERE   condition
ORDER   BY   field(s);
```

Try It Out - Using SELECT INTO

We'll create a table called OldCust which contains all the customers from Florida sorted by name.

1 Create a new query as before and replace the **SELECT DISTINCTROW**; line with:

```
SELECT *
INTO OldCust
FROM Customer
WHERE State="FL"
ORDER BY CustName;
```

2 Switch to datasheet view to see the results.

	CustKey	CustName	Address	Town	State	ZipCode	Phone	Fax	Credit	Alpha
▶	58	Jonahs Boats	The Quay	Stocksville	FL	16734	305-711-8855		$1,000	JONAH
	60	Major Records	Third Avenue	Stocksville	FL	10015	305-711-7851	305-711-853	$18,000	MAJOR
	66	Union Records	712 Main Street	Tampa	FL	51267	813-167-3520	813-167-352	$12,500	UNION
*	Number)								$0	

Query3 : Make Table Query

Record: 1 of 3

3 Now switch to design view. You will see that Access has changed the statement in Query Builder again - it has cleared the Show checkboxes. Yet switching to datasheet view still shows all the fields.

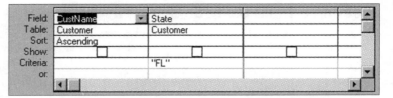

4 To keep Access happy, you need to include the table name with the asterisk, so that the statement reads:

```
SELECT Customer.*
INTO OldCust
FROM Customer
WHERE State="FL"
ORDER BY CustName;
```

Access always includes the table name in the Field row when you use an asterisk to select fields - so it expects to find Customer in the SQL statement. Using just an asterisk fools Query Builder altogether and means the column is not included in the grid. To include the column, you must write Customer.* in the SQL statement.

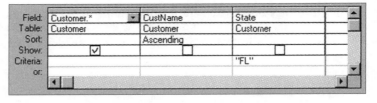

Creating a Table in a Different Database

We can also specify that the new table be created in a different database, the same as setting the Query Properties in Query Builder. If you open the Query Properties dialog, by double-clicking in the top section of the Query Builder window, you'll see entries for Destination Table and Destination DB. To place the new table in another database (we'll assume it's called **OTHERDB**) in the root of drive **C:** we would use the SQL statement:

```
SELECT *
INTO OldCust IN "C:\OTHERDB.MDB"
FROM Customer
WHERE State="FL"
ORDER BY CustName;
```

If you entered this statement in the SQL window and then switched to design view, you'd see that the Destination DB property in the Properties window is updated.

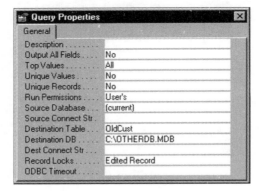

Creating a Table Using Selected Fields

As with a make table query, when we use **SELECT INTO**, we are not limited to using all the fields in the original table. We can select which fields we want, for example:

```
SELECT CustName, Address, Town, State
INTO OldCust
FROM Customer;
```

This would create a new table which contains just the address details of each customer.

We're also not limited to using one table. We'll now create a new table called ProjectList which contains the CustName, Town, Project and Date fields from the existing Customer and Project tables.

Try It Out - Creating a New Customer and Projects Table

1 Close any queries that are still open in the **WroxSoft** application and go to the Database window. Select the Queries tab and create a new query by clicking the New button, selecting Design View and clicking OK. Close the Show Table dialog without selecting any tables.

2 Switch to the SQL window and replace the existing text with:

```
SELECT CustName, Town, Project, Date
INTO ProjectList
FROM Customer
INNER JOIN Project ON Customer.CustKey = Project.CustKey
ORDER BY CustName, Date;
```

3 Go to datasheet view to see the results - Access displays a list of customers and their projects, sorted by customer then by date.

CustName	Town	Project	Date
Aardvark Ltd.	Athens	Accounts System	21-Jul-95
Aardvark Ltd.	Athens	Accounts System	07-Aug-95
Aardvark Ltd.	Athens	Accounts System	08-Aug-95
Burger Queen	Houston	Menu Generator	14-Jun-95
Cummings Intl.	Pittsburgh	Sales Tracking	03-Apr-95
Cummings Intl.	Pittsburgh	Sales Tracking	20-Apr-95
Cummings Intl.	Pittsburgh	Sales Tracking	15-May-95
Education Dept.	Chicago	School Info System	17-Jun-95
Education Dept.	Chicago	School Info System	21-Jul-95
James Builders	Phoenix	PC Support	03-Feb-95
James Builders	Phoenix	PC Support	08-Aug-95
James Builders	Phoenix	PC Support	08-Aug-95
Jonahs Boats	Stocksville	Navigation System	14-Apr-95
Le Bistro	Vancouver	Menu Generator	22-Mar-95
Le Bistro	Vancouver	Menu Generator	12-Apr-95
Major Records	Stocksville	Warehouse System	03-Mar-95

Query1 : Make Table Query

Record: 1 of 24

4 Now switch to design view - Access displays the query grid showing how the SQL statement has been translated. It's just as we would have expected.

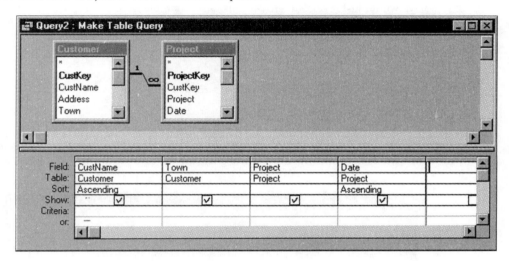

5 To create the new table, click the Run button. Access warns you that you are about to paste the rows into a new table and asks you if you are sure. Click Yes and then go to the Database window, select the Tables list and open the new ProjectList table that now exists.

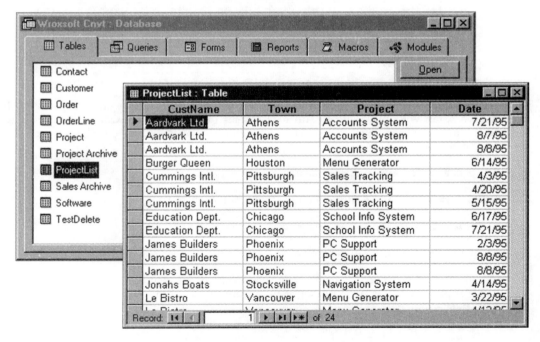

6 We've sorted the records using two fields - CustName and Date. We just place them both in the **ORDER BY** part of the statement, in the order we want them carried out. To sort by Date first, then CustName, we would just reverse them. But this raises a problem that you can see if you switch the query back to SQL view. Try editing the SQL statement so that the **ORDER BY** fields are reversed:

```
SELECT CustName, Town, Project, Date
INTO ProjectList
FROM Customer
INNER JOIN Project ON Customer.CustKey = Project.CustKey
ORDER BY Date, CustName;
```

7 Now switch to design view again. You'll see that Access has added the CustName field again after the Date field and set its sort order to Ascending, but cleared the Show checkbox. This is the only way it can sort the fields in the right order, while leaving the order of the fields in the new table the same.

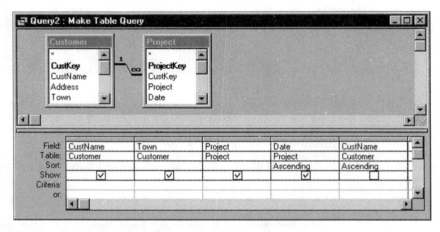

So we have found another way that, using SQL, gives us more flexibility to create exactly the recordset we want, without having to add extra copies of a field to the Query grid. If we want to sort the records in descending order, we just add the keyword **DESC** to the SQL statement, after the name of the field.

```
...  ORDER BY CustName, Date DESC;
```

This would sort by ascending customer name and descending date.

```
...  ORDER BY CustName DESC, Date DESC;
```

would sort by descending customer name and date.

So, you can see that the **SELECT INTO** statement works in an identical way to the **SELECT** statement except for the **INTO** clause. Once the recordset has been created, this simply specifies where the data should go.

Remember that when you run a **SELECT INTO** query, any existing table with the same name will be deleted before the query runs. You will, however, get a message asking you to confirm you want to delete it before it is removed.

518

The INSERT statement

The **INSERT** statement is the equivalent to an Access append query and adds the records we specify to an existing table.

It contains a standard **SELECT** statement, prefaced by the special keywords **INSERT INTO** and the details of the destination table. The syntax is as follows:

```
INSERT   INTO  table   (field  list)
SELECT   fields
FROM   tables
WHERE   condition
ORDER   BY   field(s);
```

We can convert a make table query into an append query in Query Builder by simply selecting Append... from the Query menu. Let's see what difference this makes to the query we used in the previous example.

Try It Out - Using an Append Query to Create an INSERT Statement

1 Go back to the SQL window where we created the previous query and change the sort order back to CustName, then Date. The SQL statement you need is:

```
SELECT CustName, Town, Project, Date
INTO ProjectList
FROM Customer
INNER JOIN Project ON Customer.CustKey = Project.CustKey
ORDER BY CustName, Date;
```

2 Now switch to design view and select Append.. from the Query menu. Access suggests the same table, ProjectList, as the destination. Select OK and Access replaces the Show: row with an Append To: row and sets it to the name of the fields specified for each column. (It assumes that the destination table uses the same field names.)

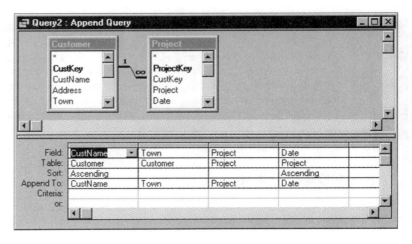

3 Switch to SQL view to see the new statement. Access has added the **INSERT INTO** keywords followed by the name of the destination table and a list of the fields we are appending. You'll see it has placed the Date field in square brackets because Date is also the name of an Access internal function. The brackets just define it as being a field name. After the **INSERT INTO** part is a standard **SELECT** statement which creates the recordset that will be appended to the new table:

```
INSERT INTO ProjectList ( CustName, Town, Project, [Date] )
SELECT Customer.CustName, Customer.Town, Project.Project, Project.Date
FROM Customer
INNER JOIN Project ON Customer.CustKey = Project.CustKey
ORDER BY Customer.CustName, Project.Date;
```

Again, you can see that Access has added the table names for us - we could equally well use the shortened form in this case:

```
INSERT INTO ProjectList ( CustName, Town, Project, [Date] )
SELECT CustName, Town, Project, Date
FROM Customer
INNER JOIN Project ON Customer.CustKey = Project.CustKey
ORDER BY CustName, Date;
```

We aren't forced to append values to all of the fields in the destination table. We can just add certain values and leave the other fields blank. Switch the query to design view and delete the Town and Date fields from the Query Builder grid. Now execute the query, using the Run button on the toolbar and open the ProjectList table to see the result. The new, appended records have a blank Town and Date field. The SQL query for this is:

```
INSERT INTO ProjectList ( CustName, Project )
SELECT CustName, Project
FROM Customer
INNER JOIN Project ON Customer.CustKey = Project.CustKey
ORDER BY CustName;
```

How an INSERT Statement Works

So an **INSERT** statement is just a **SELECT** statement preceded by the **INSERT INTO** section, which defines where the data will be appended. To work correctly, the list of fields in the **INSERT INTO** part must exactly match those created by the **SELECT** part.

FYI

Remember that when you run an **INSERT** query to add records to an existing table, you must ensure that the output of your query matches the requirements of the destination table, including the correct field names. If you break the rules of referential integrity that are specified for the destination table, or the field types are incompatible, you'll get a message warning you that some or all of the changes were unsuccessful. In particular, if you only append certain fields to an existing table, you must include a value for the primary key and any other fields which are indexed **Yes (No Duplicates)** to prevent a 'Field cannot contain Null' error occurring.

The UPDATE statement

The last of the standard Access query types is the update query. This is equivalent to the **UPDATE** statement in SQL. The basic syntax is:

```
UPDATE  table
SET  field = expression
WHERE  condition ;
```

The **SET** part of the statement defines the new values for the fields and can be used to update more than one field at a time by placing a comma between each **field = expression** section. We'll start with a simple query where we check for customers who have a credit limit greater than $10,000 and increase their credit by 15%.

Try It Out - Updating Values in the Customer Table

1 Close any queries that are still open. Create a new blank query in the usual way, without adding any tables to it.

2 Select SQL View from the Query View List to open the SQL window. We want to increase the credit limit of customers who have an existing limit of greater than 10000 by 15%. Delete the existing text and type in the following SQL statement:

```
UPDATE Customer
SET Credit = [Credit]*1.15
WHERE Credit>10000;
```

3 Switch to datasheet view to see the results - Access displays a list of Credit fields which are currently greater than 10000 - these are the ones that will be updated.

4 Go back to SQL view and click the Run button on the toolbar - Access displays a message showing the number of records in the table that will be updated.

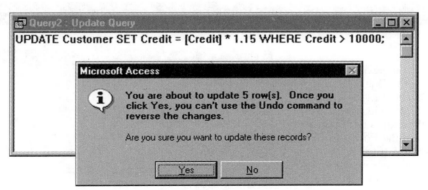

5 Click Yes and then open the table from the Database window to see the results.

521

	CustKey	CustName	Address	Town	State	ZipCode	Phone	Fax	Credit	Alpha
	51	Aardvark Ltd.	All Saints Street	Athens	OH	39812	216-376-1298	216-376-8811	$10,000	AARDV
	52	Burger Queen	Constants Avenue	Houston	TX	30517	713-771-6727	713-771-6728	$5,000	BURGE
▶	53	Education Dept	The Offices, City Square	Chicago	IL	10745	312-712-8567		$17,250	EDUCA
	55	Cummings Intl.	124th Street West	Pittsburgh	PA	17265	412-455-6104	412-455-1399	$28,750	CUMMI
	56	J.R.Higgins	The Market	Green Bay	WI	61733	414-831-8812	414-831-7293	$2,000	HIGGI
	57	James Builders	2131 New Street	Phoenix	AZ	78034	602-281-3318	602-281-7318	$7,500	JAMES
	58	Jonahs Boats	The Quay	Stocksville	FL	16734	305-711-8855		$1,000	JONAH
	59	Le Bistro	Rue Francais	Vancouver	WA	41322	206-133-8294	206-133-8295	$1,500	LEBIS
	60	Major Records	Third Avenue	Stocksville	FL	10015	305-711-7851	305-711-8531	$20,700	MAJOR
	61	Martha's Bar	Top Street	Clarksville	NY	54876			$500	MARTH
	62	Miracle Supplie	18th Avenue	Oakland	CA	10593	415-671-6633	415-671-8833	$20,125	MIRAC
	65	Pedro Mana	Calle Sebastione	St. Paul	MN	65109	612-401-1350	612-401-1388	$7,500	MANAP
	66	Union Records	712 Main Street	Tampa	FL	51267	813-167-3520	813-167-3521	$14,375	UNION
✳	Number)								$0	

Record: 3 of 13

6 Now switch the query to design view and look at the Query Builder grid. It contains a single column showing the Credit field, the expression to calculate the new value and the criteria for selecting the records to be updated.

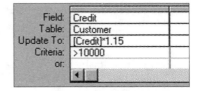

Field:	Credit
Table:	Customer
Update To:	[Credit]*1.15
Criteria:	>10000
or:	

How It Works

This SQL statement is easy enough to understand. We've updated the Customer table, **WHERE** the records have a credit value of more than $10,000. The **SET** clause is the part of the statement that actually changes the record. We simply entered an expression which multiplied the Credit value by 1.15. There are, however, some inherent dangers of the **UPDATE** statement that you must be aware of. To illustrate these, we'll try a different update this time and add the international dialing code to the numbers in our table.

Try It Out - Updating the Phone Numbers

1 Delete the existing fields from the Query Builder grid and add the Phone and Fax fields. Enter "00 1 " & [Phone] in the Update To: row of the Phone field and "00 1 " & [Fax] in the Update To: row of the Fax field. For both, add the Criteria: Is Not Null, so that we don't update empty fields.

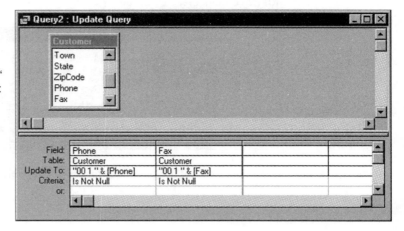

2 Switch to SQL view and look at the statement. We've got the two update sections in the **SET** part, separated by a comma and the **WHERE** part contains our compound criteria expression which ensures we only update existing numbers.

```
UPDATE Customer
SET Customer.Phone = "00 1 " & [Phone], Customer.Fax = "00 1 " & [Fax]
WHERE (((Customer.Phone)Is Not Null) AND ((Customer.Fax) Is Not Null));
```

3 Execute the query by clicking the Run button on the toolbar and then open the table to see the results. Most of our records have been updated. However, you'll notice that we slipped up - where there is only a phone number and no fax number we didn't get an update.

CustKey	CustName	Address	Town	State	ZipCode	Phone	Fax
51	Aardvark Ltd.	All Saints Street	Athens	OH	39812	00 1 216-376-1298	00 1 216-376-8811
52	Burger Queer	Constants Avenue	Houston	TX	30517	00 1 713-771-6727	00 1 713-771-6728
53	Education De	The Offices, City Sq	Chicago	IL	10745	312-712-8567	
55	Cummings Inf	124th Street West	Pittsburgh	PA	17265	00 1 412-455-6104	00 1 412-455-1399
56	J.R.Higgins	The Market	Green Bay	WI	61733	00 1 414-831-8812	00 1 414-831-7293
57	James Builde	2131 New Street	Phoenix	AZ	78034	00 1 602-281-3318	00 1 602-281-7318
58	Jonahs Boats	The Quay	Stocksville	FL	16734	305-711-8855	
59	Le Bistro	Rue Francais	Vancouver	WA	41322	00 1 206-133-8294	00 1 206-133-8295
60	Major Record	Third Avenue	Stocksville	FL	10015	00 1 305-711-7851	00 1 305-711-8531
61	Martha's Bar	Top Street	Clarksville	NY	54876		
62	Miracle Suppl	18th Avenue	Oakland	CA	10593	00 1 415-671-6633	00 1 415-671-8833
65	Pedro Mana	Calle Sebastione	St. Paul	MN	65109	00 1 612-401-1350	00 1 612-401-1388
66	Union Record	712 Main Street	Tampa	FL	51267	00 1 813-167-3520	00 1 813-167-3521

Record: 1 of 13

What Went Wrong?

Although our query may have looked perfectly reasonable, we didn't take the rules of logic into account. By setting the two Criteria: to Is Not Null, we only get a match when both of the fields contain a value. (Remember from Chapter 2 that two criteria on the same row are **AND**ed.) However, if we relax the criteria to include records with only one number, we'll get an update to the other (null) field as well, which is also undesirable.

In fact, it's the **SET** part of the query that's wrong, not the **WHERE** part. We should check each value for a null before we update it, using the expressions:

```
Phone = IIf(IsNull([Phone]),Null,"00 1 " & [Phone])
Fax = IIf(IsNull([Fax]),Null,"00 1 " & [Fax])
```

In the first line, the **IIf** function checks whether the Phone field is Null. If it is, it leaves it set to Null, otherwise it enters "00 1 " & [Phone]. If we do this then, we don't need a **WHERE** part at all - we can go through all the records and only the fields that contain a number will be updated. The SQL statement to do this is:

```
UPDATE Customer
SET Phone = IIf(IsNull([Phone]),Null,"00 1 " & [Phone]),
Fax = IIf(IsNull([Fax]),Null,"00 1 " & [Fax]);
```

and the equivalent in the Query Builder window is:

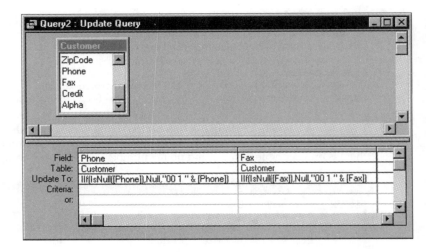

So a timely reminder. Using SQL can be just as dangerous as using Query Builder. If you fail to specify the correct expression in an SQL statement which changes the contents of tables, you can cause a lot of damage. Always back up any information, or make a copy of the original table before you run an action query or SQL statement that changes its records.

Exerting Extra Control over SQL Queries

So far, we've used relatively simple queries to illustrate the main structure of each type of SQL statement. Of course, they can become a lot more complicated, including long lists of fields and multiple **WHERE** and **SET** clauses. The great thing with SQL, though, is that the statements do follow a fixed structure - you can expand each type of statement by adding all the permissible types of clause. For example, we've seen how a **SELECT** statement can start out as simple as

```
SELECT * FROM Customer;
```

and grow to something like

```
SELECT DISTINCTROW Customer.CustKey, Customer.CustName, Contact.EMail,
Contact.ContactName, Contact.ContactAddr, Customer.Address, Customer.Town,
Customer.State FROM Customer INNER JOIN Contact ON Customer.CustKey =
Contact.CustKey WHERE ((Contact.ContactName Is Not Null) AND (Customer.State="FL"
Or Customer.State="WA")) ORDER BY Customer.State, Customer.CustName;
```

Providing you break it down into logical groups it all makes sense:

```
SELECT DISTINCTROW Customer.CustKey, Customer.CustName, Contact.EMail,
Contact.ContactName, Contact.ContactAddr, Customer.Address, Customer.Town,
Customer.State
```

```
... FROM Customer INNER JOIN Contact ON Customer.CustKey = Contact.CustKey
```

```
... WHERE ((Contact.ContactName Is Not Null) AND (Customer.State="FL" Or
Customer.State="WA"))
```

```
... ORDER BY Customer.State, Customer.CustName;
```

However, there are other optional parts to an SQL statement that we often need to include in even the most simple statements. When we looked at queries in Part 1, we discovered other aspects that allowed us to further control the results we obtained - calculated fields and the Unique Values and Unique Records properties (which are used to remove duplicate records from our recordset). We also saw how we could use parameters to allow the user to enter values for the criteria in a query as it runs, rather than 'hard-coding' them into the query ourselves.

Using Calculated Fields in an SQL Statement

One optional part of all SQL statements is the **AS** keyword which allows us to specify the name of a field in the resulting recordset (i.e. rename it) and determine how the values that fill it are calculated. For example, suppose we use the simple **SELECT** query:

```
SELECT CustName, Credit
FROM Customer;
```

However, we find that the name Credit that we gave to the field when we designed the table is unsuitable. Perhaps it clashes with the name of another object in the database, or we just find it is giving the wrong impression of the values it contains. We can use **AS** to re-name the field and call it Limit:

```
SELECT CustName, Credit AS Limit
FROM Customer;
```

In datasheet view, the recordset now uses this name for the old Credit field.

CustName	Limit
Aardvark Ltd.	$10,000
Burger Queen	$5,000
Education Dept.	$17,250
Cummings Intl.	$28,750
J.R.Higgins	$2,000
James Builders	$7,500
Jonahs Boats	$1,000
Le Bistro	$1,500
Major Records	$20,700
Martha's Bar	$500
Miracle Supplies	$20,125
Pedro Mana	$7,500
Union Records	$14,375
*	$0

Record: 1 of 13

You will recall that in several places in our earlier discussions on queries and forms and in our sample **WroxSoft** application, we used a calculated field to display the customer's full address as one line of text. We used an expression similar to:

```
IIf(IsNull([Address]),"*unknown*",[Address] & ", " & [Town] & ", " & [State] & ", "
& [ZipCode])
```

which returns the complete address separated by commas, or the string ***unknown*** if the Address field is blank.

We can incorporate this into our **SELECT** query using the **AS** keyword:

```
SELECT CustName, IIf(IsNull([Address]),"*unknown*",[Address] & ", " & [Town] & ", "
& [State] & ", " & [ZipCode]) AS FullAddr
FROM Customer;
```

This produces exactly the same results as the method we used in earlier chapters.

Specifying Unique Values and Unique Records

When we created an SQL statement to fill a Project combo box list in Part 1, we found that Access sometimes returned duplicate values in the recordset that the query produced. We cured this by changing the Unique Values property from the default No to Yes. When we use an SQL statement we can also specify this. To see how, we'll create the same query using SQL and see what Access does with the properties in the Query Builder window.

Try It Out - Controlling Duplicated Values in a Recordset

1 Close any queries you have open. Then create a new query, again without adding any table to it and switch to SQL view.

2 We'll produce a list of the types of project from the Project table. Delete the existing text and type in the following SQL statement:

```
SELECT DISTINCTROW Project.Project FROM Project;
```

3 Go to datasheet view to see the results - Access displays a list of projects and there are many duplicated records.

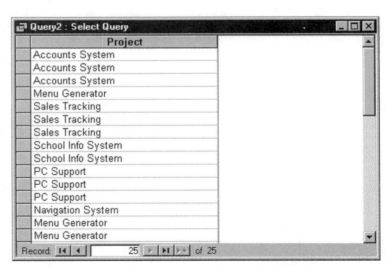

4 Now switch to design view. Double-click on the top section of the Query Builder grid to open the Query Properties window. Access has set the Unique Values property to No and the Unique Records property to Yes. These are the defaults for a new query.

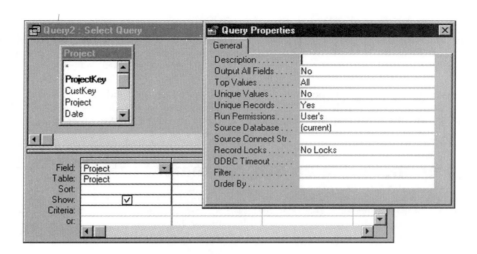

5 Back in the SQL view, delete the **DISTINCTROW** keyword from the statement, then switch back the design view. Now the Unique Records property is set to No as well. Change to datasheet view to see the results - just the same! So the **DISTINCTROW** keyword has made no difference.

6 Go back to design view and set the Unique Values property to Yes. In datasheet view, we now have what we want - each project type only appears once.

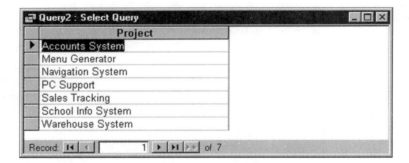

7 Switch to SQL View to see what Access has done - it's replaced the **DISTINCTROW** keyword with just **DISTINCT**. Now our query reads:

```
SELECT DISTINCT Project.Project FROM Project;
```

How It Works

We can use the two keywords **DISTINCTROW** and **DISTINCT** to control the duplication of records in our recordset. They have different effects on our data, so it's best to summarize them:

SQL keyword	Unique Records Property	Unique Values Property
DISTINCTROW	Yes	No
DISTINCT	No	Yes
(neither)	No	No

When Access executes the query, it first assembles the records that meet the criteria to keep the size of the recordset it has to manipulate to a minimum. It then removes any duplicate records if the Unique Records property is set to Yes and finally selects the fields that it needs for the result. As each of our project *records* is different, we get all the records still included at this point.

Once Access has assembled the final recordset by selecting the fields we specified, it looks at the Unique Values property. If it is No, it outputs all the records that it has assembled. It's only if we set this to Yes, by including the **DISTINCT** keyword in our SQL statement, that the duplicates are removed.

Using Parameters in an SQL Statement

If we know what a query is required to do, but the criteria can't be fixed, we often use a **parameter query** which asks the user for the missing information before it runs. In this example, we'll use a query which uses a parameter [Customer Name] to prompt for the name of the customer. By adding an asterisk to the end of the text that the user enters when they run the query, we can show all the customers whose name starts with that text. If the user enters 'M', we'll show all the customers whose name starts with 'M'.

Try It Out - Using a Parameter Query

1 Close the query from the last example and create a new one. This time select the Customer table from the Show Table dialog and drag CustName down to the Field: row. Add the expression Like ([Customer Name] & "*") to the Criteria row of the CustName field.

2 Select Parameters from the Query menu. In the Parameters dialog, type Customer Name as the parameter and select Text as the data type. We can now prompt the user for the customer's name.

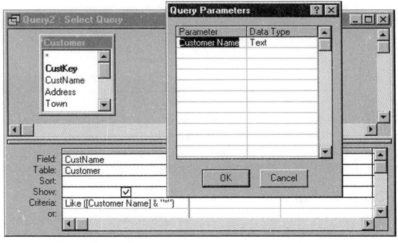

3 Open the SQL window to see the statement. It's the normal **SELECT** statement but preceded by the parameter declaration section and a semi-colon. We simply list all the parameters followed by the data type specified in the Parameters dialog.

```
PARAMETERS [Customer Name] Text;
SELECT DISTINCTROW Customer.CustName
FROM Customer
WHERE (((Customer.CustName) Like ([Customer Name] & "*")));
```

4 Switch to datasheet view to see the results of the query and enter the letter M for the parameter. You will get the following:

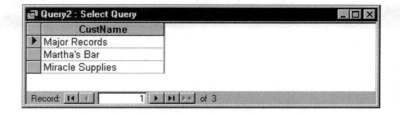

Again, Access has included all the table names and its usual selection of parentheses. We can simplify this statement with no ill effect on the query:

```
PARAMETERS [Customer Name] Text;
SELECT CustName
FROM Customer
WHERE CustName Like ([Customer Name] & "*");
```

One interesting point is that Access manages the parameters itself - you don't actually have to use the Parameters dialog to specify the data types. Go back to design view and open the Parameters dialog again. Delete the entry for the Customer Name parameter and look at the SQL statement. Now there's no **PARAMETERS** section - but if we run it, Access still prompts for the parameter.

Remember that Access automatically treats all the parts of a query which it can't identify as an expression or field name as a parameter - so it still prompts for **Customer Name** because it can't find a field with that name in the source table. However, this is peculiar to Access - if you use this expression in most other SQL situations, such as in Microsoft's SQL Server, you'll get an error, because it can't resolve the statement.

Types of JOIN in SQL Statements

So far, when we've linked tables together, we've used the original relationships between the tables. For instance, we used the Customer and Project table to see an SQL **SELECT** statement at work by using:

```
SELECT Date, CustName, Town, Phone, Project
FROM Customer
INNER JOIN Project ON Customer.CustKey = Project.CustKey
ORDER BY Date;
```

This joined the tables together on the CustKey fields, using the values in the Customer.CustKey and Project.CustKey fields. We had to define which table each field came from because the same field name is used in both tables. This is an **INNER** join.

As you might expect, there's another type of join called an **OUTER** join. This type has to be specified a little differently in an SQL statement. You'll see why in the next example. You'll recall that we have a field in our Projects table which identifies the main contact for a project. We'll use this now...

Try It Out - Exploring Join Types in an SQL Statement

1 Close the last query and create a new one. Add the Project and Contact tables by holding down *Ctrl* while you click on them. Select Add and then close the Show Table dialog.

2 Close the Show Table dialog. There is no relationship between the two tables, so before we start we need to create one. Drag the MainContactKey field from the Project table and drop it on the ContactKey field in the Contact table. Access creates the link.

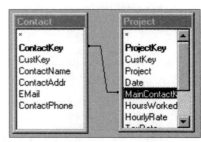

3 Drag the Project field from the Project table and the ContactName field from the Contact table to the grid. Select Ascending for the Project field's Sort order.

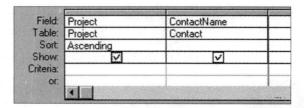

4 Switch to datasheet view to view the results - Access displays a list of projects and the main contact for each.

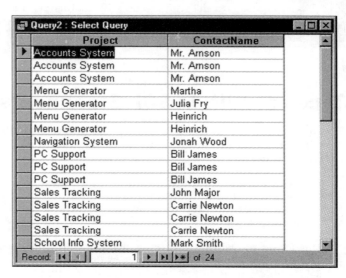

5 Switch to SQL View to see the statement. It's a normal **SELECT** statement using the **INNER JOIN** we created between the tables:

```
SELECT DISTINCTROW Project.Project, Contact.ContactName
FROM Project
INNER JOIN Contact ON Project.MainContactKey = Contact.ContactKey
ORDER BY Project.Project;
```

6 However, remember that we allow the MainContactKey field to be empty in the Project table if there is no main contact for that project. Open the Project table from the Database window and delete a few of the MainContactKey entries.

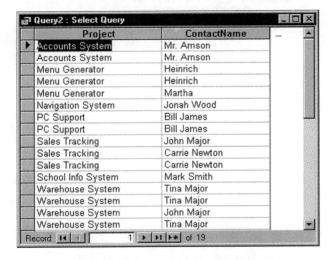

	ProjectKey	CustKey	Project	Date	MainContactKey	HoursWorked	Hour
	P 0029	51	Accounts System	07-Aug-95	3	17	
	P 0030	51	Accounts System	21-Jul-95	3	6	
▶	P 0031	51	Accounts System	08-Aug-95		3	
	P 0032	52	Menu Generator	14-Jun-95		12	
	P 0033	55	Sales Tracking	03-Apr-95	6	51	
	P 0034	55	Sales Tracking	20-Apr-95	6	7	
	P 0035	55	Sales Tracking	15-May-95		33	
	P 0036	53	School Info System	17-Jun-95		63	
	P 0037	53	School Info System	21-Jul-95	7	14	
	P 0038	57	PC Support	03-Feb-95	10	4	
	P 0039	57	PC Support	08-Aug-95		9	
	P 0040	57	PC Support	08-Aug-95	10	7	
	P 0041	58	Navigation System	14-Apr-95	12	19	
	P 0042	59	Menu Generator	22-Mar-95	13	5	
	P 0043	59	Menu Generator	12-Apr-95	13	3	

Record: 14 ◀ 3 ▶ ▶I ▶＊ of 24

7 Go back to the query and switch to datasheet view again. Now the projects with no main contact have disappeared from the list.

Project	ContactName
Accounts System	Mr. Arnson
Accounts System	Mr. Arnson
Menu Generator	Heinrich
Menu Generator	Heinrich
Menu Generator	Martha
Navigation System	Jonah Wood
PC Support	Bill James
PC Support	Bill James
Sales Tracking	John Major
Sales Tracking	Carrie Newton
Sales Tracking	Carrie Newton
School Info System	Mark Smith
Warehouse System	Tina Major
Warehouse System	Tina Major
Warehouse System	John Major
Warehouse System	Tina Major

Record: 14 ◀ 1 ▶ ▶I ▶＊ of 19

8 Back in design view, open the Join Properties dialog by clicking on the link between the tables and then double-clicking it (or right-click and select Join Properties). We have specified that Access only include rows where the joined fields from both tables are equal.

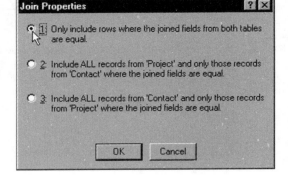

Join Properties

- ⦿ 1: Only include rows where the joined fields from both tables are equal.
- ○ 2: Include ALL records from 'Project' and only those records from 'Contact' where the joined fields are equal.
- ○ 3: Include ALL records from 'Contact' and only those records from 'Project' where the joined fields are equal.

[OK]   [Cancel]

531

> We have joined the tables on the **MainContactKey** field and where there is no value in this field in the **Project** table, Access cannot find a matching record in the **Contact** table. So these records are omitted from the recordset.

9 Select 'Include ALL records from Project and only those from Contact where the joined fields are equal' and click OK. Now the join in the query is shown with an arrow pointing to the Contact table.

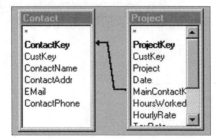

10 Switch to SQL View. The join is now specified as a **LEFT JOIN**:

```
SELECT DISTINCTROW Project.Project, Contact.ContactName
FROM Project
LEFT JOIN Contact ON Project.MainContactKey = Contact.ContactKey
ORDER BY Project.Project;
```

11 Now switch to datasheet view to see the result. We've got all the projects back, with an empty field where there is no main contact specified in the Project table.

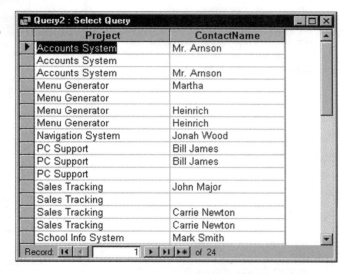

12 Now open the Join Properties dialog and select the 'Include ALL records from Contact and only those from Project where the joined fields are equal'. Then switch back to design view. This time the arrow on the join between the tables points to the Project table.

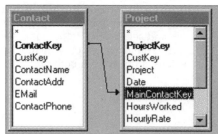

13 Switch to SQL view again and you'll see in the SQL statement that the **LEFT JOIN** has changed to **RIGHT JOIN**.

14 Switch to datasheet view to see the results of this change. Access has included all the contacts and left the Project field blank for those not linked to an existing project.

Query2 : Select Query	
Project	**ContactName**
	Davy
	Tony De Varlio
	Julia Fry
	Dave Jones
	John
	Fred James
Accounts System	Mr. Arnson
Accounts System	Mr. Arnson
Menu Generator	Heinrich
Menu Generator	Heinrich
Menu Generator	Martha
Navigation System	Jonah Wood
PC Support	Bill James
PC Support	Bill James
Sales Tracking	John Major
Sales Tracking	Carrie Newton

Record: 26 ▶ ▶I ▶* of 26

How It Works

This probably seems a little confusing, so let's look a little closer at the SQL statements we've used. In the 'normal' query we started with, we had an **INNER JOIN** - only the rows where both fields were equal were included.

```
...
FROM Project
INNER JOIN Contact ON Project.MainContactKey = Contact.ContactKey
```

When we told Access to include all the records from the Project table, it changed this to a **LEFT JOIN**:

```
...
FROM Project
LEFT JOIN Contact ON Project.MainContactKey = Contact.ContactKey
```

The new statement specifies that we include all records from the table on the **LEFT** of the **JOIN** keyword. So when we changed the Join Properties dialog again, the SQL statement changed to read:

```
...
FROM Project
RIGHT JOIN Contact ON Project.MainContactKey = Contact.ContactKey
```

Access then took all the records from the table on the **RIGHT** of the **JOIN** keyword - the Contact table.

This type of join is technically referred to as an **OUTER JOIN**, though we actually have to use the syntax **LEFT JOIN** or **RIGHT JOIN** so that we know which table we need to include all the records from.

Advanced Queries

We've seen and used all the main types of SQL statement and their Access equivalent now, but there are still a few more. We won't go into these in as much depth, but you should be aware of how they work. We'll take a look at **TRANSFORM** statements, **UNION** statements (which you've already come across) and **sub-queries**.

The TRANSFORM Statement

The SQL **TRANSFORM** statement is the equivalent of an Access crosstab query. Instead of returning rows taken from existing records, like other types of query, it combines values from one of the fields to produce a spreadsheet-like table with row and column headings.

In effect, it takes the values in one of the fields and pivots them to form the column headings - one column for each different value. We used crosstab queries in Part 1 of the book, so let's now see how we create them directly using SQL statements. The syntax of a **TRANSFORM** statement is:

```
TRANSFORM  summary_field
<SELECT  STATEMENT>
PIVOT  row_heading_field;
```

We'll create a **summary_field** by using one of the SQL aggregate functions, such as **Sum**, **Count**, **Max**, **Avg,** etc., on a field in the table. We'll then create a recordset from the source tables and specify the field which is to be used as the column heading.

Try It Out - Creating the SQL Equivalent of a Crosstab Query

1 Create a new query and, in SQL view, enter the following SQL statement:

```
TRANSFORM Sum(Project.HoursWorked) AS SumOfHoursWorked
SELECT Project.Project
FROM Project
GROUP BY Project.Project
PIVOT Project.Date;
```

2 In design view, this produces a standard Access crosstab query, using the Project table as the source of the records.

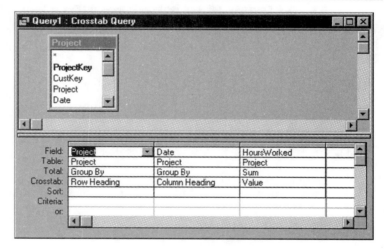

3 When we switch to datasheet view, we see the total hours worked for each project, listed in columns by the date of the project.

Project	2/3/95	2/15/95	3/3/95	3/11/95	3/22/95	4/3/95	4/12/95	4/14/95	4/20/95	5/7/95	5/15/95	5/3
Accounts System												
Menu Generator		5			5		3					
Navigation System								19				
PC Support	4											
▶ Sales Tracking						51				7	33	
School Info System												
Warehouse System			52	28						27		

Record: ◄◄ ◄ | 5 | ► ►► ►* | of 7

4 However, this is not a very neat way to display the results; it would be better to show the total hours worked for each project by month, for instance. Go back to SQL view and edit the SQL statement so that it includes a new calculated field for the columns and specifies the column headings in the order that we want them.

```
TRANSFORM Sum(Project.HoursWorked) AS SumOfHoursWorked
SELECT Project.Project
FROM Project
GROUP BY Project.Project
PIVOT Format([Date],"mmm") In ("Feb","Mar","Apr","May","Jun","Jul","Aug");
```

5 Now go to datasheet view to see the results.

Project	Feb	Mar	Apr	May	Jun	Jul	Aug
▶ Accounts System						6	20
Menu Generator	5	5	3		12		
Navigation System			19				
PC Support	4						16
Sales Tracking			58	33		14	
School Info System					63	14	
Warehouse System		80		46	26	3	

Record: ◄◄ ◄ | 1 | ► ►► ►* | of 7

How It Works

The **TRANSFORM** part of the statement uses:

```
Sum(Project.HoursWorked) AS SumOfHoursWorked
```

to create a calculated field which contains the sum of the hours worked for each date (the **PIVOT** statement specifies that the HoursWorked field is summed by date) and the new field is named SumOfHoursWorked using the **AS** keyword. Next, the **SELECT** statement selects the Project field from all the records in the Project table, sorting them in order:

```
SELECT Project.Project
FROM Project
GROUP BY Project.Project
```

535

The **GROUP BY** section simply divides the recordset into groups of each project type.

Finally, the **PIVOT** part of the statement uses the **Format** function to convert the Date field into a three letter abbreviation of the month. The column headings are then specified as the same format, so the values in the Date fields are summed by month and placed in the right column.

```
PIVOT Format([Date],"mmm") In ("Feb","Mar","Apr","May","Jun","Jul","Aug");
```

The UNION Statement

The SQL **UNION** statement is one of those that can't be created using Query Builder. We used one in our **WroxSoft** application to combine projects and sales records into one recordset, so that we could produce Statements of Account for our customers, and built it in Part 2 of the book.

The effect of a **UNION** statement is similar to what you get when you use a make table query to create a new table and then add records to it using an append query. The difference is, of course, that a union query creates its recordset in memory, not on disk like a make table query.

The syntax of a **UNION** statement is simple:

```
<SELECT   STATEMENT>
  UNION
<SELECT   STATEMENT>   ;
```

In other words, it uses normal **SELECT** statements to create the initial recordsets, then combines these 'end-to-end' to produce the final one. If there are more than two **SELECT** statements, we just list them with the **UNION** keyword in between each one. As an example, we can use the Customer and Contact tables in the **WroxSoft** database to create a single table which contains the name, address and phone number of all our customers and contacts.

Try It Out - Using the UNION Statement

1 Create a new query and, in SQL view, enter the statement:

```
SELECT CustName, Address, Phone
FROM Customer
UNION
SELECT ContactName, ContactAddr, ContactPhone
FROM Contact;
```

2 Try selecting design view - you'll see that this option is disabled. Access cannot translate this statement into Query Builder.

3 Switch to datasheet view to see the results.

Access uses the names of the fields in the first table for the fields in the new recordset. We can change the names or include calculated fields using the **AS** keyword. And, of course, we can control the way records are included from each source recordset by adding **WHERE** and **ORDER BY** clauses to the individual **SELECT** statements.

For example, the following statement changes the name of the fields in the resulting recordset and only includes records from the Contact table where the ContactPhone field is not empty.

```
SELECT CustName AS All_Name, Address AS All_Address, Phone AS All_Phone
FROM Customer
UNION
SELECT ContactName, ContactAddr, ContactPhone
FROM Contact
WHERE NOT(IsNull([ContactPhone]));
```

Using SQL Sub-Queries

When we use a query, we can include an expression to create a calculated field or as a criteria to select records. Access allows us to use an SQL statement within an expression. For example, the following SQL statement calculates the average hourly rate for all the records in our Project table using the SQL aggregate function **Avg**:

```
SELECT Avg([HourlyRate])
FROM [Project];
```

If we wanted to list the projects we worked on where we charged less than average rates, we could use this statement within the criteria - in the **WHERE** part of the SQL statement - enclosing it in parentheses:

```
SELECT Project, Date, HoursWorked, HourlyRate
FROM Project
WHERE HourlyRate < (SELECT Avg(HourlyRate) FROM Project;);
```

Although this technique is not often required, it can be a useful way to get that buried information out of your data. In the Query Builder grid, the SQL sub-query would look like this:

Field:	Project	Date	HoursWorked	HourlyRate	
Table:	Project	Project	Project	Project	
Sort:					
Show:	☑	☑	☑	☑	
Criteria:				<(SELECT Avg(HourlyRate) FROM Project;)	
or:					

FYI   Don't forget that you can always construct an SQL statement in **Query Builder** then copy it to another location. When we created the union query in Chapter 11, we used this method so that we didn't have to create each **SELECT** statement from scratch. We just created a new empty query, switched to SQL view and copied each **SELECT** statement into it, separating them with the **UNION** keyword. In the same way, you can create your sub-query then copy the SQL statement it produces into **Query Builder**, or directly into another SQL statement.

Pass-Through and Data Definition Queries

Access also includes **pass-through** and **data definition queries**, which are used when you are manipulating data in tables that are outside the Access environment. Access can attach to several types of non-native database tables, as you'll see in the next chapter, but if you are working with data stored on a non PC-based system, you'll generally have to communicate with it by sending SQL statements directly to it, allowing them to manipulate the tables and return the results to you. When you execute the query, Access simply 'passes through' the SQL statement to the other system.

A pass-through or data definition query is created in a text window by selecting SQL Specific from the Query menu and then selecting Pass-Through or Data Definition. You need to know how the system you want to communicate with works and then enter the statement using the correct syntax for it. A pass-through query is used to retrieve data or modify the contents of the tables and a data definition query is used to create or modify the structure of tables.

Summary

In this chapter, we've attempted to unravel the mysteries of SQL (Structured Query Language) and show you how it's used to gain the maximum benefits from your data. Remember, in most cases, you don't actually have to know SQL - you can always build the common statements using the Query Builder grid. However, it's worth being aware of how it works and what extra power it can offer. In fact, our **WroxSoft** application depends on one type of query that you can't create in Query Builder - the union query.

We looked at how to **SELECT** information from our tables, then we learned how to alter the information within the tables, via the **SELECT INTO**, **INSERT**, **UPDATE** and **DELETE** statements. We also looked at more specific SQL statements which help summarize and present the information more effectively. It might seem like an uphill struggle, but once you understand how SQL fits together, you can often use this knowledge to improve the performance of your application, or just solve the problem that ordinary queries just can't reach.

You have learned:

> ▶ Why it's worth learning SQL.
>
> ▶ How to use all the common SQL statements.
>
> ▶ How you can use calculated fields in a statement.
>
> ▶ How SQL statements handle parameters.
>
> ▶ How to create the inner and outer joins within an SQL statement.
>
> ▶ How to use the **TRANSFORM** and **UNION** statements and SQL subqueries.

Hopefully, you will have realized that SQL is really not that difficult. In fact, it is often quicker and easier to type in an SQL statement than create the query in the Query Grid. Remember, if you would like to find out more about SQL, have a look at *Instant SQL* from Wrox.

Now that we've considered some of the inner workings of Access, it's time to look at how we get information out of Access into other applications. This is the subject of the next chapter.

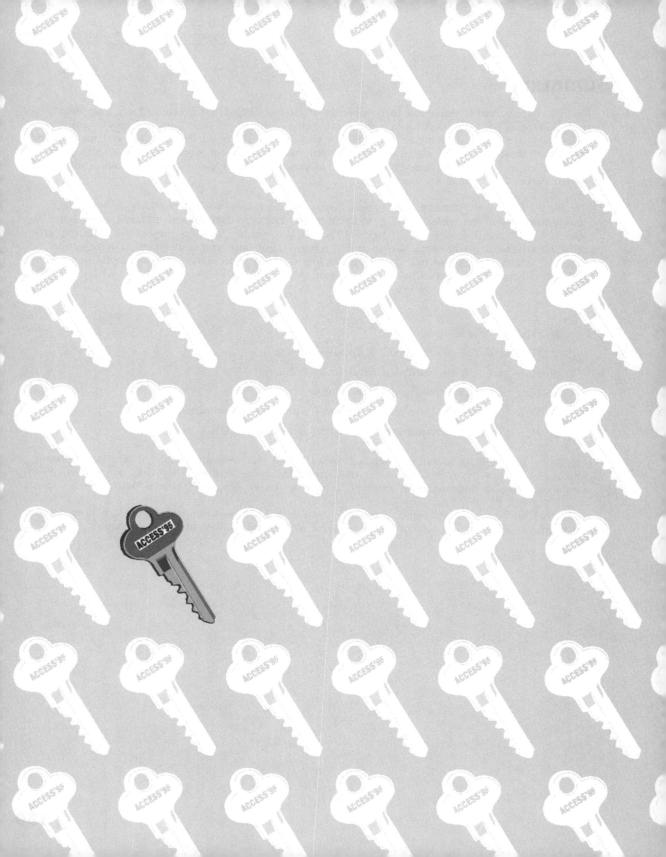

Importing And Exporting Data

When we used Access for the first time, the first thing we did was import data from our **Accounts** spreadsheet in Excel and use it to create a new database. However, you may not always be working with Microsoft products, or have the data that you wish to import into Access in the correct format. Luckily, Access has enough import options to cope with this.

In this chapter we'll look at the different types of data that Access can import and see how you can convert existing data so that Access can read it. We'll also examine how the different output formats can be used to create files that are ready to load into other applications.

We'll also look at two of today's buzz-words. First, **data warehousing** - one of the hottest new topics in the commercial world. We'll see what it is and how Access can contribute towards it. Second, we'll look at Access's **database replication** feature, which allows you to have several copies of the data available to users, yet still be able to merge them into one compound database containing all the changes to the data.

The topics we'll consider are:

- Importing data from other applications.
- Linking tables.
- Database replication.
- Exporting data to other applications.
- Data warehousing.

Importing Data from Other Applications

We started off this book by importing an Excel spreadsheet file into Access. However, if you have been keeping your customer file in a word-processor, or a contact manager like Lotus Organizer, you probably won't be able to create a spreadsheet-format file to import into Access. Similarly, if you're using another database program such as dBase or FileMaker, you may find that the file export formats are limited. And, it's most unlikely that any of these will include Microsoft Access as an option. You shouldn't worry though, because Access is capable of dealing with this.

The Need for Importing

It's not that often that you have the chance to develop a database application completely from scratch. Often when you come to use a database, it's because the application that is currently being used to store the data is no longer efficient. You will then have to decide on the system that will be the base of your new application and then design the application using this system so that it meets the needs of the users. You also have to allow for it to be developed and expanded - to grow as the needs of the users most definitely will. Having settled on Access, we went through these steps in the previous chapters, building an application which would meet all of our needs.

Once you've got the application working, the next step is to get the existing data into it. We started by importing our **Accounts** spreadsheet and used this as the foundation for our application. But often things aren't this simple - you may have data stored on a main-frame computer. Alternatively, it may be in an application package that's based on MS-DOS rather than Windows, or even on another operating system altogether. In these cases, it can be difficult to transfer the data and, in some cases, companies with huge amounts of stored information are put off changing their database application altogether simply by the task that converting the data may involve.

Access can import four categories of data - Spreadsheets, Databases, Text and SQL. Any application that you might have been using previously will be able to create a one of these file types almost without exception. We'll look at each in turn.

The Import Options Dialog

All of the Access import operations start with the <u>G</u>et External Data command on the <u>F</u>ile menu. Select <u>I</u>mport to open the Import dialog.

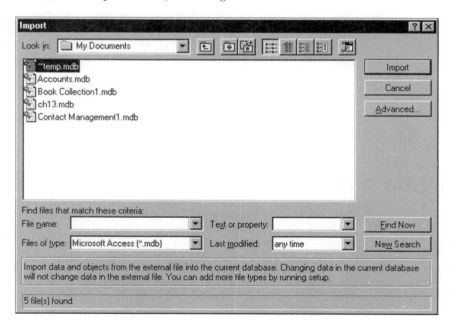

At the bottom of the window is a section where you specify the type of files you wish to show in the list. There are four main sections which you can use:

 You can tell Access the name of the file (including wild-cards, such as proj* to show all files which start with proj).

 You can enter some text or properties so that it only shows files that contain this text or match these properties.

 You can tell Access to only show files which have been modified during the last day, week, month, or at any time.

 You can select the type of file you want to import.

To see the list of data formats that Access supports directly, open the drop-down list in the Files of type: box.

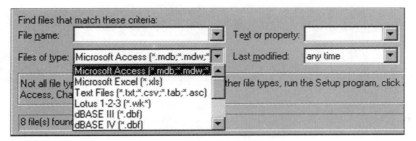

If you scroll down the list, you'll see that the import filter supports four types of database file: Access (**.mdb**), Microsoft's other database Foxpro (also ***.mdb**), dBase (versions III, IV and V) and Borland/Novell's Paradox (**.db**).

For spreadsheets there's the Excel format (**.xls**) plus the generic Lotus 1-2-3 (**.wk***) format, supporting **.wk3** and **.wk4** files as well as the original **.wks**. Text files of various types are one single option on the list - Access supports **.txt**, **.csv**, **.tab** and **.asc** files, though in the case of a text file, the extension may not always define the file format as neatly as this. You'll see more on this later.

Finally, there's the ODBC Databases option at the foot of the list, which allows Access to obtain data from any system which supports the ODBC (Open Database Connectivity) model. This allows you to import data from main-frame and mini-computers, or other mainline database applications that support this standard. We'll briefly touch upon this later on.

If you have a great many files in the list, you can use Windows Advanced Find dialog to narrow the search. Click the Advanced button and Access shows the Advanced Find dialog.

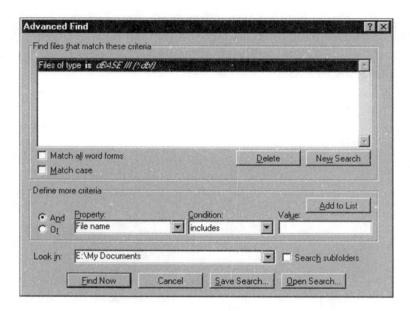

This is used in several places in Windows and allows you to specify a set of search criteria, then save this set as a 'Search' type. If you then want to repeat it, you can use the Open Search button to load the criteria again. This option is only likely to be useful where you are importing files from a large network based system, where there are many hundreds of available files to choose from.

So having selected the file, you click the Import button to start the import. From here on, the way that the process works depends on the type of file you have selected. We'll work through the different options that are available to you.

Importing from Other Databases

If you're importing to Access from another PC-based package, you should have no problems. The most common type of database file is the **.dbf** format and this is used by a great many applications, from simple database programs and contact managers to the full-featured Ashton Tate/Borland dBase and other generic *x*Base programs. This is one of the formats supported by Lotus Organizer for example, and if the application you're exporting data to Access with offers it, you should use this rather than a text file option. We've included a file on the disk called **Dbasefmt.dbf** which contains a few sample address records so that you can see it in action in the next example.

Try It Out - Importing a File from Lotus Organizer

1 Open the **Wroxsoft** database, holding down *Shift* so that the Database window appears. Open the File menu and select Get External Data, then select Import from the submenu that appears. When the Import dialog opens, we need to select the particular format we want. In our case, we are using dBase format, so select dBase III.

If there are a number of subformats and you are not sure which one to use, select the lowest. Formats are generally backwards compatible so you shouldn't have problems if you select the earliest format. The original file is left intact so you can always delete the imported table from the Access **Database** window and try again with another format if the import does not produce the results you want.

2 Select the file **Dbasefmt.dbf** from the **BegAcc95** folder, then click the Import button. The database file is imported and a message shows the success or failure of the import process.

3 Select Close to close the Import dialog and go to the Database window. Access has created a new table Dbasefmt which contains the three records we've just imported. Click the Open button to see them.

NAME	ADDRESS	TOWN	COUNTY	ZIPCODE	PHONE
Le Bistro	Rue Francais	Vancouver	WA	41322	206-133-8294
J.R.Higgins	The Market	Green Bay	WI	61733	414-831-8812
James Builders	2131,New Stree	Phoenix	AZ	78034	602-281-3318

Record: 1 of 3

4 Once you've finished looking, close down this window, highlight Dbasefmt and press the *Delete* key. When Access asks you if you're sure, select Yes. We need to delete this file, as we're going to be using it later in the database in a different format.

How It Works

A dBase format file contains all the information about the table(s) it contains - you can see that the field names are created automatically and, if you switch to design view, you'll see that Access has set them all as Text data types - as defined in the original table. However, there's no primary key or indexes. So, although you have all the data, you still need to change the properties for the new table to make it behave the way you want in Access. When you import any type of data from outside Access, you must be prepared to put some work into setting up the new tables before you can start building an application around them.

Importing Data from Another Access Database

There is one exception, however - you can import tables from another Access database and the newly imported table will retain all the properties set in the original database. We'll import tables from our own application in this example. You might want to do this is if you wanted to alter the same table, so that users without permissions couldn't see all of the information contained in one version of the table, while users who were allowed would have access to a full version of the table. There are also other ways of achieving this too, but we will discuss these in chapter 16.

Close the table and open the Import dialog again (using Get External Data from the File menu and selecting Import) and select Access Databases (*.mdb) from the list of file types. Move to the **BegAcc95** folder and select the **WroxSoft** application. Then click Import.

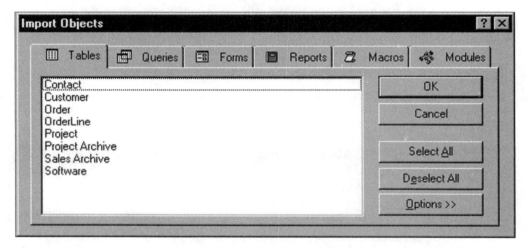

Access lists all the objects in the source database, using a window similar to the normal Database window. You can move through the lists selecting the objects you want to import, or else use the Select All and Deselect All buttons. Click the Options >> button to open another section of the window. Here you can tell Access to also import, any Relations that exist between the tables you import, and include any Custom Toolbars that are in the other database. If you want to import tables, but not include the data in them, you can also tell Access to import the Definition only. Finally, you can import the Queries either as they exist in the source database, or as tables that contain the results of running the queries.

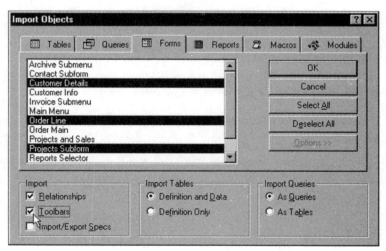

Once you've selected all the items you want, just click OK. Access starts the import process. Once it's complete, you'll see the new items listed in the Database window.

Importing Data from Spreadsheets

In Chapter 2, we imported the original **Accounts** spreadsheet from a Microsoft Excel file into Access. When we import a spreadsheet file, Access starts the Spreadsheet Import Wizard which takes us through the different steps of importing the data. The options you see in the wizard depend on the type of spreadsheet you're working with. However, you'll generally be able to specify which parts of the spreadsheet you want and how they're to be imported. This includes selecting which sheets you want to include or, if there are named ranges in the spreadsheet, which ranges you want. The wizard continuously shows the data as it will be imported from the spreadsheet so that you can see the result of your selections. We'll import part of the **Accounts.xls** spreadsheet that we imported in full in Chapter 2.

Try It Out - Importing Named Ranges or Parts of a Spreadsheet

1 Select the File menu, then the Get External Data option and then the Import option from the submenu. In the Import dialog that opens, change the Files of Type box to Microsoft Excel (*.xls). Select the **Accounts.xls** spreadsheet from the **BegAcc95** folder and click Import.

2 Import Spreadsheet Wizard opens up a new dialog. Click on the Show Named Ranges option and select the Original$_FilterDatabase range. This is the name that Excel has given to the area of the spreadsheet containing the original projects data.

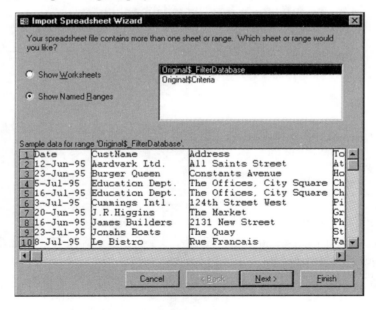

 FYI Some of the early spreadsheet formats, such as **.wks**, do not allow multiple pages in a spreadsheet, and some do not allow named ranges. In these cases, you wouldn't be offered this option.

3 Click on the Next> button. Now we need to tell the wizard that the first row contains the names to be used for the fields in the new table. Click on the First Row Contains Column Headings box so that it is ticked.

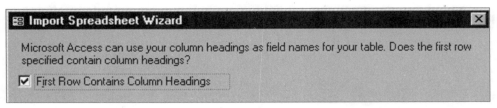

 Generally, when you import a spreadsheet, you find that the first row is used to identify the columns. If it has titles or the data is organized in columns rather than rows, then you may not have this option. In fact, you may have to do some work on the original file before you can import it into Access - removing any blank rows and adding column names - otherwise the results may be useless once imported.

4 Click the Next> button. The next screen in the wizard allows you do some of the ground-work on the new table before you actually import the data. Click on the gray selector above the Address column to select it and click on the Do not Import field box, so that it is ticked. This will omit the Address column from the spreadsheet when we create the new table.

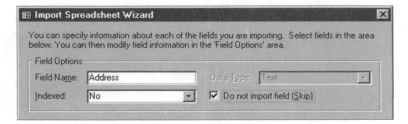

5 Click the Next> button. Now we can allow Access to create the primary key for the new table for us. We have a choice of either selecting which field to use or letting Access create a new field based on the AutoNumber data type. We want Access to add a primary key as we have no column with unique names that could easily be used as a primary key. Click on the Let Access add primary key option.

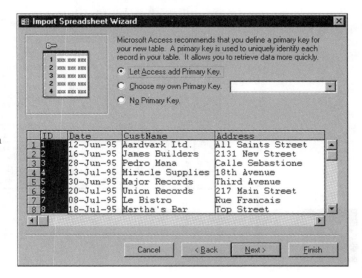

6 Click the Next> button and on the last screen the wizard confirms the name for the new table. Don't change anything - just click on Finish. The wizard then creates our new table. Afterwards, you can open it from the Database window to view the results.

ID	Date	CustName	Town	State	ZipCode	Phone	Fax	Project
1	12/06/95	Aardvark Ltd.	Athens	OH	39812	216-376-1298	216-376-8811	Accounts System
2	16/06/95	James Builders	Phoenix	AZ	78034	602-281-3318	602-281-7318	Accounts System
3	28/06/95	Pedro Mana	St. Paul	MN	65109	612-401-1350	612-401-1388	Accounts System
4	13/07/95	Miracle Supplie	Oakland	CA	10593	415-671-6633	415-671-8833	Accounts System
5	30/06/95	Major Records	Stocksville	FL	10015	305-711-7851	305-711-8531	Catalogue System
6	20/07/95	Union Records	Tampa	FL	51267	813-167-3520	813-167-3521	Catalogue System
7	08/07/95	Le Bistro	Vancouver	WA	41322	206-133-8294	206-133-8295	Menu Generator
8	18/07/95	Martha's Bar	Clarksville	NY	54876			Menu Generator

Original$_FilterDatabase : Table — Record: 1 of 16

So when we import a spreadsheet file, especially if it's been created by a modern spreadsheet application, we can select which rows and columns we want using the named ranges or sheet names and then select which columns we want to omit from that range.

Importing Text and ASCII Data

Of all the types of file you may wish to import, the ones most likely to cause problems are text or ASCII files. The reason is simple - all the other types already have some kind of structure imposed on them. Text can be completely unstructured and so we have to supply a lot more information about how Access is to interpret it when it is imported into a table.

The Access import methods support two basic types of text file: Delimited Text and Fixed Width Text. You need to match the type to the file that your application produces. In most cases, Delimited Text is the best choice - this has each item of data separated (delimited) by a special character and each row of items separated by a different character, usually *Return*. Access will accept almost any character as the field marker - you simply set up the import options to match the file. In the case of Fixed Width Text, which is generally the type of file produced by mainframe and traditional mini-computers, each row of items contains the same number of characters and we then have to tell Access where in the row each field starts and how many characters belong to each one.

Importing text or ASCII data is done through the Import dialog, by selecting the Text Files option as the Type of File. We've included three different types in the samples on the disk. All have the file extension of **.txt**, so you can see that you have to be aware of the contents before you can import the data from them successfully. The files are:

▶ **Tabdeltx.txt**   Tab delimited text file

▶ **Csvdeltx.txt**   Comma separated values (comma delimited) text file

▶ **Fixwidtx.txt**   Fixed width text file

FYI   You can see that, when you are dealing with importing and exporting data, you often need to know about file extensions. If you cannot see the file extensions (Windows 95 can hide them), turn them on by opening **My Computer** or **Explorer** and selecting **Options** from the **View** menu. Then select the **View** tab and turn off the **Hide MS-DOS file extensions...** option.

Tab Delimited Text Files

If you load the file **Tabdeltx.txt** from the **BegAcc95** folder into Microsoft Word, you will find a simple list of addresses. You'll see that each item is separated by a *Tab* character and the end of the row is marked by *Return*. The tab positions have been changed to space the entries out neatly. We have included a header row which gives the name of each of our 'fields' - this will be useful when we import the table.

Name	Address	Town	State	ZIP	Phone
James Builders	2131 New Street	Phoenix	AZ	78034	602-281-3318
Le Bistro	Rue Francais	Vancouver	WA	41322	206-133-8294
J.R.Higgins	The Market	Green Bay	WI	61733	414-831-8812

If this is how you have stored data in your word-processor, you will have no problems importing it into Access. Remember, though, that you must save it in text form, not in your word-processor's own format. Access can only import the file if it is in plain text form (a word-processor often includes lots of other information in its own proprietary file format, such as the page set-up and other formatting commands).

Comma Separated Values Files

It's also possible that, when you created the original file, you typed in the text as single lines, separating each item with a comma. This is referred to as CSV (Comma Separated Values) format and causes a slight problem. The delimiting character is a comma, but if you've included commas in the entries themselves as well, Access will become confused when it tries to break up the lines into separate fields.

```
Name,Address,Town,State,ZIP,Phone
James Builders,2131, NewStreet,Phoenix,AZ,78034,602-281-3318
Le Bistro,Rue Francais,Vancouver,WA,41322,206-133-8294
J.R.Higgins,The Market, Green Bay,WI,61733,4414-831-8812
```

For example, the first address row in the figure contains a comma in the address as well as the comma which marks the end of that 'field'. Before we can import this file, we must remove any 'extra' commas, or use a different field separator. You may be forced into editing the file quite substantially first. This example can be found in the file **Csvdeltx.txt**.

Fixed Width Files

The third file is a Fixed Width File. This type is rarely used in Windows applications since the advent of proportional fonts, which means that items do not line up correctly on screen even if padded with equal numbers of spaces. However, it can still be found in MS-DOS applications and main-frame computer files, where fixed fonts are the norm. Each line contains the same number of characters, and each 'field' starts in the same place as the previous line. For example, the figure below shows the file **Fixwidtx.txt** open in Microsoft Word after the font has been converted to Courier (which is a fixed width font). The gaps between the columns are spaces - there is an equal number of characters in each column.

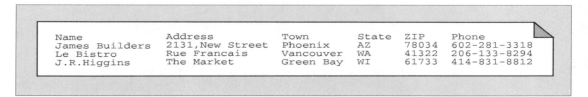

```
Name              Address          Town        State  ZIP    Phone
James Builders    2131,New Street  Phoenix     AZ     78034  602-281-3318
Le Bistro         Rue Francais     Vancouver   WA     41322  206-133-8294
J.R.Higgins       The Market       Green Bay   WI     61733  414-831-8812
```

It doesn't matter what characters you have included in this type of file as Access simply uses information on the position of each field in the line to extract the data.

We'll now walk through importing a Tab Delimited file and see how the other file types are handled afterwards. We'll be using another of Access's wizards to do this and we'll also show you how you can make future imports of the same type of data easier.

Try It Out - Importing a Tab Delimited Text File

1 In the **Wroxsoft** database, select Get External Data from the File menu and click Import to open the Import dialog. Move to the **BegAcc95** folder.

2 Select Text Files for the Files of type, then select the file **Tabdeltx.txt** and click Import. Access starts Text Import Wizard.

3 Access has decided that the file is Delimited and it's correct. However, you could change this to Fixed Width. You can see the contents of the file - the *Tab* characters are displayed as thick bars. Access uses a fixed width font for the list, so if your text was in Fixed Width format, you would see this quite clearly. Ensure the Delimited option is selected.

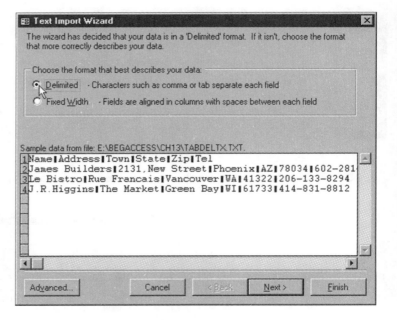

4 Click Next and now we can see how Access has interpreted the file. It's decided that the delimiting character is *Tab*. Like the Spreadsheet Import Wizard, it asks if the first row contains the names to be used for the fields in the new table. Ours does, so turn this option on. It also allows us to specify a Text Qualifier. Set this to " (a quotation mark).

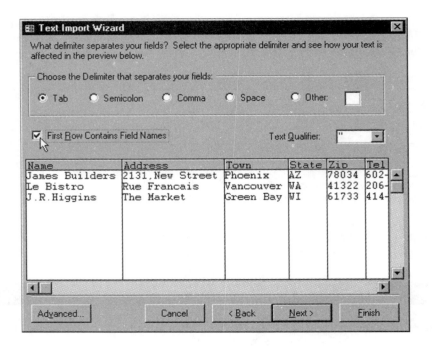

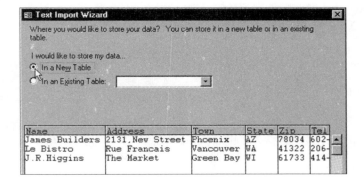

FYI Some text files created by other applications include quotation marks to differentiate text from numbers. For instance, a file exported as **Text** from a database or spreadsheet may look like this:

```
"Bracket", "Green",7.5,"Steel",210,418,"Smith & Co."
```

To translate this, you need to tell Access that the **Text Qualifier** is a quotation mark, otherwise when you import it, the fields will still contain the quotation marks themselves. The values which include quotation marks are then imported into **Text**-type fields and those that don't are imported into **Number**-type fields.

5 Click Next again. Now we have to tell Access if we want to add the data to an existing table, or create a new one. Select In a New Table.

6 Click Next. This screen is again much like the Spreadsheet Import Wizard. We can change the Name of each of the fields in the new table and specify the type of Index and the Data Type for the field. We can also elect to skip some of the fields so that they are not imported. Change the Name: for the first field to CustName and set the Indexed: entry to Yes (No Duplicates).

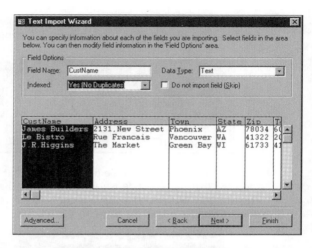

7 Click Next again. Now we set the primary key for the table. As we've set the index for CustName to Yes (No Duplicates), we can use this as the primary key. Select Choose my own Primary Key and then select CustName from the list.

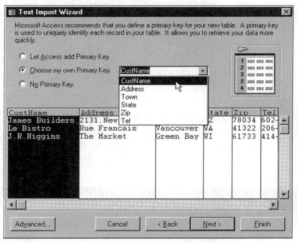

8 Click Next. Finally, we need to name the new table. Enter New Customer Table and click Finish.

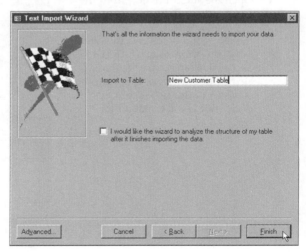

9 Access creates the new table and sets the properties we've specified, displaying a message to confirm that the data has been imported. Open and view the table from the Database window.

	CustName	Address	Town	State	Zip	Tel
▶	J.R.Higgins	The Market	Green Bay	WI	61733	414-831-8812
	James Builders	2131,New Stree	Phoenix	AZ	78034	602-281-3318
	Le Bistro	Rue Francais	Vancouver	WA	41322	206-133-8294
*						

New Customer Table : Table

Record: 14 ◀ 1 ▶ ▶I ▶* of 3

10 Switch to design view to see the properties that Access has set for each field. You can see that it's decided that the ZipCode is a number rather than a text field. We didn't specify the field type in Text Import Wizard, so it made a guess based on the contents of the file. It's also set the primary key to CustName, as we chose in the wizard.

New Customer Table : Table

Field Name	Data Type	Description
⑧▶ CustName	Text	
Address	Text	
Town	Text	
State	Text	
Zip	Number	
Tel	Text	

The Text Import Wizard windows also contain an **Advanced** button which opens another dialog. Here we can specify all the options we set in the wizard screens in one go. This can not only save time, but it also allows us to save the set of options for future use. If you have to import similar data regularly, this can be a real time-saver. We'll look at this in the next example.

Try It Out - Importing a Comma Delimited (CSV) Text File

1 Open the Import dialog from the **G**et External Data option on the **F**ile menu. Select Text Files from the list of file types and this time select the **Csvdeltx.txt** file and click Import. Access starts Text Import Wizard, showing the contents of the file. Again, it's decided it is a Delimited file.

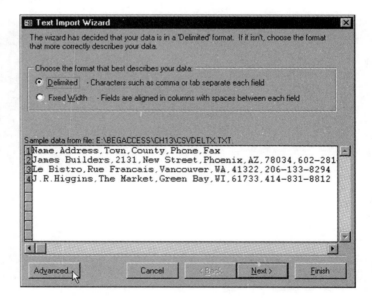

2 Click the Ad_vanced button to open another dialog. This has the title CSVDELTX Import Specification, and here we can specify all the options that Text Import Wizard uses. Set the File Format to Delimited and leave the Field Delimiter as a comma. Set the Text Qualifier to ".

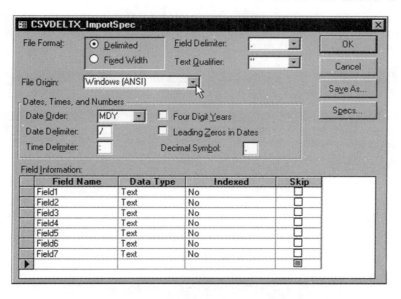

> **FYI** The **File Origin:** box tells Access whether the file was created in Windows, DOS or OS/2, or on a Macintosh computer, and changes the way that Access interprets other characters which may appear in the file. We can also change the format of dates, times and numbers to match the file we are using.

3 The lower part of the window lists the fields and shows the names, data type and indexed properties that will be used for each one. Set the options for the field names, data types and indexes to those shown in the next screenshot, and leave out the extra field (Field7) by clicking on the box under the Skip column. We'll see where this came from when we create the table.

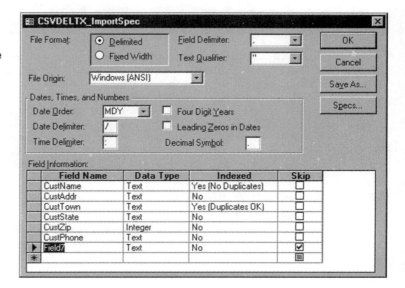

4 Now we'll save the specification for use again. Select Sa**v**e As... and click OK to save the import specification without changing the name suggested by Access.

5 Now click OK to return to Text Import Wizard and click **F**inish. We get a message to show the import is complete. But if you open the table from the Database window, you'll see why we got that extra field. Look back at the original file - it contained an extra comma in the row for James Builders and this has caused Access to break the address over two fields.

	ID	CustName	CustAddr	CustTown	CustState	CustZip	CustPhone
	1	Name	Address	Town	County		Fax
▶	2	James Builders	2131	New Street	Phoenix		78034
	3	Le Bistro	Rue Francais	Vancouver	WA		206-133-8294
	4	J.R.Higgins	The Market	Green Bay	WI		414-831-8812

CSVDELTX : Table — Record: 2 of 4

6 In the Database window is another new table called CSVDELTX_ImportErrors. Open this as well, and you can see that Access has created a list of the problems it encountered while trying to import the file. Because the fields had been shifted, we were trying to enter Text into the Number type ZipCode field. Whenever Access finds errors occurring during an import operation, it creates this table for you, so that you can see what went wrong.

Error	Field	Row
Type Conversion Failure	CustZip	1
Type Conversion Failure	CustZip	2
Type Conversion Failure	CustZip	3
Type Conversion Failure	CustZip	4

CSVDELTX_ImportErrors : Table — Record: 1 of 4

So you must be careful how you import comma delimited text like this. If we had used Text Import Wizard normally, rather than with an Import Specification, we would have seen this problem in the column view of the data that the wizard provides.

However, import specifications can be useful. If you want to try importing the **Csvdeltx.txt** file again, you can edit it in a word processor to remove the extra comma and save it back in text form. Then just open the Ad**v**anced dialog, click the S**p**ecs... button to show the existing saved specifications and select the CSVDELTX_ImportSpec. Access will set all the import options using this specification and you then just click OK and **F**inish to import the file.

Importing a Fixed Width Text File

Before we leave text files, we'll take a quick look at a Fixed Width text file. Open the Import dialog again, but this time select the **Fixwidtx.txt** file. Once Text Import Wizard has started, you'll see it has decided that it's a Fixed Width file, and this shows quite clearly in the view of the contents at the bottom of the window.

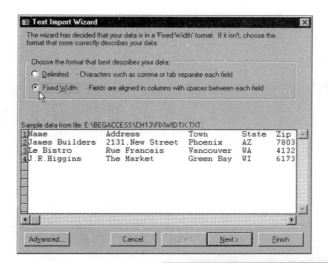

Click the **Next** button and Access shows where it thinks the beginning of each field is by placing 'break' lines in the lower window. You'll see that it numbers each column so that the text in the **Address** field, for instance, starts in column 16 and ends in column 33. In our file it's got it right, but if it doesn't you can click on a line and drag it to the correct place using the mouse.

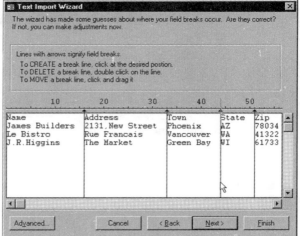

Now we go through the same process as with the other text files. Click **Next** and tell Access whether to add the data to an existing table or create a new one, and then go through the options for setting the new field names, indexes and primary key. You'll notice that Access doesn't use the first row for the field names in this case - you have to enter them yourself.

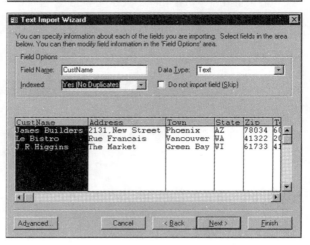

The last screen in the wizard is where we enter the name of the table we are importing to. Enter the name, but don't press Finish just yet. We have now created the specification to import this file and can save it, like we did with the comma delimited file earlier. Click the Advanced button to open the import specifications dialog.

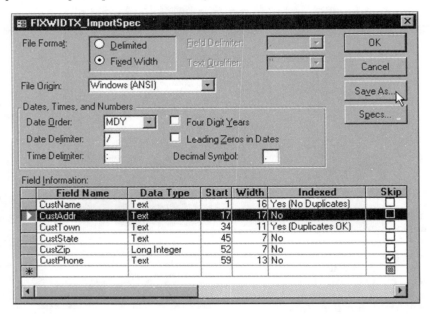

This is different from the comma separated values specification dialog. It still has the option at the top to select the file type, plus the options to tell Access whether the file was created in Windows, DOS or OS/2, or on a Macintosh computer and the meaning of the various date and number characters in the file, but the lower section also shows where in each row the fields start and how long they are. So Access can interpret the rows in the file and break them up in the correct places as it places the values in the fields of the new table. To save this specification, click the Save As.. button, then click OK and Finish to import the file.

You'll also see that the ZipCode field is specified as being of type Long Integer in the specification. There's a slight problem with this - unlike the other text formats, Access doesn't offer us the option to use the first row as field names with a fixed width file, yet that's exactly what they are. So if we carry out the import, we'll get an error because Access will try and place the value ZipCode from the first row into the Long Integer type field.

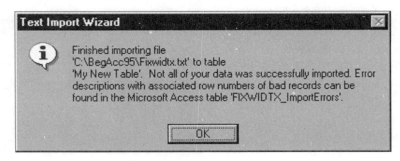

This is something that you should always be wary of when you are importing fixed width text files.

Using ODBC and SQL to Import Data

All the methods we've used so far have depended on routines within Access itself to translate the data from a file on disk into a table in our database. But if Access does not have a 'filter' to do this, we can still import the data from another source if it supports the **Open Database Connectivity** (ODBC) standard. This is a standard created by Microsoft to allow a database to be used, for example, on Access at home and then on a SQL Server (or any other database that supports ODBC) at work. This is made possible by a layer of drivers in between Access and the other database system. In fact, it even allows a user to import data from objects that have a filter using ODBC instead of the normal Import Wizard.

When you import data from an SQL Server database, you use a different technique to using filters. It is not so much a filter as a method - Access uses an SQL query and ODBC to transfer information from the data source into its tables. We do not intend to cover this here, as it's more applicable to networked situations where you can download data from a main-frame or other data server machine. It's also far too complex to cover in a short section. However, it is a powerful way to access data on other machines, and can be used to overcome the limitations of a mainframe's information retrieval by importing data and then analyzing it in Access. If you want to learn more about ODBC, look out for the forthcoming *'Revolutionary Guide to Access 95'* from Wrox Press.

Linking Tables

So far, we've been looking at ways of importing a copy of the original data into Access, so that it becomes part of our database. This is fine if we no longer intend to maintain it in the old application. If we did, we would be faced with the problem of trying to keep two different copies synchronized - changes to one must be copied into the other. Generally, we import data like this as a once-only task and abandon the original application once the new system is up and running.

However, there are cases where you want to be able to read or manipulate data which is not part of the database. Perhaps you're compiling a special report and need information stored on another computer or in another application. Importing and converting the data is fine if you only need to do it occasionally, but it becomes a headache if it's a regular job. And, of course, if you change the contents, they no longer match the data in the original application.

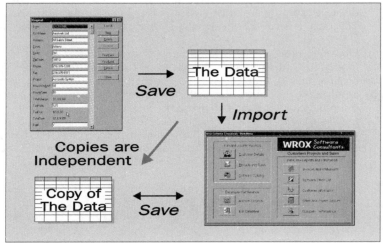

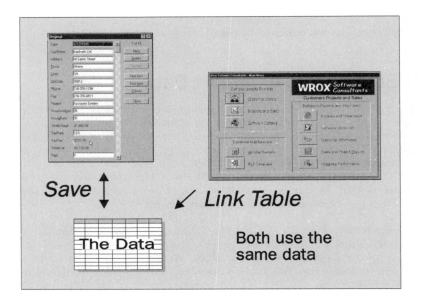

Save ↕

✓ Link Table

The Data

Both use the
same data

One of the major advances in modern databases is the ability to **link** data from another source. The tables that are part of your database are called **native** tables. By linking data, we can use it in almost exactly the same ways as we do our native tables. The great advantage is that any changes we make are made to the original data rather than to a copy inside Access. So when the original application that created the data reads it again, it contains all the changes.

Updating Linked Tables

Access can link to data in any of the applications that it supports for importing data - the database types FoxPro, dBase and Paradox, Lotus 1-2-3 and Excel spreadsheets, and even some Text file types. And, of course, you can link data that is stored in other Access databases.

You can read data in a linked data source and update it from Access - add new records or delete existing ones. Then, when the original application uses the table, it sees the updated data. The data is shared between the source application and Access.

However, working with linked data sources does impose some limits. For instance, we can freely modify the structure of a linked Access table in design view, but the changes don't affect the original table - only the way the current database 'sees' it. If you change the structure in the application that owns the table, you may find that Access no longer works correctly. For example, changing a field name or data type can cause your Access query to give an error message because it still expects the original field names and types. You then need to re-establish the link (Access offers you the option to update the link automatically, whenever you open a linked table and you can select Yes or No) and change the Access objects to use the new format.

A similar problem arises if you move the original data to a different folder - Access will not be able to find the tables when it loads. Again, you get an error message and have to re-establish the link. We'll look at how to create a link to an external table and then see what happens when we move it.

Try It Out - Linking a dBase Table to Access

1 In **WroxSoft**, close all windows and click the Database Window button.

2 Select Get External Data from the File menu and click Link Tables. Access opens the Link dialog - this is similar to the Import dialog we used earlier, except that we now have a Link button rather than an Import button.

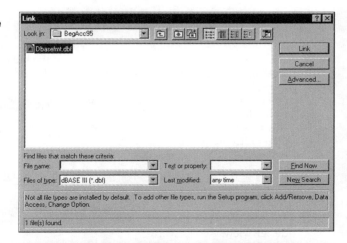

3 Change to your **BegAcc95** folder and change the Files of type: box to dBaseIII (*.dbf). Select the sample file **Dbasefmt.dbf** and click the Link button. Access opens the Select Index Files dialog.

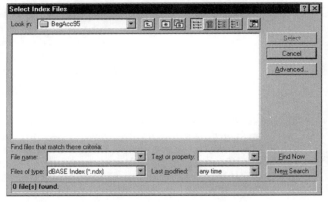

4 The dBase file format uses separate index files stored on disk, rather than including them in the database file like Access. We don't have an index for the sample table, so just click Cancel - we don't want Access to use one. If you have an index file, you can select it here and click Select.

5 Access then links the table and displays a message to show the results.

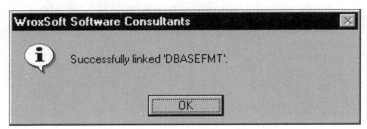

6 Click OK in the dialog box and then click the Close button to close the Import dialog. Look at the Tables list in the Database window. Access has added the table to the list and uses a special icon to show it as a linked table.

7 Click the Open button to see the contents of the table. Remember, you are looking at the contents of the original dBase file on the disk, not data that is stored in Access. But you can update the table, delete rows and add new ones, just as though it *were* part of Access.

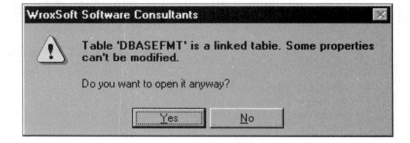

8 Now switch the table to design view. Access warns you that some of the properties of the table cannot be modified.

> **WroxSoft Software Consultants**
>
> ⚠ Table 'DBASEFMT' is a linked table. Some properties can't be modified.
>
> Do you want to open it anyway?
>
> [Yes]   [No]

9 Select Yes and then edit the name of one of the fields - change NAME to CUSTNAME for example. Then switch back to datasheet view. Access prompts you to save the table - click Yes. However, you are now warned that you can't make the change to the field name - you can't change the design of linked dBase tables. Click Yes to continue to datasheet view where you'll get a list of errors in the CUSTNAME column. You don't have to worry, though, as the changes won't have been saved.

10 Now we'll see what happens if we move the table. Make sure you have closed the table in Access and then open My Computer or Explorer and move to the folder where the sample files are stored. Select the **Dbasefmt.dbf** file and select Cut from the Edit menu (or press *Ctrl-X*). Change to a different folder and select Paste from the Edit menu (or press *Ctrl-V*).

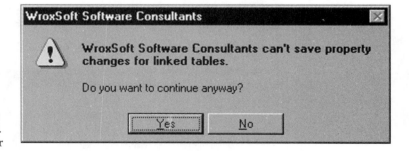

> **WroxSoft Software Consultants**
>
> ⚠ WroxSoft Software Consultants can't save property changes for linked tables.
>
> Do you want to continue anyway?
>
> [Yes]   [No]

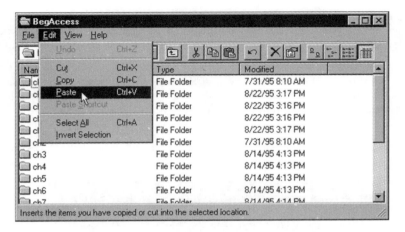

11 Go back to Access and open the table again by selecting it in the Database window and clicking Open. Access can't find the table and displays a warning message.

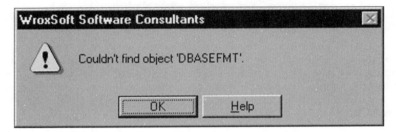

12 Click OK. Select Add-ins from the Tools menu and click Linked Table Manager.

 If **Linked Table Manager** isn't available, then you haven't installed all of the available components of Access. To install it you'll need to run the **Setup** program again. Select the **Add/Remove** components option, chose the **Select All** button and click **Continue** to add the missing components.

13 Access opens the Linked Table Manager window. This contains a list of all the tables currently linked to our database - at the moment this is just the DBASEFMT table. It shows the folder that the file should be in - but of course we've moved it.

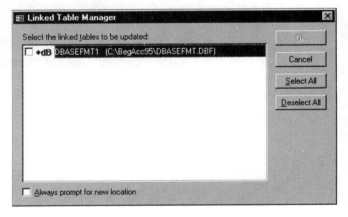

14 We need to update the link. Tick the checkbox for the DBASEFMT table and click OK. Access checks to see if there is a problem with the link, and discovers that the table is no longer where it used to be. It then opens the normal file selector window so that we can select the new location.

 FYI We can use the checkbox at the bottom of the window to force Access to prompt for the new folder for all the linked tables if there are several. This allows you to use tables from different folders. We don't need to do this, so leave it unchecked.

15 Change to the folder where you placed the table, select it, and click Open. Access refreshes the link and displays a message. The table has been successfully re-linked and will work as before.

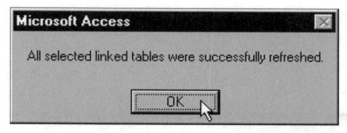

Linked tables are a useful tool if you have to work with data from a different application, but need to use it in the original application as well. By linking the data to Access, both applications always have the current data. However, the overhead you place on Access when it has to convert data from the foreign format can slow the application down. And, of course, if the other application is on a different machine, and you are accessing it over a network, this can slow the process down even more.

Splitting a Database into Two Parts

Having seen how Access can link to a foreign table in another application, we should also consider the process of linking to an Access table in a different Access database. You can do this as easily as you did with the dBase file. For example, here we've created a new database and in the Link dialog selected the **WroxSoft** database as the source of our linked tables. The Link Tables dialog opens and we can select the tables we want to link

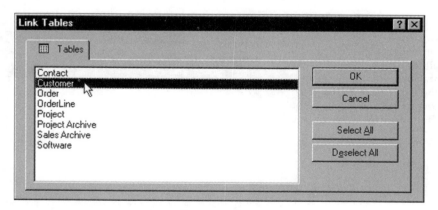

We select the Customer table and click OK. Access links to it and in the Database window it's shown as a linked Access table.

This technique is a very useful one. In fact, there are several occasions where you should seriously consider using linked tables in your database application. Access allows you to split a database into two - one part containing just the tables and the relations between them and the other containing the interface that you see and manipulate the data with.

Doing this means you can change the interface without affecting the data. Because the tables are not stored in the same database as the forms, reports, queries, and macros, you can link the interface part to a different database which contains only test data. Then when you are happy with it, you just use Linked Table Manager to change the links to point to the tables in the 'real' database.

If you are on a network, you can centralize the data by placing it on a server and each user can run their own copy of the interface database. This means that the interfaces for each user don't have to be the same - the Accounts department can use different forms, reports, etc., to the Sales department, but they both manipulate the same tables. And, of course, if you want to prevent a user being able to see a particular table, you just omit the link to that table in their interface database. This gives you extra ways to control the data that is available to each individual user.

When you are developing the application, or if you regularly update the interface, you can distribute the new versions whenever you like without having to import the original data into the new databases. The new version uses the same data in the central database as before.

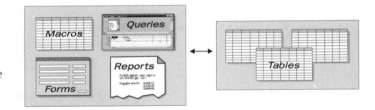

You can split an existing database by hand if you want to. The easiest way to do this is to make a second copy using My Computer or Explorer, then delete all the forms, reports, queries and macros (and modules if you have included any VBA code) from one of them - this becomes the **data** part of the database. Then you delete all the tables from the other one to create the **interface** part of the new application.

You can then open the Interface database and use the Link Tables command (select Get External Data from the File menu and click Link Tables) to link the original tables to the new Interface database. Everything works just as before.

However, before you go and try this, there is an even easier way! Access includes the Database Splitter tool which will automate the entire operation for you. We'll use this tool in the example.

Try It Out - Splitting the WroxSoft Application

Rather than use the original copy of the **WroxSoft** application, you should first make a separate copy. Simply select the file **WroxSoft.mdb** in your samples folder **C:\BegAcc95**. Press *Ctrl-C* then *Ctrl-V* to create a new copy, called **Copy of WroxSoft.mdb**.

1 Open the new **Copy of WroxSoft.mdb** file and close the main menu screen. Click the Database Window button to show the Database window. Select Add-ins from the Tools menu and click Database Splitter.

2 Access displays the introductory screen and warns you that you should make a back-up of the database first. Click Split Database.

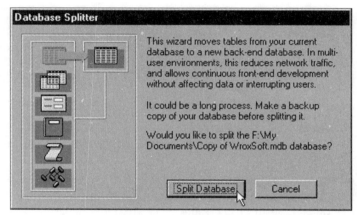

3 Next it asks for the name of the new database. Enter the name WroxSoft Split and click the Split button. Access starts the process, and displays a message when it is complete.

4 Look at the Tables list in the Database window. You can see that all the tables are now shown as Linked - they have been moved out of the current database.

We have deleted the tables that we added in this chapter from the **WroxSoft** database. You might want to do the same to keep things nice and tidy.

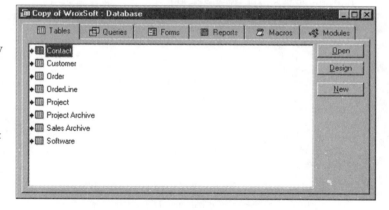

5 Just to make sure that all is working correctly, click the Forms tab in the Database window and Open the Main Menu form to start the application. You can then use it just as before - there is no obvious sign that the database is any different.

6   If you want to see the tables, close the Main Menu form and select <u>O</u>pen Database from the Access <u>F</u>ile menu. You'll see the new database WroxSoft Split that you created with Database Splitter - open it and the tables are shown as native tables in the Database window.

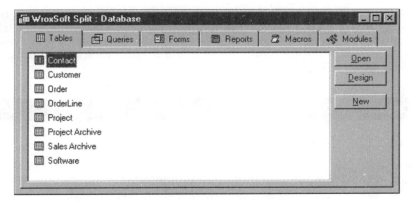

This is a much easier way to split a database into two parts. Your original database becomes the new interface section, and the new one you create just stores the data in the original tables and the relationships between them.

Database Replication

Having now seen how we can split a database into two parts, we have another situation to consider. If all your users are networked together, they will all have access to the most current data in the tables. And as each user modifies the tables, the updates are immediately available to all the other users.

But consider what happens if your users are not networked together - each has a stand-alone copy of the application. If one modifies the data, the others have no way of seeing the changes until you import the new data into their database. Though this situation may seem unlikely in an office, what about when your four sales people leave on Monday morning with a newly updated copy of the customer files on their lap-top computers? As they are all over the country, they are adding and changing information in the database every day. Meanwhile, back at head office, you're doing the same thing. So when they come back in on Friday, you have five different databases - and the task of combining them can be a real headache.

The answer is **replication** - the process of keeping the data in several databases synchronized so that they all reflect the changes made to each one. Access contains a set of tools which allow you to achieve this. The theory is that you convert the original database into a **replica design master database** and then create copies which become the **replica databases**. All these databases are then part of a single **replica set**. When you synchronize them, Access compares the replica databases against the master - updating all of the copies to contain the latest data and prompting you to select how it should reconcile any changes that conflict.

Access can also update any other **objects** in the database. So if a form or report is changed, the new version is automatically placed in the replica databases as well. However, only the design master database can be used to modify any objects other than the data in tables - changes to other objects in the replica databases are not passed through to the master design database or the other replicas in the set.

Access's database replication tools are available from the Tools menu. They use the Windows Briefcase application to synchronize the data, so if you didn't install this when you set up Windows or Access, you'll have to run Setup again.

This example creates several databases as a replica set. To make it easier to see them all, you should make a copy of your original **WroxSoft** sample application in another folder before you start. You may want to delete the copy that you split in the last example to avoid ending up with numerous copies of the database. We've created a folder called Wrox Samples in Windows' My Documents folder and used a copy located there.

Try It Out - Creating a Database Replica Set

In this Try It Out, we are using a copy of the **Wroxsoft** database called **Copy2.mdb**.

1 Open your new copy of the **WroxSoft** application and select the Create Replica.. command from the Replication section of the Tools menu. Access informs you that it must close the current database down.

2 Click Yes and Access will offer to create a back-up copy of the original database for you so that you can recover it if a problem should arise. To be safe, select the Yes button to create a back-up.

3 Next, Access converts the original database into a replica design master database, then asks for the

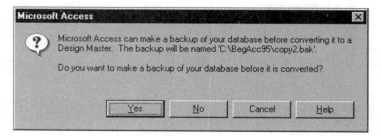

name and location of the first replica database. Access suggests the name Replica of Copy2.mdb and prompts for a location to save it. Ensure it's set to the same folder that you started with (e.g. **BegAcc95**). Click OK and Access creates the first of the replica databases. After it has completed the conversion of the original database and created the first replica database, you get a message informing you what has been done.

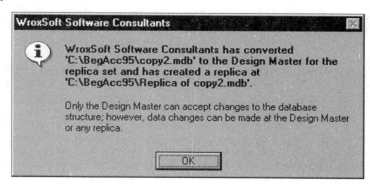

Once you've created the design master and first replica databases, you can always create more replicas using the Create Replica.. command. If fact, you can add more replicas to the replica set at any time.

Looking at a Replica Database

When you convert your database into a replica set, Access adds new tables and fields to each one. It also adds new properties and changes some of the existing properties of the tables in the database. Among these is the Replicable property. This controls whether that object will be synchronized (updated) with the other changes made to the database - you can specify this property for objects so that they are not updated when you synchronize the rest of the data and objects. To change the property, right-click on the object - say a query - in the Database window and select Properties... from the short-cut menu. If you clear the Replicated checkbox, the object will no longer be copied to, or updated with, the other databases in the replica set.

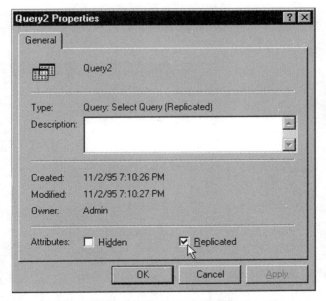

This allows you to create **local** objects in a database that are not copied into the others when the replication process is used. When you create a new object (such as a form or query) in the design master database and save it for the first time, Access adds a checkbox

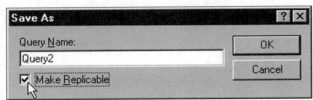

to the Save As dialog where you specify if the new object is to be replicable. The default is 'no' (unticked) and this makes the new object local to the design master database. However, if you tick this option before saving the object, you make it replicable and it *will* then be copied into all the other members of the replica set next time you synchronize them.

To see the extra *tables* that Access has added, you need to change the viewing options. Select Options... from the Tools menu and click the View tab. Turn on the Show - Hidden Objects and Show - System Objects options and click OK.

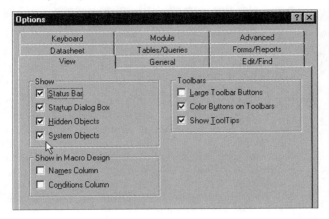

If you click on the Tables tab in the Database window, Access displays a whole list of new tables that were hidden from view before. These are both the normal system tables and the special replication tables. To see the new fields and properties that are added to the tables, select one of the original (normal) tables in the Database window and Open it. Access has added three new fields - s_Guid which is a global identifier, s_Lineage which contains information about changes made to the record, and s_Generation which holds information about the different groups of changes.

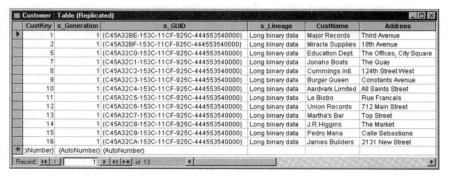

One of the major changes to the design of the table is that all fields which use the AutoNumber data type now have their New Values property changed to Random. When the databases are synchronized, the values in all the tables are identical across the set. So normally when a new record is added to that table in each database, it would assume the same number for an AutoNumber field as all the others in the set, causing conflicts in future synchronizations. For example, if there were 16 records in the copies of the database, if two users wanted to add new but differing records, then Autonumber would assign 17 to both, thus causing a conflict. By using random values for the new field, this is far less likely to happen. To see these changes switch the table you have open to design view.

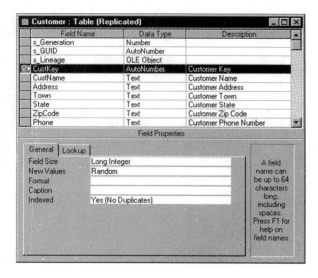

You should not change any of the new fields or properties that Access has added.

Synchronizing Databases in a Replica Set

Once you have created the replica set, you use the Synchronize Now... command to synchronize the databases (select the Tools menu, then Replication to find this command). If you have the database open, Access reminds you that once again, it has to be closed before it can perform the required operation. Click Yes and Access prompts for the name of the database you want to synchronize - it will suggest the name of the last one you used, or you can select a different one from the drop-down list. You can also use the Browse... button to open Windows' File dialog and select it there.

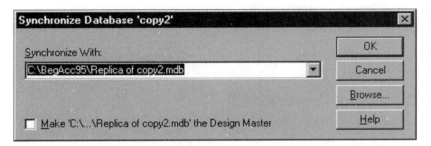

Click **OK** and Access starts the
synchronization by examining all the data
in each field of each table in the two
databases. As it does so, it displays a
progress gauge on screen. If there are a lot
of records in the tables, the process can
take some time.

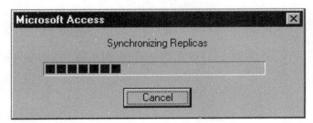

Once the process is complete,
Access displays a message. Notice
that you have to close and re-open
the database to be sure of seeing all
the changes made to the data
during synchronization. Access can
do this automatically if required -
just click the **Yes** button.

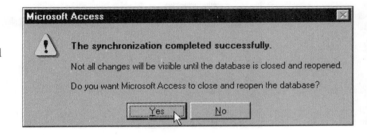

How Replication Works

The extra fields added to the tables when the database is converted into a replica hold
information about when the last changes were made to the data. If only one database contains
changes to the data made since the last synchronization, then Access simply copies these changes
into the other database. So if the customer's address and phone numbers are updated in one
copy, both will contain the new data after synchronization.

Problems arise, however, if both databases contain changes. If the changes in each database are
in different records, Access just places the record with the most recent changes in both databases.
If one database contains a new address for Jonah's Boats and the other a new address for
Cummings Intl. then after synchronization both databases will contain the latest addresses for
both customers.

But what happens if both databases contain changes to the same record? Say we've changed the
address for Cummings Intl. in one database and their phone and fax numbers in the other
database. When we open the
database we'll get a warning
that there have been changes to
the data during synchronization
and that **conflicts** exist. The
reason why the database has to
be closed and re-opened if
there are any items to be

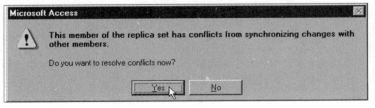

571

updated in it now becomes clear - this warning is only displayed in a database that contains conflicts when that database is opened.

Click Yes and Access attempts to resolve the conflicts and synchronize the two databases, so that they contain the latest version of the information.

Handling Conflicting Updates

Because we have changed the same record in both databases, Access has found conflicts that it cannot resolve automatically and it displays a message indicating this. It shows the tables where conflicts exist and the number of records affected. In our case it's the Customer table and there is only one record affected. You'll also see a new table has appeared in the Database window, named Customer_Conflict. This contains details of the conflicts between the two tables.

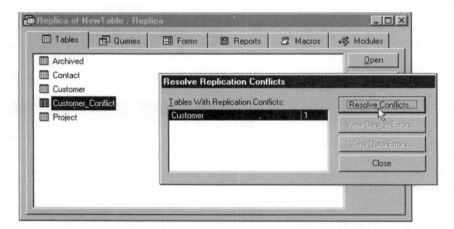

Click the Resolve Conflicts button and Access creates a form showing the two versions of the record where the conflict exists - again in our case it's just the record for Cummings Intl. in the two databases. Here we can elect to keep the existing record - the one in the current database - or overwrite it with the changed (conflict) record from the other database.

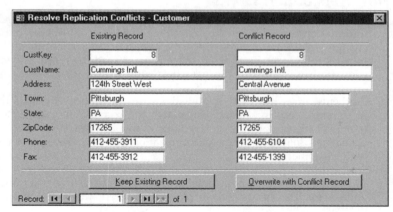

Of course, there's a third possibility, and here lies the strength of Access's replication methods. We can edit either of the records before we elect to keep that one. The Conflict Record contains the correct new address, so all we have to do is edit the Phone and Fax fields so that they contain the latest data and then click the Overwrite with Conflict Record button. Now both databases will contain the latest information for Cummings Intl.

If you don't resolve the conflicts now, you will be prompted to do so each time you open the database in the future. You can use the Resolve Conflicts... command in the Replication section of the Tools menu at any time to resolve any existing conflicts in a database.

Changing and Recovering the Design Master

You must always have one design master database in a replica set. This can be used to make changes to the design of objects, rather than just the data, in all the other databases. If you lose

the design master for any reason - such as systems failure or file corruption - you can convert one of the existing replica databases to create a new design master. Open one of the replicas and select the Recover Design Master.. command from the Replication section of the Tools menu. Access warns you that you can only have one design master database in a set. To create the new one, you click Yes. Access then prompts to see if you've synchronized all the replicas. You can cancel the change by selecting No, or set it in motion by selecting Yes.

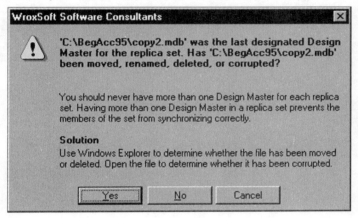

You can also change which database is the design master when you synchronize them. At the bottom of the dialog which appears when you select the Synchronize Now... option is a checkbox. If you check this, it makes the database which is not open (i.e. the other one being synchronized) the design master.

Exporting Data to Other Applications

Although Access seems to offer us all the facilities we need in a database, there are times when you need to get your data out again in a form that can be used by another application, rather than as a printed report. While you can select items in a control on a form or in the datasheet view of a table or query, and copy them using the clipboard, this is not always the most efficient way. Instead we use the Export options that are included in Access. Select the item you want to export, say the Order table from our **WroxSoft** application, and then select Save As/ Export from the File menu to open the Save As dialog.

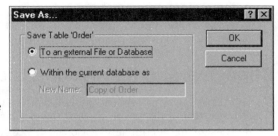

Here we can either make another copy of the selected object, or export the information it contains to an external file - this is the option we want. Then we click OK to open the Save...In dialog.

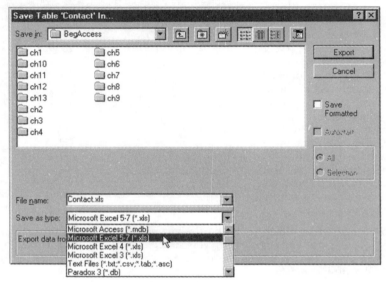

Now we select the destination folder and enter the name for the new file. Access suggests a name based on the name of the object we're exporting and shows all other files of the same type. The dialog also includes a list of file types that Access supports, shown in the Save as type: box. The list you see depends on the option you selected when you installed Access.

This list is far more specific that the import options we saw earlier in this chapter - while we could select Excel as the import type and leave it to Access to decipher the exact format (i.e. which version of Excel created the file), we can't do this when we export the data. Instead, we have to select the particular format we require. We'll take a look at the different formats that are supported.

Databases and ODBC

You can export data to a file in the correct format for Paradox 3, 4, and 5, dBase III, IV and V, and FoxPro 2.0, 2.5, 2.6 and 3.0. You also have the ODBC (Open Database Connectivity) option.

Once you have set the destination folder and file name, you just click Export and the new file is created. The one exception is the ODBC option, where Access next prompts you with the Export dialog.

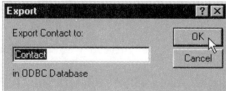

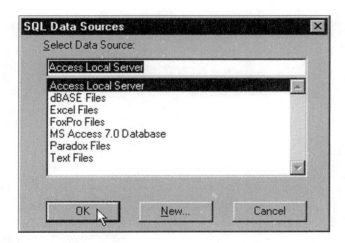

Clicking OK produces the Select Server dialog and this is followed by the Login Prompt to your server. Once connected, you can export the data using Access' drivers to other databases.

Text Files

You may have thought there were a lot of forms of text and ASCII data that you can import, but there are even more options in the Export list. Access allows you to use the generic Text format (`.txt, .csv, .tab, .asc`), Rich Text Format (`.rtf`) and Microsoft Word Merge which creates a 'Merge File'. We'll look at how the normal text file format is used to export the contents of the Customer table.

Once you click Export, Access starts Text Export Wizard. This is very similar to the Text Import Wizard we used earlier.

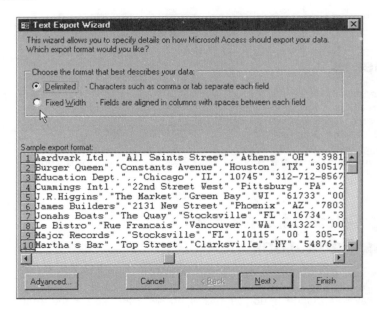

The first screen allows you to select Delimited or Fixed Width format for the new file. The next one allows you to select the Delimiter Character that you want - in the following figure we've selected *Tab*. We've also selected {none} for the Text Qualifier so that Access does not surround the text with quotation marks.

Finally, you just confirm the name for the new file, and click Finish to export it. You'll notice that the window also contains the Advanced button. Click this to open the Export Specs window where you can view and save the export specification - in the same way as we did when we imported text files earlier.

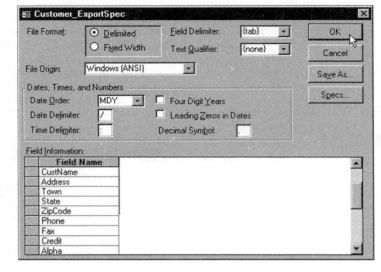

Spreadsheets

You can export data in several different spreadsheet formats - Access supports Excel format in versions 5-7, 4, and 3, plus Lotus 1-2-3 in **.wk1** and **.wk3** formats. Once you have selected the folder and file name, click the Export button to start the process. The Save...In dialog closes and the export is carried out automatically.

Exporting Selected Data and Preserving Formatting

When we export data in Text or Excel 5-7 formats, we can tell Access to preserve the formatting of the data (fonts, colors, etc.) in the new file by setting the Save Formatted option. If this is on, we can also set the Autostart option and arrange for Access to automatically start the application afterwards (either Microsoft Excel or Microsoft Word). Finally, we can also select whether to export All or just a Selection of the data using the option buttons.

If you only want to export part of a table, you use the Selection option. Here we've selected part of eight records from our Contact table, and selected Save As/Export.

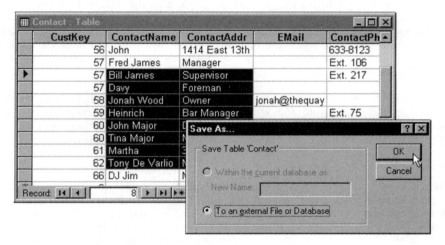

We select To an external File or Database and click OK. Access then opens the Save..In dialog. Here we set the Save Formatted and Autostart options and change the third option to Selection.

Because we specified the format as Microsoft Excel 7, Access creates the new file as a spreadsheet file and starts Excel with that file loaded. It contains only the data we selected in the table. (If we had selected a Text format, Access would have created a text file and started Microsoft Word.)

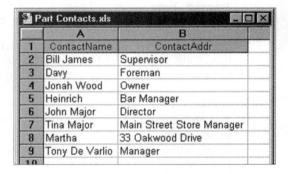

 FYI If you export the data in **Rich Text Format (.rtf)**, the formatting information is automatically included, but you can still select the **Autostart** and **All/Selection** options.

Analysis in Excel

One area where exporting data is very useful is when you need detailed analysis of it. Access doesn't support the esoteric financial functions that most spreadsheets do - if you want to carry out Consolidations, Projections or Goal Seeking you need a bit more muscle in this area than Access can offer. And, if you want to produce complex charts, then the Graph applet that Access uses falls somewhat short of 'state of the art'. So, instead we can automate the process of exporting data to an Excel spreadsheet and use its better features to get the result we need.

Exporting Data with a Macro

One of the easiest ways to do this is with a simple one-line macro. If we want to export the contents of a table, we can use the TransferSpreadsheet or OutputTo macro actions. The TransferSpreadsheet action automatically produces a spreadsheet file on disk which contains the information from the table, while the OutputTo action broadly duplicates the Export method we used earlier. There are also equivalent Transfer actions for other formats - TransferText and TransferDatabase.

When we use a macro action to export data, we have to supply all the information about the type of file we want to create and what we want to export. This information is placed in the arguments for the macro. You'll see from the arguments of the Transfer actions, that they can import data as well as export it. The arguments required are as follows:

OutputTo

Object Type	Table, query, form, report, or module.
Object Name	The name of the object in the database.
Output Format	Microsoft Excel, Rich Text Format, or MS DOS text.
Output File	The full path and name for the new file.
Auto Start	Yes or No to start the target application after exporting.

TransferSpreadsheet

Transfer Type	Choose Import, Export, or Link.
Spreadsheet Type	The application format required: Excel/Lotus 1-2-3.
Table Name	The name of the table in the database.
File Name	The full path and name for the new file.
Has Field Names	Yes, if the first row includes the names of the fields.
Range	The name of the spreadsheet range for import from.

TransferText

Transfer Type	Choose Import, Export, or Link and data type.
Spec. Name	The name of a stored specification for the import or export.
Table Name	The name of the table in the database.
File Name	The full path and name for the new file.
Has Field Names	Yes, if the first row includes the names of the fields.

TransferDatabase

Transfer Type	Choose Import, Export, or Link.
Database Type	The application format required: Access/dBase/FoxPro, etc.
Database Name	The full path and file name of the other database.
Object Type	Choose table, query, form, report, macro, or module.
Source	The name of the object in Access.
Destination	The name of the object in the other database.
Structure Only	Yes to import or export only the structure, not the data.

While there is no advantage in using the **TransferSpreadsheet** action to **export** data, remember that it can be used to **import** data from an existing spread-sheet file into an Access table.

To export to a spreadsheet, the most useful action is OutputTo. Using this to export to Excel 5-7 allows us to start Excel up once we have completed the export. The exported data is then shown immediately.

Action: OutputTo
  Object Type: Query
  Object Name: Customers By Town
  Output Format: Microsoft Excel
  Output File: E:\My Documents\Customers.xls
  Auto Start: Yes

Here we've created a macro using the OutputTo action and saved it on a macro sheet. (It doesn't matter which macro sheet it is saved to.) It specifies the Object Type as a query and the Object Name as Customers By Town - the name of a simple select query that simply sorts the customer table by the town field. We've selected Microsoft Excel as the output format and told it to start Excel once the export is complete.

Now if we close the macro window, switch to the Macros list in the Database window, select the Excel Export macro and click the Run button, Access will run the Customers By Town query in the background and export the results to the file E:\My Documents\Customers.xls. Excel will then start with that file loaded.

	A	B	C	D	E	F	G	H	I	J
1	CustKey	CustName	Address	Town	State	ZipCode	Phone	Fax	Credit	Alpha
2	51	Aardvark	All Saints Street	Athens	OH	39812	00 1 216-376-	00 1 216-376-	10000	AARD
3	53	Education		Chicago	IL	10745	312-712-8567		17250	EDUC
4	61	Martha's Bar	Top Street	Clarksvill	NY	54876			500	MART
5	56	J.R.Higgins	The Market	Green	WI	61733	00 1 414-831-	00 1 414-831-	2000	HIGGI
6	52	Burger	Constants Avenue	Houston	TX	30517	00 1 713-771-	00 1 713-771-	5000	BURG
7	62	Miracle	18th Avenue	Oakland	CA	10593	00 1 415-671-	00 1 415-671-	20125	MIRA
8	57	James	2131 New Street	Phoenix	AZ	78034	00 1 602-281-	00 1 602-281-	7500	JAME
9	55	Cummings	124th Street West	Pittsbur	PA	17265	00 1 412-455-	00 1 412-455-	17500	CUM
10	65	Pedro Mana	Calle Sebastione	St. Paul	MN	65109	00 1 612-401-	00 1 612-401-	7500	MANA
11	60	Major		Stocksvi	FL	10015	00 1 305-711-	00 1 305-711-	20700	MAJO
12	58	Jonahs	The Quay	Stocksvi	FL	16734	305-711-8855		1000	JONA
13	66	Union	712 Main Street	Tampa	FL	51267	00 1 813-167-	00 1 813-167-	14375	UNIO
14	59	Le Bistro	Rue Francais	Vancouv	WA	41322	00 1 206-133-	00 1 206-133-	1500	LEBIS
15										

Alternatively, we can use a far more complex query, and use Excel's superior charting capabilities to show the data in a better way that Access can. As an example, the Sales/Projects crosstab query in our **WroxSoft** application creates a recordset containing the total income from all the sales and project work our consultant has done. We'll output the results of this query and look a chart created from it in Excel. The macro we need is:

Action: OutputTo
  Object Type: Query
  Object Name: Sales/Projects Crosstab
  Output Format: Microsoft Excel
  Output File: E:\My Documents\Income.xls
  Auto Start: Yes

The result of running the macro is a new Excel spreadsheet file containing a row for each product, showing the total income and the income broken down by month.

	A	B	C	D	E	F	G	H	I	J
	Desc	Row Summary	Jan	Feb	Mar	Apr	May	Jun	Jul	Aug
1										
2	Accounts System	$1,690							$390	$1,3
3	Menu Generator	$1,605		$425	$325	$195		$660		
4	Navigation System	$1,615				$1,615				
5	PC Support	$800		$160						$6
6	Sales Tracking	$5,394				$2,813	$1,601		$980	
7	School Info	$5,775						$4,725	$1,050	
8	Software	$30,214		$5,589	$3,500	$2,153	$8,588	$1,247	$8,537	$5
9	Warehouse	$7,980			$4,000		$2,435	$1,395	$150	
10										

We can use this data to create a multiple-axis chart which shows the information for each project, as well as the total income, every month - this is a lot better than Access' Graph applet could manage.

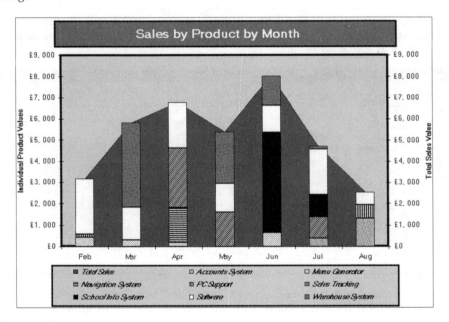

Data Warehousing Concepts

In the commercial world everyone is talking about an exciting new topic **- data warehousing**. Like many of today's buzz-words, this means different things to different people, but at the heart of it all is the principle of capturing information from the huge quantities of data that a large organization can produce. Here's an illustration of a typical commercial organization's IT system:

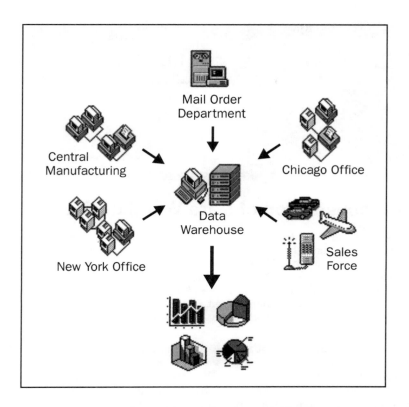

Imagine a grocery store chain - their automated checkouts with bar-code readers produce an endless stream of information on what is selling, at what time of day, in what quantity to each customer and on which day of the week. It shows the effects of special offers, local demand and even changes in the weather. If the management want to minimize stock without removing fast-selling lines or risking running out of anything, they need up to the minute information from this huge mass of numbers.

Of course, we can store all this data centrally and run queries on it whenever we like. But there is a constant danger of 'information overload' - we'll have extreme difficulty coping with the amount of data. This situation exists in many businesses today, and the constant search for competitive advantage means that a solution must be found.

Instead of storing the data within the applications that create it, we extract the useful parts and store this away from the main applications. Then we can stroll round this 'data warehouse' whenever we like, with no worry that our manipulations of the contents may affect the day-to-day processing of the original data.

We'll take as a simple example the data on sales and project work in our **WroxSoft** application. This is constantly being updated as we process orders and carry out work for our customers - the current term for this is **on-line transaction processing** (OLTP). And, of course, after a period, it is archived and ultimately deleted altogether. Our data warehouse will capture parts of this information on a regular basis and store it in a separate database. We've supplied this database as **Warehous.mdb** on the disk that accompanies this book. Open it and look at the main screen.

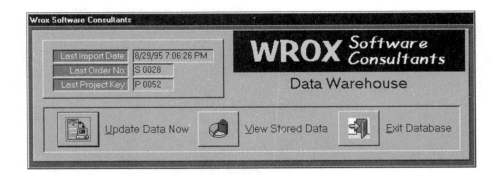

A Simple Demonstration of Data Warehousing

The main form contains three text boxes which show the date that the last access was made to the **WroxSoft** database, and the last Project Key and Order Number that were retrieved from it. There are three buttons - Update Data Now which updates the data in the application by querying the tables in the **WroxSoft** application for any data not already collected, View Stored Data which displays a graph of the data in the **Warehouse** application's tables, and Exit Database, which closes the application. When you first load this database there is no information in it, so you will have to select Update Data Now, if you want to see it working.

FYI

Because the **Warehouse** database uses links to the tables in the **WroxSoft** application, you will get an error message when you start the **Update** process if the sample files are not in the **BegAcc95** folder. Access will tell you that the tables it needs can't be found, and, if this happens, you will have to re-establish the links when you first run it. Select **Add-ins** from the **Tools** menu and click **Linked Table Manager**. This contains a list of all the tables linked to the database and shows the folder where it expects to find the **WroxSoft** application. Select all the tables and click **OK**. Access opens another window where you can select the new location. Change to the folder where you installed the sample files and select **WroxSoft.mdb**, then click **OK**. Access refreshes the links and the **Warehouse** application will now work correctly.

A macro attached to the On Click property of the Update Data Now button runs two queries - Collect Project Data and Collect Sales Data. These are append queries which access the tables in the **WroxSoft** application through links, and add the results to the IncomeDetail table.

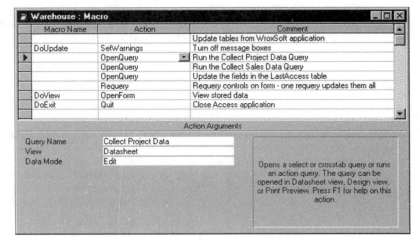

Because the table stores details of both projects and software sales, each query must convert the data to suit the layout of the table - if you open the queries and table in design view, you can see that calculated fields are used to create the totals and other entries where the data in the original table is not suitable. For instance, the Collect Sales Data query uses the calculated field:

GrossAmount: [Qty]*[Price]-([Qty]*[Price]*[Discount]/100)

to create the value for the GrossAmount field in the IncomeDetail table. To ensure that only new records are added, the query contains the Criteria for the OrderNo field:

>[Forms]![Warehouse Main]![LastOrderNo]

It therefore only returns any records with a higher order number than the value displayed on the main form. The Collect Project Data query works in a similar way - collecting only the data from new Project records.

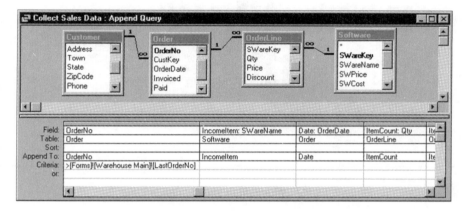

Once the data has been retrieved, an update query named Set Access Details is run against the LastAccess table. This table is the source of the values on the main form and contains only one record with three fields - LastImportDate, LastOrderNo and LastProjectKey. The query uses the **DMax** function to get the last OrderNo and ProjectKey values from the IncomeDetail table and the **Now()** function to find the current date and time. These values are then placed in the single record in the LastAccess table.

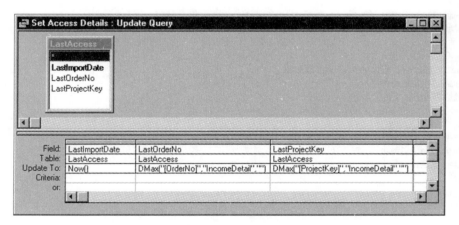

Finally, a Requery action is used to update the controls on the form to show the last record numbers and access time.

When you press the View Stored Data button, the Graph View form is opened which contains a Graph object in an OLE control. This displays a graph of the contents of the IncomeDetail table.

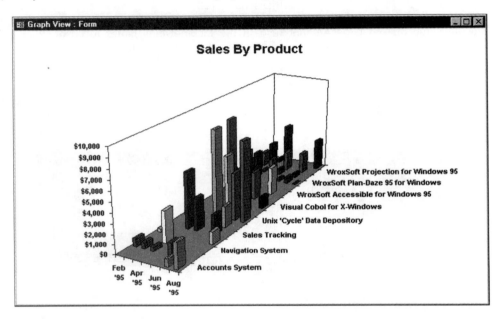

The arguments for the macros in the Warehouse macro sheet are:

Macro: DoUpdate - runs when the Update button is pressed

Action: SetWarnings
 Warnings On: No

Action: OpenQuery
 Query Name: Collect Project Data
 View: Datasheet
 Data Mode: Edit

Action: OpenQuery
 Query Name: Collect Sales Data
 View: Datasheet
 Data Mode: Edit

Action: OpenQuery
 Query Name: Set Access Details
 View: Datasheet
 Data Mode: Edit

Action: Requery
    Control Name: LastProjectKey

Macro: DoView - runs when the View button is pressed

Action: OpenForm
    Form Name: Graph View
    View: Form
    Filter Name:
    Where Condition:
    Data Mode: Edit
    Window Mode:

Macro: DoExit - runs when the Exit button is pressed

Action: Quit
    Options: Save All

Summary

This chapter has looked at how we can use Access in real world situations. A database does not exist in isolation, it has to be able to communicate with the outside world by importing and exporting data and information to and from other applications.

Access is capable of handling many popular file formats. In this chapter we've seen how it can:

- Capture data from most other types of system.
- Link to data and manipulate it without changing the form it was stored in .
- Return data to the outside world by exporting it (both as information or just as raw data).
- Combine all of these methods to convert data from one application to another, or just store and manipulate data to provide us with better information.

In multi-user and networked environments, Access provides powerful tools both to maximize the efficiency of the system and reduce maintenance effort. By using replication, we can synchronize data from different sources so that the information is always current. You'll see more about how Access is used in a network situation in the next, and final, chapter.

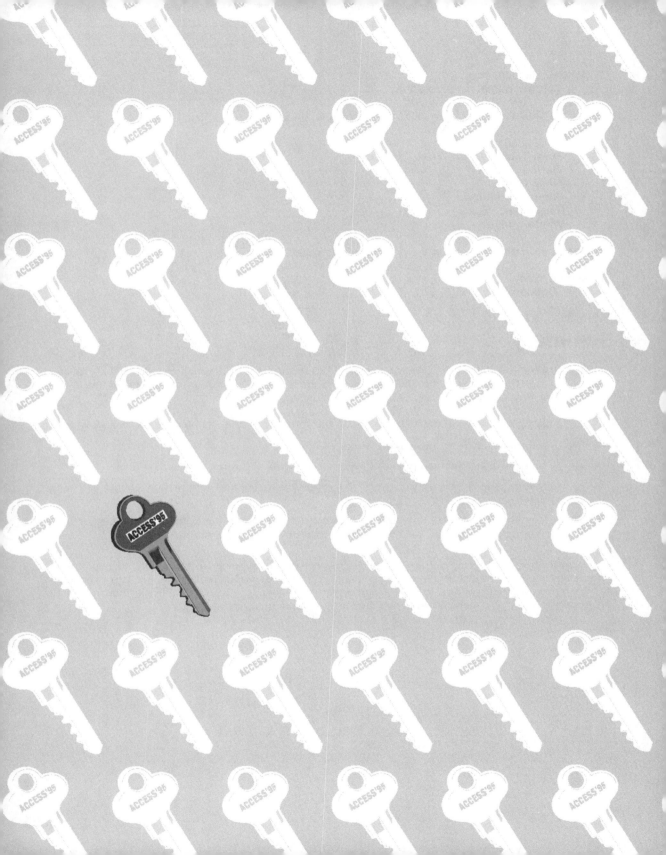

Administering A Working System

In this, the final chapter, we'll look at the tasks involved in using Access in a workgroup or multi-user environment. However, if you're using a stand-alone machine, don't think you can skip this chapter - much of what you'll meet here is still applicable to the single-user situation.

Once you have designed and built your application, there are a few final things you should consider. Access contains several tools designed to help you manage your application once it passes from the design stage into general use. It can also help you recover files if they become damaged and protect files from unauthorized changes.

So in this chapter we'll be looking at:

- ▶ Setting the properties of the database.
- ▶ Optimizing application performance.
- ▶ Repairing damaged database files.
- ▶ Compacting database files.
- ▶ Converting old Access databases.
- ▶ Managing the security of your data.
- ▶ Administering a multi-user system.

Setting the Properties of a Database

Every Access database has a set of properties that you can use to identify it by indicating the version, release date, purpose, or a myriad of other items of information. To open the Properties window, right-click on the title bar of the Database window and select Database Properties... from the short-cut menu that appears, or select Database Properties from the File menu. Access opens the Database Properties window. This is a tabbed dialog window with several pages. The first of these is the General page.

The General Page

The General page shows details about the database file on disk - including the last time it was modified or just accessed (opened). This information is maintained by Access and can't be edited.

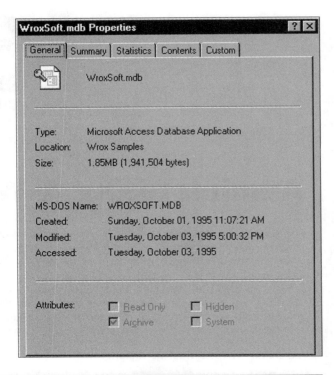

The Summary Page

The second, Summary, page contains the properties that are used to identify the database. All Microsoft applications now store their data on disk using **streams**. These are simply files that allow each application to store its data in the way best suited to that application, but they have headers or identifiers stored with them that can be read by other applications. The entries you place in the Database Properties are stored in these headers, therefore another application can identify your database and report its properties, even though it can't open the file.

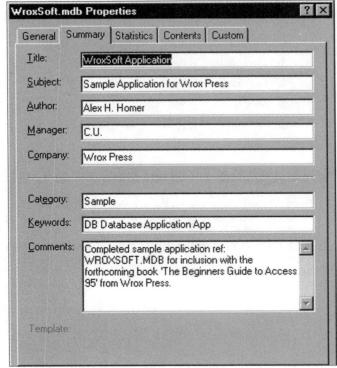

The Statistics and Contents Pages

The next two pages, Statistics and Contents, repeat the dates and times that the file was created, last modified and accessed and printed. There are also details of who last saved it, the revision number and the time taken editing it. The Contents page contains a list of all the objects in the application.

The Custom Page

Finally, there's the Custom page. Here you can create and set values for your own properties. You set a property by selecting a pre-defined one from the drop-down list, or typing the name for your own, and then selecting a data type for it. You can then enter the value you want for that property in the lower window. You can choose from Text, Number and Date types, and use almost anything for the property name. You'll see in the screenshot that we've used some of the pre-defined ones, and added one of our own. You should use it to store any information about the database that hasn't been registered elsewhere. If you wish to delete any properties you have entered simply select them in the Properties window and click the delete button to remove the entry.

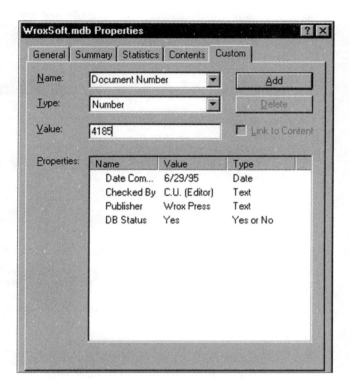

Optimizing Application Performance

Once your application is nearing completion, you should have an idea of how quickly it's performing with the current data. However, it's often the case that you only include a few records while building the application - and even during basic testing there seems little point in typing in hundreds of records. The problem comes when you start to use it in the real world - although you may have an idea of how many records may need to be stored, you can only guess at the way it will perform until you actually try it out with this number. You must also consider the different machines on which it will run. Just because you've used a Pentium 100 to design and build it doesn't mean it will fly when running on the junior accountant's 386SX!

At the best of times, Access is not a fast program - few Windows databases are, due to the amount of work they have to do loading and saving records, linking tables and querying them to produce recordsets and sending data to and from the various system databases and OLE servers. So you must make sure you introduce as few delays as possible into the process. Access provides a wizard which will analyze your whole database, or just part of it, and suggest improvements. We'll put it through its paces now.

Try It Out - Using Performance Analyzer

1 Open the **WroxSoft** application and close the Main Menu form (or any other tables, forms, queries etc. that may be open). Switch to the Database window, select Analyze from the Tools menu and click Performance.

2 Access starts **Performance Analyzer**. The first window has a drop-down list where you can select the type of object you want to analyze, and underneath there is a list of all the objects of that type. For example, the figure on the right shows all the tables in **WroxSoft**. Select All from the Object Type list. We will allow Performance Analyzer free reign over the whole of our application.

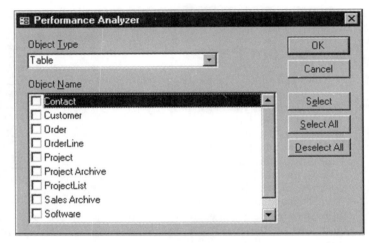

3 Performance Analyzer now shows all the objects in the database. Click the Select All button to select all the objects.

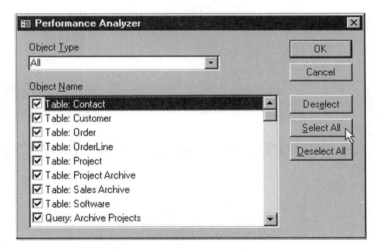

4 Now click OK and you'll see Access examining each item in the application - the names are displayed in a small message window. It takes a long time, so be prepared to put the kettle on while waiting for it. Once it is complete, you see the results in the form of a list of recommendations. This list shows a series of things that may improve the performance of our application. For example, the first suggestion is to change the data type of the ZipCode field to Long Integer. It also shows you the reasons why, how to do it and the dangers involved.

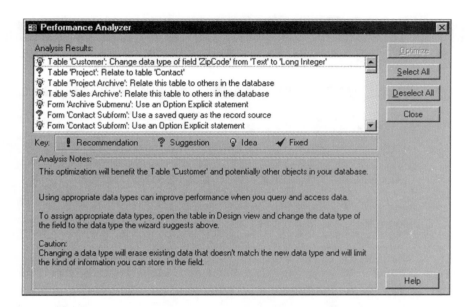

 Access suggests we change the data type of **ZipCode** because all the values in it at the moment are numbers, but we specified the field type as **Text**. Access can process numbers more efficiently. However, if we make this change, it means that we can then only store numbers in this field. If you intend to include customers from other countries, you may need to store text in this field as well as numbers.

5 Some of the suggestions are less than useful. For instance, it has suggested relating the Project Archive table to the other tables in the database. Click on this suggestion to see the Analysis Notes.

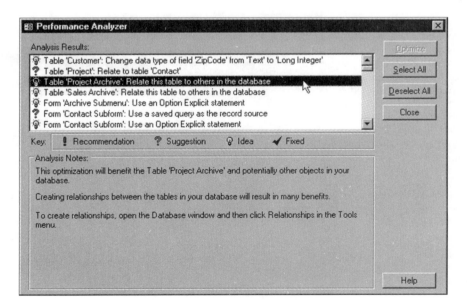

6 We purposely left this table unrelated to others because it only holds archived records. We intend to move the contents to store them elsewhere, so we don't really need to relate it to the other tables. However, click on the sixth entry - the first one regarding the Contact Subform.

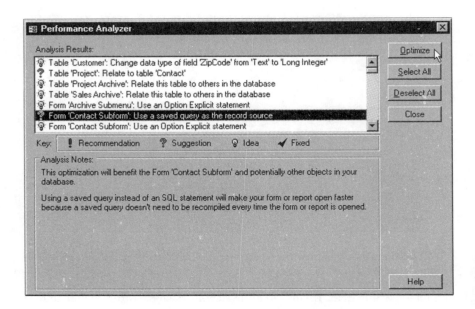

 Here Performance Analyzer suggests we use a saved query as the **Record Source** rather than the SQL statement we placed there. This can make the application more efficient, though it does clutter up the database with more saved queries.

7 We'll go along with this suggestion. If you look in the top left of the window, you'll see that Performance Analyzer has enabled the **Optimize** button. It can do the job for us automatically - so click this now. Access asks for the name for the new saved query.

8 Click OK; the new query is created and the Record Source property of the form updated. In the Performance Analyzer list, you can see that this suggestion is now marked as Fixed.

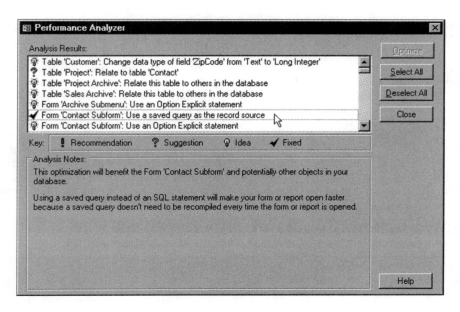

You can go through all the suggestions and decide which ones you want to accept. While Performance Analyzer cannot fix them all automatically, it will always provide some hints on how you can fix the problem yourself.

Remember, Performance Analyzer doesn't know how you will be using the application, or anything about the world it must operate in. Its suggestions are based simply on logic and fixed rules. You must interpret them yourself and decide if you want to carry them out.

Other Ways to Enhance Performance

Even though Performance Analyzer does produce some strange suggestions, there's a lot of sense in most of them. For instance, it often suggests you reduce the number of controls on a form. Even if you can't remove text boxes without reducing the usefulness of the form, you may be able to remove some of the decorative labels that contain fancy text and use lower-overhead image controls for any graphics, or even just load them into the form background itself. Reducing the color depth of any images or graphics to a maximum of 16 colors also helps to speed up loading of forms.

One thing that will make your queries run quicker is making sure you have indexed all the pertinent fields in your tables. If a field is regularly used for searching for a record - you may, for example, regularly use the **SWareName** field to search for a particular product - you should set the indexed property of that field to suit - either **Yes (No Duplicates)** or **Yes (Duplicates OK)**, depending on whether it has to be able to hold duplicate values. Remember, though, that you should only index fields where there is a high proportion of different values - indexing a field which contains the same value in most of the records is a waste of time, unless you *always* search using this field. (See Chapter 3 for more information about creating indexes.)

So, before you disregard any of the suggestions made by Performance Analyzer, sit back and spend a few moments taking a wider view. There may well be things that you can do to improve the speed and responsiveness of your application. We have considered many of these - such as the way you open and close the forms - in previous chapters.

Repair and Maintenance

Close down all your database and have a look at the Tools menu. You will see that the options available are very different from the ones you get when you have a database open. The first of them, Database Utilities, allows you to convert, compact or maintain and repair the database files on your disk.

Access stores all the objects and data in your application in a single file on disk. For example, the file **Wroxsoft.mdb** holds all the forms, reports, macros and queries that our **WroxSoft** application uses, as well as the tables and all the data stored in them. While this is a very convenient method when compared with some other database systems which store every item in a different file, it does increase the risk of substantial data loss if the file becomes corrupted.

Creating Back-up Copies of Your Database File

Before we go into detail about what you can do if a file becomes damaged, it's as well to remember that prevention is better than cure. You should have a system of creating regular back-ups of your database files - and keep at least three generations so that you can always go back to where a problem first arose. In other words, you regularly copy the file to a back-up media such as tape or disk, or to the server on a network, but don't

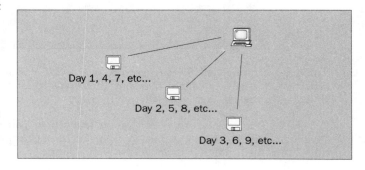

Day 1, 4, 7, etc...

Day 2, 5, 8, etc...

Day 3, 6, 9, etc...

overwrite the previous back-up copy. Instead, you keep three copies of the backup and only overwrite the oldest one each time. You can, of course, keep more copies if you wish, or use a different system of generations. The aim is the same in all cases - to make sure you have another copy which can be brought into service if the current one is lost for any reason.

Because Access stores everything in one file, you will find that it becomes very large - even with only a few sample records, the **WroxSoft** application is around 3Mb. If you use floppy disks for backing-up, you will need to compress the files to fit them on one disk, or split them over several disks. Remember that you can always export data from Access to create back-ups, as we saw in Chapter 15. For example, you can save the records from each table as spreadsheet format files, which could easily be imported back into Access if required.

As Access stores everything in a single file, each time you do a back-up you are backing up parts of the application that don't really need it - forms, reports, queries, etc., don't change as you use them. In most situations, the only changes you want to save are changes to the records in the tables. One way to make this easier is to separate the database into two sections: a code and a data section. These are often called 'front-end' and 'back-end' databases and we looked at them in detail in Chapter 15. Once you have established this type of database, where the tables are stored in a separate database file to the working parts (the forms, reports, etc.), you only need to regularly back-up the one containing the tables.

Repairing a Damaged Database File

Once Access starts to work with your database, it opens many different parts of it at one go - it has to do this to read details of each table, query, form and report as your application runs. And, of course, it has to do the same to read the contents of each record. While it's reading information, there's no real danger of the file being corrupted; it's while it's writing to the disk that problems can occur. If you suffer a machine fault, power failure, or even a mains spike at just the wrong moment, the file can be damaged because Access has written to it but not closed it properly. When you try and open it again, Access will report an error in the file. This type of error is unusual - in many cases, you find that even after a power failure, the database is still intact. However, Access provides a tool to help out for that time when it isn't.

If you experience this type of error, close any open database and select the Repair Database option from Database Utilities on the Tools menu. Access asks you to specify the location and name of the database to be repaired.

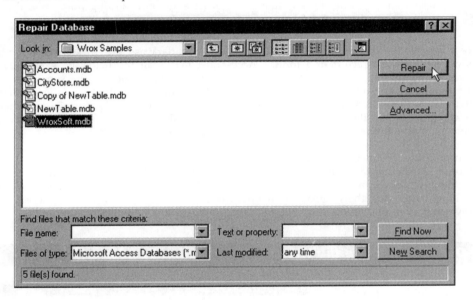

Once you select it and click Repair, Access attempts to fix the file. In the great majority of cases this is successful, though you may find that the most recent changes to the data have been lost. At the end of the process, a message is displayed to confirm the repair was successful. If Access can't fix it, just be grateful you have a recent copy in your regular back-ups....

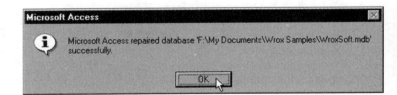

Access also carries out a check on the integrity of each database file as it is opened. If it finds an error, it displays a message and asks if you want to start the repair process.

Compacting the System

As you add and delete records in a database, or create, edit and delete objects such as forms and reports, the database file on disk starts to become **fragmented**. Fragmentation literally means what it sounds like - a fragmenting of the records over the disk which reduces the performance of the application. It plagues many systems and is caused by data and other objects in the database being saved and then deleted repeatedly.

> **Remember that unlike most other applications, Access does not attempt to load the whole file - or even contiguous parts of it - as it runs. And when you are finished with the database, you don't save it in a new file as you would in a spreadsheet or word-processor. Access simply tidies up any loose ends, writes any outstanding changes to the data back to the original file and then closes it.**

Access doesn't actually remove deleted records from a database file. In some cases, you may see this as you delete a record in a form - Access just marks all the fields as #Deleted# and flags the record so that it's not included in the table again. This improves the speed at which Access runs because it doesn't have to reorganize the file on disk each time you delete records. However, it does mean that the file grows continuously - especially during development. Queries that create and then delete tables, such as when exporting data to another application, also cause problems. These tables tend to break up the continuity of the data as well.

To solve the problem of fragmentation, you use one of Access' built-in tools to compact the database file. Before you can do this, the file must be closed by all users who may have it open on a network, and you must have your copy of Access loaded, with no database open. Once you have compacted the database, you often find it shrinks by 30% to 50%, depending on how many temporary objects (deleted records, etc.) were in it.

Try It Out - Compacting the WroxSoft Application Database File

1 Make sure you have closed any database you had open. Ensure also that all other networked users have closed **WroxSoft**.

2 Select Compact Database from Database Utilities on the Tools menu. Access asks for the name and location of the file you want to compact. Move to the folder where you installed the sample files and select **Wroxsoft.mdb**.

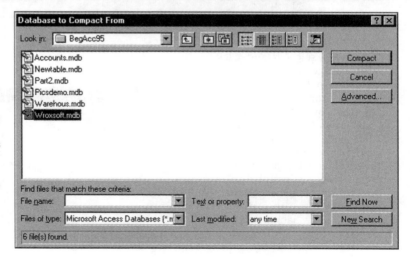

3   Click Compact and Access prompts for the name and location of the new file. You can use the same name as the file you are compacting - Access will create it as a new file and then, providing the compact is successful, delete the original one and re-name the compacted one back to the old name. We'll be cautious, though - enter WroxSoft Compacted for the name of the new file.

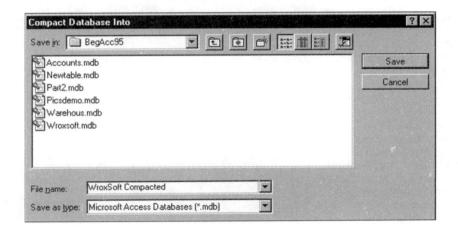

4   Click Save. Access starts to compact the file and displays its progress on the status bar at the bottom of the screen. It starts by removing temporary objects, then compacts the remaining objects.

5   Once complete, Access displays a message to tell you all went well. You can delete the original **Wroxsoft.mdb** file now if you wish. However, before you do, open My Computer or Explorer, click the All Details button to show the file sizes, and compare the two. You will see how much the compact process has removed. In this example, the database size was almost halved.

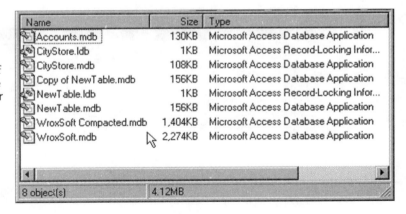

Converting Old Access Databases

If you have a database that was created in an earlier version of Access, you'll have to convert it to Access 95 format before you can use it fully in Access 95. You can open and use an Access version 2 database in Access 95, but you won't be able to change the design of any of the objects in it. You'll get a message telling you this when you open it.

However, even if you only want to read from an Access 2 database, it's still a good idea to convert it. If you use an Access 2 database in Access 95, Access has to translate all the objects to the new format each time it uses them. Depending on the objects it contains, you may find the speed loss quite noticeable.

Ultimately, you'll have to convert your databases to Access 95 format if you wish to maintain and modify them in Access 95. To convert a database, select the Database Utilities command from the Tools menu and click Convert Database. Access opens a dialog where you can select the database you want to convert.

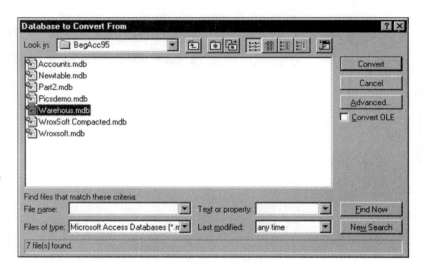

Click Convert and Access then prompts for the destination for the converted copy. Again, you can use the same name and location - Access will create it as a new file and then, providing the conversion is successful, delete the original one and re-name the converted one back to the old name. However, you should generally avoid this method and keep the old version as well, in case you need to refer to it later. Instead, choose a different folder or change the name of the database.

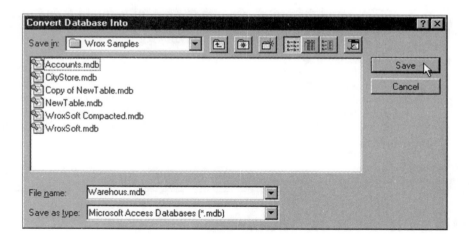

Click Save and the process starts. You'll see a series of messages in the status bar as the database is verified, compacted and each object is converted. The conversion process can take quite a while. Once it is complete, you can load and run the database as normal.

Note that you cannot convert a database back into version 2 (or earlier) format once you have converted it to Access 95. You should keep a copy of all your version 2 databases until you are absolutely sure you will never need them again!

Security and Passwords

When you first create a database application, anyone can modify both the data it contains and the design of the objects, such as the forms and reports. In our **WroxSoft** application, we made some attempt to control this by replacing the standard menu bars with our own, which only allowed the user to switch to different forms or reports and not enter design view or see the database window where all the objects are available. We also used a custom toolbar which would, in normal situations, only have buttons for the tasks you wanted to make available to your users. (We included some which allowed you to switch to design view to be able to work with the database, but normally design view wouldn't be present.)

These methods are a first-level attempt to protect the data. They also help to guide the user by only offering them the options they need. It makes the Access interface much less intimidating. But a user who is trying to break into the application, especially if they have some knowledge about how Access works, would not be put off by these methods for long.

The techniques we've seen so far work by using the Startup properties of a database - we looked at these in Chapter 13. There we defined the custom menu bars, toolbars and other aspects of the database's setup that we wanted.

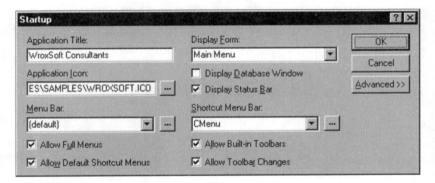

However, even if we remove all the toolbars from an application, all an intruder has to do is hold down the *Shift* key while the database is loading and all our security is gone. Access displays the normal design interface with all the objects available for editing.

To protect a database from intruders (which is especially necessary in a networked environment), we can use the range of security tools that Access includes. There are five different 'levels' to these:

- Encrypting the database
- Setting a password
- Establishing a workgroup and securing it
- Creating user groups and permissions
- Establishing user groups security

You can also take advantage of these features in a single-user situation. If you have several people who use the application, even though it is on a single machine, you can use the security tools to control what each person can do with the data. And, of course, if you are administering a network, you must do this anyway.

How far you take the establishing of security is up to you. The list above shows ascending levels of security - you should at least consider setting a password on your database if it contains any sensitive information that you don't want others to see.

Encrypting the Database

Many database systems store the data from the tables in simple text form on disk. Access uses a method that is a little more complex, but it makes little attempt to hide the data. For example, here is part of a database file loaded into Microsoft Word as a text file:

    □□□□Cummings Intl.124th Street WestPittsburgPA17265412-455-6104412-455-
    1399CUMMIWK?:8/-□□□a□□□5□□□□ Ñô□□□□□□Education Dept.The Offices, City
    SquareChicagoIL10745312-712-8567EDUCAVQQE@>7-
    □□□b□□□4□□□□δú□□□□□□Burger QueenConstants AvenueHoustonTX305177 13-771-
    6727713-771-6728BURGEWRF:53,□□□□f□□□3□□□□á δ□□□□□□Aardvark Ltd.All Saints
    StreetGreen BayWI39812216-376-1298216-376-
    8811AARDV[VJ>97.□□□□□□!+G□□□□□□□□□ñ□×□□□□□□□□□□ñ□b rudv□□ p□f|w□ufbrud
    □□□□1□□ÿÿ"□bvofpx,ufbrudv□□□sufzjrxv□ufbrud□□□□1□□ÿÿ□ bvofpx,ufbrudv□□ pf□{
    □ufbrud□□□□1□□ÿÿ
    □`xwrfl̃fb□□□□□1□□ÿ□   □buofpx□□□□□1□□ÿ□□□ buofpx,rswjrpv□□□□□2□□ÿ□
    □buofpx,rswjrpv□□□b mrvf□sufzjf{□□□□2□□ÿÿ□□ bdofpx,ufbrudv□□□□2□□ÿ□-
    □bdofpx,ufbrudv□□ vruw□a}□□p`of□□□□2□□ÿÿ-
    □bdofpx,ufbrudv□□ vruw□a}□□wr{p□□□2□□ÿÿ-□ bdofpx,ufbrudv□□ p□f|w□ufbrud□□□□
    2□□ÿÿ"□bdofpx,ufbrudv□□□sufzjrxv□ufbrud□□□□2□□ÿÿ□□ bdofpx,ufbrudv□□ pf□{□ufbru
    d□□□□2□□ÿÿ

You can clearly see the name and address details. To avoid this, the first step in securing your database is to **encrypt** it, so that the contents of the field become unreadable. This is done with the <u>E</u>ncrypt/Decrypt Database command, which can be selected from the Securi<u>t</u>y submenu on the Access <u>T</u>ools menu - you will only be able to see this if you have no database open at the time.

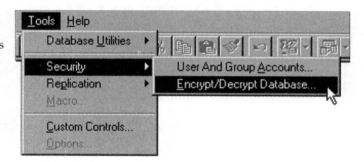

Access opens the Encrypt/Decrypt Database dialog, where you can select the database you want to encrypt.

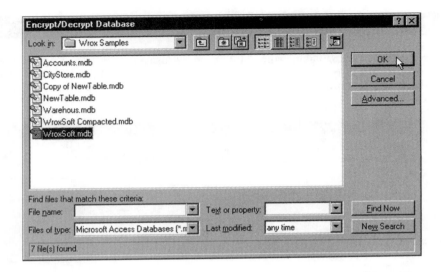

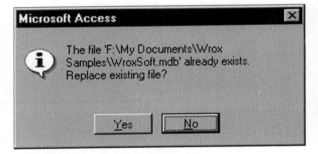

Next you tell Access the location and name of the new database and click Save - it will create a new encrypted copy and leave the original file unchanged. If you want to replace the original, you just specify the same location and name for the new database (Access will ask you to confirm this).

Once you have encrypted the database, it is stored on disk in such a way that the contents cannot be read by looking at the file in another application. However, an encrypted database may run more slowly as the data has to be decrypted each time it is read from disk. The difference can be around 10%, but on a fast machine it is not too noticeable.

To decrypt the database, you must first close all open databases and then select the Encrypt/ Decrypt Database command again. In the Encrypt/Decrypt Database dialog, select the encrypted database and click OK, then select the location and name for the new decrypted file and click Save.

Setting a Password for the Database

One way of preventing anyone from seeing the information in your database is to secure it with a password. As soon as the database is loaded, Access prompts for the password that you have set - and without it the database cannot be opened.

Try It Out - Setting a Password

1 Open up **WroxSoft.mdb**, making sure you tick the Exclusive option in the Open dialog as you do so. This option must be on if you want to set a password. It may be the default on a single-user system depending on how you have set up the Access Options, but it will not be the default in a network environment.

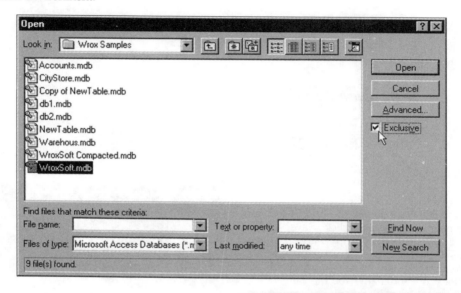

2 Close the Main menu and open the database window using the toolbar buttons. Select Security from the Tools menu and click Set Database Password... Access displays the Set Database Password dialog.

3 Type the password you want in the Password box, then repeat it in the Verify box - as you type Access displays asterisks to hide the password. You can use any combination of letters and numbers in a password, up to a maximum of 14 characters. Remember that passwords are case-sensitive, so MyPassword is different to Mypassword.

4 Click OK to set the password and close down the database. You can then try opening it - Access will display the Password Required dialog.

5   Enter the correct password and click OK to open the database.

 FYI   Note that if you forget the password, you will not be able to open the database again. Once you have set a password for a database, Access will display the **Password Required** dialog each time you open it.

6   To change or remove the password, open the database again in Exclusive mode.

7   The Security option on the Tools menu now offers an Unset Database Password option. Select this and Access displays the Unset Database Password dialog. Type the current password in to remove it.

You can then repeat the process to set a new password if you wish.

 FYI   Once you've set a password or established any other level of security and put the procedure into practice, Access automatically encrypts the database.

Establishing a Workgroup and Securing It

Setting a password for a database is useful if there is only one person using it, or if only a few users are allowed access to all the parts of it. However, in a workgroup environment, there may be many people who need to be able to use parts of the database, but not all of it. In this kind of situation, you need to be able to control the access rights of each user separately. To do this you establish **workgroup security**.

A **workgroup** in Access is a number of people who need to use the same data - usually on a network of some type. It includes the situation where several people use one machine at different times. The thing these people have in common is that their work involves basically the same data and similar tasks. For example, the sales department of a company could be a workgroup that handled all the sales inquiries, order processing, invoicing and sales management for the department.

However, the sales department database application may contain information that is not appropriate for all the users to see, or be set up so that the people who handle inquiries cannot enter orders. So each user must have access to different parts of the database. This means that they must be identified within the workgroup as they log onto Access.

 FYI   Access contains the Workgroup Administrator application which is used to set up and manage workgroups. The program file is called `Wrkgadm.exe`. This program is installed with Access and is automatically placed in your Windows 95 Start menu. If you can't see it, you'll have to run the Setup program again and re-install the files from your original program disk.

When you use a workgroup to secure your application, Access stores the details of each user, including their passwords, in a system database. The default system database is called **System.mdw**. It is through the workgroup that Access knows which user has permission for each part of the database. The **users** are generally divided up into **groups**, and each workgroup also has an **owner** - the person responsible for setting it up.

> If you have a **System.mda** in your Access program folder as well as a **System.mdw**, then this is an old Access 2 version of the system database, which will still be there if you installed Access 95 over the top of Access 2.

When creating a secure workgroup application, you can either convert your **System.mdw** or create a new one in a different folder, then make it the current system database. Changing the current system database is often referred to as choosing a workgroup, because the system database defines the workgroup itself.

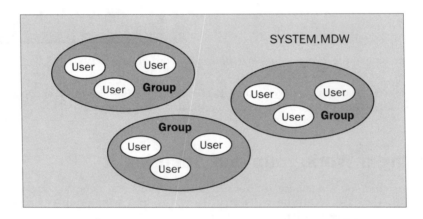

Try It Out - Changing the Workgroup

This and the next Try It Out example are complex and you should take care when you embark on them. You must start by closing Access and using Explorer or My Computer to create a copy of **System.mdw** in the **BegAcc95** samples folder which you can freely alter. Please understand that under no circumstances should you alter the original **System.mdw**!

If you do work through the following examples you will find that your system is now using this new copy of **System.mdw**. Once you have completed the examples you should run the Workgroup Administrator again and Join to the original **System.mdw**, which can be found in your Access folder, and then Exit to get the system back to its normal state. If you are unsure about what to do, please read through the sections, before trying them.

In this first Try It Out we will join to the new copy of **System.mdw** you have placed in the samples folder and then create new characteristics for it.

1 Close Access and using Explorer or My Computer, copy your **System.mdw** file into the **BegAcc95** folder. Make sure you copy rather than move the file.

2 Start the Workgroup Administrator application from the Windows 95 Start menu. When you open the Administrator, the first dialog shows the details of the current workgroup file - probably the **System.mdw** in your Access folder.

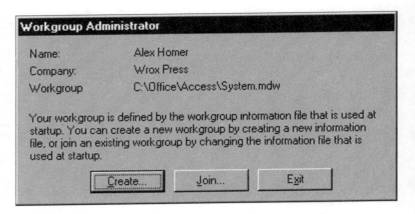

3 Select Join to open the Workgroup Information File dialog which displays the name and path of the current system database. We want to change this to use the copy of **System.mdw**. Type in the full path and name of the new system database, which is **C:\BegAcc95\System.mdw** (or whatever directory you have placed the copy in) or click Browse.. and select it from the normal file selector window that is displayed.

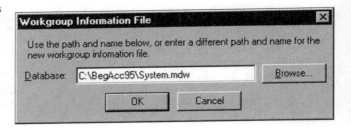

4 Click OK and Access will tell you that you have successfully joined the new work group.

5 You can then click Exit to close Workgroup Administrator. Access will now use the copy of **System.mdw** in your **BegAcc95** each time you log on, until you tell it otherwise.

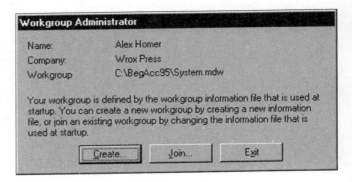

Creating Rather than Joining a Workgroup

We have made a copy of our default system database and then joined this workgroup. You could, of course, create a new one - in this case you simply click the Create button in the Workgroup Administrator window. You are presented with the Workgroup Owner Information dialog, where you would enter a workgroup ID. Each workgroup is identified by a Name and Organization Name, plus a Workgroup ID which is like a password. If you don't include a Workgroup ID when you create the workgroup, anyone can re-create it using just the Name and Organization Name information. However, like a password, you must keep the Workgroup ID safe - you will need it if you want to modify or re-build the workgroup for any reason.

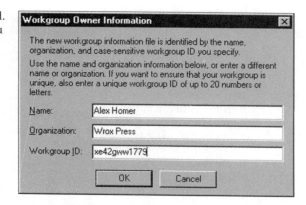

Once you click OK, Access displays the Workgroup Information File dialog where you enter the full path and name of the new system database for the workgroup.

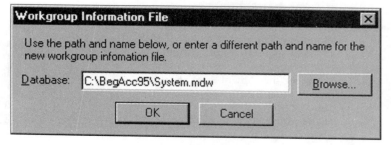

Clicking OK on this screen opens another dialog where you confirm that you want to save the details to the **System.mdw** file. You are then shown the details of the new workgroup.

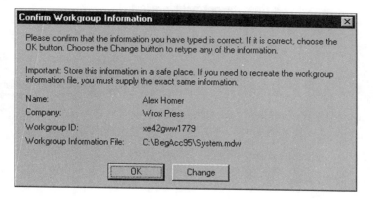

From here you click OK again to return to the Workgroup Administrator dialog and then select Exit to log out of the Workgroup Administrator.

Creating User Groups and Permissions

Having created the new workgroup and made it current, the next time you start Access it will use this workgroup. However, you won't see any signs of this, because the default workgroup allows anyone to open the databases and use them without limitation. To control the use of each part, you create user groups and user accounts and set the permissions for each one. The first step is to create the **administrator** and **owner** accounts.

Access supplies default groups called Admins and Users. It also supplies a default Admin user account. Don't confuse the two, group names are all plural, while account names are singular.

If the database is not secured, the default Admin account is used for every user. So they all have full permissions to use and modify all parts of the database. If you wish to secure a database, then this is undesirable.

To secure a database, you must first create a new administrator account which has full permissions. However, you can't create a password for a new administrator account if you are logged on as Admin - you actually have to log in using the new account first. You can then create a new copy of the database which belongs to that account - you become the **owner** and have full permissions on the database and can then set and change the security levels for all other users.

Try It Out - Creating a Secured Database Application

Note that you should make sure you have carried out the steps in the previous Try It Out *before* embarking on the following example.

In this Try It Out, you will log in as Admin and create a password for this account to secure it. Next you create an administrator account called WroxAdmin, then log on to Access as WroxAdmin and create a password for that account. You'll also remove the adminstrator permissions for the Admin account. Finally, you'll create a copy of the **WroxSoft** database which has WroxAdmin as the owner.

1 Select Security from the Tools menu. Select User And Group Accounts. Access opens the User and Group Accounts dialog, with the default Admin account shown.

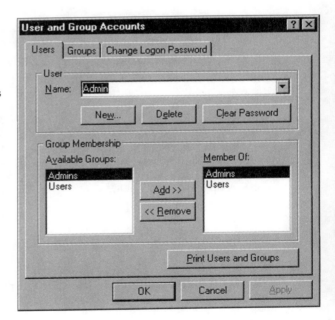

2   The first step is to enable the logon dialog. This will appear when you load Access and you are asked for a password. Click the Change Logon Password tab and enter a new password for the Admin account. Type in the same password in the Verify box. Leave the Old Password box empty (there's no password at the moment).

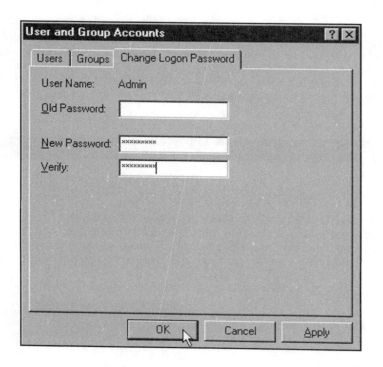

3   Go back to the Users tab. The next thing to do is to set up a new administrator account - we'll call it WroxAdmin. Click New... and enter the name of the group and a Personal ID.

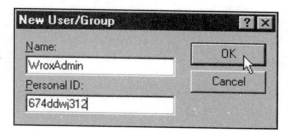

4   Click OK and you are returned to the previous dialog. Now make the new WroxAdmin user account a member of the Admins group by selecting Admins in the Available Groups list and clicking the Add>> button.

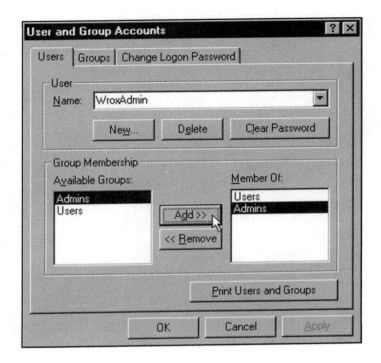

5 Click OK. Then close Access and restart it - the Logon dialog appears, with Admin already filled in. Log on as WroxAdmin instead. There's no password set for this workgroup (we set the password for Admin not WroxAdmin), so leave this blank. Click Cancel on the first screen, so that you don't open any database.

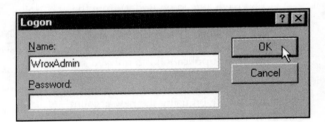

6 Now we can take control of the workgroup and the application. Select Security from the Tools menu, and click User And Group Accounts. Select the Admin account in the User Name box and click on the <<Remove option to remove it from the Admins group, which stops it being used to administer the application.

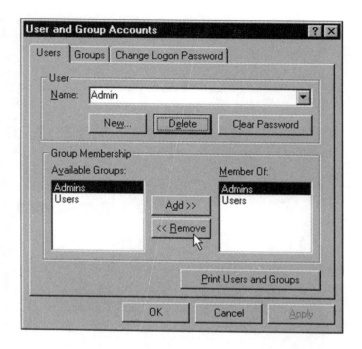

7 Select the WroxAdmin account (the one you have logged on under) from the top drop-down list box. Then select the Change Logon Password tab and enter a password, this time for WroxAdmin. Now the application can only be administered using this account and password. Close Access and open it again. Log on using the new account and password.

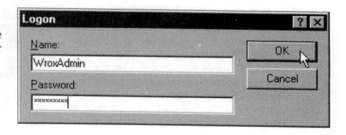

8 Now we can create a copy of the database with the WroxAdmin account as the owner. Open **Wroxsoft**, go to the Database window and select Security from the Tools menu. This time click User-Level Security Wizard. This will automatically create the new secured database - you can select which classes of objects you want to be secured. Leave them all checked and click OK.

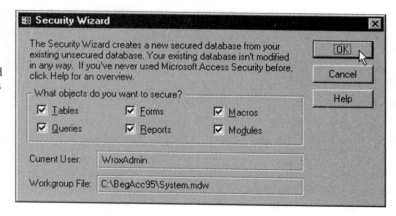

9 Access prompts you to set the path and name of the new secured database. The name must be different from the existing database - it suggests preceding the existing name with Secure. Click Save to create the new database.

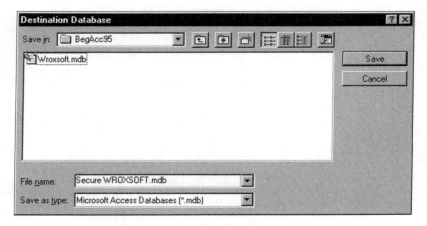

10 Once it has finished (and this may take some time on a large application or slower machine), Access displays a message showing that the new database is complete and the only accounts that have permissions to use it are the WroxAdmin account we set up and other members of the Admins group. Because we removed the default Admin account from this group before we secured the database, they do not have any permissions.

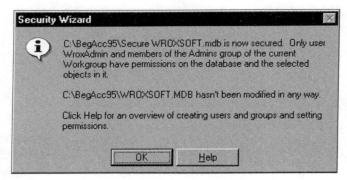

So we have created a new copy of the original application, but this new copy is owned by the WroxAdmin *user* rather than by the default Admin account. The system database file, **System.mdw** holds the information which controls the ownership and permissions within it. WroxAdmin is the only member of the Admins *group* and hence the only account that can open the database at the moment.

Establishing User Groups

Once you have established a secured workgroup and created the secured database, you can add other users and set the permissions for each one so that they only have access to the parts of the database application they need for their daily tasks or level of responsibility. However, rather than creating an individual set of permissions for each user, you can create user groups, then add each user to the appropriate group. That way you can change the permissions available to the whole group in one go. Say you introduce a different Order form and want to change the permissions on the old one - if you create individual accounts for each user, you need to change the permission for the form for each user separately, whereas if they all belong to one group you only need to change the group permission for that form.

Creating and managing user groups is done in the User And Group Accounts dialog - to get there, select Security from the Tools menu and then click User And Group Accounts. This dialog is the same as we used in the previous section to secure the **WroxSoft** application. It shows the name of all the current groups in the lower left-hand list - here we've added some more to our application.

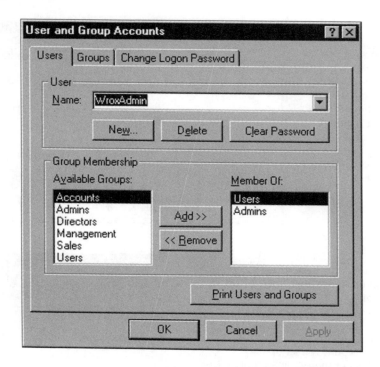

To create a new group you use the Groups page - click the Groups tab in the dialog. Then click New.. and Access opens another dialog where you can enter the Name and Personal ID for that group. The Personal ID that you use should be stored carefully - you will need it if you want to re-create the group in future.

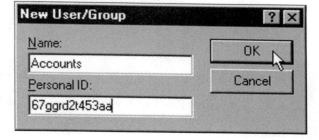

Once you have created the groups, you can then create the user accounts. To log on to Access, each user must have their own user account - they cannot log on using the group name. Click the Users tab again and now you can create new user names and allocate each to the relevant groups. Click New.. and enter a Name and Personal ID to create the user.

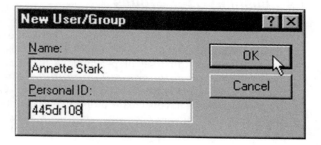

Now you can add them to one or more of the Available Groups using the Add>> button.

If you wish to delete an existing group, just select it and click the Delete button.

Access checks with you that you really do want to delete the group before removing it.

Setting User Group Permissions

To set the permissions for a user account, open the **User and Group Permissions** dialog by selecting **Security** from the **Tools** menu and clicking **User And Group Permissions**. Depending on the setting of the **List** option, the top section displays all the existing user or group names.

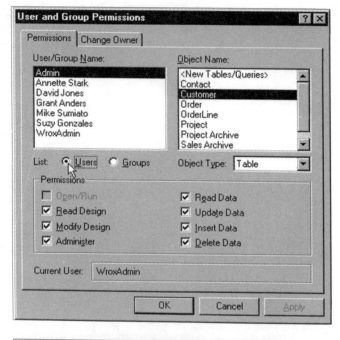

Note that all the permissions are set for the default **Admin** user - they have full access to all the objects in the database. Select any of the **Object Types** and any of the entries in the **Object Name** list to see this. However, if you select any of the other users, including our **WroxAdmin** account, they have no permissions on any of the items. Remember that our **WroxAdmin** account, like all the other accounts we have created, is a member of the **Users** group. Once you have used Sscurity Wizard to create the new secured database, the members of the **Users** group have *no* default permissions. To see the permissions for the **Users** group, click the **Groups** option below the list of **User/Group** names and select **Users**.

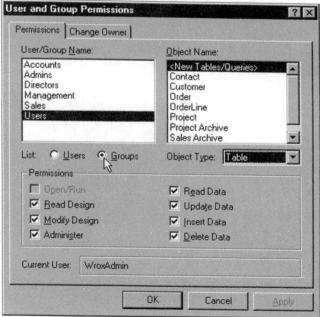

All the other groups have no permissions, so the first step is to remove any permissions from the Users group (to which every user belongs) that you don't want them to have, then add permissions to each of the other groups depending on which objects you want them to be able to use. Remember that setting the permissions for the group means each member of that group will inherit the same permissions.

To change the permissions for an object, select it using the Object Type for a list of the objects and Object Name for specific objects within the database. You can select more than one item in the Object Name list by holding down *Shift* or *Ctrl* while you click on them. Then either set or clear the checkboxes for each type of permission you want them to have. You can set permissions for:

Permission...	means that they can ...
Open/Run	Open a database, form, or report, or run a macro.
Open Exclusive	Open a database with exclusive access.
Read Design	View objects in design view.
Modify Design	View and change the design of objects, or delete them.
Administer	Have full administrator's access to objects and data.
Read Data	View data.
Update Data	View and modify, but not insert or delete data.
Insert Data	View and insert, but not modify or delete data.
Delete Data	View and delete, but not modify or insert data.

 Some permissions automatically include others - giving a user **Update Data** permission for a table for instance, means they also have **Read** permissions which are needed to actually change the data in the table.

If you want a user to have different permissions from other members of the same group, you can set individual variations by selecting the Users option to show a list of users and setting the permissions for any of the objects. These settings will only apply to that particular user.

Setting Passwords for Each User

When you create a group or user account, you have to supply a Personal ID. This is not the same as a password - the users themselves will set the password once the account is established, or you can set it for them. The Personal ID is simply a way of securing the account as it is created, and again you should make sure it is stored carefully - you will need it if you want to re-create the account in future.

Once you have completed creation of the user accounts, the passwords for these should be established. You can do this by logging in to Access using each of the user names in turn and setting their password, or by instructing each user to set their own password when they log on.

The user account password is set the same way as we set the Admin and WroxAdmin passwords earlier. Select Security form the Tools menu and click User And Group Accounts. Then click the Change Logon Password tab and enter and verify the password. You or a user can also change the existing password to a new one in the same way.

Printing a Security Report

You can print a report which lists all the groups, users and permissions by selecting Print Users and Groups in the User And Group Accounts dialog.

This opens the Print Security selector which allows you to include either Users or Groups in the report, or print one that includes both.

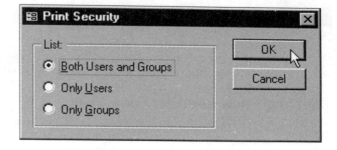

The report shows which users belong to each group, listed either by user name or group name. If you selected the first option, Access prints both of these.

Users

User Name	Groups that User Belongs To
Admin	Users
Annette Stark	Sales, Users
David Jones	Accounts, Users
Grant Anders	Accounts, Directors, Management, Sales, Users

etc...

Groups

Group Name	Users that Belong to Group
Admins	WroxAdmin
Users	Annette Stark, David Jones, Grant Anders, Mike Sumiato, Suzy Gonzales, WroxAdmin

etc...

Try It Out - Restoring your System to its Original State

We've got to the end of the examples, so you should now return your system to its original state.

1 To do this, close Access and then run the Workgroup Administrator and select the Join option. This time use Browse to find (or type in the name of) the path to your original **System.mdw** file. This should look something like **C:\MSOffice\Access\System.mdw**. (Your original **System.mdw** will be in your Access folder.) Click OK and Access will revert to using the original version of **System.mdw**.

2 Once you've set the path, just click Exit. Note that you can continue to use **WroxSoft.mdb**, but if you open Secure **WroxSoft.mdb**, you'll find that it is now read-only.

Administering a Multi-user System

If you have several users accessing the same tables, you have extra responsibilities to consider. Probably the most important concerns the problems that arise when two users are trying to edit the same records in a table - when you have more than one user this is always a possibility. Access guards against it by means of **record locking**.

As a user opens a table (or a query which draws records from a table) and begins to edit it, Access **locks** the records so that no other user can change them. This protects the integrity of the data - imagine if one person opens the table and, while they are editing a record in their form, another user changes the contents of the same record. When the first user saves their copy of the record, they won't have seen, or be aware of, the changes made by the second user. The changes made by the second user will be lost, but both will still think they have updated the record.

By applying a lock to a record when it is opened, Access prevents any other user from reading and updating that record until the first user has closed and saved it. The only problem is that Access cannot lock just one record - it locks a 'page' of records instead. So if several users are working on the same set of records, they can regularly find themselves locked out while another user is editing records on that page. (The number of records on a page depends on the size of each record and the way your system is set up.)

To minimize delays due to this, you can set properties in your forms. Each bound form has Data Entry and Record Locks properties. Setting the Data Entry property to Yes means that only new records can be added using that form. This avoids record locking problems as the current records are not locked while the form is in use. However, it is of no use when you want to use a form for updating existing records. In this case, you can use the Record Locks property. The available settings reflect how you expect the records to be used in a form - No Locks, All Records and Edited Record.

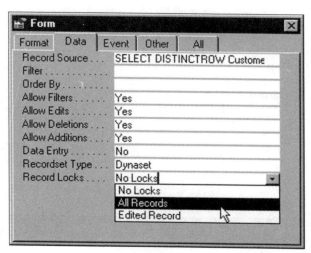

The effects of each of these is:

Value	Effect
No Locks	When you start to edit the record, Access applies no locks to it and another user can edit the same record. If this happens, you get a message when you try to save the changed record and you can either copy the record to the clipboard so that you can view the other user's changes then complete the updating, or abandon your changes to the record - in the same way as pressing the *Escape* key. This method is often called **optimistic record locking** and works best if users are rarely editing the same records at the same time. It makes the operation very efficient because Access does not have to apply and remove locks - and users can edit records on the same 'page' at the same time.
All Records	As soon as you open the form, Access locks all the records in all the underlying tables. They are locked all the time the form is open, so this method should only be used where you know no-one else will require access to them.
Edited Record	This method is used where you want to make sure all updates will succeed by preventing two users editing the same record. Once one user opens it, all other users find it is locked and cannot be opened. So the first user will always be able to save the changes without fear of the record having been changed. However, Access cannot lock individual records - in most cases, it locks a 'page' of records so other users will be locked out of these as well. This method is often called **pessimistic record locking**.

Advanced Options

You can also limit the number of conflicts that occur in a multi-user environment by setting various global Access options. Select Options from the Tools menu and click the Advanced tab.

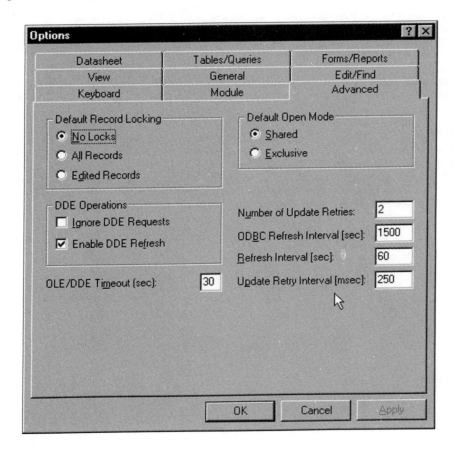

Here you can set the default value for a form's Record Locks property - this will apply to all new forms you create. You can also control how Access **updates** and **refreshes** records displayed in a form (or table).

For example, you can change the Number of Update Retries from its default value of 2 to a higher number. If the record is locked by another user, Access will try to save the changes to the record up to 10 times before displaying a message to say it cannot be saved. You can also change the delay between each update attempt - the Update Retry Interval - from zero to 1 second (1,000 msec). When combined together, these two properties help you avoid locking errors where two users are attempting to save the same record.

Another cause of record locking conflicts can be when each user is refreshing the records displayed in their forms or tables. If another user has the record locked, Access cannot read it and so the refresh can fail. You can increase the settings for Refresh Interval from the default of 60 seconds - this affects refreshes to data in native and normal attached tables. There is also an ODBC Refresh Interval setting which applies to records which are supplied to Access via an ODBC driver.

Summary

We've now reached the end of the chapter and with it, the end of the book. We've traveled a long, and sometimes tortuous, route from a simple spreadsheet in Excel to talking about database performance and administration in Access. Along the way, you have seen most of the things that Access can accomplish and how it can be adapted both for these and other less obvious tasks. You've learned how to work with the different kinds of objects so that you can build database applications of quite amazing power and ability.

Of course, there's always something more to learn. Access has some features we've hardly touched on - especially the Visual Basic for Applications code it supports. And there are many more ways of using the other more familiar objects, limited often only by your imagination.

Much of what we've done in this book is aimed towards the single user or small workgroup environment. While you are becoming familiar with Access, this is the best place to experiment. But Access is much more than this. It supports connectivity methods which allow you almost unlimited data processing opportunities. You can use SQL Server, or other proprietary methods, to link Access to almost any type of mainframe or mini computer to build company-wide information systems. This is hopefully only the beginning of your Access explorations.

List of Functions by Name

Function Name	Function Group	What it does
Abs	Mathematical	Returns the absolute value of a number.
Array	Array Handling	Returns a variant containing an array.
Asc, AscB	Text Handling	Return the ASCII code of the first letter in a string.
Atn	Mathematical	Returns the arctangent of a number.
CBool	Conversion	Converts an expression to a boolean type.
CByte	Conversion	Converts an expression to a byte type.
CCur	Conversion	Converts an expression to a currency type.
CDate, CVDate	Conversion	Converts an expression to a date type.
CDbl	Conversion	Converts an expression to a double type.
Choose	Selection	Selects a value from a list of arguments.
Chr	Text Handling	Returns the character for a specified ASCII code.
CInt	Conversion	Converts an expression to an integer type.
CLng	Conversion	Converts an expression to a long type.
CodeDB	Miscellaneous	Returns the name of the current database.
Cos	Mathematical	Returns the cosine of an angle.
CreateControl	Object Handling	Creates a control on a form.
CreateObject	Object Handling	Creates an OLE automation object.
CreateReport	Object Handling	Creates a report.
CSng	Conversion	Converts an expression to a single type.
CStr	Conversion	Converts an expression to a string type.

Table Continued on Following Page

Function Name	Function Group	What it does
CurDir	File & Disk	Returns the current drive path.
CurrentUser	Miscellaneous	Returns the name of the current user of the current database.
CVar	Conversion	Converts an expression to a variant type.
Date	Date & Time	Returns the current system date.
DateAdd	Date & Time	Adds a specified time interval to a date.
DateDiff	Date & Time	Returns the number of time intervals between two dates.
DatePart	Date & Time	Returns a specified part of a given date.
DateSerial	Date & Time	Returns a date for a given year, month and day.
DateValue	Date & Time	Returns a date type from a given string.
DAvg	Domain Aggregate	Calculates the average for a set of values.
Day	Date & Time	Returns the day of the month as a number.
DCount	Domain Aggregate	Counts the number of records in the domain.
DDB	Financial	Returns the depreciation of an asset.
DDE	DDE Commands	Define a DDE conversation.
DDEInitiate	DDE Commands	Initiates a DDE conversation.
DDERequest	DDE Commands	Request data in a DDE conversation.
DDESend	DDE Commands	Sends data in a DDE conversation.
Dir	File & Disk	Finds one or more a files or folders.
DLookup	Domain Aggregate	Returns a value from a set of records.
DMax	Domain Aggregate	Calculates the maximum for a set of values.
DMin	Domain Aggregate	Calculates the minimum for a set of values.
DoEvents	Miscellaneous	Yields execution to the operating system.
DStDev	Domain Aggregate	Calculates the standard deviation for a set of values.
DStDevP	Domain Aggregate	Calculates the standard deviation population for a set of values.
DSum	Domain Aggregate	Calculates the total for a set of values.
DVar	Domain Aggregate	Calculates the variance for a set of values.
DVarP	Domain Aggregate	Calculates the variance population for a set of values.
Environ	Miscellaneous	Returns an environment variable setting.
EOF	File & Disk	Check for the end of a file.

624

Table Continued on Following Page

Function Name	Function Group	What it does
Error	Miscellaneous	Returns the message for a given error number.
Eval	Mathematical	Evaluates an expression.
FileAttr	File & Disk	Returns information about the way a file was opened.
Fix, Int	Mathematical	Returns the integer portion of a number.
Format	Text Handling	Formats values according to instructions contained in the format expression.
FreeFile	File & Disk	Returns the next file number available.
FV	Financial	Returns the future value of an annuity.
GetObject	Object Handling	Retrieves an OLE object from a file.
Hex	Conversion	Converts a hexadecimal number to a string.
Hour	Date & Time	Returns the hour of the day as a number.
IIf	Selection	Returns one of two values, depending on the evaluation of an expression.
Input	File & Disk	Returns characters from an open disk file.
InputBox	Miscellaneous	Displays a dialog box and waits for the user to enter a value.
InStr	Text Handling	Searches for a string within another string.
IPmt	Financial	Returns the interest payment for a given period of an annuity.
IsDate	Examination	Tests whether an expression can be converted to a date.
IsEmpty	Examination	Tests whether a variable has been initialized.
IsMissing	Examination	Tests whether an optional argument has been passed to a procedure.
IsNumeric	Examination	Tests whether an expression can be evaluated as a number.
IsNull	Examination	Tests whether an expression contains valid data.
IsObject	Object Handling	Tests whether an expression references a valid OLE automation object.
IRR	Financial	Returns the internal rate of return for a series of cash flows.
LBound	Array Handling	Returns the lower bound (index) of an array.
LCase	Text Handling	Converts text to lower case.
Left	Text Handling	Returns the left part of a text string.

Table Continued on Following Page

Function Name	Function Group	What it does
Loc	File & Disk	Returns the current position within a disk file.
LOF	File & Disk	Returns the size (length) in bytes of a file.
Log	Mathematical	Returns the natural logarithm of a number.
LTrim	Text Handling	Removes leading spaces from a string.
Max	SQL Aggregate	Returns the maximum of a set of values.
Mid	Text Handling	Returns the middle part of a text string.
Min	SQL Aggregate	Returns the minimum of a set of values.
Minute	Date & Time	Returns the minute of the hour as a number.
MIRR	Financial	Returns the modified internal rate of return for a series of cash flows.
Month	Date & Time	Returns the month of the year as a number.
MsgBox	Miscellaneous	Displays a message dialog and waits for the user to press a button.
Now	Date & Time	Returns the current date and time.
NPer	Financial	Returns the number of periods for an annuity.
NPV	Financial	Returns the net present value of an investment.
Oct	Conversion	Converts an octal number to a string.
Partition	Selection	Returns a string indicating where a number occurs within a series of ranges.
Pmt	Financial	Returns the payment for an annuity.
PPmt	Financial	Returns the principal payment for an annuity.
PV	Financial	Returns the present value of an investment.
QBColor	Miscellaneous	Returns the RGB color code corresponding to a color number.
Rate	Financial	Returns the interest rate for an annuity.
RGB	Miscellaneous	Returns a whole number representing an RGB color value.
Right	Text Handling	Returns the right part of a text string.
Rnd	Miscellaneous	Returns a random number.
RTrim	Text Handling	Removes trailing spaces from a string.
Second	Date & Time	Returns the second of the minute as a number.
Seek	File & Disk	Sets the current position within a disk file.

Table Continued on Following Page

Function Name	Function Group	What it does
Sgn	Mathematical	Tests the sign of a number.
Shell	Miscellaneous	Starts another application.
Sin	Mathematical	Returns the sine of an angle.
SLN	Financial	Returns the straight-line depreciation of an asset.
Space	Text Handling	Creates a string of a given number of spaces.
Spc, Tab	Text Handling	Used to position output when printing.
Sqr	Mathematical	Returns the square root of a number.
StDev	SQL Aggregate	Returns the standard deviation.
StDevP	SQL Aggregate	Returns the standard deviation population.
Str	Text Handling	Converts a number to its string representation.
StrComp	Text Handling	Compares two strings and returns a value.
String	Text Handling	Creates a string of a given repeating character.
Sum	SQL Aggregate	Calculates the total of a set of numbers.
Switch	Selection	Returns a value for the first expression in a list that is true.
SYD	Financial	Returns the sum-of-years' digits depreciation of an asset.
SysCmd	Miscellaneous	Carries out Access status actions.
Tan	Mathematical	Returns the tangent of an angle.
Time	Date & Time	Returns the current system time.
Timer	Miscellaneous	Returns the number of seconds since midnight.
TimeSerial	Date & Time	Returns the time for a given hour, minute, and second.
TimeValue	Date & Time	Returns a date type containing the time given in a string.
Trim	Text Handling	Removes leading and trailing spaces.
UBound	Array Handling	Returns the upper bound (index) of an array.
UCase	Text Handling	Converts text to upper case.
Val	Conversion	Returns a number contained in a string.
Var	SQL Aggregate	Calculates the variance.
VarP	SQL Aggregate	Calculates the variance population.
VarType	Examination	Returns a value indicating the type of data stored in a variable.
Weekday	Date & Time	Returns the day of the week as a number.
Year	Date & Time	Returns the year part of the current date.

List of Functions by Type

	Function Name	What it does
Array Handling	Array	Returns a variant containing an array.
	LBound	Returns the lower bound (index) of an array.
	UBound	Returns the upper bound (index) of an array.
Conversion	CBool	Converts an expression to a boolean type.
	CByte	Converts an expression to a byte type.
	CCur	Converts an expression to a currency type.
	Cdate, CVDate	Converts an expression to a date type.
	CDbl	Converts an expression to a double type.
	CInt	Converts an expression to an integer type.
	CLng	Converts an expression to a long type.
	CSng	Converts an expression to a single type.
	CStr	Converts an expression to a string type.
	CVar	Converts an expression to a variant type.
	Hex	Converts a hexadecimal number to a string.
	Oct	Converts an octal number to a string.
	Val	Returns a number contained in a string.
Date & Time	Date	Returns the current system date.
	DateAdd	Adds a specified time interval to a date.
	DateDiff	Returns the number of time intervals between two dates.
	DatePart	Returns a specified part of a given date.
	DateSerial	Returns a date for a given year, month and day.
	DateValue	Returns a date type from a given string.
	Day	Returns the day of the month as a number.
	Hour	Returns the hour of the day as a number.
	Minute	Returns the minute of the hour as a number.
	Month	Returns the month of the year as a number.
	Now	Returns the current date and time.

Table Continued on Following Page

	Function Name	What it does
	Second	Returns the second of the minute as a number.
	Time	Returns the current system time.
	TimeSerial	Returns the time for a given hour, minute and second.
	TimeValue	Returns a date type containing the time given in a string.
	Weekday	Returns the day of the week as a number.
	Year	Returns the year part of the current date.
DDE Commands	DDE	Defines a DDE conversation.
	DDEInitiate	Initiates a DDE conversation.
	DDERequest	Requests data in a DDE conversation.
	DDESend	Sends data in a DDE conversation.
Domain Aggregate	DAvg	Calculates the average for a set of values.
	DCount	Counts the number of records in the domain.
	DLookup	Returns a value from a set of records.
	DMax	Calculates the maximum for a set of values.
	DMin	Calculates the minimum for a set of values.
	DStDev	Calculates the standard deviation for a set of values.
	DStDevP	Calculates the standard deviation population for a set of values.
	DSum	Calculates the total for a set of values.
	DVar	Calculates the variance for a set of values.
	DVarP	Calculates the variance population for a set of values.
Examination	IsDate	Tests whether an expression can be converted to a date.
	IsEmpty	Tests whether a variable has been initialized.
	IsMissing	Tests whether an optional argument has been passed to a procedure.
	IsNumeric	Tests whether an expression can be evaluated as a number.
	IsNull	Tests whether an expression contains valid data.
	VarType	Returns a value indicating the type of data stored in a variable.

Table Continued on Following Page

629

	Function Name	*What it does*
File & Disk	CurDir	Returns the current drive path.
	Dir	Finds one or more a files or folders.
	EOF	Checks for the end of a file.
	FileAttr	Returns information about the way a file was opened.
	FreeFile	Returns the next file number available.
	Input	Returns characters from an open disk file.
	Loc	Returns the current position within a disk file.
	LOF	Returns the size (length) in bytes of a file.
	Seek	Sets the current position within a disk file.
Financial	DDB	Returns the depreciation of an asset.
	FV	Returns the future value of an annuity.
	IPmt	Returns the interest payment for a given period of an annuity.
	IRR	Returns the internal rate of return for a series of cash flows.
	MIRR	Returns the modified internal rate of return for a series of cash flows.
	NPer	Returns the number of periods for an annuity.
	NPV	Returns the net present value of an investment.
	Pmt	Returns the payment for an annuity.
	PPmt	Returns the principal payment for an annuity.
	PV	Returns the present value of an investment.
	Rate	Returns the interest rate for an annuity.
	SLN	Returns the straight-line depreciation of an asset.
	SYD	Returns the sum-of-years' digits depreciation of an asset.
Mathematical	Abs	Returns the absolute value of a number.
	Atn	Returns the arctangent of a number.
	Cos	Returns the cosine of an angle.
	Eval	Evaluates an expression.
	Fix, Int	Returns the integer portion of a number.

Table Continued on Following Page

	Function Name	What it does
	Log	Returns the natural logarithm of a number.
	Sgn	Tests the sign of a number.
	Sin	Returns the sine of an angle.
	Sqr	Returns the square root of a number.
	Tan	Returns the tangent of an angle.
Miscellaneous	CodeDB	Returns the name of the current database.
	CurrentUser	Returns the name of the current user of the current database.
	DoEvents	Yields execution to the operating system.
	Environ	Returns an environment variable setting.
	Error	Returns the message for a given error number.
	InputBox	Displays a dialog box and waits for the user to enter a value.
	MsgBox	Displays a message dialog and waits for the user to press a button.
	QBColor	Returns the RGB color code corresponding to a color number.
	RGB	Returns a whole number representing an RGB color value.
	Rnd	Returns a random number.
	Shell	Starts another application.
	SysCmd	Carry out Access status actions.
	Timer	Returns the number of seconds since midnight.
Object Handling	CreateControl	Creates a control on a form.
	CreateObject	Creates an OLE automation object.
	CreateReport	Creates a report.
	GetObject	Retrieves an OLE object from a file.
	IsObject	Tests whether an expression references a valid OLE automation object.
Selection	Choose	Selects a value from a list of arguments.

Table Continued on Following Page

	Function Name	What it does
	IIf	Returns one of two values, depending on the evaluation of an expression.
	Partition	Returns a string indicating where a number occurs within a series of ranges.
	Switch	Returns a value for the first expression in a list that is True.
SQL Aggregate	Max	Returns the maximum of a set of values.
	Min	Returns the minimum of a set of values.
	StDev	Returns the standard deviation.
	StDevP	Returns the standard deviation population.
	Sum	Calculates the total of a set of numbers.
	Var	Calculates the variance.
	VarP	Calculates the variance population.
Text Handling	Spc, Tab	Used to position output when printing.
	Asc, AscB	Returns the ASCII code of the first letter in a string.
	Chr	Returns the character for a specified ASCII code.
	Format	Formats values according to instructions contained in the format expression.
	InStr	Searches for a string within another string.
	LCase	Converts text to lower case.
	Left	Returns the left part of a text string.
	LTrim	Removes leading spaces from a string.
	Mid	Returns the middle part of a text string.
	Right	Returns the right part of a text string.
	RTrim	Removes trailing spaces from a string.
	Space	Creates a string of a given number of spaces.
	Str	Converts a number to its string representation.
	StrComp	Compares two strings and returns a value.
	String	Creates a string of a given repeating character.
	Trim	Removes leading and trailing spaces.
	UCase	Converts text to upper case.

Access Macro Actions

Task	Macro Actions
Apply or remove a filter	ApplyFilter, ShowAllRecords
Move around a recordset	FindNext, FindRecord, GoToRecord
Move around in a form or report	GoToControl, GoToPage
Carry out a menu command	DoMenuItem
Execute a query or SQL statement	OpenQuery, RunSQL
Run a macro or VBA procedure	RunCode, RunMacro
Run another application	RunApp
Stop execution	CancelEvent, StopAllMacros, StopMacro
Close a database	Quit
Export Access objects to other applications	OutputTo, SendObject
Export data to other applications	TransferDatabase, TransferSpreadsheet, TransferText
Copy, save or rename an object	CopyObject, Rename, Save
Delete an object	DeleteObject
Move or resize a window	Maximize, Minimize, MoveSize, Restore
Open or close an object	Close, OpenForm, OpenModule, OpenQuery, OpenReport, OpenTable
Open an object	OpenForm, OpenQuery, OpenReport
Print an object	PrintOut
Select an object	SelectObject
Set the value of a field, control or property	SetValue
Update data or the screen	RepaintObject, Requery
Create a custom menu bar for a form	AddMenu, SetMenuItem
Display information on screen	Echo, Hourglass, MsgBox, SetWarnings
Generate keystrokes	SendKeys
Display or hide the toolbar	ShowToolbar
Sound a beep	Beep

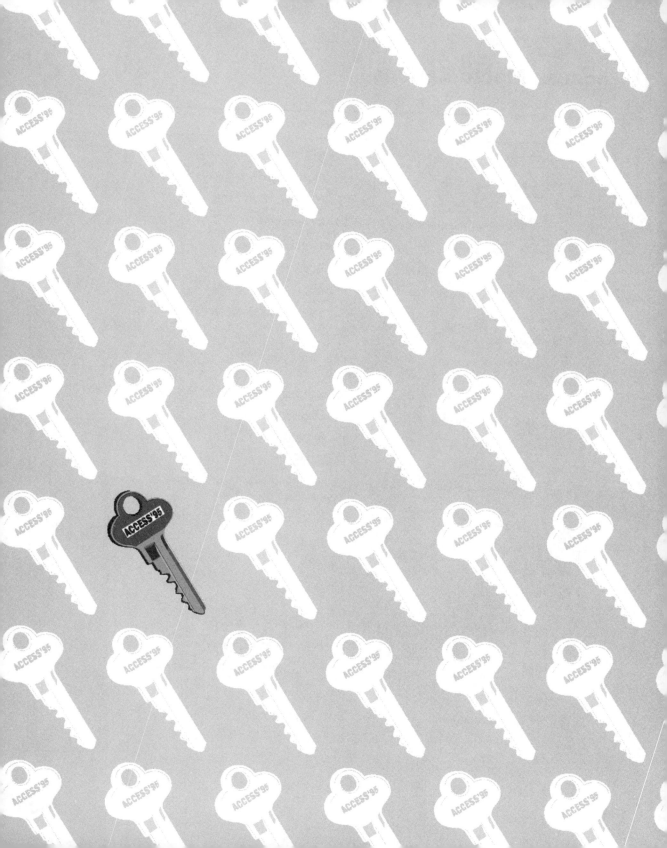

The Beginner's Guide to

Access 95

Index

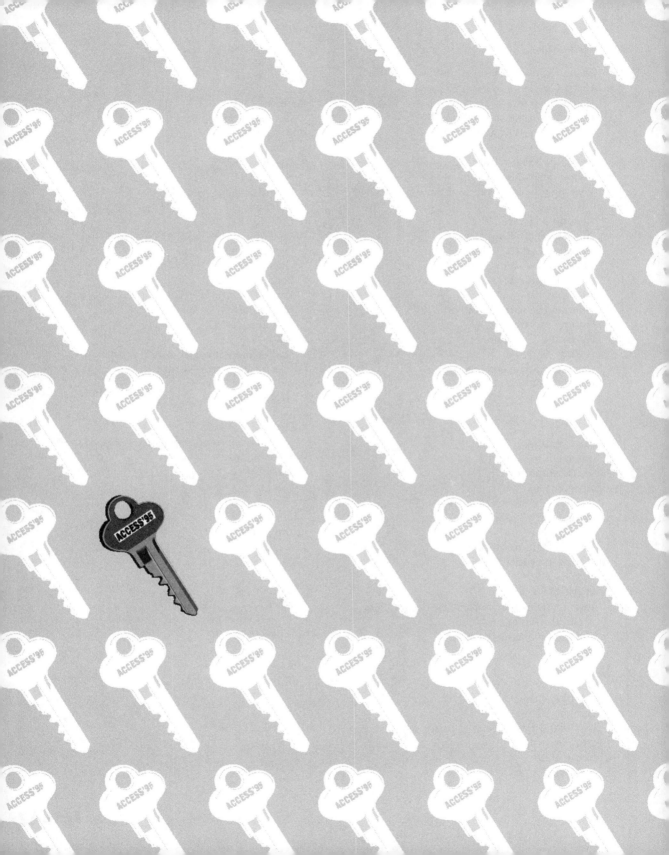

INSTANT DELPHI PROGRAMMING

This book provides a fast guide to the essentials of Borland's new development tool. Borland have put together fast executable Pascal code with a truly intuitive event-driven environment. The result is a powerful, yet easy to use program, and this book caters for programmers who want to master its fundamental advantages. Taking developers through the strengths of the innovative Object Pascal code, its access to a database engine, as well as advanced features such as using VBX controls, this book will help programmers from many different backgrounds move successfully into Borland's strong new package.

AUTHOR: Dave Jewell   ISBN: 1-874416-57-5   PRICE: $24.95 C$34.95 £22.99

THE REVOLUTIONARY GUIDE TO WIN 32 PROGRAMMING WITH VISUAL C++

This book is the definitive guide to programming the 32 bit editions of Windows with Visual C++ 2.1. Comprehensive coverage of the MFC 3.1 provides the programmer with all the tools required to take advantage of the 32bit architectures of Win32s, Windows NT 3.51 and the forthcoming Windows'95 (aka Chicago). Written by one of the leading members of Microsoft's Visual C++ team, it is a must for Visual C++ developers. The book assumes that the reader is familiar with the concepts of object-oriented programming and comes complete with a CD-ROM containing all source code, a full hypertext version of the book and various third party tools and samples.

AUTHOR: Mike Blaszczak   ISBN: 1-874416-47-8   PRICE: $44.95 C$62.95 £41.99

OTHER WROX PRESS TITLES	ISBN:	PRICE:	RELEASE:
The Beginner's Guide to **Visual Basic 4.0**	1-874416-55-9	**$34.95 C$48.95 £32.99**	Out Now
The Beginner's Guide to **Access Programming**	1-874416-64-8	**$34.95 C$48.95 £32.99**	Feb '96
Instant **UNIX**	1-874416-65-6	**$24.95 C$34.95 £22.99**	Out Now
Instant **SQL Programming**	1-874416-50-8	**$29.95 C$41.95 £27.99**	Out Now
Instant **C Programming**	1-874416-24-9	**$24.95 C$34.95 £22.99**	Out Now
The Revolutionary Guide to **PowerBuilder**	1-874416-60-5	**$49.95 C$69.95 £46.99**	Out Now
The Revolutionary Guide to **QBasic**	1-874416-20-6	**$34.95 C$48.95 £32.99**	Jan '96
The Revolutionary Guide to **Visual Basic 4 Professional**	1-874416-37-0	**$44.95 C$62.95 £41.99**	Jan '96

WIN FREE BOOKS

TELL US WHAT YOU THINK!

Complete and return the bounce back card and you will:

- Help us create the books you want.
- Receive an update on all Wrox titles.
- Enter the draw for 5 Wrox titles of your choice.

FILL THIS OUT to enter the draw for free Wrox titles

Name _____

Address _____

_____

_____

_____ Postcode/Zip _____

Occupation _____

How did you hear about this book?

☐ Book review (name) _____

☐ Advertisement (name) _____

☐ Recommendation

☐ Catalogue

☐ Other _____

Where did you buy this book?

☐ Bookstore (name) _____

☐ Computer Store (name) _____

☐ Mail Order

☐ Other _____

I would be interested in receiving information about Wrox Press titles by email in future. My email/Internet address is:

_____

What influenced you in the purchase of this book?

☐ Cover Design

☐ Contents

☐ Other (please specify) _____

What did you find most useful about this book? _____

What did you find least useful about this book? _____

Please add any additional comments. _____

What other subjects will you buy a computer book on soon? _____

What is the best computer book you have used this year? _____

How did you rate the overall contents of this book?

☐ Excellent   ☐ Good

☐ Average   ☐ Poor

Note: This information will only be used to keep you updated about new Wrox Press titles and will not be used for any other purpose or passed to any other third party.

WROX

WROX PRESS INC.

Wrox writes books for you. Any suggestions, or
ideas about how you want information given in
your ideal book will be studied by our team.
Your comments are always valued at WROX.

Free phone in USA 800 814 4527
Fax (312) 465 4063

Compuserve 100063,2152.
UK Tel. (44121) 706 6826   Fax   (44121) 706 2967

——— *Computer Book Publishers* ———

NB. If you post the bounce back card below in the UK, please send it to:
Wrox Press Ltd. Unit 16, Sapcote Industrial Estate, 20 James Road, Birmingham, B11 2BA